AMERICAN
VISIONS

AMERICAN VISIONS

Multicultural Literature for Writers

DOLORES LAGUARDIA
University of San Francisco

HANS P. GUTH
Santa Clara University

Mayfield Publishing Company
Mountain View, California
London • *Toronto*

For Dorian, Justin, Ingrid, Michael, Susan, and Paul

LIBRARY OF CONGRESS CATALOGING-IN-PUBLICATION DATA
LaGuardia, Dolores.
    American visions : multicultural literature for writers / Dolores laGuardia, Hans P. Guth.
        p.   cm.
    ISBN 1-55934-322-2
    1. Readers—Social sciences. 2. United States—Ethnic relations—Problems, exercises, etc. 3. Ethnic groups—United States—Problems, exercises, etc. 4. Pluralism (Social sciences)—Problems, exercises, etc. 5. English language—Rhetoric.
    6. College readers.   I. Guth, Hans Paul.   II. Title.
    PE1127.S6L34   1994
    810.8—dc20   94-6444
                                                                          CIP

Manufactured in the United States of America
10 9 8 7 6 5 4 3 2

Mayfield Publishing Company
1280 Villa Street
Mountain View, California 94041

Sponsoring editor, James Bull; production editor, April Wells-Hayes; manuscript editor, Loralee Windsor; art director, Jeanne M. Schreiber; text design, TS Design Group; cover designer, Donna Davis; manufacturing manager, Martha Branch. The text was set in 10.5/12 Bembo by Thompson Type and printed on 45# New Era Matte by the Maple-Vail Book Manufacturing Group.

Cover image: Jasper Johns, *Map.* 1961. Oil on canvas, 6'6" × 10'3⅛".
© Jasper Johns/VAGA, New York. Photograph courtesy Leo Castelli Gallery.

Acknowledgments appear on pages 733–737, which constitute an extension of the copyright page.

TO THE INSTRUCTOR

History . . . does not refer merely, or even principally to the past. On the contrary, the great force of history comes from the fact that we carry it within us, we are unconsciously controlled by it in many ways, and history is literally present in all that we do.

James Baldwin

American Visions aims at giving teachers and students a fuller, richer multicultural definition of the American literary tradition. The book is designed to help students discover their cultural history through the study of imaginative literature. We invite students to discover and interact with writers who, in the words of one reviewer, try "to make sense of America." Focusing on the diversity of the American heritage, the book explores the historical context and contemporary relevance of major themes that have shaped our consciousness as a nation. The fiction, poetry, drama, and nonfiction printed here explore the forces that have played a major role in the American experience.

American Visions is designed to help students become more alert and responsive readers, more fully aware of the social contexts and human meaning of imaginative literature. The apparatus promotes interaction between the literature and the reader in discussion, writing, and collaborative work.

The Goals of *American Visions*

A SENSE OF HISTORY This book is organized around major themes that help explain who and what Americans are as a nation. To help our students develop a sense of history, we need to remember that chronology is not history and that bit facts do not bring the past to life. This book uses a combined historical and thematic approach—presenting major themes in historical perspective. To help students understand the presence of the past, it traces major strands that make up the fabric of the American experience. It focuses on major concerns and shifts in consciousness, such as the idea of America as the land of promise, the search for a national identity, the reclaiming of the Native American past, the lure and limitations of American individualism, the challenges to American optimism, the trauma of slavery, the glory and decline of the American city, the search for personal fulfillment, the emergence of a new multicultural consciousness, and the rediscovery of nature.

REDEFINING THE HERITAGE   This book helps readers move toward a new multicultural definition of the American heritage. An authentic vision of a shared American culture moves beyond the boundaries of region, gender, and ethnicity. Over the years, a fuller, richer vision of the American experience has emerged: The flourishing of Southern and American Jewish literature put the New England tradition in a larger national context. African American writers from Frederick Douglass to James Baldwin and Alice Walker, and Native American writers from N. Scott Momaday to Louise Erdrich, have found a large audience for the unheard voices of America's minorities. Feminist readers and feminist critics have rediscovered eloquent women writers of the past and championed women writing in the present. In recent years, bilingual American writers—Latinos, American Chinese, American Japanese—have begun to make a significant contribution to our national literature.

THE RELEVANCE OF LITERATURE   This book is designed to help students become more responsive and more sophisticated readers. We do not want them to see image and metaphor and symbol as ends in themselves; instead, we want them to see how the elements of literature serve its human meaning. In the words of Tillie Olsen, we should make available to our students literature that is close to the "human condition"; that recognizes great capacities "in everyday use"; that "makes us profoundly conscious of what harms, degrades, denies development, destroys"; and that reminds us how much human potential "is unrealized, unlived."

THE RESPONSIVE READER   As teachers of literature today we do not expect the student reader to be like a blank page. We recognize and validate what students bring to their reading—their background, allegiances, questionings, ideals, and disillusionments. We expect not only to engage the students' intelligence but also to bring their emotions and imagination into play. Many of the poems and stories dramatize concerns that involve and engage young readers: probing tensions between the generations, searching for meaning in our lives, asserting independence from wrongful authority, searching for self-worth, challenging the barriers that prejudice erects in the path of self-realization, or trying to counteract the human capacity for violence.

LITERATURE FOR DISCUSSION AND WRITING   The after-selection apparatus in this book provides a rich range of stimuli for discussion and writing. The "Thinking About Connections" strand guides students to revealing juxtapositions. A final chapter devoted to writing about literature includes guidelines for journal writing, writing about a poem, writing about character, writing about theme, and comparing and contrasting related selections.

SPECIAL FEATURES   Our headnotes go beyond routine author biography to place a selection in the context of a historical dialectic and to dramatize an author's roots and commitments. In lieu of footnotes, these headnotes often include help with the author's language and range of allusion.

Acknowledgments

We owe a special debt to the students at the University of San Francisco, San Jose State University, and Santa Clara University who have kept alive our faith in the native intelligence, mother wit, and imagination of the current generation. We are grateful to the teachers in both four-year and two-year colleges who have shared with us their experiences, their doubts, and their enthusiasms.

We also wish to thank the following reviewers for their thoughtful comments: Janice Albert, Las Positas College; Linda Bensel-Meyers, University of Tennessee, Knoxville; Denise David, Niagara Community College; Marvin Diogenes, University of Arizona; Russell Durst, University of Cincinnati; Kenneth Fox, University of Iowa; John Hanes, Duquesne University; Mary Ann Latimer, California State University, Chico; Frances Leonard, West Los Angeles College; James C. McDonald, University of Southwestern Louisiana; Jeri Ohmart, California State University, Chico; Kathleen Shine Cain, Merrimack College; and William Smith, Western Washington University.

TO THE STUDENT

This book asks you to understand America by looking in the mirror of its imaginative literature. Since before the beginning of history, human beings have used poem, song, and story to leave a record of who they were and how they saw their world. Since before the formal founding of this nation, Americans have used the spoken and written word to give voice to feelings of love, pride, belonging, or isolation; to their hopes, fears, grievances, and aspirations. Today as in the past, people with the gift of language put their thoughts and feelings into words that can bring the past to life and illuminate the present.

The readings in this book are organized around major themes in the cultural history of this country. These themes are deeply rooted concerns, pervasive trends, or nagging preoccupations that have helped shape how we as Americans envision our country and ourselves. They have helped form our national identity; they are part of what it means to be an American today. Writers engaged with these themes dramatize the legacies, the promises, the choices, the traumas, and the liabilities that come with being American.

Here is a preview of the themes explored in the documents, speeches, poems, stories, and plays in this book:

1 NEW WORLD: The Promise of America

To millions here and abroad, America meant the promise of a new beginning. Those who formulated the goals and aspirations of the new nation meant to leave behind an oppressive past: the rigid class distinctions of old-world societies, the use of religion in the service of the state. They envisioned a new world where all were "created equal," with equal opportunities and equal rights. All were to be "free to profess and by argument to maintain, their opinions in matters of religion" (Thomas Jefferson). Later generations have judged this nation by how successfully it has translated its ideals into reality. Have they remained for too many an unkept promise?

2 NEW NATION: The One and the Many

From the beginning, America was a coming together of many nationalities to form a new nation. "Here is not a nation but a teeming nation of nations," said Walt Whitman, the poet of democracy. English, Irish, and Germans, followed by Italians, Czechs, Jews, Poles and others, made for a new ethnic and cultural mix. Mexicans came into the Union in the conquered territories of the Southwest, and Chinese were brought in as "coolie" labor in the West. Would the jostling mix of nationalities develop a shared identity? Would a new national character emerge from the diversity of backgrounds, traditions, and religions?

3 NATIVE AMERICANS: Reclaiming the Past

The white settlers spreading throughout North America did not move into "virgin territory." They drove back a native population of a million or more who were decimated by massacre, starvation, and disease. A remnant survived on the reservations, with their religion and rituals banned, their way of life destroyed. In recent years, Native American writers have begun to rewrite their history and "to celebrate the miracle of survival of those remaining Native people, religions, cultures, language, legal systems, medicine, and values" (Suzan Harjo). What was the culture of the Native Americans? What is the sense of identity of their descendants? How do they see their role in the larger culture today?

4 AMERICAN INDIVIDUALISM: A Different Drummer

American culture has glorified the self-reliant individual. Bred into Americans is the distrust of government and of institutions. ("That government is best which governs least," said the New England maverick Henry David Thoreau.) The American folk hero has been the lone rider, the self-made man, the nonconformist. The great names in American literature—Thoreau, Melville, Dickinson—are writers whose individual voice expresses a unique vision of the world. Is individuality being lost in a homogenized mass culture? Is the individualism of the frontier and pioneer days an anachronism in our modern world?

5 BEYOND OPTIMISM: The End of Innocence

Americans have a reputation for being optimists. They want to believe that people of good will can live together in peace, fight off famine, and defeat epidemics. They teach that honest effort pays, and they like to believe that private greed in the end serves the common good. Mark Twain, America's greatest humorist, was not the first to tell bitter truths at odds with the gospel of optimism. ("When you pick up a starving dog and make him prosperous, he will not bite you," he said. "That is the principal difference between a dog and a man.") Greed, lawlessness, and lynch justice; the loss of faith in the capitalist system during the Great Depression; genocidal totalitarian regimes—all these have sorely tested the optimistic American belief in the power of good. Is it still possible to believe in the "perfectibility" of humankind?

6 BLACK IDENTITY: Let My People Go

For many, slavery has been the fall from grace that brought sin into the American Eden. From the Civil War to the civil rights movement, the challenge to the nation has been to bring its professed ideals into harmony with its treatment of its oppressed and disenfranchised black minority. African American writers have generated a rich literature of protest against racism and of search for black pride. Alice Walker, author of *The Color Purple*, has said that her heritage as a black writer from the South was "a trust in humanity beyond our knowledge of evil" and "an abiding love of justice." What does it mean to be black in white America? What does it mean to be a black woman in a male-dominated culture?

7 CITYSCAPES: Contexts for Living

Boosters of the burgeoning American cities celebrated them as bastions of prosperity and of American economic might. American city architecture, with its towers of glass and steel, testified to the capacity of a modern technological civilization for monumental creative achievement. At the same time, however, artists and writers chronicled the other side of city life, looking into city faces "Tired of wishes,/Empty of dreams" (Carl Sandburg). Today, the decaying, violence-ridden cities are often the place where the American Dream turns into a nightmare. How does the urban environment shape the lives and outlook of Americans? Does the city have a future?

8 DESPERATE GLORY: War and Its Aftermath

War is the great unsolved problem of human civilization. What role has it played in the history and self-awareness of the American nation? The Revolutionary War and the Civil War, or War between the States, tested the new nation's visions of sovereignty and union. For many writers, the great later conflicts—from the war against Mexico through the two World Wars to the war in Vietnam—called into question their faith in humanity and their loyalty to the war machine. "There died a myriad/And of the best," said the American poet Ezra Pound after World War I, "for a botched civilization." What do the protests of writers and artists avail?

9 INNER QUEST: The Searching Self

"It's intellectual devastation/of everybody/to avoid emotional commitment," says the black poet Nikki Giovanni in her "Woman Poem." A persistent subtext in American literature has been the lack of emotional fulfillment—the failure of people to lead fulfilled lives in accordance with their inner needs. The "Unlighted Lamps" in the title of a short story by Sherwood Anderson are symbolic of a capacity for love and joy that has remained unused. In poem, story, and play, we see characters whose true selves have been repressed. What is at fault—a lingering Puritan suspicion of sin, the stifling effect of small-town respectability, loneliness in the faceless city, the emotional wasteland of suburbia? The disregard of a male-dominated patriarchal culture for the emotional needs of women? Does mainstream middle-class American culture render people unable to tap their feelings?

10 AMERICAN MOSAIC: Multicultural America

Recent decades have seen a mass influx of new Americans from culturally diverse backgrounds. Mexicans, Puerto Ricans, and Cubans have brought a Latin feeling to cities and neighborhoods. Chinese and Vietnamese immigrants have revitalized decaying downtowns. Immigrants from countries like the Philippines, India, and Pakistan are living in new immigrant ghettos. Are old mechanisms of assimilation and acculturation breaking down? How do the new Americans see themselves in relation to mainstream society?

11 INVISIBLE WALLS: The Untapped Potential

Americans pride themselves on their sympathy for the unfortunate. Recent years have seen a crusade to integrate the disabled and enable them to lead rewarding lives. Growing awareness or consciousness raising is helping to end the outgrouping of outsiders. Often we are asked to rethink what were once considered liabilities. At the same time, we are sometimes accused of encouraging people to think of themselves as victims. Is the right of people to a full life regardless of barriers or handicaps still part of the American credo?

12 REGAINED ROOTS: Encountering Nature

In the eighteenth century, European intellectuals saw in the untamed wilderness of the American continent an answer to congested, corrupt city civilization. Nature remained for many later writers a counterpoint to the triumph of a technology-driven, technocratic culture. The ecological movement of the twentieth century has fostered a renewed respect for our natural roots and a new cult of the outdoors as the antidote to urban sprawl, pollution, and nuclear accidents. How close to nature or how alienated from it are Americans today?

CONTENTS IN BRIEF

CONTENTS

Reading Multicultural Literature

I hear the sound I love, the sound of the human voice,
I hear all sounds running together, combined, fused or following,
Sounds of the city and sounds out of the city, sounds of the day and
night.

Walt Whitman

One day, some identifiable life form will come to Earth and ask: Who
are these people . . . these Black Americans? And we will proudly pre-
sent our songs, stories, plays, speeches, and poetry. We will proudly say:
We are the people who believe in the possibilities.

Nikki Giovanni

May God keep us
From single vision.
William Blake

Imaginative literature is like a mirror in which we recognize ourselves and our world. Poets, writers of fiction, and playwrights have a special gift for taking in what they see and hear. It is as if they had more wide open eyes and more alert ears than others. They are shrewd observers. At the same time, they have a special gift for putting into words thoughts and feelings that might be confused or inarticulate in our minds. They know the language of the emotions. They have words for our desires and hopes and fears. The mirror these writers hold up to life sees more than the hurried observer, and it probes beyond the polite or deliberately casual faces people present to others.

THE LITERATURE OF DIVERSITY

Writers of multicultural literature hold up the mirror to the diversity of the life around us. The people who make up this country were not all cast from the same mold. They include the descendants of Native Americans, white settlers, and African slaves. The ethnic and religious strands in our common heritage include Puritan English and Catholic Irish; German or Scandinavian Lutheran as well as Orthodox Jew; Spanish-speaking Americans of Mexican, Cuban, or Puerto Rican ancestry; and Asians with roots in the traditional cultures of China, Japan, and Vietnam. The big cities of this country have been strongholds of the "white ethnics," including Poles, Italians, and Lithuanians. Quakers, Buddhists, Mormons, Muslims, and Baptists have their own places of worship and their own ways of looking at the world.

The literature of America reflects the diversity and vitality of its people. At one time, reading American literature meant reading first of all the literature of New England—Nathaniel Hawthorne, Ralph Waldo Emerson, Herman Melville, Emily Dickinson, Henry David Thoreau. Slowly the established canon—the "approved" list of widely admired and taught books—broadened to reflect the true sweep of the American experience. In the twentieth century, Southern writers sharing a collective memory of slavery and a lost war helped change the geography of American literature. Southerners from William Faulkner and Flannery O'Connor to Alice Walker have long been among the heavyweights of American fiction. Writers close to the traditions and traumas of Jewish culture—Bernard Malamud, Arthur Miller, Saul Bellow—have played a major role in the literature of twentieth-century America.

Throughout our history, writers have asked: "What is an American?" Whatever the answer, it is no longer "white Anglo heterosexual male." Some of the giants of American literature—Walt Whitman, Tennessee Williams —have been gay. Lesbian poets like Adrienne Rich, Audre Lord, and Judy Grahn are widely read. Feminist critics have brought about the reappraisal or rediscovery of pioneering women writers from Kate Chopin and Charlotte Perkins Gilman to Edith Wharton. Today Native American, African American, Chinese American, and Spanish American (Hispanic or Latino) writers are among our best-selling authors.

In a country of diverse cultural traditions, imaginative literature plays a special humanizing role. Literature broadens our range of imaginative sympathy. A poem, a short story, or a play can take you beyond your own limited experience. It can help you imagine what it was like to be a plantation owner or a fugitive slave. It can make you imagine yourself a pioneer trekking across uncharted desert or a survivor of the death camps. It can help you imagine the world from a different point of view—that of a foreigner eyed suspiciously by the natives perhaps, or of a woman locked into a stifling marriage.

A poem or a story may ask you to walk in someone else's shoes. That experience can be uplifting or depressing. It may make you happy, or it may make you angry. It will be only natural if you relate better to some of the readings in this book better than to others. Together, however, they should leave you with a better understanding of what it means to be an American in today's world.

READING IMAGINATIVE LITERATURE

Literature is a mirror, but it is a special kind of mirror. It selects and shapes reality. The magic mirror of literature can make people seem taller or smaller than they are. It can uncover hidden ugliness, but it can also transform sorrow to make us find the beauty in suffering. In literature you see life not through the cold lens of a surveillance camera but through the eyes of a thinking, feeling human being. Each selection you read represents the vision of a creative individual.

The poems, the short stories, and the plays you will read in this book each represent a different kind, or genre, of imaginative literature. Poets, writers of fiction, and playwrights honor (and often bend or defy) different traditions and conventions. However, most of the writers you will encounter in this book illustrate three qualities—three gifts they share:

THE LOVE OF LANGUAGE For the writer of imaginative literature, language is not a throwaway item. Words are not just for immediate practical use and disposable thereafter. Language makes us human; it is the medium of our desires, fears, struggles, and aspirations. It is something to be cherished, to be appreciated, to be used with care and wonder. The words of great writers linger in our memory. "A blade of grass is the journey-work of the stars," says Walt Whitman. "Evil is the result of collaboration," says Stephen Crane. "Love / cracked me open / and I'm / alive to / tell the tale," says Denise Levertov.

THE POWER OF ATTENTION Imaginative writers have the gift of cutting through the blur and static of ordinary experience. They sift and sort out. They know how to bring something into focus so we can do it justice. They concentrate our attention on what matters. While we are listening to them, some part of life has a chance to become less confusing, more understandable.

THE SEARCH FOR PATTERN Imaginative writers often possess to a high degree the human instinct for shaping, for bringing order out of chaos. They search for pattern, structure, design. Style in its largest sense is the result of the creative human spirit leaving its imprint on formless raw reality. Pattern, design, or style in creative uses of language fills the same human need it fills in other areas of life. Nikki Giovanni says,

> Style has profound meaning to Black Americans. If we can't drive we will invent walks and the world will envy the dexterity of our feet. If we can't have ham we will boil chitterlings; if we are given rotten peaches we will make cobblers; if given scraps we will make quilts; take away our drums and we will clap our hands. We prove the human spirit will prevail.

RESPONDING TO A POEM

Let poetry be like a key
Opening a thousand doors.
Vicente Huidobro

Writers of imaginative literature use words as their tools, the way a painter uses colors and shapes. They use our common language, but they use more of it than we usually do, and they use it with more loving attention to the shapes and flavors and impact of words. Poets in particular make special, more intense use of our common language. The words they use seem richer in meaning. The images they present seem more vividly imprinted on our senses. In the constant flow of verbal communication that surrounds us, a poem marks off a message worth lingering over, worth remembering and thinking about.

The following is the best-known poem of a Mexican American poet who still uses the Spanish words she heard in her childhood when she talks about the scenes and people of her youth. The last line of the poem repeats in Spanish the preceding line about the "ship that will never dock"—that will never reach safe harbor. How is the statement the poem makes different from the kind of statement you might read in a report on bilingual education?

Lorna Dee Cervantes
Refugee Ship

Like wet cornstarch, I slide   *1*
past my grandmother's eyes. Bible
at her side, she removes her glasses.
The pudding thickens.
Mama raised me without language,   *5*

I'm orphaned from my Spanish name.
The words are foreign, stumbling
on my tongue. I see in the mirror
My reflection: bronzed skin, black hair.

I feel I am a captive   *10*
aboard the refugee ship.
The ship that will never dock.
El barco que nunca atraca.

Every poem is different and creates its own world of meaning. Nevertheless, most poems share features that you can come to recognize and that will help you "get into" a poem. What do most of the short poems that you will encounter have in common?

What meets the eye is that poems are laid out differently on the page. The lines of a poem are usually shorter than those of ordinary prose. They are set off one from the other, as if we are expected to dwell on them more, going on to the next only after the preceding one has sunk in. (This does not mean, however, that they are cut off like slices of cheese. The poet may pull us from one line into the other, as with "Bible / at her side" or "stumbling / on my tongue.") Lines, as in this poem, may be grouped together in sets of perhaps four or five, called **stanzas.** Each separate stanza invites you to dwell on it, to take it in as a whole. The poet expects you to pay attention. She expects you to stay with the poem longer and remember it longer than you would a routine memo or newspaper article.

When you take the time to pay attention to what the poet says, you will take in clues like the following to the poem's meaning or intention:

FOCUS   The poet brings something into focus. Everyday life is a series of miscellaneous, often disjointed impressions. A poet may ask you to focus on a situation, a person, an issue. You will then be able to concentrate, to do justice to one thing. The speaker in this poem sees her grandmother— and then thinks of her mother. Something happened in the passage from one generation to the other. The contrast between the two makes her ponder who or what she is. This question is at the heart of the poem.

IMAGE   The poet takes you into a world of concrete images. Whatever thoughts and feelings the poem brings into play are anchored to things you can visualize: the grandmother's Bible and glasses; the grandchild's "bronzed skin" and "black hair" in the mirror. The poem is not just going to tell you about problems of identity in general terms, the way a sociologist or psychologist would. It acts out what it talks about; it translates it into what you can see or hear. To take in the meaning of the poem, you have to enter into the experience of the speaker in the poem. A poem will typically give you things to see, hear, or feel.

FIGURATIVE LANGUAGE   Much of the time a poet uses imaginative rather than **literal language.** We are literally orphaned when we lose our parents. How can the poet be orphaned from her Spanish name? She is not literally orphaned, but she is cut off from something as important as a parent. She is cut off from the language and culture of her Mexican ancestors. Like many immigrant parents, her mother decided to raise her child "without language"—that is, without the Spanish language that to the parent might have seemed a handicap for the child in school and in the world of work. The implied *like* or *as* or *as if* is the key to figurative language— language that uses imaginative comparisons to help the poet put thoughts and feelings into words. (When the *like* or *as if* is spelled out, we call the figurative expression a **simile**—the poet slides past the grandmother's eyes "*like* wet cornstarch." When the *like* or *as if* is only implied, we call the figurative expression a **metaphor**—the Spanish words, having become foreign, are "stumbling" on her tongue as if they were clumsy intruders.)

SYMBOL The poet knows the power of symbols. The symbol that gives the poem its name is the refugee ship. Refugee ships took the boat people of Vietnam to places like Hong Kong—where they were not wanted and from where many were sent back to the country they had tried to escape. A ship with Jewish refugees from Nazi Germany was turned back when it reached New York Harbor. The refugee ship here becomes a powerful symbol of the fate of millions in our modern world. These are people who have left behind the culture they were born into but who have never become fully integrated into the societies in which they hoped to forge a new identity. They have become the alien, the "other."

PATTERN The poem has a shape; it starts somewhere and finishes somewhere else. We enter the poem at one point and come out at another. This poem is given shape and direction by the succession of three generations. This sequence is an archetypal pattern that is deeply ingrained in our shared human experience. The poem starts with the image of the grandmother, with her bible and cornstarch pudding. She seems to stand for the traditional ways—the religion and language of the past. Why does the grandchild "slide past" the grandmother's eyes instead of talking to her? The mother cut the connection with tradition and the old-country language. The child representing the third generation is left stranded. Her dark skin and hair make her look like her ancestors. But, as with many second-generation children of immigrants, her command of the old-country language and her knowledge of old-country ways are fading.

THEME The theme of a poem is the answer that the poem as a whole seems to give to the question it asks or to the issues it raises in the reader's mind. This poem seems pervaded by a sense of loss. The speaker feels caught between two worlds, fully belonging to neither. This sense of loss could help explain why many Americans in recent years set out in search of their roots, trying to rediscover a lost heritage.

Many readers find that the full meaning of a poem unfolds for them on second or third reading. They find layers of meaning in language rich in images, metaphors, and symbols. They begin to see a pattern emerge that may lead them from an open question to a satisfying close. However, reading a poem is not a one-way communication from poet to reader. Much depends on what you as the reader bring to the poem. Can you find a personal connection? For instance, does the idea of contradictory influences on your life mean anything to you? Have you ever felt pushed in different directions? Have you ever felt a sense of loss—a lost heritage, lost traditions, lost opportunities? Have you ever puzzled about the connection between how you look and who you really are? What do you know or care about refugees? (Could you say, as one student reader said, that the speaker in the poem "reminds me of the girl I see in the mirror every day"?)

Comparing your own personal reading with those of others can help you respond more fully to a poem that may at first be puzzling. Be sure to hear a poem read aloud, and volunteer to read a poem to a group.

POETIC FORM Traditionally, poems rhymed and had a strong regular beat, or **meter.** Most modern poems, like "Refugee Ship," do without rhyme and meter. What is the difference? What are the pros and cons of traditional form and of the "open form" preferred by many modern poets? The following short poem by a poet of the Harlem Renaissance of the thirties and forties uses conventional end rhyme: *seed/creed; rain/again.* It has the basic **iambic** beat of much traditional English poetry—stress on each second syllable: teDUM-teDUM- teDUM (or DeTROIT-DeTROIT-DeTROIT).

What pleases the ear about the use of traditional rhyme and meter in this poem? At the same time, do they make the poem seem more finished, more packaged, more "artificial?" Does the modern form of the Cervantes poem seem more open-ended? Does it appeal to our modern dislike of formal constraints? (Be sure you hear both poems read out loud.)

Countee Cullen
For My Grandmother

This lovely flower fell to seed;   *1*
Work gently sun and rain.
She held it as her dying creed
That she would grow again.

The iambic beat (This LOVEly FLOWer FELL to SEED) is by far the most common meter in traditional English poetry. It is most often used in a five-beat line, or iambic pentameter (named after the Greek word for five, also used in *pentagon*). Perfectly regular iambic pentameter has five segments, or **feet,** of two syllables each. Other traditional meters are the **trochaic** (BOSton—BOSton—BOSton), the **dactylic** (ALbany—ALbany—ALbany) and the **anapestic** meter (New RoCHELLE—New RoCHELLE—New RoCHELLE).

Segments, or feet, employing these alternate beats are most often used to introduce variations or counterrhythms into iambic verse. In the following opening lines from a poem by Edna St. Vincent Millay, the second line is regular iambic pentameter. However, in the first line the very first word (PITy) reverses the iambic pattern. This trochaic reversal emphasizes a key word repeated several times later in the poem.

PITy me NOT beCAUSE the LIGHT of DAY
at CLOSE of DAY no LONger WALKS the SKY

A later line of the poem has three such trochaic feet, with one of them serving to highlight the word *love*—the central word of the poem.

THIS have I KNOWN ALways: LOVE is no MORE
than the wide blossom that the wind assails

RESPONDING TO A SHORT STORY

Short stories are not about issues; they are about people in the flush of
actual living.

Gary Soto

The short story is the most native kind, or **genre,** of American literature. The typical short story puts one or more characters in a setting and sets
them in motion. Something happens—whether a major confrontation or a
subtle change in attitude. Two or more characters may come into conflict. A
challenge may arise and be met or fail to be met. A segment of human life is
played out for us as the readers—for us to enter into, contemplate, and
interpret. The reader's inborn curiosity about people—how they talk, how
they act, how they think—has provided large audiences for American storytellers from Mark Twain and Ernest Hemingway to Flannery O'Connor and
Alice Walker.

There is no formula for a successful story. Every story creates its own
world. However, some familiar elements go into the making of most stories
you will read. The following is a **short short**—an exceptionally *short* short
story. It nevertheless illustrates many features that give readers clues to the
meaning or intention of a story. What is the story about? Why have many
readers found it worth reading? How do you react to it?

Mary Robison
Yours

Allison struggled away from her white Renault, limping with the   *1*
weight of the last of the pumpkins. She found Clark in the twilight on
the twig-and-leaf-littered porch behind the house.

He wore a wool shawl. He was moving up and back in a padded
glider, pushed by the ball of his slippered foot.

Allison lowered a big pumpkin, let it rest on the wide floorboards.

Clark was much older—seventy-eight to Allison's thirty-five. They
were married. They were both quite tall and looked something alike in
their facial features. Allison wore a natural-hair wig. It was a thick blond
hood around her face. She was dressed in bright-dyed denims today.
She wore durable clothes, usually, for she volunteered afternoons at a
children's day-care center.

She put one of the smaller pumpkins on Clark's long lap. "Now,   *5*
nothing surreal," she told him. "Carve just a *regular* face. These are for
kids."

In the foyer, on the Hepplewhite desk, Allison found the maid's
chore list with its cross-offs, which included Clark's supper. Allison
went quickly through the day's mail: a garish coupon packet, a bill from

Jamestown Liquors, November's pay-TV program guide, and the worst thing, the funniest, an already opened, extremely unkind letter from Clark's relations up North. "You're an old fool," Allison read, and, "You're being cruelly deceived." There was a gift check for Clark enclosed, but it was uncashable, signed, as it was, "Jesus H. Christ."

Late, late into this night, Allison and Clark gutted and carved the pumpkins together, at an old table set on the back porch, over newspaper after soggy newspaper, with paring knives and with spoons and with a Swiss Army knife Clark used for exact shaping of tooth and eye and nostril. Clark had been a doctor, an internist, but also a Sunday watercolorist. His four pumpkins were expressive and artful. Their carved features were suited to the sizes and shapes of the pumpkins. Two looked ferocious and jagged. One registered surprise. The last was serene and beaming.

Allison's four faces were less deftly drawn, with slits and areas of distortion. She had cut triangles for noses and eyes. The mouths she had made were just wedges—two turned up and two turned down.

By one in the morning they were finished. Clark, who had bent his long torso forward to work, moved back over to the glider and look out sleepily at nothing. All the lights were out across the ravine.

Clark stayed. For the season and time, the Virginia night was warm. *10* Most leaves had been blown away already, and the trees stood unbothered. The moon was round above them.

Allison cleaned up the mess.

"Your jack-o'-lanterns are much, much better than mine," Clark said to her.

"Like hell," Allison said.

"Look at me," Clark said, and Allison did.

She was holding a squishy bundle of newspapers. The papers reeked *15* sweetly with the smell of pumpkin guts.

"Yours are *far* better," he said.

"You're wrong. You'll see when they're lit," Allison said.

She went inside, came back with yellow vigil candles. It took her a while to get each candle settled, and then to line up the results in a row on the porch railing. She went along and lit each candle and fixed the pumpkin lids over the little flames.

"See?" she said.

They sat together a moment and looked at the orange faces. *20*

"We're exhausted. It's good night time," Allison said. "Don't blow out the candles. I'll put in new ones tomorrow."

That night, in their bedroom, a few weeks earlier in her life than had been predicted, Allison began to die. "Don't look at me if my wig comes off," she told Clark. "Please."

Her pulse cords were fluttering under his fingers. She raised her knees and kicked away the comforter. She said something to Clark about the garage being locked.

At the telephone, Clark had a clear view out back and down to the porch. He wanted to get drunk with his wife once more. He wanted to tell her, from the greater perspective he had, that to own only a little talent, like his, was an awful, plaguing thing; that being only a little special meant you expected too much, most of the time, and liked yourself too little. He wanted to assure her that she had missed nothing.

He was speaking into the phone now. He watched the jack-o'- 25 lanterns. The jack-o'-lanterns watched him.

To make the most of a story, you may want to keep in mind questions like the following:

SETTING   Where are we? A story creates its own setting in place and time. Often the setting matters. The people in Robison's story do not live in a highrise. They live somewhere where people can still sit on a porch that is littered with twigs and leaves from the surrounding trees. They live somewhere where people still carve pumpkins into jack-o'-lanterns for Halloween. They can see the moon at night. They live close to a ravine. They are closer to nature than most urban and suburban Americans.

CHARACTER   Who are the people? The characters in a story have a history. They have agendas; they may have ties with other people. All of these can help us understand what the characters say and do. The people in this story are married. The husband is old and retired; he is an artist of sorts. The woman is much younger. She seems to be gone much of the day, working as a volunteer at a day-care center. We have early hints of her illness; she wears a wig, since she apparently has lost her hair after chemotherapy. Relatives disapprove of the May-December relationship, saying nasty things in their letters.

PLOT   What happens? Most stories have a story line: They create a situation that carries with it the potential for conflict or action. This story heads for the wife's death, which occurs earlier than expected. But before it happens, the couple share a loving, caring experience that the writer recreates for us in rich detail. In spite of the hateful relatives, in spite of impending doom, the two enjoy the yearly ritual of carving the pumpkins and setting them up for others to see and enjoy.

POINT OF VIEW   Who is telling the story? Through whose eyes do we see what happens? Much writing is autobiography, or thinly veiled autobiography. The storyteller, or narrator, may be at the center of the story, speaking in the first person (*I, my, myself*) about his or her own experiences, challenges, or traumas. Or the "I" of the story may be in the story as an observer of what the main characters do. In "Yours," the point of view is more objective. The writer tells us about other people, using the third person (*he, she, they*). The story may be based on something the writer has observed or experienced, but she stays out of the story. However, the narrator's attitude toward the couple guides much of our reaction to what we read. She is sympathetic toward the two. (How can you tell? Would you agree that the story gives short shrift to the spiteful relatives?)

SYMBOL   What in the story has a special significance? What acquires a symbolic meaning beyond its practical or prosaic role in the story? The pumpkins loom large in "Yours." They are in the first sentence as well as in the last. In the words of one student reader, they are "a last sweet harvest." The newspapers "reeked sweetly with the smell of pumpkin guts." The pumpkins, like life or people, can be made to look mean and threatening or happy and relaxed. They become a symbol of the richness and potential of life. At the very end of the story, the bereaved husband is still watching the carved pumpkins, and they are watching him.

THEME   What does the story make you think? As with a poem or a play, the theme is the answer the story as a whole seems to give to the question or questions it raises. This story raises questions about aging and death. How are we going to deal with them? The young woman has accepted the age of the person she loves. The old man accepts her illness without murmuring. They both make the best of the time they have together. Perhaps the theme of the story is that we should cherish those we love in spite of encroaching age and impending death. We face a **paradox** when both sides of a contradiction turn out to be each in its own way true. Paradoxically, in this story, life is threatened but also precious.

STYLE   How is the story told? For instance, does it play up or play down emotion? In this story, we hear no passionate lamentation or eloquent tributes to the dead. The sad ending is told in understated, short sentences:

"It's good night time."

"Don't look at me if my wig comes off."

She said something to Clark about the garage being locked.

He was speaking into the phone now.

He watched the jack-o'lanterns.

The jack-o'lanterns watched him.

The story is written in the modern tradition of **understatement,** presenting faithfully what is there without a great show of feeling. The readers can supply the appropriate emotions. Modern writers have generally been suspicious of grand gestures and emotional display, which can too easily be faked. They have been suspicious of sentimentality, which allows people to feel sorry for themselves and to bask in a warm glow of self-approving emotions. The understated style is in keeping with the prevailing sense of **irony** in the story. Irony makes us respond with a wry smile when events go counter to our ordinary superficial assumptions. In our unthinking moments, we expect old people to die first. Ironically, people often die young. In this story, as often in real life, a young person dies, upsetting our smug assumptions but also making us think, "I should have known."

Readers vary in how much they allow themselves to be drawn into a story. If you have recently had to come to terms with someone's death, with the threat of serious illness, or with the precariousness of love, you may be more open to what this story has to say than would others. But a writer like Robison has the power to draw us into her story on a what-if basis. What if we were to fall in love with someone separated from us by age, ethnic background, status, or wealth? (Would we listen to relatives who call us fools?) What if a person we love develops a serious illness? (Would we weep and lament? Would we quarrel with fate?)

To get the most out of your reading, try to get into the spirit of a story. Give it the benefit of the doubt. At times we all fight a story because something about it seems slanted or unreal or wrongheaded. We may find ourselves saying in the middle of a story: "No, that's not the way it is at all!" However, it is usually worth looking for what other readers saw in the story and found rewarding. This does not mean that you have to abdicate your right to approve or disapprove. Often a great story leaves us with unanswered questions, making us weigh the pros and cons. You owe it to the writer to read the story well enough to know what you are questioning and why.

RESPONDING TO A PLAY

When you watch a play, it is as if someone else had read a story for you and brought it to life. Directors, actors, costumers, and designers take the bare bones of a script and flesh it out, creating the illusion of real-life action. The magic of the stage for a few hours makes you share in other lives. It tests your ability to enter imaginatively into the experience of others. When you read a play instead of watching it in the theater, you are doing the job of director, actor, and designer, bringing the play to life in the theater of the mind.

Like a story, drama puts characters in a setting, and we watch a chain of events unfold as the playwright sets the characters in motion. What is the audience expected to get out of the following opening passage of a play? What are you as a responsive reader meant to take in? The excerpt is from *The Dance and the Railroad* by the Chinese American playwright David Henry Whang. We are on a mountaintop near the transcontinental railroad being constructed by Chinese "coolie" laborers. One of these laborers, his hair in the traditional pigtail, is practicing the dance steps of traditional Chinese opera, while another is watching him in hiding but finally approaches cautiously.

David Henry Hwang
The Dance and the Railroad

Scene 1

A mountaintop. LONE *is practicing opera steps. He swings his pigtail around like a fan.* MA *enters, cautiously, watches from a hidden spot.* MA *approaches* LONE.

LONE: So, there are insects hiding in the bushes.
MA: Hey, listen, we haven't met, but—
LONE: I don't spend time with insects.

> (LONE *whips his hair into* MA's *face;* MA *backs off;* LONE *pursues him, swiping at* MA *with his hair*)

MA: What the—? Cut it out!

> (MA *pushes* LONE *away*)

LONE: Don't push me.
MA: What was that for?
LONE: Don't ever push me again.
MA: You mess like that, you're gonna get pushed.
LONE: Don't push me.
MA: You started it. I just wanted to watch.
LONE: You "just wanted to watch." Did you ask my permission?
MA: What?
LONE: Did you?
MA: C'mon.
LONE: You can't expect to get in for free.
MA: Listen. I got some stuff you'll wanna hear.
LONE: You think so?
MA: Yeah. Some advice.
LONE: Advice? How old are you, anyway?
MA: Eighteen.
LONE: A child.
MA: Yeah. Right. A child. But listen—
LONE: A child who tries to advise a grown man—
MA: Listen, you got this kind of attitude.
LONE: —is a child who will never grow up.
MA: You know, the ChinaMen down at camp, they can't stand it.
LONE: Oh?
MA: Yeah. You gotta watch yourself. You know what they say? They call you "Prince of the Mountain." Like you're too good to spend time with them.
LONE: Perceptive of them.
MA: After all, you never sing songs, never tell stories. They say you act like your spit is too clean for them, and they got ways to fix that.

LONE: Is that so?

MA: Like they're gonna bury you in the shit buckets, so you'll have more to clean than your nails.

LONE: But I don't shit.

MA: Or they're gonna cut out your tongue, since you never speak to them.

LONE: There's no one here worth talking to.

MA: Cut it out, Lone. Look, I'm trying to help you, all right? I got a solution.

LONE: So young yet so clever.

MA: That stuff you're doing—it's beautiful. Why don't you do it for the guys at camp? Help us celebrate?

LONE: What will "this stuff" help celebrate?

MA: C'mon. The strike, of course. Guys on a railroad gang, we gotta stick together, you know.

LONE: This is something to celebrate?

MA: Yeah. Yesterday, the weak-kneed ChinaMen, they were running around like chickens without a head: "The white devils are sending their soldiers! Shoot us all!" But now, look—day four, see? Still in one piece. Those soldiers—we've never seen a gun or a bullet.

LONE: So you're all warrior-spirits, huh?

MA: They're scared of us, Lone—that's what it means.

LONE: I appreciate your advice. Tell you what—you go down—

MA: Yeah?

LONE: Down to the camp—

MA: Okay.

LONE: To where the men are—

MA: Yeah?

LONE: Sit there—

MA: Yeah?

LONE: And wait for me.

MA: Okay. (*Pause*) That's it? What do you think I am?

LONE: I think you're an insect interrupting my practice. So fly away. Go home.

What would the ideal reader make of this passage? How is reading it different from reading a short story or nonfiction prose?

Thinking about the following features of drama may help you make sense of a play:

DIALOGUE Although there may at times be violent action on the stage, the truth is that plays are mostly talk. We have to listen more attentively than usual to what the characters are saying. They are the ones explaining who and what they are; they create for us the world in which they live. The basic medium of the stage is **dialogue,** alerting us to what is at stake as we listen to characters share information, trade off challenges, or reveal their plans and motives. (When a single character holds forth at length, dialogue turns into a **monologue**.) In this opening scene, there is some pushing and shoving, but what is really happening is talk setting the scene and bringing key issues into focus.

CHARACTER   The action in a play proceeds in large part from the characters—their history, their needs and wants, their agendas. Without the benefit of the lengthy explanations and commentaries furnished by a writer of fiction, we need to listen to them attentively, especially when they are speaking as if to themselves (**soliloquies**) or making remarks for the benefit of the audience (**asides**). Early in the play especially, we listen for clues to what kind of people they are and what they might do. For instance, both of the characters in this sample scene seem to be proud people who don't like to "get pushed." Lone can be very insulting, calling the secret watcher an insect. Ma seems to have more feelings of solidarity with his fellow workers. He is trying to head off an ugly confrontation between Lone and the other workers, and he is trying to make Lone join the other workers in their defiance of their white overseers.

CONFLICT   Conflict is at the heart of drama. Events take a dramatic turn when opposites clash or when dream and reality meet. We already see the seeds of conflict in this short conversation between the two characters. There is a latent conflict between the artist—a perfectionist in his demanding calling—and the populace. Lone seems to be a loner, with a haughty superior attitude toward his fellow laborers. These seem ready to retaliate for his insolence, threatening great bodily harm. At the same time, the Chinese railroad workers are on strike against the "white devils" exploiting their labor.

PLOT   How are the conflicts going to be resolved? Unresolved problems or unmet challenges create suspense. The plot of a play may slowly bring a conflict to a boil until the play reaches a high point, or **climax.** There may be a turning point where good fortune abruptly ends or a key player makes a momentous decision. However, many modern playwrights are suspicious of gratuitous plot effects—a rich uncle dies at the right moment, or a skinflint employer has a miraculous change of heart.

STYLE   Audiences watching Shakespeare's *Romeo and Juliet* or *Macbeth* expect the characters to talk about love or ambition in an elevated formal style. ("O she doth teach the torches to burn bright.") Even so, Shakespeare was a master at playing off the solemn formal language of high tragic moments against the irreverent and often coarse talk of comic interludes. Much modern drama takes the audience close to ordinary reality by having the characters talk everyday language, without embellishment. ("You mess like that, you're gonna get pushed.") Apart from the use of language in a play, the playwright may aim at a realistic or documentary effect, making us think,

"This is how it was," or "This is how it is." But the writer may also expose and heighten weakness or folly, holding them up to ridicule. Luis Valdez, in *Los Vendidos,* is writing **satire,** using humor as a weapon against hypocrisy.

Like modern imaginative literature generally, much modern drama is experimental, defying conventions. Therefore you should not be surprised when you encounter a poem, story, or play that does not fit the descriptions you have just read. In reading a play, you may find that nothing really happens, or that the characters seem to be talking nonsense, or that they take turns making long speeches at the audience. This does not mean that all our usual critical terms or literary categories will prove irrelevant. The meaningless chatter may symbolize the emptiness of much social intercourse. The characters presenting long monologues may merely be taking the possibilities of self-revelation to extreme lengths. Their presentations together may explore dimensions of a common theme.

1

New World:
The Promise
of America

Haply the swords I know may indeed be turned to reaping tools.
Walt Whitman

Reconciling our high-minded rhetoric as a nation with our actual behavior as citizens continues to be the pivotal issue in the two-hundred-year-old argument over our identity as a nation and the meaning of democracy.
Wesley Brown and Amy Ling

I think that between the Negroes of the South and the women at the North all talking about rights, the white men will be in a fix pretty soon.
Sojourner Truth

LITERATURE IN CONTEXT

Scholars call "national narratives" those works of literature that shape a people's sense of identity as a nation. Throughout history, nations have had poets and prophets that made them envision a shared destiny. Three thousand years ago, Homer's *Iliad* did more than tell the story of the Trojan war, when the Greeks assembled a fleet of "a thousand ships" and traveled across the sea to lay siege to the fabled trading city of Troy. Homer's epic, a poem commemorating victories and defeats of a ten-year war, gave the splintered, feuding Greek tribes a sense of common purpose. Four hundred years ago, Shakespeare's theater did the same for the English nation state emerging from an era of dynastic quarrels and civil war. His history plays did not just stage a bloody pageant of loyalty and treachery, of high hopes and astonishing reversals of fortune. His plays acted out the ritual of a strong leader—who would

17

bring peace and prosperity—emerging from centuries of civil war that pitted "brother against brother, self against self."

What were the documents that helped give the new American nation its sense of identity and its sense of destiny? Our early national documents are not heroic narratives celebrating the deeds of great men on magnificent horses. They are political documents like Thomas Jefferson's revolutionary *Declaration of Independence.* Jefferson wrote at a time when the new ideology of the Enlightenment was calling the "divine right" of kings into question. It challenged the privileges of a hereditary aristocracy. No longer would the many bow and scrape while the pampered few squandered the fruits of other people's labor. Jefferson's manifesto asserted that God had not created masters and servants, aristocrats and commoners, or master races and lesser breeds. All had been "created equal." All were entitled to human dignity.

The promise of a land where people could make a new start without the crushing inequalities of the feudal societies of Europe and Asia made America a beacon of hope around the world. For millions everywhere, America became the land of promise. It became the *goldene medinah,* the distant golden shore. The religious dissenters that came here to escape persecution were only the first boat people making it to these shores. Millions of Irish left a land blighted by potato disease and British landlords. To come here, Russian Jews defied first the czar's police and later Soviet apparatchiks. Mexicans defied the Immigration Service. Refugees from failed revolutions and lost wars found their way past restrictive immigration laws. One refugee from Hitler's Europe called "to start all over again" the most American of all American expressions.

Throughout American history, the promise of equality before the law and in the eyes of God has been invoked by groups denied their place in the sun. Harriet Beecher Stowe's novel *Uncle Tom's Cabin,* which was read by millions around the world, asserted that the African slaves who were brought to this country in chains were our sisters and brothers. Therefore slavery was an abomination in the sight of God. Early feminists insisted that the promise of equal rights and human dignity for all was meaningless without equal rights for women. Is it true that for many Americans the promise of America has remained an unkept promise?

TO THE WESTERN WORLD
Louis Simpson

Blurred by the hate and favor of the interested parties,
his picture shifts and changes in recorded history.
Friedrich Schiller

> *The Italian adventurer Christopher Columbus left the seaport of Palos in Spain in 1492 with three caravels, or timbered three-masted sailing ships, to cross the uncharted western ocean. The voyage he undertook turned out to be one of the most momentous in human history. Columbus had lobbied Queen Isabella of Spain for years to persuade her to sponsor and fund a project testing the theories of the new science and the new astronomy. If the earth was round and not flat, travelers from Europe should theoretically be able to reach the ancient civilizations of China and India not merely by going east, following the interminable traditional land routes or navigating around the southern tip of Africa. They should be able to reach the East by going west across the uncharted ocean.*
>
> *Columbus had no way of knowing that the land he reached after a grueling voyage with a near-mutinous crew was a huge unknown continent barring the way to the west. He was still thousands of miles from the fabled "Cathay" (or China) of the following poem or from the India rich in jewels and spices that were his supposed destinations. In fact he had reached an island in the Gulf of Mexico, the "Mexique Bay" of the poem.*
>
> *Columbus' achievement has been seen through a multifaceted prism of conflicting interpretations. He was long celebrated as the discoverer of the New World, bringing to it the blessings of Christian civilization. He has more recently been seen as the symbol of genocide, leading the way for the Spaniards who in their greed for gold enslaved and massacred whole populations. He was an unwitting player in a great ecological catastrophe that saw millions of people dying from epidemics caused by the white man's diseases—smallpox, tuberculosis—against which the native populations of America had no immunity.*
>
> *What is the perspective on the voyage of Columbus in the following poem by a twentieth-century American poet?*

A siren sang, and Europe turned away   1
From the high castle and the shepherd's crook.
Three caravels went sailing to Cathay
On the strange ocean, and the captains shook
Their banners out across the Mexique Bay.   5

And in our early days we did the same.
Remembering our fathers in their wreck
We crossed the sea from Palos where they came

And saw, enormous to the little deck,
A shore in silence waiting for a name.   *10*

The treasures of Cathay were never found.
In this America, this wilderness
Where the ax echoes with a lonely sound,
The generations labor to possess
And grave by grave we civilize the ground.   *15*

The Responsive Reader

1. Why is the "shepherd's crook" or shepherd's staff in this poem a symbol
   of the church authority the early Americans left behind in the Old
   World? What is the other symbol of the Old World in this poem?
   What for the poet is a symbol of the civilization the colonists built in
   America?
2. The poet thinks of the voyagers that came with Columbus as the
   prototype of later travelers. ("And in our early days we did the same.")
   What is the essential parallel? How well does the parallel hold?
3. Why or how did the lure of the unknown turn out to be a "siren
   song?" What is the basic contrast in this poem between expectation
   and reality?

Thinking, Talking, Writing

4. In recent years, the concept of civilization, and especially of Western
   civilization, has come in for much debate and revision. For you, what
   ideas and associations cluster around the term *civilization?* Why or how
   has it become controversial?

FIVE AZTEC POEMS
Stephen Berg

The white invaders obliterated most of the art and oral traditions of the native peoples of the Americas. The conquistadores razed the temples and melted down the sacred objects for gold. The destruction of native life and culture has made it difficult for us to hear the authentic voices of the conquered. Sympathetic early accounts of the history of the conquered nations of the South were written by scribes steeped in the world view of the Catholic church. Famous speeches by native chiefs in the North that American students used to read in schoolbooks were heavily edited by translators (if not simply made up by the whites who first printed them). The Aztecs of Mexico and the Maya of Guatemala still speak to us through the ruins of their temples and the remnants of their art that escaped destruction at the hands of the European conquerors. However, what their sculptures and hieroglyphics tell us about their religious rituals, their social structure, and their ways of waging war is debated by archeologists. How much is myth or legend? How much is a depiction of everyday reality?

The following is a modern poet's attempt at recreating imaginatively poems that the Aztecs knew before the arrival of the Spaniards.

1

now my friends   1
listen
the dream I am singing
is
each spring life   5
in the corn
puts on a collar of rare stones

2

my soul fills to the brim with what I say
Oh friends
I am going to let my heart roam the earth   10
looking for peace
looking for good luck
no one is born twice

3

Oh nothing will cut down the flower of war
there it is on the edges of the river   15
here it is opening its petals

flower of the tiger flower of the shield
dust rises over the bells

4

until today my heart was happy
I hear this song I see a flower   20
if only they would never wither

5

we disappear
eagles tigers
nothing in the gold
nothing in the emeralds   25
nothing in the feathers
nothing in the word

The Responsive Reader

1. Interpret the metaphors for life and death and war in these poems.
   Which seem unusual? How are they different from what you might
   expect?
2. What details help the poet evoke the New World setting and the pre-
   Columbian past? How successful are these poems in helping you imagine the feelings and attitudes of a different time and place?

Thinking, Talking, Writing

3. How would you sum up the attitude toward life in these poems? What
   thoughts or feelings here seem "universal?" Do any of them sound
   more European than Native American to you?

Collaborative Projects

4. Do you have access to pictures or slides of pre-Columbian—Aztec,
   Maya, Inca—architecture and art? Working with a group, you may
   want to help assemble a slide show or other presentation exploring
   what the surviving structures and artifacts tell us about these early
   American civilizations.

TO THE MEMORY OF MY FATHER

Anne Bradstreet

The spring is a lively emblem of the resurrection. After a long winter, we see the leafless trees and dry stocks at the approach of the sun resume their former vigor and beauty . . . so shall it be at that great day when the sun of righteousness shall appear. Those dry bones shall arise in far more glory than that which they lost at their creation.

Anne Bradstreet

Anne Bradstreet is one of America's earliest poets. Early colonial Americans took religion more seriously than many do today. The devout spent much time in worship and prayer, and their diaries chronicle their experiences with the workings of divine goodness and the deceitfulness of Satan. They saw the hand of God and the wiles of the devil in everyday events. They had an intense anguished consciousness of sin—what the author of one colonial autobiography called the "sense of my wickedness." Sermons like Jonathan Edwards' "Sinners in the Hands of an Angry God" made them picture a wrathful God dropping sinners into the fires of hell like odious vermin.

The earliest communities in New England were established by Puritans— radical Protestants who saw it as their mission to cleanse the Christian faith of the pomp and ritual of other churches. In England they had been dissenters from the Anglican state church—the Church of England—a "middle way" between the Roman Catholic church and the extreme Protestant sects. Anglicans had rejected the Pope's authority but kept much of the traditional ritual and a many-layered church hierarchy, with an archbishop and bishops. At the other pole of the religious spectrum were dissident sects like the Quakers, considered too radical and persecuted even by the Puritans. The Quakers took the Protestant rejection of traditional institutions and priestly authority a step further. They subscribed to the Lutheran tenet that personal faith alone was sufficient for salvation. They met not in splendid churches but in plain meeting houses. They did not have a minister preach a prepared sermon from the pulpit but kept silent till the spirit moved a member of the congregation to speak. Scandalizing their contemporaries, they broke with the patriarchal tradition by allowing women to preach.

America eventually became a sanctuary for many sects and denominations. Anne Bradstreet represents the central Puritan tradition that did much to shape the American national consciousness. The Puritans followed the lead of Calvin, who had developed the theory of "election"—the belief that God alone chooses regardless of our own puny human efforts who is to be saved and who is to be damned. As Bradstreet says, God "chooses when and where and whom he pleases." Nevertheless, we should walk in "fear and trembling" lest we "through unbelief fall short of a promise."

One of thy founders him, New England, know,   *1*
Who stayed° thy feeble sides when thou wast low   *supported*
Who spent his state°, his strength, and years with care   *wealth*
That after-comers in them might have share.
True patriot of this little commonweal—   *5*
Who is't can tax thee ought° but for thy zeal? *blame you for anything*
Truth's friend thou wert, to errors still a foe,
Which caused apostates° to malign thee so.   *traitors to faith*
Thy love to true religion ever shall shine.
My father's God—be God of me and mine.   *10*
Upon the earth he did not build his nest
But as a pilgrim what he had a possessed.
High thoughts he gave no harbor in his heart,
Nor honors puffed° him when he had a part—   *went to his head*
Those titles he loathed which some too much do love,   *15*
For truly his ambition lay above. . . .
No wonder it was, low things never much did move°   *tempt him*
For he a mansion had prepared above,
For which he sighed and prayed and longed full sore° *very badly*
He might be clothed upon for evermore—   *20*
Oft spoke of death, and with a smiling cheer
He did exult his end was drawing near.
Now fully ripe, as shock of wheat that's grown,
Death like a sickle has him fully mown
And in celestial barn has housed him high,   *25*
Were storms nor showers nor ought can damnify.°   *do damage*

The Responsive Reader

1. To the Puritan world view, life on earth was a battle between truth and falsehood, good and evil. Where or how does this perspective show in this excerpt from a longer poem?
2. What is the attitude toward death in this poem?
3. The Puritan poets of New England often used homely everyday metaphors and analogies to help their readers visualize spiritual truths. Where or how does Bradstreet do so in this poem?

Thinking, Talking, Writing

4. Traditional eulogies tell only the best of the deceased and none of the worst. Try your hand at writing a eulogy that a representative modern child might write for a parent.

TO THOMAS JEFFERSON, ESQUIRE
Archibald MacLeish

> *When Thomas Jefferson was president of the United States, he sponsored the Lewis and Clark expedition of 1803–1806. The following poem recreates the spirit of their exploration of the Western frontier at the onset of the large-scale settlement of the American heartland. In the American popular imagination, the wide open spaces out west became a key to the difference between the American experience and the European past. They became the focus of the central American myth of unlimited opportunity, of a life away from the crowded cities for those not wanting to be fenced in.*
>
> *Archibald MacLeish was an American poet who played an active role in the political events of his time and served as assistant secretary of state during World War II. He had earlier written* Conquistador *(1932), a long poem about the Spanish conquest of the New World.*

"To Thos. Jefferson Esq. his obd't serv't   1
M. Lewis: captain: detached:
                                    Sir:

Having in mind your repeated commands in this matter,
And the worst half of it done and the streams mapped,   5

And we here on the back of this beach beholding the
Other ocean—two years gone and the cold

Breaking with rain for the third spring since St. Louis,
The crows at the fishbones on the frozen dunes,

The first cranes going over from south north,   10
And the river down by a mark of the pole since the morning,

And time near to return, and a ship (Spanish)
Lying in for the salmon: and fearing chance or the

Drought or the Sioux should deprive you of these discoveries—
Therefore we send by sea in this writing.   15

                                    Above the
Platte there were long plains and a clay country:
Rim of the sky far off, grass under it,

Dung for the cook fires by the sulphur licks.
After that there were low hills and the sycamores,   20

And we poled up by the Great Bend in the skiffs:
The honey bees left us after the Osage River.

The wind was west in the evenings, and no dew and the
Morning Star larger and whiter than usual—

The winter rattling in the brittle haws.   25
The second year there was sage and the quail calling.

All that valley is good land by the river:
Three thousand miles and the clay cliffs and
Rue and beargrass by the water banks
And many birds and the brant° going over and tracks of   *wild geese*   30

Bear, elk, wolves, marten: the buffalo
Numberless so that the cloud of their dust covers them:

The antelope fording the fall creeks, and the mountains and
Grazing lands and the meadow lands and the ground

Sweet and open and well-drained.   35
                              We advise you to
Settle troops at the forks and to issue licenses:

Many men will have living on these lands.
There is wealth in the earth for them all and the wood standing

And wild birds on the water where they sleep.   40
There is stone in the hills for the towns of a great people . . .”

The Responsive Reader

1. The beckoning yet perilous open spaces on the Western frontier have
   played a major role in shaping the American national consciousness.
   How does this modern poem mirror the lure or the mystique of
   the West?
2. Where are the native populations of the land in this poem? How does
   this poem echo the popular belief in America's "manifest destiny?"

Thinking, Talking, Writing

3. Has the myth of the wide open spaces as the alternative to crowded
   city life lost its appeal for the current generation? Has the West ceased
   to be the symbol of opportunity?

THE MAYFLOWER COVENANT

Many came to America to find a place where they could practice a religion persecuted in their own country. They came to worship according to the faith of their own choice, although many were slow to grant that same freedom of worship to others. When the Mayflower *brought the Pilgrims to New England in 1620, about a third of the passengers were Puritans—religious dissidents. They were fundamentalist Protestants who had been discriminated against by the official state church of England in their home country.*

These early Americans were strict in their insistence on conformity to their own doctrine and observances. They declared themselves "loyal subjects" of King James I of England. At the same time, however, they established the tradition of self-government that was to make America different from the monarchies of the Old World. At the very beginning of the country, they established the idea "that the citizens of a society could join freely and agree to govern themselves by making laws for the common good" (Diane Ravitch).

The following covenant, or contract, was signed by most of the male passengers of the Mayflower before they disembarked in 1620 at Cape Cod. Women did not have political rights. The members signing the declaration became the governing body of the Plymouth colony.

Having undertaken, for the glory of God and advancement of the Christian faith and honor of our king and country, a voyage to plant the first colony in the northern parts of Virginia, do by these presents solemnly and mutually in the presence of God, and one of another, covenant and combine ourselves together into a civil body politic, for our better ordering and preservation and furtherance of the ends aforementioned, and by virtue hereof to enact, constitute, and frame such just and equal laws, ordinances, acts, conditions, and offices from time to time as shall be thought most meet and convenient for the general good of the colony, unto which we promise all due submissions and obedience.

The Responsive Reader

1. This brief document uses weighty words that are still part of our vocabulary of politics. What for you are the meanings and associations of terms like *covenant, body politic,* or *the common good?* How and where do we still use them?
2. Until recently at least, Britishers tended to refer to themselves as "British subjects," whereas Americans referred to themselves as "American citizens." What is the difference?
3. What are the differences between laws, ordinances, and constitutions?

Thinking, Talking, Writing

4. What makes the proposed commonwealth different from a society ruled by a traditional aristocracy, a military junta, or a totalitarian government? What are the key differences? What to you is the essence of self-government in the American tradition?
5. What makes laws "just and equal?"

Collaborative Projects

6. Imagine that you and your classmates are members of a constitutional convention asked to redefine the purpose and mission of your country. Collaborate in drawing up a paragraph that would sum up the foundations and purposes of the body politic.

THE DECLARATION OF INDEPENDENCE

Thomas Jefferson

Thomas Jefferson symbolizes for many both the promise and the contradictions of America's historical heritage. Like other founders of the country, he was a landowner, builder, and political leader with a substantial stake in the community. He was also a thinker steeped in the philosophy of the eighteenth-century Enlightenment, which saw humanity emerging from dark ages of superstition toward a more rational and humane future. For Jefferson and many contemporaries, the world was the creation of an all-benevolent Supreme Being. What mattered most about people was not whether they were Christian, Muslim, or Jew but whether they were kind and decent human beings. As author of the original draft of the Declaration of Independence, Jefferson helped the emerging new nation formulate the principles that provided the rallying cries of the American Revolution.

Although the founders were landowners and men of standing in the community, they were profoundly influenced by the political ideology of the Enlightenment. European intellectuals such as Rousseau and Voltaire were challenging the foundations of the old order. They were questioning the rule of what Jefferson called the "tinsel-aristocracy"—the pampered upper classes who built the rich ostentatious palaces of Versailles or Dresden while their lice- and disease-ridden subjects lived in hovels. As the lifestyle of the upper class became more sumptuous, the misery of the masses was becoming more of a scandal. As the Scottish poet Robert Burns said, it was time to do away with the gross inequalities of rank and inherited privilege: "A man's man for all that." He said, "See yonder strutting lord," all beribboned and bewigged—he's "just a fool for all that." Many of the clichés of Fourth of July orators—liberty, equal rights, and respect for human dignity—were in the eighteenth century rousing slogans, promising a new dawn to the exploited common people.

Jefferson was a plantation owner from Virginia who became the third president of the new country. He engaged in ambitious building projects at Monticello and Poplar Forest. Like later American farmers, he was heavily in debt to the banks. He unsuccessfully looked for an alternative crop to tobacco, which he raised with continual bad luck as the result of rain, hail, and fire. His plantations were worked by Negro slaves. During his presidency, his political enemies published charges that he had several children with one of his slaves, Sally Hemings. Several prominent African Americans today claim to be descendants of Jefferson, with their oral family history tracing their ancestry to this relationship. Sally Hemings is generally believed to have been the half-sister of Jefferson's wife.

In recent years, the debate over Jefferson's owning of slaves and his relationship with a woman of mixed white and African ancestry has for many become a dramatic example of the tension between the nation's ideals and the realities of American life. Jefferson himself warned his fellow Americans that the practice of slavery was brutalizing and degrading for both master and slave. He foresaw as an eventual result of the American Revolution the "total emancipation" of the slaves with the consent of their masters.

Jefferson wrote the first draft of the declaration with the assistance of Benjamin Franklin and John Adams. The following text is the version edited by the Continental Congress and published as the unanimous declaration of the thirteen original United States of America on July 4, 1776.

When in the Course of human events, it becomes necessary for one people to dissolve the political bands which have connected them with another, and to assume among the Powers of the earth, the separate and equal station to which the Laws of Nature and of Nature's God entitle them, a decent respect to the opinions of mankind requires that they should declare the causes which impel them to the separation.—We hold these truths to be self-evident, that all men are created equal, that they are endowed by their Creator with certain unalienable Rights, that among these are Life, Liberty and the pursuit of Happiness.—That to secure these rights, Governments are instituted among Men, deriving their just powers from the consent of the governed,—That whenever any Form of Government becomes destructive of these ends, it is the Right of the People to alter or to abolish it, and to institute new Government, laying its foundation on such principles and organizing its powers in such form, as to them shall seem most likely to effect their Safety and Happiness. Prudence, indeed, will dictate that Governments long established should not be changed for light and transient causes; and accordingly all experience hath shewn, that mankind are more disposed to suffer, while evils are sufferable, than to right themselves by abolishing the forms to which they are accustomed. But when a long train of abuses and usurpations, pursing invariably the same Object evinces a design to reduce them under absolute Despotism, it is their right, it is their duty, to throw off such Government, and to provide new Guards for their future security.— Such has been the patient sufferance of these Colonies; and such is now the necessity which constrains them to alter their former Systems of Government. The history of the present King of Great Britain is a history of repeated injuries and usurpations, all having in direct object the establishment of an absolute Tyranny over these States. To prove this, let Facts be submitted to a candid world.—He has refused his Assent to Laws, the most wholesome and necessary for the public good.—He has forbidden his Governors to pass Laws of immediate and pressing importance, unless suspended in their operation till his Assent should be obtained; and when so suspended, he has utterly neglected to attend to them.—He has refused to pass other Laws for the accommodation of large districts of people, unless those people would relinquish the right of Representation in the Legislature, a right inestimable to them and formidable to tyrants only.—He has called together legislative bodies at places unusual, uncomfortable, and distant from the depository of their public Records, for the sole purpose of fatiguing them into compliance with his measures.—He has dissolved Representative Houses repeatedly, for opposing with manly firmness his invasions of the rights of the people.—He has refused for a long time, after such dissolutions, to cause others to be elected; whereby the Legislative powers, incapable of Annihilation, have returned to the People at large for their exercise; the State remaining in the mean time exposed to all the dangers of invasion from without, and convulsions within.—He has endeavoured to prevent the population of these States; for that purpose obstructing the Laws for Naturalization of Foreigners; refusing to pass others to encourage their migrations hither, and raising the conditions of new Appropriations of Lands.—He has obstructed the Administration of Justice, by refusing his Assent to Laws for establishing Judiciary powers.—He has made Judges dependent on his Will alone, for the tenure of their offices, and the amount and payment of their salaries.—He has erected a multitude of New Offices, and sent hither swarms of Officers to harrass our people, and eat out their substance.—He has kept among us, in times of peace, Standing Armies without the Consent of our legislatures.— He has affected to render the Military independent of and superior to the Civil power.—He has combined with others to subject us to a jurisdiction foreign to our constitution, and unacknowledged by our laws; giving his Assent to their Acts of pretended Legislation:—For quartering large bodies of armed troops among us:—For protecting them, by a mock Trial, from punishment for any Murders which they should commit on the Inhabitants of these States:—For cutting off our Trade with all parts of the world:—For imposing Taxes on us without our Consent:—For depriving us in many cases, of the benefits of Trial by Jury:—For transporting us beyond Seas to be tried for pretended offences:—For abolishing the free System of English Laws in a neighbouring Province, establishing therein an Arbitrary government, and enlarging its Boundaries so as to render it at once an example and fit instrument for introducing the same absolute rule into these Colonies:— For taking away our Charters, abolishing our most valuable Laws, and altering fundamentally the Forms of our Governments:—For suspending our own Legislatures, and declaring themselves invested with power to legislate for us in all cases whatsoever.—He has abdicated Government here, by declaring us out of his Protection and waging War againt us.—He has plundered our seas, ravaged our Coasts, burnt our towns, and destroyed the Lives of our people.—He is at this time transporting large Armies of foreign Mercenaries to complete the works of death, desolation and tyranny, already begun with circumstances of Cruelty and perfidy scarcely paralleled in the most barbarous ages, and totally unworthy the Head of a civilized nation.— He has constrained our fellow Citizens taken Captive on the high Seas to bear Arms against their Country, to become the executioners of their friends and Brethren, or to fall themselves by their Hands.—He has excited domestic insurrections amongst us, and has endeavoured to bring on the inhabitants of our frontiers, the merciless Indian Savages, whose known rule of warfare, is an undistinguished destruction of all ages, sexes, and conditions. In every stage of these Oppressions We have Petitioned for Redress in the most humble terms: Our repeated Petitions have been answered only by repeated injury. A Prince, whose character is thus marked by every act which may define a Tyrant, is unfit to be the ruler of a free people. Nor have We been wanting in attentions to our British brethren. We have warned them from time to time of attempts by their legislature to extend an unwarrantable jurisdiction over us. We have reminded them of the circumstances of our emigration and settlement here. We have appealed to their native justice and magnanimity, and we have conjured them by the ties of our common kindred to disavow these usurpations, which, would inevitably interrupt our connections and correspondence. They too have been deaf to the voice of justice and of consanguinity. We must, therefore, acquiesce in the necessity, which denounces our Separation, and hold them, as we hold the rest of mankind, Enemies in War, in Peace Friends.—

We, therefore, the Representatives of the *United States of America,* in General Congress, Assembled, appealing to the Supreme Judge of the world for the rectitude of our intentions, do, in the Name, and by Authority of the good People of these Colonies, solemnly publish and declare, That these United Colonies are, and of Right ought to be *Free and Independent States;* that they are Absolved from all Allegiance to the British Crown, and that all political connection between them and the State of Great Britain, is and ought to be totally dissolved; and that as Free and Independent States, they have full Power to levy War, conclude Peace, contract Alliances, establish Commerce, and to do all other Acts and Things which Independent States may of right do.—And for the support of this Declaration, with a firm reliance on the protection of divine Providence, we mutually pledge to each other our Lives, our Fortunes and our sacred Honor.

The Responsive Reader

1. The declaration embodies eighteenth-century ideas of the origin and purposes of government. It invokes hallowed principles like equality, liberty, the right to revolution, the social contract, and the consent of the governed. How would you explain these to someone who has grown up under a "tyrannical" or "despotic" government?
2. Where and how does the declaration deal with principles like the following that have become part of the American tradition:

   - separation of powers and independence of the judiciary
   - subordination of the military to civilian control

Thinking, Talking, Writing

3. Revolutionaries have often divided into moderate and radical factions. Do you see the declaration as moderate or radical in spirit? In content? In tone?
4. Do Americans today still believe in the right to revolution?
5. The colonists especially resented the king's use of mercenaries. Have Americans abandoned the ideal of a citizen army?

Collaborative Projects

6. The American Revolution and the French Revolution derived from some of the same ideological currents and used similar slogans. You may want to farm out topics like the following to different groups or to different members of your group: What was the involvement of American revolutionaries like Tom Paine and Benjamin Franklin in the French Revolution? How did Jefferson and his contemporaries see the French Revolution?

JEFFERSON AND THE EQUALITY OF MEN

Douglas L. Wilson

History is not a blind-folded figure impartially weighing evidence in the balance any more than Justice is. History is written and published by the survivors, by the victors, by those in power. American children would have different history books if the South had won the Civil War. Russian students will get a different picture of Stalin and Trotzky and Lenin now that the official Soviet encyclopedia is going out of print.

In modern times especially, the job of historians has often been to rewrite *history. They have often been revisionists—revising familiar accounts and judgments, not just in the light of new evidence, but in accordance with changing standards and assumptions. The Jefferson scholar who authored the following article uses the term* presentism *to describe our tendency to judge historical figures, not by the standards of their own time, but by the standards of the present. This way, we impose "today's meanings on yesterday."*

This article focuses on a key issue for many modern readers: What was Jefferson's stand on the issue of slavery? Was he insincere when he wrote that "all men are created equal?"

How could the man who wrote that "all men are created equal" own   *1*
slaves? This, in essence, is the question most persistently asked of those who write about Thomas Jefferson, and by all indications it is the thing that contemporary Americans find most vexing about him. In a recent series of some two dozen radio talk shows, I was asked this question on virtually every program, either by the host or by a caller. Most often, those who point to this problem admire Jefferson, and they appear as reluctant to give up their admiration as they would be to give up the principle of equality itself. But they are genuinely baffled by the seeming contradiction.

The question carries a silent assumption that because he practiced slaveholding, Jefferson must have somehow believed in it, and must therefore have been a hypocrite. My belief is that this way of asking the question . . . is essentially backward, and reflects the pervasive presentism of our time. Consider, for example, how different the question appears when inverted and framed in more historical terms: How did a man who was born into a slaveholding society, whose family and admired friends owned slaves, who inherited a fortune that was dependent on slaves and slave labor, decide at an early age that slavery was morally wrong and forcefully declare that it ought to be abolished?

Though stating the same case, these are obviously different questions, focusing on different things, but one is framed in a historical context and the other ignores historical circumstances. The rephrased question reveals that what is truly remarkable is that Jefferson went against his society and his own self-interest to denounce slavery and urge its abolition. And, crucially, there is no hidden assumption that he must in some way have believed in or tacitly accepted the morality of slavery.

But when the question is explained in this way, another invariably follows: If Jefferson came to believe that holding slaves was wrong, why did he continue to hold them? This question, because of its underlying assumptions, is both harder and easier than the first. It is harder because we are at such a great remove from the conditions of eighteenth-century Virginia that no satisfactory explanation can be given in a nutshell. To come to terms with the tangle of legal restrictions and other obstacles faced by the eighteenth-century Virginia slaveholder who might have wished freedom for his slaves, together with the extraordinary difficulties of finding them viable places of residence and means of livelihood, requires a short course in early American history. But the question is easier in that there is no doubt that these obstacles to emancipation in Jefferson's Virginia were formidable, and the risk was demonstrably great that emancipated slaves would enjoy little, if any, real freedom and would, unless they could pass as white, be more likely to come to grief in a hostile environment. In short, the master whose concern extended beyond his own morality to the well-being of his slaves was caught on the horns of a dilemma. Thus the question of why Jefferson didn't free his slaves only serves to illustrate how presentism involves us in mistaken assumptions about historical conditions—in this case that an eighteenth-century slaveholder wanting to get out from under the moral stigma of slavery and improve the lot of his slaves had only to set them free.

The inevitable question about slavery and equality partly reflects the   5
fact that most Americans are only vaguely familiar with the historical Jefferson, but delving into his writings and attempting to come to terms with the character of his thought, though illuminating, can create further consternation. The college student confronting Jefferson's one published book, *Notes on the State of Virginia,* is nowadays unprepared for and often appalled at what the author of the Declaration of Independence had to say about race. Thirty years ago college students were shocked to find Jefferson referring to the slave populations as "blacks," a term that to them suggested racial insensitivity. But to those born after the civil-rights acts of the 1960s, it comes as a shock to discover that Jefferson, while firmly in favor of general emancipation, held out no hope for racial integration. Believing that an amalgamation of the races was not desirable and would not work, he advocated a plan of gradual emancipation and resettlement. Present-day students are even more shocked to find Jefferson concluding, albeit as "a suspicion only," that the blacks he had observed were "inferior to the whites in the endowments both of body and mind." Even his positive finding that blacks appeared to be superior to

whites in musical ability rankles, for it comes through to students of the current generation as an early version of a familiar stereotype.

At a time like the present, when relations between the races are in the forefront of public discussion and desegregation is the law of the land, it is not surprising that college students should be sensitive to discrepancies between what they understand to be the prevailing ideals of their country and the views of its most prominent Founding Father. National ideals, however, spring not only from the beliefs and aspirations of founders but also, as this essay attempts to show, from the experience and efforts of subsequent generations. Though he foresaw that slavery could not prevail ("Nothing is more certainly written in the book of fate than that these people are to be free"), Jefferson can hardly be counted bigoted or backward for seriously doubting that a racially integrated society of white Europeans and black Africans was truly feasible. As the Harvard historian Bernard Bailyn has written, "It took a vast leap of the imagination in the eighteenth century to consider integrating into the political community the existing slave population, whose very 'nature' was the subject of puzzled inquiry and who had hitherto been politically non-existent." Interestingly, the reasons that Jefferson gave for doubting the possibility of integration—"deep rooted prejudices entertained by the whites; ten ·thousand recollections, by the blacks, of the injuries they have sustained; new provocations; [and] the real distinctions which nature has made"—are the same reasons often cited by black separatists, who entertain the same misgivings.

But if Jefferson's being a separatist can be accounted for, what can be said about his invidious comparison of the natural endowments of blacks with those of whites, or with those of American Indians, whom he found to be on a par with whites? His own testimony suggests an answer, for he admitted that his acquaintance with blacks did not extend to the African continent and embraced only black people who had been born in and forced to live under the degrading conditions of slavery. "It will be right to make great allowances for the difference of condition, of education, of conversation, of the sphere in which they move," Jefferson wrote, but it is evident in the hindsight of two hundred years that his estimate of the capabilities of blacks failed to make sufficient allowances, particularly for the things he himself named. It is perhaps poetic justice that posterity should be liable to the same kind of mistake in judging him.

But if Jefferson's beliefs add up to a kind of racism, we must specify two important qualifications. First, that Jefferson offered his conclusions as a hypothesis only, acknowledging that his own experience was not a sufficient basis on which to judge an entire race. Had he lived long enough to meet the ex-slave Frederick Douglass or hear the searing eloquence of his oratory, he would have recognized intellectual gifts in a black man that were superior to those of most whites. Douglass's oratory brings us to the second qualification, which is a telling one. Attacking the justifications for slavery in 1854, Douglass observed,

Ignorance and depravity, and the inability to rise from degradation to civilization and respectability, are the most usual allegations against the oppressed. The evils most fostered by slavery and oppression are precisely those which slaveholders and oppressors would transfer from their system to the inherent character of their victims. Thus the very crimes of slavery become slavery's best defence. By making the enslaved a character fit only for slavery, they excuse themselves for refusing to make the slave a freeman.

Although we may find Jefferson guilty of failing to make adequate allowance for the conditions in which blacks were forced to live, Jefferson did not take the next step of concluding that blacks were fit only for slavery. This rationalization of slavery was indeed the common coin of slaveholders and other whites who condoned or tolerated the "peculiar" institution, but it formed no part of Jefferson's thinking. In fact, he took the opposite position: that having imposed the depredations of slavery on blacks, white Americans should not only emancipate them but also educate and train them to be self-sufficient, provide them with necessary materials, and establish a colony in which they could live as free and independent people.

But if going back to original sources and historical contexts is essential in discerning the meanings that Today has imposed on Yesterday, it is equally important in determining how Yesterday's meanings have colored Today's. The concept of equality that is universally recognized in our own time as a fundamental principle of American society only had its beginnings in the eighteenth century; it did not emerge full-blown from the Declaration of Independence.

Whenever he sent correspondents a copy of the Declaration, Jefferson *10* transcribed the text in such a way as to show what the Continental Congress had added to his draft and what it had cut out. The process of congressional emendation was clearly a painful memory for him, and the deletion about which he probably felt the most regret was also the most radical of the passages, for it undertook to blame the King of England directly for the African slave trade. It begins,

He has waged cruel war against human nature itself, violating it's most sacred rights of life and liberty in the persons of a distant people who never offended him, captivating & carrying them into slavery in another hemisphere, or to incur miserable death in their transportation thither. . . . Determined to keep open a market where MEN should be bought & sold, he has prostituted his negative for suppressing every legislative attempt to prohibit or to restrain this execrable commerce.

Had this passage been ratified as part of the official Declaration, then a question often raised in the nineteenth century—Did Jefferson mean to include blacks in the language of the Declaration?—would have been susceptible of a clear-cut and demonstrable answer. For, as the political scientist Jean Yarbrough has recently pointed out, this passage says unmistakably that the Africans captured into slavery were not a separate category of beings but men, with the sacred rights of life and liberty that are said in the prologue of the Declaration to be the natural endowments of all men. It is precisely in having these same rights that the prologue asserts that all men are created equal.

This deleted passage also provides an answer to a question often raised in the twentieth century: Did Jefferson mean to include women in the phrase "all men are created equal"? Implicit in the passage is that "men" is being used in the broader sense of "mankind," for those who were cruelly transported to be "bought & sold" on the slave market were certainly female as well as male.

That blacks and women were meant to be included in the affirmations of Jefferson's Declaration at a time when they enjoyed nothing remotely like political and social equality underscores a source of continuing confusion for contemporary Americans—the difference between a philosophical conception of natural rights and a working system of laws and societal values which allows for the fullest expression of those rights. In our own time the stubbornly persistent disparity between these two is often a source of cynicism and despair, but a Jeffersonian perspective would put more emphasis on the considerable progress made in closing the gap. Jefferson himself was sustained by a profound belief in progress. His unshakable conviction that the world was steadily advancing, not only in the material but also in the moral sphere, is abundantly evident in his writings. Though sometimes criticized as being naive in this regard, he was fully aware that his belief embraced the prospect of recurrent political and social transformations. Writing from retirement at the age of seventy-three, he told a correspondent that "laws and institutions must go hand in hand with the progress of the human mind."

> As that becomes more developed, more enlightened, as new discoveries are made, new truths disclosed, and manners and opinions change with the change of circumstances, institutions must advance also, and keep pace with the times. We might as well require a man to wear still the coat which fitted him when a boy, as civilized society to remain ever under the regimen of their barbarous ancestors.

One way of looking at American history from Jefferson's day down to our own is as the series of changes and adjustments in our laws and institutions necessitated by the ideals implicit in Jefferson's Declaration. Sometimes the effect of these ideals has been simply to prevent other, incompatible ideals from gaining ascendancy, as in the case of Social Darwinism, whose notions of the natural inferiority of certain racial and social groups were impeded by the prevalence and familiarity of the Declaration's precepts. But without doubt the most important event in the development of the American ideal of equality, after Jefferson's Declaration, was Abraham Lincoln's address at

Gettysburg. Without any warrant from the founders themselves or from sub-sequent interpreters or historians, Lincoln declared that not only the essential meaning of the Civil War but also the national purpose itself was epitomized in Jefferson's phrase "all men are created equal."

As Garry Wills has cogently argued, Lincoln at Gettysburg was practic- *15* ing not presentism but futurism. In the most stunning act of statesmanship in our history, he invested Jefferson's eighteenth-century notion of equality with an essentially new meaning and projected it onto the future of the nation. Transfigured in the context of civil war, and transformed by Lincoln into a larger and more consequential ideal, Jefferson's formulation would never be the same. Thanks in large part to Lincoln, Americans no longer understand the prologue of the Declaration as a philosophical expression of natural rights, but rather take it to be a statement about the social and political conditions that ought to prevail.

Jefferson's Declaration is thus remarkable not only for its durability— its ability to remain meaningful and relevant—but also for its adaptability to changing conditions. At a time when natural rights are widely proclaimed a nullity, the language of the Declaration is universally understood as affirming human rights, and is resorted to even by those who do not consciously associate their ideas or aspirations with Jefferson. When the black separatist Malcolm X underwent a change of heart about white people and publicly renounced the "sweeping indictments of one race," he told an audience in Chicago, "I am not a racist and do not subscribe to any of the tenets of racism. In all honesty and sincerity it can be stated that I wish nothing but freedom, justice, and equality; life, liberty, and the pursuit of happiness—for all people." Simply to name the most basic American ideals is to invoke the words of Jefferson.

"Today, makes Yesterday mean." In the light of the foregoing at least one more meaning for Emily Dickinson's evocative phrase emerges: that the constantly shifting conditions of the present serve to revivify the past, offering it up as a subject for renewed exploration. Thus we can never hope to say the last word about our history—about Thomas Jefferson, for example— because we are continually having to re-open the past and consider its trans-actions anew in the light of an unforeseen and unforeseeable present.

A page from Jefferson's draft of the Declaration of Independence, with his condemnation of slavery. (A transcription appears on page 41.)

[he has incited treasonable insurrections of our fellow citizens, with the allurements of forfeiture & confiscation of our property, he has constrained others in captivity on the high seas to bear arms against their country, to become the executioners of their friends and brethren, or to fall themselves by their hands, he has waged cruel war against human nature itself, violating its most sacred rights of life & liberty in the persons of a distant people who never offended him, captivating & carrying them into slavery in another hemisphere, or to incur miserable death in their transportation thither. This piratical warfare, the opprobrium of infidel powers, is the warfare of the Christian king of Great Britain. determined to keep open a market where MEN should be bought & sold: he has prostituted his negative for suppressing every legislative attempt to prohibit or to restrain this execrable commerce: and that this assemblage of horrors might want no fact of distinguished die, he is now exciting those very people to rise in arms among us, and to purchase that liberty of which he has deprived them, by murdering the people upon whom he also obtruded them; thus paying off former crimes committed against the liberties of one people, with crimes which he urges them to commit against the lives of another.]

The Responsive Reader

1. At the beginning of this selection from a larger article, Wilson asks you to look at the question of Jefferson's stand on slavery from a different perspective. How? Does he succeed in making you reconsider the question?
2. Key evidence in this article is a passage written by Jefferson and indicting slavery that his contemporaries in the Continental Congress were not ready to adopt. What did the deleted passage say? How did Jefferson intend to use it in the Declaration? How does it affect your answer to the basic question raised in this article?
3. In recent years, feminists have challenged the "generic" use of the terms *man* and *men* to mean human beings generally, including both men and women. According to feminist critics, terms like *mankind* or phrases like *history of man*, while allegedly covering both sexes, in practice tend to downplay or exclude women. In this connection, what is Wilson's argument concerning the use of *men* in the Declaration?

Thinking, Talking, Writing

4. Have you seen other evidence of *presentism*—retroactively applying our own contemporary standards to the people and events of the past? Are we unfair when we judge the past by our own changing standards? Or, on the contrary, do we excuse or condone crimes or immorality of the past by saying that the people involved thought they were justified by the standards of their time?

5. In a book about Jefferson, Fawn M. Brodie accepted his liaison with Hemings as fact and described it as a "serious passion that brought Jefferson and the slave woman much private happiness over a period lasting over thirty-eight years." Wilson commented that in earlier days such an affair would have been considered scandalous and shameful but that today public opinion would be much more tolerant. "For most," he claimed, "such a liaison is apparently not objectionable" but in fact may work in Jefferson's favor, showing him not to have been a "stuffy moralist." Do you think Wilson is right about the prevailing moral climate in our society today?

6. Are Americans or the media too hard on today's political leaders or public figures?

Collaborative Projects

7. According to critics like Wilson, our tendency to debunk the heroes of the past has shifted the emphasis to the failures and problems of the leading figures of our history. Working with a group, explore how this revisionist tendency has affected our image of a leading figure in America's past.

INDEPENDENCE DAY SPEECH
Frederick Douglass

You have seen how a man was made a slave; you shall see how a slave was made a man.

Frederick Douglass

The Autobiography *(1845) of Frederick Douglass told the story of an escaped former slave who became a leader in the movement to abolish slavery. His eloquence as a writer and orator convinced many that slavery was an abomination in a country that considered itself a Christian nation and the home of the free. Although Douglass had had some experience with kindhearted slaveowners, most of his account bore witness to unspeakable meanness and brutality. Slaves were forced to do backbreaking labor from sunup to sundown. They were subjected to sadistic whippings; a "good overseer" to the slaves was one who beat them without enjoying it. Douglass had witnessed the shooting of a slave in cold blood for refusing to obey an order. He described a slaveowner's wife beating a young babysitter to death for falling asleep from exhaustion.*

Douglass never knew his parents and was raised by his grandmother on a Maryland plantation. He went to work as a house slave at eight and was taught to read by his owner when helping slaves to become literate was still illegal. After working as a field hand on a plantation, he escaped to the North and became a featured speaker at meetings of antislavery societies. He eventually purchased his freedom with money earned on a lecture tour abroad and started his own abolitionist newspaper, the North Star.

The following is the concluding part of a speech Douglass gave in Rochester, New York, on Independence Day in 1852. Like other eloquent black writers and speakers after him, he made himself the voice of the excluded, of the unheard. He practiced a solemn style of oratory, steeped in the language of the Bible.

Fellow citizens, pardon me, allow me to ask, why am I called upon to   *1* speak here today? What have I, or those I represent, to do with your national independence? Are the great principles of political freedom and of natural justice, embodied in that Declaration of Independence, extended to us? and am I, therefore, called upon to bring our humble offering to the national altar, and to confess the benefits and express devout gratitude for the blessings resulting from your independence to us?

Would to God, both for your sakes and ours, that an affirmative answer could be truthfully returned to these questions! Then would my task be light, and my burden easy and delightful. For who is there so cold that a nation's sympathy could not warm him? Who so obdurate and dead to the claims of gratitude that would not thankfully acknowledge such priceless benefits? Who so stolid and selfish that would not give his voice to swell the hallelujahs of a nation's jubilee, when the chains of servitude had been torn from his limbs? I am not that man. In a case like that the dumb might eloquently speak and the "lame man leap as an hart."

But such is not the state of the case. I say it with a sad sense of the disparity between us. I am not included within the pale of this glorious anniversary! Your high independence only reveals the immeasurable distance between us. The blessings in which you, this day, rejoice are not enjoyed in common. The rich inheritance of justice, liberty, prosperity, and independence bequeathed by your fathers is shared by you, not by me. The sunlight that brought light and healing to you has brought stripes and death to me. This Fourth of July is yours, not mine. You may rejoice, I must mourn. To drag a man in fetters into the grand illuminated temple of liberty, and call upon him to join you in joyous anthems, were inhuman mockery and sacrilegious irony. Do you mean, citizens, to mock me by asking me to speak today? If so, there is a parallel to your conduct. And let me warn you that it is dangerous to copy the example of a nation whose crimes, towering up to heaven, were thrown down by the breath of the Almighty, burying that nation in irrevocable ruin! I can today take up the plaintive lament of a peeled and woe-smitten people!

> By the rivers of Babylon, there we sat down. Yea! we wept when we remembered Zion. We hanged our harps upon the willows in the midst thereof. For there, they that carried us away captive, required of us a song; and they who wasted us required of us mirth, saying, Sing us one of the songs of Zion. How can we sing the Lord's song in a strange land? If I forget thee, O Jerusalem, let my right hand forget her cunning. If I do not remember thee, let my tongue cleave to the roof of my mouth.

Fellow citizens, above your national, tumultuous joy, I hear the mournful wail of millions! whose chains, heavy and grievous yesterday, are, today, rendered more intolerable by the jubilee shouts that reach them. If I do forget, if I do not faithfully remember those bleeding children of sorrow this day, "may my right hand forget her cunning, and may my tongue cleave to the roof of my mouth"! To forget them, to pass lightly over their wrongs, and to chime in with the popular theme would be treason most scandalous and shocking, and would make me a reproach before God and the world. My subject, then, fellow citizens, is *American slavery*. I shall see this day and its popular characteristics from the slave's point of view. Standing there identified with the American bondman, making his wrongs mine. I do not hesitate to declare with all my soul that the character and conduct of this nation never looked blacker to me than on this Fourth of July! Whether we turn to the declarations of the past or to the professions of the present, the conduct of the nation seems equally hideous and revolting. America is false to the past, false to the present, and solemnly binds herself to be false to the future. Standing with God and the crushed and bleeding slave on this occasion, I will, in the name of humanity which is outraged, in the name of liberty which is fettered, in the name of the Constitution and the Bible which are disregarded and trampled upon, dare to call in question and to denounce, with all the emphasis I can command, everything that serves to perpetuate slavery—the great sin and shame of America! "I will not equivocate, I will not excuse"; I will use the severest language I can command; and yet not one word shall escape me that any man, whose judgment is not blinded by prejudice, or who is not at heart a slaveholder, shall not confess to be right and just.

But I fancy I hear someone of my audience say, "It is just in this circumstance that you and your brother abolitionists fail to make a favorable impression on the public mind. Would you argue more and denounce less, would you persuade more and rebuke less, your cause would be much more likely to succeed." But, I submit, where all is plain, there is nothing to be argued. What point in the antislavery creed would you have me argue? On what branch of the subject do the people of this country need light? Must I undertake to prove that the slave is a man? That point is conceded already. Nobody doubts it. The slaveholders themselves acknowledge it in the enactment of laws for their government. They acknowledge it when they punish disobedience on the part of the slave. There are seventy-two crimes in the state of Virginia which, if committed by a black man (no matter how ignorant he be), subject him to the punishment of death; while only two of the same crimes will subject a white man to the like punishment. What is this but the acknowledgment that the slave is a moral, intellectual, and responsible being? The manhood of the slave is conceded. It is admitted in the fact that the Southern statute books are covered with enactments forbidding, under severe fines and penalties, the teaching of the slave to read or to write. When you can point to any such laws in reference to the beasts of the field, then I may consent to argue the manhood of the slave. When the dogs in your streets, when the fowls of the air, when the cattle on your hills, when the fish of the sea and the reptiles that crawl shall be unable to distinguish the slave from a brute, then will I argue with you that the slave is a man!

For the present, it is enough to affirm the equal manhood of the Negro race. Is it not astonishing that, while we are plowing, planting, and reaping, using all kinds of mechanical tools, erecting houses, constructing bridges, building ships, working in metals of brass, iron, copper, silver, and gold: that, while we are reading, writing, and ciphering, acting as clerks, merchants, and secretaries, having among us lawyers, doctors, ministers, poets, authors, editors, orators, and teachers; that, while we are engaged in all manner of enterprises common to other men, digging gold in California, capturing the whale in the Pacific, feeding sheep and cattle on the hillside, living, moving, acting, thinking, planning, living in families as husbands, wives, and children, and, above all, confessing and worshipping the Christian's God, and looking hopefully for life and immortality beyond the grave, we are called upon to prove that we are men!

Would you have me argue that man is entitled to liberty? That he is the rightful owner of his own body? You have already declared it. Must I argue the wrongfulness of slavery? Is that a question for republicans? Is it to be settled by the rules of logic and argumentation, as a matter beset with great difficulty, involving a doubtful application of the principle of justice, hard to be understood? How should I look today, in the presence of Americans, dividing and subdividing a discourse, to show that men have a natural right to freedom? speaking of it relatively and positively, negatively and affirmatively? To do so would be to make myself ridiculous and to offer an insult to your understanding. There is not a man beneath the canopy of heaven that does not know that slavery is wrong for him.

What, am I to argue that it is wrong to make men brutes, to rob them of their liberty, to work them without wages, to keep them ignorant of their relations to their fellow men, to beat them with sticks, to flay their flesh with the lash, to load their limbs with irons, to hunt them with dogs, to sell them at auction, to sunder their families, to knock out their teeth, to burn their flesh, to starve them into obedience and submission to their masters? Must I argue that a system thus marked with blood, and stained with pollution, is wrong? No! I will not. I have better employment for my time and strength than such arguments would imply.

What, then, remains to be argued? Is it that slavery is not divine: that God did not establish it; that our doctors of divinity are mistaken? There is blasphemy in the thought. That which is inhuman cannot be divine! Who can reason on such a proposition? They that can may: I cannot. The time for such argument is past.

At a time like this, scorching iron, not convincing argument, is needed. 10 O! had I the ability, and could I reach the nation's ear, I would today pour out a fiery stream of biting ridicule, blasting reproach, withering sarcasm, and stern rebuke. For it is not light that is needed, but fire; it is not the gentle shower, but thunder. We need the storm, the whirlwind, and the earthquake. The feeling of the nation must be quickened; the conscience of the nation must be roused; the propriety of the nation must be startled; the hypocrisy of the nation must be exposed; and its crimes against God and man must be proclaimed and denounced.

What, to the American slave, is your Fourth of July? I answer: a day that reveals to him, more than all other days in the year, the gross injustice and cruelty to which he is the constant victim. To him, your celebration is a sham; your boasted liberty, an unholy license; your national greatness, swelling vanity; your sounds of rejoicing are empty and heartless; your denunciation of tyrants, brass-fronted impudence; your shouts of liberty and equality, hollow mockery; your prayers and hymns, your sermons and thanksgivings, with all your religious parade and solemnity, are, to Him, mere bombast, fraud, deception, impiety, and hypocrisy—a thin veil to cover up crimes which would disgrace a nation of savages. There is not a nation on the earth guilty of practices more shocking and bloody than are the people of the United States at this very hour.

Go where you may, search where you will, roam through all the monarchies and despotisms of the Old World, travel through South America, search out every abuse, and when you have found the last, lay your facts by the side of the everyday practices of this nation, and you will say with me that, for revolting barbarity and shameless hypocrisy, America reigns without a rival.

The Responsive Reader

1. How does Douglass in the opening paragraphs heighten the contrast between the promise of Independence Day and the reality of slavery? What are striking images? What sentences offer powerful variations on his theme of "This Fourth of July is yours, not mine"?

2. African American oratory and spirituals have often invoked the parallel between the black experience and the Babylonian captivity of the Jews. How and why? How does Douglass do so in this speech? With what effect?

3. If "all men are created equal," what were the consequences for Douglass's America once it was acknowledged that blacks were full human beings? How does Douglass deal with the question of the "equal manhood of the Negro race"? (How does he turn the tables on the many legal restrictions imposed on black Americans?)

4. Why does Douglass refuse to argue that liberty and basic principles of humanity apply to black Americans? What is his rhetorical strategy here?

Thinking, Talking, Writing

5. For Douglass, the practice of slavery meant that the Constitution and the Bible were "disregarded and trampled upon." Do you think most Americans today would acknowledge that he was right? Would they acknowledge that the historical legacy of slavery and racism continue to call the nation's political ideals and religious values into question?

6. Today, do you think the best strategy for correcting injustice is to "call in question and to denounce, with all the emphasis" possible—without equivocating and making excuses? Or would it "make a more favorable impression on the public mind" to "denounce less" and "persuade more?" Which do you think works better—the more radical or the more moderate approach? (Do you agree that not "light" is needed but "fire"?)

Collaborative Projects

7. Is the tradition of eloquent oratory dead? You may want to join class-mates in staging a dramatic reading of selected passages from Jefferson, Douglass, and Stanton.

ADDRESS ON WOMEN'S RIGHTS
Elizabeth Cady Stanton

Elizabeth Cady Stanton advocated the cause of equal rights for women and, with Susan B. Anthony, became one of the foremost leaders of the nineteenth-century women's movement. Daughter of a conservative jurist and wife of an abolitionist lawyer, Stanton worked to help pass legislation giving property rights to married women in New York State in 1848. In 1854 she went to the New York State legislature in Albany to deliver the speech on women's rights from which Diane Ravitch selected the following excerpts for her collection, The American Reader. *Fifty thousand copies of the speech were printed for circulation as tracts.*

European feminists had early insisted that Rousseau's eighteenth-century slogan of the "equality of men" was incomplete unless it included the equality of women. In 1792 Mary Wollstonecraft had asked men to "snap our chains and be content with rational fellowship instead of slavish obedience." During its early decades, the American women's moment devoted much of its energy to the struggle for the right to vote, which finally bore fruit in 1922.

The early suffragists, or advocates of a woman's right to vote, had a long way to go. In 1900 President Grover Cleveland declared, "The relative positions to be assumed by man and woman in the working out of our civilization were assigned long ago by a higher intelligence than ours." Only slowly the voices of less traditional males were beginning to be heard. Mark Twain, America's foremost humorist, said, "If women could vote, they would vote on the side of morality . . . and set up some candidates fit for decent human beings to vote for."

Look at the position of woman as woman. It is not enough for us that by your laws we are permitted to live and breathe, to claim the necessaries of life from our legal protectors—to pay the penalty of our crimes; we demand the full recognition of all our rights as citizens of the Empire State. We are persons; native, freeborn citizens; property-holders, tax-payers; yet are we denied the exercise of our right to the elective franchise. We support ourselves, and, in part, your schools, colleges, churches, your poor-houses, jails, prisons, the army, the navy, the whole machinery of government, and yet we have no voice in your councils. We have every qualification required by the Constitution, necessary to the legal voter, but the one of sex. . . .

Can it be that here, where we acknowledge no royal blood, no apostolic descent, that you, who have declared that all men were created equal—that governments derive their just powers from the consent of the governed, would willingly build up an aristocracy that places the ignorant and vulgar above the educated and refined—the alien and the ditch digger above the authors and poets of the day—an aristocracy that would raise the sons above the mothers that bore them? . . .

Look at the position of woman as wife. Your laws relating to marriage—founded as they are on the old common law of England, a compound of barbarous usages, but partially modified by progressive civilization—are in open violation of our enlightened ideas of justice, and of the holiest feelings of our nature. If you take the highest view of marriage, as a Divine relation, which love alone can constitute and sanctify, then of course human legislation can only recognize it. Men can neither bind nor loose its ties, for that prerogative belongs to God alone, who makes man and woman, and the laws of attraction by which they are united. But if you regard marriage as a civil contract, then let it be subject to the same laws which control all other contracts. Do not make it a kind of half-human, half-divine institution, which you may build up, but can not regulate. Do not, by your special legislation for this one kind of contract, involve yourselves in the grossest absurdities and contradictions.

So long as by your laws no man can make a contract for a horse or piece of land until he is twenty-one years of age, and by which contract he is not bound if any deception has been practiced, or if the party contracting has not fulfilled his part of the agreement—so long as the parties in all mere civil contracts retain their identity and all the power and independence they had before contracting, with the full right to dissolve all partnerships and contracts for any reason, at the will and option of the parties themselves, upon what principle of civil jurisprudence do you permit the boy of fourteen and the girl of twelve, in violation of every natural law, to make a contract more momentous in importance than any other, and then hold them to it come what may, the whole of their natural lives, in spite of disappointment, deception, and misery? Then, too, the signing of this contract is instant civil death to one of the parties. The woman who but yesterday was sued on bended knee, who stood so high in the scale of being as to make an agreement on equal terms with a proud . . . man, to-day has no civil existence, no social freedom. The wife who inherits no property holds about the same legal position that does the slave of the Southern plantation. She can own nothing, sell nothing. She has no right even to the wages she earns; her person, her time, her services are the property of another.

Many times and oft it has been asked us, with unaffected seriousness,   5 "What do you women want? What are you aiming at?" Many have manifested a laudable curiosity to know what the wives and daughters could complain of in republican America, where their sires and sons have so bravely fought for freedom and gloriously secured their independence, trampling all tyranny, bigotry, and caste in the dust, and declaring to a waiting world the divine truth that all men are created equal. What can woman want under such a government? Admit a radical difference in sex, and you demand different spheres—water for fish, and air for birds.

It is impossible to make the Southern planter believe that his slave feels and reasons just as he does—that injustice and subjection are as galling as to him—that the degradation of living by the will of another, the mere dependent on his caprice, at the mercy of his passions, is as keenly felt by him as his master. If you can force on his unwilling vision a vivid picture of the negro's wrongs, and for a moment touch his soul, his logic brings him instant consolation. He says, the slave does not feel this as I would. Here, gentlemen, is our difficulty: When we plead our cause before the law-makers and savants of the republic, they can not take in the idea that men and women are alike; and so long as the mass rest in this delusion, the public mind will not be so much startled by the revelations made of the injustice and degradation of woman's position as by the fact that she should at length wake up to a sense of it. . . . .

But if, gentlemen, you take the ground that the sexes are alike, and, therefore, you are our faithful representatives—then why all these special laws for woman? Would not one code answer for all of like needs and wants? Christ's golden rule is better than all the special legislation that the ingenuity of man can devise: "Do unto others as you would have others do unto you." This, men and brethren, is all we ask at your hands. We ask no better laws than those you have made for yourselves. We need no other protection than that which your present laws secure to you.

In conclusion, then, let us say, in behalf of the women of this State, we ask for all that you have asked for yourselves in the progress of your development, since the *Mayflower* cast anchor beside Plymouth rock; and simply on the ground that the rights of every human being are the same and identical. You may say that the mass of the women of this State do not make the demand; it comes from a few sour, disappointed old maids and childless women.

You are mistaken; the mass speak through us. A very large majority of the women of this State support themselves and their children, and many their husbands too. . . . .

Now, do you candidly think these wives do not wish to control the 10 wages they earn—to own the land they buy—the houses they build? to have at their disposal their own children, without being subject to the constant interference and tyranny of an idle, worthless profligate? Do you suppose that any woman is such a pattern of devotion and submission that she willingly stitches all day for the small sum of fifty cents, that she may enjoy the unspeakable privilege, in obedience to your laws, of paying for her husband's tobacco and rum? Think you the wife of the confirmed, beastly drunkard would consent to share with him her home and bed, if law and public sentiment would release her from such gross companionship? Verily, no! . . .

For all these, then, we speak. If to this long list you add the laboring women who are loudly demanding remuneration for their unending toil; those women who teach in our seminaries, academies, and public schools for a miserable pittance; the widows who are taxed without mercy; the unfortunate ones in our work-houses, poor-houses, and prisons; who are they that we do not now represent? But a small class of the fashionable butterflies, who, through the short summer days, seek the sunshine and the flowers; but the cool breezes of autumn and the hoary frosts of winter will soon chase all these away; then they too, will need and seek protection, and through other lips demand in their turn justice and equity at your hands.

The Responsive Reader

1. In the opening paragraphs, what for you are strong points or telling arguments in Stanton's plea for "full recognition of our rights as citizens?"
2. How is the unequal status of men and women like the aristocratic European system that Americans had left behind? For Stanton, what is the irony of women being put on a pedestal during courtship, being sued to "on bended knee?"
3. What for Stanton is the parallel between the mentality that makes possible slavery and the mentality that disenfranchises women?
4. What is Stanton's answer to the charge that feminists like her do not speak for the large majority of women?

Thinking, Talking, Writing

5. In the words of the cigarette ad, do you think today's women "have come a long way" since Stanton's time?
6. What are common themes in Stanton's speech and in the speeches of other early advocates of women's rights, such as Susan B. Anthony and Sojourner Truth?

Thinking about Connections

7. Observers early noted parallels between the arguments and slogans of the Civil Rights movement and the women's movement. Do the speeches of Douglass and Stanton share common assumptions? Do they use similar appeals or similar strategies?

2

New Nation:
The One and the Many

Here is not a nation but a teeming nation of nations.
                                                    Walt Whitman

*To the extent that one's own self-esteem has been damaged by racism,
it is good and often necessary to become whole by interacting with
members of one's own group. This having been achieved, however, it is
self-defeating for individuals of any nationality to define the circle of
acquaintance primarily by race.*

                                            David Henry Hwang

*The price the immigrants had to pay for coming to America is that they
had to become Americans.*

                                                Amiri Baraka

LITERATURE IN CONTEXT

Countless millions came to America across the oceans on crowded,
smelly ships. Many were penniless. A poor woman immigrant was likely to
find herself in debt for her transportation, spending years paying off the debt
as a wage slave or "indentured servant." While most of the early immigrants
came from England and Scotland, America slowly became a magnet for the
poor and disenfranchised from Ireland and Germany, from Italy and Poland
and Russia, and eventually from the rest of the world.

The miracle of America was that here many nationalities lived in peace.
Irish and English, Germans and Jews, Poles and Russians, Serbs and Croats,
Turks and Armenians coexisted. Nationalities divided by murderous age-old
feuds worked together without planting bombs in front of one another's
stores. This is not to say that there was not prejudice and ethnic strife.
Bigoted parents frowned when a son or daughter wanted to marry one who
was "not one of theirs." (Why would a nice Jewish boy want to marry an
English girl?) Irish youths encountered signs that said "No Irish need apply."

Jewish newspaper vendors had their newspaper stands trashed by gentile thugs. At various times, anti-Irish, anti-German, anti-Japanese, or simply anti-foreign sentiment ran high.

Many Americans have special ties with a culture or a language other than that of mainstream America. Millions of Americans have always been bilingual. Becoming an American has often meant reconciling pride in old-world or old-country bonds with a new national identity that transcends religious, ethnic, or racial divisions. Many second-generation Americans have had to forge their own identity in the clash of cultural traditions. They have often lived in a world of old-country ways and old-country food at home and in a world of baseball, hot dogs, and Coke at school or among their peers.

For America's racial minorities, the tension between a separate and a larger national identity has been especially strong. As the Chinese American playwright David Henry Hwang says, unlike Old World countries, "America—at least in principle—subscribes to the notion that whoever takes residence on these shores may call them home." Asian Americans, then, like other minorities, tend to go through an "assimilationist" phase. They try to assimilate—to become like everyone else, "to out-white the whites." However, they find that, like other people of color, "we are never completely accepted as Americans; we are perpetual foreigners." The "inability to become white" may in fact "produce terrible self-loathing." Often the next stage has been a "separatist" phase of defiant self-assertion: African Americans shed their Anglo names for African names or join Black nationalist organizations. Mexican Americans declare solidarity with *la raza*. Asian Americans work with and write mainly for other Asian Americans.

Foreign observers often stress the leveling influence of American mass culture. The shopping centers, the way young people dress, and the hits on local radio stations seem the same from coast to coast. Jeans, McDonalds, popular music seem to define American culture. However, many Americans have always had to come to terms with a dual identity. They have had ties to a language, a religion, or a culture different from that of the mainstream. "Who am I?" has been a recurrent theme in American autobiographical writing.

I UNDERSTAND THE LARGE HEARTS OF HEROES

Walt Whitman (1819-1892)

I resist anything better than my own diversity.
> Walt Whitman

Walt Whitman said in the preface to the 1855 edition of his monumental, sprawling Leaves of Grass, *"The United States themselves are essentially the greatest poem." In the poems collected in that volume, he championed the full range of common humanity and celebrated America as a new world giving them the scope to realize their talents. In long chanting poems that read like a roll call of the American nation, he embraced the native and the foreign, the trapper and the farmer, the builder and the merchant, the shipwrecked sailor and the runaway slave, the preaching Quakeress and the preaching Methodist minister, the Yankee and the Southerner, men and women, young and old. He said early in the 1855 preface,*

> *The genius of the United States is not best or most in its executives or legislatures, nor in its ambassadors or authors or colleges or churches or parlors, nor even in its newspapers or inventors . . . but always in the common people. Their manners, speech, dress, friendships—the freshness and candor of their physiognomy—the picturesque looseness of their carriage . . . their deathless attachment to freedom . . . the practical acknowledgment of the citizens of one state by the citizens of all other states—the fierceness of their roused resentment—their curiosity and welcome of novelty—their self-esteem and wonderful sympathy—their susceptibility to a slight—the air they have of persons who never knew how it felt to stand in the presence of superiors . . . their good temper and openhandedness . . . the President's taking off his hat to them, not they to him—these too are unrhymed poetry.*

Whitman was the "poet of democracy," the voice of American democratic idealism. Born on Long Island, Whitman grew up in Brooklyn and worked there and in Manhattan as a journalist. He gloried in the diversity of the American nation while at the same time envisioning it as animated by a common spirit. He celebrated the nation's vital energy, enterprise, generosity, and equality, including the "perfect equality of the female with the male." He said that the opposition to slavery "shall never cease till it ceases or the speaking of tongues and the moving of lips cease." Whitman's "When Lilacs Last in the Dooryard Bloomed," his elegy on the death of President Lincoln, was his tribute to a leader he revered.

Whitman had to an uncommon degree the ability to identify with others. ("In all people I see myself, none more and not one a barleycorn less.") How does this gift for empathy show in the following selection from Leaves of Grass?

I understand the large hearts of heroes,   1
The courage of present times and all times,
How the skipper saw the crowded and rudderless wreck of the steam-ship,
    and Death chasing it up and down the storm,
How he knuckled tight and gave not back an inch, and was faithful of days
    and faithful of nights,
And chalked in large letters on a board, *Be of good cheer, we will not desert*   5
    you;
How he followed with them and tacked with them three days and would
    not give it up,
How he saved the drifting company at last,
How the lank loose-gowned women looked when boated from the side of
    their prepared graves,
How the silent old-faced infants and the lifted sick, and the sharp-lipp'd
    unshaven men;
All this I swallow, it tastes good, I like it well, it becomes mine,   10
I am the man, I suffered, I was there.

The disdain and calmness of martyrs,
The mother of old, condemned for a witch, burnt with dry wood, her
    children gazing on,
The hounded slave that flags in the race, leans by the fence, blowing,
    covered with sweat,
The twinges that sting like needles his legs and neck, the murderous   15
    buckshot and the bullets,
All these I feel or am.

I am the hounded slave, I wince at the bite of the dogs,
Hell and despair are upon me, crack and again crack the marksmen,
I clutch the rails of the fence, my gore dribs, thinned with the ooze of my
    skin,
I fall on the weeds and stones,   20
The riders spur their unwilling horses, haul close,
Taunt my dizzy ears and beat me violently over the head with whipstocks.

Agonies are one of my changes of garments,
I do not ask the wounded person how he feels, I myself become the
    wounded person,
My hurts turn livid upon me as I lean on a cane and observe.   25

I am the mashed fireman with breast-bone broken,
Tumbling walls buried me in their debris,
Heat and smoke I inspired, I heard the yelling shouts of my comrades.
I heard the distant click of their picks and shovels,
They have cleared the beams away, they tenderly lift me forth.   30

I lie in the night air in my red shirt, the pervading hush is for my sake,
Painless after all I lie exhausted but not so unhappy,
White and beautiful are the faces around me, the heads are bared of their
    fire-caps,
The kneeling crowd fades with the light of the torches.

Distant and dead resuscitate,   35
They show as the dial or move as the hands of me, I am the clock myself.

I am an old artillerist, I tell of my fort's bombardment,
I am there again.

Again the long roll of the drummers,
Again the attacking cannon, mortars,   40
Again to my listening ears the cannon responsive.

I take part, I see and hear the whole.

The Responsive Reader

1. Is there a common denominator for the people Whitman includes in this selection from his poem? Is there a common focus?
2. Does Whitman succeed in helping you identify with the people he describes? What details are for you most real or most striking? Where, for you, is he most successful? Where least and why?
3. How is Whitman's way of dealing with disaster and suffering similar to or different from their treatment in television news or newspaper coverage?
4. Whitman's free-flowing verse, breaking with the tradition of regular meter and rhyme, has seemed to many readers fitting for the sweep of his democratic vision. How should this poem be read? What should be the tone? What kind of person is speaking?

Thinking, Talking, Writing

5. Some people seem exceptionally callous about the suffering of others while others seem oversensitive to it. What makes the difference? (Toward which extreme do you tend yourself and why?) Is there an ideal middle ground?
6. Have you ever witnessed the kind of solidarity or received the kind of compassionate support Whitman describes?
7. Which of the American traits that Whitman lists in his preface do you recognize? Which do you think survive most strongly in our own time? For which could you do the best job of citing current examples? (You may want to concentrate on one and discuss it in detail.) What has happened to some of the others and why?

LEGACY II
Leroy V. Quintana

The first European settlements in North America were established by Spanish explorers. Large areas of the American West and Southwest were once part of Mexico, and Spanish is still the first language of many of its inhabitants. People who spoke Spanish founded many of the towns and cities: Santa Fe, San Antonio, El Paso, San Diego, Los Angeles. Missions first built by Spanish priests still dot the royal highway, or El Camino Real.

Leroy Quintana grew up with the Mexican traditions and folklore of the Southwest. He has described himself as "basically a small-town New Mexico boy carrying on the oral tradition." Born in Albuquerque, Quintana was raised by his grandparents and is a graduate of the University of New Mexico. In 1976 he published a book of poems called Hijo del Pueblo—Son of the Pueblo. *He won the Before Columbus Foundation American Book Award for* Sangre *(1982) and again for* The History of Home *(1993). With Victor Hernandez Cruz and Virgil Suarez, he edited an anthology of Latino poetry entitled* Paper Dance: 53 Latino Poets *(1994).*

Grandfather never went to school   1
spoke only a few words of English,
a quiet man; when he talked
talked about simple things
planting corn or about the weather   5
sometimes about herding sheep as a child.
One day pointed to the four directions
taught me their names

        El Norte
Poniente   Oriente   10
        El Sur

He spoke their names as if they were
one of only a handful of things
a man needed to know

Now I look back   15
only two generations removed
realize I am nothing but a poor fool
who went to college

trying to find my way back
to the center of the world   20
where Grandfather stood
that day

The Responsive Reader

1. In what sense did the grandfather stand "at the center of the world?"
2. In "concrete poetry," words are laid out on the page in a way that mirrors or suggests their meaning. How would the poem be different if the names of the four directions had been printed as a regular line of print?

Thinking, Talking, Writing

3. Is the grandfather's simple world gone forever, or is it still possible for people to approximate it? What kind of world would you find yourself in if you could go two generations back in your own family?
4. If you had to select "a handful of things" that people needed to know, what would you include and why?

AFTER THE FUNERAL

Joan I. Siegel

> *During the nineteenth century, large numbers of Jewish immigrants came to the United States, many from Poland and Russia. The Yiddish they spoke has left its imprint on American English; New York City life and politics have been strongly colored by the Jewish influence. Large areas of American life—science, medicine, psychiatry, business, comedy, music—are hard to imagine without the leadership of America's Jewish citizens. The outlook of many of today's Jewish Americans has been strongly affected by the memory of the Holocaust and by their support for the Jewish state in Israel.*
>
> *Joan I. Siegel teaches at Orange County Community College in the state of New York. Her poetry has appeared in many periodicals and in* Rage Before Pardon: Poems on the Holocaust *(1993). What is specifically Jewish about the following poem? What is universal?*

It rained later. 1

At noon, the sun shone.
The rabbi said Kaddish
beneath the canopy.
We followed along
on our printed cards. 5
Then we laid flowers,
dropped a handful of dirt
and stones and walked
away. 10

He told us not to look
back.

At the house
we took off our shoes
and lit the candle that burns 15
eight days and eight nights.

Our bodies ached
as though we'd been carrying
something heavy
and had put it down. 20

We sat around the table:
  a mother
  two daughters
  two husbands

         two grandchildren.   *25*
We ate sandwiches
as the sky went grey,
waiting for the doorbell to ring,
for someone
a friend, a relative   *30*
to bring honeycake,
condolences

waiting
for my father
to walk in from the rain.   *35*

The Responsive Reader

1. What do you know about American Jewish culture? What do you learn about American Jewish culture from this poem?
2. Does a reader have to be Jewish to appreciate this poem?

Thinking, Talking, Writing

3. People's lives used to be shaped by customs, ritual, tradition. How much of that influence is still at work in your own life?

Collaborative Projects

4. Yiddish has influenced American English in several ways; including vocabulary (*kibitz, schlock, schmaltz, kibosh*); idiom, or characteristic ways of talking ("frail-shmail!"); and word order ("on him it looks good," "that you call a lining?") Working with a group, you may want to explore the influence of Yiddish on American English or the influence of Jewish humor in American life.

MARRIAGE WAS A FOREIGN COUNTRY

Mitsuye Yamada

> *Mitsuye Yamada was born in Japan and raised in Seattle. Like many other Japanese Americans, she was interned in a relocation camp during World War II. She published her* Camp Notes and Other Poems *in 1976. Her poems often deal with the perspective of Americans who see the traditional culture of their immigrant parents at one remove while being considered a "minority" in their own country. The following poem focuses on one of the thousands of women from Japan, China, or India who came to this country as the dependents of immigrant workers through arranged marriages, often waiting many years to join their spouses. Often, as "picture brides," they knew their intended husbands only from photographs.*

I come to be here   1
because
they say I must
follow my husband

so I come.   5

My grandmother cried:
you are not cripple
why
to America?

When we land the boat full   10
of new brides
lean over railing
with wrinkled glossy pictures
they hold inside hand
like this   15
so excited
down there a dock full of men
they do same thing
hold pictures
look up and down   20
like this
they find faces to
match pictures.

Your father I see him on the dock
he come to Japan to marry   25
and leave me
I was not a picture bride
I only was afraid.

The Responsive Reader

1. How does the speaker in the poem feel about her arrival in the new country? What was the attitude of those she left behind?
2. Do you recognize features of the immigrant's English used by the speaker in the poem?

Thinking, Talking, Writing

3. Are arranged marriages a thing of the past? Do couples today marry for practical considerations or for love?
4. The speaker in the poem says, "They say I must follow my husband." Is this still true of wives today?

Collaborative Projects

5. Bring to class and share with your classmates old photographs of women (grandmothers, great-grandmothers) in your family or in the community. What can these pictures tell you about women's lives?

WHAT IS AN AMERICAN?

St. Jean de Crèvecoeur

> *St. Jean de Crèvecoeur's* Letters from an American Farmer, *published in 1782, were one of the first attempts to define the identity and the soul of the new nation. Although he came from an aristocratic French family and had served as an officer in the French army in Canada, he described himself as a "humble American planter, a simple cultivator of the earth." He saw colonial America as a haven set up by Providence for ever-growing numbers of European emigrants, driven from their homes by the "severity of taxes, the injustice of laws, the tyranny of the rich, and the oppressive avarice of the church." He painted a picture of a country that offered plentiful fishing, forests yielding the best lumber, and land everywhere for cattle and bountiful crops. At the same time, he was one of the first writers to paint an ideal picture of his Native American neighbors as uncorrupted children of nature. He said, "without temples, without priests, without kings, and without laws, they are in many instances superior to us," bearing hardships with patience and living without the corroding anxieties of white civilization.*
>
> *By the time his letters were published, Crèvecoeur's optimistic vision of the American future had been badly shaken by the hatreds engendered by the War of Revolution. He saw both sides inflict barbaric cruelties on accused traitors or suspected backsliders and their helpless families. Suspected of Tory sympathies by the revolutionaries, he eventually returned to live in France, except for some years of service as a French consul in the East.*
>
> *The following selection represents the first part of the most famous of Crèvecoeur's letters. At the time, he wrote, the colonies were still part of "British America." Harvard, the first colonial college, had been founded in 1636 and was already over a hundred years old.*

I wish I could be acquainted with the feelings and thoughts which 1 must agitate the heart and present themselves to the mind of an enlightened Englishman when he first lands on this continent. He must greatly rejoice that he lived at a time to see this fair country discovered and settled; he must necessarily feel a share of national pride when he views the chain of settlements which embellish these extended shores. When he says to himself, "This is the work of my countrymen, who, when convulsed by factions, afflicted by a variety of miseries and wants, restless and impatient, took refuge here. They brought along with them their national genius, to which they principally owe what liberty they enjoy and what substance they possess." Here he sees the industry of his native country displayed in a new manner and traces in their works the embryos of all the arts, sciences, and ingenuity which flourish in Europe. Here he beholds fair cities, substantial villages, extensive fields, an immense country filled with decent houses, good roads, orchards, meadows, and bridges where a hundred years ago all was wild, woody, and uncultivated! What a train of pleasing ideas this fair spectacle must suggest; it is a prospect which must inspire a good citizen with the most heart-felt pleasure. The difficulty consists in the manner of viewing so extensive a scene. He is arrived on a new continent; a modern society offers itself to his contemplation, different from what he had hitherto seen. It is not composed, as in Europe, of great lords who possess everything and of a herd of people who have nothing. Here are no aristocratic families, no courts, no kings, no bishops, no ecclesiastical dominion, no invisible power giving to a few a very visible one, no great manufactures employing thousands, no great refinements of luxury. The rich and the poor are not so far removed from each other as they are in Europe. Some few towns excepted, we are all tillers of the earth, from Nova Scotia to West Florida. We are a people of cultivators scattered over an immense territory, communicating with each other by means of good roads and navigable rivers, united by the silken bands of mild government, all respecting the laws without dreading their power, because they are equitable. We are all animated with the spirit of an industry which is unfettered and unrestrained, because each person works for himself. If he travels through our rural districts, he views not the hostile castle and the haughty mansion, contrasted with the clay-built hut and miserable cabin, where cattle and men help to keep each other warm and dwell in meanness, smoke, and indigence. A pleasing uniformity of decent competence appears throughout our habitations. The meanest of our log houses is a dry and comfortable habitation. Lawyer or merchant are the fairest titles our towns afford; that of a farmer is the only appellation of the rural inhabitants of our country. It must take some time before he can reconcile himself to our dictionary, which is but short in words of dignity and names of honor. There, on a Sunday, he sees a congregation of respectable farmers and their wives, all clad in neat homespun, well mounted, or riding in their own humble wagons. There is not among them an esquire, save the unlettered magistrate. There he sees a parson as simple as his flock, a farmer who does not riot on the labor of others. We have no princes for whom we toil, starve, and bleed; we are the most perfect society now existing in the world. Here man is free as he ought to be, nor is this pleasing equality so transitory as many others are. Many ages will not see the shores of our great lakes replenished with inland nations, nor the unknown bounds of North America entirely peopled. Who can tell how far it extends? Who can tell the millions of men whom it will feed and contain? For no European foot has as yet traveled half the extent of this mighty continent!

The next wish of this traveler will be to know whence came all these people. They are a mixture of English, Scotch, Irish, French, Dutch, Germans, and Swedes. From this promiscuous breed, that race now called Americans have arisen. The eastern provinces must indeed be excepted as being the unmixed descendants of Englishmen. I have heard many wish that they had been more intermixed also; for my part, I am no wisher and think it much better as it has happened. They exhibit a most conspicuous figure in this great and variegated picture; they too enter for a great share in the pleasing perspective displayed in these thirteen provinces. I know it is fashionable to reflect on them, but I respect them for what they have done; for the accuracy and wisdom with which they have settled their territory; for the decency of their manners; for their early love of letters; their ancient college, the first in this hemisphere; for their industry, which to me who am but a farmer is the criterion of everything. There never was a people, situated as they are, who with so ungrateful a soil have done more in so short a time. . . .

In this great American asylum, the poor of Europe have by some means met together, and in consequence of various causes; to what purpose should they ask one another what countrymen they are? Alas, two thirds of them had no country. Can a wretch who wanders about, who works and starves, whose life is a continual scene of sore affliction or pinching penury—can that man call England or any other kingdom his country? A country that had no bread for him, whose fields procured him no harvest, who met with nothing but the frowns of the rich, the severity of the laws, with jails and punishments, who owned not a single foot of the extensive surface of this planet? No! Urged by a variety of motives, here they came. Everything has tended to regenerate them: new laws, a new mode of living, a new social system; here they are become men: in Europe they were as so many useless plants, wanting vegetative mould and refreshing showers. They withered and were mowed down by want, hunger, and war, but now, by the power of transplantation, like all other plants they have taken root and flourished! Formerly they were not numbered in any civil lists of their country, except in those of the poor; here they rank as citizens. By what invisible power has this surprising metamorphosis been performed? By that of the laws and that of their industry. The laws, the indulgent laws, protect them as they arrive, stamping on them the symbol of adoption. They receive ample rewards for their labors; these accumulated rewards procure them lands; those lands confer on them the title of freemen, and to that title every benefit is affixed which men can possibly require. This is the great operation daily performed by our laws. Whence proceed these laws? From our government. Whence that government? It is derived from the original genius and strong desire of the people ratified and confirmed by the crown. This is the great chain which links us all, this is the picture which every province exhibits, Nova Scotia excepted. There the crown has done all; either there were no people who had genius or it was not much attended to; the consequence is that the province is very thinly inhabited indeed; the power of the crown in conjunction with the mosquitoes has prevented men from settling there. Yet some parts of it flourished once, and it contained a mild, harmless set of people. But for the fault of a few leaders, the whole was banished. The greatest political error the crown ever committed in America was to cut off men from a country which wanted nothing but men!

What attachment can a poor European emigrant have for a country where he had nothing? The knowledge of the language, the love of a few kindred as poor as himself, were the only cords that tied him; his country is now that which gives him his land, bread, protection, and consequence; *Ubi panis ibi patria* [My country is where I earn my bread] is the motto of all emigrants. What, then, is the American, this new man? He is either an European or the descendant of an European; hence that strange mixture of blood, which you will find in no other country. I could point out to you a family whose grandfather was an Englishman, whose wife was Dutch, whose son married a French woman, and whose present four sons have now four wives of different nations. *He* is an American, who, leaving behind him all his ancient prejudices and manners, receives new ones from the new mode of life he has embraced, the new government he obeys, and the new rank he holds. He becomes an American by being received in the broad lap of our great Alma Mater. Here individuals of all nations are melted into a new race of men, whose labors and posterity will one day cause great changes in the world. Americans are the western pilgrims who are carrying along with them that great mass of arts, sciences, vigor, and industry which began long since in the East; they will finish the great circle. The Americans were once scattered all over Europe; here they are incorporated into one of the finest systems of population which has ever appeared, and which will hereafter become distinct by the power of the different climates they inhabit. The American ought therefore to love this country much better than that wherein either he or his forefathers were born. Here the rewards of his industry follow with equal steps the progress of his labor; his labor is founded on the basis of nature, self-interest; can it want a stronger allurement? Wives and children, who before in vain demanded of him a morsel of bread, now, fat and frolicsome, gladly help their father to clear those fields whence exuberant crops are to arise to feed and to clothe them all, without any part being claimed, either by a despotic prince, a rich abbot, or a mighty lord. Here religion demands but little of him: a small voluntary salary to the minister and gratitude to God. Can he refuse these? The American is a new man, who acts upon new principles; he must therefore entertain new ideas and form new opinions. From involuntary idleness, servile dependence, penury, and useless labor, he has passed to toils of a very different nature, rewarded by ample subsistence. This is an American.

British America is divided into many provinces, forming a large association scattered along a coast of 1,500 miles extent and about 200 wide. This society I would fain examine, at least such as it appears in the middle provinces; if it does not afford that variety of tinges and gradations which may be observed in Europe, we have colors peculiar to ourselves. For instance, it is natural to conceive that those who live near the sea must be very different from those who live in the woods; the intermediate space will afford a separate and distinct class. 5

Men are like plants; the goodness and flavor of the fruit proceeds from the peculiar soil and exposition in which they grow. We are nothing but what we derive from the air we breathe, the climate we inhabit, the government we obey, the system of religion we profess, and the nature of our employment. Here you will find but few crimes; these have acquired as yet no root among us. I wish I were able to trace all my ideas; if my ignorance prevents me from describing them properly, I hope I shall be able to delineate a few of the outlines, which is all I propose.

Those who live near the sea feed more on fish than on flesh and often encounter that boisterous element. This renders them more bold and enterprising; this leads them to neglect the confined occupations of the land. They see and converse with a variety of people; their intercourse with mankind becomes extensive. The sea inspires them with a love of traffic, a desire of transporting produce from one place to another, and leads them to a variety of resources which supply the place of labor. Those who inhabit the middle settlements, by far the most numerous, must be very different; the simple cultivation of the earth purifies them, but the indulgences of the government, the soft remonstrances of religion, the rank of independent freeholders, must necessarily inspire them with sentiments, very little known in Europe among a people of the same class. What do I say? Europe has no such class of men; the early knowledge they acquire, the early bargains they make, give them a great degree of sagacity. As freemen, they will be litigious; pride and obstinacy are often the cause of lawsuits; the nature of our laws and governments may be another. As citizens, it is easy to imagine that they will carefully read the newspapers, enter into every political disquisition, freely blame or censure governors and others. As farmers, they will be careful and anxious to get as much as they can, because what they get is their own. As northern men, they will love the cheerful cup. As Christians, religion curbs them not in their opinions; the general indulgence leaves every one to think for themselves in spiritual matters. The law inspects our actions; our thoughts are left to God. Industry, good living, selfishness, litigiousness, country politics, the pride of freemen, religious indifference, are their characteristics. If you recede still farther from the sea, you will come into more modern settlements; they exhibit the same strong lineaments, in a ruder appearance. Religion seems to have still less influence, and their manners are less improved.

Now we arrive near the great woods, near the last inhabited districts; there men seem to be placed still farther beyond the reach of government, which in some measure leaves them to themselves. How can it pervade every corner, as they were driven there by misfortunes, necessity of beginnings, desire of acquiring large tracks of land, idleness, frequent want of economy, ancient debts; the reunion of such people does not afford a very pleasing spectacle. When discord, want of unity and friendship, when either drunkenness or idleness prevail in such remote districts, contention, inactivity, and wretchedness must ensue. There are not the same remedies to these evils as in a long-established community. The few magistrates they have are in general little better than the rest. They are often in a perfect state of war, that of man against man, sometimes decided by blows, sometimes by means of the law; that of man against every wild inhabitant of these venerable woods, of which they are come to dispossess them. There men appear to be no better than carnivorous animals of a superior rank, living on the flesh of wild animals when they can catch them, and when they are not able, they subsist on grain. He who would wish to see America in its proper light and have a true idea of its feeble beginnings and barbarous rudiments must visit our extended line of frontiers, where the last settlers dwell and where he may see the first labors of settlement, the mode of clearing the earth, in all their different appearances, where men are wholly left dependent on their native tempers and on the spur of uncertain industry, which often fails when not sanctified by the efficacy of a few moral rules. There, remote from the power of example and check of shame, many families exhibit the most hideous parts of our society. They are a kind of forlorn hope, preceding by ten or twelve years the most respectable army of veterans which come after them. In that space, prosperity will polish some, vice and the law will drive off the rest, who, uniting again with others like themselves, will recede still farther, making room for more industrious people, who will finish their improvements, convert the log-house into a convenient habitation, and rejoicing that the first heavy labors are finished, will change in a few years that hitherto barbarous country into a fine, fertile, well-regulated district. Such is our progress; such is the march of the Europeans toward the interior parts of this continent. In all societies there are off-casts; this impure part serves as our precursors or pioneers. My father himself was one of that class, but he came upon honest principles and was therefore one of the few who held fast; by good conduct and temperance, he transmitted to me his fair inheritance, when not above one in fourteen of his contemporaries had the same good fortune.

Forty years ago, this smiling country was thus inhabited; it is now purged, a general decency of manners prevails throughout, and such has been the fate of our best countries.

Exclusive of those general characteristics, each province has its own, *10* founded on the government, climate, mode of husbandry, customs, and peculiarity of circumstances. Europeans submit insensibly to these great powers and become, in the course of a few generations, not only Americans in general, but either Pennsylvanians, Virginians, or provincials under some other name. Whoever traverses the continent must easily observe those strong differences, which will grow more evident in time. The inhabitants of Canada, Massachusetts, the middle provinces, the southern ones, will be as different as their climates; their only points of unity will be those of religion and language.

As I have endeavored to show you how Europeans become Americans, it may not be disagreeable to show you likewise how the various Christian sects introduced wear out and how religious indifference becomes prevalent.

When any considerable number of a particular sect happen to dwell contiguous to each other, they immediately erect a temple and there worship the Divinity agreeably to their own peculiar ideas. Nobody disturbs them. If any new sect springs up in Europe, it may happen that many of its professors will come and settle in America. As they bring their zeal with them, they are at liberty to make proselytes if they can and to build a meeting and to follow the dictates of their consciences; for neither the government nor any other power interferes. If they are peaceable subjects and are industrious, what is it to their neighbors how and in what manner they think fit to address their prayers to the Supreme Being? But if the sectaries are not settled close together, if they are mixed with other denominations, their zeal will cool for want of fuel, and will be extinguished in a little time. Then, the Americans become as to religion what they are as to country, allied to all. In them the name of Englishman, Frenchman, and European is lost, and in like manner, the strict modes of Christianity as practised in Europe are lost also.

The Responsive Reader

1. In the opening pages, what does Crèvecoeur see as the key contrasts between Europe and the new world? Why, for instance, does he make a special point of the absence of titles, of "words of dignity and names of honor?" What evidence does he give to support his thesis that "we are the most perfect society now existing in the world"?

2. In spite of his generally critical view of Europe, what parts of the European tradition or inheritance does the author credit with making America what it is? In particular, where and how does he pay tribute to the English contribution to the new nation?

3. What picture does Crèvecoeur give you of the early immigrants who came to America—their class background, their motives? What, according to him, was their relationship or attitude toward the "old country"?

4. How does Crèvecoeur shed light on the traditional "melting pot" view of American culture? What according to him was the ethnic mix of the early immigrants? How or how soon did they come to see themselves as Americans?

5. What account does this letter give of regional differences? What is its account of life on the Western frontier?

6. What light does this letter shed on the American tradition of religious tolerance?

Thinking, Talking, Writing

7. What to you is the essence of Crèvecoeur's answer to "What Is an American?" How much of his answer to you think is still true or relevant today?

8. Do you agree that "My country is where I earn my bread"?

9. Try your hand at an updated definition of what it means to be an American.

Thinking about Connections

10. Jefferson's Declaration of Independence," Crèvecoeur's "What Is an American?" and Whitman's "I Understand the Large Hearts of Heroes" embody much of what was promising and hopeful about the new nation. What values or expectations do they share? How do they help you define the promise of America?

ONLY YESTERDAY

Ellen Glasgow

What were the people like who first settled in the eastern part of the continent? Ellen Glasgow's novel Vein of Iron *takes the reader to Appalachian Virginia, to the valleys of the Blue Ridge and Alleghenies, where descendants of the early settlers lived in scattered farmhouses with weathered tin or shingle roofs. Their ancestors had been Scotch Presbyterians: A great-great-grandfather was a Presbyterian minister who brought the elders and deacons and other members of his church across the Atlantic with him in a crossing that took 118 days in a small ship. In the early days, the newcomers had lived in a state of intermittent small-scale warfare with the tribes in whose lands they had settled and to whom they referred as "heathens" or "savages."*

The following short excerpts from the novel focus on Grandmother Fincastle, who is a tower of strength to the family in Glasgow's novel. The grandmother reminisces about her own life and about people and places she has known or heard about. One of these is Great-great-grandmother Tod, who as a ten-year-old girl was captured by the Shawnees during one of their raids on white settlements. When she was sixteen, she was married to a young Shawnee chief. Under the peace treaty that ended Pontiac's war in 1766, she was returned to her original family.

What follows are Grandmother Fincastle's memories of pioneer life and of her family history. A few references remind us of the role of religion in the family's life. Sunday is called the Sabbath. When a young person is admitted to "sealing ordinances," she becomes a full member of the church and is eligible for sacraments such as Holy Communion. The congregation sings the "doxology," a hymn of praise that is part of the church ritual.

Her youth had suffered from hardships; she had spent her childhood in   1
a log cabin, yet she had not been ashamed. When she was five years old her father was called to a mission on Wildcat Mountain, and from that time she had not seen a railway train until she was grown. Mr. Fincastle had met her when he came to preach at the mission, and he had felt from the first minute, he told her afterwards, that this also was appointed. That was the Sabbath she was admitted to sealing ordinances. But even before she had reached the years of discretion, her faith had been strong. When she was no bigger than a slip of a girl she had felt that she was ready to do or die, or even to be damned, if it would redound to the greater glory of God.

Though she knew that bricks are no more than straws in the sight of the Lord, she would always remember how wonderful the manse had appeared to her, as a bride, when she had first seen it on a spring morning. Everything had seemed to her to be provided; the grove of oaks to cast shade; the vegetable garden at the back of the house; the well so close to the kitchen porch; the springhouse at the bottom of the yard under the big willow; and the house inside, with the solid furniture, the rows of books that had always been there, and the shining pewter plates, so bright you could see your face in them, on the sideboard. She could imagine nothing more luxurious than eating in a dining room, with a cloth on the table, and having hot water to wash in. As a bride she used to say that she praised the Lord whenever she took up that big kettle from the trivet in front of the fire. . . .

How in the world, Grandmother still asked herself, had those early settlers been able to enjoy living without such simple comforts as featherbeds and kettles of hot water? In fear, too, whenever they had taken time to stop and think, of the savages. Yet they also had loved life. They had loved it the more because it was fugitive; they had loved it for the sake of the surprise, the danger, the brittleness of the moment. Her husband, she knew, had felt this, though what he had said sounded so different. Life will yield up its hidden sweetness, she had heard him preach from the pulpit, only when it is being sacrificed to something more precious than life.

They had believed this in the old days. Time and again, they had risen from the ruins of happiness. Yet they had gone on; they had rebuilt the ruins; they had scattered life more abundantly over the ashes. There was a near neighbor of her grandfather who had held his cabin twice when others fled to the stockade. For the sake of his crop, he had held his ground. All within the space of ten years, he had seen two wives and two families of children scalped and killed by the savages. He himself had once been left to die, and a second time he had escaped from an Indian village and made his way home through the wilderness. For the rest of his life he had worn a handkerchief tied over his head, and one Sunday morning, while the congregation sang the Doxology, he had fallen down in a fit. In his later years he had married a third wife and had brought up a new family, after the manner of Job, to inherit the land. Though he had seen men burned at the stake, he had never lost his trust in Divine goodness.

And nearer still, there was her own grandmother, Martha Tod. She had liked the young chief too well, people had whispered. He was a noble figure; he had many virtues; she had wept when they came to redeem her. One story ran that her Indian husband had come to the settlement in search of her, and that her two brothers had killed him in the woods, from ambush, and had hidden his body. This may have been true, and again it may not have been. The age was a wild one. Many of the men who had come to the wilderness to practice religion appeared to have forgotten its true nature. Whatever happened, Martha Tod's lips were sealed tight. No one, not even her mother, had ever won her confidence again, or heard her speak of her life with the Shawnees. But as long as she lived, after her marriage to an elder in the church, she had suffered from spells of listening, a sort of wildness, which would steal upon her in the fall of the year, especially in the blue haze of weather they called Indian summer. Then she would leap up at the hoot of an owl or the bark of a fox and disappear into the forest. When she returned from these flights, her husband would notice a strange stillness in her eyes, as if she were listening to silence. But gradually, as her children grew up, ten of them in all, fine, sturdy, professing Christians, her affliction became lighter. To the end of her days, even after her reason had tottered, she could still card, spin, weave, dye, or knit as well as the best of them. Grandmother had heard that when she was dying, her youth, with the old listening look, had flashed back into her face, and she had tried to turn toward the forest. But that was too much to credit. It couldn't have happened. Not when her mind was addled, not when she was well over a hundred. Grandmother remembered her well . . .

A closed memory unfolded as a fan in her thoughts. She saw the pale red loop of the road round the manse on a spring morning, the narrow valley, deep as a river, and the lofty Endless Mountains thronging beneath the April blue of the sky. It was more than fifty years ago, but it seemed only yesterday!

The Responsive Reader

1. On the basis of these excerpts, try to piece together a picture of what the life of a typical pioneer family may have been like.
2. In many accounts of pioneer life, we get only glimpses of the Native Americans into whose lands the white settlers were moving. What glimpses of the Native Americans do you get here? From what perspective are they seen?
3. What kind of women do you see in these excerpts? Are they similar to or different from what you would have expected to see in this kind of society and this point in history?

Thinking, Talking, Writing

4. How much do you know of your own family history? Where can you turn to learn more? Prepare a family history that you can present to the other members of your class.

Collaborative Projects

5. Working as a group, you may want to select and edit family histories for a class publication.

EILEEN

Mary Gordon

Along with the English and the Germans, the Irish were one of the large early immigrant groups that helped shape the American national character. Discriminated against at first, they came to play a dominant role in the ward politics of Boston and other large cities. The Irish pub, the Irish cop on the beat, and Irish song and story became part of American folklore. Mary Gordon's fiction is often set in the context of Irish America. She has written novels including Final Payments *and* The Other Side. *The following short story appeared in a collection of her stories called* Temporary Shelter *(1987). Gordon lives in New York City, traditionally a hub of immigrant life.*

In this story, Irish immigrants struggle to move up out of poverty. As in Italian or Polish neighborhoods, Catholicism is strong. Nuns teach the young and offer their charitable services to the sick or disabled. As in American cities of later years, random violence and murderous gunplay are already the bane of American city life.

"There's some that just can't take it," Bridget said. "No matter what they do or you do for them, they just don't fit in."

"You certainly were good to her, Kathleen," said Nettie, "when she first came over. No one could have been better when she first came over."

"That was years ago," Kathleen said. "We never kept up with her."

Nora thought of Eileen Foley when she had first come over, twelve years ago, when Nora was eleven and Eileen, twenty-one. They'd had to share a bed, and Kathleen had apologized. "There's no place for her, only here. I don't know what they were thinking of, sending her over, with no one to vouch for her, only the nuns. The Foleys were like that, the devil take the hindmost, every one of them. You'd see why she wanted to get out."

But Nora hadn't minded. She liked Eileen's company, and her body was no intrusion in the bed. Her flesh was pleasant, fragrant. Though she was large, she was careful not to take up too much room. They joked about it. "Great cow that I am, pray God I don't roll over one fine night and crush you. How'd yer mam forgive me if I should do that."

And they would laugh, excluding Nora's brothers, as they excluded them with all their talk about the future, Eileen's and Nora's both. It was adult talk; the young boys had no place in it. It was female too, but it was different from the way that Nora's mother and aunts, Bridget and Nettie, spoke, because it had belief and hope, and the older women's conversation began with a cheerful, skeptical, accepting resignation and could move—particularly when Bridget took the lead—to a conviction of injustice and impossibility and the inevitable folly of expecting one good thing.

They talked every night about what had happened to Eileen at work. She was a cook at a school for the blind run for the Presentation sisters. It was in the Bronx. In Limerick, she'd worked at the sisters' orphanage; she was grateful they had recommended her over here. She was proud of her work, she liked the people, worshipped the nuns that ran the place. She said she would have loved to be a nun, only for her soft nature. She was right about herself; she had a penchant for small luxuries: lavender sachets to perfume her underclothes, honey-flavored lozenges that came in a tin box with a picture of a beautiful blond child, a clothesbrush with an ivory handle, a hatpin that pushed its point into the dull black felt of Eileen's hat and left behind a butterfly of yellow and red stones. She would take these things out secretly and show them first to Nora, so that Nora felt that she possessed them too and considered herself doubly blessed: with the friendship of one so much older and with the passion of her observation of these objects she could covet, and could prize but need not own.

The nuns, Eileen told Nora often, had a terrible hard life. They slept on wooden pallets and were silent after dark; they woke at dawn, ate little and were not permitted to have friends. Not even among each other; no, they had to be particularly on their guard for that. "Particular friendships, it's called," Eileen told Nora proudly. "They're forbidden particular friendships." She told Nora she'd learned all this from Sister Mary Rose who ran the kitchen. It was not her praise that mattered to Eileen, though, but the words of Sister Catherine Benedict, the superior.

"She came up to me once, that quiet, I didn't know she was behind me. I was cutting up some cod for boiling, you know the blind ones have to have soft foods, as they can't cut, of course—and Sister must have been watching me over my shoulder all the time. 'You are particularly careful, Eileen Foley, and the Blessed Mother sees that, and she will reward you, mark my words. A bone left in a piece of fish could mean death for one of the children, so to cut up each piece with the utmost care is like a Corporal Work of Mercy for the poor little souls.' "

Eileen said that Sister Catherine Benedict had come from Galway city. *10* "You could tell she comes from money. But she gave it up. For God." At Christmas time, Sister had given Eileen a holy picture of her patron saint, Saint Catherine of Siena and on the back had signed her name with a cross in front of it. Nora and Eileen would look at the picture; it seemed to them a sign of something that they valued but could not find or even name in the world that they inhabited; excellence, simplicity. One day, Eileen promised, she would bring Nora to the home so that she could meet Sister Catherine for herself. But it never happened, there was never time.

Because, really, Eileen hadn't lived with the Derencys very long, six months perhaps. Nora tried to remember how long it was; at twenty-three the seasons of an eleven-year-old seemed illusory: what could possibly have happened then to mark one month from another, or one year? Each day of her adulthood seemed like the dropping down of coins into a slot: a sound fixed, right and comforting accompanied her aging, the sound of money in the bank. Childhood was no gift to a cripple, she'd often thought, with its emphasis on physical speed, with those interminable hours which required for their filling senseless, interminable games of jumping, running, catching, following, scaling, shinnying, those various and diffuse verbs that spelled her failure. Even now, in her well-cut suit, her perfumed handkerchief shaped like a fan tucked in her pocket, the gold compact she had bought herself with her first wages, even now she could think of those childhood games and bring back once again the fear, the anger, the thin high smell that was the anguish of exclusion. Even now, though her success at Mr. Riordan's law office was breathtaking, even now she could bring back the memory of her body's defeat.

Even now, at twenty-three, as she stood in the kitchen drinking black coffee while her mother cooked and her aunts lounged over their boiled eggs, even now Nora could feel the misery. She thought of Eileen and of the pleasure it had been to have her; one of her few physical pleasures as a child. She thought about Eileen's abundant flesh that seemed to have much more in common with a food than with an object of sexual desire: the white flesh of an apple came to mind or milk, a peach in its first blush of ripeness, the swell of a firm, mild delicious cheese. Nothing dark, secretive or inexplicably responsive seemed to be a part of Eileen's body life. And Nora prized Eileen because it seemed to her that Eileen was as definitely cut off from coupling as she, although she could not quite say why. For it was Nora's body's bro- kenness that always would exclude her from the desiring eye of men, whereas with Eileen it was excessive wholeness that would turn men's eyes away: nothing could be broken into, broken up.

Six months it must have been, thought Nora, that she lived here. After that she moved into the convent. She felt embarrassed, she'd confessed to Nora, to be living with the family. She'd offered money for her board, but Kathleen had refused it. And she hated the remarks that Bridget made about her family. Family passion and its underside, the family shame, could make Eileen's high color mottle, and her perfect skin appear sickish and damp. She knew what her family was, but after all, she said, they tried their best, their luck had been against them.

"You make your own luck," Bridget had said when Nora tried, just after Eileen had left them, to defend the Foleys. She'd mentioned their bad luck. "Every greenhorn in America came here through nothing but bad luck. If it was good luck that we had, we'd be back home in great fine houses."

"Still there's some like the Foleys that God's eye doesn't shine on," said   *15* Kathleen.

"God's eye, my eye, 'tis nothing wrong with them but laziness and drink, the same old song, and no new verses added," Bridget said.

"But what about the mother?" Nettie said. The two sisters looked sharply at her, warning her to silence.

"That was never proved," said Kathleen.

"What was never proved?" eleven-year-old Nora had asked.

"Time enough for you to be knowing that kind of story. Hanging   20
about the way you do, you know far too much as it is," Bridget said.

I know more than you'll know when you're a hundred, Nora wanted
to say to her aunt, whom she despised for her bad nature and yet feared. She
felt that Bridget blamed her for her leg, as if, if she'd wanted it, she could be
outside running with the other children. There was some truth in that, there
always was in Bridget's black predictions and malevolent reports. It was the
partial truths in what she said that made her dangerous.

It was only recently that they'd explained about Eileen's mother. Nora
tried now to remember what the circumstances might have been that would
have made the sisters talk about it. She could not. It wasn't that they'd seen
Eileen, they hadn't, not since Nora's high school graduation which was six
years ago now. They had known the Foleys' house, so it was real to them,
the news, when it came from her cousin Anna Fogarty, who had stayed on
at home. Mrs. Foley, Eileen's mother, who everyone had thought was queer,
had burned the house down and she herself and her youngest baby, a boy of
six months, had both perished. Everyone believed that she had set the fire.
Nora felt she saw it, the fixed face of the mother as her life burned up
around her, the green skeleton of the boy baby, left to be gone over like the
ruined clothes, the spoons, the pots and pans.

Eileen's father had married again, which just showed, Bridget said, the
foolishness of some young girls. All the sisters thought of marriage as a sign
of weakness: they made only partial exceptions for themselves. But the young
girl who'd married Eileen's father seemed to prove the sisters' point. She'd
left her family where she had considered herself unhappy, thinking she was
moving out to something better. The parish had helped Jamesie Foley build
a new house: that had turned the young girl's head. But what she got for her
pains was a drunken husband and a brood of someone else's children whom
she tormented until Eileen couldn't bear to see it and left to work in the
orphanage in Limerick, where the nuns, knowing her wishes, got the place
for her in their house in New York.

The sisters in both convents knew her dreams were for her brother
Tom. Tom was twelve years younger than Eileen, the youngest living child.
He was wonderfully intelligent, Eileen told Nora, and had an angel's nature.
Every penny of her salary she could she put into the bank to bring him over;
that was why she took the sister's offer of her living in the convent instead of
with the Derencys, she could save her carfare. That was what she said to the
Derencys, but Nora knew there was more to it. Her pride, which couldn't
tolerate Kathleen not taking any money. Nora could tell that Eileen worshipped Kathleen. And it troubled her that there was nothing she could do
for Kathleen when Kathleen did so much for her.

As Kathleen's life had blurred, Nora's had been pressed into sharp focus.   25

She had wanted to become a teacher, and her teachers encouraged her. Austere and yet maternal Protestants, romantic from the books they read, they treasured the pretty crippled girl with her devotion to the plays of Shakespeare and to Caesar's Gallic Wars, to anything, in fact, that they suggested she should read. Nora had been accepted at the Upstate Normal School on the basis of her grades and of her teachers' letters. But none of them had mentioned Nora's deformity; she'd been born with one leg shorter than the other. She realized they hadn't known, the moment she arrived, nervous to the point of sickness, driven by her nervous mother. How shocked those men were, in the office of the Dean, when they beheld her with her high shoe and her crutch. They blamed the teachers. "No one has informed us . . . You must see, of course, it's quite impossible . . . We must think first about the safety of potential children who might be in your charge. Imagine if there were a fire or a similar emergency . . ." They talked as if they were reading what they said from a book. They did not look at her. They said that it was most regrettable, but they were sure she understood, and understood that it was no reflection—not-a-tall—on her. They were just sorry she had had to make the trip.

She drove back with her mother in shamed silence, as if she'd been left at the altar and in all her wedding finery was making her way home. That was the way her father behaved, as if she had been jilted. He said he and some of his friends whose names he wouldn't mention would drive themselves up there and teach a lesson to those Yankee bastards. It was a free country, he said; you didn't get away with that kind of behavior here. He was very angry at his wife.

"Did you say nothing to them, Kathleen? Did you just walk out with your tail between your legs like some bog trotter thrown off the land by an English thief? Was that the way of it?"

Nora saw her mother's shame. She knew her father was just talk; he would have done no better. She herself had remained silent, and she bore her own shame in her heart. She would not let her mother feel the weight of it.

"I think, you know, Dad, it's a blessing in disguise. I'd make three times the money in an office. You were right, Dad, all along. I should have taken the commercial course."

"I was not right. You went where you belonged, there in the academic. You've twice the brains of any of them. Reading Latin like a priest. French too. I'm that proud of you."

She wanted to tell him that her education had been nothing, foolishness, Latin she was already forgetting, French she couldn't speak, history that meant not one thing to her, plays and poems about nothing to do with her life. She felt contempt, then, for her teachers and the things they stood for. She felt they'd conspired against her and made her look a fool. They could have fought for her against the men who sat behind the desks there in the office of the Normal School. But they did not fight for her, they kept their silence, as she had and as her mother had. And they had counted on that silence, those men in that office; it gave them the confidence to say the things they said, "regret" and "understanding" and "upon reflection." They had counted on the silence that surrounded people like Nora and her family, fell upon them like a cloak, swallowed them up and made them disappear so quickly that by the time Nora and her mother had stopped in Westchester for a cup of tea they could forget that they had ever seen her.

She determined that she would be successful in the business world. She finished senior year with the high grades she had begun with: she owed her parents that. But her attention was on the girls she knew who worked in offices: the way they dressed and spoke and carried themselves. She would be one of them; she would be better than any one of them. She would take trains and manicure her nails. Every muscle in her body she would devote to an appearance of efficiency and competence, with its inevitable edges of contempt.

Her one regret was that she had to ask her father for the money for her business-school tuition. He was glad to give it to her, she could tell he felt that he was making something up to her, making it all right. She was first in her class in every subject. Easily, within a week of graduation, she was hired by the firm of MacIntosh and Riordan, where she thrived.

She almost became the thing she wanted. She grew impatient with home life, in love with the world that required of her what she so easily, so beautifully could give. The years of all the anger which her family had not acknowledged or allowed she put into a furious, commercial energy. Soon Mr. Riordan had only to give her a brief idea of the contents of a letter; she herself composed those sentences that shone like music to her: threatening or clarifying, setting straight. This new person she had become had no place in her life for Eileen Foley, or for her brother Tom, whom she had finally brought over after six hard years.

He was fifteen when he arrived in New York; two years younger than Nora, but he was a child, and she a woman of the world. Eileen brought him to the Derencys to ask advice about his schooling; she was determined he be educated, although everyone advised against it, even Sister Catherine Benedict. And certainly Bridget advised against it.

"Vanity, vanity, all is vanity," she said, and everyone grew silent. Any kind of quote abashed them all.

"Well, what would you say, Nora, with your education?" Eileen asked.

It was a terrible word to Nora, education, all that she had had violently, cruelly to turn her back on, all that had betrayed her, caused her shame. Yet even in her bitterness, she saw it need not be the same for Tommy Foley. He would not want what she had wanted, Latin and the poetry, the plays. He would want, and Eileen wanted for him, merely a certificate. What he would learn would never touch him; therefore it would never hurt him. He wanted, simply, a good job.

Nora felt her mother's eyes hard on her, wanting her to give encouragement to Eileen. She understood why. Eileen's desire for her brother's prospering was so palpable, so dangerous almost, that it should not be balked.

"Why not try?" said Nora in her new, sharp way. Her parents did not   *40*
know she'd begun smoking; if she'd dared, it would have been a perfect time to light a cigarette.

Eileen was constantly afraid that her ambitions for her brother would be ruined by the influences of the neighborhood. For her they were contagious, like the plague; the greenhorn laziness, the fecklessness, the wish for fun. Nora's success made Eileen worshipful; she grew in Nora's presence deferential, asking her advice on everything, ravenously listening to every word she said, and urging Tom to listen, too.

Nora knew enough of the world not to overvalue the position that the Foleys had invented for her. She knew her place; it was a good place, near the top. And yet she knew that she would never be precisely at the top. She saw in the hallway of the office building where she worked a hundred girls like her. She was not the best of them; her bad leg meant she could not make the picture whole. She could not stride off, her high heels making that exciting sound of purpose on the wooden floors. She could not rise purposefully from her typewriter and move to the file cabinet, closing the drawers like a prime minister conferring an ambassadorship, as Flo Ziegler or Celie Kane, the partners' secretaries, did. To play the part she coveted required speed and line, like a good sailboat. Nora knew that her high shoe, her skirts cut full and long to hide it, detracted from her appearance of efficiency. Her work, the quickness of her mind might earn the highest place for her, but she would always be encumbered and slowed down by what John Riordan, a kind man, called her "affliction." Even so, even though she would never be at the very top, she knew herself above Eileen and her brother; there was no place for them in her new life, except the place forced free by charity.

She tried to joke Eileen out of her subservience, reminding her of when they had shared Eileen's secret trove of almond, nougat, crystallized ginger. But perhaps she didn't try wholeheartedly; her daily striving to achieve her dream of herself exhausted her; there was a kind of ease in lying back against the bolster of Eileen's adoration. Eileen had an idea of the game Nora was playing, even if she was mistaken about the nature of the stakes. Nora's parents and Aunt Nettie had no knowledge of the game. But Bridget did; she was contemptuous and mocking; when she saw Nora ironing, with passionate devotion, her blouses, handkerchiefs or skirt; when she came upon Nora polishing her nails, she sniffed and walked by, loose and ill-defined in her practical nurse's uniform, trailing the scorn of her belief in the futility of every effort Nora made.

Eileen kept hinting that Nora should be on the lookout for a place in Mr. Riordan's office that Tommy could fill. She'd heard about boys who started in law offices as messengers and worked their way up till eventually they studied on their own, sat for the bar exam and became lawyers.

"Well, I've heard of it. I've never seen a case myself," said Nora, smoking cynically. "You'd have to have an awful lot of push."

And this was what Tom Foley lacked completely: push. Pale, with hair that would never look manly and blue eyes that hid expression or else were supplicating, he was nearly silent except when he and Eileen talked about home. He could go then from silence to a frightening ebullience about some detail of their childhood: a cow with one horn only, a dog that barked when anybody sang, pears that fell from a tree once as they sat below it, soft, heavy as footballs, damaging themselves before they hit the ground. Then he would grow embarrassed at his outburst, would blush and look more childish than ever. It was quite impossible; she didn't understand why Eileen couldn't see it, he was not the office type and never would be. Right off the boat Eileen had put him with the Christian brothers; he lived there while Eileen lived with the nuns. In the summer on her week's vacation they went to a boarding house three hours from the city in the mountains, a house run by an Irish woman they had known from home. But Tom had never spoken to a soul outside his school except in Eileen's company, and Nora doubted that he could. She'd never mentioned him to Mr. Riordan, it would not work out and in the end would just make everyone look bad.

She suspected Eileen resented her for not doing anything for Tom. They stopped seeing one another; when the family got the news of Eileen they hadn't heard a word from her in longer than a year. She phoned to tell them Tommy had died. He'd got a job working for Western Union, as a messenger to start, but his bosses had said he's shown great promise. He was delivering a wire and had walked by a saloon. There was a fight inside, and a wild gunshot had come through the window. The bullet landed in his heart.

Eileen said this in the kitchen drinking tea with Nora and her mother and her father and her aunts. As she spoke, her cup did not tremble. They had no way of knowing what she felt about the terrible thing that had happened; she would give no sign. She met no one's eye; her voice, which had been musical, was flat and tired. What they could see was that the life had gone out of her flesh. What had been her richness had turned itself to stone; her body life, which once had given her and all around her pleasure, had poured itself into a mold of dreadful bitter piety. She talked about the will of God and punishment for her ambitions. It was this country, she said, the breath of God had left it if it ever had been here. Money was God here, and success, and she had bent the knee. Her brother had died of it.

So she was going home, she said. She cursed the day she ever left, she cursed the day she'd listened to the lying tongues, the gold-in-the-street stories, the palaver about starting over, making good. It was the worst day of her life, she said, the day she'd come here. But she wanted them to know that she was grateful for the way they'd helped her when she first was over; she would not forget. She told them she was going back to her old job at the orphanage in Limerick. She said that she would write them, but they all knew she would not.

When she walked out the door, they felt one of the dead had left them, *50* and they looked among themselves like murderers and could find no relief. When Bridget tried to blame Eileen or blame the Foleys, no one listened. They could hardly bear each other's company.

Nora went upstairs to her room and lay down on her bed, still in her work skirt. It would be terribly wrinkled; before the night was over she would have to press it. But not now. Now she lay back on her bed and knew what would be her life: to rise from it each morning and to make her way to work. Each morning she would join the others on the train, and in the evening, tired out but not exhausted, and with no real prospects that could lead to pleasure, with the others, she would make her way back home.

The Responsive Reader

1. What do we gradually learn in the story about Eileen's family history? How do we know? Why doesn't the author tell us straight out? What has brought Eileen (like millions of other Irish immigrants) to America? What had she heard or been told about the New World? When do we find out?

2. What is the relationship between Nora and Eileen as the two key characters in this story? How does it change or develop? What do they have in common? What if anything comes between them? Does the author seem to take sides, identifying more with one than with the other? Do *you* find yourself taking sides?

3. What other minor or secondary characters play a role in the story? How important are they to the story? How are the nuns treated in the story?

4. Why does Eileen go back to Ireland at the end? How does she explain her bitterness or her disillusionment? How do you react?

Thinking, Talking, Writing

5. Upward mobility—doing better than the parents' generation—has long been part of the American Dream. To judge from this story, what are factors that help determine the individual's success or failure?

6. If you had only one sentence to sum up what the story as a whole says about Eileen, what would you say?

7. If you had the option, would you send children to a private religious school rather than to a public school? What would be the reasons for your decision? Are there arguments pro and con?

Collaborative Projects

8. What role does a strong religious presence—Catholicism, Judaism, Islam—play in ethnic neighborhoods? How does it affect the lives of the young? How does it shape the outlook of the people? Working with a group, conduct a study of an ethnic neighborhood—for instance, Italian American, Polish American, Arab American, African American—where religion plays a highly visible role. You may want to draw on the personal testimony of classmates, on interviews with residents, on talks with ministers or rabbis or other religious functionaries, and on relevant material in local newspapers or other publications.

MERICANS

Sandra Cisneros

What's in a name? Spanish-speaking Americans are the largest ethnic group that has tended to keep its own language and maintain close ties with the traditional culture. Members of the group have in recent years had second thoughts about the quasi-official term Hispanic, *because it seems to emphasize the role of the Spanish conquistadores in the history of peoples of mixed Spanish and Native American ancestry. Many now prefer the term* Latino *(*Latina *for a woman) after the common Latin roots of the Spanish spoken by Mexican Americans, Puerto Ricans, and Nicaraguans alike. When minority groups commonly used hyphenated labels like Mexican-American, Italian-American, Irish-American, or Polish-American, the English-only, America-first politicians were fond of saying that there was no room in this country for hyphenated Americans. (A prominent Mexican-American once said that the children of immigrant parents find themselves precariously perched on the hyphen, tilting one way or the other sooner or later.) Today, in the days of ethnic revival, many Mexican Americans or Irish Americans have abandoned the hyphen, thus perhaps affirming their belief that it is possible to be Mexican and American, or Irish and American, at the same time.*

In the West and Southwest, American writers of Mexican ancestry, like Gary Soto or Luis Valdez, call themselves Chicanos *(short for* Mexicanos). *Sandra Cisneros is a Chicana author who was born and raised in Chicago. She first became well-known for her collection* The House on Mango Street. *The following story is from her collection of stories called* Woman Hollering Creek *(1991). Many of the Spanish phrases or references to Mexico's history in the story are more or less self-explanatory.* La Virgen de Guadalupe *is the Virgin Mary of Guadalupe; the first PRI elections, which installed Mexico's ruling party, left many of the more radical supporters of the Mexican revolution disillusioned.*

We're waiting for the awful grandmother who is inside dropping pesos into *la ofrenda* box before the altar to La Divina Providencia. Lighting votive candles and genuflecting. Blessing herself and kissing her thumb. Running a crystal rosary between her fingers. Mumbling, mumbling, mumbling.

There are so many prayers and promises and thanks-be-to-God to be given in the name of the husband and the sons and the only daughter who never attend mass. It doesn't matter. Like La Virgen de Guadalupe, the awful grandmother intercedes on their behalf. For the grandfather who hasn't believed in anything since the first PRI elections. For my father, El Periquín, so skinny he needs his sleep. For Auntie Light-skin, who only a few hours before was breakfasting on brain and goat tacos after dancing all night in the pink zone. For Uncle Fat-face, the blackest of the black sheep—*Always*

1

remember your Uncle Fat-face in your prayers. And Uncle Baby—*You go for me, Mamá—God listens to you.*

The awful grandmother has been gone a long time. She disappeared behind the heavy leather outer curtain and the dusty velvet inner. We may stay near the church entrance. We must not wander over to the balloon and punch-ball vendors. We cannot spend our allowance on fried cookies or Familia Burrón comic books or those clear cone-shaped suckers that make everything look like a rainbow when you look through them. We cannot run off and have our picture taken on the wooden ponies. We must not climb the steps up the hill behind the church and chase each other through the cemetery. We have promised to stay right where the awful grandmother left us until she returns.

There are those walking to church on their knees. Some with fat rags tied around their legs and others with pillows, one to kneel on, and one to flop ahead. There are women with black shawls crossing and uncrossing themselves. There are armies of penitents carrying banners and flowered arches while musicians play tinny trumpets and tinny drums.

La Virgen de Guadalupe is waiting inside behind a plate of thick glass.   5
There's also a gold crucifix bent crooked as a mesquite tree when someone once threw a bomb. La Virgen de Guadalupe on the main altar because she's a big miracle, the crooked crucifix on a side altar because that's a little miracle.

But we're outside in the sun. My big brother Junior hunkered against the wall with his eyes shut. My little brother Keeks running around in circles.

Maybe and most probably my little brother is imagining he's a flying feather dancer, like the ones we saw swinging high up from a pole on the Virgin's birthday. I want to be a flying feather dancer too, but when he circles past me he shouts, "I'm a B-Fifty-two bomber, you're a German," and shoots me with an invisible machine gun. I'd rather play flying feather dancers, but if I tell my brother this, he might not play with me at all.

"*Girl.* We can't play with a *girl.*" *Girl.* It's my brothers' favorite insult now instead of "sissy." "You *girl,*" they yell at each other. "You throw that ball like a *girl.*"

I've already made up my mind to be a German when Keeks swoops past again, this time yelling "I'm Flash Gordon. You're Ming the Merciless and the Mud People." I don't mind being Ming the Merciless, but I don't like being the Mud People. Something wants to come out of the corners of my eyes, but I don't let it. Crying is what *girls* do.

I leave Keeks running around in circles—"I'm the Lone Ranger, you're   10
Tonto." I leave Junior squatting on his ankles and go look for the awful grandmother.

Why do churches smell like the inside of an ear? Like incense and the dark and candles in blue glass? And why does holy water smell of tears? The awful grandmother makes me kneel and fold my hands. The ceiling high and everyone's prayers bumping up there like balloons.

If I stare at the eyes of the saints long enough, they move and wink at me, which makes me a sort of saint too. When I get tired of winking saints, I count the awful grandmother's mustache hairs while she prays for Uncle Old, sick from the worm, and Auntie Cuca, suffering from a life of troubles that left half her face crooked and the other half sad.

There must be a long, long list of relatives who haven't gone to church. The awful grandmother knits the names of the dead and the living into one long prayer fringed with the grandchildren born in that barbaric country with its barbarian ways.

I put my weight on one knee, then the other, and when they both grow fat as a mattress of pins, I slap them each awake. *Micaela, you may wait outside with Alfredito and Enrique.* The awful grandmother says it all in Spanish, which I understand when I'm paying attention. "What?" I say, though it's neither proper nor polite. "What?" which the awful grandmother hears as "¿Guat?" But she only gives me a look and shoves me toward the door.

After all that dust and dark, the light from the plaza makes me squinch   15
my eyes like if I just came out of the movies. My brother Keeks is drawing squiggly lines on the concrete with a wedge of glass and the heel of his shoe. My brother Junior squatting against the entrance, talking to a lady and man.

They're not from here. Ladies don't come to church dressed in pants. And everybody knows men aren't supposed to wear shorts.

"*¿Quieres chicle?*" the lady asks in a Spanish too big for her mouth.

"*Gracias.*" The lady gives him a whole handful of gum for free, little cellophane cubes of Chiclets, cinnamon and aqua and the white ones that don't taste like anything but are good for pretend buck teeth.

"*Por favor,*" says the lady. "*¿Un foto?*" pointing to her camera.

"*Sí.*"   20

She's so busy taking Junior's picture, she doesn't notice me and Keeks.

"Hey, Michele, Keeks. You guys want gum?"

"But you speak English!"

"Yeah," my brother says, "we're Mericans."

We're Mericans, we're Mericans, and inside the awful grandmother   25
prays.

The Responsive Reader

1. What picture does this story give you of the traditional Mexican culture represented by the older generation? How do the glimpses you get here confirm what you thought you knew? Do they in any way change your assumptions? (What role does the word *barbarian* play in this story? What is its history?)

2. To what extent are the children "Americanized"? What role does American popular culture play in their world? What is their attitude toward the Spanish spoken by their elders?

3. What is the author's attitude toward the picture-taking tourist lady? How can you tell?
4. What is the point of the story?

Thinking, Talking, Writing

5. Do people ever ask you, "What are you?" Do they ever ask you "Where are you from" because they think you are different? (Or have others you know had this experience?) How do you react to this kind of question?
6. Have you (or people you know well) ever been identified with a group with which you did not want to be identified? Have you ever *joined* a group because it seemed to be in tune with who or what you are?
7. Students of language claim that when we learn a language, we do not just learn new words for familiar things. We enter into a different culture, a new way of looking at the world. We learn a different set of manners, of likes and dislikes. Have you encountered any evidence for this view?

Collaborative Projects

8. Millions of Americans have always been bilingual. What role does a language other then English play in the lives of people in your school or community?

THE DANCE AND THE RAILROAD
David Henry Hwang

David Henry Hwang is a Chinese American playwright whose Tony Award-winning M. Butterfly *(1988) was performed in both the United States and Europe. Part of the classical repertory of European opera, Puccini's* Madame Butterfly *had set to lush music the story of a Japanese geisha girl who marries an American naval officer and commits suicide when he abandons her and sends his American wife to collect their love child. Hwang's play attacked and mocked the stereotype of the meek, submissive, and self-sacrificing Asian female. His* Madame Butterfly *is a Chinese opera singer who is a male playing female roles and who works for the Chinese government as a spy.*

Hwang was born in Los Angeles in 1957 and studied at Stanford University and the Yale School of Drama. His plays explore and validate the experiences of countless Asian Americans whose lives and struggles were in danger of being forgotten. In the words of Maxine Hong Kingston, Hwang's plays give life to the tradition of the Chinese American theater, which "started out with a bang—fire crackers, drums," but which was in danger of dying out. Hwang's plays look at what it means to be Chinese in America from changing provocative perspectives. A familiar figure in his plays in the FOB, the naive newly arrived immigrant "Fresh Off the Boat" who still marvels at everything in his new country and still believes much of what Americans or earlier immigrants tell him.

Hwang's The Dance and the Railroad *is essentially a dialogue between two imported Chinese laborers who, as the song says, are "working on the railroad all the livelong day." In this play, Whang writes about the ChinaMen who were brought to this country as cheap coolie labor. They built the railroads that linked the two coasts of the continent and helped make America one nation. They came from villages threatened by starvation to the "Gold Mountain"—the legendary land across the ocean from which they hoped to return rich, honored by their families and neighbors.*

We tend to think of the masses of anonymous immigrants, legal or illegal, as faceless illiterate individuals glad to do the menial jobs we assign them. However, the Chinese laborers in the following play brought with them ties with several thousand years of Chinese culture, including the tradition of Chinese opera and dance that plays a role in the following scenes. Hwang said about this play,

An actual incident, the Chinese railroad workers' strike of 1867, provides the background of this piece. So often "coolie" laborers have been characterized in America as passive and subservient, two stereotypes often attached to Asians. The strike is important because it reminds us that in historical fact these were assertive men who stood up for their rights in the face of great adversity.

Characters
LONE, twenty years old, *ChinaMan railroad worker.*
MA, eighteen years old, *ChinaMan railroad worker.*

Place *A mountaintop near the transcontinental railroad.*

Time *June, 1867.*

Synopsis of Scenes
Scene 1. *Afternoon.*
Scene 2. *Afternoon, a day later.*
Scene 3. *Late afternoon, four days later.*
Scene 4. *Late that night.*
Scene 5. *Just before the following dawn.*

Scene 1

A mountaintop. LONE *is practicing opera steps. He swings his pigtail around like a fan.* MA *enters, cautiously, watches from a hidden spot.* MA *approaches* LONE.

LONE: So, there are insects hiding in the bushes.
MA: Hey, listen, we haven't met, but—
LONE: I don't spend time with insects.

> (LONE *whips his hair into* MA'S *face;* MA *backs off;* LONE *pursues him, swiping at* MA *with his hair*)

MA: What the—? Cut it out!

> (MA *pushes* LONE *away*)

LONE: Don't push me.
MA: What was that for?
LONE: Don't ever push me again.
MA: You mess like that, you're gonna get pushed.
LONE: Don't push me.
MA: You started it. I just wanted to watch.
LONE: You "just wanted to watch." Did you ask my permission?
MA: What?
LONE: Did you?
MA: C'mon.
LONE: You can't expect to get in for free.
MA: Listen. I got some stuff you'll wanna hear.
LONE: You think so?
MA: Yeah. Some advice.
LONE: Advice? How old are you, anyway?

MA: Eighteen.

LONE: A child.

MA: Yeah. Right. A child. But listen—

LONE: A child who tries to advise a grown man—

MA: Listen, you got this kind of attitude.

LONE: —is a child who will never grow up.

MA: You know, the ChinaMen down at camp, they can't stand it.

LONE: Oh?

MA: Yeah. You gotta watch yourself. You know what they say? They call you "Prince of the Mountain." Like you're too good to spend time with them.

LONE: Perceptive of them.

MA: After all, you never sing songs, never tell stories. They say you act like your spit is too clean for them, and they got ways to fix that.

LONE: Is that so?

MA: Like they're gonna bury you in the shit buckets, so you'll have more to clean than your nails.

LONE: But I don't shit.

MA: Or they're gonna cut out your tongue, since you never speak to them.

LONE: There's no one here worth talking to.

MA: Cut it out, Lone. Look, I'm trying to help you, all right? I got a solution.

LONE: So young yet so clever.

MA: That stuff you're doing—it's beautiful. Why don't you do it for the guys at camp? Help us celebrate?

LONE: What will "this stuff" help celebrate?

MA: C'mon. The strike, of course. Guys on a railroad gang, we gotta stick together, you know.

LONE: This is something to celebrate?

MA: Yeah. Yesterday, the weak-kneed ChinaMen, they were running around like chickens without a head: "The white devils are sending their soldiers! Shoot us all!" But now, look—day four, see? Still in one piece. Those soldiers—we've never seen a gun or a bullet.

LONE: So you're all warrior-spirits, huh?

MA: They're scared of us, Lone—that's what it means.

LONE: I appreciate your advice. Tell you what—you go down—

MA: Yeah?

LONE: Down to the camp—

MA: Okay.

LONE: To where the men are—

MA: Yeah?

LONE: Sit there—

MA: Yeah?

LONE: And wait for me.

MA: Okay. (*Pause*) That's it? What do you think I am?

LONE: I think you're an insect interrupting my practice. So fly away. Go home.

MA: Look, I didn't come here to get laughed at.

LONE: No, I suppose you didn't.

MA: So just stay up here. By yourself. You deserve it.

LONE: I do.

MA: And don't expect any more help from me.

LONE: I haven't gotten any yet.

MA: If one day, you wake up and your head is buried in the shit can—

LONE: Yes?

MA: You can't find your body, your tongue is cut out—

LONE: Yes.

MA: Don't worry, 'cuz I'll be there.

LONE: Oh.

MA: To make sure your mother's head is sitting right next to yours.

(MA *exits*)

LONE: His head is too big for this mountain.

(*Returns to practicing*)

Scene 2

Mountaintop. Next day. LONE *is practicing.* MA *enters.*

MA: Hey.

LONE: You? Again?

MA: I forgive you.

LONE: You . . . what?

MA: For making fun of me yesterday. I forgive you.

LONE: You can't—

MA: No. Don't thank me.

LONE: You can't forgive me.

MA: No. Don't mention it.

LONE: You—! I never asked for your forgiveness.

MA: I know. That's just the kinda guy I am.

LONE: This is ridiculous. Why don't you leave? Go down to your friends and play soldiers, sing songs, tell stories.

MA: Ah! See? That's just it. I got other ways I wanna spend my time. Will you teach me the opera?

LONE: What?

MA: I wanna learn it. I dreamt about it all last night.

LONE: No.

MA: The dance, the opera—I can do it.

LONE: You think so?

MA: Yeah. When I get outa here, I wanna go back to China and perform.

LONE: You want to become an actor?

MA: Well, I wanna perform.

LONE: Don't you remember the story about the three sons whose parents send them away to learn a trade? After three years, they return. The first one says, "I have become a coppersmith." The parents say, "Good. Second son, what have you become?" "I've become a silversmith." "Good—and youngest son, what about you?" "I have become an actor." When the parents hear that their son has become only an actor, they are very sad. The mother beats her head against the ground until the ground, out of pity, opens up and swallows her. The father is so angry he can't even speak, and the anger builds up inside him until it blows his body to pieces—little bits of his skin are found hanging from trees days later. You don't know how you endanger your relatives by becoming an actor.

MA: Well, I don't wanna become an "actor." That sounds terrible. I just wanna perform. Look, I'll be rich by the time I get out of here, right?

LONE: Oh?

MA: Sure. By the time I go back to China, I'll ride in gold sedan chairs, with twenty wives fanning me all around.

LONE: Twenty wives? This boy is ambitious.

MA: I'll give out pigs on New Years's and keep a stable of small birds to give to any woman who pleases me. And in my spare time, I'll perform.

LONE: Between your twenty wives and your birds, where will you find a free moment?

MA: I'll play Gwan Gung and tell stories of what life was like on the Gold Mountain.

LONE: Ma, just how long have you been in "America"?

MA: Huh? About four weeks.

LONE: You are a big dreamer.

MA: Well, all us ChinaMen here are—right? Men with little dreams—have little brains to match. They walk with their eyes down, trying to find extra grains of rice on the ground.

LONE: So, you know all about "America"? Tell me, what kind of stories will you tell?

MA: I'll say, "We laid tracks like soldiers. Mountains? We hung from cliffs in baskets and the winds blew us like birds. Snow? We lived underground like moles for days at a time. Deserts? We—"

LONE: Wait. Wait. How do you know these things after only four weeks?

MA: They told me—the other ChinaMen on the gang. We've been telling stories ever since the strike began.

LONE: They make it sound like it's very enjoyable.

MA: They said it is.

LONE: Oh? And you believe them?

MA: They're my friends. Living underground in winter—sounds exciting, huh?

LONE: Did they say anything about the cold?

MA: Oh, I already know about that. They told me about the mild winters and the warm snow.

LONE: Warm snow?

MA: When I go home, I'll bring some back to show my brothers.

LONE: Bring some—? On the boat?

MA: They'll be shocked—they never seen American snow before.

LONE: You can't. By the time you get snow to the boat, it'll have melted, evaporated, and returned as rain already.

MA: No.

LONE: No?

MA: Stupid.

LONE: Me?

MA: You been here awhile, haven't you?

LONE: Yes. Two years.

MA: Then how come you're so stupid? This is the Gold Mountain. The snow here doesn't melt. It's not wet.

LONE: That's what they told you?

MA: Yeah. It's true.

LONE: Did anyone show you any of this snow?

MA: No. It's not winter.

LONE: So where does it go?

MA: Huh?

LONE: Where does it go, if it doesn't melt? What happens to it?

MA: The snow? I dunno. I guess it just stays around.

LONE: So where is it? Do you see any?

MA: Here? Well, no, but . . . (*Pause*) This is probably one of those places where it doesn't snow—even in winter.

LONE: Oh.

MA: Anyway, what's the use of me telling you what you already know? Hey, c'mon—teach me some of that stuff. Look—I've been practicing the walk—how's this? (*Demonstrates*)

LONE: You look like a duck in heat.

MA: Hey—it's a start, isn't it?

LONE: Tell you what—you want to play some *die siu?*

MA: *Die siu?* Sure.

LONE: You know, I'm pretty good.

MA: Hey, I play with the guys at camp. You can't be any better than Lee— he's really got it down.

(LONE *pulls out a case with two dice*)

LONE: I used to play till morning.

MA: Hey, us too. We see the sun start to rise, and say, "Hey, if we got to sleep now, we'll never get up for work." So we just keep playing.

LONE: (*Holding out dice*) Die or *siu?*

MA: *Siu.*

LONE: You sure?

MA: Yeah!

LONE: All right. (*He rolls*) *Die!*

MA: *Siu!*

(*They see the result*)

MA: Not bad.

(*They continue taking turns rolling through the following section;* MA *always loses*)

LONE: I haven't touched these in two years.

MA: I gotta practice more.

LONE: Have you lost much money?

MA: Huh? So what?

LONE: Oh, you have gold hidden in all your shirt linings, huh?

MA: Here in "America"—losing is no problem. You know—End of the Year Bonus?

LONE: Oh, right.

MA: After I get that, I'll laugh at what I lost.

LONE: Lee told you there was a bonus, right?

MA: How'd you know?

LONE: When I arrived here, Lee told me there was a bonus, too.

MA: Lee teach you how to play?

LONE: Him? He talked to me a lot.

MA: Look, why don't you come down and start playing with the guys again?

LONE: "The guys."

MA: Before we start playing, Lee uses a stick to write "Kill!" in the dirt.

LONE: You seem to live for your nights with "the guys."

MA: What's life without friends, huh?

LONE: Well, why do *you* think I stopped playing?

MA: Hey, maybe you were the one getting killed, huh?

LONE: What?

MA: Hey, just kidding.

LONE: Who's getting killed here?

MA: Just a joke.

LONE: That's not a joke, it's blasphemy.

MA: Look, obviously you stopped playing 'cause you wanted to practice the opera.

LONE: Do you understand that discipline?

MA: But, I mean, you don't have to overdo it either. You don't have to treat 'em like dirt. I mean, who are you trying to impress?

(*Pause.* LONE *throws dice into the bushes*)

LONE: Oooops. Better go see who won.

MA: Hey! C'mon! Help me look!

LONE: If you find them, they are yours.

MA: You serious?

LONE: Yes.

MA: Here.

(*Finds the dice*)

LONE: Who won?

MA: I didn't check.

LONE: Well, no matter. Keep the dice. Take them and go play with your friends.

MA: Here. (*He offers them to* LONE) A present.

LONE: A present? This isn't a present!

MA: They're mine, aren't they? You gave them to me, right?

LONE: Well, yes, but—

MA: So now I'm giving them to you.

LONE: You can't give me a present. I don't want them.

MA: You wanted them enough to keep them two years.

LONE: I'd forgotten I had them.

MA: See, I know, Lone. You wanna get rid of me. But you can't. I'm paying for lessons.

LONE: With my dice.

MA: Mine now. (*He offers them again*) Here.

(*Pause.* LONE *runs* MA's *hand across his forehead*)

LONE: Feel this.

MA: Hey!

LONE: Pretty wet, huh?

MA: Big deal.

LONE: Well, it's not from playing *die siu*.

MA: I know how to sweat. I wouldn't be here if I didn't.

LONE: Yes, but are you willing to sweat after you've finished sweating? Are you willing to come up after you've spent the whole day chipping half an inch off a rock, and punish your body some more?

MA: Yeah. Even after work, I still—

LONE: No, you don't. You want to gamble, and tell dirty stories, and dress up like women to do shows.

MA: Hey, I never did that.

LONE: You've only been here a month. (*Pause*) And what about "the guys"? They're not going to treat you so well once you stop playing with them. Are you willing to work all day listening to them whisper, "That one—let's put spiders in his soup"?

MA: They won't do that to me. With you, it's different.

LONE: Is it?

MA: You don't have to act that way.

LONE: What way?

MA: Like you're so much better than them.

LONE: No. You haven't even begun to understand. To practice every day, you must have a fear to force you up here.

MA: A fear? No—it's 'cause what you're doing is beautiful.

LONE: No.

MA: I've seen it.

LONE: It's ugly to practice when the mountain has turned your muscles to ice. When my body hurts too much to come here, I look at the other ChinaMen and think, "They are dead. Their muscles work only because the white man forces them. I live because I can still force my muscles to work for me." Say it. "They are dead."

MA: No. They're my friends.

LONE: Well, then, take your dice down to your friends.

MA: But I want to learn—

LONE: This is your first lesson.

MA: Look, it shouldn't matter—

LONE: It does.

MA: It shouldn't matter what I think.

LONE: Attitude is everything.

MA: But as long as I come up, do the exercises—

LONE: I'm not going to waste time on a quitter.

MA: I'm not!

LONE: Then say it.—"They are dead men."

MA: I can't.

LONE: Then you will never have the dedication.

MA: That doesn't prove anything.

LONE: I will not teach a dead man.

MA: What?

LONE: If you can't see it, then you're dead too.

MA: Don't start pinning—

LONE: Say it!

MA: All right.

LONE: What?

MA: All right. I'm one of them. I'm a dead man too.

(*Pause*)

LONE: I thought as much. So, go. You have your friends.

MA: But I don't have a teacher.

LONE: I don't think you need both.

MA: Are you sure?

LONE: I'm being questioned by a child.

(LONE *returns to practicing. Silence*)

MA: Look, Lone, I'll come up here every night—after work—I'll spend my time practicing, okay? (*Pause*) But I'm not gonna say that they're dead. Look at them. They're on strike; dead men don't go on strike, Lone. The white devils—they try and stick us with a ten-hour day. We want a return to eight hours and also a fourteen-dollar-a-month raise. I learned the demon English—listen: "Eight hour a day good for white man, all same good for ChinaMan." These are the demands of live ChinaMen, Lone. Dead men don't complain.

LONE: All right, this is something new. No one can judge the ChinaMen till after the strike.

MA: They say we'll hold out for months if we have to. The smart men will live on what we've hoarded.

LONE: A ChinaMan's mouth can swallow the earth. (*He takes the dice*) While the strike is on, I'll teach you.

MA: And afterwards?

LONE: Afterwards—we'll decide then whether these are dead or live men.

MA: When can we start?

LONE: We've already begun. Give me your hand.

Scene 3

LONE *and* MA *are doing physical exercises.*

MA: How long will it be before I can play Gwan Gung?

LONE: How long before a dog can play the violin?

MA: Old Ah Hong—have you heard him play the violin?

LONE: Yes. Now, he should take his violin and give it to a dog.

MA: I think he sounds okay.

LONE: I think he caused that avalanche last winter.

MA: He used to play for weddings back home.

LONE: Ah Hong?

MA: That's what he said.

LONE: You probably heard wrong.

MA: No.

LONE: He probably said he played for funerals.

MA: He's been playing for the guys down at camp.

LONE: He should play for the white devils—that will end this stupid strike.

MA: Yang told me for sure—it'll be over by tomorrow.

LONE: Eight days already. And Yang doesn't know anything.

MA: He said they're already down to an eight-hour day and five-dollar raise at the bargaining sessions.

LONE: Yang eats too much opium.

MA: That doesn't mean he's wrong about this.

LONE: You can't trust him. One time—last year—he went around camp looking in everybody's eyes and saying, "Your nails are too long.

They're hurting my eyes." This went on for a week. Finally, all the men clipped their nails, made a big pile, which they wrapped in leaves and gave to him. Yang used the nails to season his food—he put it in his soup, sprinkled it on his rice, and never said a word about it again. Now tell me—are you going to trust a man who eats other men's fingernails?

MA: Well, all I know is we won't go back to work until they meet all our demands. Listen, teach me some Gwan Gung steps.

LONE: I should have expected this. A boy who wants to have twenty wives is the type who demands more than he can handle.

MA: Just a few.

LONE: It takes years before an actor can play Gwan Gung.

MA: I can do it. I spend a lot of time watching the opera when it comes around. Every time I see Gwan Gung, I say, "Yeah. That's me. The god of fighters. The god of adventurers. We have the same kind of spirit."

LONE: I tell you, if you work very hard, when you return to China, you can perhaps be the Second Clown.

MA: Second Clown?

LONE: If you work hard.

MA: What's the Second Clown?

LONE: You can play the *p'i p'a,* and dance and jump all over.

MA: I'll buy them.

LONE: Excuse me?

MA: I'm going to be rich, remember? I'll buy a troupe and force them to let me play Gwan Gung.

LONE: I hope you have enough money, then, to pay audiences to sit through your show.

MA: You mean, I'm going to have to practice here every night—and in return, all I can play is the Second Clown?

LONE: If you word hard.

MA: Am I that bad? Maybe I shouldn't even try to do this. Maybe I should just go down.

LONE: It's not you. Everyone must earn the right to play Gwan Gung. I entered opera school when I was ten years old. My parents decided to sell me for ten years to this opera company. I lived with eighty other boys and we slept in bunks four beds high and hid our candy and rice cakes from each other. After eight years, I was studying to play Gwan Gung.

MA: Eight years?

LONE: I was one of the best in my class. One day, I was summoned by my master, who told me I was to go home for two days because my mother had fallen very ill and was dying. When I arrived home, Mother was standing at the door waiting, not sick at all. Her first words to me, the son away for eight years, were, "You've been playing while your village has starved. You must go to the Gold Mountain and work."

MA: And you never returned to school?

LONE: I went from a room with eighty boys to a ship with three hundred men. So, you see, it does not come easily to play Gwan Gung.

MA: Did you want to play Gwan Gung?

LONE: What a foolish question!

MA: Well, you're better off this way.

LONE: What?

MA: Actors—they don't make much money. Here, you make a bundle, then go back and be an actor again. Best of both worlds.

LONE: "Best of both worlds."

MA: Yeah!

(LONE *drops to the ground, begins imitating a duck, waddling and quacking*)

MA: Lone? What are you doing? (Lone *quacks*) You're a duck? (LONE *quacks*) I can see that. (LONE *quacks*) Is this an exercise? Am I supposed to do this? (LONE *quacks*) This is dumb. I never seen Gwan Gung waddle. (LONE *quacks*) Okay. All right. I'll do it. (MA *and* LONE *quack and waddle*) You know, I never realized before how uncomfortable a duck's life is. And you have to listen to yourself quacking all day. Go crazy! (LONE *stands up straight*) Now, what was that all about?

LONE: No, no. Stay down there, duck.

MA: What's the—

LONE: (*Prompting*) Quack, quack, quack.

MA: I don't—

LONE: Act your species!

MA: I'm not a duck!

LONE: Nothing worse than a duck that doesn't know his place.

MA: All right. (*Mechanically*) Quack, quack.

LONE: More.

MA: Quack.

LONE: More!

MA: Quack, quack, quack!

(MA *now continues quacking, as* LONE *gives commands*)

LONE: Louder! It's your mating call! Think of your twenty duck wives! Good! Louder! Project! More! Don't slow down! Put your tail feathers into it! They can't hear you!

(MA *is now quacking up a storm.* LONE *exits, unnoticed by* MA)

MA: Quack! Quack! Quack! Quack. Quack . . . quack.
(*He looks around*) Quack . . . quack . . . Lone? . . . Lone?
(*He waddles around the stage looking*) Lone, where are you?

Where'd you go? (*He stops, scratches his left leg with his right foot*) C'mon—stop playing around. What is this? (LONE *enters as a tiger, unseen by* MA) Look, let's call it a day, okay? I'm getting hungry. (MA *turns around, notices* LONE *right before* LONE *is to bite him*) Aaaaah! Quack, quack, quack!

(*They face off, in character as animals. Duck-*MA *is terrified*)

LONE: Grrrr!

MA: (*As a cry for help*) Quack, quack, quack!

(LONE *pounces on* MA. *They struggle, in character.* MA *is quacking madly, eyes tightly closed.* LONE *stands up straight.* MA *continues to quack*)

LONE: Stand up.

MA: (*Eyes still closed*) Quack, quack, quack!

LONE: (*Louder*) Stand up!

MA: (*Opening his eyes*) Oh.

LONE: What are you?

MA: Huh?

LONE: A ChinaMan or a duck?

MA: Huh? Gimme a second to remember.

LONE: You like being a duck?

MA: My feet fell asleep.

LONE: You change forms so easily.

MA: You said to.

LONE: What else could you turn into?

MA: Well, you scared me—sneaking up like that.

LONE: Perhaps a rock. That would be useful. When the men need to rest, they can sit on you.

MA: I got carried away.

LONE: Let's try . . . a locust. Can you become a locust?

MA: No. Let's cut this, okay?

LONE: Here. It's easy. You just have to know how to hop.

MA: You're not gonna get me—

LONE: Like this.

(*He demonstrates*)

MA: Forget it, Lone.

LONE: I'm a locust.

(*He begins jumping toward* MA)

MA: Hey! Get away!

LONE: I devour whole fields.

MA: Stop it.

LONE: I starve babies before they are born.

MA: Hey, look, stop it!

LONE: I cause famines and destroy villages.

MA: I'm warning you! Get away!

LONE: What are you going to do? You can't kill a locust.

MA: You're not a locust.

LONE: You kill one, and another sits on your hand.

MA: Stop following me.

LONE: Locusts always trouble people, If not, we'd feel useless. Now, if you became a locust, too . . .

MA: I'm not going to become a locust.

LONE: Just stick your teeth out!

MA: I'm not gonna be a bug! It's stupid!

LONE: No man who's just been a duck has the right to call anything stupid.

MA: I thought you were trying to teach me something.

LONE: I am. Go ahead.

MA: All right. There. That look right?

LONE: Your legs should be a little lower. Lower! There. That's adequate. So how does it feel to be a locust?

(LONE *gets up*)

MA: I dunno. How long do I have to do this?

LONE: Could you do it for three years?

MA: Three years? Don't be—

LONE: You couldn't, could you? Could you be a duck for that long?

MA: Look, I wasn't born to be either of those.

LONE: Exactly. Well, I wasn't born to work on a railroad, either. "Best of both worlds." How can you be such an insect!

(*Pause*)

MA: Lone . . .

LONE: Stay down there! Don't move! I've never told anyone my story— the story of my parents' kidnapping me from school. All the time we were crossing the ocean, the last two years here—I've kept my mouth shut. To you, I finally tell it. And all you can say is, "Best of both worlds." You're a bug to me, a locust. You think you understand the dedication one must have to be in the opera? You think it's the same as working on a railroad.

MA: Lone, all I was saying is that you'll go back too, and—

LONE: You're no longer a student of mine.

MA: What?

LONE: You have no dedication.

MA: Lone, I'm sorry.

LONE: Get up.

MA: I'm honored that you told me that.

LONE: Get up.

MA: No.

LONE: No?

MA: I don't want to. I want to talk.

LONE: Well, I've learned from the past. You're stubborn. You don't go. All right. Stay there. If you want to prove to me that you're dedicated, be a locust till morning. I'll go.

MA: Lone, I'm really honored that you told me.

LONE: I'll return in the morning.

(*Exits*)

MA: Lone? Lone, that's ridiculous. You think I'm gonna stay like this? If you do, you're crazy. Lone? Come back here.

Scene 4

Night. MA, *alone, as a locust.*

MA: Locusts travel in huge swarms, so large that when they cross the sky, they block out the sun, like a storm. Second Uncle—back home—when he was a young man, his whole crop got wiped out by locusts one year. In the famine that followed, Second Uncle lost his eldest son and his second wife—the one he married for love. Even to this day, we look around before saying the word "locust," to make sure Second Uncle is out of hearing range. About eight years ago, my brother and I discovered Second Uncle's cave in back of the stream near our house. We saw him come out of it one day around noon. Later, just before the sun went down, we sneaked in. We only looked once. Inside, there must have been hundreds—maybe five hundred or more—grasshoppers in huge bamboo cages—and around them—stacks of grasshopper legs, grasshopper heads, grasshopper antennae, grasshoppers with one leg, still trying to hop but toppling like trees coughing, grasshoppers wrapped around sharp branches rolling from side to side, grasshoppers legs cut off grasshopper bodies, then tied around grasshoppers and tightened till grasshoppers died. Every conceivable kind of grasshopper in every conceivable stage of life and death, subject to every conceivable grasshopper torture. We ran out quickly, my brother and I—we knew an evil place by the thickness of the air. Now, I think of Second Uncle. How sad that the locusts forced him to take out his agony on innocent grasshoppers. What if Second Uncle could see me now? Would he cut off my legs? He might as well. I can barely feel them. But then again, Second Uncle never tortured actual locusts, just weak grasshoppers.

Scene 5

Night. MA *still as a locust.*

LONE: (*Off, singing*)

> Hit your hardest
> Pound out your tears
> The more you try
> The more you'll cry
> At how little I've moved
> And how large I loom
> By the time the sun goes down

MA: You look rested.

LONE: Me?

MA: Well, you sound rested.

LONE: No, not at all.

MA: Maybe I'm just comparing you to me.

LONE: I didn't even close my eyes all last night.

MA: Aw, Lone, you didn't have to stay up for me. You coulda just come up here and—

LONE: For you?

MA: —apologized and everything woulda been—

LONE: I didn't stay up for you.

MA: Huh? You didn't?

LONE: No.

MA: Oh. You sure?

LONE: Positive. I was thinking, that's all.

MA: About me?

LONE: Well . . .

MA: Even a little?

LONE: I was thinking about the ChinaMen—and you. Get up, Ma.

MA: Aw, do I have to? I've gotten to know these grasshoppers real well.

LONE: Get up. I have a lot to tell you.

MA: What'll they think? They take me in, even though I'm a little large, then they find out I'm a human being. I stepped on their kids. No trust. Gimme a hand, will you? (LONE *helps* MA *up, but* MA's *legs can't support him*) Aw, shit. My legs are coming off.

(*He lies down and tries to straighten them out*)

LONE: I have many surprises. First, you will play Gwan Gung.

MA: My legs will be sent home without me. What'll my family think? Come to port to meet me and all they get is two legs.

LONE: Did you hear me?

MA: Hold on. I can't be in agony and listen to Chinese at the same time.

LONE: Did you hear my first surprise?

MA: No. I'm too busy screaming.

LONE: I said, you'll play Gwan Gung.

MA: Gwan Gung?

LONE: Yes.

MA: Me?

LONE: Yes.

MA: Without legs?

LONE: What?

MA: That might be good.

LONE: Stop that!

MA: I'll become a legend. Like the blind man who defended Amoy.

LONE: Did you hear?

MA: "The legless man who played Gwan Gung."

LONE: Isn't this what you want? To play Gwan Gung?

MA: No, I just wanna sleep.

LONE: No, you don't. Look. Here. I brought you something.

MA: Food?

LONE: Here. Some rice.

MA: Thanks, Lone. And duck?

LONE: Just a little.

MA: Where'd you get the duck?

LONE: Just bones and skin.

MA: We don't have duck. And the white devils have been blockading the food.

LONE: Sing—he had some left over.

MA: Sing? That thief?

LONE: And something to go with it.

MA: What? Lone, where did you find whiskey?

LONE: You know, Sing—he has almost anything.

MA: Yeah. For a price.

LONE: Once, even some thousand-day-old eggs.

MA: He's a thief. That's what they told me.

LONE: Not if you're his friend.

MA: Sing don't have any real friends. Everyone talks about him bein' tied in to the head of the klan in San Francisco. Lone, you didn't have to do this. Here. Have some.

LONE: I had plenty.

MA: Don't gimme that. This cost you plenty, Lone.

LONE: Well, I thought if we were going to celebrate, we should do it as well as we would at home.

MA: Celebrate? What for? Wait.

LONE: Ma, the strike is over.

MA: Shit, I knew it. And we won, right?

LONE: Yes, the ChinaMen have won. They can do more than just talk.

MA: I told you. Didn't I tell you?

LONE: Yes. Yes, you did.

MA: Yang told me it was gonna be done. He said—

LONE: Yes, I remember.

MA: Didn't I tell you? Huh?

LONE: Ma, eat your duck.

MA: Nine days, we civilized the white devils. I knew it. I knew we'd hold out till their ears started twitching. So that's where you got the duck, right? At the celebration?

LONE: No, there wasn't a celebration.

MA: Huh? You sure? ChinaMen—they look for any excuse to party.

LONE: But I thought *we* should celebrate.

MA: Well, that's for sure.

LONE: So you will play Gwan Gung.

MA: God, nine days. Shit, it's finally done. Well, we'll show them how to party. Make noise. Jump off rocks. Make the mountain shake.

LONE: We'll wash your body, to prepare you for the role.

MA: What role?

LONE: Gwan Gung. I've been telling you.

MA: I don't wanna play Gwan Gung.

LONE: You've shown the dedication required to become my student, so—

MA: Lone, you think I stayed up last night 'cause I wanted to play Gwan Gung?

LONE: You said you were like him.

MA: I am. Gwan Gung stayed up all night once to prove his loyalty. Well, now I have too. Lone, I'm honored that you told me your story.

LONE: Yes . . . That is like Gwan Gung.

MA: Good. So let's do an opera about *me*.

LONE: What?

MA: You wanna party or what?

LONE: About you?

MA: You said I was like Gwan Gung, didn't you?

LONE: Yes, but—

MA: Well, look at the operas he's got. I ain't even got one.

LONE: Still, you can't—

MA: You tell me, is that fair?

LONE: You can't do an opera about yourself.

MA: I just won a victory, didn't I? I deserve an opera in my honor.

LONE: But it's not traditional.

MA: Traditional? Lone, you gotta figure any way I could do Gwan Gung wasn't gonna be traditional anyway. I may be as good a guy as him, but he's a better dancer. (*Sings*)

Old Gwan Gung, just sits about
Till the dime-store fighters have had it out
Then he pitches his peach pit
Combs his beard
Draws his sword
And they scatter in fear

LONE: What are you talking about?

MA: I just won a great victory. I get—whatcha call it?—poetic license. C'mon. Hit the gongs. I'll immortalize my story.

LONE: I refuse. This goes against all my training. I try and give you your wish and—

MA: Do it. Gimme my wish. Hit the gongs.

LONE: I never—I can't.

MA: Can't what? Don't think I'm worth an opera? No, I guess not. I forgot—you think I'm just one of those dead men.

(*Silence.* LONE *pulls out a gong.* MA *gets into position.* LONE *hits the gong. They do the following in a mock-Chinese-opera style*)

MA: I am Ma. Yesterday, I was kicked out of my house by my three elder brothers, calling me the lazy dreamer of the family. I am sitting here in front of the temple trying to decide how I will avenge this indignity. Here comes the poorest beggar in this village. (*He cues* LONE) He is called Fleaman because his body is the most popular meeting place for fleas from around the province.

LONE: (*Singing*)

Fleas in love,
Find your happiness
In the gray scraps of my suit

MA: Hello, Flea—

LONE: (*Continuing*)

Fleas in need,
Shield your families
In the gray hairs of my beard

MA: Hello, Flea—

(LONE *cuts* MA *off, continues an extended improvised aria*)

MA: Hello, Fleaman.

LONE: Hello, Ma. Are you interested in providing a home for these fleas?

MA: No!

LONE: This couple here—seeking to start a new home. Housing today is so hard to find. How about your left arm?

MA: I may have plenty of my own fleas in time. I have been thrown out by my elder brothers.

LONE: Are you seeking revenge? A flea epidemic on your house? (*To a flea*) Get back there. You should be asleep. Your mother will worry.

MA: Nothing would make my brothers angrier than seeing me rich.

LONE: Rich? After the bad crops of the last three years, even the fleas are thinking of moving north.

MA: I heard a white devil talk yesterday.

LONE: Oh—with hair the color of a sick chicken and eyes round as eggs? The fleas and I call him Chicken-Laying-an-Egg.

MA: He said we can make our fortunes on the Gold Mountain, where work is play and the sun scares off snow.

LONE: Don't listen to chicken-brains.

MA: Why not? He said gold grows like weeds.

LONE: I have heard that it is slavery.

MA: Slavery? What do you know, Fleaman? Who told you? The fleas? Yes, I will go to Gold Mountain.

(*Gongs.* MA *strikes a submissive pose to* LONE)

LONE: "The one hundred twenty-five dollars passage money is to be paid to the said head of said Hong, who will make arrangements with the coolies, that their wages shall be deducted until the debt is absorbed."

(MA *bows to* LONE. *Gongs. They pick up fighting sticks and do a water-crossing dance. Dance ends. They stoop next to each other and rock*)

MA: I have been in the bottom of this boat for thirty-six days now. Tang, how many have died?

LONE: Not me. I'll live through this ride.

MA: I didn't ask how you are.

LONE: But why's the Gold Mountain so far?

MA: We left with three hundred and three.

LONE: My family's depending on me.

MA: So tell me, how many have died?

LONE: I'll be the last one alive.

MA: That's not what I wanted to know.

LONE: I'll find some fresh air in this hole.

MA: I asked, how many have died.

LONE: Is that a crack in the side?

MA: Are you listening to me?

LONE: If I had some air—

MA: I asked, don't you see—?

LONE: The crack—over there—

MA: Will you answer me, please?

LONE: I need to get out.

MA: The rest here agree—

LONE: I can't stand the smell.

MA: That a hundred eighty—

LONE: I can't see the air—

MA: Of us will not see—

LONE: And I can't die.

MA: Our Gold Mountain dream.

(LONE/TANG *dies;* MA *throws his body overboard. The boat docks.* MA *exits, walks through the streets. He picks up one of the fighting sticks, while* LONE *becomes the mountain*)

MA: I have been given my pickax. Now I will attack the mountain.

(MA *does a dance of labor.* LONE *sings*)

LONE:

Hit your hardest
Pound out your tears
The more you try
The more you'll cry
At how little I've moved
And how large I loom
By the time the sun goes down

(*Dance stops*)

MA: This mountain is clever. But why shouldn't it be? It's fighting for its life, like we fight for ours.

(*The* MOUNTAIN *picks up a stick.* MA *and the* MOUNTAIN *do a battle dance. Dance ends*)

MA: This mountain not only defends itself—it also attacks. It turns our strength against us.

(LONE *does* MA*'s labor dance, while* MA *plants explosives in midair. Dance ends*)

MA: This mountain has survived for millions of years. Its wisdom is immense.

(LONE *and* MA *begin a second battle dance. This one ends with them working the battle sticks together.* LONE *breaks away, does a warrior strut*)

LONE: I am a white devil! Listen to my stupid language: "Wha che doo doo blah blah." Look at my wide eyes—like I have drunk seventy-two pots of tea. Look at my funny hair—twisting, turning, like a snake telling lies. (*To* MA) Bla bla doo doo tee tee.
MA: We don't understand English.
LONE: (*Angry*) Bla bla doo doo tee tee!
MA: (*With Chinese accent*) Please you-ah speak-ah Chinese?
LONE: Oh. Work—uh—one—two—more—work—two—
MA: Two hours more? Stupid demons. As confused as your hair. We will strike!

(*Gongs.* MA *is on strike*)

MA: (*In broken English*) Eight hours day good for white man, all same good for ChinaMan.

LONE: The strike is over! We've won!

MA: I knew we would.

LONE: We forced the white devil to act civilized.

MA: Tamed the Barbarians!

LONE: Did you think—

MA: Who woulda thought?

LONE: —it could be done?

MA: Who?

LONE: But who?

MA: Who could tame them?

MA *and* LONE: Only a ChinaMan!

(*They laugh*)

LONE: Well, c'mon.

MA: Let's celebrate!

LONE: We have.

MA: Oh.

LONE: Back to work.

MA: But we've won the strike.

LONE: I know. Congratulations! And now—

MA: —back to work?

LONE: Right.

MA: No.

LONE: But the strike is over.

(LONE *tosses* MA *a stick. They resume their stick battle as before, but* MA *is heard over* LONE's *singing*)

LONE:	MA:
Hit your hardest	Wait.
Pound out your	I'm tired of this!
tears	How do we end it?
The more you try	Let's stop now, all
The more you'll cry	right?
At how little I've	Look, I said enough!
moved	
And how large I	
loom	
By the time the	
sun goes down.	

(MA *tosses his stick away, but* LONE *is already aiming a blow toward it, so that* LONE *hits* MA *instead and knocks him down*)

MA: Oh! Shit . . .

LONE: I'm sorry! Are you all right?

MA: Yeah. I guess.

LONE: Why'd you let go? You can't just do that.

MA: I'm bleeding.

LONE: That was stupid—where?

MA: Here.

LONE: No.

MA: Ow!

LONE: There will probably be a bump.

MA: I dunno.

LONE: What?

MA: I dunno why I let go.

LONE: It was stupid.

MA: But how were we going to end the opera?

LONE: Here. (*He applies whiskey to* MA*'s bruise*) I don't know.

MA: Why didn't we just end it with the celebration? Ow! Careful.

LONE: Sorry. But Ma, the celebration's not the end. We're returning to work. Today. At dawn.

MA: What?

LONE: We've already lost nine days of work. But we got eight hours.

MA: Today? That's terrible.

LONE: What do you think we're here for? But they listened to our demands. We're getting a raise.

MA: Right. Fourteen dollars.

LONE: No. Eight.

MA: What?

LONE: We had to compromise. We got an eight-dollar raise.

MA: But we wanted fourteen. Whey didn't we get fourteen?

LONE: It was the best deal they could get. Congratulations.

MA: Congratulations? Look, Lone, I'm sick of you making fun of the ChinaMen.

LONE: Ma, I'm not. For the first time. I was wrong. We got eight dollars.

MA: We wanted fourteen.

LONE: But we got eight hours.

MA: We'll go back on strike.

LONE: Why?

MA: We could hold out for months.

LONE: And lose all that work?

MA: But we just gave in.

LONE: You're being ridiculous. We got eight hours. Besides, it's already been decided.

MA: I didn't decide. I wasn't there. You made me stay up here.

LONE: The heads of the gangs decide.

MA: And that's it?

LONE: It's done.

MA: Back to work? That's what they decided? Lone, I don't want to go back to work.

LONE: Who does?

MA: I forgot what it's like.

LONE: You'll pick up the technique again soon enough.

MA: I mean, what it's like to have them telling you what to do all the time. Using up your strength.

LONE: I thought you said even after work, you still feel good.

MA: Some days. But others . . . (*Pause*) I get so frustrated sometimes. At the rock. The rock doesn't give in. It's not human. I wanna claw it with my fingers, but that would just rip them up. I wanna throw myself head first onto it, but it'd just knock my skull open. The rock would knock my skull open, then just sit there, still, like nothing had happened, like a faceless Buddha. (*Pause*) Lone, when do I get out of here?

LONE: Well, the railroad may get finished—

MA: It'll never get finished.

LONE: —or you may get rich.

MA: Rich. Right. This is the Gold Mountain. (*Pause*) Lone, has anyone ever gone home rich from here?

LONE: Yes. Some.

MA: But most?

LONE: Most . . . do go home.

MA: Do you still have the fear?

LONE: The fear?

MA: That you'll become like them—dead men?

LONE: Maybe I was wrong about them.

MA: Well, I do. You wanted me to say it before. I can say it now: "They are dead men." Their greatest accomplishment was to win a strike that's gotten us nothing.

LONE: They're sending money home.

MA: No.

LONE: It's not much, I know, but it's something.

MA: Lone, I'm not even doing that. If I don't get rich here, I might as well die here. Let my brothers laugh in peace.

LONE: Ma, you're too soft to get rich here, naïve—you believed the snow was warm.

MA: I've got to change myself. Toughen up. Take no shit. Count my change. Learn to gamble. Learn to win. Learn to stare. Learn to deny. Learn to look at men with opaque eyes.

LONE: You want to do that?

MA: I will. 'Cause I've got the fear. You've given it to me.

(*Pause*)

LONE: Will I see you here tonight?

MA: Tonight?

LONE: I just thought I'd ask.

MA: I'm sorry, Lone. I haven't got time to be the Second Clown.

LONE: I thought you might not.

MA: Sorry.

LONE: You could have been a . . . fair actor.

MA: You coming down? I gotta get ready for work. This is gonna be a terrible day. My legs are sore and my arms are outa practice.

LONE: You go first. I'm going to practice some before work. There's still time.

MA: Practice? But you said you lost your fear. And you said that's what brings you up here.

LONE: I guess I was wrong about that, too. Today, I am dancing for no reason at all.

MA: Do whatever you want. See you down at camp.

LONE: Could you do me a favor?

MA: A favor?

LONE: Could you take this down so I don't have to take it all?

(LONE *points to a pile of props*)

MA: Well, okay. (*Pause*) But this is the last time.

LONE: Of course, Ma. (MA *exits*) See you soon. The last time. I suppose so.

(LONE *resumes practicing. He twirls his hair around as in the beginning of the play. The sun begins to rise. It continues rising until* LONE *is moving and seen only in shadow*)

Curtain

The Responsive Reader

1. What kind of people are the two characters in the play? Do you like one better than the other, and why? Prepare a written or oral capsule portrait of one or the other.
2. What is the relationship between the two characters? Does it change or evolve during the play?
3. What is the role of the phrase "best of both worlds" in this play? Who uses it first and how? Who echoes it and with what effect?

Thinking, Talking, Writing

4. Participate in group effort to act out some key scenes and to pantomine the animal characters that have a role in the play. Does such active involvement help you get into the spirit of the play?
5. Why do you think we hear about the strike only at second hand? Do you see any connection between Lone's dedication to his artistry and the strike of the workers?

6. Do you think the audience needs to be Asian American to understand this play fully or to appreciate it truly? Why or why not?
7. Write the story of what happened in this play as told from the point of view of one of the two characters or of one of their fellow laborers who remain offstage. What does it all mean to the person telling his version of the story?

Collaborative Projects

8. Cesar Chavez died in 1993 after a lifetime of unionizing migrant agricultural workers and of organizing strikes and boycotts designed to advance their cause. Working with a group, study tributes and obituaries assessing his work or achievement. Are there recurrent issues or themes? Is there a consensus?

3

Native Americans: Reclaiming the Past

On the mainland of America, the Wampanoags of Massasoit and King Philip had vanished, along with the Chesapeakes, the Chickahominys, and the Potomacs of the great Powhatan confederacy. . . . Scattered or reduced to remnants were the Pequots, Montauks, Nanticokes, Machapungas, Catawbas, Cheraws, Miamis, Hurons, Eries, Mohawks, Senecas, and Mohegans. . . . Their musical names remained forever fixed on the American land, but their bones were forgotten in a thousand burned villages or lost in forests fast disappearing before the axes of twenty million invaders.

Dee Brown

As a young girl I used to look at myself in the mirror, trying to find a clue as to who and what I was. My face is very Indian, and so are my eyes and my hair, but my skin is very light. Always I waited for the summer, for the prairie sun, the Badlands sun, to tan me and make me into a real skin.

Mary Crow Dog

> *Because who would believe*
> *the fantastic and terrible story of all of our survival*
> *those who were never meant*
>   *to survive?*
>   *Joy Harjo, "Anchorage"*

LITERATURE IN CONTEXT

A new generation of Native Americans has tried to reclaim the tribal past and give their people a new sense of pride. Writers and artists have worked to create a new sense of identity that would point beyond the poverty, the hopelessness, and the squalor of reservation life. They have revived the outlawed religious ceremonies. They have rediscovered their ancestors' reverence for life and closeness to nature as antidotes to the ills of a sterile, plastic technological civilization.

Varying estimates place up to a million Native Americans in what is now U.S. territory at the time the first immigrant ships came to New England and Virginia. The original inhabitants were divided into tribes ranging from small bands to nations or confederacies of perhaps twenty thousand people. Like the people who built the Aztec, Maya, and Inca civilizations of Central and South America, they were descended from immigrants who had crossed the Bering Straits from Asia perhaps fifty thousand years ago. The population of North America spoke many different languages, or dialects that had drifted so far apart that they were no longer mutually intelligible. Some of these are being recorded and studies by linguists before the last speakers die out.

We know about Native American life from the fragmentary testimony of survivors, from the stories brought back by whites who lived for a time in tribal villages, and from the work of painters and photographers concerned to leave a documentary record of a threatened civilization. Tribal communities had elaborate gradations of rank and of honor and disgrace. Horses and firearms, both brought to the Americas by the Spaniards, were prized possessions. In some tribes, women were treated as inferiors; others were "mother-centered, mother-right people" (Paula Gunn Allen). Tribes from the Iroquois and Sioux to the Apache cultivated a warrior ethic that made bravery in battle or in raids against enemy tribes a test of manliness. They enforced the warrior ethic through ridicule of cowardice and through cruel reprisals against the families of those of their own who were killed in battle.

When Lewis and Clark observed the villages of related but often feuding tribes along the Missouri River in 1804, smallpox, brought by the whites, was already taking its toll. Broken treaties and forcible removal, together with the extermination of the buffalo, would increasingly deny the native population the means to live. By 1860, perhaps 300,000 Native Americans were left, driven from their lands by the rising tide of white settlement. The fate of the tribes was essentially the same, regardless of what strategies they adopted for dealing with the "grim, unrelenting advance of the U.S. Cavalry" (N. Scott Momaday). In the end, it did not matter whether they were "hostile," or tried to live side by side with the white settlers, or, like the Cherokee, adopted the white man's ways, becoming farmers and converting to Christianity. Two centuries of "ethnic cleansing" left a legacy of tribes decimated by massacre, hunger, and disease. Where millions of buffalo had roamed the prairies sustaining life for the Plains Indians, there was only "an endless desolation of bones and skulls and rotting hooves" (Dee Brown). Forced conversion, forced assimilation, unemployment, alcoholism, and poverty were the gifts of white civilization for the survivors.

The Native Americans had a rich tradition of storytelling and song and dance. They conducted elaborate religious ceremonies, like the Kiowa sun dance or the sweat baths and ghost dances of the Sioux. However, much of what survives of their oral tradition comes to us filtered through translation and adaptation by white interpreters and missionaries. When writers and historians today try to honor and recreate the past, they find themselves enmeshed in debates over the true meaning of the Native American experience.

For centuries the original inhabitants of the continent were seen in the distorting mirror of white expectations and assumptions. Columbus had described the native Carribbean population that he enslaved and brutalized in his search for gold as generous and without guile, endowed with acute intelligence. The Spaniards colonizing the Southwest for a time debated whether the Indios had souls (and were therefore worthy of conversion and salvation). The white settlers of the North, after initial friendly contacts, gradually came to stereotype the Native Americans as children of the devil and bloodthirsty savages. At the same time, among writers and artists a countermyth idealized the native population as innocent children of nature. The "noble savage" was painted as uncorrupted by the greed and materialism of white civilization. Educated, tolerant eighteenth-century writers like William Byrd of Virginia claimed that the natives proved the Enlightenment theory of a universal natural religion. Without the benefit of revelation, nature had taught them such basics as belief in a God, knowledge of good and evil, and faith in an afterlife.

Today, Native Americans are often described as the first conservationists, the first ecologists, who "knew that life was equated with the earth and its resources." Dee Brown, in his spectacularly successful and widely translated *Bury My Heart at Wounded Knee* (1970) paints a picture of the last free tribes living "the way they had always lived" among the remaining buffalo in close harmony with nature:

> The Indians killed only enough animals to supply their needs for winter—stripping the meat carefully to dry in the sun, storing marrow and fat in skins, treating the sinews for bowstring and thread, making spoons and cups of the horns, weaving the hair into ropes and belts, curing the hides for tepee covers, clothing and moccasins. Before the beginning of the Yellow Leaves Moon, the floor of the canyon along the creek was a forest of tepees—Kiowa, Comanche, and Cheyenne—all well stocked with food to last until spring. Almost two thousand horses shared the rich grass with the buffalo. Without fear, the women went about their tasks and the children played along the streams.

NEW WORLD

N. Scott Momaday

> *N. Scott Momaday, Pulitzer Prize–winning poet and novelist, is a Kiowa from Oklahoma who became a professor of English at the University of California at Santa Barbara and at the University of New Mexico. In his widely reprinted autobiographical essay "The Way to Rainy Mountain" (1967), he tells the story of his personal search for roots. He traced the history of his ancestors, to whom "war was their sacred business" and who, in alliance with the Comanches, "had ruled the whole Southern plains." The poet's grandmother had as a young child participated in the last sun dances, and she had kept "a reverence for the sun, a holy regard that is now all but gone" out of humankind. Momaday has tried to keep alive the attitudes of wonder and reverence toward the land that were part of the ceremonies and oral literature of his people.*
>
> *Momaday's novel* The House Made of Dawn *won the Pulitzer Prize in 1969. Many of his poems appear in his collection* The Gourd Dancer *(1976).*
>
> *(To preserve the original arrangement of this poem, it appears on the opposite page instead of immediately following.)*

The Responsive Reader

1. For the poet, what is the keynote or characteristic feeling for each stage of the daily cycle? What details for him best create the characteristic mood or feeling of each stage? Do any seem particularly appropriate to you?
2. Why would the poet focus on something as obvious or familiar as the daily cycle of dawn, noon, and dusk? Why would he ask the first human being to become aware of or attuned to this basic rhythm?

Thinking, Talking, Writing

3. Is it true that our technological civilization has to a large extent isolated us from the rhythms of nature? Have we lost the sense of the daily cycle? Have we lost our sense of the cycle of the seasons?

Collaborative Projects

4. Terms like *genesis* and *creation* activate basic questions about the origin, nature, and purpose of life. They play a central role in the myths and religions of different cultures. Working in groups, your class may want to explore the traditions, ideas, associations, and controversies that cluster around these terms. (What creation myths have your classmates encountered? What views of the world are implied in the accounts of genesis in different religions?)

1

First Man, *1*
behold:
the earth
glitters
with leaves; *5*
the sky
glistens
with rain.

2

Pollen   At dawn   *20*
is borne *10* eagles
on winds   hie and
that low   hover
and lean   above
upon   the plain *25*
mountains. *15* where light
Cedars   gathers
blacken   in pools.
the slopes—   Grasses
and pines.   shimmer *30*
                and shine.
                Shadows
                withdraw
                and lie
                away *35*
                like smoke.

3

At noon
turtles
enter
slowly *40*
into
the warm
dark loam.
Bees hold
the swarm. *45*
Meadows
recede
through planes
of heat
and pure *50*
distance.

4

At dusk
the gray
foxes
stiffen *55*
in cold;
blackbirds
are fixed
in the
branches. *60*
Rivers
follow
the moon,
the long
white track *65*
of the
full moon.

MOVING CAMP TOO FAR

nila northSun

> *nila northSun was born in Nevada of Shoshoni-Chippewa heritage. She is
> the coauthor of* After the Drying Up of the Water *and* Diet Pepsi *and*
> Nacho Cheese. *She has written with bitter irony about white men who came
> to the reservations to develop mines that would make them, but not the
> tribespeople, rich and to father children they would later abandon. She has
> written about the mixed feelings of those leaving the reservation behind: "god
> how I hated living on the reservation / but now / it doesn't look so bad"
> ("Up and Out"). An editor called the following poem "a mourning song, as
> it is one of a stunted and trivialized vision made to fit a pop-culture conception
> of the Indian."*

i can't speak of   *1*
    many moons
    moving camp on travois
i can't tell of
    the last great battle   *5*
    counting coup or
    taking scalp
i don't know what it
    was to hunt buffalo
    or do the ghost dance   *10*
but
i can see an eagle
    almost extinct
    on slurpee plastic cups
i can travel to powwows   *15*
    in campers & winnebagos
i can eat buffalo meat
    at the tourist burger stand
i can dance to indian music
    rock-n-roll hey-a-hey-o   *20*
i can
    & unfortunately
    i do

The Responsive Reader

1. What is the meaning of the title? What other echoes of Native American life or history play a role in this poem? (What is the meaning of
   travois and *counting coup?*) How does the poet show the native heritage
   to have been "trivialized" in American pop culture?

2. What is the poet's own relation to her heritage and its trivialization or exploitation? Do you understand her feelings? Is there an answer to the poet's frustration?

Thinking, Talking, Writing

3. Have you seen evidence of other cultural traditions becoming trivialized or commercialized? Have you ever reacted negatively to part of your own heritage being misrepresented or exploited?

SURE YOU CAN ASK ME A PERSONAL QUESTION

Diane Burns

No, we are not extinct.
Diane Burns

> *Diane Burns is of Ojibwa and Cheemehuevi ancestry. A painter and illustrator, she studied at the Institute of American Indian Art at Santa Fe and at Barnard College. Her first book of poetry,* Riding the One-Eyed Ford, *appeared in 1981. In the following dialogue, do any of the questions or comments directed at the poet have a familiar ring?*

How do you do?   1
    No, I am not Chinese.
No, not Spanish.
    No, I am American Indi-uh, Native American.
No, not from India.   5
    No, not Apache.
No, not Navajo.
    No, not Sioux.
No, we are not extinct.
    Yes, Indin.   10
Oh?
    So that's where you got those high cheekbones.
Your great grandmother, huh?
    An Indian Princess, huh?
Hair down to there?   15
    Let me guess. Cherokee?
Oh, so you've had an Indian friend?
    That close?
Oh, so you've had an Indian lover?
    That tight?   20
Oh, so you've had an Indian servant?
    That much?
Yeah, it was awful what you guys did to us.
    It's real decent of you to apologize.
No, I don't know where you can get peyote.   25
    No, I don't know where you can get Navajo rugs real cheap.
No, I didn't make this. I bought it at Bloomingdale's.
    Thank you. I like your hair too.
I don't know if anyone knows whether or not Cher is really Indian.
    No, I didn't make it rain tonight.   30

Yeah. Uh-huh. Spirituality.
    Uh-huh. Yeah. Spirituality. Uh-huh. Mother
Earth. Yeah. Uh'huh. Uh'huh. Spirituality.
    No, I didn't major in archery.
Yeah, a lot of us drink too much.   *35*
    Some of us can't drink enough.
This ain't no stoic look.
    This is my face.

The Responsive Reader

1. What stereotypes about Native Americans does Burns satirize in this poem? (How many can you identify? How does she deal with them?)
2. Where does the poet allude to what the African American writer Shelby Steele has called "white guilt"? What is her response?

Thinking, Talking, Writing

3. Americans from culturally diverse backgrounds sometimes feel alternately defensive and assertive about their distinct identity. Can you understand how they feel? Does this poem fit this pattern? How or why?
4. Some people adopt a special "telephone voice" when they talk on the telephone. Do you adopt a special way of speaking or acting when you are around people from a minority background?

Collaborative Projects

5. You and your classmates may want to work in pairs writing and presenting imaginary dialogues—each between a person who tends to think in stereotypes and a member of a group that is often stereotyped.

LEAVING

Joy Harjo

> *Joy Harjo was born in Tulsa, Oklahoma, and is of the Creek tribe. Her poems have appeared in a wide range of periodicals and have been collected in* The Last Song *and* What Moon Drove Me to This. *They have been reprinted in anthologies of Native American literature and of women's poetry. Harjo has degrees from the University of New Mexico and the Iowa Writers Workshop and has taught Native American Literature and Creative Writing at the Institute of American Indian Arts and Arizona State University. The following poem appeared in* She Had Some Horses *(1983). One reviewer said of this book, it is "an opening into woman light, into hatching, into awakening. The ruined and dismembered, imprisoned, dispossessed, ride out on a bright thundering of horses in a light of illumination and love" (Meridel Le Sueur).*

Four o'clock this morning there was a call.   1
She talked Indian, so it was probably her mother.
It was. Something not too drastic, tone of voice,
no deaths or car wrecks. But something. I was
out of the sheets, unwrapped from the blankets,   5
fighting to stay in sleep. Slipped in and out of her
voice, her voice on the line.
She came back to me. Lit cigarette blurred in the dark.
All lights off but that. Laid
down next to me, empty, these final hours   10
before my leaving.

Her sister was running away from her boyfriend and
was stranded in Calgary, Alberta. Needed money
and comfort for the long return back home.

I dreamed of a Canadian plain, and warm arms around me,   15
the soft skin of the body's landscape. And I dreamed
of bear, and a thousand mile escape homeward.

The Responsive Reader

1. What is the situation in this poem? What in the poem is specifically related to the poet's ancestry and to her lifestyle?
2. Is there a keynote or recurrent underlying theme in this poem?

Thinking, Talking, Writing

3. Do you ever dream about "escaping homeward"?

4. Harjo often writes about members of a younger generation who leave behind the "aboriginal music" of their origins and go to the cities to "live in another language." What is it like to "live in another language"? How is it different from just speaking another language?

WHEN I WAS A CHILD I PLAYED WITH THE BOYS

Mary Mackey

The epic struggle between the native tribes and the white invaders has had a special hold on the popular imagination both in this country and around the world. It has inspired the scenarios of countless books and movies pitting settlers and the cavalry against the doomed warriors of the forests and the plains. For writers probing the paradoxes of our civilization, the opposition of red man and white man became fraught with symbolic meanings. How does the poet use the archetypal conflict in the following poem?

Mary Mackey is a novelist and poet who has worked as a journalist and teacher and is a founder of the Feminist Writers Guild. The poem is from her collection Split Ends *(1974).*

when I was a child   1
I played with the boys
and (because I was only a girl)
they made me
be   5
the Indians

my name was Fox Woman
and they hunted me
like dogs

my name was   10
White Bird
and I flew to escape them

my name was
Last Star
the last   15
of my people

my name was
Sunset
for they caught me
and burned me   20

my name was
Won't Talk
for I never
betrayed us

time after time   *25*
the boys shot me down
and I came back
Red Witch
wild and chanting

came back   *30*
Ghost Dance
came back
Can't Forget
and Crazy-With-Grief

I know where they went   *35*
those boys with their guns
they're still hunting Indians

look
you can see
their names are   *40*
Spills Blood
and Kills-Without-Mercy

The Responsive Reader

1. What image or mystique of the Native American is acted out in this poem? What parts or features of it do you recognize?
2. Who are the "boys" in this poem? Do they stand symbolically for present-day white civilization?
3. How does the poem draw a parallel between the Native American as victim and woman as victim? How persuasive or justified is the parallel?

Thinking, Talking, Writing

4. If asked to choose sides, would you choose to be with the Indians or with the Indian-hunting whites?

LIVES FAR CHILD

Craig Strete

Craig Kay Strete is a Native American storyteller who knows how to evoke the spirit of the past while keeping a sharp satirical eye on the present. Strete has worked as a scriptwriter and as a teacher of creative writing. He has written about the comic adventures of the minority person navigating among liberals who are compensating for white guilt, befriending a Native American writer or artist to cement their good standing in the world of radical chic. However, he has also written haunting fiction taking the reader back to the world of native storytelling, as in the following ghost story from his volume Death Chants *(1988). The Argentinian writer Jorge Luis Borges has said about Strete that he "can construct a universe within the skull, to rival the real."*

"It was the beatings," was all Lives Far would say, and she knelt down by the bed with the red and blue Navaho blanket and wept.   1

"Seems to me, you married a hard one," said Navana, her father. He sat cross-legged by the door of the hogan. His hands were busy carving a small whistle out of elk bone.

"I don't mind the beatings so much," said Lives Far, "but it is not good for my children to see. It shows them the wrong path in life."

Navana watched her with vague unease. Lives Far was five years old, just five, but she was a strange, strange child.

Navana blew the bone scrapings off the whistle and put it to his lips.   5
He blew gently on it and it made a pleasing birdlike trill.

Lives Far turned and looked in his direction, her eyes brightening in spite of the tears.

He held it out to her. "I made this for you, little one."

She came toward him eagerly and took it from his hands. Her face was still wet with tears.

"Make it sing, Lives Far," said Navana and his face lit with a brief hope.

She started to put it to her lips, delight in her eyes, but something   10
stopped the delight and she became solemn and her hands closed in a fist over the whistle.

"I'll keep it and give it to my children," she said. "They are waiting for me outside."

Navana's second wife, Winter Gatherer, stood in the doorway. She was of another tribe and her ways were sometimes hard.

"That child must be punished!" she said bitterly. "We have heard enough of her lies."

Navana put his hand over the small child fist that held the elk bone whistle.

He smiled down at the child with sadness in his eyes.   15

"My people teach that lies are blackhearted and a child would be beaten if it talked like . . ." Winter Gatherer started again.

Navana turned on her angrily.

"I have heard enough about your people and your ways! We do not beat our little ones! Always gentleness, always respect and understanding, so I have been raised and so I will raise my children! Our way is better."

"A stupid way to raise children," she said. "But something will have to be done about her, if you're too cowardly to beat her."

"Go outside and play," Navana told the child.

"Yes. I've got washing to do and corn to weed and hoe," said Lives Far. "And I better see to fixing supper for Thomas or he'll beat me again."

She went outside, moving slowly, like an old woman bent under the burdens of a lifetime.

At birth, Lives Far was a child unlike other children. Her mother, Navana's first wife, slowly bleeding to death under the birth blankets, had looked into the tiny red face and feared greatly what she saw. Her own death, red and inevitable beneath the Pendleton blanket, did not scare her.

Death was an old friend but the things she saw in her child's eyes were older than anything that ever moved in her world.

When Navana had come at last into the quickening room, he saw the obscene birds of birth and death perched on the same withered branch of his living tree. His wife took his face in her hands when he bent down over her. Gently she turned him away so that he might not look upon the face of the child at her breast. For children at birth cannot hide themselves from the world until life is strong in their bodies.

And she feared that seeing the child for what it might be, he might wish to destroy it.

"I call this child, Lives Far," she said speaking prophecy, and she kept Navana busy with her own death until the child had taken enough of the world's wind into its body, enough living strength to hide its true self. The old ones say such a happening is an evil birth, evil when the greedy child sucks the life out of its own mother. But the child came into the world, evil or not, and was loved and grew under Navana's nurturing wing.

Navana knew Lives Far never played as other children played. She just sat in the sun and talked to people who were not there.

Lives Far, so she said, was married to a white man and had two children by him. His name was Thomas Morgan and he drank and beat her and was evil. Yes, that was what she said. And she described him in great detail, in a way no child of five could possibly know.

"Thomas burns with drink and it burns his head inside, burns some-place deep until his hair no longer feels like hair, but like a scalp of ashes."

"Poor Thomas," she said and her child's voice seemed to forgive him everything. "The drink burns his tongue in the roof of his mouth so the words of his war nightmares can't escape as he sleeps. It started not just with his liking it, but his needing it, the drink, always the drink, because it is the water of war and it made one forget to be afraid and promised other kinds of forgetfulness."

Navana had felt like screaming in the face of such solemn, straight-faced gibberish, if a part of him had not been a little shocked by it, and a little frightened of it as well.

For though Navana did not heed the words of the old ones, who would have seen this child, Lives Far, who took her own mother out of this world, destroyed as an evil thing, still Navana was disturbed and uneasy sometimes when the child was acting this way. He loved her with all his heart but his mind sometimes saw shadows lurking all about her, and a darkness he could not fathom.

"But the forgetfulness must have been too deep or not deep enough. The Thomas Morgan that I married never came back from the war."

Her face was full of sorrow. "He doesn't sleep with me anymore," she   35
confided in a childish whisper. "I've begged him, pleaded with him, but he won't touch me now. He just drinks now and sometimes beats me and always, always, has nightmares. He used to be so sweet when he made love to me. Now he's a stranger to my bed."

Coming from the lips of a five-year-old, it was a tiny, almost mad horror.

Navana brushed the elk bone shavings off his lap.

Winter Gatherer remained in the doorway, looking out at the squash garden. Her beauty was like a weapon, her sharp tongue the point of her spear.

"She's just sitting there like always, Navana, talking to her invisible family. She's head-sick," said Winter Gatherer, fingering a beaded choker around her neck.

"She was always a big-eyed child. Always in a dream," remembered   40
Navana. "The sky is full of rabbits, yellow and brown ones, she would tell me. Or fish are swimming in my ears, Father, make them stop."

"Childish dreams are one thing," said Winter Gatherer. "But these strange dreams have grown to truth in her mind. She is like one possessed."

"Many were the strange dreams I myself had as a child, but as time moved me down the path of life, those dreams left me and new and proper ones came to take their place. So it will be with her, if we give her time," said Navana, but there was very little hope in his voice as much as he wanted to believe it.

Lives Far screamed.

Navana and Winter Gatherer ran outside.

They expected danger but saw none.   45

Just Lives Far alone, her eyes red with weeping, sprawled in a heap in the dust.

"What's wrong, little one? Spider bite you? See a snake?" asked Navana with loving concern, suddenly conscious of clenched fists and relaxing them.

"He's dead," she said.

"Who's dead?" said Winter Gatherer suspiciously, her eyes flashing darkly.

"My husband, Thomas," said Lives Far. "Mostly it's the drink I blame.   *50*
It's what caused most of our trouble too. I always said it would be the death of him. And now it's taken him away forever. But he wouldn't listen to me. He just wouldn't listen, so he got into a fight in a bar and another white man stabbed him. Left me and the children all alone."

Navana wiped his face with his hand, anxiety plain in his face.

"Now I have to ask you if we can go bring the children to stay with us. It isn't right that the children should be home alone when I work. I know I'll have to work. Thomas fed us at least, but with him gone, it'll be up to me," said Lives Far solemnly, regarding each of them gravely.

"I'm sorry to hear he's dead," said Navana, not sure if he liked this sudden turn of events. If this meant an end to her strange make-believe and a return to being his little five-year-old girl, then Navana was all for it. But he had little real hope.

"We have to go get the children," insisted Lives Far.

"You don't have a husband and you don't have any damn children!"   *55*
said Winter Gatherer, arms thrust out angrily at her side. She was like an angry snake, coiled to strike.

Navana looked at his wife, shaking his head no. "I'll handle this."

He bent down and put his arm around the frail child. He gently wiped the tears from her eyes.

"Listen to me, Lives Far. If we go to find your children, and there are no children, no Thomas, dead or otherwise, will you put aside this dream once and for all?"

"What dream?" asked Lives Far. "Please, Father, they are blood of your blood. You have to go with me to pick them up."

Navana decided to take the challenge.   *60*

"All right, little one, do you know the road to take?"

"West," said Lives Far. "Until we reach the great rock shaped like a turtle, there we turn left and then follow the stream bed. That's where they buried Thomas this morning. And my children will be just down the road from there."

Navana stood up, looked to the west and then nodded once, having come to a decision.

"Then west we shall go."

"Leave me out of the we," said Winter Gatherer. "I'm sick of the whole   *65*
business."

Navana looked at her for a moment as if seeing her for the first time, and not exactly liking what he saw.

"No need for you to come," said Navana. "I'll saddle up just the one horse for me and Lives Far."

"Eat supper first. Man's going to be a damn fool, he ought to at least have a full belly first."

"I've got a full belly of something already," he said and he took Lives Far by the hand and led her to the barn.

While they were saddling up the horse, they heard the back door of *70* the house slam.

"Isn't Winter Gatherer coming to see her grandchildren?" asked Lives Far.

"No," said Navana grimly, tightening the cinch strap under the belly of the horse. "I figure she's heading into the trading post. Probably to visit a couple relatives of hers that live in bottles. We don't need her anyway."

"How far do you reckon this place is?" said Navana, leading the horse out of the barn.

Lives Far trotted along at his side. "Years and years in Indian time," said Lives Far. "It's not far at all."

Navana swung up easily into the saddle. He bent down, reached for *75* the child and swung her up gracefully behind him on the horse.

They trotted down the long dusty road to the west. The sun walked across the sky. The air was as dry as dust under a dead snake and the heat rose off the road in waves. Sweat soaked them both and they swayed dizzily in the saddle with the heat.

As the afternoon moved toward evening, Navana noticed that Lives Far was blood-red with the sun and the heat. She was barely conscious, her arms loosening moment by moment around his waist.

"I've been down this road a thousand times, little one, as far west as it goes and I've never seen a rock shaped like a turtle."

With an effort the child opened her eyes, and moved her head so that she could see past him.

"There!" she cried. "There it is! Just like I said." *80*

Navana turned and his eyes widened in horror.

A landslide had dumped a pile of rocks across one side of the road as it entered Devil's Canyon. Seen from a distance, the tumbled heap of stones did indeed look very much like a turtle.

"Funny nobody ever told me about that landslide," said Navana, shaking his head in bewilderment. "I was through here just last week and there was nothing like this."

"This is where we turn," said Lives Far. "Hurry, Father. We're almost there."

Reluctantly, with no sense of the make-believe coming to an end, *85* Navana turned the horse and they moved on.

The horse almost stumbled as it moved down into the bed of a long-dry stream.

"Now just follow the stream bed and we'll be there soon," said Lives Far. "I can't wait to see my children!"

Heartsick and feeling a growing uneasiness, Navana let the horse follow the stream bed at a walk.

The light of day was beginning to fade. The long shadows of night began marching across the sky. Now the stream bed seemed to melt under their feet and the sky was vanishing into darkness.

"Child, in all my years, I don't recall a stream being here. It's near dark and getting hard to see the way. We ought to be home. Maybe we better turn back now."   *90*

"But we're almost there," cried Lives Far. "See over there, that's the graveyard!"

She was pointing off to the right.

Navana turned in horror and saw a small area of ground, fenced off with wrought iron. It was the kind of fence the white men used around their burying places. Navana felt raw pulsing terror rising in him.

Lives Far let go of his waist and slid off the horse. She hit hard, over-balanced and fell forward on her face. She bounced to her feet, ignoring her injuries, and began running toward the graveyard.

"Thomas!" she cried.   *95*

"Wait!" screamed Navana. "Come back!"

Lives Far ran through the front gate and dashed through the rows of tombstones, thrusting up into the night like the pale white stone fingers of dead men.

Navana jumped down off the horse and ran after her, screaming for her to stop.

She was lost to sight from him somewhere in the cold gray rows of stone.

He stumbled through the growing dark, calling out her name.   *100*

He couldn't find her anywhere.

His terror and panic grew. Each step seemed to take him deeper into darkness. He passed by a group of small tombstones at the far end of the graveyard and then he heard her voice.

"Poor Thomas. I loved you once." That was Lives Far's voice coming eerily from somewhere off to the right.

He staggered toward her.

"Lives Far!" he screamed.   *105*

A cloud passed overhead and the new moon cast a gray light on the graveyard.

In the distance he thought he saw her hunched over a small tombstone, her back to him.

"Lives Far, come away from there! You are disturbing the dead and doing them a dishonor! None of our people are buried here. Come away, child. I know you are sick in your mind. Very sick, Lives Far, and I am going to take you home now!"

Resolutely, he moved toward her, past the ice palaces of cold speechless stone.

"Don't you want to pay your respects to Thomas, Father?"   *110*

He came and stood over her, like a sad shadow in the moonlight.

"My poor little one," he said and he bent down to take her in his arms. But as he stooped over, the moon plainly illuminated the lettering on the gravestone.

HERE LIES THOMAS MORGAN
BELOVED HUSBAND OF LIVES FAR MORGAN
1830–1873

Navana backed away in terror.

"Where am I? Where is this place?"

"Father," said Lives Far. "We have to go now. My children are just *115* down the way."

"No, child," said Navana, his voice high with fear. "We must go back the way we came!"

"But I don't want to go back," said Lives Far. "I don't want to be a child back there. I belong here."

"Where is here?" asked Navana.

"Why, 1873 of course," said Lives Far. "This year I lost my husband, Thomas."

"We have to go back!" he cried, terror etching the lines of his face. He *120* turned and looked at the lettering on the gravestone. He knew that the date had to be right, but it could not be! When he had gotten up that morning, it was as the white men had numbered it, 1845, not 1873!

"I can't leave my children," said Lives Far. "You can't make me go back! I won't go! You're dead anyway now."

Lives Far started to back away from him.

"Wait! Listen to me!" he cried but she turned and began to run from him. "Go back!" she said. "You're dead here. And my children need me."

Navana wanted to run after her but terror held him like a dark mother embracing a night child.

She seemed to grow as she ran away from him. Gone were the short *125* little legs of a child, coltish and awkward. Now she ran with the grace of a young girl, as if now seeking the first ground-devouring strides of womanhood.

And then as she passed finally into the distance, she seemed to run with the full-legged gait of a woman.

"LIVES FAR!" His anguished cry chased her all through the moonlit night.

The child was gone.

As much as he wanted to run after her, a certainty as black as night itself, held him back.

He knew that on the other side of that graveyard, somewhere in 1873, *130* his child was a woman grown with children of her own and he was a tree of nothing but bones, shaking no more wind in its white branches.

Navana stood there like a lost deer in the night wind.

He looked back the way he had come and thought now of the childless house back there waiting for him, the empty maternal rooms, the dust gathering on soon-to-be-forgotten toys.

Could a life be lived in that house now? His thoughts turned unhappily to Winter Gatherer and to the rest of their journey of days together.

What did he have to go back to, with Lives Far gone from him?

A man without children was no better than a wind in the grave.   *135*

He squared his shoulders and began to walk in the direction Lives Far had gone. If the living can see the dead, then the dead can see the living, this was in his mind.

He stepped outside the back gate of the cemetery and his feet began to sink into the ground.

So this is what death is like, he thought.

Then he made a great effort to straighten his shoulders once more and again walk in the direction Lives Far had gone. With each step, he sank deeper as the dark earth reached up to pull the white bones down through his skin. His skin seemed to run away like water into the thirsty earth, seeking its own level.

He did not die as he left the cemetery. He could not die.   *140*

In Lives Far Woman's world, for five cold long years, he had already been dead.

The Responsive Reader

1. What kind of person is the father in this story? What goes on in his mind? How do you react to him?
2. Ghost stories often have a skeptic in them—someone who champions common sense and refuses to go along with the story. Who plays this role in this story and how? Why do you think ghost stories often include this kind of character?
3. Stories like this one require of the reader "a willing suspension of disbelief." Does this story work for you? Why or why not?

Thinking, Talking, Writing

4. What sidelights does the story of "Lives Far Child" offer on Native American life of the past?
5. Do you enjoy ghost stories? Why or why not?

Collaborative Projects

6. Recent years have seen many collections of traditional Native American stories, such as stories in which the coyote as trickster or firebringer plays a central role. Your class may want to prepare a mini-festival of Native American myth and legend, with oral presentations or dramatizations of traditional story material.

WHERE I COME FROM IS LIKE THIS

Paula Gunn Allen

In recent years, Native American women have written eloquently about their search for the native heritage in an attempt to define who and what they are. They have written about the clash of widely differing cultural traditions and assumptions as they move between the white world and the tribal world. Paula Gunn Allen was born in New Mexico of Native American (Laguna, Sioux) and Mexican American ancestry. She became known for her poetry and her novel The Woman Who Owned the Shadows. *She has taught at universities including UC Berkeley and UCLA. The following autobiographical essay is from her collection* The Sacred Hoop: Recovering the Feminine in American Indian Traditions *(1986).*

I

Modern American Indian women, like their non-Indian sisters, are deeply engaged in the struggle to redefine themselves. In their struggle they must reconcile traditional tribal definitions of women with industrial and postindustrial non-Indian definitions. Yet while these definitions seem to be more or less mutually exclusive, Indian women must somehow harmonize and integrate both in their own lives.

An American Indian woman is primarily defined by her tribal identity. In her eyes, her destiny is necessarily that of her people, and her sense of herself as a woman is first and foremost prescribed by her tribe. The definitions of woman's roles are as diverse as tribal cultures in the Americas. In some she is devalued, in others she wields considerable power. In some she is a familial/clan adjunct, in some she is as close to autonomous as her economic circumstances and psychological traits permit. But in no tribal definitions is she perceived in the same way as are women in Western industrial and postindustrial cultures.

In the West, few images of women form part of the cultural mythos, and these are largely sexually charged. Among Christians, the Madonna is the female prototype, and she is portrayed as essentially passive: her contribution is simply that of birthing. Little else is attributed to her and she certainly possesses few of the characteristics that are attributed to mythic figures among Indian tribes. This image is countered (rather than balanced) by the witch-goddess/whore characteristics designed to reinforce cultural beliefs about women, as well as Western adversarial and dualistic perceptions of reality.

The tribes see women variously, but they do not question the power of femininity. Sometimes they see women as fearful, sometimes peaceful, sometimes omnipotent and omniscient, but they never portray women as mindless, helpless, simple, or oppressed. And while the women in a given tribe, clan, or band may be all these things, the individual woman is provided with a variety of images of women from the interconnected supernatural, natural, and social worlds she lives in.

As a half-breed American Indian woman, I cast about in my mind for negative images of Indian women, and I find none that are directed to Indian women alone. The negative images I do have are of Indians in general and in fact are more often of males than of females. All these images come to me from non-Indian sources, and they are always balanced by a positive image. My ideas of womanhood, passed on largely by my mother and grandmothers, Laguna Pueblo women, are about practicality, strength, reasonableness, intelligence, wit, and competence. I also remember vividly the women who came to my father's store, the women who held me and sang to me, the women at Feast Day, at Grab Days, the women in the kitchen of my Cubero home, the women I grew up with; none of them appeared weak or helpless, none of them presented herself tentatively. I remember a certain reserve on those lovely brown faces; I remember the direct gaze of eyes framed by bright-colored shawls draped over their heads and cascading down their backs. I remember the clean cotton dresses and carefully pressed hand-embroidered aprons they always wore; I remember laughter and good food, especially the sweet bread and the oven bread they gave us. Nowhere in my mind is there a foolish woman, a dumb woman, a vain woman, or a plastic woman, though the Indian women I have known have shown a wide range of personal style and demeanor.

My memory includes the Navajo woman who was badly beaten by her Sioux husband; but I also remember that my grandmother abandoned her Sioux husband long ago. I recall the stories about the Laguna woman beaten regularly by her husband in the presence of her children so that the children would not believe in the strength and power of femininity. And I remember the women who drank, who got into fights with other women and with the men, and who often won those battles. I have memories of tired women, partying women, stubborn women, sullen women, amicable women, selfish women, shy women, and aggressive women. Most of all I remember the women who laugh and scold and sit uncomplaining in the long sun on feast days and who cook wonderful food on wood stoves, in beehive mud ovens, and over open fires outdoors.

Among the images of women that come to me from various tribes as well as my own are White Buffalo Woman, who came to the Lakota long ago and brought them the religion of the Sacred Pipe which they still practice; Tinotzin the goddess who came to Juan Diego to remind him that she still walked the hills of her people and sent him with her message, her demand, and her proof to the Catholic bishop in the city nearby. And from Laguna I take the images of Yellow Woman, Coyote Woman, Grandmother Spider (Spider Old Woman), who brought the light, who gave us weaving and medicine, who gave us life. Among the Keres she is known as

Thought Woman who created us all and who keeps us in creation even now. I remember Iyatiku, Earth Woman, Corn Woman, who guides and counsels the people to peace and who welcomes us home when we cast off this coil of flesh as huskers cast off the leaves that wrap the corn. I remember Iyatiku's sister, Sun Woman, who held metals and cattle, pigs and sheep, highways and engines and so many things in her bundle, who went away to the east saying that one day she would return.

II

Since the coming of the Anglo-Europeans beginning in the fifteenth century, the fragile web of identity that long held tribal people secure has gradually been weakened and torn. But the oral tradition has prevented the complete destruction of the web, the ultimate disruption of tribal ways. The oral tradition is vital; it heals itself and the tribal web by adapting to the flow of the present while never relinquishing its connection to the past. Its adaptability has always been required, as many generations have experienced. Certainly the modern American Indian woman bears slight resemblance to her forebears—at least on superficial examination—but she is still a tribal woman in her deepest being. Her tribal sense of relationship to all that is continues to flourish. And though she is at times beset by her knowledge of the enormous gap between the life she lives and the life she was raised to live, and while she adapts her mind and being to the circumstances of her present life, she does so in tribal ways, mending the tears in the web of being from which she takes her existence as she goes.

My mother told me stories all the time, though I often did not recognize them as that. My mother told me stories about cooking and childbearing; she told me stories about menstruation and pregnancy; she told me stories about gods and heroes, about fairies and elves, about goddesses and spirits; she told me stories about the land and the sky, about cats and dogs, about snakes and spiders; she told me stories about climbing trees and exploring the mesas; she told me stories about going to dances and getting married; she told me stories about dressing and undressing, about sleeping and waking; she told me stories about herself, about her mother, about her grandmother. She told me stories about grieving and laughing, about thinking and doing; she told me stories about school and about people; about darning and mending; she told me stories about turquoise and about gold; she told me European stories and Laguna stories; she told me Catholic stories and Presbyterian stories; she told me city stories and country stories; she told me political stories and religious stories. She told me stories about living and stories about dying. And in all of those stories she told me who I was, who I was supposed to be, whom I came from, and who would follow me. In this way she taught me the meaning of the words she said, that all life is a circle and everything has a place within it. That's what she said and what she showed me in the things she did and the way she lives.

Of course, through my formal, white, Christian education, I discovered   *10* that other people had stories of their own—about women, about Indians, about fact, about reality—and I was amazed by a number of startling suppositions that others made about tribal customs and beliefs. According to the un-Indian, non-Indian view, for instance, Indians barred menstruating women from ceremonies and indeed segregated them from the rest of the people, consigning them to some space specially designed for them. This showed that Indians considered menstruating women unclean and not fit to enjoy the company of decent (nonmenstruating) people, that is, men. I was surprised and confused to hear this because my mother had taught me that white people had strange attitudes toward menstruation: they thought something was bad about it, that it meant you were sick, cursed, sinful, and weak and that you had to be very careful during that time. She taught me that menstruation was a normal occurrence, that I could go swimming or hiking or whatever else I wanted to do during my period. She actively scorned women who took to their beds, who were incapacitated by cramps, who "got the blues."

As I struggled to reconcile these very contradictory interpretations of American Indians' traditional beliefs concerning menstruation, I realized that the menstrual taboos were about power, not about sin or filth. My conclusion was later borne out by some tribes' own explanations, which, as you may well imagine, came as quite a relief to me.

The truth of the matter as many Indians see it is that women who are at the peak of their fecundity are believed to possess power that throws male power totally out of kilter. They emit such force that, in their presence, any male-owned or -dominated ritual or sacred object cannot do its usual task. For instance, the Lakota say that a menstruating woman anywhere near a yuwipi man, who is a special sort of psychic, spirit-empowered healer, for a day or so before he is to do his ceremony will effectively disempower him. Conversely, among many if not most tribes, important ceremonies cannot be held without the presence of women. Sometimes the ritual woman who empowers the ceremony must be unmarried and virginal so that the power she channels is unalloyed, unweakened by sexual arousal and penetration by a male. Other ceremonies require tumescent women, others the presence of mature women who have borne children, and still others depend for empowerment on postmenopausal women. Women may be segregated from the company of the whole band or village on certain occasions, but on certain occasions men are also segregated. In short, each ritual depends on a certain balance of power, and the positions of women within the phases of womanhood are used by tribal people to empower certain rites. This does not derive from a male-dominant view; it is not a ritual observance imposed on women by men. It derives from a tribal view of reality that distinguishes tribal people from feudal and industrial people.

Among the tribes, the occult power of women, inextricably bound to our hormonal life, is thought to be very great; many hold that we possess innately the blood-given power to kill—with a glance, with a step, or with a judicious mixing of menstrual blood into somebody's soup. Medicine women among the Pomo of California cannot practice until they are sufficiently mature; when they are immature, their power is diffuse and is likely to interfere with their practice until time and experience have it under control. So women of the tribes are not especially inclined to see themselves as poor helpless victims of male domination. Even in those tribes where something akin to male domination was present, women are perceived as powerful, socially, physically, and metaphysically. In times past, as in times present, women carried enormous burdens with aplomb. We were far indeed from the "weaker sex," the designation that white aristocratic sisters unhappily earned for us all.

I remember my mother moving furniture all over the house when she wanted it changed. She didn't wait for my father to come home and help— she just went ahead and moved the piano, a huge upright from the old days, the couch, the refrigerator. Nobody had told her she was too weak to do such things. In imitation of her, I would delight in loading trucks at my father's store with cases of pop or fifty-pound sacks of flour. Even when I was quite small I could do it, and it gave me a belief in my own physical strength that advancing middle age can't quite erase. My mother used to tell me about the Acoma Pueblo women she had seen as a child carrying huge ollas (water pots) on their heads as they wound their way up the tortuous stairwell carved into the face of the "Sky City" mesa, a feat I tried to imitate with books and tin buckets. ("Sky City" is the term used by the chamber of commerce for the mother village of Acoma, which is situated atop a high sandstone table mountain.) I was never very successful, but even the attempt reminded me that I was supposed to be strong and balanced to be a proper girl.

Of course, my mother's Laguna people are Keres Indian, reputed to be the last extreme mother-right people on earth. So it is no wonder that I got notably nonwhite notions about the natural strength and prowess of women. Indeed, it is only when I am trying to get non-Indian approval, recognition, or acknowledgment that my "weak sister" emotional and intellectual ploys get the better of my tribal woman's good sense. At such times I forget that I just moved the piano or just wrote a competent paper or just completed a financial transaction satisfactorily or have supported myself and my children for most of my adult life. 15

Nor is my contradictory behavior atypical. Most Indian women I know are in the same bicultural bind: we vacillate between being dependent and strong, self-reliant and powerless, strongly motivated and hopelessly insecure. We resolve the dilemma in various ways: some of us party all the time; some of us drink to excess; some of us travel and move around a lot; some of us land good jobs and then quit them; some of us engage in violent exchanges; some of us blow our brains out. We act in these destructive ways because we suffer from the societal conflicts caused by having to identify with two hopelessly opposed cultural definitions of women. Through this destructive dissonance we are unhappy prey to the self-disparagement common to, indeed demanded of, Indians living in the United States today. Our situation is caused by the exigencies of a history of invasion, conquest, and colonization whose searing marks are probably ineradicable. A popular bumper sticker on many Indian cars proclaims: "If You're Indian You're In," to which I always find myself adding under my breath, "Trouble."

No Indian can grow to any age without being informed that her people were "savages" who interfered with the march of progress pursued by respectable, loving, civilized white people. We are the villains of the scenario when we are mentioned at all. We are absent from much of white history except when we are calmly, rationally, succinctly, and systematically dehumanized. On the few occasions we are noticed in any way other than as howling, bloodthirsty beings, we are acclaimed for our noble quaintness. In this definition, we are exotic curios. Our ancient arts and customs are used to draw tourist money to state coffers, into the pocketbooks and bank accounts of scholars, and into support of the American-in-Disneyland promoters' dream.

As a Roman Catholic child I was treated to bloody tales of how the savage Indians martyred the hapless priests and missionaries who went among them in an attempt to lead them to the one true path. By the time I was through high school I had the idea that Indians were people who had benefited mightily from the advanced knowledge and superior morality of the Anglo-Europeans. At least I had, perforce, that idea to lay beside the other one that derived from my daily experience of Indian life, an idea less dehumanizing and more accurate because it came from my mother and the other Indian people who raised me. That idea was that Indians are a people who don't tell lies, who care for their children and their old people. You never see an Indian orphan, they said. You always know when you're old that someone will take care of you—one of your children will. Then they'd list the old folks who were being taken care of by this child or that. No child is ever considered illegitimate among the Indians, they said. If a girl gets pregnant, the baby is still part of the family, and the mother is too. That's what they said, and they showed me real people who lived according to those principles.

Of course the ravages of colonization have taken their toll; there are orphans in Indian country now, and abandoned, brutalized old folks; there are even illegitimate children, though the very concept still strikes me as absurd. There are battered children and neglected children, and there are battered wives and women who have been raped by Indian men. Proximity to the "civilizing" effects of white Christians has not improved the moral quality of life in Indian country, though each group, Indian and white, explains the situation differently. Nor is there much yet in the oral tradition that can enable us to adapt to these inhuman changes. But a force is growing in that direction, and it is helping Indian women reclaim their lives. Their power, their sense of direction and of self will soon be visible. It is the force of the women who speak and work and write, and it is formidable.

Through all the centuries of war and death and cultural and psychic   20
destruction have endured the women who raise the children and tend the fires, who pass along the tales and the traditions, who weep and bury the dead, who are the dead, and who never forget. There are always the women, who make pots and weave baskets, who fashion clothes and cheer their children on at powwow, who make fry bread and piki bread, and corn soup and chili stew, who dance and sing and remember and hold within their hearts the dream of their ancient peoples—that one day the woman who thinks will speak to us again, and everywhere there will be peace. Meanwhile we tell the stories of fun and scandal and laugh over all manner of things that happen every day. We watch and we wait.

My great-grandmother told my mother: Never forget you are Indian. And my mother told me the same thing. This, then, is how I have gone about remembering, so that my children will remember too.

The Responsive Reader

1. How does the white culture expect Native Americans to envision their history? What image of Native Americans did Gunn encounter during her white-oriented education? How does she correct the traditional stereotypes? (Do these stereotypes survive in schoolbooks or in popular culture?)
2. Much feminist writing has explored matriarchal, woman-centered traditions as an alternative to the dominant patriarchal, male-oriented culture. What self-image of women did Gunn encounter in her own tribal culture? What are striking features or details? What glimpses does she give you of the role of women in other tribal tradition and myth?
3. How did the view of women's roles in Gunn's tribal background clash with the view of women she sees in the traditional white culture? (How is the view of women in the Western tradition "dualistic"?)
4. How did Gunn resolve the conflict between the two opposed influences on her self-image as a woman? How did the conflict shape her personality?
5. What does Gunn see as the legacy of the white conquest for today's Native Americans?

Thinking, Talking, Writing

6. Have you encountered any parallels to Gunn's family tradition of strong, independent women in your own experience? In what cultural context?
7. What do you know about the role of women in religion and myth?

8. Have you encountered clashing cultural traditions that proved "more or less mutually exclusive"? Have you had experience trying to "harmonize and integrate" such conflicting influences in your own life?

Collaborative Projects

9. Among older people you know, is the oral tradition still alive? What kind of stories did they hear when growing up? Working with a group, you may want to pool and compare oral traditions from different cultural strands.

PRIVATE PROPERTY

Leslie Marmon Silko

> *Leslie Marmon Silko was born in Albuquerque, New Mexico, and grew up on the Laguna Pueblo reservation. She became known for her* Ceremony *(1977), a novel about reservation life. In 1981 she published* Storyteller, *a collection of her poems and stories. Silko is of Native American, Mexican, and white ancestry. Some of her stories deal with simple events in the lives of farm families tending their livestock and attending to seasonal chores. However, other stories revolve around the misunderstandings caused by different cultural traditions affecting people's lives.*

All Pueblo Tribes have stories about such a person—a young child, an orphan. Someone has taken the child and has given it a place by the fire to sleep. The child's clothes are whatever the people no longer want. The child empties the ashes and gathers wood. The child is always quiet, sitting in its place tending the fire. They pay little attention to the child as they complain and tell stories about one another. The child listens although it has nothing to gain or lose in anything they say. The child simply listens. Some years go by and great danger stalks the village—in some versions of the story it is a drought and great famine, other times it is a monster in the form of a giant bear. And when all the others have failed and even the priests doubt the prayers, this child, still wearing old clothes, goes out. The child confronts the danger and the village is saved. Among the Pueblo people the child's reliability as a narrator is believed to be perfect.

Etta works with the wind at her back. Sand and dust roll down the road. She feels scattered drops of rain and sometimes flakes of snow. What they have been saying about her all these years is untrue. They are angry because she left. Old leaves and weed stalks lie in gray drifts at the corners of the old fence. Part of an old newspaper is caught in the tumbleweeds; the wind presses it into brittle yellow flakes. She rakes the debris as high as her belly. They continue with stories about her. Going away has changed her. Living with white people has changed her. Fragments of glass blink like animal eyes. The wind pushes the flames deep into the bones and old manure heaped under the pile of dry weeds. The rake drags out a shriveled work shoe and then the sleeve torn from a child's dress. They burn as dark and thick as hair. The wind pushes her off balance. Flames pour around her and catch the salt bushes. The yard burns bare. The sky is the color of stray smoke. The next morning the wind is gone. The ground is crusted with frost and still the blackened bones smolder.

The horses trot past the house before dawn. The sky and earth are the same color then—dense gray of the night burned down. At the approach of the sun, the east horizon bleeds dark blue. Reyna sits up in her bed suddenly and looks out the window at the horses. She has been dreaming she was stolen by Navajos and was taken away in their wagon. The sound of the horses' hooves outside the window had been the wagon horses of her dreams. The white one trots in the lead, followed by the gray. The little sorrel mare is always last. The gray sneezes at their dust. They are headed for the river. Reyna wants to remember this, and gets up. The sky is milky. Village dogs are barking in the distance. She dresses and finds her black wool cardigan. The dawn air smells like rain but it has been weeks since the last storm. The crickets don't feel the light. The mockingbird is in the pear tree. The bare adobe yard is swept clean. A distance north of the pear tree there is an old wire fence caught on gray cedar posts that lean in different directions. Etta has come back after many years to live in the little stone house.

The sound of the hammer had been Reyna's first warning. She blames herself for leaving the old fence posts and wire. The fence should have been torn down years ago. The old wire had lain half-buried in the sand that had drifted around the posts. Etta was wearing men's gloves that were too large for her. She pulled the strands of wire up and hammered fence staples to hold the wire to the posts. Etta has made the fence the boundary line. She has planted morning glories and hollyhocks all along it. She waters them every morning before it gets hot. Reyna watches her. The morning glories and hollyhocks are all that hold up the fence posts anymore.

Etta is watching Reyna from the kitchen window of the little stone house. She fills the coffee pot without looking at the level of water. Reyna is walking the fence between their yards. She paces the length of the fence as if she can pull the fence down with her walking. They had been married to brothers, but the men died long ago. They don't call each other "sister-in-law" anymore. The fire in the cookstove is cracking like rifle shots. She bought a pickup load of pinon wood from a Navajo. The little house has one room, but the walls are rock and adobe mortar two feet thick. The one who got the big house got the smaller yard. That is how Etta remembers it. Their mother-in-law had been a kind woman. She wanted her sons and daughters-in-law to live happily with each other. She followed the old ways. She believed houses and fields must always be held by the women. There had been no nieces or daughters. The old woman stood by the pear tree with the daughters-in-law and gave them each a house, and the yard to divide. She pointed at the little stone house. She said the one who got the little house got the bigger share of the yard. Etta remembers that.

Cheromiah drives up in his white Ford pickup. He walks to the gate smiling. He wears his big belly over his Levi's like an apron. Reyna is gathering kindling at the woodpile. The juniper chips are hard and smooth as flint. She rubs her hands together although there is no dust. "They came through this morning before it was even daylight." She points in the direction of the river. "They were going down that way." He frowns, then he smiles. "I've been looking for them all week," he says. The old woman shakes her head. "Well, if you hurry, they might still be there." They are his horses. His father-in-law gave him the white one when it was a colt. Its feet are as big around as pie pans. The gray is the sorrel mare's colt. The horses belong to Cheromiah, but the horses don't know that. "Nobody told them," that's what people say and then they laugh. The white horse leans against corral planks until they give way. It steps over low spots in old stone fences. The gray and little sorrel follow.

"The old lady said to share and love one another. She said we only make use of these things as long as we are here. We don't own them. Nobody owns anything." Juanita nods. She listens to both of her aunts. The two old women are quarreling over a narrow strip of ground between the two houses. The earth is hard-packed. Nothing grows there. Juanita listens to her Aunt Reyna and agrees that her Aunt Etta is wrong. Too many years living in Winslow. Aunt Etta returns and she wants to make the yard "private property" like white people do in Winslow. Juanita visits both of her aunts every day. She visits her Aunt Etta in the afternoon while her Aunt Reyna is resting. Etta and Reyna know their grandniece must visit both her aunts. Juanita has no husband or family to look after. She is the one who looks after the old folks. She is not like her brothers or sister who have wives or a husband. She doesn't forget. She looked after Uncle Joe for ten years until he finally died. He always told her she would have the house because women should have the houses. He didn't have much. Just his wagon horses, the house and a pig. He was the oldest and believed in the old ways. Aunt Reyna was right. If her brother Joe were alive he would talk to Etta. He would remind her that this is the village, not Winslow, Arizona. He would remind Etta how they all must share. Aunt Reyna would have more space for her woodpile then.

Most people die once, but "old man Joe he died twice," that's what people said, and then they laughed. Juanita knew they joked about it, but still she held her head high. She was the only one who even tried to look after the old folks. That November, Uncle Joe had been sick with pneumonia. His house smelled of Vicks and Ben-Gay. She checked on him every morning. He was always up before dawn the way all the old folks were. They greeted the sun and prayed for everybody. He was always up and had a fire in his little pot belly stove to make coffee. But that morning she knocked and there was no answer. Her heart was beating fast because she knew what she would find. The stove was cold. She stood by his bed and watched. He did not move. She touched the hand on top of the blanket and the fingers were as cold as the room. Juanita ran all the way to Aunt Reyna's house with the news. They sent word. The nephews and the clansmen came with picks and shovels. Before they went to dress him for burial, they cooked the big meal always prepared for the gravediggers. Aunt Reyna rolled out the tortillas and cried. Joe had always been so good to her. Joe had always loved her best after their parents died.

Cheromiah came walking by that morning while Juanita was getting more firewood. He was dragging a long rope and leather halter. He asked if she had seen any sign of his horses. She shook her head and then she told him Uncle Joe had passed away that morning. Tears came to her eyes. Cheromiah stood quietly for a moment. "I will miss the old man. He taught me everything I know about horses." Juanita nodded. Her arms were full of juniper wood. She looked away toward the southeast. "I saw your gray horse up in the sandhills the other day." Cheromiah smiled and thanked her. Cheromiah's truck didn't start in cold weather. He didn't feel like walking all the way up to the sand hills that morning. He took the road around the far side of the village to get home. It took him past Uncle Joe's place. The pig was butting its head against the planks of the pen making loud smacking sounds. The wagon horses were eating corn stalks the old man had bundled up after harvest for winter feed. Cheromiah wondered which of the old man's relatives was already looking after the livestock. He heard someone chopping wood on the other side of the house. The old man saw him and waved in the direction of the river. "They were down there last evening grazing in the willows." Cheromiah dropped the halter and rope and gestured with both hands. "Uncle Joe! They told me you died! Everyone thinks you are dead! They already cooked the gravediggers lunch!"

From that time on Uncle Joe didn't get up before dawn like he once did. But he wouldn't let them tease Juanita about her mistake. Behind her back, Juanita's cousins and in-laws were saying that she was in such a hurry to collect her inheritance. They didn't think she should get everything. They thought all of it should be shared equally. The following spring, Uncle Joe's wagon horses went down Paguate Hill too fast and the wagon wheel hit a big rock. He was thrown from the wagon and a sheepherder found him. Uncle Joe was unconscious for two days and then he died. "This time he really *is* dead, poor thing," people would say and then they'd smile.

The trouble over the pig started on the day of the funeral. Juanita caught her brother's wife at the pig pen. The wife held a large pail in both hands. The pail was full of a yellowish liquid. There were bones swimming in it. Corn tassels floated like hair. She looked Juanita in the eye as she dumped the lard pail into the trough. The pig switched its tail and made one push through the liquid with its snout. It looked up at both of them. The snout kept moving. The pig would not eat. Juanita had already fed the pigs scraps from the gravediggers' plates. She didn't want her brothers' wives feeding the pig. They would claim, they had fed the pig more than she had. They would say that whoever fed the pig the most should get the biggest share of meat. At butchering time they would show up to collect half. "It won't eat slop," Juanita said, "don't be feeding it slop."

10

The stories they told about Etta always came back to the same thing.

While the other girls learn cooking and sewing at the Indian School, Etta works in the greenhouse. In the evenings the teacher sits with her on the sofa. They repeat the names of the flowers. She teaches Etta the parts of the flower. On Saturdays while the dormitory matrons take the others to town, Etta stays with the teacher. Etta kneels beside her in the garden. They press brown dirt over the gladiola bulbs. The teacher runs a hot bath for her. The teacher will not let her return to the dormitory until she has cleaned Etta's fingernails. The other girls tell stories about Etta.

The white gauze curtains are breathing in and out. The hollyhocks bend around the fence posts and lean over the wire. The buds are tight and press between the green lips of the sheath. The seed had been saved in a mason jar. Etta found it in the pantry behind a veil of cobwebs. She planted it the length of the fence to mark the boundary. She had only been a child the first time, but she can still remember the colors—reds and yellows swaying above her head, tiny black ants in the white eyes of pollen. Others were purple and dark red, almost black as dried blood. She planted the seeds the teacher had given her. She saved the seeds from the only year the hollyhocks grew. Etta doesn't eat pork. She is thinking about the row of tamarisk trees she will plant along the fence so people cannot see her yard or house. She does not want to spend her retirement with everyone in the village minding her business the way they always have. Somebody is always fighting over something. The years away taught her differently. She knows better now. The yard is hers. They can't take it just because she has lived away from the village all those years. A person could go away and come back again. The village people don't understand fences. At Indian School she learned fences tell you where you stand. In Winslow, white people built fences around their houses, otherwise something might be lost or stolen. There were rumors about her the whole time she lived in Winslow. The gossip was not true. The teacher had written to her all the years Etta was married. It was a job to go to after her husband died. The teacher was sick and old. Etta went because she loved caring for the flowers. It was only a job, but people like to talk. The teacher was sick for a long time before she died.

"What do you want with those things," the clanswoman scolded, 15 "wasting water on something we can't eat." The old woman mumbled to herself all the way across the garden. Etta started crying. She sat on the ground by the hollyhocks she had planted, and held her face. She pressed her fingers into her eyes. The old woman had taken her in. It was the duty of the clan to accept orphans.

Etta tells her she is not coming back from Indian School in the summer. She has a job at school caring for the flowers. She and the clanswoman are cleaning a sheep stomach, rinsing it under the mulberry tree. The intestines are coiled in a white enamel pan. They are bluish gray, the color of the sky before snow. Strands of tallow branch across them like clouds. "You are not much good to me anyway. I took you because no one else wanted to. I have tried to teach you, but the white people at that school have ruined you. You waste good water growing things we cannot eat."

The first time Etta returned from Winslow for a visit, Reyna confided there was gossip going on in the village. Etta could tell by the details that her sister-in-law was embroidering stories about her too. They did not speak to each other after that. People were jealous of her because she had left. They were certain she preferred white people. But Etta spoke only to the teacher. White people did not see her when she walked on the street.

The heat holds the afternoon motionless. The sun does not move. It has parched all color from the sky and left only the fine ash. The street below is empty. Down the long dim hall there are voices in English and, more distantly, the ticking of a clock. The room is white and narrow. The shade is pulled. It pulses heat the texture of pearls. The water in the basin is the color of garnets. Etta waits in a chair beside the bed. The sheets are soaked with her fever. She murmurs the parts of the flowers—she whispers that the bud is swelling open, but that afternoon was long ago.

Ruthie's husband is seeing that other woman in the cornfield. The cornfield belongs to her and to her sister, Juanita. Their mother left it to both of them. In the morning her husband walks to the fields with the hoe on his shoulder. Not long after, the woman appears with a coal bucket filled with stove ashes. The woman follows the path toward the trash pile, but when she gets to the far corner of the cornfield she stops. When she thinks no one is watching she sets the bucket down. She gathers up the skirt of her dress and steps over the fence where the wire sags.

Ruthie would not have suspected anything if she had not noticed the rocks. He was always hauling rocks to build a new shed or corral. But this time there was something about the colors of the sandstone. The reddish pink and orange yellow looked as if they had been taken from the center of the sky as the sun went down. She had never seen such intense color in sandstone. She had always remembered it being shades of pale yellow or peppered white-colors for walls and fences. But these rocks looked as if rain had just fallen on them. She watched her husband. He was unloading the rocks from the old wagon and stacking them carefully next to the woodpile. When he had finished it was dark and she could not see the colors of the sandstone any longer. She thought about how good-looking he was, the kind of man all the other women chase.

Reyna goes with them. She takes her cane but carries it ready in her hand like a rabbit club. Her grandnieces have asked her to go with them. Ruthie's husband is carrying on with another woman. The same one as before. They are going after them together—the two sisters and the old aunt.

20

Ruthie told Juanita about it first. It was their mother's field and now it is theirs. If Juanita had a husband he would work there too. "The worst thing is them doing it in the cornfield. It makes the corn sickly, it makes the beans stop growing. If they want to do it they can go down to the trash and lie in the tin cans and broken glass with the flies," that's what Reyna says.

They surprise them lying together on the sandy ground in the shade of the tall corn plants. Last time they caught them together they reported them to the woman's grandmother, but the old woman didn't seem to care. They told that woman's husband too. But he has a job in Albuquerque, and men don't bother to look after things. It is up to women to take care of everything. He is supposed to be hoeing weeds in their field, but instead he is rolling around on the ground with that woman, killing off all their melons and beans.

Her breasts are long and brown. They bounce against her like potatoes. She runs with her blue dress in her hand. She leaves her shoes. They are next to his hoe. Ruthie stands between Juanita and Aunt Reyna. They gesture with their arms and yell. They are not scolding him. They don't even look at him. They are scolding the rest of the village over husband-stealing and corn that is sickly. Reyna raps on the fence post with her cane. Juanita calls him a pig. Ruthie cries because the beans won't grow. He kneels to lace his work shoes. He kneels for a long time. His fingers move slowly. They are not talking to him. They are talking about the other woman. The red chili stew she makes is runny and pale. They pay no attention to him. He goes back to hoeing weeds. Their voices sift away in the wind. Occasionally he stops to wipe his forehead on his sleeve. He looks up at the sky or over the sand hills. Off in the distance there is a man on foot. He is crossing the big sand dune above the river. He is dragging a rope. The horses are grazing on yellow rice grass at the foot of the dune. They are down wind from him. He inches along, straining to crouch over his own stomach. The big white horse whirls suddenly, holding its tail high. The gray half-circles and joins it, blowing loudly through its nostrils. The little sorrel mare bolts to the top of the next dune before she turns.

Etta awakens and the yard is full of horses. The gray chews a hollyhock. Red petals stream from its mouth. The sorrel mare watches her come out the door. The white horse charges away, rolling his eyes at her nightgown. Etta throws a piece of juniper from the woodpile. The gray horse presses hard against the white one. They tremble in the corner of the fence, strings of blue morning glories trampled under their hooves. Etta yells and the sorrel mare startles, crowding against the gray. They heave forward against the fence, and the posts make slow cracking sounds. The wire whines and squeaks. It gives way suddenly and the white horse stumbles ahead tangled in wire. The sorrel and the gray bolt past, and for an instant the white horse hesitates, shivering at the wire caught around its forelegs and neck. Then the white horse leaps forward, rusty wire and fence posts trailing behind like a broken necklace.

The Responsive Reader

1. How does Silko recreate for the reader the physical setting of reservation life? What details help make the setting real for you?
2. What do you learn from this story about the traditions and customs that shape reservation life? What traditions regarding the care of orphans, of old people, or the settling of inheritances play a role in the story?
3. What are the sources of conflict in this story? Where and how do the old ways and white people's ways come into conflict? With what results?
4. What makes the people in this story seem strange to you? What makes them seem very human?

Thinking, Talking, Writing

5. Have you encountered different attitudes toward property, toward boundaries, toward fences?
6. What version of the Cinderella tale is part of this story? How is it different from other versions? How is it the same? Do you know other similar stories? What is their shared appeal?

THE RED CONVERTIBLE
Louise Erdrich

> Of Chippewa and German-American descent, Louise Erdrich grew up on a reservation in North Dakota where her grandfather had been tribal chair and where her father taught. She studied at Dartmouth College and Johns Hopkins University and has published prize-winning poetry and fiction. Her writing has been praised for "conveying unflinchingly the funkiness, humor, and great unspoken sadness of the Indian reservations, and a people exiled to a no-man's-land between two worlds" (Peter Matthiessen). Her best-selling Love Medicine (1984) was a series of intermeshing stories about the lives of two reservation families. In the following example, the narrator tells the story of a brother who went to serve in Vietnam and was never the same after his return. Erdrich continued exploring the histories of the fictional families in these stories in Beet Queen (1986) and Tracks (1988).

Lyman Lamartine

I was the first one to drive a convertible on my reservation. And of course it was red, a red Olds. I owned that car along with my brother Henry Junior. We owned it together until his boots filled with water on a windy night and he bought out my share. Now Henry owns the whole car, and his younger brother Lyman (that's myself), Lyman walks everywhere he goes.

How did I earn enough money to buy my share in the first place? My one talent was I could always make money. I had a touch for it, unusual in a Chippewa. From the first I was different that way, and everyone recognized it. I was the only kid they let in the American Legion Hall to shine shoes, for example, and one Christmas I sold spiritual bouquets for the mission door to door. The nuns let me keep a percentage. Once I started, it seemed the more money I made the easier the money came. Everyone encouraged it. When I was fifteen I got a job washing dishes at the Joliet Café, and that was where my first big break happened.

It wasn't long before I was promoted to busing tables, and then the short-order cook quit and I was hired to take her place. No sooner than you know it I was managing the Joliet. The rest is history. I went on managing. I soon became part owner, and of course there was no stopping me then. It wasn't long before the whole thing was mine.

After I'd owned the Joliet for one year, it blew over in the worst tornado ever seen around here. The whole operation was smashed to bits. A total loss. The fryalator was up in a tree, the grill torn in half like it was paper. I was only sixteen. I had it all in my mother's name, and I lost it quick, but before I lost it I had every one of my relatives, and their relatives, to dinner, and I also bought that red Olds I mentioned, along with Henry.

The first time we saw it! I'll tell you when we first saw it. We had   5
gotten a ride up to Winnipeg, and both of us had money. Don't ask me why,
because we never mentioned a car or anything, we just had all our money.
Mine was cash, a big bankroll from the Joliet's insurance. Henry had two
checks—a week's extra pay for being laid off, and his regular check from the
Jewel Bearing Plant.

We were walking down Portage anyway, seeing the sights, when we
saw it. There it was, parked, large as life. Really as *if* it was alive. I thought
of the word *repose,* because the car wasn't simply stopped, parked, or whatever. That car reposed, calm and gleaming, a FOR SALE sign in its left front
window. Then, before we had thought it over at all, the car belonged to us
and our pockets were empty. We had just enough money for gas back home.

We went places in that car, me and Henry. We took off driving all one
whole summer. We started off toward the Little Knife River and Mandaree
in Fort Berthold and then we found ourselves down in Wakpala somehow,
and then suddenly we were over in Montana on the Rocky Boy, and yet the
summer was not even half over. Some people hang on to details when they
travel, but we didn't let them bother us and just lived our everyday lives here
to there.

I do remember this one place with willows. I remember I laid under
those trees and it was comfortable. So comfortable. The branches bent down
all around me like a tent or a stable. And quiet, it was quiet, even though
there was a powwow close enough so I could see it going on. The air was
not too still, not too windy either. When the dust rises up and hangs in the
air around the dancers like that, I feel good. Henry was asleep with his arms
thrown wide. Later on, he woke up and we started driving again. We were
somewhere in Montana, or maybe on the Blood Reserve—it could have
been anywhere. Anyway it was where we met the girl.

All her hair was in buns around her ears, that's the first thing I noticed
about her. She was posed alongside the road with her arm out, so we
stopped. That girl was short, so short her lumber shirt looked comical on
her, like a nightgown. She had jeans on and fancy moccasins and she carried
a little suitcase.

"Hop on in," says Henry. So she climbs in between us.   10
"We'll take you home," I says. "Where do you live?"
"Chicken," she says.
"Where the hell's that?" I ask her.
"Alaska."
"Okay," says Henry, and we drive.   15

We got up there and never wanted to leave. The sun doesn't truly set
there in summer, and the night is more a soft dusk. You might doze off,
sometimes, but before you know it you're up again, like an animal in nature.
You never feel like you have to sleep hard or put away the world. And things
would grow up there. One day just dirt or moss, the next day flowers and

long grass. The girl's name was Susy. Her family really took to us. They fed us and put us up. We had our own tent to live in by their house, and the kids would be in and out of there all day and night. They couldn't get over me and Henry being brothers, we looked so different. We told them we knew we had the same mother, anyway.

One night Susy came in to visit us. We sat around in the tent talking of this and that. The season was changing. It was getting darker by that time, and the cold was even getting just a little mean. I told her it was time for us to go. She stood up on a chair.

"You never seen my hair," Susy said.

That was true. She was standing on a chair, but still, when she unclipped her buns the hair reached all the way to the ground. Our eyes opened. You couldn't tell how much hair she had when it was rolled up so neatly. Then my brother Henry did something funny. He went up to the chair and said, "Jump on my shoulders." So she did that, and her hair reached down past his waist, and he started twirling, this way and that, so her hair was flung out from side to side.

"I always wondered what it was like to have long pretty hair," Henry says. Well we laughed. It was a funny sight, the way he did it. The next morning we got up and took leave of those people.   [20]

On to greener pastures, as they say. It was down through Spokane and across Idaho then Montana and very soon we were racing the weather right along under the Canadian border through Columbus, Des Lacs, and then we were in Bottineau County and soon home. We'd made most of the trip, that summer, without putting up the car hood at all. We got home just in time, it turned out, for the army to remember Henry had signed up to join it.

I don't wonder that the army was so glad to get my brother that they turned him into a Marine. He was built like a brick outhouse anyway. We liked to tease him that they really wanted him for his Indian nose. He had a nose big and sharp as a hatchet, like the nose on Red Tomahawk, the Indian who killed Sitting Bull, whose profile is on signs all along the North Dakota highways. Henry went off to training camp, came home once during Christmas, then the next thing you know we got an overseas letter from him. It was 1970, and he said he was stationed up in the northern hill country. Whereabouts I did not know. He wasn't such a hot letter writer, and only got off two before the enemy caught him. I could never keep it straight, which direction those good Vietnam soldiers were from.

I wrote him back several times, even though I didn't know if those letters would get through. I kept him informed all about the car. Most of the time I had it up on blocks in the yard or half taken apart, because that long trip did a hard job on it under the hood.

I always had good luck with numbers, and never worried about the draft myself. I never even had to think about what my number was. But Henry was never lucky in the same way as me. It was at least three years before Henry came home. By then I guess the whole war was solved in the government's mind, but for him it would keep on going. In those years I'd put his car into almost perfect shape. I always thought of it as his car while he was gone, even though when he left he said, "Now it's yours," and threw me his key.

"Thanks for the extra key," I'd said. "I'll put it up in your drawer just   25 in case I need it." He laughed.

When he came home, though, Henry was very different, and I'll say this: the change was no good. You could hardly expect him to change for the better, I know. But he was quiet, so quiet, and never comfortable sitting still anywhere but always up and moving around. I thought back to times we'd sat still for whole afternoons, never moving a muscle, just shifting our weight along the ground, talking to whoever sat with us, watching things. He'd always had a joke, then, too, and now you couldn't get him to laugh, or when he did it was more the sound of a man choking, a sound that stopped up the throats of other people around him. They got to leaving him alone most of the time, and I didn't blame them. It was a fact: Henry was jumpy and mean.

I'd bought a color TV set for my mom and the rest of us while Henry was away. Money still came very easy. I was sorry I'd ever bought it though, because of Henry. I was also sorry I'd bought color, because with black-and-white the pictures seem older and farther away. But what are you going to do? He sat in front of it, watching it, and that was the only time he was completely still. But it was the kind of stillness that you see in a rabbit when it freezes and before it will bolt. He was not easy. He sat in his chair gripping the armrests with all his might, as if the chair itself was moving at a high speed and if he let go at all he would rocket forward and maybe crash right through the set.

Once I was in the room watching TV with Henry and I heard his teeth click at something. I looked over, and he'd bitten through his lip. Blood was going down his chin. I tell you right then I wanted to smash that tube to pieces. I went over to it but Henry must have known what I was up to. He rushed from his chair and shoved me out of the way, against the wall. I told myself he didn't know what he was doing.

My mom came in, turned the set off real quiet, and told us she had made something for supper. So we went and sat down. There was still blood going down Henry's chin, but he didn't notice it and no one said anything, even though every time he took a bite of his bread his blood fell onto it until he was eating his own blood mixed in with the food.

While Henry was not around we talked about what was going to   30 happen to him. There were no Indian doctors on the reservation, and my mom couldn't come around to trusting the old man, Moses Pillager, because he courted her long ago and was jealous of her husbands. He might take revenge through her son. We were afraid that if we brought Henry to a regular hospital they would keep him.

"They don't fix them in those places," Mom said; "they just give them drugs."

"We wouldn't get him there in the first place," I agreed, "so let's just forget about it."

Then I thought about the car.

Henry had not even looked at the car since he'd gotten home, though like I said, it was in tip-top condition and ready to drive. I thought the car might bring the old Henry back somehow. So I bided my time and waited for my chance to interest him in the vehicle.

One night Henry was off somewhere. I took myself a hammer. I went   35
out to that car and I did a number on its underside. Whacked it up. Bent the tail pipe double. Ripped the muffler loose. By the time I was done with the car it looked worse than any typical Indian car that has been driven all its life on reservation roads, which they always say are like government promises— full of holes. It just about hurt me, I'll tell you that! I threw dirt in the carburetor and I ripped all the electric tape off the seats. I made it look just as beat up as I could. Then I sat back and waited for Henry to find it.

Still, it took him over a month. That was all right, because it was just getting warm enough, not melting, but warm enough to work outside.

"Lyman," he says, walking in one day, "that red car looks like shit."

"Well it's old," I says, "You got to expect that."

"No way!" says Henry. "That car's a classic! But you went and ran the piss right out of it, Lyman, and you know it don't deserve that. I kept that care in A-one shape. You don't remember. You're too young. But when I left, that car was running like a watch. Now I don't even know if I can get it to start again, let alone get it anywhere near its old condition."

"Well you try," I said, like I was getting mad, "but I say it's a piece of   40
junk."

Then I walked out before he could realize I knew he'd strung together more than six words at once.

After that I thought he'd freeze himself to death working on that car. He was out there all day, and at night he rigged up a little lamp, ran a cord out the window, and had himself some light to see by while he worked. He was better than he had been before, but that's still not saying much. It was easier for him to do the things the rest of us did. He ate more slowly and didn't jump up and down during the meal to get this or that or look out the window. I put my hand in the back of the TV set, I admit, and fiddled around with it good, so that it was almost impossible now to get a clear picture. He didn't look at it very often anyway. He was always out with that car or going off to get parts for it. By the time it was really melting outside, he had it fixed.

I had been feeling down in the dumps about Henry around this time. We had always been together before. Henry and Lyman. But he was such a loner now that I didn't know how to take it. So I jumped at the chance one day when Henry seemed friendly. It's not that he smiled or anything. He just said, "Let's take that old shitbox for a spin." Just the way he said it made me think he could be coming around.

We went out to the car. It was spring. The sun was shining very bright. My only sister, Bonita, who was just eleven years old, came out and made us stand together for a picture. Henry leaned his elbow on the red car's windshield, and he took his other arm and put it over my shoulder, very carefully, as though it was heavy for him to lift and he didn't want to bring the weight down all at once.

"Smile," Bonita said, and he did. *45*

That picture. I never look at it anymore. A few months ago, I don't know why, I got his picture out and tacked it on the wall. I felt good about Henry at the time, close to him. I felt good having his picture on the wall, until one night when I was looking at television. I was a little drunk and stoned. I looked up at the wall and Henry was staring at me. I don't know what it was, but his smile had changed, or maybe it was gone. All I know is I couldn't stay in the same room with that picture. I was shaking. I got up, closed the door, and went into the kitchen. A little later my friend Ray came over and we both went back into that room. We put the picture in a brown bag, folded the bag over and over tightly, then put it way back in a closet.

I still see that picture now, as if it tugs at me, whenever I pass that closet door. The picture is very clear in my mind. It was so sunny that day Henry had to squint against the glare. Or maybe the camera Bonita held flashed like a mirror, blinding him, before she snapped the picture. My face is right out in the sun, big and round. But he might have drawn back, because the shadows on his face are deep as holes. There are two shadows curved like little hooks around the ends of his smile, as if to frame it and try to keep it there—that one, first smile that looked like it might have hurt his face. He has his field jacket on and the worn-in clothes he'd come back in and kept wearing ever since. After Bonita took the picture, she went into the house and we got into the car. There was a full cooler in the trunk. We started off, east, toward Pembina and the Red River because Henry said he wanted to see the high water.

The trip over there was beautiful. When everything starts changing, drying up, clearing off, you feel like your whole life is starting. Henry felt it, too. The top was down and the car hummed like a top. He'd really put it back in shape, even the tape on the seats was very carefully put down and glued back in layers. It's not that he smiled again or even joked, but his face looked to me as if it was clear, more peaceful. It looked as though he wasn't thinking of anything in particular except the bare fields and windbreaks and houses we were passing.

The river was high and full of winter trash when we got there. The sun was still out, but it was colder by the river. There were still little clumps of dirty snow here and there on the banks. The water hadn't gone over the banks yet, but it would, you could tell. It was just at its limit, hard swollen, glossy like an old gray scar. We made ourselves a fire, and we sat down and watched the current go. As I watched it I felt something squeezing inside me and tightening and trying to let go all at the same time. I knew I was not just feeling it myself; I knew I was feeling what Henry was going through at that moment. Except that I couldn't stand it, the closing and opening. I jumped to my feet. I took Henry by the shoulders and I started shaking him. "Wake up," I says, "wake up, wake up, wake up!" I didn't know what had come over me. I sat down beside him again.

His face was totally white and hard. Then it broke, like stones break all 50
of a sudden when water boils up inside them.

"I know it," he says. "I know it. I can't help it. It's no use."

We start talking. He said he knew what I'd done with the car. It was obvious it had been whacked out of shape and not just neglected. He said he wanted to give the car to me for good now, it was no use. He said he'd fixed it just to give it back and I should take it.

"No way," I says. "I don't want it."

"That's okay," he says, "you take it."

"I don't want it, though," I says back to him, and then to empha- 55
size, just to emphasize, you understand, I touch his shoulder. He slaps my hand off.

"Take that car," he says.

"No," I say. "Make me," I say, and then he grabs my jacket and rips the arm loose. That jacket is a class act, suede with tags and zippers. I push Henry backwards, off the log. He jumps up and bowls me over. We go down in a clinch and come up swinging hard, for all we're worth, with our fists. He socks my jaw so hard I feel like it swings loose. Then I'm at his rib cage and land a good one under his chin so his head snaps back. He's dazzled. He looks at me and I look at him and then his eyes are full of tears and blood and at first I think he's crying. But no, he's laughing. "Ha! Ha!" he says. "Ha! Ha! Take good care of it."

"Okay," I says. "Okay, no problem. Ha! Ha!"

I can't help it, and I start laughing, too. My face feels fat and strange, and after a while I get a beer from the cooler in the trunk, and when I hand it to Henry he takes his shirt and wipes my germs off. "Hoof-and-mouth disease," he says. For some reason this cracks me up, and so we're really laughing for a while, and then we drink all the rest of the beers one by one and throw them in the river and see how far, how fast, the current takes them before they fill up and sink.

"You want to go on back?" I ask after a while. "Maybe we could snag *60*
a couple nice Kashpaw girls."

He says nothing. But I can tell his mood is turning again.

"They're all crazy, the girls up here, every damn one of them."

"You're crazy too," I say, to jolly him up. "Crazy Lamartine boys!"

He looks as though he will take this wrong at first. His face twists, then
clears, and he jumps on his feet. "That's right!" he says. "Crazier 'n hell.
Crazy Indians!"

I think it's the old Henry again. He throws off his jacket and starts *65*
springing his legs up from the knees like a fancy dancer. He's down doing
something between a grass dance and a bunny hop, no kind of dance I ever
saw before, but neither has anyone else on all this green growing earth. He's
wild. He wants to pitch whoopee! He's up and at me and all over. All this
time I'm laughing so hard, so hard my belly is getting tied up in a knot.

"Got to cool me off!" he shouts all of a sudden. Then he runs over to
the river and jumps in.

There's boards and other things in the current. It's so high. No sound
comes from the river after the splash he makes, so I run right over. I look
around. It's getting dark. I see he's halfway across the water already, and I
know he didn't swim there but the current took him. It's far. I hear his voice,
though, very clearly across it.

"My boots are filling," he says.

He says this in a normal voice, like he just noticed and he doesn't know
what to think of it. Then he's gone. A branch comes by. Another branch.
And I go in.

By the time I get out of the river, off the snag I pulled myself onto, the *70*
sun is down. I walk back to the car, turn on the high beams, and drive it up
the bank. I put it in first gear and then I take my foot off the clutch. I get
out, close the door, and watch it plow softly into the water. The headlights
reach in as they go down, searching, still lighted even after the water swirls
over the back end. I wait. The wires short out. It is all finally dark. And then
there is only the water, the sound of it going and running and going and
running and running.

The Responsive Reader

1. In retrospect, how is the opening paragraph an example of the storyteller's wry humor? What kind of persona, or fictional identity, does
   Erdrich create for the brother telling the story?
2. Foreign observers often say that the typical American has a love affair
   with his or her car. How do the two brothers in this story live up to
   this reputation?
3. What is the story of Henry's experience in the army? What did the
   experience do to him? (We learn many details as the narrator men-

tions them casually, almost in passing. What is the reason for this casual style? What is its effect on you as the reader?)

4. What was the younger brother's strategy for dealing with his brother's change? Was it successful?
5. Erdrich has a gift for bringing a story to life with haunting detail. What is the role in the story of the girl hitchhiker, of the picture taken of the brothers by Bonita?
6. What is happening in the climactic final confrontation between the two brothers? What is going on in their minds? Why do they fight? Is anything settled or resolved?

Thinking, Talking, Writing

7. Is the red convertible a central symbol in this story? What does it symbolize? What role does it play in the story?
8. Does this story confirm or challenge assumptions you have about reservation life?

Collaborative Projects

9. Is it true that in recent times America's minorities have had a disproportionate share of military service and of service to this country's wars? How could you and your classmates find out?

Thinking about Connections

10. Spokespersons for minorities sometimes charge that too many accounts of minority experience reflect too negative an image of America's minorities. On balance, do you think Gunn, Silko, and Erdrich are accentuating the positive or the negative?

4

American Individualism: A Different Drummer

If a man does not keep pace with his own companions, perhaps it is because he hears a different drummer.

Henry David Thoreau

I have always strenuously supported the right of every man to his opinion, however different that opinion might be to mine.

Tom Paine

As long as possible live free and uncommitted.

Henry David Thoreau

LITERATURE IN CONTEXT

Traditionally, America has honored the individual. The American folk hero is the individual who paddles his or her own canoe and who has the right to be wrong. A familiar figure of American folklore is the maverick who refuses to follow meekly a party line, a company directive, or a dress code. Deeply engrained in the collective memory are the millions who came here on their own initiative and had to make it on their own. They tried to make a go of it in one place and then, when things didn't work out, they pulled up stakes and moved on. Rather than being aided by the authorities in their search for a new life, many left the old country one jump ahead of the police. They then had to work their way past immigration when they arrived here with defective papers, with banned diseases, and without a dime.

Some of the most widely heard voices of the new country preached self-reliance. "Trust thyself," said Ralph Waldo Emerson, a Boston minister who quit the Unitarian church to preach his own ideas in his own way. "Nothing is at last sacred but the integrity of your own mind," he wrote in his essay on "Self-reliance" in 1841. He ridiculed men and women who gave up after their first failure at a job (or their first failure to find a job when fresh out of college): "A sturdy lad from New Hampshire or Vermont, who in turn tries all the professions, who teams it, farms it, peddles, keeps a school, preaches, edits a newspaper, goes to Congress, buys a township, and so forth, in successive years, and always, like a cat, falls on his feet, is worth a hundred of these city dolls."

For much of American history, the frontier beckoned the nonconformist. The open spaces of the West offered scope for individual effort. Even though the open range may have long since been fenced in, in American folklore the loner, the lone rider, survives as a mythical figure. Even though real cowboys work long hours for little pay and for demanding bosses, the cowboy roaming the open spaces became the archetypal figure of American popular entertainment.

Today, many Americans are anonymous numbers in the computer of a large corporation or institution. Even so, the American folk hero is not really the employee who is a willing cog in the machine. Many admire the maverick, the whistleblower, or the woman who sues the man in charge. The popular prints love the second-in-command of a large corporation who pulls up stakes and starts up a separate company next door. Readers love a story like that of Gretel Ehrlich, who left a media career behind to move to the wide open spaces of Wyoming and herd sheep.

Is individualism obsolete? Is the spirit of sturdy individualism a relic of the past? Does it keep us from developing a sense of human solidarity with others? Does it hamper the sense of community and common purpose that we need to master the problems of today? Do we have too much distrust of collective effort, too much impatience with the mechanisms that produce consent and political action?

FIVE POEMS
Emily Dickinson

Experiment escorts us last—
His pungent company
Will not allow an Axiom
An Opportunity.
>   Emily Dickinson

    Emily Dickinson was the great nonconformist of nineteenth-century American poetry. Now widely considered America's greatest poet, she managed to publish only a few of her poems during her lifetime. Her editors thought her work willfully different and strange. When they did publish her poems, they made them rhyme, smoothed out the irregular beat, and replaced puzzling provocative words with dull predictable ones. Dickinson was brought up in a strictly religious household but stopped going to church, because in the privacy of her solitude a "better clergyman" (namely God) preached better and shorter sermons. She read the great women novelists—George Eliot, Charlotte Brontë—who were beginning to challenge the conventions of an uptight moralistic society. There has been much speculation about why she increasingly cut herself off from the outside world.

    Dickinson had an uncanny gift for looking at life afresh, without the blinders of convention, and for finding spiritual meaning in the observations of common everyday existence. Her observations of a butterfly launching into flight, of a snake slithering in the grass of the garden, of a bird hopping down a walk, or of a relative dying send shudders of recognition down the reader's spine. In thousands of poems found and published after her death, she serves her readers as a scout for a deeper and more meaningful reality that underlies the tired clichés of people with ordinary minds. The poems appear here in the original form restored by Thomas H. Johnson in The Collected Poems of Emily Dickinson.

A Bird came down the Walk

A Bird came down the Walk—   *1*
He did not know I saw—
He bit an Angleworm in halves
And ate the fellow, raw,

And then he drank a Dew   *5*
From a convenient Grass—
And then hopped sidewise to the Wall
To let a Beetle pass—

He glanced with rapid eyes
That hurried all around—   10
They looked like frightened Beads, I thought—
He stirred his Velvet Head

Like one in danger. Cautious,
I offered him a Crumb
And he unrolled his feathers   15
And rowed him softer home—

Than Oars divide the Ocean,
Too silver for a seam°—   *seamless like silver*
Or Butterflies, off Banks of Noon
Leap, splashless° as they swim.   *without a splash*   20

"Hope" is the thing with feathers

"Hope" is the thing with feathers—   1
That perches in the soul—
And sings the tune without the words—
And never stops—at all—

And sweetest—in the Gale—is heard—   5
And sore must be the storm—
That could abash° the little Bird   *subdue and silence*
That kept so many warm—

I've heard it in the chillest land—
And on the strangest Sea—   10
Yet, never, in Extremity,°   *in extreme danger or adversity*
It asked a crumb—of Me.

The Soul selects her own Society

The Soul selects her own Society—   1
Then—shuts the Door—

To her divine Majority—
Present no more—

Unmoved—she notes the Chariots—pausing   5
At her low Gate—
Unmoved—an Emperor be kneeling
Upon her Mat—

I've known her—from an ample nation—
Choose One—   10
Then—close the Valves of her attention—
Like Stone—

I'm Nobody! Who are you?

I'm Nobody! Who are you?   *1*
Are you—Nobody—Too?
Then there's a pair of us?
Don't tell! They'd advertise—you know!

How dreary—to be—Somebody!   *5*
How public—like a Frog—
To tell one's name—the livelong June—
To an admiring Bog!

Much Madness is divinest Sense

Much Madness is divinest Sense—   *1*
To a discerning Eye—
Much Sense—the starkest Madness—
'Tis the Majority
In this, as All, prevail—   *5*
Assent—and you are sane—
Demur°—you're straightway dangerous—   *disagree*
And handled with a Chain—

The Responsive Reader

1. ("A Bird Came Down the Walk") What phrases or details make the bird seem almost human? Which remind us that it is a creature alien to us? Which do most to make you visualize a real bird? What could be symbolized by the contrast between the hurried, frightened hopping of the bird on the ground and its effortless gliding through the air? Why are swimming and rowing appropriate metaphors for flight?
2. ("'Hope' Is the Thing with Feathers") Jot down the ideas, images, and associations that the word *hope* might normally bring to your mind. How is the treatment of hope different or unusual in this poem? In how many ways is hope like a bird? Why is its song sweetest in a gale? In what way is it true that it never asks for a crumb?
3. ("The Soul Selects Her Own Society") In how many ways does this poem make the individual soul seem independent, superior, invulnerable, sublime?
4. ("I'm Nobody! Who Are You?") How does this poem turn the tables on the common desire to "be somebody"?
5. ("Much Madness Is Divinest Sense") Is it true that the majority decides what is sane and insane? Do you know of people who were thought mad by many but who made sense on a higher plane or when seen from a different perspective?

Thinking, Talking, Writing

6. How do these poems together assert the uniqueness and independence of the individual? How do they champion the one against the many?

Thinking about Connections

7. Dickinson is perhaps the most reclusive and Whitman the most extrovert of American poets. Compare and contrast the attitude toward others or the perspective on fellow humanity in Whitman's "I Understand the Large Heart of Heroes" and in one or more of the poems by Dickinson.

WHERE I LIVED, AND WHAT I LIVED FOR

Henry David Thoreau

I went to the woods because I wished to live deliberately, to front only the essential facts of life, and see if I could not learn what it had to teach, and not, when I came to die, discover that I had not lived.

Henry David Thoreau

Thoreau is for many the most eloquent voice of the New England tradition of individualism. He lived in Concord, a few miles from where the first shots of the War of Independence were fired. He studied at Harvard College and was a friend of Emerson and other leading scholars and writers of his time. His essay "On the Duty of Civil Disobedience" (1849), a classic in the literature of dissent, remained for a century the manifesto of readers determined to resist authority and to challenge the tyranny of the majority. "That government is best which governs least," said Thoreau, preaching "cheerful self-reliance" and "progress toward a true respect for the individual." The great liberal causes of the day were opposition to slavery and to the war against Mexico, which brought California and large areas of the Southwest into the Union as the country moved toward its "Manifest Destiny." For Thoreau, the war was an aggressive, imperialistic war on the discredited European model, and he was briefly jailed for refusing to pay taxes to support it. Thoreau's example inspired later proponents of nonviolent resistance from Mahatma Gandhi in British India to Martin Luther King Jr. in the American South.

Thoreau had written his first book about trips and hikes to explore the New England countryside. The following selection from his later Walden *(1854) is his account of his two-year "experiment" in living close to nature, freeing himself of most of the trappings of civilization. "I lived alone in the woods," he said, "a mile from any neighbor, in a house which I had built myself, on the shore of Walden Pond, in Concord, Massachusetts, and earned a living by the labor of my hands only."*

Thoreau's allusions include brief references to mythology or history that may escape the modern reader: The Vedas are part of the sacred writings of ancient India; the Harivansa is a Hindu epic. Mount Olympus is the dwelling place of the Greek gods; Aurora is the Greek goddess of the dawn. Germany was in Thoreau's time splintered into many petty principalities; Don Carlos, Don Pedro, and the Infanta (or daughter of the king) were all at one time in the running for the next monarch of Spain. A cimeter is a Turkish sword. A "Nilometer" would measure the level of the River Nile, whose annual flooding assured the fertility of the central valley of Egypt.

When first I took up my abode in the woods, that is, began to spend *1* my nights as well as days there, which, by accident, was on Independence day, or the Fourth of July, 1845, my house was not finished for winter, but was merely a defense against the rain, without plastering or chimney, the walls being of rough weather-stained boards, with wide chinks, which made it cool at night. The upright white hewn studs and freshly planed door and window casings gave it a clean and airy look, especially in the morning, when its timbers were saturated with dew, so that I fancied that by noon some sweet gum would exude from them. To my imagination it retained throughout the day more or less of this auroral character, reminding me of a certain house on a mountain which I had visited a year before. This was an airy and unplastered cabin, fit to entertain a travelling god, and where a goddess might trail her garments. The winds which passed over my dwelling were such as sweep over the ridges of mountains, bearing the broken strains, or celestial parts only, of terrestrial music. The morning wind forever blows, the poem of creation is uninterrupted; but few are the ears that hear it. Olympus is but the outside of the earth everywhere.

The only house I had been the owner of before, if I except a boat, was a tent, which I used occasionally when making excursions in the summer, and this is still rolled up in my garret; but the boat, after passing from hand to hand, has gone down the stream of time. With this more substantial shelter about me, I had made some progress toward settling in the world. This frame, so slightly clad, was a sort of crystallization around me, and reacted on the builder. It was suggestive somewhat as a picture in outlines. I did not need to go outdoors to take the air, for the atmosphere within had lost none of its freshness. It was not so much within doors as behind a door where I sat, even in the rainiest weather. The Harivansa says, "An abode without birds is like a meat without seasoning." Such was not my abode, for I found myself suddenly neighbor to the birds; not by having imprisoned one, but having caged myself near them. I was not only nearer to some of those which commonly frequent the garden and the orchard, but to those wilder and more thrilling songsters of the forest which never, or rarely, serenade a villager—the wood-thrush, the veery, the scarlet tanager, the field-sparrow, the whippoorwill, and many others.

I was seated by the shore of a small pond, about a mile and a half south of the village of Concord and somewhat higher than it, in the midst of an extensive wood between that town and Lincoln, and about two miles south of that our only field known to fame, Concord Battle Ground; but I was so low in the woods that the opposite shore, half a mile off, like the rest, covered with wood, was my most distant horizon. For the first week, whenever I looked out on the pond it impressed me like a tarn high up on the side of a mountain, its bottom far above the surface of other lakes, and, as the sun arose, I saw it throwing off its nightly clothing of mist, and here and there, by degrees, its soft ripples or its smooth reflecting surface was revealed, while the mists, like ghosts, were stealthily withdrawing in every direction into the woods, as at the breaking up of some nocturnal conventicle. The very dew seemed to hang upon the trees later into the day than usual, as on the sides of mountains.

This small lake was of most value as a neighbor in the intervals of a gentle rain storm in August, when both air and water being perfectly still, but the sky overcast, mid-afternoon had all the serenity of evening, and the wood-thrush sang around, and was heard from shore to shore. A lake like this is never smoother than at such a time; and the clear portion of the air above it being shallow and darkened by clouds, the water, full of light and reflections, becomes a lower heaven itself so much the more important. From a hill top near by, where the wood had been recently cut off, there was a pleasing vista southward across the pond, through a wide indentation in the hills which form the shore there, where their opposite sides sloping toward each other suggested a stream flowing out in that direction through a wooded valley, but stream there was none. That way I looked between and over the near green hills to some distant and higher ones in the horizon, tinged with blue. Indeed, by standing on tiptoe I could catch a glimpse of some of the peaks of the still bluer and more distant mountain ranges in the north-west, those true-blue coins from heaven's own mint, and also of some portion of the village. But in other directions, even from this point, I could not see over or beyond the woods which surrounded me. It is well to have some water in your neighborhood, to give buoyancy to and float the earth. One value even of the smallest well is, that when you look into it you see that earth is not continent but insular. This is as important as that it keeps butter cool. When I looked across the pond from this peak toward the Sudbury meadows, which in time of flood I distinguished elevated perhaps by a mirage in their seething valley, like a coin in a basin, all the earth beyond the pond appeared like a thin crust insulated and floated even by this small sheet of intervening water, and I was reminded that this on which I dwelt was but *dry land*.

Though the view from my door was still more contracted, I did not feel crowded or confined in the least. There was pasture enough for my imagination. The low shrub-oak plateau to which the opposite shore arose, stretched away toward the prairies of the West and the steppes of Tartary, affording ample room for all the roving families of men. "There are none happy in the world but beings who enjoy freely a vast horizon,"—said Damodara, when his herds required new and larger pastures.

Both place and time were changed, and I dwelt nearer to those parts of the universe and to those eras in history which had most attracted me. Where I lived was as far off as many a region viewed nightly by astronomers. We are wont to imagine rare and delectable places in some remote and more celestial corner of the system, behind the constellation of Cassiopeia's Chair, far from noise and disturbance. I discovered that my house actually had its site in such a withdrawn, but forever new and unprofaned, part of the universe. If it were worth the while to settle in those parts near to the Pleiades or the Hyades, to Aldebaran or Altair, then I was really there, or at an equal remoteness from the life I had left behind, dwindled and twinkling with as fine a ray to my nearest neighbor, and to be seen only in moonless nights by him. Such was that part of creation where I had squatted—

> There was a shepherd that did live,
>   And held his thoughts as high
> As were the mounts whereon his flocks
>   Did hourly feed him by.

What should we think of the shepherd's life if his flocks always wandered to higher pastures than his thoughts?

Every morning was a cheerful invitation to make my life of equal simplicity, and I may say innocence, with Nature herself. I have been as sincere a worshipper of Aurora as the Greeks. I got up early and bathed in the pond; that was a religious exercise, and one of the best things which I did. They say that characters were engraven on the bathing tub of King Tching-thang to this effect: "Renew thyself completely each day; do it again, and again, and forever again." I can understand that. Morning brings back the heroic ages. I was as much affected by the faint hum of a mosquito making its invisible and unimaginable tour through my apartment at earliest dawn, when I was sitting with door and windows open, as I could be by any trumpet that ever sang of fame. It was Homer's requiem; itself an Iliad and Odyssey in the air, singing its own wrath and wanderings. There was something cosmical about it; a standing advertisement, till forbidden, of the ever-lasting vigor and fertility of the world. The morning, which is the most memorable season of the day, is the awakening hour. Then there is least somnolence in us; and for an hour, at least, some part of us awakes which slumbers all the rest of the day and night. Little is to be expected of that day, if it can be called a day, to which we are not awakened by our Genius, but by the mechanical nudgings of some servitor, are not awakened by our newly-acquired force and aspirations from within, accompanied by the undulations of celestial music, instead of factory bells, and a fragrance filling the air—to a higher life than we fell asleep from; and thus the darkness bear its fruit, and prove itself to be good, no less than the light. That man who does not believe that each day contains an earlier, more sacred, and auroral hour than he has yet profaned, has despaired of life, and is pursuing a descending and darkening way. After a partial cessation of his sensuous life, the soul of man, or its organs rather, are reinvigorated each day, and his Genius tries again what noble life it can make. All memorable events, I should say, transpire in morning time and in a morning atmosphere. The Vedas say, "All intelligences awake with the morning." Poetry and art, and the fairest and most memorable of the actions of men, date from such an hour. All poets and heroes, like Memnon, are the children of Aurora, and emit their music at sunrise. To him whose elastic and vigorous thought keeps pace with the sun, the day is a perpetual morning. It matters not what the clocks say or the attitudes and labors of men. Morning is when I am awake and there is a dawn in me. Moral reform is the effort to throw off sleep. Why is it that men give so poor an account of their day if they have not been slumbering? They are not such poor calculators. If they had not been overcome with drowsiness they would have performed something. The millions are awake enough for physical labor; but only one in a million is awake enough for effective intellectual exertion, only one in a hundred millions to a poetic or divine life. To be awake is to be alive. I have never yet met a man who was quite awake. How could I have looked him in the face?

We must learn to reawaken and keep ourselves awake, not by mechanical aids, but by an infinite expectation of the dawn, which does not forsake us in our soundest sleep. I know of no more encouraging fact than the unquestionable ability of man to elevate his life by a conscious endeavor. It is something to be able to paint a particular picture, or to carve a statue, and so to make a few objects beautiful; but it is far more glorious to carve and paint the very atmosphere and medium through which we look, which morally we can do. To affect the quality of the day, that is the highest of arts. Every man is tasked to make his life, even in its details, worthy of the contemplation of his most elevated and critical hour. If we refused, or rather used up, such paltry information as we get, the oracles would distinctly inform us how this might be done.

I went to the woods because I wished to live deliberately, to front only the essential facts of life, and see if I could not learn what it had to teach, and not, when I came to die, discover that I had not lived. I did not wish to live what was not life, living is so dear; nor did I wish to practice resignation, unless it was quite necessary. I wanted to live deep and suck out all the marrow of life, to live so sturdily and Spartanlike as to put to rout all that was not life, to cut a broad swath and shave close, to drive life into a corner, and reduce it to its lowest terms, and, if it proved to be mean, why then to get the whole and genuine meanness of it, and publish its meanness to the world; or if it were sublime, to know it by experience, and be able to give a true account of it in my next excursion. For most men, it appears to me, are in a strange uncertainty about it, whether it is of the devil or of God, and have *somewhat hastily* concluded that it is the chief end of man here to "glorify God and enjoy him forever."

Still we live meanly, like ants; though the fable tells us that we were   10
long ago changed into men; like pygmies we fight with cranes; it is error upon error, and clout upon clout, and our best virtue has for its occasion a superfluous and inevitable wretchedness. Our life is frittered away by detail. An honest man has hardly need to count more than his ten fingers, or in extreme cases he may add his ten toes, and lump the rest. Simplicity, simplicity, simplicity! I say, let your affairs be as two or three, and not a hundred or a thousand; instead of a million count half a dozen, and keep your accounts on your thumb nail. In the midst of this chopping sea of civilized life, such are the clouds and storms and quicksands and thousand-and-one items to be allowed for, that a man has to live, if he would not founder and go to the

bottom and not make his port at all, by dead reckoning, and he must be a great calculator indeed who succeeds. Simplify, simplify. Instead of three meals a day, if it be necessary eat but one; instead of a hundred dishes, five; and reduce other things in proportion. Our life is like a German Confederacy, made up of petty states, with its boundary forever fluctuating, so that even a German cannot tell you how it is bounded at any moment. The nation itself, with all its so-called internal improvements, which, by the way, are all external and superficial, is just such an unwieldy and overgrown establishment, cluttered with furniture and tripped up by its own traps, ruined by luxury and heedless expense, by want of calculation and a worthy aim, as the million households in the land; and the only cure for it as for them is in a rigid economy, a stern and more than Spartan simplicity of life and elevation of purpose. It lives too fast. Men think that it is essential that the *Nation* have commerce, and export ice, and talk through a telegraph, and ride thirty miles an hour, without a doubt, whether *they* do or not; but whether we should live like baboons or like men is a little uncertain. If we do not get our sleepers, and forge rails, and devote days and nights to the work, but go to tinkering upon our *lives* to improve *them,* who will build railroads? And if railroads are not built, how shall we get to heaven in season? But if we stay at home and mind our business, who will want railroads? We do not ride on the railroad; it rides upon us. Did you ever think what those sleepers are that underlie that railroad? Each one is a man, an Irishman, or a Yankee man. The rails are laid on them, and they are covered with sand, and the cars run smoothly over them. They are sound sleepers, I assure you. And every few years a new lot is laid down and run over; so that, if some have the pleasure of riding on a rail, others have the misfortune to be ridden upon. And when they run over a man that is walking in his sleep, a supernumerary sleeper in the wrong position, and wake him up, they suddenly stop the cars, and make a hue and cry about it, as if this were an exception. I am glad to know that it takes a gang of men for every five miles to keep the sleepers down and level in their beds as it is, for this is a sign that they may sometime get up again.

Why should we live with such hurry and waste of life? We are determined to be starved before we are hungry. Men say that a stitch in time saves nine, and so they take a thousand stitches today to save nine tomorrow. As for *work,* we haven't any of consequence. We have the Saint Vitus' dance, and cannot possibly keep our heads still. If I should only give a few pulls at the parish bell-rope, as for a fire, that is, without setting the bell, there is hardly a man on his farm in the outskirts of Concord, notwithstanding that press of engagements which was his excuse so many times this morning, nor a boy, nor a woman, I might almost say, but would forsake all and follow that sound, not mainly to save property from the flames, but, if we will confess the truth, much more to see it burn, since burn it must, and we, be it known, did not set it on fire—or to see it put out, and have a hand in it, if that is done as handsomely; yes, even if it were the parish church itself. Hardly a man takes a half hour's nap after dinner, but when he wakes he holds up his head and asks, "What's the news?" as if the rest of mankind had stood his sentinels. Some give directions to be waked every half hour, doubtless for no other purpose; and then, to pay for it, they tell what they have dreamed. After a night's sleep the news is as indispensable as the breakfast. "Pray tell me anything new that has happened to a man anywhere on this globe"—and he reads it over his coffee and rolls that a man has had his eyes gouged out this morning on the Wachito River; never dreaming the while that he lives in the dark unfathomed mammoth cave of this world, and has but the rudiment of an eye himself.

For my part, I could easily do without the post office. I think that there are very few important communications made through it. To speak critically, I never received more than one or two letters in my life—I wrote this some years ago—that were worth the postage. The penny-post is, commonly, an institution through which you seriously offer a man that penny for his thoughts which is so often safely offered in jest. And I am sure that I never read any memorable news in a newspaper. If we read of one man robbed, or murdered, or killed by accident, or one house burned, or one vessel wrecked, or one steamboat blown up, or one cow run over on the Western Railroad, or one mad dog killed, or one lot of grasshoppers in the winter, we never need read of another. One is enough. If you are acquainted with the principle, what do you care for a myriad instances and applications? To a philosopher all *news,* as it is called, is gossip, and they who edit and read it are old women over their tea. Yet not a few are greedy after this gossip. There was such a rush, as I hear, the other day at one of the offices to learn the foreign news by the last arrival, that several large squares of plate glass belonging to the establishment were broken by the pressure—news which I seriously think a ready wit might write a twelvemonth or twelve years beforehand with sufficient accuracy. As for Spain, for instance, if you know how to throw in Don Carlos and the Infanta, and Don Pedro and Seville and Granada, from time to time in the right proportions—they may have changed the names a little since I saw the papers—and serve up a bull-fight when other entertainments fail, it will be true to the letter, and give us as good an idea of the exact state of ruin of things in Spain as the most succinct and lucid reports under this head in the newspapers: and as for England, almost the last significant scrap of news from that quarter was the revolution of 1649; and if you have learned the history of her crops for an average year, you never need attend to that thing again, unless your speculations are of a merely pecuniary character. If one may judge who rarely looks into the newspapers, nothing new does ever happen in foreign parts, a French revolution not excepted.

What news! how much more important to know what that is which was never old! "Kieou-he-yu (great dignitary of the state of Wei) sent a man to Khoung-tseu to know his news. Khoung-tseu caused the messenger to be seated near him, and questioned him in these terms: What is your master doing? The messenger answered with respect: My master desires to diminish the number of his faults, but he cannot come to the end of them. The messenger being gone, the philosopher remarked: What a worthy messenger; What a worthy messenger!" The preacher, instead of vexing the ears of drowsy farmers on their day of rest at the end of the week—for Sunday is the fit conclusion of an ill-spent week, and not the fresh and brave beginning of a new one—with this one other draggle-tail of a sermon, should shout with thundering voice,—"Pause! Avast! Why so seeming fast, but deadly slow?"

Shams and delusions are esteemed for soundest truths, while reality is fabulous. If men would steadily observe realities only, and not allow themselves to be deluded, life, to compare it with such things as we know, would be like a fairy tale and the Arabian Nights' Entertainments. If we respected only what is inevitable and has a right to be, music and poetry would resound along the streets. When we are unhurried and wise, we perceive that only great and worthy things have any permanent and absolute existence,—that petty fears and petty pleasures are but the shadow of the reality. This is always exhilarating and sublime. By closing the eyes and slumbering, and consenting to be deceived by shows, men establish and confirm their daily life of routine and habit everywhere, which still is built on purely illusory foundations. Children, who play life, discern its true law and relations more clearly than men, who fail to live it worthily, but who think that they are wiser by experience, that is, by failure. I have read in a Hindu book, that "there was a king's son, who, being expelled in infancy from his native city, was brought up by a forester, and, growing up to maturity in that state, imagined himself to belong to the barbarous race with which he lived. One of his father's ministers having discovered him, revealed to him what he was, and the misconception of his character was removed, and he knew himself to be a prince. So soul," continues the Hindu philosopher, "from the circumstances in which it is placed, mistakes its own character, until the truth is revealed to it by some holy teacher, and then it knows itself to be *Brahme*." I perceive that we inhabitants of New England live this mean life that we do because our vision does not penetrate the surface of things. We think that that *is* which *appears* to be. If a man should walk through this town and see only the reality, where, think you, would the "Mill-dam" go to? If he should give us an account of the realities he beheld there, we should not recognize the place in his description. Look at a meeting house, or a courthouse, or a jail, or a shop, or a dwelling house, and say what that thing really is before a true gaze, and they would all go to pieces in your account of them. Men esteem truth remote, in the outskirts of the system, behind the farthest star, before Adam and after the last man. In eternity there is indeed something true and sublime. But all these times and places and occasions are now and here. God himself culminates in the present moment, and will never be more divine in the lapse of all the ages. And we are enabled to apprehend at all what is sublime and noble only by the perpetual instilling and drenching of the reality that surrounds us. The universe constantly and obediently answers to our conceptions; whether we travel fast or slow, the track is laid for us. Let us spend our lives in conceiving then. The poet or the artist never yet had so fair and noble a design but some of his posterity at least could accomplish it.

Let us spend one day as deliberately as Nature, and not be thrown off 15 the track by every nutshell and mosquito's wing that falls on the rails. Let us rise early and fast, or break fast, gently and without perturbation; let company come and let company go, let the bells ring and the children cry— determined to make a day of it. Why should we knock under and go with the stream? Let us not be upset and overwhelmed in that terrible rapid and whirlpool called a dinner, situated in the meridian shallows. Weather this danger and you are safe, for the rest of the way is down hill. With unrelaxed nerves, with morning vigor, sail by it, looking another way, tied to the mast like Ulysses. If the engine whistles, let it whistle till it is hoarse for its pains. If the bell rings, why should we run? We will consider what kind of music they are like. Let us settle ourselves, and work and wedge our feet downward through the mud and slush of opinion, and prejudice, and tradition, and delusion, and appearance, that alluvion which covers the globe, through Paris and London, through New York and Boston and Concord, through church and state, through poetry and philosophy and religion, till we come to a hard bottom and rocks in place, which we can call *reality,* and say, This is, and no mistake; and then begin, having a *point d'appui* [a firm support], below freshet and frost and fire, a place where you might found a wall or a state, or set a lamp-post safely, or perhaps a gauge, not a Nilometer, but a Realometer, that future ages might know how deep a freshet of shams and appearances had gathered from time to time. If you stand right fronting and face to face to a fact, you will see the sun glimmer on both its surfaces, as if it were a cimeter, and feel its sweet edge dividing you through the heart and marrow, and so you will happily conclude your mortal career. Be it life or death, we crave only reality. If we are really dying, let us hear the rattle in our throats and feel cold in the extremities; if we are alive, let us go about our business.

Time is but the stream I go a-fishing in. I drink at it; but while I drink I see the sandy bottom and detect how shallow it is. Its thin current slides away, but eternity remains. I would drink deeper; fish in the sky, whose bottom is pebbly with stars. I cannot count one. I know not the first letter of the alphabet. I have always been regretting that I was not as wise as the day I was born. The intellect is a cleaver; it discerns and rifts its way into the secret of things. I do not wish to be any more busy with my hands than is necessary. My head is hands and feet. I feel all my best faculties concentrated in it. My instinct tells me that my head is an organ for burrowing, as some creatures use their snout and forepaws, and with it I would mine and burrow my way through these hills. I think that the richest vein is somewhere here- abouts; so by the divining rod and thin rising vapors I judge; and here I will begin to mine.

The Responsive Reader

1. Thoreau's thesis was "Simplicity! Simplicity! Simplicity!" How did he try to implement this program during his experiment of living in the woods?
2. Thoreau looked at the world from a strongly personal, individual point of view. For instance, in his time the rapidly expanding railroads were for many the symbol of the triumphant new technology of the industrial age. What does Thoreau mean when he says, "We do not ride on the railroad; it rides on us"? What is his unconventional perspective on subjects like newspapers and news, the arts, or what makes a person rich?
3. What does Thoreau mean when he says, "God himself culminates in the present moment"? What seems to be the essence of his sense of the spiritual dimension of life? How is his definition of "reality" different from more familiar ones?

Thinking, Talking, Writing

4. Is something like Thoreau's scheme for escaping from the complexities of modern civilization still feasible today?
5. Is Thoreau's religious perspective compatible with the religious faith or outlook with which you are most familiar?
6. Where is the line between an individualist, a maverick, and a crank? Are they basically the same people?

Collaborative Projects

7. Some people like to update proverbs, giving them a modern twist. ("If you strike while the iron is hot, you'll get a third-degree burn.") Do the same for some of Thoreau's **aphorisms**—statements that sum up a general truth in a pointed, memorable way. Working with a group, cull the best modern rewrites of sentences like the following:

> A man is rich in proportion to the number of things he can afford to let alone.

> As long as possible live free and uncommitted.

> To a philosopher all news, as it is called, is gossip.

> We do not ride on the railroad; it rides on us.

> To affect the quality of the day, that is the highest of arts.

> The intellect is a cleaver; it discerns and rifts its way into the secret of things.

> Shams and delusions are esteemed for soundest truths, while reality is fabulous.

THE TALL MEN
William Faulkner

William Faulkner became a dominant figure in modern American fiction with his series of intermeshing novels set in the post–Civil War South. Many of his books are set in his fictional Yoknapatawpha County, modeled on Lafayette County in northern Mississippi, where he lived much of his life at Oxford. Millions here and abroad have read The Sound and the Fury *(1929),* Sanctuary *(1931),* Light in August *(1932),* Absalom, Absalom! *(1936), and* Intruder in the Dust *(1948) among others. Faulkner received the Nobel Prize in 1950 and became widely recognized as a giant among the Southern writers who shaped much of the American literary tradition in the twentieth century.*

Faulkner himself thought of his work as a saga of the Old South in transition to the modern world. His characters run the gamut from faded gentility through rapacious upstarts to poor whites, with black people always present on the fringes of a white society rife with tension and latent violence. While often struggling to keep up genteel appearances, Faulkner's people tend to be tortured souls beset by memories of wealth and status lost in a changing society, haunted by family secrets, driven by violent antagonisms or vindictiveness, or doomed by destructive passion. His difficult, many-layered sentences try to capture the contradictory thoughts and violent emotions in the consciousness of his characters. Flashbacks and shifts in point of view complicate his story lines, which slowly unravel rather than develop in linear fashion. Faulkner's densely packed prose reminds us that the world each of us sees is a fiction: We see the world as in a distorting mirror, in which the memory of the past and the obsessions of the present create their own hallucinatory reality.

They passed the dark bulk of the cotton gin. Then they saw the lamplit house and the other car, the doctor's coupé, just stopping at the gate, and they could hear the hound baying.   1

"Here we are," the old deputy marshal said.

"What's that other car?" the younger man said, the stranger, the state draft investigator.

"Doctor Schofield's," the marshal said. "Lee McCallum asked me to send him out when I telephoned we were coming."

"You mean you warned them?" the investigator said. "You telephoned   5 ahead that I was coming out with a warrant for these two evaders? Is this how you carry out the orders of the United States Government?"

The marshal was a lean, clean old man who chewed tobacco, who had been born and lived in the country all his life.

"I understood all you wanted was to arrest these two McCallum boys and bring them back to town," he said.

"It was!" the investigator said. "And now you have warned them, given them a chance to run. Possibly put the Government to the expense of hunting them down with troops. Have you forgotten that you are under a bond yourself?"

"I ain't forgot it," the marshal said. "And ever since we left Jefferson I been trying to tell you something for you not to forget. But I reckon it will take these McCallums to impress that on you. . . . Pull in behind the other car. We'll try to find out first just how sick whoever it is that is sick is."

The investigator drew up behind the other car and switched off and blacked out his lights. "These people," he said. Then he thought, *But this doddering, tobacco-chewing old man is one of them, too, despite the honor and pride of his office, which should have made him different.* So he didn't speak it aloud, removing the keys and getting out of the car, and then locking the car itself, rolling the windows up first, thinking, *These people who lie about and conceal the ownership of land and property in order to hold relief jobs which they have no intention of performing, standing on their constitutional rights against having to work, who jeopardize the very job itself through petty and transparent subterfuge to acquire a free mattress which they intend to attempt to sell; who would relinquish even the job, if by so doing they could receive free food and a place, any rathole, in town to sleep in; who, as farmers, make false statements to get seed loans which they will later misuse, and then react in loud vituperative outrage and astonishment when caught at it. And then, when at long last a suffering and threatened Government asks one thing of them in return, one thing simply, which is to put their names down on a selective-service list, they refuse to do it.*

The old marshal had gone on. The investigator followed, through a stout paintless gate in a picket fence, up a broad brick walk between two rows of old shabby cedars, toward the rambling and likewise paintless sprawl of the two-story house in the open hall of which the soft lamplight glowed and the lower story of which, as the investigator now perceived, was of logs.

He saw a hall full of soft lamplight beyond a stout paintless gallery running across the log front, from beneath which the same dog which they had heard, a big hound, came booming again, to stand foursquare facing them in the walk, bellowing, until a man's voice spoke to it from the house. He followed the marshal up the steps onto the gallery. Then he saw the man standing in the door, waiting for them to approach—a man of about forty-five, not tall, but blocky, with a brown, still face and horseman's hands, who looked at him once, brief and hard, and then no more, speaking to the marshal, "Howdy, Mr. Gombault. Come in."

"Howdy, Rafe," the marshal said. "Who's sick?"

"Buddy," the other said. "Slipped and caught his leg in the hammer mill this afternoon."

"Is it bad?" the marshal said.

"It looks bad to me," the other said. "That's why we sent for the doctor instead of bringing him in to town. We couldn't get the bleeding stopped."

"I'm sorry to hear that," the marshal said. "This is Mr. Pearson." Once

10

15

more the investigator found the other looking at him, the brown eyes still, courteous enough in the brown face, the hand he offered hard enough, but the clasp quite limp, quite cold. The marshal was still speaking. "From Jackson. From the draft board." Then he said, and the investigator could discern no change whatever in his tone: "He's got a warrant for the boys."

The investigator could discern no change whatever anywhere. The limp hard hand merely withdrew from his, the still face now looking at the marshal. "You mean we have declared war?"

"No," the marshal said.

"That's not the question, Mr. McCallum," the investigator said. "All required of them was to register. Their numbers might not even be drawn this time; under the law of averages, they probably would not be. But they refused—failed, anyway—to register." 20

"I see," the other said. He was not looking at the investigator. The investigator couldn't tell certainly if he was even looking at the marshal, although he spoke to him, "You want to see Buddy? The doctor's with him now."

"Wait," the investigator said. "I'm sorry about your brother's accident, but I—" The marshal glanced back at him for a moment, his shaggy gray brows beetling, with something at once courteous yet a little impatient about the glance, so that during the instant the investigator sensed from the old marshal the same quality which had been in the other's brief look. The investigator was a man of better than average intelligence; he was already becoming aware of something a little different here from what he had expected. But he had been in relief work in the state several years, dealing almost exclusively with country people, so he still believed he knew them. So he looked at the old marshal, thinking, *Yes. The same sort of people, despite the office, the authority and responsibility which should have changed him.* Thinking again, *These people. These people.* "I intend to take the night train back to Jackson," he said. "My reservation is already made. Serve the warrant and we will—"

"Come along," the old marshal said. "We are going to have plenty of time."

So he followed—there was nothing else to do—fuming and seething, attempting in the short length of the hall to regain control of himself in order to control the situation, because he realized now that if the situation were controlled, it would devolve upon him to control it; that if their departure with their prisoners were expedited, it must be himself and not the old marshal who would expedite it. He had been right. The doddering old officer was not only at bottom one of these people, he had apparently been corrupted anew to his old, inherent, shiftless sloth and unreliability merely by entering the house. So he followed in turn, down the hall and into a bedroom; whereupon he looked about him not only with amazement but with something very like terror. The room was a big room, with a bare unpainted floor, and besides the bed, it contained only a chair or two and one other piece of old-fashioned furniture. Yet to the investigator it seemed so filled with tremendous men cast in the same mold as the man who had met them that the very walls themselves must bulge. Yet they were not big, not tall, and it was not vitality, exuberance, because they made no sound, merely looking quietly at him where he stood in the door, with faces bearing an almost identical stamp of kinship—a thin, almost frail old man of about seventy, slightly taller than the others; a second one, white-haired, too, but otherwise identical with the man who had met them at the door; a third one about the same age as the man who had met them, but with something delicate in his face and something tragic and dark and wild in the same dark eyes; the two absolutely identical blue-eyed youths; and lastly the blue-eyed man on the bed over which the doctor, who might have been any city doctor, in his neat city suit, leaned—all of them turning to look quietly at him and the marshal as they entered. And he saw, past the doctor, the slit trousers of the man on the bed and the exposed, bloody, mangled leg, and he turned sick, stopping just inside the door under that quiet, steady regard while the marshal went up to the man who lay on the bed, smoking a cob pipe, a big, old-fashioned, wicker-covered demijohn, such as the investigator's grandfather had kept his whisky in, on the table beside him.

"Well, Buddy," the marshal said, "this is bad." 25

"Ah, it was my own damn fault," the man on the bed said. "Stuart kept warning me about that frame I was using."

"That's correct," the second old one said.

Still the others said nothing. They just looked steadily and quietly at the investigator until the marshal turned slightly and said, "This is Mr. Pearson. From Jackson. He's got a warrant for the boys."

Then the man on the bed said, "What for?"

"That draft business, Buddy," the marshal said. 30

"We're not at war now," the man on the bed said.

"No," the marshal said. "It's that new law. They didn't register."

"What are you going to do with them?"

"It's a warrant, Buddy. Swore out."

"That means jail." 35

"It's a warrant," the old marshal said. Then the investigator saw that the man on the bed was watching him, puffing steadily at the pipe.

"Pour me some whisky, Jackson," he said.

"No," the doctor said. "He's had too much already."

"Pour me some whisky, Jackson," the man on the bed said. He puffed steadily at the pipe, looking at the investigator. "You come from the Government?" he said.

"Yes," the investigator said. "They should have registered. That's all 40 required of them yet. They did not—" His voice ceased, while the seven pairs of eyes contemplated him, and the man on the bed puffed steadily.

"We would have still been here," the man on the bed said. "We wasn't going to run." He turned his head. The two youths were standing side by side at the foot of the bed. "Anse, Lucius," he said.

To the investigator it sounded as if they answered as one, "Yes, father."

"This gentleman has come all the way from Jackson to say the Government is ready for you. I reckon the quickest place to enlist will be Memphis. Go upstairs and pack."

The investigator started, moved forward. "Wait!" he cried.

But Jackson, the eldest, had forestalled him. He said, "Wait," also, and   *45* now they were not looking at the investigator. They were looking at the doctor.

"What about his leg?" Jackson said.

"Look at it," the doctor said. "He almost amputated it himself. It won't wait. And he can't be moved now. I'll need my nurse to help me, and some ether, provided he hasn't had too much whisky to stand the anesthetic too. One of you can drive to town in my car. I'll telephone—"

"Ether?" the man on the bed said. "What for? You just said yourself it's pretty near off now. I could whet up one of Jackson's butcher knives and finish it myself, with another drink or two. Go on. Finish it."

"You couldn't stand any more shock," the doctor said. "This is whisky talking now."

"Shucks," the other said. "One day in France we was running through   *50* a wheat field and I saw the machine gun, coming across the wheat, and I tried to jump it like you would jump a fence rail somebody was swinging at your middle, only I never made it. And I was on the ground then, and along toward dark that begun to hurt, only about that time something went whang on the back of my helmet, like when you hit a anvil, so I never knowed nothing else until I woke up. There was a heap of us racked up along a bank outside a field dressing station, only it took a long time for the doctor to get around to all of us, and by that time it was hurting bad. This here ain't hurt none to speak of since I got a-holt of this johnny-jug. You go on and finish it. If it's help you need, Stuart and Rafe will help you. . . . Pour me a drink, Jackson."

This time the doctor raised the demijohn and examined the level of the liquor. "There's a good quart gone," he said. "If you've drunk a quart of whisky since four o'clock, I doubt if you could stand the anesthetic. Do you think you could stand it if I finished it now?"

"Yes, finish it. I've ruined it; I want to get shut of it."

The doctor looked about at the others, at the still, identical faces watching him. "If I had him in town, in the hospital, with a nurse to watch him, I'd probably wait until he got over this first shock and got the whisky out of his system. But he can't be moved now, and I can't stop the bleeding like this, and even if I had ether or a local anesthetic—"

"Shucks," the man on the bed said. "God never made no better local nor general comfort or anesthetic neither than what's in this johnny-jug. And this ain't Jackson's leg nor Stuart's nor Rafe's nor Lee's. It's mine. I done started it; I reckon I can finish cutting it off any way I want to."

But the doctor was still looking at Jackson. "Well, Mr. McCallum?" he   *55* said. "You're the oldest."

But it was Stuart who answered. "Yes," he said. "Finish it. What do you want? Hot water, I reckon."

"Yes," the doctor said. "Some clean sheets. Have you got a big table you can move in here?"

"The kitchen table," the man who had met them at the door said. "Me and the boys—"

"Wait," the man on the bed said. "The boys won't have time to help you." He looked at them again. "Anse, Lucius," he said.

Again it seemed to the investigator that they answered as one, "Yes, father."   60

"This gentleman yonder is beginning to look impatient. You better start. Come to think of it, you won't need to pack. You will have uniforms in a day or two. Take the truck. There won't be nobody to drive you to Memphis and bring the truck back, so you can leave it at the Gayoso Feed Company until we can send for it. I'd like for you to enlist into the old Sixth Infantry, where I used to be. But I reckon that's too much to hope, and you'll just have to chance where they send you. But it likely won't matter, once you are in. The Government done right by me in my day, and it will do right by you. You just enlist wherever they want to send you, need you, and obey your sergeants and officers until you find out how to be soldiers. Obey them, but remember your name and don't take nothing from no man. You can go now."

"Wait!" the investigator cried again; again he started, moved forward into the center of the room. "I protest this! I'm sorry about Mr. McCallum's accident. I'm sorry about the whole business. But it's out of my hands and out of his hands now. This charge, failure to register according to law, has been made and the warrant issued. It cannot be evaded this way. The course of the action must be completed before any other step can be taken. They should have thought of this when these boys failed to register. If Mr. Gombault refuses to serve this warrant, I will serve it myself and take these men back to Jefferson with me to answer this charge as made. And I must warn Mr. Gombault that he will be cited for contempt!"

The old marshal turned, his shaggy eyebrows beetling again, speaking down to the investigator as if he were a child, "Ain't you found out yet that me or you neither ain't going nowhere for a while?"

"What?" the investigator cried. He looked about at the grave faces once more contemplating him with that remote and speculative regard. "Am I being threatened?" he cried.

"Ain't anybody paying any attention to you at all," the marshal said.   65
"Now you just be quiet for a while, and you will be all right, and after a while we can go back to town."

So he stopped again and stood while the grave, contemplative faces freed him once more of that impersonal and unbearable regard, and saw the two youths approach the bed and bend down in turn and kiss their father on the mouth, and then turn as one and leave the room, passing him without even looking at him. And sitting in the lamplit hall beside the old marshal, the bedroom door closed now, he heard the truck start up and back and turn and go down the road, the sound of it dying away, ceasing, leaving the still, hot night—the Mississippi Indian summer, which had already outlasted half of November—filled with the loud last shrilling of the summer's cicadas, as though they, too, were aware of the imminent season of cold weather and of death.

"I remember old Anse," the marshal said pleasantly, chattily, in that tone in which an adult addresses a strange child. "He's been dead fifteen-sixteen years now. He was about sixteen when the old war broke out, and he walked all the way to Virginia to get into it. He could have enlisted and fought right here at home, but his ma was a Carter, so wouldn't nothing do him but to go all the way back to Virginia to do his fighting, even though he hadn't never seen Virginia before himself; walked all the way back to a land he hadn't never even seen before and enlisted in Stonewall Jackson's army and stayed in it all through the Valley, and right up to Chancellorsville, where them Carolina boys shot Jackson by mistake, and right on up to that morning in 'Sixty-five when Sheridan's cavalry blocked the road from Appomattox to the Valley, where they might have got away again. And he walked back to Mississippi with just about what he had carried away with him when he left, and he got married and built the first story of this house—this here log story we're in right now—and started getting them boys—Jackson and Stuart and Raphael and Lee and Buddy.

"Buddy come along late, late enough to be in the other war, in France in it. You heard him in there. He brought back two medals, an American medal and a French one, and no man knows till yet how he got them, just what he done. I don't believe he even told Jackson and Stuart and them. He hadn't hardly got back home, with them numbers on his uniform and the wound stripes and them two medals, before he had found him a girl, found her right off, and a year later them twin boys was born, the livin', spittin' image of old Anse McCallum. If old Anse had just been about seventy-five years younger, the three of them might have been thriblets. I remember them—two little critters exactly alike, and wild as spikehorn bucks, running around here day and night both with a pack of coon dogs until they got big enough to help Buddy and Stuart and Lee with the farm and the gin, and Rafe with the horses and mules, when he would breed and raise and train them and take them to Memphis to sell, right on up to three, four years back, when they went to the agricultural college for a year to learn more about whiteface cattle.

"That was after Buddy and them had quit raising cotton. I remember that too. It was when the Government first begun to interfere with how a man farmed his own land, raised his cotton. Stabilizing the price, using up the surplus, they called it, giving a man advice and help, whether he wanted it or not. You may have noticed them boys in yonder tonight; curious folks almost, you might call them. That first year, when county agents was trying to explain the new system to farmers, the agent come out here and tried to explain it to Buddy and Lee and Stuart, explaining how they would cut down the crop, but that the Government would pay farmers the difference, and so they would actually be better off than trying to farm by themselves.

" 'Why, we're much obliged,' Buddy says. 'But we don't need no help. We'll just make the cotton like we always done; if we can't make a crop of it, that will just be our lookout and our loss, and we'll try again.' 70

"So they wouldn't sign no papers nor no cards nor nothing. They just went on and made the cotton like old Anse had taught them to; it was like they just couldn't believe that the Government aimed to help a man whether he wanted help or not, aimed to interfere with how much of anything he could make by hard work on his own land, making the crop and ginning it right here in their own gin, like they had always done, and hauling it to town to sell, hauling it all the way into Jefferson before they found out they couldn't sell it because, in the first place, they had made too much of it and, in the second place, they never had no card to sell what they would have been allowed. So they hauled it back. The gin wouldn't hold all of it, so they put some of it under Rafe's mule shed and they put the rest of it right here in the hall where we are setting now, where they would have to walk around it all winter and keep themselves reminded to be sho and fill out that card next time.

"Only next year they didn't fill out no papers neither. It was like they still couldn't believe it, still believed in the freedom and liberty to make or break according to a man's fitness and will to work, guaranteed by the Government that old Anse had tried to tear in two once and failed, and admitted in good faith he had failed and taken the consequences, and that had give Buddy a medal and taken care of him when he was far away from home in a strange land and hurt.

"So they made that second crop. And they couldn't sell it to nobody neither because they never had no cards. This time they built a special shed to put it under, and I remember how in that second winter Buddy come to town one day to see Lawyer Gavin Stevens. Not for legal advice how to sue the Government or somebody into buying the cotton, even if they never had no card for it, but just to find out why. 'I was for going ahead and signing up for it,' Buddy says. 'If that's going to be the new rule. But we talked it over, and Jackson ain't no farmer, but he knowed father longer than the rest of us, and he said father would have said no, and I reckon now he would have been right.'

"So they didn't raise any more cotton; they had a plenty of it to last a while—twenty-two bales, I think it was. That was when they went into whiteface cattle, putting old Anse's cotton land into pasture, because that's what he would have wanted them to do if the only way they could raise cotton was by the Government telling them how much they could raise and how much they could sell it for, and where, and when, and then pay them for not doing the work they didn't do. Only even when they didn't raise cotton, every year the county agent's young fellow would come out to measure the pasture crops they planted so he could pay them for that, even if they never had no not-cotton to be paid for. Except that he never measured no crop on this place. 'You're welcome to look at what we are doing,' Buddy says. 'But don't draw it down on your map.'

" 'But you can get money for this,' the young fellow says. 'The Government wants to pay you for planting all this.' *75*

" 'We are aiming to get money for it,' Buddy says. 'When we can't, we will try something else. But not from the Government. Give that to them that want to take it. We can make out.'

"And that's about all. Them twenty-two bales of orphan cotton are down yonder in the gin right now, because there's room for it in the gin now because they ain't using the gin no more. And them boys grew up and went off a year to the agricultural college to learn right about whiteface cattle, and then come back to the rest of them—these here curious folks living off here to themselves, with the rest of the world all full of pretty neon lights burning night and day both, and easy, quick money scattering itself around everywhere for any man to grab a little, and every man with a shiny new automobile already wore out and throwed away and the new one delivered before the first one was even paid for, and everywhere a fine loud grabble and snatch of AAA and WPA and a dozen other three-letter reasons for a man not to work. Then this here draft comes along, and these curious folks ain't got around to signing that neither, and you come all the way up from Jackson with your paper all signed and regular, and we come out here, and after a while we can go back to town. A man gets around, don't he?"

"Yes," the investigator said. "Do you suppose we can go back to town now?"

"No," the marshal told him in that same kindly tone, "not just yet. But we can leave after a while. Of course you will miss your train. But there will be another one tomorrow."

He rose, though the investigator had heard nothing. The investigator *80* watched him go down the hall and open the bedroom door and enter and close it behind him. The investigator sat quietly, listening to the night sounds and looking at the closed door until it opened presently and the marshal came back, carrying something in a bloody sheet, carrying it gingerly.

"Here," he said. "Hold it a minute."

"It's bloody," the investigator said.

"That's all right," the marshal said. "We can wash when we get through." So the investigator took the bundle and stood holding it while he watched the old marshal go back down the hall and on through it and vanish and return presently with a lighted lantern and a shovel. "Come along," he said. "We're pretty near through now."

The investigator followed him out of the house and across the yard, carrying gingerly the bloody, shattered, heavy bundle in which it still seemed to him he could feel some warmth of life, the marshal striding on ahead, the lantern swinging against his leg, the shadow of his striding scissoring and enormous along the earth, his voice still coming back over his shoulder, chatty and cheerful, "Yes, sir. A man gets around and he sees a heap; a heap of folks in a heap of situations. The trouble is, we done got into the habit of confusing the situations with the folks. Take yourself, now," he said in that same kindly tone, chatty and easy; "you mean all right. You just went and got yourself all fogged up with rules and regulations. That's our trouble. We done invented ourselves so many alphabets and rules and recipes that we can't see anything else; if what we see can't be fitted to an alphabet or a rule, we are lost. We have come to be like critters doctor folks might have created in laboratories, that have learned how to slip off their bones and guts and still live, still be kept alive indefinite and forever maybe even without even knowing the bones and the guts are gone. We have slipped our backbone; we have about decided a man don't need a backbone any more; to have one is old-fashioned. But the groove where the backbone used to be is still there, and the backbone has been kept alive, too, and someday we're going to slip back onto it. I don't know just when nor just how much of a wrench it will take to teach us, but someday."

They had left the yard now. They were mounting a slope; ahead of them the investigator could see another clump of cedars, a small clump, somehow shaggily formal against the starred sky. The marshal entered it and stopped and set the lantern down and, following with the bundle, the investigator saw a small rectangle of earth enclosed by a low brick coping. Then he saw the two graves, or the headstones—two plain granite slabs set upright in the earth.

"Old Anse and Mrs. Anse," the marshal said. "Buddy's wife wanted to be buried with her folks. I reckon she would have been right lonesome up here with just McCallums. Now, let's see." He stood for a moment, his chin in his hand; to the investigator he looked exactly like an old lady trying to decide where to set out a shrub. "They was to run from left to right, beginning with Jackson. But after the boys was born, Jackson and Stuart was to come up here by their pa and ma, so Buddy could move up some and make room. So he will be about here." He moved the lantern nearer and took up the shovel. Then he saw the investigator still holding the bundle. "Set it down," he said. "I got to dig first."

"I'll hold it," the investigator said.

"Nonsense, put it down," the marshal said. "Buddy won't mind."

So the investigator put the bundle down on the brick coping and the marshal began to dig, skillfully and rapidly, still talking in that cheerful, interminable voice, "Yes, sir. We done forgot about folks. Life has done got cheap, and life ain't cheap. Life's a pretty durn valuable thing. I don't mean just getting along from one WPA relief check to the next one, but honor and pride and discipline that make a man worth preserving, make him of any value. That's what we got to learn again. Maybe it takes trouble, bad trouble, to teach it back to us; maybe it was the walking to Virginia because that's where his ma come from, and losing a war and then walking back, that taught it to old Anse. Anyway, he seems to learned it, and to learned it good enough to bequeath it to his boys. Did you notice how all Buddy had to do was to tell them boys of his it was time to go, because the Government had sent them word? And how they told him good-by? Growned men kissing one another without hiding and without shame. Maybe that's what I am trying to say. . . . There." he said. "That's big enough."

He moved quickly, easily; before the investigator could stir, he had lifted the bundle into the narrow trench and was covering it, covering it as rapidly as he had dug, smoothing the earth over it with the shovel. Then he stood up and raised the lantern—a tall, lean old man, breathing easily and lightly. 90

"I reckon we can go back to town now," he said.

The Responsive Reader

1. This story centers on the different perspectives of the state investigator and of the marshal. What assumptions about the local people does the investigator bring to his job? What are his complaints about them? Do his charges remind you of stereotypes about these or other people on the margin of modern society?
2. What do we learn about the McCallums at first hand? What is their lifestyle? How do they define their relation to society? How do they feel about government interference? What is their definition of freedom?
3. How does draft registration become the test case for the different attitudes toward life and society that contend in this story? Are the McCallums antidraft or antiwar? What role do memories of past wars play in the story?
4. What role do the accident and the amputation play in the story? Do they seem a distraction or detour in the course of the plot? What do they tell the reader about the characters?
5. What is the marshal's role in the story? How does he clash with the investigator? How does he see the story of the McCallums as part of larger patterns of social or cultural change?

Thinking, Talking, Writing

6. Faulkner says that the local people in the story were "not big, not tall." Why then does he call the story "The Tall Men"?
7. Are the McCallums cut off from the modern world? Is their outlook or mentality a thing of the past?

Collaborative Projects

8. Are rural people likely to be more independent than city dwellers? Working with a group, organize some interviews or a survey that might shed light on this question.

Thinking about Connections

9. Erdrich's "The Red Convertible" and Faulkner's "Tall Men" both focus on people who are misfits from the viewpoint of mainstream society. What makes the characters in each story outsiders? Is there a common thread? Are there key differences?

A SEPARATE ROAD

Richard Wright

Richard Wright could not learn his role. Nor could he learn to be secure in the traditional consolation of the oppressed—the hope of a better world here- after. *Black Boy* is the story of self-education achieved in rebellion against the conventions of Negro society.

John Reilly

Richard Wright was for many later African American writers a towering figure to emulate and to try to go beyond. Wright once said that even as a young boy he knew about "the hunger of the human heart," the "thirst of the human spirit to conquer and transcend the implacable limitations of human life." He was a taboo breaker whose searing novels explored the odyssey of the young black male trying to "merge himself with others and be a part of this world, to lose himself in it so he could find himself, to be allowed a chance to live like others, even though he was black."

Wright was born as the son of a sharecropper in Natchez, Mississippi, and he early rebelled against a strict religious upbringing. He struggled with poverty and racism and worked as ditch digger, delivery boy, dishwasher, and hospital worker. He read widely on his own, discovering the class-consciousness and the radical ideologies of the Depression era. He became a member of the Commu- nist-sponsored John Reed Club, joined the Communist party, and became Har- lem editor of The Daily Worker. *Like other disillusioned black writers and artists, he eventually broke with the party when he saw white radicals exploiting the black community for their own political ends. Wright traveled the archetypal journey from the rural South to the city (Memphis), from the South north to Chicago, and from there to life as an expatriate in Paris, France, where he was lionized by European intellectuals.*

His novel Native Son *(1940) dramatized the anger and pent-up violence that he saw as the heritage of a history of oppression. It told the story of a poor black patronized by radical whites and a rich employer and hunted down by police and vigilantes after the murder of a white woman. The following excerpt is from his autobiographical novel* Black Boy *(1945). It describes a time when the boy and his partially paralyzed mother are living with his authoritarian aunt and grandmother.*

I went to school, feeling that my life depended not so much upon my   *1* learning as upon getting into another world of people.

Until I entered Jim Hill public school, I had had but one year of unbroken study. With the exception of one year at the church school, each time I had begun a school term something happened to disrupt it. Already my personality was lopsided. My knowledge of feeling was far greater than my knowledge of fact. Though I was not aware of it, the next four years were to be the only opportunity for formal study in my life.

The first school day presented the usual problem and I was emotionally prepared to meet it. Upon what terms would I be allowed to remain upon the school grounds? With pencil and tablet, I walked nonchalantly into the schoolyard, wearing a cheap, brand-new straw hat. I mingled with the boys, hoping to pass unnoticed, but knowing that sooner or later I would be spotted for a newcomer. And trouble came quickly. A black boy bounded past me, thumping my straw hat to the ground, and yelling:

"Straw katy!"

I picked up my hat and another boy ran past, slapping my hat even   5
harder.

"Straw katy!"

Again I picked up my hat and waited. The cry spread. Boys gathered around, pointing, chanting:

"Straw katy! Straw katy!"

I did not feel that I had been really challenged so far. No particular boy had stood his ground and taunted me. I was hoping that the teasing would cease, and tomorrow I would leave my straw hat at home. But the boy who had begun the game came close.

"Mama bought me a straw hat," he sneered.   10

"Watch what you're saying," I warned him.

"Oh, look! He talks!" the boy said.

The crowd howled with laughter, waiting, hoping.

"Where you from?" the boy asked me.

"None of your business," I said.   15

"Now, look, don't you go and get sassy, or I'll cut you down," he said.

"I'll say what I please," I said.

The boy picked up a tiny rock and put it on his shoulder and walked close again.

"Knock it off," he invited me.

I hesitated for a moment, then acted. I brushed the rock from his   20
shoulder and ducked and grabbed him about the legs and dumped him to the ground. A volcano of screams erupted from the crowd. I jumped upon the fallen boy and started pounding him. Then I was jerked up. Another boy had begun to fight me. My straw hat had been totally crushed and forgotten.

"Don't you hit my brother!" the new boy yelled.

"Two fighting one ain't fair!" I yelled.

Both of them now closed in on me. A blow landed on the back of my head. I turned and saw a brick rolling away and I felt blood oozing down my back. I looked around and saw several brickbats scattered about. I scooped up a handful. The two boys backed away. I took aim as they circled me; I made a motion as if to throw and one of the boys turned and ran. I let go with the brick and caught him in the middle of his back. He screamed. I chased the other halfway around the schoolyard. The boys howled their delight; they crowded around me, telling me that I had fought with two bullies. Then suddenly the crowd quieted and parted. I saw a woman teacher bearing down upon me. I dabbed at the blood on my neck.

"Was it you who threw that brick?" she asked.

"Two boys were fighting me," I told her.   *25*

"Come," she said, taking my hand.

I entered school escorted by the teacher, under arrest. I was taken to a room and confronted with the two brothers.

"Are these the boys?" she asked.

"Both of 'em fought me," I said. "I had to fight back."

"He hit me first!" one brother yelled.   *30*

"You're lying!" I yelled back.

"Don't you use that language in here," the teacher said.

"But they're not telling the truth," I said, "I'm new here and they tore up my hat."

"He hit me first," the boy said again.

I reached around the teacher, who stood between us, and smacked the   *35* boy. He screamed and started at me. The teacher grabbed us.

"The very idea of you!" the teacher shouted at me. "You are trying to fight right in school! What's the matter with you?"

"He is not telling you the truth," I maintained.

She ordered me to sit down; I did, but kept my eyes on the two brothers. The teacher dragged them out of the room and I sat until she returned.

"I'm in a good mind not to let you off this time," she said.

"It wasn't my fault," I said.   *40*

"I know. But you hit one of those boys right in here," she said.

"I'm sorry."

She asked me my name and sent me to a room. For a reason I could not understand, I was assigned to the fifth grade. Would they detect that I did not belong there? I sat and waited. When I was asked my age I called it out and was accepted.

I studied night and day and within two weeks I was promoted to the sixth grade. Overjoyed, I ran home and babbled the news. The family had not thought it possible. How could a bad, bad boy do that? I told the family emphatically that I was going to study medicine, engage in research, make discoveries. Flushed with success, I had not given a second's thought to how I would pay my way through a medical school. But since I had leaped a grade in two weeks, anything seemed possible, simple, easy.

I was now with boys and girls who were studying, fighting, talking. It   *45* revitalized my being, whipped my senses to a high, keen pitch of receptivity. I knew that my life was revolving about a world that I had to encounter and fight when I grew up. Suddenly the future loomed tangibly for me, as tangible as a future can loom for a black boy in Mississippi.

Most of my schoolmates worked mornings, evenings, and Saturdays.

They earned enough to buy their clothes and books, and they had money in their pockets at school. To see a boy go into a grocery store at noon recess and let his eyes roam over filled shelves and pick out what he wanted—even a dime's worth—was a hairbreadth short of a miracle to me. But when I broached the idea of my working to Granny, she would have none of it; she laid down the injunction that I could not work on Saturdays while I slept under her roof. I argued that Saturdays were the only days on which I could earn any worthwhile sum, and Granny looked me straight in the eyes and adamantly quoted Scripture:

But the seventh day is the sabbath of the Lord thy God: in it thou shalt not do any work, thou, nor thy son, nor thy daughter, nor thy manservant, nor thy maidservant, nor thine ox, nor thine ass, nor any of thy cattle, nor thy stranger that is within thy gates; that thy manservant and thy maidservant may rest as well as thou . . .

And that was the final word. Though we lived just on the borders of actual starvation, I could not bribe Granny with a promise of half or two-thirds of my salary. Her answer was no and never. Her refusal wrought me up to a high pitch of nervousness and I cursed myself for being made to live a different and crazy life. I told Granny that she was not responsible for my soul, and she replied that I was a minor, that my soul's fate rested in her hands, that I had no word to say in the matter.

To protect myself against pointed questions about my home and my life, to avoid being invited out when I knew that I could not accept, I was reserved with the boys and girls at school, seeking their company but never letting them guess how much I was being kept out of the world in which they lived, valuing their casual friendships but hiding it, acutely self-conscious but covering it with a quick smile and a ready phrase. Each day at noon I would follow the boys and girls into the corner store and stand against a wall and watch them buy sandwiches, and when they would ask me: "Why don't you eat a lunch?" I would answer with a shrug of my shoulders: "Aw, I'm not hungry at noon, ever." And I would swallow my saliva as I saw them split open loaves of bread and line them with juicy sardines. Again and again I vowed that someday I would end this hunger of mine, this apartness, this eternal difference; and I did not suspect that I would never get intimately into their lives, that I was doomed to live with them but not of them, that I had my own strange and separate road, a road which in later years would make them wonder how I had come to tread it.

I now saw a world leap to life before my eyes because I could explore it, and that meant not going home when school was out, but wandering, watching, asking, talking. Had I gone home to eat my plate of greens, Granny would not have allowed me out again, so the penalty I paid for roaming was to forfeit my food for twelve hours. I would eat mush at eight in the morning and greens at seven or later at night. To starve in order to learn about my environment was irrational, but so were my hungers. With my books slung over my shoulder, I would tramp with a gang into the woods, to rivers, to creeks, into the business district, to the doors of pool-rooms, into the movies when we could slip in without paying, to neighbor-hood ball games, to brick kilns, to lumberyards, to cottonseed mills to watch men work. There were hours when hunger would make me weak, would make me sway while walking, would make my heart give a sudden wild spurt of beating that would shake my body and make me breathless; but the happiness of being free would lift me beyond hunger, would enable me to discipline the sensations of my body to the extent that I could temporarily forget. . . .

As summer waned I obtained a strange job. Our next-door neighbor, a   *50* janitor, decided to change his profession and become an insurance agent. He was handicapped by illiteracy and he offered me the job of accompanying him on trips into the delta plantation area to write and figure for him, at wages of five dollars a week. I made several trips with Brother Mance, as he was called, to plantation shacks, sleeping on shuck mattresses, eating salt pork and black-eyed peas for breakfast, dinner, and supper; and drinking, for once, all the milk I wanted.

I had all but forgotten that I had been born on a plantation and I was astonished at the ignorance of the children I met. I had been pitying myself for not having books to read, and now I saw children who had never read a book. Their chronic shyness made me seem bold and city-wise. A black mother would try to lure her brood into the room to shake hands with me and they would linger at the jamb of the door, peering at me with one eye, giggling hysterically. At night, seated at a crude table, with a kerosene lamp spluttering at my elbow, I would fill out insurance applications, and a share-cropper family, fresh from laboring in the fields, would stand and gape. Brother Mance would pace the floor, extolling my abilities with pen and paper. Many of the naïve black families bought their insurance from us because they felt that they were connecting themselves with something that would make their children "write 'n speak lak dat pretty boy from Jackson." . . .

I returned home with a pocketful of money that melted into the bot-tomless hunger of the household. My mother was proud; even Aunt Addie's hostility melted temporarily. To Granny, I had accomplished a miracle and some of my sinful qualities evaporated, for she felt that success spelled the reward of righteousness and that failure was the wages of sin. But God called Brother Mance to heaven that winter and, since the insurance company would not accept a minor as an agent, my status reverted to a worldly one. The holy household was still burdened with a wayward boy to whom, in spite of all, sin somehow insisted upon clinging.

School opened and I began the seventh grade. My old hunger was still with me and I lived on what I did not eat. Perhaps the sunshine, the fresh air, and the pot liquor from greens kept me going. Of an evening I would sit in my room reading, and suddenly I would become aware of smelling meat frying in a neighbor's kitchen and would wonder what it was like to eat as much meat as one wanted. My mind would drift into a fantasy and I would imagine myself a son in a family that had meat on the table at each meal; then I would become disgusted with my futile daydreams and would rise and shut the window to bar the torturing scent of meat.

When I came downstairs one morning and went into the dining room for my bowl of mush and lard gravy I felt at once that something serious was happening in the family. Grandpa, as usual, was not at the table; he always had his meals in his room. Granny nodded me to my seat; I sat and bowed my head. From under my brows I saw my mother's tight face. Aunt Addie's eyes were closed, her forehead furrowed, her lips trembling. Granny buried her face in her hands. I wanted to ask what had happened, but I knew that I would not get an answer.

Granny prayed and invoked the blessings of God for each of us, asking   55
Him to guide us if it was His will, and then she told God that "my poor old husband lies sick this beautiful morning" and asked God, if it was His will, to heal him. That was how I learned of Grandpa's final illness. On many occasions I learned of some event, a death, a birth, or an impending visit, some happening in the neighborhood, at her church, or at some relative's home, first through Granny's informative prayers at the breakfast or dinner table.

Grandpa was a tall, black, lean man with a long face, snow-white teeth, and a head of woolly white hair. In anger he bared his teeth—a habit, Granny said, that he had formed while fighting in the trenches of the Civil War— and hissed, while his fists would clench until the veins swelled. In his rare laughs he bared his teeth in the same way, only now his teeth did not flash long and his body was relaxed. Grandpa owned a sharp pocketknife—which I had been forbidden to touch—and sat for long hours in the sun, whittling, whistling quietly, or maybe, if he was feeling well, humming some strange tune.

I had often tried to ask him about the Civil War, how he had fought, how he had felt, had he seen Lincoln, but he would never respond.

"You, git 'way from me, you young'un," was all that he would ever say.

From Granny I learned—over a course of years—that he had been wounded in the Civil War and had never received his disability pension, a fact which he hugged close to his heart with bitterness. I never heard him speak of white people; I think he hated them too much to talk of them. In the process of being discharged from the Union Army, he had gone to a white officer to seek help in filling out his papers. In filling out the papers, the white officer misspelled Grandpa's name, making him Richard Vinson instead of Richard Wilson. It was possible that Grandpa's southern accent and his illiteracy made him mispronounce his own name. It was rumored that the white officer had been a Swede and had had a poor knowledge of English. Another rumor had it that the white officer had been a Southerner and had deliberately falsified Grandpa's papers. Anyway, Grandpa did not discover that he had been discharged in the name of Richard Vinson until years later; and when he applied to the War Department for a pension, no trace could be found of his ever having served in the Union Army under the name of Richard Wilson.

I asked endless questions about Grandpa's pension, but information was   *60* always denied me on the grounds that I was too young to know what was involved. For decades a long correspondence took place between Grandpa and the War Department; in letter after letter Grandpa would recount events and conversations (always dictating these long accounts to others); he would name persons long dead, citing their ages and descriptions, reconstructing battles in which he had fought, naming towns, rivers, creeks, roads, cities, villages, citing the names and numbers of regiments and companies with which he had fought, giving the exact day and the exact hour of the day of certain occurrences, and send it all to the War Department in Washington.

I used to get the mail early in the morning and whenever there was a long, businesslike envelope in the stack, I would know that Grandpa had got an answer from the War Department and I would run upstairs with it. Grandpa would lift his head from the pillow, take the letter from me and open it himself. He would stare at the black print for a long time, then reluctantly, distrustfully hand the letter to me.

"Well?" he would say.

And I would read him the letter—reading slowly and pronouncing each word with extreme care—telling him that his claims for a pension had not been substantiated and that his application had been rejected. Grandpa would not blink an eye, then he would curse softly under his breath.

"It's them rebels," he would hiss.

As though doubting what I had read, he would dress up and take the   *65* letter to at least a dozen of his friends in the neighborhood and ask them to read it to him; finally he would know it from memory. At last he would put the letter away carefully and begin his brooding again, trying to recall out of his past some telling fact that might help him get his pension. Like "K" of Kafka's novel, *The Castle,* he tried desperately to persuade the authorities of his true identity right up to the day of his death, and failed.

Often, when there was no food in the house, I would dream of the Government's sending a letter that would read something like this:

Dear Sir:

   Your claim for a pension has been verified. The matter of your name has been satisfactorily cleared up. In accordance with official regulations, we are hereby instructing the Secretary of the Treasury to compile and compute and send to you, as soon as it is convenient, the total amount of all moneys past due, together with interest, for the past— years, the amount being $——.

   We regret profoundly that you have been so long delayed in this matter. You may be assured that your sacrifice has been a boon and a solace to your country.

But no letter like that ever came, and Grandpa was so sullen most of the time that I stopped dreaming of him and his hopes. Whenever he walked into my presence I became silent, waiting for him to speak, wondering if he were going to unbraid me for something. I would relax when he left. My will to talk to him gradually died. . . .

I came in from school one afternoon and Aunt Addie met me in the hallway. Her face was trembling and her eyes were red.

"Go upstairs and say good-bye to your grandpa," she said.

"What's happened?"

She did not answer. I ran upstairs and was met by Uncle Clark, who had come from Greenwood. Granny caught my hand.

"Come and say good-bye to your grandpa," she said.

She led me to Grandpa's room; he was lying fully dressed upon the bed, looking as well as he ever looked. His eyes were open, but he was so still that I did not know if he was dead or alive.

"Papa, here's Richard," Granny said softly.

Grandpa looked at me, flashed his white teeth for a fraction of a second.

"Good-bye, grandpa," I whispered.

"Good-bye, son," he spoke hoarsely. "Rejoice, for God has picked out my s-s-e . . . in-in h-heaven . . ."

His voice died. I had not understood what he had said and I wondered if I should ask him to repeat it. But Granny took my hand and led me from the room. The house was quiet; there was no crying. My mother sat silent in her rocking chair, staring out the window; now and then she would lower her face to her hands. Granny and Aunt Addie moved silently about the house. I sat mute, waiting for Grandpa to die. I was still puzzled about what he had tried to say to me. It seemed important that I should understand his final words. I followed Granny into the kitchen.

"Granny, what did Grandpa say? I didn't quite hear him," I whispered.

She whirled and gave me one of her backhanded slaps across my mouth.

"Shut up! The angel of death's in the house!"

"I just wanted to know," I said, nursing my bruised lips.

She looked at me and relented.

"He said that God had picked out his seat in heaven," she said. "Now you know. So sit down and quit asking fool questions."

When I awakened the next morning my mother told me that Grandpa had "gone home."

"Get on your hat and coat," Granny said.

"What do you want me to do?" I asked.

"Quit asking questions and do what you are told," she said.

I dressed for the outdoors.

"Go to Tom and tell him that Papa's gone home. Ask him to come here and take charge of things," Granny said.

Tom, her eldest son, had recently moved from Hazelhurst to Jackson and lived near the outskirts of town. Feeling that I was bearing an important message, I ran every inch of the two miles; I thought that news of a death should be told at once. I came in sight of my uncle's house with a heaving chest; I bounded up the steps and rapped on the door. My little cousin, Maggie, opened the door.

"Where's Uncle Tom?" I asked.

"He's sleeping," she said.

I ran into his room, went to his bed, and shook him.

"Uncle Tom, Granny says to come at once. Grandpa's dead," I panted.

He stared at me a long time.   *95*

"You certainly are a prize fool," he said quietly. "Don't you know that that's no way to tell a person that his father's dead?"

I stared at him, baffled, panting.

"I ran all the way out here," I gasped. "I'm out of breath. I'm sorry."

He rose slowly and began to dress, ignoring me; he did not utter a word for five minutes.

"What're you waiting for?" he asked me.   *100*

"Nothing," I said.

I walked home slowly, asking myself what on earth was the matter with me, why it was I never seemed to do things as people expected them to be done. Every word and gesture I made seemed to provoke hostility. I had never been able to talk to others, and I had to guess at their meanings and motives. I had not intentionally tried to shock Uncle Tom, and yet his anger at me seemed to outweigh his sorrow for his father. Finding no answer, I told myself that I was a fool to worry about it, that no matter what I did I would be wrong somehow as far as my family was concerned.

I was not allowed to go to Grandpa's funeral; I was ordered to stay home "and mind the house." I sat reading detective stories until the family returned from the graveyard. They told me nothing and I asked no questions. The routine of the house flowed on as usual. For me there was sleep, mush, greens, school, study, loneliness, yearning, and then sleep again.

My clothing became so shabby that I was ashamed to go to school. Many of the boys in my class were wearing their first long-pants suits. I grew so bitter that I decided to have it out with Granny; I would tell her that if she did not let me work on Saturdays, I would leave home. But when I opened the subject, she would not listen. I followed her about the house, demanding the right to work on Saturday. Her answer was no and no and no.

"Then I'll quit school," I declared.   *105*

"Quit then. See how much I care," she said.

"I'll go away from here and you'll never hear from me!"

"No, you won't," she said tauntingly.

"How can I ever learn enough to get a job?" I asked her, switching my tactics. I showed her my ragged stockings, my patched pants. "Look, I won't go to school like this! I'm not asking you for money or to do anything. I only want to work!"

"I have nothing to do with whether you go to school or not," she said. *110*
"You left the church and you are on your own. You are with the world.
You're dead to me, dead to Christ."

"That old church of yours is messing up my life," I said.

"Don't you say that in his house!"

"It's true and you know it!"

"God's punishing you," she said. "And you're too proud to ask Him
for help."

"I'm going to get a job anyway." *115*

"Then you can't live here," she said.

"Then I'll leave," I countered, trembling violently.

"You won't leave," she repeated.

"You think I'm joking, don't you?" I asked, determined to make her
know how I felt. "I'll leave this minute!"

I ran to my room, got a battered suitcase, and began packing my ragged *120*
clothes. I did not have a penny, but I was going to leave. She came to
the door.

"You little fool! Put that suitcase down!"

"I'm going where I can work!"

She snatched the suitcase out of my hands; she was trembling.

"All right," she said. "If you want to go to hell, then go. But God'll
know that it was not my fault. He'll forgive me, but He won't forgive you."

Weeping, she rushed from the door. Her humanity had triumphed over *125*
her fear. I emptied the suitcase, feeling spent. I hated these emotional out-
bursts, these tempests of passion, because they always left me tense and weak.
Now I was truly dead to Granny and Aunt Addie, but my mother smiled
when I told her that I had defied them. She rose and hobbled to me on her
paralytic legs and kissed me.

The Responsive Reader

1. During his first day at the new school, what is the narrator's experience
   with injustice? Is there something about this brush with injustice that
   makes it similar to experiences many other young people are likely to
   have encountered?

2. What made the first job important to the boy? How did this experience compare with his experiences at school? How do you think it
   changed his outlook or affected him as a person?

3. Many black writers have written about the heritage of bitterness
   against the white world that they saw as the birthright of every black
   American. What is the story of the narrator's grandfather? How did his
   grievance against the army color the setting in which the boy found
   himself?

4. What is the basic conflict between the boy and his strict religious
   relatives? What is the story of the climactic final confrontation? What
   is the outcome? What do you think was the lasting effect on the boy?

Thinking, Talking, Writing

5. Among the formative influences that shape a person's personality, psychologists and sociologists debate the relative importance of the individual (or the person's character), the family environment, and the larger society. What is the role and relative importance of each of these in Wright's account?

6. Have you ever resisted the pressure to conform? Do you yourself have a story about a first defiance of authority? Have you ever rebelled against oppressive rules, customs, or traditions?

Collaborative Projects

7. Richard Wright is still one of the most widely known and most widely discussed African American writers here and abroad. Working with a group, you may want to study his reputation and influence as reflected in critical discussions of his work and in new editions of his books.

THE ONES WHO WALK AWAY FROM OMELAS:
Variations on a theme by William James

Ursula K. Le Guin

Ursula K. Le Guin is an essayist, novelist, and science fiction writer who has raised a strongly individual voice in support of causes she cherishes: her love of the land, her engagement for the environment, her support for Native American culture, her anger at censors and anti-abortionists. She has spoken and written eloquently about empowering the unheard. She has urged women to find their own language, saying that in a male-dominated society "when women speak truly they speak subversively—they can't help it: if you're underneath, if you're kept down, you break out, you subvert." Her essays and speeches were collected in Dancing at the Edge of the World *in 1989.*

Born in Berkeley, California, and educated at Radcliffe and Columbia, Le Guin is best known as the author of the Earthsea *Trilogy (1968–1972) and other science fiction books and stories. Her science fiction does without space age gadgetry and alien invaders but instead takes us out of our daily routine to make us ponder basic human needs and dilemmas. The following story at first seems to take us to utopia—an ideal future society where war, unhappiness, and misery have disappeared. However, individuality and dissent have also disappeared, and only a few misfits or outsiders depart from the norm.*

With a clamor of bells that set the swallows soaring, the Festival of Summer came to the city Omelas, bright-towered by the sea. The rigging of the boats in harbor sparkled with flags. In the streets between houses with red roofs and painted walls, between old moss-grown gardens and under avenues of trees, past great parks and public buildings, processions moved. Some were decorous: old people in long stiff robes of mauve and grey, grave master workmen, quiet, merry women carrying their babies and chatting as they walked. In other streets the music beat faster, a shimmering of gong and tambourine, and the people went dancing, the procession was a dance. Children dodged in and out, their high calls rising like the swallows' crossing flights over the music and the singing. All the processions wound toward the north side of the city, where on the great water-meadow called the Green Fields boys and girls, naked in the bright air, with mud-stained feet and ankles and long, lithe arms, exercised their restive horses before the race. The horses wore no gear at all but a halter without bit. Their manes were braided with streamers of silver, gold, and green. They flared their nostrils and pranced and boasted to one another; they were vastly excited, the horse being the only animal who has adopted our ceremonies as his own. Far off to the north and west the mountains stood up half encircling Omelas on her bay. The air of morning was so clear that the snow still crowning the Eighteen Peaks burned with white-gold fire across the miles of sunlit air, under the dark blue of the sky. There was just enough wind to make the banners that marked the racecourse snap and flutter now and then. In the silence of the broad green meadows one could hear the music winding through the city streets, farther and nearer and ever approaching, a cheerful faint sweetness of the air that from time to time trembled and gathered together and broke out into the great joyous clanging of the bells.

Joyous! How is one to tell about joy? How describe the citizens of Omelas?

They were not simple folk, you see, though they were happy. But we do not say the words of cheer much any more. All smiles have become archaic. Given a description such as this one tends to make certain assumptions. Given a description such as this one tends to look next for the King, mounted on a splendid stallion and surrounded by his noble knights, or perhaps in a golden litter borne by great-muscled slaves. But there was no king. They did not use swords, or keep slaves. They were not barbarians. I do not know the rules and laws of their society, but I suspect that they were singularly few. As they did without monarchy and slavery, so they also got on without the stock exchange, the advertisement, the secret police, and the bomb. Yet I repeat that these were not simple folk, nor dulcet shepherds, noble savages, bland utopians. They were not less complex than us. The trouble is that we have a bad habit, encouraged by pedants and sophisticates, of considering happiness as something rather stupid. Only pain is intellectual, only evil interesting. This is the treason of the artist: a refusal to admit the banality of evil and the terrible boredom of pain. If you can't lick 'em, join 'em. If it hurts, repeat it. But to praise despair is to condemn delight, to embrace violence is to lose hold of everything else. We have almost lost hold, we can no longer describe a happy man, nor make any celebration of joy. How can I tell you about the people of Omelas? They were not naïve and happy children—though their children were, in fact, happy. They were mature, intelligent, passionate adults whose lives were not wretched. O miracle! but I wish I could describe it better. I wish I could convince you. Omelas sounds in my words like a city in a fairy tale, long ago and far away, once upon a time. Perhaps it would be best if you imagined it as your own fancy bids, assuming it will rise to the occasion, for certainly I cannot suit you all. For instance, how about technology? I think that there would be no cars or helicopters in and above the streets; this follows from the fact that the people of Omelas are happy people. Happiness is based on a just discrimination of what is necessary, what is neither necessary nor destructive, and what is destructive. In the middle category, however—that of the unnecessary but undestructive, that of comfort, luxury, exuberance, etc.—they could perfectly well have central heating, subway trains, washing machines, and all kinds of marvelous devices not yet invented here, floating light-sources, fuelless power, a cure for the common cold. Or they could have none of that: it doesn't matter. As you like it. I incline to think that people from towns up and down the coast have been coming in to Omelas during the last days before the Festival on very fast little trains and double-decked trams, and that the train station of Omelas is actually the handsomest building in town, though plainer than the magnificent Farmers' Market. But even granted trains, I fear that Omelas so far strikes some of you as goody-goody. Smiles, bells, parades, horses, bleh. If so, please add an orgy. If an orgy would help, don't hesitate. Let us not, however, have temples from which issue beautiful nude priests and priestesses already half in ecstasy and ready to copulate with any man or woman, lover or stranger, who desires union with the deep godhead of the blood, although that was my first idea. But really it would be better not to have any temples in Omelas—at least, not manned temples. Religion yes, clergy no. Surely the beautiful nudes can just wander about, offering themselves like divine soufflés to the hunger of the needy and the rapture of the flesh. Let them join the processions. Let tambourines be struck above the copulations, and the glory of desire be proclaimed upon the gongs, and (a not unimportant point) let the offspring of these delightful rituals be beloved and looked after by all. One thing I know there is none of in Omelas is guilt. But what else should there be? I thought at first there were no drugs, but that is puritanical. For those who like it, the faint insistent sweetness of *drooz* may perfume the ways of the city, *drooz* which first brings a great lightness and brilliance to the mind and limbs, and then after some hours a dreamy languor, and wonderful visions at last of the very arcana and inmost secrets of the Universe, as well as exciting the pleasure of sex beyond all belief; and it is not habit-forming. For more modest tastes I think there ought to be beer. What else, what else belongs in the joyous city? The sense of victory, surely, the celebration of courage. But as we did without clergy, let us do without soldiers. The joy built upon successful slaughter is not the right kind of joy; it will not do; it is fearful and it is trivial. A boundless and generous contentment, a magnanimous triumph felt not against some outer enemy but in communion with the finest and fairest in the souls of all men everywhere and the splendor of the world's summer: this is what swells the hearts of the people of Omelas, and the victory they celebrate is that of life. I really don't think many of them need to take *drooz*.

Most of the procession have reached the Green Fields by now. A marvelous smell of cooking goes forth from the red and blue tents of the provisioners. The faces of small children are amiably sticky; in the benign grey beard of a man a couple of crumbs of rich pastry are entangled. The youths and girls have mounted their horses and are beginning to group around the starting line of the course. An old woman, small, fat, and laughing, is passing out flowers from a basket, and tall young men wear her flowers in their shining hair. A child of nine or ten sits at the edge of the crowd, alone, playing on a wooden flute. People pause to listen, and they smile, but they do not speak to him, for he never ceases playing and never sees them, his dark eyes wholly rapt in the sweet, thin magic of the tune.

He finishes, and slowly lowers his hands holding the wooden flute.   *5*

As if that little private silence were the signal, all at once a trumpet sounds from the pavilion near the starting line: imperious, melancholy, piercing. The horses rear on their slender legs, and some of them neigh in answer. Sober-faced, the young riders stroke the horses' necks and soothe them, whispering, "Quiet, quiet, there my beauty, my hope. . . ." They begin to form in rank along the starting line. The crowds along the racecourse are like a field of grass and flowers in the wind. The Festival of Summer has begun.

Do you believe? Do you accept the festival, the city, the joy? No? Then let me describe one more thing.

In a basement under one of the beautiful public buildings of Omelas, or perhaps in the cellar of one of its more spacious private homes, there is a room. It has one locked door, and no window. A little light seeps in dustily between cracks in the boards, secondhand from a cobwebbed window somewhere across the cellar. In one corner of the little room a couple of mops, with stiff, clotted, foul-smelling heads, stand near a rusty bucket. The floor is dirt, a little damp to the touch, as cellar dirt usually is. The room is about three paces long and two wide: a mere broom closet or disused tool room. In the room a child is sitting. It could be a boy or a girl. It looks about six, but actually is nearly ten. It is feeble-minded. Perhaps it was born defective, or perhaps it has become imbecile through fear, malnutrition, and neglect. It picks its nose and occasionally fumbles vaguely with its toes or genitals, as it sits hunched in the corner farthest from the bucket and the two mops. It is afraid of the mops. It finds them horrible. It shuts its eyes, but it knows the mops are still standing there; and the door is locked; and nobody will come. The door is always locked; and nobody ever comes, except that sometimes— the child has no understanding of time or interval—sometimes the door rattles terribly and opens, and a person, or several people, are there. One of them may come in and kick the child to make it stand up. The others never come close, but peer in at it with frightened, disgusted eyes. The food bowl and the water jug are hastily filled, the door is locked, the eyes disappear. The people at the door never say anything, but the child, who has not always lived in the tool room, and can remember sunlight and its mother's voice, sometimes speaks. "I will be good," it says. "Please let me out. I will be good!" They never answer. The child used to scream for help at night, and cry a good deal, but now it only makes a kind of whining "eh-haa, eh-haa," and it speaks less and less often. It is so thin there are no calves to its legs; its belly protrudes; it lives on a half-bowl of corn meal and grease a day. It is naked. Its buttocks and thighs are a mass of festered sores, as it sits in its own excrement continually.

They all know it is there, all the people of Omelas. Some of them have come to see it, others are content merely to know it is there. They all know that it has to be there. Some of them understand why, and some do not, but they all understand that their happiness, the beauty of their city, the tenderness of their friendships, the health of their children, the wisdom of their scholars, the skill of their makers, even the abundance of their harvest and the kindly weathers of their skies, depend wholly on this child's abominable misery.

This is usually explained to children when they are between eight and twelve, whenever they seem capable of understanding; and most of those who come to see the child are young people, though often enough an adult comes, or comes back, to see the child. No matter how well the matter has been explained to them, these young spectators are always shocked and sickened at the sight. They feel disgust, which they had thought themselves superior to. They feel anger, outrage, impotence, despite all the explanations. They would like to do something for the child. But there is nothing they can do. If the child were brought up into the sunlight out of the vile place, if it were cleaned and fed and comforted, that would be a good thing, indeed; but if it were done, in that day and hour all the prosperity and beauty and delight of Omelas would wither and be destroyed. Those are the terms. To exchange all the goodness and grace of every life in Omelas for that single, small improvement: to throw away the happiness of thousands for the chance of the happiness of one: that would be to let guilt within the walls indeed.

The terms are strict and absolute; there may not even be a kind word spoken to the child.

Often the young people go home in tears, or in a tearless rage, when they have seen the child and faced this terrible paradox. They may brood over it for weeks or years. But as time goes on they begin to realize that even if the child could be released, it would not get much good of its freedom: a little vague pleasure of warmth and food, no doubt, but little more. It is too degraded and imbecile to know any real joy. It has been afraid too long ever to be free of fear. Its habits are too uncouth for it to respond to humane treatment. Indeed, after so long it would probably be wretched without walls about it to protect it, and darkness for its eyes, and its own excrement to sit in. Their tears at the bitter injustice dry when they begin to perceive the terrible justice of reality, and to accept it. Yet it is their tears and anger, the trying of their generosity and the acceptance of their helplessness, which are perhaps the true source of the splendor of their lives. Theirs is no vapid, irresponsible happiness. They know that they, like the child, are not free. They know compassion. It is the existence of the child, and their knowledge of its existence, that makes possible the nobility of their architecture, the poignancy of their music, the profundity of their science. It is because of the child that they are so gentle with children. They know that if the wretched one were not there snivelling in the dark, the other one, the flute-player, could make no joyful music as the young riders line up in their beauty for the race in the sunlight of the first morning of summer.

Now do you believe in them? Are they not more credible? But there is one more thing to tell, and this is quite incredible.

At times one of the adolescent girls or boys who go to see the child does not go home to weep or rage, does not, in fact, go home at all. Sometimes also a man or woman much older falls silent for a day or two, and then leaves home. These people go out into the street, and walk down the street alone. They keep walking, and walk straight out of the city of Omelas, through the beautiful gates. They keep walking across the farmlands of Omelas. Each one goes alone, youth or girl, man or woman. Night falls; the traveler must pass down village streets, between the houses with yellow-lit windows, and on out into the darkness of the fields. Each alone, they go west or north, toward the mountains. They go on. They leave Omelas, they walk ahead into the darkness, and they do not come back. The place they go toward is a place even less imaginable to most of us than the city of happiness. I cannot describe it at all. It is possible that it does not exist. But they seem to know where they are going, the ones who walk away from Omelas.

The Responsive Reader

1. What makes Omelas a utopia of happiness and delight? What is the nature and spirit of its festivals? How would you describe the attitude of the people toward politics, technology, and drugs?
2. Why does Le Guin say that her readers should probably fill in the features of this Utopian society in accordance with their own desires?
3. Why is it crucial to this story that the people of Omelas do not have a sense of guilt?
4. What explanations are the young people of Omelas given for the treatment of the imprisoned child? How do the young people react to these explanations? How is the existence of the child supposedly related to the joy and beauty of their society? What does the child symbolize for you?
5. Who are the ones who walk away from Omelas? Do you think you would have been one of them? Why or why not?

Thinking, Talking, Writing

6. For you, was there anything wrong with the happy society of Omelas before you learned of the existence of the abused child? Did you think you could have been happy there? Is it a perfect society except for one basic flaw?
7. If you could design a happier society of the future, what features would it share with Omelas? What would be different?
8. Can you think of any parallels in the present or in the past to the few who walked away from Omelas?
9. Le Guin tells her readers that today we live in a society where it is considered unsophisticated to believe in happiness and where only evil and violence are considered interesting. Is she right?

A GOOD MAN IS HARD TO FIND

Flannery O'Connor

"The dragon is by the side of the road,
watching those who pass. Beware lest he
devour you. We go to the father of souls,

Born and educated in Georgia, Flannery O'Connor was a devout Catholic in the Baptist South. In the fifties and sixties, she published puzzling, disturbing, widely admired short stories populated by quirky individuals who refuse to fit into ready-made categories and stereotypes. Some of her most memorable characters are drifters, misfits, and loners outside the norms of polite society. They often verge on the freakish or grotesque, being frightening and comic at the same time. She once explained that to recognize the freakish element in humanity we had to have a conception of the whole and complete person intended by God—which would enable us to see how far we fell short.

O'Connor's outlook was affected by a long debilitating illness. She wrote from a devoutly religious perspective, and she chronicled the eccentricities and backslidings of her characters with the charity with which a priest might look on the antics of sinners. She often talked about redemption through divine love, although many of her readers failed to sense that promise in her actual stories.

Taking place in a deceptively everyday setting, O'Connor's stories often take a violent turn, with tensions building up to a climactic resolution. However, she never intended violence to be an end in itself. She once said, "It is the extreme situation that best reveals what we are essentially, and I believe these are the times when writers are more interested in what we are essentially than in the tenor of our daily lives." Alice Walker, author of The Color Purple, *said about O'Connor that "whether one 'understands' her stories or not, one knows her characters are new and wondrous creations in the world . . . After her great stories of sin, damnation, prophecy, and revelation, the stories one reads casually in the average magazine seem to be about love and roast beef."*

The grandmother didn't want to go to Florida. She wanted to visit some of her connections in east Tennessee and she was seizing every chance to change Bailey's mind. Bailey was the son she lived with, her only boy. He was sitting on the edge of his chair at the table, bent over the orange sports section of the *Journal*. "Now look here, Bailey," she said, "see here, read this," and she stood with one hand on her thin hip and the other rattling the newspaper at his bald head. "Here this fellow that calls himself The Misfit is aloose from the Federal Pen and headed toward Florida and you read here what it says he did to these people. Just you read it. I wouldn't take my children in any direction with a criminal like that aloose in it. I couldn't answer to my conscience if I did."

Bailey didn't look up from his reading so she wheeled around then and faced the children's mother; a young woman in slacks, whose face was as broad and innocent as a cabbage and was tied around with a green headkerchief that had two points on the top like rabbit's ears. She was sitting on the sofa, feeding the baby his apricots out of a jar. "The children have been to Florida before," the old lady said. "You all ought to take them somewhere else for a change so they would see different parts of the world and be broad. They never have been to east Tennessee."

The children's mother didn't seem to hear her, but the eight-year-old boy, John Wesley, a stocky child with glasses, said, "If you don't want to go to Florida, why dontcha stay at home?" He and the little girl, June Star, were reading the funny papers on the floor.

"She wouldn't stay at home to be queen for a day," June Star said without raising her yellow head.

"Yes, and what would you do if this fellow, The Misfit, caught you?"   5
the grandmother asked.

"I'd smack his face," John Wesley said.

"She wouldn't stay at home for a million bucks," June Star said. "Afraid she'd miss something. She has to go everywhere we go."

"All right, Miss," the grandmother said. "Just remember that the next time you want me to curl your hair."

June Star said her hair was naturally curly.

The next morning the grandmother was the first one in the car, ready   10
to go. She had her big black valise that looked like the head of a hippopotamus in one corner, and underneath it she was hiding a basket with Pitty Sing, the cat, in it. She didn't intend for the cat to be left alone in the house for three days because he would miss her too much and she was afraid he might brush against one of the gas burners and accidentally asphyxiate himself. Her son, Bailey, didn't like to arrive at a motel with a cat.

She sat in the middle of the back seat with John Wesley and June Star on either side of her. Bailey and the children's mother and the baby sat in the front and they left Atlanta at eight forty-five with the mileage on the car at 55890. The grandmother wrote this down because she thought it would be interesting to say how many miles they had been when they got back. It took them twenty minutes to reach the outskirts of the city.

The old lady settled herself comfortably, removing her white cotton gloves and putting them up with her purse on the shelf in front of the back window. The children's mother still had on slacks and still had her head tied up in a green kerchief, but the grandmother had on a navy blue straw sailor hat with a bunch of white violets on the brim and a navy blue dress with a small white dot in the print. Her collar and cuffs were white organdy trimmed with lace and at her neckline she had pinned a purple spray of cloth violets containing a sachet. In case of an accident, anyone seeing her dead on the highway would know at once that she was a lady.

She said she thought it was going to be a good day for driving, neither too hot nor too cold, and she cautioned Bailey that the speed limit was fifty-five miles an hour and that the patrolmen hid themselves behind billboards and small clumps of trees and sped out after you before you had a chance to slow down. She pointed out interesting details of the scenery: Stone Mountain; the blue granite that in some places came up to both sides of the highway; the brilliant red clay banks slightly streaked with purple; and the various crops that made rows of green lace-work on the ground. The trees were full of silver-white sunlights and the meanest of them sparkled. The children were reading comic magazines and their mother had gone back to sleep.

"Let's go through Georgia fast so we won't have to look at it much," John Wesley said.

"If I were a little boy," said the grandmother, "I wouldn't talk about my native state that way. Tennessee has the mountains and Georgia has the hills." 15

"Tennessee is just a hillbilly dumping ground," John Wesley said, "and Georgia is a lousy state too."

"You said it," June Star said.

"In my time," said the grandmother, folding her thin veined fingers, "children were more respectful of their native states and their parents and everything else. People did right then. Oh look at the cute little pickaninny!" she said and pointed to a Negro child standing in the door of a shack. "Wouldn't that make a picture, now?" she asked and they all turned and looked at the little Negro out of the back window. He waved.

"He didn't have any britches on," June Star said.

"He probably didn't have any," the grandmother explained. "Little niggers in the country don't have things like we do. If I could paint, I'd paint that picture," she said. 20

The children exchanged comic books.

The grandmother offered to hold the baby and the children's mother passed him over the front seat to her. She set him on her knee and bounced him and told him about the things they were passing. She rolled her eyes and screwed up her mouth and stuck her leathery thin face into his smooth bland one. Occasionally he gave her a faraway smile. They passed a large cotton field with five or six graves fenced in the middle of it, like a small island. "Look at the graveyard!" the grandmother said, pointing it out. "That was the old family burying ground. That belonged to the plantation."

"Where's the plantation?" John Wesley asked.

"Gone With the Wind," said the grandmother. "Ha. Ha."

When the children finished all the comic books they had brought, they opened the lunch and ate it. The grandmother ate a peanut butter sandwich and an olive and would not let the children throw the box and the paper napkins out the window. When there was nothing else to do they played a game by choosing a cloud and making the other two guess what shape it suggested. John Wesley took one the shape of a cow and June Star guessed a cow and John Wesley said, no, an automobile, and June Star said he didn't play fair, and they began to slap each other over the grandmother. 25

The grandmother said she would tell them a story if they would keep quiet. When she told a story, she rolled her eyes and waved her head and was very dramatic. She said once when she was a maiden lady she had been courted by a Mr. Edgar Atkins Teagarden from Jasper, Georgia. She said he was a very good-looking man and a gentleman and that he brought her a watermelon every Saturday afternoon with his initials cut in it, E.A.T. Well, one Saturday, she said, Mr. Teagarden brought the watermelon and there was nobody at home and he left it on the front porch and returned in his buggy to Jasper, but she never got the watermelon, she said, because a nigger boy ate it when he saw the initials, E.A.T.! This story tickled John Wesley's funny bone and he giggled and giggled but June Star didn't think it was any good. She said she wouldn't marry a man that just brought her a watermelon on Saturday. The grandmother said she would have done well to marry Mr. Teagarden because he was a gentleman and had bought Coca-Cola stock when it first came out and that he had died only a few years ago, a very wealthy man.

They stopped at The Tower for barbecued sandwiches. The Tower was a part-stucco and part-wood filling station and dance hall set in a clearing outside of Timothy. A fat man named Red Sammy Butts ran it and there were signs stuck here and there on the building and for miles up and down the highway saying, TRY RED SAMMY'S FAMOUS BARBECUE. NONE LIKE FAMOUS RED SAMMY'S! RED SAM! THE FAT BOY WITH THE HAPPY LAUGH. A VETERAN! RED SAMMY'S YOUR MAN!

Red Sammy was lying on the bare ground outside The Tower with his head under a truck while a gray monkey about a foot high, chained to a small chinaberry tree, chattered nearby. The monkey sprang back into the tree and got on the highest limb as soon as he saw the children jump out of the car and run toward him.

Inside, The Tower was a long dark room with a counter at one end and tables at the other and dancing space in the middle. They all sat down at a broad table next to the nickelodeon and Red Sam's wife, a tall burnt-brown woman with hair and eyes lighter than her skin, came and took their order. The children's mother put a dime in the machine and played "The Tennessee Waltz," and the grandmother said that tune always made her want to dance. She asked Bailey if he would like to dance but he only glared at her. He didn't have a naturally sunny disposition like she did and trips made him nervous. The grandmother's brown eyes were very bright. She swayed her head from side to side and pretended she was dancing in her chair. June Star said play something she could tap to so the children's mother put in another dime and played a fast number and June Star stepped out onto the dance floor and did her tap routine.

"Ain't she cute?" Red Sam's wife said, leaning over the counter. "Would you like to come be my little girl?" 30

"No, I certainly wouldn't," June Star said. "I wouldn't live in a broken-down place like this for a million bucks!" and she ran back to the table.

"Ain't she cute?" the woman repeated, stretching her mouth politely.

"Aren't you ashamed?" hissed the grandmother.

Red Sam came in and told his wife to quit lounging on the counter and hurry up with these people's order. His khaki trousers reached just to his hip bones and his stomach hung over them like a sack of meal swaying under his shirt. He came over and sat down at a table nearby and let out a combination sigh and yodel. "You can't win," he said. "You can't win," and he wiped his sweating red face off with a gray handkerchief. "These days you don't know who to trust," he said. "Ain't that the truth?"

"People are certainly not nice like they used to be," said the grandmother. 35

"Two fellers come in here last week," Red Sammy said, "driving a Chrysler. It was an old beat-up car but it was a good one and these boys looked all right to me. Said they worked at the mill and you know I let them fellers charge the gas they bought? Now why did I do that?"

"Because you're a good man!" the grandmother said at once.

"Yes'm, I suppose so," Red Sam said as if he were struck with this answer.

His wife brought the orders, carrying the five plates all at once without a tray, two in each hand and one balanced on her arm. "It isn't a soul in this green world of God's that you can trust," she said. "And I don't count nobody out of that, not nobody," she repeated, looking at Red Sammy.

"Did you read about that criminal, The Misfit, that's escaped?" asked 40 the grandmother.

"I wouldn't be a bit surprised if he didn't attack this place right here," said the woman. "If he hears about it being here, I wouldn't be none surprised to see him. If he hears it's two cent in the cash register, I wouldn't be a tall surprised if he . . ."

"That'll do," Red Sam said. "Go bring these people their Co'-Colas," and the woman went off to get the rest of the order.

"A good man is hard to find," Red Sammy said. "Everything is getting terrible. I remember the day you could go off and leave your screen door unlatched. Not no more."

He and the grandmother discussed better times. The old lady said that in her opinion Europe was entirely to blame for the way things were now. She said the way Europe acted you would think we were made of money and Red Sam said it was no use talking about it, she was exactly right. The children ran outside into the white sunlight and looked at the monkey in the lacy chinaberry tree. He was busy catching fleas on himself and biting each one carefully between his teeth as if it were a delicacy.

They drove off again into the hot afternoon. The grandmother took 45 cat naps and woke up every few minutes with her own snoring. Outside of Toombsboro she woke up and recalled an old plantation that she had visited in this neighborhood once when she was a young lady. She said the house had six white columns across the front and that there was an avenue of oaks leading up to it and two little wooden trellis arbors on either side in front where you sat down with your suitor after a stroll in the garden. She recalled exactly which road to turn off to get to it. She knew that Bailey would not be willing to lose any time looking at an old house, but the more she talked about it, the more she wanted to see it once again and find out if the little twin arbors were still standing. "There was a secret panel in this house," she said craftily, not telling the truth but wishing that she were, "and the story went that all the family silver was hidden in it when Sherman came through but it was never found . . ."

"Hey!" John Wesley said. "Let's go see it! We'll find it! We'll poke all the woodwork and find it! Who lives there? Where do you turn off at? Hey Pop, can't we turn off there?"

"We never have seen a house with a secret panel!" June Star shrieked. "Let's go to the house with the secret panel! Hey, Pop, can't we go see the house with the secret panel!"

"It's not far from here, I know," the grandmother said. "It wouldn't take over twenty minutes."

Bailey was looking straight ahead. His jaw was as rigid as a horseshoe. "No," he said.

The children began to yell and scream that they wanted to see the *50* house with the secret panel. John Wesley kicked the back of the front seat and June Star hung over her mother's shoulder and whined desperately into her ear that they never had any fun even on their vacation, that they could never do what THEY wanted to do. The baby began to scream and John Wesley kicked the back of the seat so hard that his father could feel the blows in his kidney.

"All right!" he shouted and drew the car to a stop at the side of the road. "Will you all shut up? Will you all just shut up for one second? If you don't shut up, we won't go anywhere."

"It would be very educational for them," the grandmother murmured.

"All right," Bailey said, "but get this. This is the only time we're going to stop for anything like this. This is the one and only time."

"The dirt road that you have to turn down is about a mile back," the grandmother directed. "I marked it when we passed."

"A dirt road," Bailey groaned. *55*

After they had turned around and were headed toward the dirt road, the grandmother recalled other points about the house, the beautiful glass over the front doorway and the candle lamp in the hall. John Wesley said that the secret panel was probably in the fireplace.

"You can't go inside this house," Bailey said. "You don't know who lives there."

"While you all talk to the people in front, I'll run around behind and get in a window," John Wesley suggested.

"We'll all stay in the car," his mother said.

They turned onto the dirt road and the car raced roughly along in a *60* swirl of pink dust. The grandmother recalled the times when there were no paved roads and thirty miles was a day's journey. The dirt road was hilly and there were sudden washes in it and sharp curves on dangerous embankments. All at once they would be on a hill, looking down over the blue tops of trees for miles around, then the next minute, they would be in a red depression with the dust-coated trees looking down on them.

"This place had better turn up in a minute," Bailey said, "or I'm going to turn around."

The road looked as if no one had traveled on it in months.

"It's not much farther," the grandmother said and just as she said it, a horrible thought came to her. The thought was so embarrassing that she turned red in the face and her eyes dilated and her feet jumped up, upsetting her valise in the corner. The instant the valise moved, the newspaper top she had over the basket under it rose with a snarl and Pitty Sing, the cat, sprang onto Bailey's shoulder.

The children were thrown to the floor and their mother, clutching the baby, was thrown out the door onto the ground; the old lady was thrown into the front seat. The car turned over once and landed right-side-up in a gulch on the side of the road. Bailey remained in the driver's seat with the cat—gray-striped with a broad white face and an orange nose—clinging to his neck like a caterpillar.

As soon as the children saw they could move their arms and legs, they scrambled out of the car, shouting, "We've had an ACCIDENT!" The grandmother was curled up under the dashboard, hoping she was injured so that Bailey's wrath would not come down on her all at once. The horrible thought she had had before the accident was that the house she had remembered so vividly was not in Georgia but in Tennessee.

Bailey removed the cat from his neck with both hands and flung it out the window against the side of a pine tree. Then he got out of the car and started looking for the children's mother. She was sitting against the side of the red gutted ditch, holding the screaming baby, but she only had a cut down her face and a broken shoulder. "We've had an ACCIDENT!" the children screamed in a frenzy of delight.

"But nobody's killed," June Star said with disappointment as the grandmother limped out of the car, her hat still pinned to her head but the broken front brim standing up at a jaunty angle and the violet spray hanging off the side. They all sat down in the ditch, except the children, to recover from the shock. They were all shaking.

"Maybe a car will come along," said the children's mother hoarsely.

"I believe I have injured an organ," said the grandmother, pressing her side, but no one answered her. Bailey's teeth were clattering. He had on a yellow sport shirt with bright blue parrots designed in it and his face was as yellow as the shirt. The grandmother decided that she would not mention that the house was in Tennessee.

The road was about ten feet above and they could see only the tops of the trees on the other side of it. Behind the ditch they were sitting in there were more woods, tall and dark and deep. In a few minutes they saw a car some distance away on top of a hill, coming slowly as if the occupants were watching them. The grandmother stood up and waved both arms dramatically to attract their attention. The car continued to come on slowly, disappeared around a bend and appeared again, moving even slower, on top of the hill they had gone over. It was a big black battered hearselike automobile. There were three men in it.

It came to a stop over them and for some minutes, the driver looked down with a steady expressionless gaze to where they were sitting, and didn't speak. Then he turned his head and muttered something to the other two and they got out. One was a fat boy in black trousers and a red sweat shirt with a silver stallion embossed on the front of it. He moved around on the right side of them and stood staring, his mouth partly open in a kind of loose grin. The other had on khaki pants and a blue striped coat and a gray hat pulled down very low, hiding most of his face. He came around slowly on the left side. Neither spoke.

The driver got out of the car and stood by the side of it, looking down at them. He was an older man than the other two. His hair was just beginning to gray and he wore silver-rimmed spectacles that gave him a scholarly look. He had a long creased face and didn't have on any shirt or undershirt. He had on blue jeans that were too tight for him and was holding a black hat and a gun. The two boys also had guns.

"We've had an ACCIDENT!" the children screamed.

The grandmother had the peculiar feeling that the bespectacled man was someone she knew. His face was as familiar to her as if she had known him all her life but she could not recall who he was. He moved away from the car and began to come down the embankment, placing his feet carefully so that he wouldn't slip. He had on tan and white shoes and no socks, and his ankles were red and thin. "Good afternoon," he said. "I see you all had you a little spill."

"We turned over twice!" said the grandmother.   75

"Oncet," he corrected. "We seen it happen. Try their car and see will it run, Hiram," he said quietly to the boy with the gray hat.

"What you got that gun for?" John Wesley asked. "Whatcha gonna do with that gun?"

"Lady," the man said to the children's mother, "would you mind calling them children to sit down by you? Children make me nervous. I want all you all to sit down right together there were you're at."

"What are you telling us what to do for?" June Star asked.

Behind them the line of woods gaped like a dark open mouth. "Come   80
here," said their mother.

"Look here now," Bailey began suddenly, "we're in a predicament! We're in . . ."

The grandmother shrieked. She scrambled to her feet and stood staring.

"You're The Misfit!" she said. "I recognized you at once!"

"Yes'm," the man said, smiling slightly as if he were pleased in spite of himself to be known, "but it would have been better for all of you, lady, if you hadn't of reckernized me."

Bailey turned his head sharply and said something to his mother that shocked even the children. The old lady began to cry and The Misfit reddened.

"Lady," he said, "don't you get upset. Sometimes a man says things he don't mean. I don't reckon he meant to talk to you thataway."

"You wouldn't shoot a lady, would you?" the grandmother said and removed a clean handkerchief from her cuff and began to slap at her eyes with it.

The Misfit pointed the toe of his shoe into the ground and made a little hole and then covered it up again. "I would hate to have to," he said.

"Listen," the grandmother almost screamed, "I know you're a good man. You don't look a bit like you have common blood. I know you must come from nice people!"

"Yes mam," he said, "finest people in the world." When he smiled he showed a row of strong white teeth. "God never made a finer woman than my mother and my daddy's heart was pure gold," he said. The boy with the red sweat shirt had come around behind them and was standing with his gun at his hip. The Misfit squatted down on the ground. "Watch them children, Bobby Lee," he said. "You know they make me nervous." He looked at the six of them huddled together in front of him and he seemed to be embarrassed as if he couldn't think of anything to say. "Ain't a cloud in the sky," he remarked, looking up at it. "Don't see no sun but don't see no cloud neither."

"Yes, it's a beautiful day," said the grandmother. "Listen," she said, "you shouldn't call yourself The Misfit because I know you're a good man at heart. I can just look at you and tell."

"Hush!" Bailey yelled. "Hush! Everybody shut up and let me handle this!" He was squatting in the position of a runner about to spring forward but he didn't move.

"I pre-chate that, lady," The Misfit said and drew a little circle in the ground with the butt of his gun.

"It'll take a half a hour to fix this here car," Hiram called, looking over the raised hood of it.

"Well, first you and Bobby Lee get him and that little boy to step over yonder with you," The Misfit said, pointing to Bailey and John Wesley. "The boys want to ask you something," he said to Bailey. "Would you mind stepping back in them woods there with them?"

"Listen," Bailey began, "we're in a terrible predicament! Nobody realizes what this is," and his voice cracked. His eyes were as blue and intense as the parrots in his shirt and he remained perfectly still.

The grandmother reached up to adjust her hat brim as if she were going to the woods with him but it came off in her hand. She stood staring at it and after a second she let it fall on the ground. Hiram pulled Bailey up by the arm as if he were assisting an old man. John Wesley caught hold of his father's hand and Bobby Lee followed. They went off toward the woods and just as they reached the dark edge, Bailey turned and supporting himself against a gray naked pine trunk, he shouted, "I'll be back in a minute, Mamma, wait on me!"

"Come back this instant!" his mother shrilled but they all disappeared into the woods.

"Bailey Boy!" the grandmother called in a tragic voice but she found she was looking at The Misfit squatting on the ground in front of her. "I just know you're a good man," she said desperately. "You're not a bit common!"

"Nome, I ain't a good man," The Misfit said after a second as if he had *100* considered her statement carefully, "but I ain't the worst in the world neither. My daddy said I was a different breed of dog from my brothers and sisters. 'You know,' Daddy said, 'it's some that can live their whole life out without asking about it and it's others has to know why it is, and this boy is one of the latters. He's going to be into everything!'" He put on his black hat and looked up suddenly and then away deep into the woods as if he were embarrassed again. "I'm sorry I don't have on a shirt before you ladies," he said, hunching his shoulders slightly. "We buried our clothes that we had on when we escaped and we're just making do until we can get better. We borrowed these from some folks we met," he explained.

"That's perfectly all right," the grandmother said. "Maybe Bailey has an extra shirt in his suitcase."

"I'll look and see terrectly," The Misfit said.

"Where are they taking him?" the children's mother screamed.

"Daddy was a card himself," The Misfit said. "You couldn't put anything over on him. He never got in trouble with the Authorities though. Just had the knack of handling them."

"You could be honest too if you'd only try," said the grandmother. *105* "Think how wonderful it would be to settle down and live a comfortable life and not have to think about somebody chasing you all the time."

The Misfit kept scratching in the ground with the butt of his gun as if he were thinking about it. "Yes'm, somebody is always after you," he murmured.

The grandmother noticed how thin his shoulder blades were just behind his hat because she was standing up looking down on him. "Do you ever pray?" she asked.

He shook his head. All she saw was the black hat wiggle between his shoulder blades. "Nome," he said.

There was a pistol shot from the woods, followed closely by another. Then silence. The old lady's head jerked around. She could hear the wind move through the tree tops like a long satisfied insuck of breath. "Bailey Boy!" she called.

"I was a gospel singer for a while," The Misfit said. "I been most *110* everything. Been in the arm service, both land and sea, at home and abroad, been twict married, been an undertaker, been with the railroads, plowed Mother Earth, been in a tornado, seen a man burnt alive oncet," and he looked up at the children's mother and the little girl who were sitting close together, their faces white and their eyes glassy; "I even seen a woman flogged," he said.

"Pray, pray," the grandmother began, "pray, pray . . ."

"I never was a bad boy that I remember of," The Misfit said in an almost dreamy voice, "but somewheres along the line I done something wrong and got sent to the penitentiary. I was buried alive," and he looked up and held her attention to him by a steady stare.

"That's when you should have started to pray," she said. "What did you do to get sent to the penitentiary that first time?"

"Turn to the right, it was a wall," The Misfit said, looking up again at the cloudless sky. "Turn to the left, it was a wall. Look up it was a ceiling, look down it was a floor. I forget what I done, lady. I set there and set there, trying to remember what it was I done and I ain't recalled it to this day. Oncet in a while, I would think it was coming to me, but it never come."

"Maybe they put you in by mistake," the old lady said vaguely. $\qquad$ *115*

"Nome," he said. "It wasn't no mistake. They had the papers on me."

"You must have stolen something," she said.

The Misfit sneered slightly. "Nobody had nothing I wanted," he said. "It was a head-doctor at the penitentiary said what I had done was kill my daddy but I known that for a lie. My daddy died in nineteen ought nineteen of the epidemic flu and I never had a thing to do with it. He was buried in the Mount Hopewell Baptist churchyard and you can go there and see for yourself."

"If you would pray," the old lady said, "Jesus would help you."

"That's right," The Misfit said. $\qquad$ *120*

"Well then, why don't you pray?" she asked trembling with delight suddenly.

"I don't want no hep," he said, "I'm doing all right by myself."

Bobby Lee and Hiram came ambling back from the woods. Bobby Lee was dragging a yellow shirt with bright blue parrots in it.

"Throw me that shirt, Bobby Lee," The Misfit said. The shirt came flying at him and landed on his shoulder and he put it on. The grandmother couldn't name what the shirt reminded her of. "No, lady," The Misfit said while he was buttoning up, "I found out the crime don't matter. You can do one thing or you can do another, kill a man or take a tire off his car, because sooner or later you're going to forget what it was you done and just be punished for it."

The children's mother had begun to make heaving noises as if she *125* couldn't get her breath. "Lady," he asked, "would you and that little girl like to step off yonder with Bobby Lee and Hiram and join your husband?"

"Yes, thank you," the mother said faintly. Her left arm dangled helplessly and she was holding the baby, who had gone to sleep, in the other. "Help that lady up, Hiram," The Misfit said as she struggled to climb out of the ditch, "and Bobby Lee, you hold onto that little girl's hand."

"I don't want to hold hands with him," June Star said. "He reminds me of a pig."

The fat boy blushed and laughed and caught her by the arm and pulled her off into the woods after Hiram and her mother.

Alone with The Misfit, the grandmother found that she had lost her voice. There was not a cloud in the sky nor any sun. There was nothing around her but woods. She wanted to tell him that he must pray. She opened and closed her mouth several times before anything came out. Finally she found herself saying, "Jesus, Jesus," meaning, Jesus will help you, but the way she was saying it, it sounded as if she might be cursing.

"Yes'm," The Misfit said as if he agreed. "Jesus thrown everything off *130* balance. It was the same case with Him as with me except He hadn't committed any crime and they could prove I had committed one because they had the papers on me. Of course," he said, "they never shown me my papers. That's why I sign myself now. I said long ago, you get you a signature and sign everything you do and keep a copy of it. Then you'll know what you done and you can hold up the crime to the punishment and see do they match and in the end you'll have something to prove you ain't been treated right. I call myself The Misfit," he said, "because I can't make what all I done wrong fit what all I gone through in punishment."

There was a piercing scream from the woods, followed closely by a pistol report. "Does it seem right to you, lady, that one is punished a heap and another ain't punished at all?"

"Jesus!" the old lady cried. "You've got good blood! I know you wouldn't shoot a lady! I know you come from nice people! Pray! Jesus, you ought not to shoot a lady. I'll give you all the money I've got!"

"Lady," The Misfit said, looking beyond her far into the woods, "there never was a body that give the undertaker a tip."

There were two more pistol reports and the grandmother raised her head like a parched old turkey hen crying for water and called, "Bailey Boy, Bailey Boy!" as if her heart would break.

"Jesus was the only One that ever raised the dead," The Misfit con- *135* tinued, "and He shouldn't have done it. He thrown everything off balance. If He did what He said, then it's nothing for you to do but throw away everything and follow Him, and if He didn't then it's nothing for you to do but enjoy the few minutes you got left the best way you can—by killing somebody or burning down his house or doing some other meanness to him. No pleasure but meanness," he said and his voice had become almost a snarl.

"Maybe He didn't raise the dead," the old lady mumbled, not knowing what she was saying and feeling so dizzy that she sank down in the ditch with her legs twisted under her.

"I wasn't there so I can't say He didn't," the Misfit said. "I wisht I had of been there," he said, hitting the ground with his fist. "It ain't right I wasn't there because if I had of been there I would of known. Listen lady," he said in a high voice, "if I had of been there I would of known and I wouldn't be like I am now." His voice seemed about to crack and the grandmother's head cleared for an instant. She saw the man's face twisted close to her own as if he were going to cry and she murmured, "Why, you're one of my babies. You're one of my own children!" She reached out and touched him on the shoulder. The Misfit sprang back as if a snake had bitten him and shot her three times through the chest. Then he put his gun down on the ground and took off his glasses and began to clean them.

Hiram and Bobby Lee returned from the woods and stood over the ditch, looking down at the grandmother who half sat and half lay in a puddle of blood with her legs crossed under her like a child's and her face smiling up at the cloudless sky.

Without his glasses, The Mitfit's eyes were red-rimmed and pale and defenseless-looking. "Take her off and throw her where you thrown the others," he said, picking up the cat that was rubbing itself against his leg.

"She was a talker, wasn't she?" Bobby Lee said, sliding down the ditch *140* with a yodel.

"She would of been a good woman," The Misfit said, "if it had been somebody there to shoot her every minute of her life."

"Some fun!" Bobby Lee said.

"Shut up, Bobby Lee," The Misfit said. "It's no real pleasure in life."

The Responsive Reader

1. If you were asked to sum up what happens in this story, what would you include? What are major turning points or waystations in the story? What are key details?
2. O'Connor called the grandmother the "heroine" of the story. What do you think she meant? Do you think of the grandmother as ordinary or as freakish, eccentric? Does your perception of her change as the story develops? How would you sum up her role in the story?
3. What kind of people are the rest of the family? What roles do they play in the story? Would you call them ordinary? pathetic? strange? Are they like or unlike people you know?
4. Would it make any difference to the story if the stop at the "fat man's" barbecue had been omitted?
5. What is the story of The Misfit? (And how much of it do you believe?) What kind of person is he? How do you think the author expected you to react to him? What do you make of his talk about justice and about Jesus? What for you is the clue to his behavior or personality?

6. What do you make of the climactic confrontation between the grandmother and the Misfit? To you, does it seem to have a symbolic meaning? Does it seem to have a religious meaning?

Thinking, Talking, Writing

7. Was what happened to the people in this story meant to happen? Or
   was it a meaningless accident?
8. For you, how much of this story is grounded in common human
   nature? How much seems freakish or unheard of?
9. Is society responsible for its misfits? How should it deal with someone
   like The Misfit in this story?

Thinking about Connections

10. William Faulkner and Flannery O'Connor are two Southern writers
    known for their creation of strong eccentric characters. Are the major
    characters in Faulkner's "The Tall Men" misfits in a similar sense as
    the Misfit in O'Connor's story?

5

Beyond Optimism: The End of Innocence

Everyone is a moon and has a dark side which he never shows to anybody.

Mark Twain

No writer is a pessimist; the very act of writing is an optimistic act.
Flannery O'Connor

LITERATURE IN CONTEXT

Americans have traditionally been optimists, believing in the possibility of a better future. This country was founded in the eighteenth century, when educated people believed in the "perfectibility" of humankind. Emerging from centuries of ignorance and oppression, humanity would move toward a more enlightened future. America promised freedom from tyrannical authority, equality of opportunity for all, and good will toward one's fellow human beings. These ideals now sound like clichés from the speeches of politicians. However, at the time, they translated into English the rallying cries of the French Revolution, which in 1796 was to overthrow the old aristocratic regime: *liberté, egalité, fraternité*. Liberty, equality, brotherhood.

For downtrodden millions around the world, America conjured up visions of upward mobility blocked in the status–conscious, ossified societies of Europe or Asia. A descendant of penniless Irish immigrants, driven from their land by famine and absentee landlords, could become a millionaire and a US ambassador. One of his sons in turn could become a member of the best clubs at Harvard and a president of the United States. Descendants of serfs and tenant farmers whose lives at home had been ground into the dust by aristocratic bloodsuckers could start their own shops, homestead their own farms, or build their own commercial empires. In this new America, nationalities that had been feuding for centuries could live in peace. Germans and Russians could shop at Jewish delicatessens without plotting progroms against their owners. Turks and Armenians could break bread together without perpetuating a history of assassination, massacre, and paranoia.

America long served as a beacon toward a better future. In our century, this vision of America as a force for good survived most strongly in American popular culture. In countless Western movies—as popular around the world as in Peoria—outlaws terrorized a community during the first four reels until finally at high noon a long-suffering, soft-spoken sheriff put the bullies under. In endless *Star Trek* reruns, a science fiction version of the myth is played out: Captain Kirk and his crew beam down on a planet riddled with violence and oppression. In spite of the intergalactic Federation's nonintervention directive, they become an influence for the good—planting the seeds of democracy or thwarting the evil Klingon empire.

Americans love to think of themselves as a force for good in the world. However, throughout American history, there has been a strong, more pessimistic counterpoint to the tradition of optimism. In many of the great American novels of the nineteenth century, the myth of American innocence and good will came in for rethinking. Nathaniel Hawthorne, a descendant of witch-hunting Puritans, probed the Puritan obsession with hidden sin, with the human capacity for depravity rather than the human potential for good. His *The Scarlet Letter* (1850) tells the story of a Puritan minister betraying his calling, his secret lover, and his illegitimate child. Mark Twain's *Huckleberry Finn,* one of the great mythical American books, plays off native-born innocence against worldly wise experience. On the surface, it tells the nostalgic tale of the naive runaway Huck, who escapes from adults who want to "sivilize" him to travel on a raft down the great legendary Mississippi River with his friend Jim, an escaped slave. But the two innocents—the lovable country boy and his trusting black friend—are played off by the embittered author against a pageant of violence and corruption. The two witness families being destroyed in a blood feud growing out of a petty quarrel. They travel for a time with two all-American con men who prey on the gullible and bereaved and who in turn are savaged by the moral majority. At the very beginning of the novel, Huck barely escapes with his life from his last encounter with his brutish, drunken, abusive father.

A persistent strand in American literature makes us discover the serpent in the garden of the American Eden. It focuses on the worm in the apple. It points forward to a skeptical modern view of Americans as a nation inflicting or condoning evil with the best intentions.

FROG AUTUMN
Sylvia Plath

Sylvia Plath became known for powerful, disturbing poems projecting her dark vision of life. Daughter of an Austrian-born father, she was a brilliant student at Smith College and went to England on a Fulbright grant, where she married the British poet Ted Hughes. She had a history of hospitalizations and ultimately took her own life. Her collection of poems The Colossus *(1960) appeared a few years before her death. In her quasi-autobiographical novel* The Bell Jar, *she told the story of a young woman rebelling desperately against the banality of suburbia, becoming disillusioned with the surface glamor of work as a magazine editor in the big city, and fighting a losing battle against suicidal depression. Plath became an icon, or revered symbolic figure, for readers sympathizing with her radical alienation from her world, and her poetry has continued to exercise its fascination for the critics. One of them said that Plath "lived on a knife-edge, in the presence of a tremendous attraction to death and nothingness" (David Young).*

Summer grows old, cold-blooded mother.   *1*
The insects are scant, skinny.
In these palustral° homes we only   *swampy*
Croak and wither.

Mornings dissipate in somnolence.°   *sleepiness*   *5*
The sun brightens tardily
Among the pithless° reeds. Flies fail us.   *weak-stemmed*
The fen° sickens.   *bog, swamp*

Frost drops even the spider. Clearly
The genius of plenitude°   *bountifulness* *10*
Houses himself elsewhere. Our folk thin
Lamentably.

The Responsive Reader

1. How does the poem invite you to think of the frogs as fellow creatures, capable of almost human thoughts and feelings? On the other hand, what helps you remember that these are real frogs?
2. What is the implied parallel with human life in this poem? What stage in human life or what developments in society do you think the poet may have had in mind?

Thinking, Talking, Writing

3. Do you think of frogs and reptiles as alien? Do we tend to limit our sympathy for animals to mammals? (If we are to feel close to animals, do they have to be furry and cuddly?)
4. Do you or people you know believe in the "genius of plenitude?" Or do the people you know best tend to lament the thinness or scantness of what life has to offer?

CHILDHOOD IS THE KINGDOM WHERE NOBODY DIES

Edna St. Vincent Millay

After the first death there is no other.
                    Dylan Thomas

> *Edna St. Vincent Millay was known in the twenties and thirties for her bittersweet poems of fugitive love, but she lost favor with critics when a more detached, intellectualized kind of poetry became fashionable. She has been rediscovered by feminist critics who value her for her command of the language of the emotions and for giving voice to the woman's feelings in the traditional male-dominated love relationship.*

Childhood is not from birth to a certain age and at a certain age   1
The child is grown, and puts away childish things.
Childhood is the kingdom where nobody dies.

Nobody that matters, that is. Distant relatives of course
Die, whom one never has seen or has seen for an hour,   5
And they gave one candy in a pink-and-green striped bag, or a jack-knife,
And went away, and cannot really be said to have lived at all.

And cats die. They lie on the floor and lash their tails,
And their reticent fur is suddenly all in motion
With fleas that one never knew were there,   10
Polished and brown, knowing all there is to know,
Trekking off into the living world.
You fetch a shoe-box, but it's much too small, because she won't curl up
    now:
So you find a bigger box, and bury her in the yard, and weep.

But you do not wake up a month from then, two months,   15
A year from then, two years, in the middle of the night
And weep, with your knuckles in your mouth, and say Oh, God! Oh, God!
Childhood is the kingdom where nobody dies that matters,—mothers and
    fathers don't die.

And if you have said, "For heaven's sake, must you always be kissing a
    person?"
Or, "I do wish to gracious you'd stop tapping on the window with your   20
    thimble!"
Tomorrow, or even the day after tomorrow if you're busy having fun,
Is plenty of time to say, "I'm sorry, mother."

To be grown up is to sit at the table with people who have died, who
  neither listen nor speak;
Who do not drink their tea, though they always said
Tea was such a comfort.   25

Run down into the cellar and bring up the last jar of raspberries; they are
  not tempted.
Flatter them, ask them what was it they said exactly
That time, to the bishop, or to the overseer, or to Mrs. Mason;
They are not taken in.
Shout at them, get red in the face, rise,   30
Drag them up out of their chairs by their stiff shoulders and shake them and
  yell at them;
They are not startled, they are not even embarrassed; they slide back into
  their chairs.

Your tea is cold now.
You drink it standing up,
And leave the house.   35

The Responsive Reader

1. The passage from childhood to adulthood has often been the crucial
   rite of passage in both poetry and fiction. How does the poet contrast
   the child's attitude toward death with the perspective of the adult? How
   does she make the feelings of the child and those of the adult real for
   the reader?
2. What feelings toward the dead are expected or approved in our society?
   What makes Millay's poem nonstereotypical or unconventional?
3. What is the symbolism of the tea at the end of the poem?

Thinking, Talking, Writing

4. Many people have talked about an event like the assassination of JFK
   as the end of a period of hope or optimism during their growing up.
   Have you ever observed or experienced an event that for you meant
   the loss of innocence?
5. Is it true that our society is becoming too callous about death?

Collaborative Projects

6. Working in groups, what can you and your classmates find out about
   past and present styles and rituals of mourning?

THE POSSESSIVE

Sharon Olds

Born in San Francisco, Sharon Olds studied at Stanford and Columbia. During the eighties she became a leading practitioner of a new frankly personal poetry contrasting with the fashionably ironic and detached poetry of an earlier cycle. Her major aim has been to find an authentic voice for the self, for the person behind the persona speaking in the poem. She has written with sharp wit and emotional intensity about being a child in a dysfunctional family, about the tension between mother and daughter, and about sexual desire and fulfillment. One reader said about Olds that "she writes with astonishing frankness about being a child, a woman, and a mother."

My daughter—as if I   1
owned her—that girl with the
hair wispy as a frayed bellpull

has been to the barber, that knife grinder,
and had the edge of her hair sharpened.   5

Each strand now cuts
both ways. The blade of new bangs
hangs over her red-brown eyes
like carbon steel.

   All the little   10
spliced ropes are sliced. The curtain of
dark paper-cuts veils the face that
started from next to nothing in my body—

My body. My daughter. I'll have to find
another word. In her bright helmet   15
she looks at me as if across a
great distance. Distant fires can be
glimpsed in the resin light of her eyes:

the watch fires of an enemy, a while before
the war starts.   20

The Responsive Reader

1. What are our usual idealized or socially approved expectations of how a mother and daughter should feel about each other? How is this poem different?
2. How does the daughter's new haircut activate a whole series of metaphors related to weaponry or warfare? How many of these can you

find? What thoughts and emotions are left in the reader's mind by the concluding metaphor of the watch fires at night?

3. *My* is a possessive pronoun; it shows to whom something belongs— who owns it. Why and how does the use of the pronoun become an issue in this poem?

Thinking, Talking, Writing

4. Do you think the tension or antagonism between parent and offspring that is the subject of this poem is a natural stage of growing up?

Collaborative Projects

5. Working with a group, check a week's issues of a local or national newspaper for news reports or articles involving parents and children. What are recurrent themes or characteristic preoccupations?

Thinking about Connections

6. In recent years, many readers have noted that conventional poetry anthologies used to be dominated by dead white males. Plath, Millay, and Olds are among the best known of America's women poets. Do the poems reprinted here have something in common? For instance, is a special female sensitivity or perspective on life reflected in these poems?

LATIN NIGHT AT THE PAWN SHOP

Martin Espada

Martin Espada, North American of Puerto Rican ancestry, grew up in a Brooklyn housing project and became a lawyer and a poet. He received the 1991 Peterson Poetry Prize for Rebellion Is the Circle of a Lover's Hands. *His aim as a poet is to "use the power of the word" to fight against what he considers wrong. One reader said of him that he "brings to life his love for his people while etching haunting pictures that create lasting images" in his readers' minds.*

Chelsea, Massachusetts
Christmas, 1987

The apparition of a salsa band   *1*
gleaming in the Liberty Loan
pawnshop window:

Golden trumpet.
silver trombone,   *5*
congas, maracas, tambourine,
all with price tags dangling
like the city morgue ticket
on a dead man's toe.

The Responsive Reader

1. What is sad about pawnshops? What images and associations do they bring to mind? What is sad and ironic about the name of the pawnshop in this poem? What is sad about the time of year?
2. Why does the poet use words like *gleaming, golden,* and *silver* to describe the instruments?
3. What made the poet take the imaginative leap from the pawnshop window to the city morgue? What emotions does the concluding simile evoke in you as the reader?

Thinking, Talking, Writing

4. What difference does it make to the poem that the instruments belonged to a salsa band? What difference does it make that it is "Latin Night" at the pawnshop and not "Irish Night?"

A DAY IN ARKANSAW

Mark Twain

Mark Twain is America's greatest humorist . . . because his humor served to point up errors in American life—its gaucheries, pretenses, and political debilities—and at the same time expressed a faith in the American dream, optimistic and unquenchable.

George Perkins

If you pick up a starving dog and make him prosperous, he will not bite you. This is the principal difference between a dog and a man.

Mark Twain

Mark Twain (pen name of Samuel Clemens) is legendary around the world as the most American of American authors. His best-loved books act out the daydreams of young people everywhere: to quit school, to escape from their nagging families, to run away, to become a steamboat pilot on the mighty Mississippi river, for instance. His characters are often innocents who refuse to become jaded or cynical. They refuse to believe that the callousness and violence they see around them is merely the way things are. They are naive in the honorable sense: They look at every act of stupidity or violence as if it were happening for the first time. If we get into the spirit of their adventures, we find ourselves saying with them: "Tell me it's not so! Human beings are not meant to act this way."

Mark Twain grew up in Missouri—in Hannibal on the Mississippi in pre–Civil War days. The loyalties of his family were divided between the North and the South. He trained as a pilot for the steamboats that carried passengers, trade, news, and entertainment up and down the river. ("Mark Twain" was a boatsman's cry signaling that the water was at least two fathom deep and thus safe for passage.) He told the story of the colorful life of the river pilot in Life on the Mississippi *(1883). After the war, he went west and described the rugged West of stagecoach days in* Roughing It *(1872). He loved the tall tale, telling whoppers with a straight face and deadpan humor. However, his observations of human callousness and greed left him with the bitterness that shows in his last published stories:* The Man That Corrupted Hadleyburg *(1900) and* The Mysterious Stranger *(1916).*

Mark Twain's masterpiece is The Adventures of Huckleberry Finn *(1885). In it, Huck tells the story of his raft trip down the Mississippi River with his friend Jim, an escaped slave. Huck has left behind a drunken abusive father and the well-meaning Widow Douglas, and Jim is on the run from slavecatchers who would love to turn him in for a reward. Their stops along the river become waystations in a mythical pageant of human folly and gullibility. The following selection from the book is a vignette, or self-contained episode, that occurs when Huck and Jim for a time travel with two down-at-heel wandering actors and con men who prey on the local populace. This interlude, like the book as a whole, is alive with drama, wonder, and laughter. At the same time, we are made to ponder what makes people violent and inhuman and what makes them decent, caring human beings.*

In recent years, Mark Twain has been criticized for the way he portrays the escaped slave Jim in his book. Twain freely uses racial labels that were used by both white and black people of his time but that have become offensive in ours. In the book we often laugh at both Huck and Jim for their ignorance of the ways of the world. However, Twain was way ahead of the rest of society in his empathy for slaves trying to escape from their masters and for families torn asunder as slaves were bought and sold. James Baldwin once said that the essence of the race issue in this country is that black people want to be treated like human beings. On this score, Mark Twain was ahead of his time and of ours.

One morning, when we was pretty well down the state of Arkansaw, we come in sight of a little one-horse town in a big bend; so we tied up about three-quarters of a mile above it, in the mouth of a crick which was shut in like a tunnel by the cypress trees, and all of us but Jim took the canoe and went down there to see if there was any chance in that place for our show.

We struck it mighty lucky; there was going to be a circus there that afternoon, and the country-people was already beginning to come in, in all kinds of old shackly wagons, and on horses. The circus would leave before night, so our show would have a pretty good chance. The duke he hired the court-house, and we went around and stuck up our bills. They read like this:

Shaksperean Revival ! ! !
Wonderful Attraction!
For One Night Only!
The world renowned tragedians,
David Garrick the younger, of Drury Lane Theatre, London,
and
Edmund Kean the elder, of the Royal Haymarket Theatre,
Whitechapel, Pudding Lane, Piccadilly, London, and the
Royal Continental Theatres, in their sublime

MARK TWAIN

Shaksperean Spectacle entitled
The Balcony Scene
in
Romeo and Juliet ! ! !

Romeo..Mr. Garrick
Juliet ....Mr. Kean
Assisted by the whole strength of the company!
New costumes, new scenery, new appointments!
Also:
The thrilling, masterly, and blood-curdling

Broad–sword conflict
In Richard III. ! ! !

Richard III...Mr. Garrick
Richmond ....Mr. Kean

Also:
(by special request)
Hamlet's Immortal Soliloquy ! !
By the Illustrious Kean!
Done by him 300 consecutive nights in Paris!
For One Night Only,
On account of imperative European engagements!
Admission 25 cents; children and servants, 10 cents.

Then we went loafing around town. The stores and houses was most all old, shackly, dried-up frame concerns that hadn't ever been painted; they was set up three or four foot above ground on stilts, so as to be out of reach of the water when the river was overflowed. The houses had little gardens around them, but they didn't seem to raise hardly anything in them but jimpson-weeds, and sunflowers, and ashpiles, and old curled-up boots and shoes, and pieces of bottles, and rags, and played-out tinware. The fences was made of different kinds of boards, nailed on at different times; and they leaned every which way, and had gates that didn't generly have but one hinge—a leather one. Some of the fences had been whitewashed some time or another, but the duke said it was in Columbus's time, like enough. There was generly hogs in the garden, and people driving them out.

All the stores was along one street. They had white domestic awnings in front, and the country-people hitched their horses to the awning-posts. There was empty dry-goods boxes under the awnings, and loafers roosting on them all day long, whittling them with their Barlow knives; and chawing tobacco, and gaping and yawning and stretching—a mighty ornery lot. They generly had on yellow straw hats most as wide as an umbrella, but didn't wear no coats nor waistcoats; they called one another Bill, and Buck, and Hank, and Joe, and Andy, and talked lazy and drawly, and used considerable many cuss-words. There was as many as one loafer leaning up against every awning-post, and he most always had his hands in his britches pockets, except when he fetched them out to lend a chaw of tobacco or scratch. What a body was hearing amongst them all the time was:

"Gimme a chaw 'v tobacker, Hank."

"Cain't; I hain't got but one chaw left. Ask Bill."

Maybe Bill he gives him a chaw; maybe he lies and says he ain't got none. Some of them kinds of loafers never has a cent in the world, nor a chaw of tobacco of their own. They get all their chawing by borrowing; they say to a fellow, "I wisht you'd len' me a chaw, Jack, I jist this minute give Ben Thompson the last chaw I had"—which is a lie pretty much every time; it don't fool nobody but a stranger; but Jack ain't no stranger, so he says:

5

"*You* give him a chaw, did you? So did your sister's cat's grandmother. You pay me back the chaws you've awready borry'd off'n me, Lafe Buckner, then I'll loan you one or two ton of it, and won't charge you no back intrust, nuther."

"Well, I *did* pay you back some of it wunst."

"Yes, you did—'bout six chaws. You borry'd store tobacker and paid   10
back nigger-head."

Store tobacco is flat black plug, but these fellows mostly chaws the natural leaf twisted. When they borrow a chaw they don't generly cut it off with a knife, but set the plug in between their teeth, and gnaw with their teeth and tug at the plug with their hands till they get it in two; then sometimes the one that owns the tobacco looks mournful at it when it's handed back, and says, sarcastic:

"Here, gimme the *chaw*, and you take the *plug*."

All the streets and lanes was just mud; they warn't nothing else *but* mud—mud as black as tar and nigh about a foot deep in some places, and two or three inches deep in *all* the places. The hogs loafed and grunted around everywheres. You'd see a muddy sow and a litter of pigs come lazying along the street and whollop herself right down in the way, where folks had to walk around her, and she'd stretch out and shut her eyes and wave her ears whilst the pigs was milking her, and look as happy as if she was on salary. And pretty soon you'd hear a loafer sing out, "Hi! *so* boy! sick him, Tige!" and away the sow would go, squealing most horrible, with a dog or two swinging to each ear, and three or four dozen more a-coming; and then you would see all the loafers get up and watch the thing out of sight, and laugh at the fun and look grateful for the noise. Then they'd settle back again till there was a dog-fight. There couldn't anything wake them up all over, and make them happy all over, like a dog-fight—unless it might be putting turpentine on a stray dog and setting fire to him, or tying a tin pan to his tail and see him run himself to death.

On the river-front some of the houses was sticking out over the bank, and they was bowed and bent, and about ready to tumble in. The people had moved out of them. The bank was caved away under one corner of some others, and that corner was hanging over. People lived in them yet, but it was dangersome, because sometimes a strip of land as wide as a house caves in at a time. Sometimes a belt of land a quarter of a mile deep will start in and cave along and cave along till it all caves into the river in one summer. Such a town as that has to be always moving back, and back, and back, because the river's always gnawing at it.

The nearer it got to noon that day the thicker and thicker was the   15
wagons and horses in the streets, and more coming all the time. Families fetched their dinners with them from the country, and eat them in the wagons. There was considerable whisky-drinking going on, and I seen three fights. By and by somebody sings out:

"Here comes old Boggs!—in from the country for his little old monthly drunk; here he comes, boys!"

All the loafers looked glad; I reckoned they was used to having fun out of Boggs. One of them says:

"Wonder who he's a-gwyne to chaw up this time. If he'd a-chawed up all the men he's ben a-gwyne to chaw up in the last twenty year he'd have considerable ruputation now."

Another one says, "I wisht old Boggs 'd threaten me, 'cuz then I'd know I warn't gwyne to die for a thousan' year."

Boggs comes a-tearing along on his horse, whooping and yelling like   20
an Injun, and singing out:

"Cler the track, thar. I'm on the waw-path, and the price uv coffins is a-gwyne to raise."

He was drunk, and weaving about in his saddle; he was over fifty year old, and had a very red face. Everybody yelled at him and laughed at him and sassed him, and he sassed back, and said he'd attend to them and lay them out in their regular turns, but he couldn't wait now because he'd come to town to kill old Colonel Sherburn, and his motto was, "Meat first, and spoon vittles to top off on."

He see me, and rode up and says:

"Whar'd you come f'm, boy? You prepared to die?"

Then he rode on. I was scared, but a man says: 25

"He don't mean nothing; he's always a-carryin' on like that when he's drunk. He's the best-naturedest old fool in Arkansaw—never hurt nobody, drunk nor sober."

Boggs rode up before the biggest store in town, and bent his head down so he could see under the curtain of the awning and yells:

"Come out here, Sherburn! Come out and meet the man you've swindled. You're the houn' I'm after, and I'm a-gwyne to have you, too!"

And so he went on, calling Sherburn everything he could lay his tongue to, and the whole street packed with people listening and laughing and going on. By and by a proud-looking man about fifty-five—and he was a heap the best-dressed man in that town, too—steps out of the store, and the crowd drops back on each side to let him come. He says to Boggs, mighty ca'm and slow—he says:

"I'm tired of this, but I'll endure it till one o'clock. Till one o'clock,   30
mind—no longer. If you open your mouth against me only once after that time you can't travel so far but I will find you."

Then he turns and goes in. The crowd looked mighty sober; nobody stirred, and there warn't no more laughing. Boggs rode off blackguarding Sherburn as loud as he could yell, all down the street; and pretty soon back he comes and stops before the store, still keeping it up. Some men crowded around him and tried to get him to shut up, but he wouldn't; they told him it would be one o'clock in about fifteen minutes, and so he *must* go home— he must go right away. But it didn't do no good. He cussed away with all his might, and throwed his hat down in the mud and rode over it, and pretty soon away he went a-raging down the street again, with his gray hair a-flying. Everybody that could get a chance at him tried their best to coax him off of his horse so they could lock him up and get him sober; but it warn't no use—up the street he would tear again, and give Sherburn another cussing. By and by somebody says:

"Go for his daughter!—quick, go for his daughter; sometimes he'll listen to her. If anybody can persuade him, she can."

So somebody started on a run. I walked down street a ways and stopped. In about five or ten minutes here comes Boggs again, but not on his horse. He was a-reeling across the street towards me, bareheaded, with a friend on both sides of him a-holt of his arms and hurrying him along. He was quiet, and looked uneasy; and he warn't hanging back any, but was doing some of the hurrying himself. Somebody sings out:

"Boggs!"

I looked over there to see who said it, and it was that Colonel Sherburn. He was standing perfectly still in the street, and had a pistol raised in his right hand—not aiming it, but holding it out with the barrel tilted up towards the sky. The same second I see a young girl coming on the run, and two men with her. Boggs and the men turned round to see who called him, and when they see the pistol the men jumped to one side, and the pistol-barrel come down slow and steady to a level—both barrels cocked. Boggs throws up both of his hands and says, "O Lord, don't shoot!" Bang! goes the first shot, and he staggers back, clawing at the air—bang! goes the second one, and he tumbles backwards onto the ground, heavy and solid, with his arms spread out. That young girl screamed out and comes rushing, and down she throws herself on her father, crying, and saying, "Oh, he's killed him, he's killed him!" The crowd closed up around them, and shouldered and jammed one another, with their necks stretched, trying to see, and people on the inside trying to shove them back and shouting, "Back, back! give him air, give him air!"

Colonel Sherburn he tossed his pistol onto the ground, and turned around on his heels and walked off.

They took Boggs to a little drug store, the crowd pressing around just the same, and the whole town following, and I rushed and got a good place at the window, where I was close to him and could see in. They laid him on the floor and put one large Bible under his head, and opened another one and spread it on his breast; but they tore open his shirt first, and I seen where one of the bullets went in. He made about a dozen long gasps, his breast lifting the Bible up when he drawed in his breath, and letting it down again when he breathed it out—and after that he laid still; he was dead. Then they pulled his daughter away from him, screaming and crying, and took her off. She was about sixteen, and very sweet and gentle looking, but awful pale and scared.

Well, pretty soon the whole town was there, squirming and scrounging and pushing and shoving to get at the window and have a look, but people that had the places wouldn't give them up, and folks behind them was saying all the time, "Say, now, you've looked enough, you fellows; 'tain't right and 'tain't fair for you to stay thar all the time, and never give nobody a chance; other folks has their rights as well as you."

There was considerable jawing back, so I slid out, thinking maybe there was going to be trouble. The streets was full, and everybody was excited. Everybody that seen the shooting was telling how it happened, and there was a big crowd packed around each one of these fellows, stretching their necks and listening. One long, lanky man, with long hair and a big white fur stovepipe hat on the back of his head, and a crooked-handled cane, marked out the places on the ground where Boggs stood and where Sherburn stood, and the people following him around from one place to t'other and watching everything he done, and bobbing their heads to show they understood, and stooping a little and resting their hands on their thighs to watch him mark the places on the ground with his cane; and then he stood up straight and stiff where Sherburn had stood, frowning and having his hat-brim down over his eyes, and sung out, "Boggs!" and then fetched his cane down slow to a level, and says "Bang!" staggered backwards, says "Bang!" again, and fell down flat on his back. The people that had seen the thing said he done it perfect; said it was just exactly the way it all happened. Then as much as a dozen people got out their bottles and treated him.

Well, by and by somebody said Sherburn ought to be lynched. In about a minute everybody was saying it; so away they went, mad and yelling, and snatching down every clothes-line they come to do the hanging with.   *40*

They swarmed up towards Sherburn's house, a-whooping and raging like Injuns, and everything had to clear the way or get run over and tromped to mush, and it was awful to see. Children was heeling it ahead of the mob, screaming and trying to get out of the way; and every window along the road was full of women's heads, and there was nigger boys in every tree, and bucks and wenches looking over every fence; and as soon as the mob would get nearly to them they would break and skaddle back out of reach. Lots of the women and girls was crying and taking on, scared most to death.

They swarmed up in front of Sherburn's palings as thick as they could jam together, and you couldn't hear yourself think for the noise. It was a little twenty-foot yard. Some sung out "Tear down the fence! tear down the fence!" Then there was a racket of ripping and tearing and smashing, and down she goes, and the front wall of the crowd begins to roll in like a wave.

Just then Sherburn steps out onto the roof of his little front porch, with a double-barrel gun in his hand, and takes his stand, perfectly ca'm and deliberate, not saying a word. The racket stopped, and the wave sucked back.

Sherburn never said a word—just stood there, looking down. The stillness was awful creepy and uncomfortable. Sherburn run his eye slow along the crowd; and wherever it struck the people tried a little to outgaze him, but they couldn't; they dropped their eyes and looked sneaky. Then pretty soon Sherburn sort of laughed; not the pleasant kind, but the kind that makes you feel like when you are eating bread that's got sand in it.

Then he says, slow and scornful: 45

"The idea of *you* lynching anybody! It's amusing. The idea of you thinking you had pluck enough to lynch a *man!* Because you're brave enough to tar and feather poor friendless cast-out women that come along here, did that make you think you had grit enough to lay your hands on a *man?* Why, a *man's* safe in the hands of ten thousand of your kind—as long as it's daytime and you're not behind him.

"Do I know you? I know you clear through. I was born and raised in the South, and I've lived in the North; so I know the average all around. The average man's a coward. In the North he lets anybody walk over him that wants to, and goes home and prays for a humble spirit to bear it. In the South one man, all by himself, has stopped a stage full of men in the daytime, and robbed the lot. Your newspapers call you a brave people so much that you think you *are* braver than any other people—whereas you're just *as* brave, and no braver. Why don't your juries hang murderers? Because they're afraid the man's friends will shoot them in the back, in the dark—and it's just what they *would* do.

"So they always acquit; and then a *man* goes in the night, with a hundred masked cowards at his back, and lynches the rascal. Your mistake is, that you didn't bring a man with you; that's one mistake, and the other is that you didn't come in the dark and fetch your masks. You brought *part* of a man—Buck Harkness, there—and if you hadn't had him to start you, you'd 'a' taken it out in blowing.

"You didn't want to come. The average man don't like trouble and danger. *You* don't like trouble and danger. But if only *half* a man—like Buck Harkness, there—shouts 'Lynch him! lynch him!' you're afraid to back down—afraid you'll be found out to be what you are—*cowards*—and so you raise a yell, and hang yourselves onto that half-a-man's coat-tail, and come raging up here, swearing what big things you're going to do. The pitifulest thing out is a mob; that's what an army is—a mob; they don't fight with courage that's born in them, but with courage that's borrowed from their mass, and from their officers. But a mob without any *man* at the head of it is *beneath* pitifulness. Now the thing for *you* to do is to droop your tails and go home and crawl in a hole. If any real lynching's going to be done it will be done in the dark, Southern fashion; and when they come they'll bring their masks, and fetch a *man* along. Now *leave*—and take your half-a-man with you"—tossing his gun up across his left arm and cocking it when he says this.

The crowd washed back sudden, and then broke all apart, and went   50
tearing off every which way, and Buck Harkness he heeled it after them, looking tolerable cheap. I could 'a' stayed if I wanted to, but I didn't want to.

I went to the circus and loafed around the back side till the watchman went by, and then dived in under the tent. I had my twenty-dollar gold piece and some other money, but I reckoned I better save it, because there ain't no telling how soon you are going to need it, away from home and amongst strangers that way. You can't be too careful. I ain't opposed to spending money on circuses when there ain't no other way, but there ain't no use in *wasting* it on them.

It was a real bully circus. It was the splendidest sight that ever was when they all come riding in, two and two, and gentleman and lady, side by side, the men just in their drawers and undershirts, and no shoes nor stirrups, and resting their hands on their thighs easy and comfortable—there must 'a' been twenty of them—and every lady with a lovely complexion, and perfectly beautiful, and looking just like a gang of real sure-enough queens, and dressed in clothes that cost millions of dollars, and just littered with diamonds. It was a powerful fine sight; I never see anything so lovely. And then one by one they got up and stood, and went a-weaving around the ring so gentle and wavy and graceful, the men looking ever so tall and airy and straight, with their heads bobbing and skimming along, away up there under the tent-roof, and every lady's rose-leafy dress flapping soft and silky around her hips, and she looking like the most loveliest parasol.

And then faster and faster they went, all of them dancing, first one foot out in the air and then the other, the horses leaning more and more, and the ringmaster going round and round the center pole, cracking his whip and shouting "Hi!—hi!" and the clown cracking jokes behind him; and by and by all hands dropped the reins, and every lady put her knuckles on her hips and every gentleman folded his arms, and then how the horses did lean over and hump themselves! And so one after the other they all skipped off into the ring, and made the sweetest bow I ever see, and then scampered out, and everybody clapped their hands and went just about wild.

Well, all through the circus they done the most astonishing things; and all the time that clown carried on so it most killed the people. The ringmaster couldn't ever say a word to him but he was back at him quick as a wink with the funniest things a body ever said; and how he ever *could* think of so many of them, and so sudden and so pat, was what I couldn't no way understand. Why, I couldn't 'a' thought of them in a year. And by and by a drunken man tried to get into the ring—said he wanted to ride; said he could ride as well as anybody that ever was. They argued and tried to keep him out, but he wouldn't listen, and the whole show come to a standstill. Then the people begun to holler at him and make fun of him, and that made him mad, and he begun to rip and tear; so that stirred up the people, and a lot of men begun to pile down off of the benches and swarm toward the ring, saying, "Knock him down! throw him out!" and one or two women begun to scream. So, then, the ringmaster he made a little speech, and said he hoped there wouldn't be no disturbance, and if the man would promise he wouldn't make no more trouble he would let him ride if he thought he could stay on the horse. So everybody laughed and said all right, and the man got on. The minute he was on, the horse begun to rip and tear and jump and cavort around, with two circus men hanging on to his bridle trying to hold him, and the drunken man hanging on to his neck, and his heels flying in the air every jump, and the whole crowd of people standing up shouting and laughing till tears rolled down. And at last, sure enough, all the circus men could do, the horse broke loose, and away he went like the very nation, round and round the ring, with that sot laying down on him and hanging to his neck, with first one leg hanging most to the ground on one side, and then t'other one on t'other side, and the people just crazy. It warn't funny to me, though; I was all of a tremble to see his danger. But pretty soon he struggled up astraddle and grabbed the bridle, a-reeling this way and that; and the next minute he sprung up and dropped the bridle and stood! and the horse a-going like a house afire, too. He just stood up there, a-sailing around as easy and comfortable as if he warn't ever drunk in his life—and then he begun to pull off his clothes and sling them. He shed them so thick they kind of clogged up the air, and altogether he shed seventeen suits. And, then, there he was, slim and handsome, and dressed the gaudiest and prettiest you ever saw, and he lit into that horse with his whip and made him fairly hum—and finally skipped off, and made his bow and danced off to the dressing room, and everybody just a-howling with pleasure and astonishment.

Then the ringmaster he see how he had been fooled, and he *was* the 55 sickest ringmaster you ever see, I reckon. Why, it was one of his own men! He had got up that joke all out of his own head, and never let on to nobody. Well, I felt sheepish enough to be took in so, but I wouldn't 'a' been in that ringmaster's place, not for a thousand dollars. I don't know; there may be bullier circuses than what that one was, but I never struck them yet. Anyways, it was plenty good enough for *me;* and wherever I run across it, it can have all of *my* custom every time.

Well, that night we had *our* show; but there warn't only about twelve people there—just enough to pay expenses. And they laughed all the time, and that made the duke mad; and everybody left, anyway, before the show was over, but one boy which was asleep. So the duke said these Arkansaw lunkheads couldn't come up to Shakespeare; what they wanted was low comedy—and maybe something ruther worse than low comedy, he reckoned. He said he could size their style. So next morning he got some big sheets of wrapping-paper and some black paint, and drawed off some handbills, and stuck them up all over the village. The bills said:

AT THE COURT HOUSE!
FOR 3 NIGHTS ONLY!
The World-Renowned Tragedians
DAVID GARRICK THE YOUNGER!
AND
EDMUND KEAN THE ELDER!

Of the London and Continental
Theatres,
In their Thrilling Tragedy of
THE KING'S CAMELEOPARD,
OR
THE ROYAL NONESUCH ! ! !
Admission 50 cents.

Then at the bottom was the biggest line of all, which said:

LADIES AND CHILDREN NOT ADMITTED

"There," says he, "if that line don't fetch them, I don't know Arkansaw!"

The Responsive Reader

1. The Boggs incident is one of several instances of murderous violence that young Huck witnesses on his trip down the great river. What if anything are we supposed to learn from it? Who or what is to blame? Have we left this kind of "senseless violence" behind?
2. Lynch justice or lynch law was long a blemish on this country's record as a civilized nation. What do you know about lynching as an American institution? What is Mark Twain's comment on lynch justice in this excerpt?
3. How do you react to Huck's account of his afternoon in the circus? Why do you think Mark Twain juxtaposed the circus interlude with the murder of Boggs?

Talking, Thinking, Writing

4. How do you react to Huck's use of his down-home Southern country dialect? Is it supposed to make him sound ignorant, uneducated, or what?
5. To judge from this excerpt, what is the secret of Mark Twain's humor and worldwide appeal? (Is his kind of humor obsolete in today's world?)
6. Tell an episode from your own experience or observation in Huck's innocent, naive country-boy style.

Collaborative Projects

7. Mark Twain loved to create dramatic situations, and he played them to the hilt. Working with a group, you may want to dramatize key scenes from this excerpt and present them to an audience of classmates. For instance, you might choose one of the following parts to act out:

   - Be one of the loafers and tell your audience about your one-horse town and some of its prominent citizens.
   - Impersonate the swaggering, threatening Boggs.

- Act out the way Boggs' daughter might have pleaded with her father if she had had a chance.
- Be one of the bystanders telling the story of how Boggs died.
- Play the role of Sherburn facing down the lynch mob.
- Play the role of Huck telling about his visit to the circus.

THE BLUE HOTEL
Stephen Crane

A man said to the universe:
"Sir, I exist!"
"However," replied the universe,
"The fact has not created in me
A sense of obligation."
    Stephen Crane, "The Man and the Universe"

Stephen Crane was one of America's leading practitioners of naturalism—a literary movement aiming at an unretouched picture of life. Its followers wanted to paint life as it was and not as seen through a fog of rosy sentiments and uplifting abstractions. Naturalistic writers wrote in an age when Charles Darwin's theory of evolution had focused attention on the struggle for existence. Nature, "red in tooth and claw," was an arena where only the fittest survived. The enemy of naturalism was sentimentality—basking in a warm glow of self-approving emotions, fooling oneself about the human capacity for savagery or about the cruelty of nature.

Crane's best-known short story is the partly autobiographical "The Open Boat" (1897), about the ordeal of shipwrecked sailors in a lifeboat who discover that their will to live means nothing to the pitiless ocean. Nature in this story is far from being a refuge or a healing influence in people's lives. The sailors discover that the only thing they can pit against the indifference of the universe is their sense of brotherhood, their sense of human solidarity, their loyalty to one another.

Crane was the fourteenth child of a Methodist minister, and he scraped together a living as a freelance journalist. He often looks at harsh reality from the vantage point of the impartial reporter. His first novel, Maggie: A Girl of the Streets *(1893) took a look at a subject considered taboo in polite society. In his classic Civil War novel,* The Red Badge of Courage *(1895), Crane showed not flag-waving patriots but young men sickened by fear and tormented by feelings of guilt.*

The following short story by Crane, published in 1898, is a parable of guilt and justice. What we call "senseless violence" is in reality often the end result of a chain of events. As in many of his stories, Crane here traces such a chain of events in patient, honest detail. He does little preaching or editorializing till the end. At the end, however, he forces us to confront the question: "Whose fault?"

I

The Palace Hotel at Fort Romper was painted a light blue, a shade that   *1*
is on the legs of a kind of heron, causing the bird to declare its position
against any background. The Palace Hotel, then, was always screaming and
howling in a way that made the dazzling winter landscape of Nebraska seem
only a gray swampish hush. It stood alone on the prairie, and when the snow
was falling the town two hundred yards away was not visible. But when the
traveller alighted at the railway station he was obliged to pass the Palace Hotel
before he could come upon the company of low clapboard houses which
composed Fort Romper, and it was not to be thought that any traveller could
pass the Palace Hotel without looking at it. Pat Scully, the proprietor, had
proved himself a master of strategy when he chose his paints. It is true that
on clear days, when the great transcontinental expresses, long lines of swaying Pullmans, swept through Fort Romper, passengers were overcome at the
sight, and the cult that knows the brown-reds and the subdivisions of the
dark greens of the East expressed shame, pity, horror, in a laugh. But to the
citizens of this prairie town and to the people who would naturally stop
there, Pat Scully had performed a feat. With this opulence and splendor,
these creeds, classes, egotisms, that streamed through Romper on the rails
day after day, they had no color in common.

As if the display delights of such a blue hotel were not sufficiently
enticing, it was Scully's habit to go every morning and evening to meet the
leisurely trains that stopped at Romper and work his seductions upon any
man that he might see wavering, gripsack in hand.

One morning, when a snow-crusted engine dragged its long string of
freight cars and its one passenger coach to the station, Scully performed the
marvel of catching three men. One was a shaky and quick-eyed Swede, with
a great shining cheap valise; one was a tall bronzed cowboy, who was on his
way to a ranch near the Dakota line; one was a little silent man from the
East, who didn't look it, and didn't announce it. Scully practically made them
prisoners. He was so nimble and merry and kindly that each probably felt it
would be the height of brutality to try to escape. They trudged off over the
creaking board sidewalks in the wake of the eager little Irishman. He wore a
heavy fur cap squeezed tightly down on his head. It caused his two red ears
to stick out stiffly, as if they were made of tin.

At last, Scully, elaborately, with boisterous hospitality, conducted them
through the portals of the blue hotel. The room which they entered was
small. It seemed to be merely a proper temple for an enormous stove, which,
in the center, was humming with godlike violence. At various points on its
surface the iron had become luminous and glowed yellow from the heat.
Beside the stove Scully's son Johnnie was playing High-Five with an old
farmer who had whiskers both gray and sandy. They were quarrelling. Frequently the old farmer turned his face toward a box of sawdust—colored
brown from tobacco juice—that was behind the stove, and spat with an air

of great impatience and irritation. With a loud flourish of words Scully destroyed the game of cards, and bustled his son upstairs with part of the baggage of the new guests. He himself conducted them to three basins of the coldest water in the world. The cowboy and the Easterner burnished themselves fiery red with this water, until it seemed to be some kind of metal polish. The Swede, however, merely dipped his fingers gingerly and with trepidation. It was notable that throughout this series of small ceremonies the three travellers were made to feel that Scully was very benevolent. He was conferring great favors upon them. He handed the towel from one to another with an air of philanthropic impulse.

Afterward they went to the first room, and, sitting about the stove, listened to Scully's officious clamor at his daughters, who were preparing the midday meal. They reflected in the silence of experienced men who tread carefully amid new people. Nevertheless, the old farmer, stationary, invincible in his chair near the warmest part of the stove, turned his face from the sawdust-box frequently and addressed a glowing commonplace to the strangers. Usually he was answered in short but adequate sentences by either the cowboy or the Easterner. The Swede said nothing. He seemed to be occupied in making furtive estimates of each man in the room. One might have thought that he had the sense of silly suspicion which comes to guilt. He resembled a badly frightened man.

Later, at dinner, he spoke a little, addressing his conversation entirely to Scully. He volunteered that he had come from New York, where for ten years he had worked as a tailor. These facts seemed to strike Scully as fascinating, and afterward he volunteered that he had lived at Romper for fourteen years. The Swede asked about the crops and the price of labor. He seemed barely to listen to Scully's extended replies. His eyes continued to rove from man to man.

Finally, with a laugh and a wink, he said that some of these Western communities were very dangerous; and after his statement he straightened his legs under the table, tilted his head, and laughed again, loudly. It was plain that the demonstration had no meaning to the others. They looked at him wondering and in silence.

II

As the men trooped heavily back into the front room, the two little windows presented views of a turmoiling sea of snow. The huge arms of the wind were making attempts—mighty, circular, futile—to embrace the flakes as they sped. A gate-post like a still man with a blanched face stood aghast amid this profligate fury. In a hearty voice Scully announced the presence of a blizzard. The guests of the blue hotel, lighting their pipes, assented with grunts of lazy masculine contentment. No island of the sea could be exempt in the degree of this little room with its humming stove. Johnnie, son of Scully, in a tone which defined his opinion of his ability as a card player, challenged the old farmer of both gray and sandy whiskers to a game of High-Five. The farmer agreed with a contemptuous and bitter scoff. They sat close to the stove, and squared their knees under a wide board. The cowboy and the Easterner watched the game with interest. The Swede remained near the window, aloof, but with a countenance that showed signs of an inexplicable excitement.

The play of Johnnie and the gray-beard was suddenly ended by another quarrel. The old man arose while casting a look of heated scorn at his adversary. He slowly buttoned his coat, and then stalked with fabulous dignity from the room. In the discreet silence of all the other men the Swede laughed. His laughter rang somehow childish. Men by this time had begun to look at him askance, as if they wished to inquire what ailed him.

A new game was formed jocosely. The cowboy volunteered to become   *10* the partner of Johnnie, and they all then turned to ask the Swede to throw in his lot with the little Easterner. He asked some questions about the game, and, learning that it wore many names, and that he had played it when it was under an alias, he accepted the invitation. He strode toward the men nervously, as if he expected to be assaulted. Finally, seated, he gazed from face to face and laughed shrilly. This laugh was so strange that the Easterner looked up quickly, the cowboy sat intent and with his mouth open, and Johnnie paused, holding the cards with still fingers.

Afterward there was a short silence. Then Johnnie said, "Well, let's get at it. Come on now!" They pulled their chairs forward until their knees were bunched under the board. They began to play, and their interest in the game caused the others to forget the manner of the Swede.

The cowboy was a board-whacker. Each time that he held superior cards he whanged them, one by one, with exceeding force, down upon the improvised table, and took the tricks with a glowing air of prowess and pride that sent thrills of indignation into the hearts of his opponents. A game with a board-whacker in it is sure to become intense. The countenances of the Easterner and the Swede were miserable whenever the cowboy thundered down his aces and kings, while Johnnie, his eyes gleaming with joy, chuckled and chuckled.

Because of the absorbing play none considered the strange ways of the Swede. They paid strict heed to the game. Finally, during a lull caused by a new deal, the Swede suddenly addressed Johnnie: "I suppose there have been a good many men killed in this room." The jaws of the others dropped and they looked at him.

"What in hell are you talking about?" said Johnnie.

The Swede laughed again his blatant laugh, full of a kind of false cour-   *15* age and defiance. "Oh, you know what I mean all right," he answered.

"I'm a liar if I do!" Johnnie protested. The card was halted, and the men stared at the Swede. Johnnie evidently felt that as the son of the proprietor he should make a direct inquiry. "Now, what might you be drivin' at, mister?" he asked. The Swede winked at him. It was a wink full of cunning.

His fingers shook on the edge of the board. "Oh, maybe you think I have been to nowheres. Maybe you think I'm a tenderfoot?"

"I don't know nothin' about you," answered Johnnie, "and I don't give a damn where you've been. All I got to say is that I don't know what you're driving at. There hain't never been nobody killed in this room."

The cowboy, who had been steadily gazing at the Swede, then spoke: "What's wrong with you, mister?"

Apparently it seemed to the Swede that he was formidably menaced. He shivered and turned white near the corners of his mouth. He sent an appealing glance in the direction of the little Easterner. During these moments he did not forget to wear his air of advanced pot-valor. "They say they don't know what I mean," he remarked mockingly to the Easterner.

The latter answered after prolonged and cautious reflection. "I don't understand you," he said, impassively.   20

The Swede made a movement then which announced that he thought he had encountered treachery from the only quarter where he had expected sympathy, if not help. "Oh, I see you are all against me. I see—"

The cowboy was in a state of deep stupefaction. "Say," he cried, as he tumbled the deck violently down upon the board, "say, what are you gittin' at, hey?"

The Swede sprang up with the celerity of a man escaping from a snake on the floor. "I don't want to fight!" he shouted. "I don't want to fight!"

The cowboy stretched his long legs indolently and deliberately. His hands were in his pockets. He spat into the sawdust-box. "Well, who the hell thought you did?" he inquired.

The Swede backed rapidly toward a corner of the room. His hands   25
were out protectingly in front of his chest, but he was making an obvious struggle to control his fright. "Gentlemen," he quavered, "I suppose I am going to be killed before I can leave this house! I suppose I am going to be killed before I can leave this house!" In his eyes was the dying-swan look. Through the windows could be seen the snow turning blue in the shadow of dusk. The wind tore at the house, and some loose thing beat regularly against the clapboards like a spirit tapping.

A door opened, and Scully himself entered. He paused in surprise as he noted the tragic attitude of the Swede. Then he said, "What's the matter here?"

The Swede answered him swiftly and eagerly: "These men are going to kill me."

"Kill you!" ejaculated Scully. "Kill you! What are you talkin'?"

The Swede made the gesture of a martyr.

Scully wheeled sternly upon his son. "What is this, Johnnie?"   30

The lad had grown sullen. "Damned if I know," he answered. "I can't make no sense to it." He began to shuffle the cards, fluttering them together with an angry snap. "He says a good many men have been killed in this room, or something like that. And he says he's goin' to be killed here too. I don't know what ails him. He's crazy, I shouldn't wonder."

Scully then looked for explanation to the cowboy, but the cowboy simply shrugged his shoulders.

"Kill you?" said Scully again to the Swede. "Kill you? Man, you're off your nut."

"Oh, I know," burst out the Swede. "I know what will happen. Yes, I'm crazy—yes. Yes, of course, I'm crazy—yes. But I know one thing—" There was a sort of sweat of misery and terror upon his face. "I know I won't get out of here alive."

The cowboy drew a deep breath, as if his mind was passing into the last   *35* stages of dissolution. "Well, I'm doggoned," he whispered to himself.

Scully wheeled suddenly and faced his son. "You've been troublin' this man!"

Johnnie's voice was loud with its burden of grievance. "Why, good Gawd, I ain't done nothin' to 'im."

The Swede broke in. "Gentlemen, do not disturb yourselves. I will leave this house. I will go away, because"—he accused them dramatically with his glance—"because I do not want to be killed."

Scully was furious with his son. "Will you tell me what is the matter, you young divil? What's the matter, anyhow? Speak out!"

"Blame it!" cried Johnnie in despair, "don't I tell you I don't know?   *40* He—he says we want to kill him, and that's all I know. I can't tell what ails him."

The Swede continued to repeat: "Never mind, Mr. Scully; never mind. I will leave this house. I will go away, because I do not wish to be killed. Yes, of course, I am crazy—yes. But I know one thing! I will go away. I will leave this house. Never mind, Mr. Scully; never mind. I will go away."

"You will not go 'way," said Scully. "You will not go 'way until I hear the reason of this business. If anybody has troubled you I will take care of him. This is my house. You are under my roof, and I will not allow any peaceable man to be troubled here." He cast a terrible eye upon Johnnie, the cowboy, and the Easterner.

"Never mind, Mr. Scully; never mind. I will go away. I do not wish to be killed." The Swede moved toward the door which opened upon the stairs. It was evidently his intention to go at once for his baggage.

"No, no," shouted Scully peremptorily; but the white-faced man slid by him and disappeared. "Now," said Scully severely, "what does this mane?"

Johnnie and the cowboy cried together: "Why, we didn't do nothin'   *45* to 'im!"

Scully's eyes were cold. "No," he said, "you didn't?"

Johnnie swore a deep oath. "Why, this is the wildest loon I ever see. We didn't do nothin' at all. We were jest sittin' here playin' cards, and he—"

The father suddenly spoke to the Easterner. "Mr. Blanc," he asked, "what has these boys been doin'?"

The Easterner reflected again. "I didn't see anything wrong at all," he said at last, slowly.

Scully began to howl. "But what does it mane?" He stared ferociously   *50*
at his son. "I have a mind to lather you for this, my boy."

Johnnie was frantic. "Well, what have I done?" he bawled at his father.

III

"I think you are tongue-tied," said Scully finally to his son, the cowboy,
and the Easterner; and at the end of this scornful sentence he left the room.

Upstairs the Swede was swiftly fastening the straps of his great valise.
Once his back happened to be half turned toward the door, and, hearing a
noise there, he wheeled and sprang up, uttering a loud cry. Scully's wrinkled
visage showed grimly in the light of the small lamp he carried. This yellow
effulgence, streaming upward, colored only his prominent features, and left
his eyes, for instance, in mysterious shadow. He resembled a murderer.

"Man! man!" he exclaimed, "have you gone daffy?"

"Oh, no! Oh, no!" rejoined the other. "There are people in this world   *55*
who know pretty nearly as much as you do—understand?"

For a moment they stood gazing at each other. Upon the Swede's
deathly pale cheeks were two spots brightly crimson and sharply edged, as
if they had been carefully painted. Scully placed the light on the table and
sat himself on the edge of the bed. He spoke ruminatively. "By cracky, I
never heard of such a thing in my life. It's a complete muddle. I can't, for
the soul of me, think how you ever got this idea into your head." Presently
he lifted his eyes and asked: "And did you sure think they were going to
kill you?"

The Swede scanned the old man as if he wished to see into his mind.
"I did," he said at last. He obviously suspected that this answer might precipitate an outbreak. As he pulled on a strap his whole arm shook, the elbow
wavering like a bit of paper.

Scully banged his hand impressively on the footboard of the bed. "Why,
man, we're goin' to have a line of ilictric street-cars in this town next spring."

" 'A line of electric street-cars,' " repeated the Swede, stupidly.

"And," said Scully, "there's a new railroad goin' to be built down from   *60*
Broken Arm to here. Not to mintion the four churches and the smashin'
big brick schoolhouse. Then there's the big factory, too. Why, in two years
Romper'll be a met-tro-*pol*-is."

Having finished the preparation of his baggage, the Swede straightened
himself. "Mr. Scully," he said, with sudden hardihood, "how much do I
owe you?"

"You don't owe me anythin'," said the old man, angrily.

"Yes, I do," retorted the Swede. He took seventy-five cents from his
pocket and tendered it to Scully; but the latter snapped his fingers in disdainful refusal. However, it happened that they both stood gazing in a strange
fashion at three silver pieces on the Swede's open palm.

"I'll not take your money," said Scully at last. "Not after what's been goin' on here." Then a plan seemed to strike him. "Here," he cried, picking up his lamp and moving toward the door. "Here! Come with me a minute."

"No," said the Swede, in overwhelming alarm. 65

"Yes," urged the old man. "Come on! I want you to come and see a picter—just across the hall—in my room."

The Swede must have concluded that his hour was come. His jaw dropped and his teeth showed like a dead man's. He ultimately followed Scully across the corridor, but he had the step of one hung in chains.

Scully flashed the light high on the wall of his own chamber. There was revealed a ridiculous photograph of a little girl. She was leaning against a balustrade of gorgeous decoration, and the formidable bang to her hair was prominent. The figure was as graceful as an upright sled-stake, and, withal, it was of the hue of lead. "There," said Scully, tenderly, "that's the picter of my little girl that died. Her name was Carrie. She had the purtiest hair you ever saw! I was that fond of her, she—"

Turning then, he saw that the Swede was not contemplating the picture at all, but, instead, was keeping keen watch on the gloom in the rear.

"Look, man!" cried Scully, heartily. "That's the picter of my little gal 70 that died. Her name was Carrie. And then here's the picter of my oldest boy. Michael. He's a lawyer in Lincoln, an' doin' well. I gave that boy a grand eddication, and I'm glad for it now. He's a fine boy. Look at 'im now. Ain't he bold as blazes, him there in Lincoln, an honored an' respicted gintleman! An honored and respicted gintleman," concluded Scully with a flourish. And, so saying, he smote the Swede jovially on the back.

The Swede faintly smiled.

"Now," said the old man, "there's only one more thing." He dropped suddenly to the floor and thrust his head beneath the bed. The Swede could hear his muffled voice. "I'd keep it under me piller if it wasn't for that boy Johnnie. Then there's the old woman— Where is it now? I never put it twice in the same place. Ah, now come out with you!"

Presently he backed clumsily from under the bed, dragging with him an old coat rolled into a bundle. "I've fetched him," he muttered. Kneeling on the floor, he unrolled the coat and extracted from its heart a large yellow-brown whiskey-bottle.

His first maneuver was to hold the bottle up to the light. Reassured, apparently, that nobody had been tampering with it, he thrust it with a generous movement toward the Swede.

The weak-kneed Swede was about to eagerly clutch this element of 75 strength, but he suddenly jerked his hand away and cast a look of horror upon Scully.

"Drink," said the old man affectionately. He had risen to his feet, and now stood facing the Swede.

There was a silence. Then again Scully said: "Drink!"

The Swede laughed wildly. He grabbed the bottle, put it to his mouth; and as his lips curled absurdly around the opening and his throat worked, he kept his glance, burning with hatred, upon the old man's face.

IV

After the departure of Scully the three men, with the card-board still upon their knees, preserved for a long time an astounded silence. Then Johnnie said: "That's the doddangedest Swede I ever see."

"He ain't no Swede," said the cowboy, scornfully.

"Well, what is he then?" cried Johnnie. "What is he then?"

"It's my opinion," replied the cowboy deliberately, "he's some kind of a Dutchman." It was a venerable custom of the country to entitle as Swedes all light-haired men who spoke with a heavy tongue. In consequence the idea of the cowboy was not without its daring. "Yes, sir," he repeated. "It's my opinion this feller is some kind of a Dutchman."

"Well, he says he's a Swede, anyhow," muttered Johnnie, sulkily. He turned to the Easterner: "What do you think, Mr. Blanc?"

"Oh, I don't know," replied the Easterner.

"Well, what do you think makes him act that way?" asked the cowboy.

"Why, he's frightened." The Easterner knocked his pipe against a rim of the stove. "He's clear frightened out of his boots."

"What at?" cried Johnnie and the cowboy together.

The Easterner reflected over his answer.

"What at?" cried the others again.

"Oh, I don't know, but it seems to me this man has been reading dime novels, and he thinks he's right out in the middle of it—the shootin' and stabbin' and all."

"But," said the cowboy, deeply scandalized, "this ain't Wyoming, ner none of them places. This is Nebrasker."

"Yes," added Johnnie, "an' why don't he wait till he gits *out West*?"

The travelled Easterner laughed. "It isn't different there even—not in these days. But he thinks he's right in the middle of hell."

Johnnie and the cowboy mused long.

"It's awful funny," remarked Johnnie at last.

"Yes," said the cowboy. "This is a queer game. I hope we don't git snowed in, because then we'd have to stand this here man bein' around with us all the time. That wouldn't be no good."

"I wish pop would throw him out," said Johnnie.

Presently they heard a loud stamping on the stairs, accompanied by ringing jokes in the voice of old Scully, and laughter, evidently from the Swede. The men around the stove stared vacantly at each other. "Gosh!" said the cowboy. The door flew open, and old Scully, flushed and anecdotal, came into the room. He was jabbering at the Swede, who followed him, laughing bravely. It was the entry of two roisterers from a banquet hall.

"Come now," said Scully sharply to the three seated men, "move up and give us a chance at the stove." The cowboy and the Easterner obediently sidled their chairs to make room for the newcomers. Johnnie, however, simply arranged himself in a more indolent attitude, and then remained motionless.

"Come! Git over, there," said Scully.   *100*

"Plenty of room on the other side of the stove," said Johnnie.

"Do you think we want to sit in the draught?" roared the father.

But the Swede here interposed with a grandeur of confidence. "No, no. Let the boy sit where he likes," he cried in a bullying voice to the father.

"All right! All right!" said Scully, deferentially. The cowboy and the Easterner exchanged glances of wonder.

The five chairs were formed in a crescent about one side of the stove. *105* The Swede began to talk; he talked arrogantly, profanely, angrily. Johnnie, the cowboy, and the Easterner maintained a morose silence, while old Scully appeared to be receptive and eager, breaking in constantly with sympathetic ejaculations.

Finally the Swede announced that he was thirsty. He moved in his chair, and said that he would go for a drink of water.

"I'll git it for you," cried Scully at once.

"No," said the Swede, contemptuously. "I'll get it for myself." He arose and stalked with the air of an owner off into the executive parts of the hotel.

As soon as the Swede was out of hearing Scully sprang to his feet and whispered intensely to the others: "Upstairs he thought I was tryin' to poison 'im."

"Say," said Johnnie, "this makes me sick. Why don't you throw 'im out *110* in the snow?"

"Why, he's all right now," declared Scully. "It was only that he was from the East, and he thought this was a tough place. That's all. He's all right now."

The cowboy looked with admiration upon the Easterner. "You were straight," he said. "You were on to that there Dutchman."

"Well," said Johnnie to his father, "he may be all right now, but I don't see it. Other time he was scared, but now he's too fresh."

Scully's speech was always a combination of Irish brogue and idiom, Western twang and idiom, and scraps of curiously formal diction taken from the story-books and newspapers. He now hurled a strange mass of language at the head of his son. "What do I keep? What do I keep? What do I keep?" he demanded, in a voice of thunder. He slapped his knee impressively, to indicate that he himself was going to make reply, and that all should heed. "I keep a hotel," he shouted. "A hotel, do you mind? A guest under my roof has sacred privileges. He is to be intimidated by none. Not one word shall he hear that would prijudice him in favor of goin' away. I'll not have it. There's no place in this here town where they can say they ever took in a guest of mine because he was afraid to stay here." He wheeled suddenly upon the cowboy and the Easterner. "Am I right?"

"Yes, Mr. Scully," said the cowboy, "I think you're right."   115

"Yes, Mr. Scully," said the Easterner, "I think you're right."

V

At six-o'clock supper, the Swede fizzed like a fire-wheel. He sometimes seemed on the point of bursting into riotous song, and in all his madness he was encouraged by old Scully. The Easterner was encased in reserve; the cowboy sat in wide-mouthed amazement, forgetting to eat, while Johnnie wrathily demolished great plates of food. The daughters of the house, when they were obliged to replenish the biscuits, approached as warily as Indians, and, having succeeded in their purpose, fled with ill-concealed trepidation. The Swede domineered the whole feast, and he gave it the appearance of a cruel bacchanal. He seemed to have grown suddenly taller, he gazed, brutally disdainful, into every face. His voice rang through the room. Once when he jabbed out harpoon-fashion with his fork to pinion a biscuit, the weapon nearly impaled the hand of the Easterner, which had been stretched quietly out for the same biscuit.

After supper, as the men filed toward the other room, the Swede smote Scully ruthlessly on the shoulder. "Well, old boy, that was a good, square meal." Johnnie looked hopefully at his father; he knew that shoulder was tender from an old fall; and, indeed, it appeared for a moment as if Scully was going to flame out over the matter, but in the end he smiled a sickly smile and remained silent. The others understood from his manner that he was admitting his responsibility for the Swede's new view-point.

Johnnie, however, addressed his parent in an aside. "Why don't you license somebody to kick you downstairs?" Scully scowled darkly by way of reply.

When they were gathered about the stove, the Swede insisted on   120 another game of High-Five. Scully gently deprecated the plan at first, but the Swede turned a wolfish glare upon him. The old man subsided, and the Swede canvassed the others. In his tone there was always a great threat. The cowboy and the Easterner both remarked indifferently that they would play. Scully said that he would presently have to go to meet the 6.58 train, and so the Swede turned menacingly upon Johnnie. For a moment their glances crossed like blades, and then Johnnie smiled and said, "Yes, I'll play."

They formed a square, with the little board on their knees. The Easterner and the Swede were again partners. As the play went on, it was noticeable that the cowboy was not board-whacking as usual. Meanwhile, Scully, near the lamp, had put on his spectacles and, with an appearance curiously like an old priest, was reading a newspaper. In time he went out to meet the 6.58 train, and, despite his precautions, a gust of polar wind whirled into the room as he opened the door. Besides scattering the cards, it chilled the players to the marrow. The Swede cursed frightfully. When Scully returned, his entrance disturbed a cosy and friendly scene. The Swede again cursed. But presently they were once more intent, their heads bent forward and their hands moving swiftly. The Swede had adopted the fashion of board-whacking.

Scully took up his paper and for a long time remained immersed in matters which were extraordinarily remote from him. The lamp burned badly, and once he stopped to adjust the wick. The newspaper, as he turned from page to page, rustled with a slow and comfortable sound. Then suddenly he heard three terrible words: "You are cheatin'!"

Such scenes often prove that there can be little of dramatic import in environment. Any room can present a tragic front; any room can be comic. This little den was now hideous as a torture-chamber. The new faces of the men themselves had changed it upon the instant. The Swede held a huge fist in front of Johnnie's face, while the latter looked steadily over it into the blazing orbs of his accuser. The Easterner had grown pallid; the cowboy's jaw had dropped in that expression of bovine amazement which was one of his important mannerisms. After the three words, the first sound in the room was made by Scully's paper as it floated forgotten to his feet. His spectacles had also fallen from his nose, but by a clutch he had saved them in air. His hand, grasping the spectacles, now remained poised awkwardly and near his shoulder. He stared at the card-players.

Probably the silence was while a second elapsed. Then, if the floor had been suddenly twitched out from under the men they could not have moved quicker. The five had projected themselves headlong toward a common point. It happened that Johnnie, in rising to hurl himself upon the Swede, had stumbled slightly because of his curiously instinctive care for the cards and the board. The loss of the moment allowed time for the arrival of Scully, and also allowed the cowboy time to give the Swede a great push which sent him staggering back. The men found tongue together, and hoarse shouts of rage, appeal, or fear burst from every throat. The cowboy pushed and jostled feverishly at the Swede, and the Easterner and Scully clung wildly to Johnnie; but through the smoky air, above the swaying bodies of the peace-compellers, the eyes of the two warriors ever sought each other in glances of challenge that were at once hot and steely.

Of course the board had been overturned, and now the whole company of cards was scattered over the floor, where the boots of the men trampled the fat and painted kings and queens as they gazed with their silly eyes at the war that was waging above them.

Scully's voice was dominating the yells. "Stop now! Stop, I say! Stop, now—"

Johnnie, as he struggled to burst through the rank formed by Scully and the Easterner, was crying, "Well, he says I cheated! He says I cheated! I won't allow no man to say I cheated! If he says I cheated, he's a — —!"

The cowboy was telling the Swede, "Quit, now! Quit, d'ye hear—"

The screams of the Swede never ceased: "He did cheat! I saw him! I saw him—"

As for the Easterner, he was importuning in a voice that was not heeded: "Wait a moment, can't you? Oh, wait a moment. What's the good of a fight over a game of cards? Wait a moment—" 130

In this tumult no complete sentences were clear. "Cheat"—"Quit"—"He says"—these fragments pierced the uproar and rang out sharply. It was remarkable that, whereas Scully undoubtedly made the most noise, he was the least heard of any of the riotous band.

Then suddenly there was a great cessation. It was as if each man had paused for breath; and although the room was still lighted with the anger of men, it could be seen that there was no danger of immediate conflict, and at once Johnnie, shouldering his way forward, almost succeeded in confronting the Swede. "What did you say I cheated for? What did you say I cheated for? I don't cheat, and I won't let no man say I do!"

The Swede said, "I saw you! I saw you!"

"Well," cried Johnnie, "I'll fight any man what says I cheat!"

"No, you won't," said the cowboy. "Not here." 135

"Ah, be still, can't you?" said Scully, coming between them.

The quiet was sufficient to allow the Easterner's voice to be heard. He was repeating, "Oh, wait a moment, can't you? What's the good of a fight over a game of cards? Wait a moment!"

Johnnie, his red face appearing above his father's shoulder, hailed the Swede again. "Did you say I cheated?"

The Swede showed his teeth. "Yes."

"Then," said Johnnie, "we must fight." 140

"Yes, fight," roared the Swede. He was like a demoniac. "Yes, fight! I'll show you what kind of a man I am! I'll show you who you want to fight! Maybe you think I can't fight! Maybe you think I can't! I'll show you, you skin, you card-sharp! Yes, you cheated! You cheated! You cheated!"

"Well, let's go at it, then, mister," said Johnnie, coolly.

The cowboy's brow was beaded with sweat from his efforts in intercepting all sorts of raids. He turned in despair to Scully. "What are you goin' to do now?"

A change had come over the Celtic visage of the old man. He now seemed all eagerness; his eyes glowed.

"We'll let them fight," he answered, stalwartly. "I can't put up with it any longer. I've stood this damned Swede till I'm sick. We'll let them fight." 145

VI

The men prepared to go out-of-doors. The Easterner was so nervous that he had great difficulty in getting his arms into the sleeves of his new leather coat. As the cowboy drew his fur cap down over his ears his hands trembled. In fact, Johnnie and old Scully were the only ones who displayed no agitation. These preliminaries were conducted without words.

Scully threw open the door. "Well, come on," he said. Instantly a terrific wind caused the flame of the lamp to struggle at its wick, while a puff of black smoke sprang from the chimney-top. The stove was in mid-current of the blast, and its voice swelled to equal the roar of the storm. Some of the scarred and bedabbled cards were caught up from the floor and dashed helplessly against the farther wall. The men lowered their heads and plunged into the tempest as into a sea.

No snow was falling, but great whirls and clouds of flakes, swept up from the ground by the frantic winds, were streaming southward with the speed of bullets. The covered land was blue with the sheen of an unearthly satin, and there was no other hue save where, at the low, black railway station—which seemed incredibly distant—one light gleamed like a tiny jewel. As the men floundered into a thigh-deep drift, it was known that the Swede was bawling out something. Scully went to him, put a hand on his shoulder, and projected an ear. "What's that you say?" he shouted.

"I say," bawled the Swede again, "I won't stand much show against this gang. I know you'll all pitch on me."

Scully smote him reproachfully on the arm. "Tut, man!" he yelled. The *150* wind tore the words from Scully's lips and scattered them far alee.

"You are all a gang of—" boomed the Swede, but the storm also seized the remainder of this sentence.

Immediately turning their backs upon the wind, the men had swung around a corner to the sheltered side of the hotel. It was the function of the little house to preserve here, amid this great devastation of snow, an irregular V-shape of heavily encrusted grass, which crackled beneath the feet. One could imagine the great drifts piled against the windward side. When the party reached the comparative peace of this spot it was found that the Swede was still bellowing.

"Oh, I know what kind of a thing this is! I know you'll all pitch on me. I can't lick you all!"

Scully turned upon him panther-fashion. "You'll not have to whip all of us. You'll have to whip my son Johnnie. An' the man what troubles you durin' that time will have me to dale with."

The arrangements were swiftly made. The two men faced each other, *155* obedient to the harsh commands of Scully, whose face, in the subtly luminous gloom, could be seen set in the austere impersonal lines that are pictured on the countenances of the Roman veterans. The Easterner's teeth were chattering, and he was hopping up and down like a mechanical toy. The cowboy stood rock-like.

The contestants had not stripped off any clothing. Each was in his ordinary attire. Their fists were up, and they eyed each other in a calm that had the elements of leonine cruelty in it.

During this pause, the Easterner's mind, like a film, took lasting impressions of three men—the iron-nerved master of the ceremony; the Swede, pale, motionless, terrible; and Johnnie, serene yet ferocious, brutish yet heroic. The entire prelude had in it a tragedy greater than the tragedy of action, and this aspect was accentuated by the long, mellow cry of the blizzard, as it sped the tumbling and wailing flakes into the black abyss of the south.

"Now!" said Scully.

The two combatants leaped forward and crashed together like bullocks. There was heard the cushioned sound of blows, and of a curse squeezing out from between the tight teeth of one.

As for the spectators, the Easterner's pent-up breath exploded from him 160 with a pop of relief, absolute relief from the tension of the preliminaries. The cowboy bounded into the air with a yowl. Scully was immovable as from supreme amazement and fear at the fury of the fight which he himself had permitted and arranged.

For a time the encounter in the darkness was such a perplexity of flying arms that it presented no more detail than would a swiftly revolving wheel. Occasionally a face, as if illumined by a flash of light, would shine out, ghastly and marked with pink spots. A moment later, the men might have been known as shadows, if it were not for the involuntary utterance of oaths that came from them in whispers.

Suddenly a holocaust of warlike desire caught the cowboy, and he bolted forward with the speed of a broncho. "Go it, Johnnie! go it! Kill him! Kill him!"

Scully confronted him. "Kape back," he said; and by his glance the cowboy could tell that this man was Johnnie's father.

To the Easterner there was a monotony of unchangeable fighting that was an abomination. This confused mingling was eternal to his sense, which was concentrated in a longing for the end, the priceless end. Once the fighters lurched near him, and as he scrambled hastily backward he heard them breathe like men on the rack.

"Kill him, Johnnie! Kill him! Kill him! Kill him!" The cowboy's face 165 was contorted like one of those agony masks in museums.

"Keep still," said Scully, icily.

Then there was a sudden loud grunt, incomplete, cut short, and Johnnie's body swung away from the Swede and fell with sickening heaviness to the grass. The cowboy was barely in time to prevent the mad Swede from flinging himself upon his prone adversary. "No, you don't," said the cowboy, interposing an arm. "Wait a second."

Scully was at his son's side. "Johnnie! Johnnie, me boy!" His voice had a quality of melancholy tenderness. "Johnnie! Can you go on with it?" He looked anxiously down into the bloody, pulpy face of his son.

There was a moment of silence, and then Johnnie answered in his ordinary voice, "Yes, I—it—yes."

Assisted by his father he struggled to his feet. "Wait a bit now till you *170*
git your wind," said the old man.

A few paces away the cowboy was lecturing the Swede. "No, you
don't! Wait a second!"

The Easterner was plucking at Scully's sleeve. "Oh, this is enough," he
pleaded. "This is enough! Let it go as it stands. This is enough!"

"Bill," said Scully, "git out of the road." The cowboy stepped aside.
"Now." The combatants were actuated by a new caution as they advanced
toward collision. They glared at each other, and then the Swede aimed a
lightning blow that carried with it his entire weight. Johnny was evidently
half stupid from weakness, but he miraculously dodged, and his fist sent the
over-balanced Swede sprawling.

The cowboy, Scully, and the Easterner burst into a cheer that was like
a chorus of triumphant soldiery, but before its conclusion the Swede had
scuffled agilely to his feet and come in berserk abandon at his foe. There was
another perplexity of flying arms, and Johnnie's body again swung away and
fell, even as a bundle might fall from a roof. The Swede instantly staggered
to a little wind-waved tree and leaned upon it, breathing like an engine,
while his savage and flame-lit eyes roamed from face to face as the men bent
over Johnnie. There was a splendor of isolation in his situation at this time
which the Easterner felt once when, lifting his eyes from the man on the
ground, he beheld that mysterious and lonely figure, waiting.

"Are you any good yet, Johnnie?" asked Scully in a broken voice. *175*

The son gasped and opened his eyes languidly. After a moment he
answered, "No—I ain't—any good—any—more." Then, from shame and
bodily ill, he began to weep, the tears furrowing down through the bloodstains on his face. "He was too—too—too heavy for me."

Scully straightened and addressed the waiting figure. "Stranger," he said,
evenly, "it's all up with our side." Then his voice changed into that vibrant
huskiness which is commonly the tone of the most simple and deadly an-
nouncements. "Johnnie is whipped."

Without reply, the victor moved off on the route to the front door of
the hotel.

The cowboy was formulating new and unspellable blasphemies. The
Easterner was startled to find that they were out in a wind that seemed to
come direct from the shadowed arctic floes. He heard again the wail of the
snow as it was flung to its grave in the south. He knew now that all this time
the cold had been sinking into him deeper and deeper, and he wondered
that he had not perished. He felt indifferent to the condition of the van-
quished man.

"Johnnie, can you walk?" asked Scully. *180*

"Did I hurt—hurt him any?" asked the son.

"Can you walk, boy? Can you walk?"

Johnnie's voice was suddenly strong. There was a robust impatience in
it. "I asked you whether I hurt him any!"

"Yes, yes, Johnnie," answered the cowboy, consolingly; "he's hurt a good deal."

They raised him from the ground, and as soon as he was on his feet he went tottering off, rebuffing all attempts at assistance. When the party rounded the corner they were fairly blinded by the pelting of the snow. It burned their faces like fire. The cowboy carried Johnnie through the drift to the door. As they entered, some cards again rose from the floor and beat against the wall.

The Easterner rushed to the stove. He was so profoundly chilled that he almost dared to embrace the glowing iron. The Swede was not in the room. Johnnie sank into a chair and, folding his arms on his knees, buried his face in them. Scully, warming one foot and then the other at a rim of the stove, muttered to himself with Celtic mournfulness. The cowboy had removed his fur cap, and with a dazed and rueful air he was running one hand through his tousled locks. From overhead they could hear the creaking of boards, as the Swede tramped here and there in his room.

The sad quiet was broken by the sudden flinging open of a door that led toward the kitchen. It was instantly followed by an inrush of women. They precipitated themselves upon Johnnie amid a chorus of lamentation. Before they carried their prey off to the kitchen, there to be bathed and harangued with that mixture of sympathy and abuse which is a feat of their sex, the mother straightened herself and fixed old Scully with an eye of stern reproach. "Shame be upon you, Patrick Scully!" she cried. "Your own son, too. Shame be upon you!"

"There, now! Be quiet, now!" said the old man, weakly.

"Shame be upon you, Patrick Scully!" The girls, rallying to this slogan, sniffed disdainfully in the direction of those trembling accomplices, the cowboy and the Easterner. Presently they bore Johnnie away, and left the three men to dismal reflection.

VII

"I'd like to fight this here Dutchman myself," said the cowboy, breaking a long silence. Scully wagged his head sadly. "No, that wouldn't do. It wouldn't be right. It wouldn't be right."

"Well, why wouldn't it?" argued the cowboy. "I don't see no harm in it."

"No," answered Scully, with mournful heroism. "It wouldn't be right. It was Johnnie's fight, and now we mustn't whip the man just because he whipped Johnnie."

"Yes, that's true enough," said the cowboy; "but—he better not get fresh with me, because I couldn't stand no more of it."

"You'll not say a word to him," commanded Scully, and even then they heard the tread of the Swede on the stairs. His entrance was made theatric. He swept the door back with a bang and swaggered to the middle of the room. No one looked at him. "Well," he cried, insolently, at Scully, "I s'pose you'll tell me now how much I owe you?"

The old man remained stolid. "You don't owe me nothin'."

"Huh!" said the Swede, "huh! Don't owe 'im nothin'."

The cowboy addressed the Swede. "Stranger, I don't see how you come to be so gay around here."

Old Scully was instantly alert. "Stop!" he shouted, holding his hand forth, fingers upward. "Bill, you shut up!"

The cowboy spat carelessly into the sawdust-box. "I didn't say a word, did I?" he asked.

"Mr. Scully," called the Swede, "how much do I owe you?" It was seen that he was attired for departure, and that he had his valise in his hand.

"You don't owe me nothin'," repeated Scully in the same imperturbable way.

"Huh!" said the Swede. "I guess you're right. I guess if it was any way at all, you'd owe me somethin'. That's what I guess." He turned to the cowboy. " 'Kill him! Kill him! Kill him!' " he mimicked, and then guffawed victoriously. " 'Kill him!' " He was convulsed with ironical humor.

But he might have been jeering the dead. The three men were immovable and silent, staring with glassy eyes at the stove.

The Swede opened the door and passed into the storm, giving one derisive glance backward at the still group.

As soon as the door was closed, Scully and the cowboy leaped to their feet and began to curse. They trampled to and fro, waving their arms and smashing into the air with their fists. "Oh, but that was a hard minute!" wailed Scully. "That was a hard minute! Him there leerin' and scoffin'! One bang at his nose was worth forty dollars to me that minute! How did you stand it, Bill?"

"How did I stand it?" cried the cowboy in a quivering voice. "How did I stand it? Oh!"

The old man burst into sudden brogue. "I'd loike to take that Swede," he wailed, "and hould 'im down on a shtone flure and bate 'im to a jelly wid a shtick!"

The cowboy groaned in sympathy. "I'd like to git him by the neck and ha-ammer him"—he brought his hand down on a chair with a noise like a pistol-shot—"hammer that there Dutchman until he couldn't tell himself from a dead coyote!"

"I'd bate 'im until he—"

"I'd show *him* some things—"

And then together they raised a yearning, fanatic cry—"Oh-o-oh! if we only could—"

"Yes!"

"Yes!"

"And then I'd—"

"O-o-oh!"

195

200

205

210

215

VIII

The Swede, tightly gripping his valise, tacked across the face of the storm as if he carried sails. He was following a line of little naked, gasping trees which, he knew, must mark the way of the road. His face, fresh from the pounding of Johnnie's fists, felt more pleasure than pain in the wind and the driving snow. A number of square shapes loomed upon him finally, and he knew them as the houses of the main body of the town. He found a street and made travel along it, leaning heavily upon the wind whenever, at a corner, a terrific blast caught him.

He might have been in a deserted village. We picture the world as thick with conquering and elated humanity, but here, with the bugles of the tempest pealing, it was hard to imagine a peopled earth. One viewed the existence of man then as a marvel, and conceded a glamor of wonder to these lice which were caused to cling to a whirling, fire-smitten, ice-locked, disease-stricken, space-lost bulb. The conceit of man was explained by this storm to be the very engine of life. One was a coxcomb not to die in it. However the Swede found a saloon.

In front of it an indomitable red light was burning, and the snowflakes were made blood-color as they flew through the circumscribed territory of the lamp's shining. The Swede pushed open the door of the saloon and entered. A sanded expanse was before him, and at the end of it four men sat about a table drinking. Down one side of the room extended a radiant bar, and its guardian was leaning upon his elbows listening to the talk of the men at the table. The Swede dropped his valise upon the floor and, smiling fraternally upon the barkeeper, said, "Gimme some whiskey, will you?" The man placed a bottle, a whiskey-glass, and a glass of ice-thick water upon the bar. The Swede poured himself an abnormal portion of whiskey and drank it in three gulps. "Pretty bad night," remarked the bartender, indifferently. He was making the pretension of blindness which is usually a distinction of his class, but it could have been seen that he was furtively studying the half-erased bloodstains on the face of the Swede. "Bad night," he said again.

"Oh, it's good enough for me," replied the Swede, hardily, as he poured himself some more whiskey. The barkeeper took his coin and maneuvered it through its reception by the high nickelled cash-machine. A bell rang; a card labelled "20 cts." had appeared.

"No," continued the Swede, "this isn't too bad weather. It's good enough for me."

"So?" murmured the barkeeper, languidly.

The copious drams made the Swede's eyes swim, and he breathed a trifle heavier. "Yes, I like this weather. I like it. It suits me." It was apparently his design to impart a deep significance to these words.

"So?" murmured the bartender again. He turned to gaze dreamily at the scroll-like birds and bird-like scrolls which had been drawn with soap upon the mirrors in back of the bar.

"Well, I guess I'll take another drink," said the Swede, presently. "Have something?"

"No, thanks; I'm not drinkin'," answered the bartender. Afterward he 225 asked, "How did you hurt your face?"

The Swede immediately began to boast loudly. "Why, in a fight. I thumped the soul out of a man down here at Scully's hotel."

The interest of the four men at the table was at last aroused.

"Who was it?" said one.

"Johnnie Scully," blustered the Swede. "Son of the man what runs it. He will be pretty near dead for some weeks, I can tell you. I made a nice thing of him, I did. He couldn't get up. They carried him in the house. Have a drink?"

Instantly the men in some subtle way encased themselves in reserve. 230 "No, thanks," said one. The group was of curious formation. Two were prominent local business men; one was the district attorney; and one was a professional gambler of the kind known as "square." But a scrutiny of the group would not have enabled an observer to pick the gambler from the men of more reputable pursuits. He was, in fact, a man so delicate in manner, when among people of fair class, and so judicious in his choice of victims, that in the strictly masculine part of the town's life he had come to be explicitly trusted and admired. People called him a thoroughbred. The fear and contempt with which his craft was regarded were undoubtedly the reason why his quiet dignity shone conspicuous above the quiet dignity of men who might be merely hatters, billiard-markers, or grocery-clerks. Beyond an occasional unwary traveller who came by rail, this gambler was supposed to prey solely upon reckless and senile farmers, who, when flush with good crops, drove into town in all the pride and confidence of an absolutely invulnerable stupidity. Hearing at times in circuitous fashion of the despoilment of such a farmer, the important men of Romper invariably laughed in contempt of the victim, and if they thought of the wolf at all, it was with a kind of pride at the knowledge that he would never dare think of attacking their wisdom and courage. Besides, it was popular that this gambler had a real wife and two real children in a neat cottage in a suburb, where he led an exemplary home life; and when anyone even suggested a discrepancy in his character, the crowd immediately vociferated descriptions of this virtuous family circle. Then men who led exemplary home lives, and men who did not lead exemplary home lives, all subsided in a bunch, remarking that there was nothing more to be said.

However, when a restriction was placed upon him—as, for instance, when a strong clique of members of the new Pollywog Club refused to permit him, even as a spectator, to appear in the rooms of the organization— the candor and gentleness with which he accepted the judgment disarmed many of his foes and made his friends more desperately partisan. He invariably distinguished between himself and a respectable Romper man so quickly and frankly that his manner actually appeared to be a continual broadcast compliment.

And one must not forget to declare the fundamental fact of his entire position in Romper. It is irrefutable that in all affairs outside his business, in all matters that occur eternally and commonly between man and man, this thieving card-player was so generous, so just, so moral, that, in a contest, he could have put to flight the consciences of nine tenths of the citizens of Romper.

And so it happened that he was seated in this saloon with the two prominent local merchants and the district attorney.

The Swede continued to drink raw whiskey, meanwhile babbling at the barkeeper and trying to induce him to indulge in potations. "Come on. Have a drink. Come on. What—no? Well, have a little one, then. By gawd, I've whipped a man tonight, and I want to celebrate. I whipped him good, too. Gentlemen," the Swede cried to the men at the table, "have a drink?"

"Ssh!" said the barkeeper.   235

The group at the table, although furtively attentive, had been pretending to be deep in talk, but now a man lifted his eyes toward the Swede and said, shortly, "Thanks. We don't want any more."

At this reply the Swede ruffled out his chest like a rooster. "Well," he exploded, "it seems I can't get anybody to drink with me in this town. Seems so, don't it? Well!"

"Ssh!" said the barkeeper.

"Say," snarled the Swede, "don't you try to shut me up. I won't have it. I'm a gentleman, and I want people to drink with me. And I want 'em to drink with me now. Now—do you understand?" He rapped the bar with his knuckles.

Years of experience had calloused the bartender. He merely grew sulky.   240
"I hear you," he answered.

"Well," cried the Swede, "listen hard then. See those men over there? Well, they're going to drink with me, and don't you forget it. Now you watch."

"Hi!" yelled the barkeeper, "this won't do!"

"Why won't it?" demanded the Swede. He stalked over to the table, and by chance laid his hand upon the shoulder of the gambler. "How about this?" he asked wrathfully. "I asked you to drink with me."

The gambler simply twisted his head and spoke over his shoulder. "My friend, I don't know you."

"Oh, hell!" answered the Swede, "come and have a drink."   245

"Now, my boy," advised the gambler, kindly, "take your hand off my shoulder and go 'way and mind your own business." He was a little, slim man, and it seemed strange to hear him use this tone of heroic patronage to the burly Swede. The other men at the table said nothing.

"What! You won't drink with me, you little dude? I'll make you, then! I'll make you!" The Swede had grasped the gambler frenziedly at the throat, and was dragging him from his chair. The other men sprang up. The bar-keeper dashed around the corner of his bar. There was a great tumult, and then was seen a long blade in the hand of the gambler. It shot forward, and a human body, this citadel of virtue, wisdom, power, was pierced as easily as if it had been a melon. The Swede fell with a cry of supreme astonishment.

The prominent merchants and the district attorney must have at once tumbled out of the place backward. The bartender found himself hanging limply to the arm of a chair and gazing into the eyes of a murderer.

"Henry," said the latter, as he wiped his knife on one of the towels that hung beneath the bar rail, "you tell 'em where to find me. I'll be home, waiting for 'em." Then he vanished. A moment afterward the barkeeper was in the street dinning through the storm for help and moreover, com-panionship.

The corpse of the Swede, alone in the saloon, had its eyes fixed upon 250 a dreadful legend that dwelt atop of the cash-machine: "This registers the amount of your purchase."

IX

Months later, the cowboy was frying pork over the stove of a little ranch near the Dakota line, when there was a quick thud of hoofs outside, and presently the Easterner entered with the letters and the papers.

"Well," said the Easterner at once, "the chap that killed the Swede has got three years. Wasn't much, was it?"

"He has? Three years?" The cowboy poised his pan of pork, while he ruminated upon the news. "Three years. That ain't much."

"No. It was a light sentence," replied the Easterner as he unbuckled his spurs. "Seems there was a good deal of sympathy for him in Romper."

"If the bartender had been any good," observed the cowboy, thought- 255 fully, "he would have gone in and cracked that there Dutchman on the head with a bottle in the beginnin' of it and stopped all this here murderin'."

"Yes, a thousand things might have happened," said the Easterner, tartly.

The cowboy returned his pan of pork to the fire, but his philosophy continued. "It's funny, ain't it? If he hadn't said Johnnie was cheatin' he'd be alive this minute. He was an awful fool. Game played for fun, too. Not for money. I believe he was crazy."

"I feel sorry for that gambler," said the Easterner.

"Oh, so do I," said the cowboy. "He don't deserve none of it for killin' who he did."

"The Swede might not have been killed if everything had been square." 260

"Might not have been killed?" exclaimed the cowboy. "Everythin' square? Why, when he said that Johnnie was cheatin' and acted like such a jackass? And then in the saloon he fairly walked up to git hurt?" With these arguments the cowboy browbeat the Easterner and reduced him to rage.

"You're a fool!" cried the Easterner, viciously. "You're a bigger jackass than the Swede by a million majority. Now let me tell you one thing. Let me tell you something. Listen! Johnnie *was* cheating!"

" 'Johnnie,' " said the cowboy, blankly. There was a minute of silence, and then he said, robustly, "Why, no. The game was only for fun."

"Fun or not," said the Easterner, "Johnnie was cheating. I saw him. I know it. I saw him. And I refused to stand up and be a man. I let the Swede fight it out alone. And you—you were simply puffing around the place and wanting to fight. And then old Scully himself! We are all in it! This poor gambler isn't even a noun. He is kind of an adverb. Every sin is the result of a collaboration. We, five of us, have collaborated in the murder of this Swede. Usually there are from a dozen to forty women really involved in every murder, but in this case it seems to be only five men—you, I, Johnnie, old Scully; and that fool of an unfortunate gambler came merely as a culmination, the apex of a human movement, and gets all the punishment."

The cowboy, injured and rebellious, cried out blindly into this fog of 265 mysterious theory: "Well, I didn't do anythin', did I?"

The Responsive Reader

1. How does the host show his friendliness, his good intentions, his warmly emotional nature? Why is it ironic that the host in this story should be a well-intentioned, well-meaning person?

2. What is wrong with the Swede? What makes him strange? What makes him a problem to the other people early in the story? How would you describe or explain the phases he goes through while at the blue hotel?

3. Would you call Johnny a bad person? Would you call him "lawless"? What makes him fight? (Why does Crane say that in this setting the words "You are cheatin'!" are "terrible words"?) Is there any code or are there unspoken rules to govern the way the locals act during the quarreling and fighting?

4. Did the fate of the Swede at the end of the story surprise you? Did he "have it coming"? How and why does he come to a bad end? (What is the meaning of the message showing on the cash register?)

5. What kind of person is the Easterner, and what is his role in the story? Why did he keep quiet as long as he did? At the end, what is his comment on the events of the story? What is his theory of evil? How well is it supported by what happened in the story? (Why does he have the last word in the story?)

Thinking, Talking, Writing

6. The media today are under attack for sensationalizing and glorifying brutal violence. Is Crane's treatment of violence in this story sensational or exploitative?

7. Some writers have come to think of Americans as an inherently violence-prone nation. Do you think this conclusion is justified, or is it unfair?

8. In your own experience and reading, have you encountered support for the view that "evil is the result of collaboration?" How does this view of evil compare with other theories of good and evil that you know?

Collaborative Projects

9. Who is guilty in this story, and who is innocent? You may want to help set up a panel of judges who would determine to what extent each character in the story is implicated in the murder of the Swede.

THE HOUSE OF MORGAN *and* VAG

John Dos Passos

Now the stone house on the lakefront is finished and the workmen
    are beginning the fence.
The palings are made of iron bars with steel points that can stab
    the life out of any man who falls on them.
As a fence it is a masterpiece, and will shut off the rabble and all
    vagabonds and hungry men and all wandering children
    looking for a place to play.

Carl Sandburg, "A Fence"

For a whole generation—the grandparents of today's young adults—the Great Depression of the early thirties was the formative experience of their lives. Millions of rural Americans were driven off their farms when the banks foreclosed on loans gone bad. Other millions—who had been lured off the farm by the promise of electric lights, indoor toilets, and factory jobs—joined the ranks of the unemployed. The great industrial civilization that had promised prosperity to all who were willing to work was revealed as a soulless machine with no program for helping the countless Americans whose lives were being ground into the dust. Americans learned a lesson already well known to earlier ages: Social systems are often constructed so that the toil of the exploited many will finance the luxuries of the corrupt few. Writers and artists began to ask radical questions about the economic and political structures that seemed to have failed the nation. They turned to socialism, communism, and lesser-known ideologies in the search for alternatives to the get-rich-quick mentality that had led the world's richest nation into a quagmire of unemployment, poverty, and despair.

John Dos Passos is one of the great chroniclers of the Depression era. Although he was educated at a private school and attended Harvard, he early developed a sympathy for the underdog and the Marxist criticism of the capitalist system. He saw war at first hand in World War I as a medic, first as a volunteer with the French and Italians and then as a private in the US medical corps. His books paint unforgettable portraits of the bankers, entrepreneurs, go-getters, and corrupt politicians who had been the heroes of the bankrupt capitalist ideology. He pays tribute to those standing up to the timeservers and yes men who sold their souls to the system. He honors the designers, inventors, engineers, workers, and teachers who created wealth and knowledge rather than manipulating them for private gain. Finally, like other left-leaning writers of the thirties, from the novelist John Steinbeck (Grapes of Wrath) to the dramatist Arthur Miller, Dos Passos wrote eloquent passages voicing his solidarity with the down and out.

The following two selections were printed independently as magazine pieces in the thirties and later incorporated into his great panoramic novels of early-twentieth-century America: The 42nd Parallel, 1919, *and* The Big Money.

Dos Passos' original readers were closer to the historical events and personages he alludes to than we are today: The wars that financiers like the Morgans helped finance included not only World War I (1914–1918) but also the earlier war between France and Prussia in 1870–1871; the great builders of business empires, like Carnegie and Gary, were still remembered, as were some of the critics of Big Business, such as J. S. Coxey, who led "Coxey's army" of the unemployed to Washington, DC, to demonstrate for government-financed make-work projects in times of economic depression.

The House of Morgan

I commit my soul into the hands of my savior, wrote John Pierpont Morgan   *1*
in his will, *in full confidence that having redeemed it and washed it in His most precious blood, He will present it faultless before my heavenly father, and I intreat my children to maintain and defend at all hazard and at any cost of personal sacrifice the blessed doctrine of complete atonement for sin through the blood of Jesus Christ once offered and through that alone,*
and into the hands of the House of Morgan represented by his son,
he committed,
when he died in Rome in 1913,
the control of the Morgan interests in New York, Paris and London,   *5*
four national banks, three trust companies, three life insurance companies, ten railroad systems, three street railway companies, an express company, the International Mercantile Marine,
power,
on the cantilever principle, through interlocking directorates
over eighteen other railroads, U.S. Steel, General Electric, American Tel and Tel, five major industries;
the interwoven cables of the Morgan Stillman Baker combination held credit up like a suspension bridge, thirteen percent of the banking resources of the world.

The first Morgan to make a pool was Joseph Morgan, a hotelkeeper in   *10*
Hartford Connecticut who organized stagecoach lines and bought up Ætna Life Insurance stock in a time of panic caused by one of the big New York fires in the 1830's;
his son Junius followed in his footsteps, first in the drygoods business, and then as a partner to George Peabody, a Massachusetts banker who built up an enormous underwriting and mercantile business in London and became a friend of Queen Victoria;
Junius married the daughter of John Pierpont, a Boston preacher, poet, eccentric, and abolitionist; and their eldest son,
John Pierpont Morgan
arrived in New York to make his fortune

after being trained in England, going to school at Vevey, proving him-   *15*
self a crack mathematician at the University of Göttingen,
a lanky morose young man of twenty,
just in time for the panic of '57.
(war and panics on the stock exchange, bankruptcies, warloans, good
growing weather for the House of Morgan.)

When the guns started booming at Fort Sumter, young Morgan turned
some money over reselling condemned muskets to the U.S. army and began to make himself felt in the gold room in downtown New York; there
was more in trading in gold than in trading in muskets; so much for the
Civil War.

During the Franco-Prussian war Junius Morgan floated a huge bond   *20*
issue for the French government at Tours.

At the same time young Morgan was fighting Jay Cooke and the
German-Jew bankers in Frankfort over the funding of the American war
debt (he never did like the Germans or the Jews).

The panic of '75 ruined Jay Cooke and made J. Pierpont Morgan the
boss croupier of Wall Street; he united with the Philadelphia Drexels and
built the Drexel building where for thirty years he sat in his glassedin office,
redfaced and insolent, writing at his desk, smoking great black cigars, or, if
important issues were involved, playing solitaire in his inner office; he was
famous for his few words, Yes or No, and for his way of suddenly blowing
up in a visitor's face and for that special gesture of the arm that meant, *What
do I get out of it?*

In '77 Junius Morgan retired; J. Pierpont got himself made a member
of the board of directors of the New York Central railroad and launched
the first *Corsair.* He liked yachting and to have pretty actresses call him
Commodore.

He founded the Lying-in Hospital on Stuyvesant Square, and was fond
of going into St. George's church and singing a hymn all alone in the afternoon quiet.

In the panic of '93   *25*
at no inconsiderable profit to himself
Morgan saved the U.S. Treasury; gold was draining out, the country
was ruined, the farmers were howling for a silver standard, Grover Cleveland
and his cabinet were walking up and down in the blue room at the White
House without being able to come to a decision, in Congress they were
making speeches while the gold reserves melted at the Subtreasuries; poor
people were starving; Coxey's army was marching to Washington; for a long
time Grover Cleveland couldn't bring himself to call in the representative
of the Wall Street moneymasters; Morgan sat in his suite at the Arlington
smoking cigars and quietly playing solitaire until at last the president sent
for him;
he had a plan all ready for stopping the gold hemorrhage.

After that what Morgan said went; when Carnegie sold out he built the Steel Trust.

J. Pierpont Morgan was a bullnecked irascible man with small black magpie's eyes and a growth on his nose; he let his partners work themselves to death over the detailed routine of banking, and sat in his back office smoking black cigars; when there was something to be decided he said Yes or No or just turned his back and went back to his solitaire.

Every Christmas his librarian read him Dickens' *A Christmas Carol* from the original manuscript.

He was fond of canarybirds and pekinese dogs and liked to take pretty actresses yachting. Each *Corsair* was a finer vessel than the last.

When he dined with King Edward he sat at His Majesty's right; he ate with the Kaiser tête-à-tête; he liked talking to cardinals or the pope, and never missed a conference of Episcopal bishops;

Rome was his favorite city.

He liked choice cookery and old wines and pretty women and yachting, and going over his collections, now and then picking up a jewelled snuffbox and staring at it with his magpie's eyes.

He made a collection of the autographs of the rulers of France, owned glass cases full of Babylonian tablets, seals, signets, statuettes, busts.

Gallo-Roman bronzes,

Merovingian jewels, miniatures, watches, tapestries, porcelains, cuneiform inscriptions, paintings by all the old masters, Dutch, Italian, Flemish, Spanish,

manuscripts of the gospels and the Apocalypse,

a collection of the works of Jean-Jacques Rousseau,

and the letters of Pliny the Younger.

His collectors bought anything that was expressive or rare or had the glint of empire on it, and he had it brought to him and stared hard at it with his magpie's eyes. Then it was put in a glass case.

The last year of his life he went up the Nile on a dahabiyeh and spent a long time staring at the great columns of the Temple of Karnak.

The panic of 1907 and the death of Harriman, his great opponent in railroad financing, in 1909, had left him the undisputed ruler of Wall Street, most powerful private citizen in the world;

an old man tired of the purple, suffering from gout, he had deigned to go to Washington to answer the questions of the Pujo Committee during the Money Trust Investigation: Yes, I did what seemed to me to be for the best interests of the country.

So admirably was his empire built that his death in 1913 hardly caused a ripple in the exchanges of the world: the purple descended to his son, J. P. Morgan,

who had been trained at Groton and Harvard and by associating with
the British ruling class

to be a more constitutional monarch: *J. P. Morgan suggests . . .*

By 1917 the Allies had borrowed one billion, nine hundred million
dollars through the House of Morgan: we went overseas for democracy and
the flag;

and by the end of the Peace Conference the phrase *J. P. Morgan suggests*   50
had compulsion over a power of seventyfour billion dollars.

J. P. Morgan is a silent man, not given to public utterances, but during
the great steel strike, he wrote Gary: *Heartfelt congratulations on your stand for
the open shop, with which I am, as you know, absolutely in accord. I believe American
principles of liberty are deeply involved, and must win if we stand firm.*

(Wars and panics on the stock exchange,
machinegunfire and arson,
bankruptcies, warloans,
starvation, lice, cholera and typhus: 55
good growing weather for the House of Morgan.)

Vag

The young man waits at the edge of the concrete, with one hand he   1
grips a rubbed suitcase of phony leather, the other hand almost making a fist,
thumb up

that moves in ever so slight an arc when a car slithers past, a truck roars
clatters; the wind of cars passing ruffles his hair, slaps grit in his face.

Head swims, hunger has twisted the belly tight,

he has skinned a heel through the torn sock, feet ache in the broken
shoes, under the threadbare suit carefully brushed off with the hand, the torn
drawers have a crummy feel, the feel of having slept in your clothes; in the
nostrils lingers the staleness of discouraged carcasses crowded into a transient
camp, the carbolic stench of the jail, on the taut cheeks the shamed flush
from the boring eyes of cops and deputies, railroadbulls (they eat three
squares a day, they are buttoned into well-made clothes, they have wives to
sleep with, kids to play with after supper, they work for the big men who
buy their way, they stick their chests out with the sureness of power behind
their backs). Git the hell out, scram. Know what's good for you, you'll make
yourself scarce. Gittin' tough, eh? Think you kin take it, eh?

The punch in the jaw, the slam on the head with the nightstick, the   5
wrist grabbed and twisted behind the back, the big knee brought up sharp
into the crotch,

the walk out of town with sore feet to stand and wait at the edge of
the hissing speeding string of cars where the reek of ether and lead and gas
melts into the silent grassy smell of the earth.

Eyes black with want seek out the eyes of the drivers, a hitch, a hundred miles down the road.

Overhead in the blue a plane drones. Eyes follow the silver Douglas that flashes once in the sun and bores its smooth way out of sight into the blue.

(The transcontinental passengers sit pretty, big men with bank-accounts, highlypaid jobs, who are saluted by doormen; telephone-girls say goodmorning to them. Last night after a fine dinner, drinks with friends, they left Newark. Roar of climbing motors slanting up into the inky haze. Lights drop away. An hour staring along a silvery wing at a big lonesome moon hurrying west through curdling scum. Beacons flash in a line across Ohio.

At Cleveland the plane drops banking in a smooth spiral, the string of lights along the lake swings in a circle. Climbing roar of the motors again; slumped in the soft seat drowsing through the flat moonlight night.

Chi. A glimpse of the dipper. Another spiral swoop from cool into hot air thick with dust and the reek of burnt prairies.

Beyond the Mississippi dawn creeps up behind through the murk over the great plains. Puddles of mist go white in the Iowa hills, farms, fences, silos, steel glint from a river. The blinking eyes of the beacons reddening into day. Watercourses vein the eroded hills.

Omaha. Great cumulus clouds, from coppery churning to creamy to silvery white, trail brown skirts of rain over the hot plains. Red and yellow badlands, tiny horned shapes of cattle.

Cheyenne. The cool high air smells of sweetgrass.

The tightbaled clouds to westward burst and scatter in tatters over the strawcolored hills. Indigo mountains jut rimrock. The plane breasts a huge crumbling cloudbank and toboggans over bumpy air across green and crimson slopes into the sunny dazzle of Salt Lake.

The transcontinental passenger thinks contracts, profits, vacation-trips, mighty continent between Atlantic and Pacific, power, wires humming dollars, cities jammed, hills empty, the indiantrail leading into the wagonroad, the macadamed pike, the concrete skyway; trains, planes: history the billion-dollar speedup,

and in the bumpy air over the desert ranges towards Las Vegas

sickens and vomits into the carton container the steak and mushrooms he ate in New York. No matter, silver in the pocket, greenbacks in the wallet, drafts, certified checks, plenty restaurants in L. A.)

The young man waits on the side of the road; the plane has gone; thumb moves in a small arc when a car tears hissing past. Eyes seek the driver's eyes. A hundred miles down the road. Head swims, belly tightens, wants crawl over his skin like ants:

went to school, books said opportunity, ads promised speed, own your home, shine bigger than your neighbor, the radiocrooner whispered girls, ghosts of platinum girls coaxed from the screen, millions in winnings were chalked up on the boards in the offices, paychecks were for hands willing to work, the cleared desk of an executive with three telephones on it;

waits with swimming head, needs knot the belly, idle hands numb, beside the speeding traffic.
      A hundred miles down the road.

The Responsive Reader

1. Why does Dos Passos start by quoting the elder John Pierpont Morgan's religious sentiments from his will? What kind of person emerges from Dos Passos' portrait? How does the author use references to Morgan's personal life and personal style?
2. How does Dos Passos explain the tremendous wealth that the Morgans accumulated? What for Dos Passos were the key factors in the growth of their financial power, and how did these factors operate? What according to this account made for good "growing weather" for the Morgan financial empire?
3. Like other legendary tycoons such as the newspaper magnate Hearst, Morgan was a great patron and collector of the arts. How does Dos Passos view these activities?
4. How does Dos Passos' portrait of the vagabond counteract stereotypes about hoboes or drifters?

Thinking, Talking, Writing

5. How would you sum up Dos Passos's indictment of the capitalistic system that the Morgans represented? What in the indictment is familiar to you, and what is new? What parts of it do you find persuasive, and what parts seem biased to you?
6. Does the mystique of the entrepreneur or builder of business empires survive in our society today?
7. Do the media hold forth a promise of economic success and the good life that for many in our society remains a mirage?

Collaborative Projects

8. Your class may want to assign groups to explore specific political and economic questions raised by these two selections. For instance, how do stock market panics work, and why do they offer special opportunities for speculators? Why was the "open shop" a special thorn in the side to Dos Passos and other friends of organized labor? (How was it justified by voices of business such as the later J. P. Morgan?) In American society, do business and religion tend to be allied?

Thinking about Connections

9. Stephen Crane's "The Blue Hotel" takes place in a preindustrial small town setting. How is the vision of evil in his story different from that in Dos Passos' vignettes of industrial America?

THE LOTTERY

Shirley Jackson

I hoped, by setting a particularly brutal ancient rite in the present and in my own village, to shock the story's readers with a graphic dramatization of the pointless violence and general inhumanity in their own lives.

Shirley Jackson

At one time, Shirley Jackson's "The Lottery" could have won the title of "most unpopular short story" of the first half of the twentieth century. When it was published in the New Yorker *on June 28, 1948, it ignited a firestorm of hate mail, anonymous letters, and canceled subscriptions. The author said that she considered herself lucky to be living in Vermont, where "no one in our small town had ever heard of the* New Yorker, *much less read my story."*

"The Lottery" takes its readers to a small village where the villagers act out a traditional ritual. Each year one of their number is selected by lot as a harvest sacrifice. ("Lottery in June, corn be heavy soon" is a folk saying in the village.) Jackson's story presented a vision of evil that should not have come as a surprise to New Yorker *readers. Records of human sacrifice are well-known to anthropologists, historians, and students of early religions. The thirties and forties had seen the rise of Nazism and Stalinism, and millions of victims were sacrificed on the altar of a murderous ideology. A feature of both the Nazi and the Stalinist terror was that it was futile to argue the guilt or innocence of the individual. Individual guilt was not the issue. People were destroyed because they were Jews, landowners, gypsies, homosexuals—members of groups that had suddenly and irrationally been declared "undesirable."*

What infuriated many New Yorker *readers was that "The Lottery" does not take place in a prehistoric village or on a railroad siding outside the Auschwitz death camp. It takes place in a village in New England, with a post office and a bank. In fact, Jackson later identified it as North Bennington, where she lived while her husband taught at Bennington College.*

The morning of June 27th was clear and sunny, with the fresh warmth of a full-summer day; the flowers were blossoming profusely and the grass was richly green. The people of the village began to gather in the square, between the post office and the bank, around ten o'clock; in some towns there were so many people that the lottery took two days and had to be started on June 26th, but in this village, where there were only about three hundred people, the whole lottery took less than two hours, so it could begin at ten o'clock in the morning and still be through in time to allow the villagers to get home for noon dinner.

The children assembled first, of course. School was recently over for the summer, and the feeling of liberty sat uneasily on most of them; they tended to gather together quietly for a while before they broke into boister-ous play, and their talk was still of the classroom and the teacher, of books and reprimands. Bobby Martin had already stuffed his pockets full of stones, and the other boys soon followed his example, selecting the smoothest and roundest stones; Bobby and Harry Jones and Dickie Delacroix—the villagers pronounced this name "Dellacroy"—eventually made a great pile of stones in one corner of the square and guarded it against the raids of the other boys. The girls stood aside, talking among themselves, looking over their shoulders at the boys, and the very small children rolled in the dust or clung to the hands of their older brothers or sisters.

Soon the men began to gather, surveying their own children, speaking of planting and rain, tractors and taxes. They stood together, away from the pile of stones in the corner, and their jokes were quiet and they smiled rather than laughed. The women, wearing faded house dresses and sweaters, came shortly after their menfolk. They greeted one another and exchanged bits of gossip as they went to join their husbands. Soon the women, standing by their husbands, began to call to their children, and the children came reluc-tantly, having to be called four or five times. Bobby Martin ducked under his mother's grasping hand and ran, laughing, back to the pile of stones. His father spoke up sharply, and Bobby came quickly and took his place between his father and his oldest brother.

The lottery was conducted—as were the square dances, the teenage club, the Halloween program—by Mr. Summers, who had time and energy to devote to civic activities. He was a round-faced, jovial man and he ran the coal business, and people were sorry for him, because he had no children and his wife was a scold. When he arrived in the square, carrying the black wooden box, there was a murmur of conversation among the villagers, and he waved and called, "Little late today, folks." The postmaster, Mr. Graves, followed him, carrying a three-legged stool, and the stool was put in the center of the square and Mr. Summers set the black box down on it. The villagers kept their distance, leaving a space between themselves and the stool, and when Mr. Summers said, "Some of you fellows want to give me a hand?" there was a hesitation before two men, Mr. Martin and his oldest son, Baxter, came forward to hold the box steady on the stool while Mr. Summers stirred up the papers inside it.

The original paraphernalia for the lottery had been lost long ago, and the black box now resting on the stool had been put into use even before Old Man Warner, the oldest man in town, was born. Mr. Summers spoke frequently to the villagers about making a new box, but no one liked to upset even as much tradition as was represented by the black box. There was a story that the present box had been made with some pieces of the box that had preceded it, the one that had been constructed when the first people settled down to make a village here. Every year, after the lottery, Mr. Sum-mers began talking again about a new box, but every year the subject was allowed to fade off without anything's being done. The black box grew

5

shabbier each year; by now it was no longer completely black but splintered badly along one side to show the original wood color, and in some places faded or stained.

Mr. Martin and his oldest son, Baxter, held the black box securely on the stool until Mr. Summers had stirred the papers thoroughly with his hand. Because so much of the ritual had been forgotten or discarded, Mr. Summers had been successful in having slips of paper substituted for the chips of wood that had been used for generations. Chips of wood, Mr. Summers had argued, had been all very well when the village was tiny, but now that the population was more than three hundred and likely to keep on growing, it was necessary to use something that would fit more easily into the black box. The night before the lottery, Mr. Summers and Mr. Graves made up the slips of paper and put them in the box, and it was then taken to the safe of Mr. Summers' coal company and locked up until Mr. Summers was ready to take it to the square next morning. The rest of the year, the box was put away, sometimes one place, sometimes another; it had spent one year in Mr. Graves's barn and another year underfoot in the post office, and sometimes it was set on a shelf in the Martin grocery and left there.

There was a great deal of fussing to be done before Mr. Summers declared the lottery open. There were the lists to make up—of heads of families, heads of households in each family, members of each household in each family. There was the proper swearing-in of Mr. Summers by the postmaster, as the official of the lottery; at one time, some people remembered, there had been a recital of some sort, performed by the official of the lottery, a perfunctory, tuneless chant that had been rattled off duly each year; some people believed that the official of the lottery used to stand just so when he said or sang it, others believed that he was supposed to walk among the people, but years and years ago this part of the ritual had been allowed to lapse. There had been, also, a ritual salute, which the official of the lottery had had to use in addressing each person who came up to draw from the box, but this also had changed with time, until now it was felt necessary only for the official to speak to each person approaching. Mr. Summers was very good at all this; in his clean white shirt and blue jeans, with one hand resting carelessly on the black box, he seemed very proper and important as he talked interminably to Mr. Graves and the Martins.

Just as Mr. Summers finally left off talking and turned to the assembled villagers, Mrs. Hutchinson came hurriedly along the path to the square, her sweater thrown over her shoulders, and slid into place in the back of the crowd. "Clean forgot what day it was," she said to Mrs. Delacroix, who stood next to her, and they both laughed softly. "Thought my old man was out back stacking wood," Mrs. Hutchinson went on, "and then I looked out the window and the kids was gone, and then I remembered it was the twenty-seventh and came a-running." She dried her hands on her apron, and Mrs. Delacroix said, "You're in time, though. They're still talking away up there."

Mrs. Hutchinson craned her neck to see through the crowd and found her husband and children standing near the front. She tapped Mrs. Delacroix on the arm as a farewell and began to make her way through the crowd. The people separated good-humoredly to let her through; two or three people said, in voices just loud enough to be heard across the crowd, "Here comes your Missus, Hutchinson," and "Bill, she made it after all." Mrs. Hutchinson reached her husband, and Mr. Summers, who had been waiting, said cheerfully, "Thought we were going to have to get on without you, Tessie." Mrs. Hutchinson said, grinning, "Wouldn't have me leave m'dishes in the sink, now, would you, Joe?" and soft laughter ran through the crowd as the people stirred back into position after Mrs. Hutchinson's arrival.

"Well, now," Mr. Summers said soberly, "guess we better get started,   10
get this over with, so's we can go back to work. Anybody ain't here?"

"Dunbar," several people said, "Dunbar, Dunbar."

Mr. Summers consulted his list. "Clyde Dunbar," he said. "That's right. He's broke his leg, hasn't he? Who's drawing for him?"

"Me, I guess," a woman said, and Mr. Summers turned to look at her. "Wife draws for her husband," Mr. Summers said. "Don't you have a grown boy to do it for you, Janey?" Although Mr. Summers and everyone else in the village knew the answer perfectly well, it was the business of the official of the lottery to ask such questions formally. Mr. Summers waited with an expression of polite interest while Mrs. Dunbar answered.

"Horace's not but sixteen yet," Mrs. Dunbar said regretfully. "Guess I gotta fill in for the old man this year."

"Right," Mr. Summers said. He made a note on the list he was holding.   15
Then he asked, "Watson boy drawing this year?"

A tall boy in the crowd raised his hand. "Here," he said. "I'm drawing for m'mother and me." He blinked his eyes nervously and ducked his head as several voices in the crowd said things like "Good fellow, Jack," and "Glad to see your mother's got a man to do it."

"Well," Mr. Summers said, "guess that's everyone. Old Man Warner make it?"

"Here," a voice said, and Mr. Summers nodded.

A sudden hush fell on the crowd as Mr. Summers cleared his throat and looked at the list. "All ready?" he called. "Now, I'll read the names—heads of families first—and the men come up and take a paper out of the box. Keep the paper folded in your hand without looking at it until everyone has had a turn. Everything clear?"

The people had done it so many times that they only half listened to   20
the directions; most of them were quiet, wetting their lips, not looking around. Then Mr. Summers raised one hand high and said, "Adams." A man disengaged himself from the crowd and came forward. "Hi, Steve," Mr. Summers said, and Mr. Adams said, "Hi, Joe." They grinned at one another humorlessly and nervously. Then Mr. Adams reached into the black box and

took out a folded paper. He held it firmly by one corner as he turned and went hastily back to his place in the crowd, where he stood a little apart from his family, not looking down at his hand.

"Allen," Mr. Summers said. "Anderson. . . . Bentham."

"Seems like there's no time at all between lotteries any more," Mrs. Delacroix said to Mrs. Graves in the back row. "Seems like we got through with the last one only last week."

"Time sure goes fast," Mrs. Graves said.

"Clark. . . . Delacroix."

"There goes my old man," Mrs. Delacroix said. She held her breath   25
while her husband went forward.

"Dunbar," Mr. Summers said, and Mrs. Dunbar went steadily to the box while one of the women said, "Go on, Janey," and another said, "There she goes."

"We're next," Mrs. Graves said. She watched while Mr. Graves came around from the side of the box, greeted Mr. Summers gravely, and selected a slip of paper from the box. By now, all through the crowd there were men holding the small folded papers in their large hands, turning them over and over nervously. Mrs. Dunbar and her two sons stood together, Mrs. Dunbar holding the slip of paper.

"Harburt. . . . Hutchinson."

"Get up there, Bill," Mrs. Hutchinson said, and the people near her laughed.

"Jones."   30

"They do say," Mrs. Adams said to Old Man Warner, who stood next to him, "that over in the north village they're talking of giving up the lottery."

Old Man Warner snorted. "Pack of crazy fools," he said. "Listening to the young folks, nothing's good enough for *them*. Next thing you know, they'll be wanted to go back to living in caves, nobody work any more, live *that* way for a while. Used to be a saying about 'Lottery in June, corn be heavy soon.' First thing you know, we'd all be eating stewed chickweed and acorns. There's *always* been a lottery," he added petulantly. "Bad enough to see young Joe Summers up there joking with everybody."

"Some places have already quit lotteries," Mrs. Adams said.

"Nothing but trouble in *that*," Old Man Warner said stoutly. "Pack of young fools."

"Martin." And Bobby Martin watched his father go forward. "Over-   35
dyke. . . . Percy."

"I wish they'd hurry," Mrs. Dunbar said to her older son. "I wish they'd hurry."

"They're almost through," her son said.

"You get ready to run tell Dad," Mrs. Dunbar said.

Mr. Summers called his own name and then stepped forward precisely and selected a slip from the box. Then he called, "Warner."

"Seventy-seventh year I been in the lottery," Old Man Warner said as   40
he went through the crowd. "Seventy-seventh time."

"Watson." The tall boy came awkwardly through the crowd. Someone said, "Don't be nervous, Jack," and Mr. Summers said, "Take your
time, son."

"Zanini."

After that, there was a long pause, a breathless pause, until Mr. Summers, holding his slip of paper in the air, said, "All right, fellows." For a
minute, no one moved, and then all the slips of paper were opened. Suddenly, all the women began to speak at once, saying, "Who is it?," "Who's
got it?," "Is it the Dunbars?," "Is it the Watsons?" Then the voices began to
say, "It's Hutchinson. It's Bill," "Bill Hutchinson's got it."

"Go tell your father," Mrs. Dunbar said to her older son.

People began to look around to see the Hutchinsons. Bill Hutchinson   45
was standing quiet staring down at the paper in his hand. Suddenly, Tessie
Hutchinson shouted to Mr. Summers, "You didn't give him time enough to
take any paper he wanted. I saw you. It wasn't fair."

"Be a good sport, Tessie," Mrs. Delacroix called, and Mrs. Graves said,
"All of us took the same chance."

"Shut up, Tessie," Bill Hutchinson said.

"Well, everyone," Mr. Summers said, "that was done pretty fast, and
now we've got to be hurrying a little more to get done in time." He consulted his next list. "Bill," he said, "you draw for the Hutchinson family. You
got any other households in the Hutchinsons?"

"There's Don and Eva," Mrs. Hutchinson yelled. "Make *them* take their
chance!"

"Daughters draw for their husbands' families, Tessie," Mr. Summers said   50
gently. "You know that as well as anyone else."

"It wasn't *fair*," Tessie said.

"I guess not, Joe," Bill Hutchinson said regretfully. "My daughter draws
with her husband's family, that's only fair. And I've got no other family
except the kids."

"Then, as far as drawing for families is concerned, it's you." Mr. Summers said in explanation, "and as far as drawing for households is concerned,
that's you, too. Right?"

"Right," Bill Hutchinson said.

"How many kids, Bill?" Mr. Summers asked formally.   55

"Three," Bill Hutchinson said. "There's Bill, Jr., and Nancy, and little
Dave. And Tessie and me."

"All right, then," Mr. Summers said. "Harry, you got their tickets back?"

Mr. Graves nodded and held up the slips of paper. "Put them in the
box, then," Mr. Summers directed. "Take Bill's and put it in."

"I think we ought to start over," Mrs. Hutchinson said, as quietly as she could, "I tell you it wasn't *fair.* You didn't give him time enough to choose. *Every*body saw that."

Mr. Graves had selected the five slips and put them in the box, and he dropped all the papers but those onto the ground, where the breeze caught them and lifted them off. 60

"Listen, everybody," Mrs. Hutchinson was saying to the people around her.

"Ready, Bill?" Mr. Summers asked, and Bill Hutchinson, with one quick glance around at his wife and children, nodded.

"Remember," Mr. Summers said, "take the slips and keep them folded until each person has taken one. Harry, you help little Dave." Mr. Graves took the hand of the little boy, who came willingly with him up to the box. "Take a paper out of the box, Davy," Mr. Summers said. Davy put his hand into the box and laughed. "Take just *one* paper," Mr. Summers said. "Harry, you hold it for him." Mr. Graves took the child's hand and removed the folded paper from the tight fist and held it while little Dave stood next to him and looked up at him wonderingly.

"Nancy next," Mr. Summers said. Nancy was twelve, and her school friends breathed heavily as she went forward, switching her skirt, and took a slip daintily from the box. "Bill, Jr.," Mr. Summers said, and Billy, his face red and his feet over-large, nearly knocked the box over as he got a paper out. "Tessie," Mr. Summers said. She hesitated for a minute, looking around defiantly, and then set her lips and went up to the box. She snatched a paper out and held it behind her.

"Bill," Mr. Summers said, and Bill Hutchinson reached into the box and felt around, bringing his hand out at last with the slip of paper in it. 65

The crowd was quiet. A girl whispered, "I hope it's not Nancy," and the sound of the whisper reached the edges of the crowd.

"It's not the way it used to be," Old Man Warner said clearly. "People ain't the way they used to be."

"All right," Mr. Summers said. "Open the papers. Harry, you open little Dave's."

Mr. Graves opened the slip of paper and there was a general sigh through the crowd as he held it up and everyone could see that it was blank. Nancy and Bill, Jr. opened theirs at the same time, and both beamed and laughed, turning around to the crowd and holding their slips of paper above their heads.

"Tessie," Mr. Summers said. There was a pause, and then Mr. Summers looked at Bill Hutchinson, and Bill unfolded his paper and showed it. It was blank. 70

"It's Tessie," Mr. Summers said, and his voice was hushed. "Show us her paper, Bill."

Bill Hutchinson went over to his wife and forced the slip of paper out of her hand. It had a black spot on it, the black spot Mr. Summers had made the night before with the heavy pencil in the coal-company office. Bill Hutchinson held it up, and there was a stir in the crowd.

"All right, folks," Mr. Summers said. "Let's finish quickly."

Although the villagers had forgotten the ritual and lost the original black box, they still remembered to use stones. The pile of stones the boys had made earlier was ready; there were stones on the ground with the blowing scraps of paper that had come out of the box. Mrs. Delacroix selected a stone so large she had to pick it up with both hands and turned to Mrs. Dunbar. "Come on," she said. "Hurry up."

Mrs. Dunbar had small stones in both hands, and she said, gasping   *75* for breath, "I can't run at all. You'll have to go ahead and I'll catch up with you."

The children had stones already, and someone gave little Davy Hutchinson a few pebbles.

Tessie Hutchinson was in the center of a cleared space by now, and she held her hands out desperately as the villagers moved in on her. "It isn't fair," she said. A stone hit her on the side of the head.

Old Man Warner was saying, "Come on, come on, everyone." Steve Adams was in the front of the crowd of villagers, with Mrs. Graves beside him.

"It isn't fair, it isn't right," Mrs. Hutchinson screamed, and then they were upon her.

The Responsive Reader

1. What are some of the many details that help make the setting seem like an ordinary village with ordinary people? What kind of person is the man in charge of conducting the lottery? How does he go about his business? Why do you think the author goes out of her way to make the people of the village seem ordinary rather than monstrous?
2. What are the first hints of something ominous? When do you first fully realize that something is amiss?
3. How does the victim behave? How does her family act? How do the bystanders act? (Do the villagers *differ* in their attitude toward the ritual or toward the victims?) Do you feel you understand the way both the villagers and victims think and feel in this story?
4. What is basically wrong here? Who is responsible? Who or what is to blame?

Thinking, Talking, Writing

5. Do you object to or resent the story, as many of the original readers did? Why or why not?
6. What does the story as a whole say about the psychology or the psy-

chological mechanisms of persecution? Does it make a statement about mob psychology?

7. In our society today, do you think there are people who are being treated unjustly without cause or reason, as if by lottery?

Thinking about Connections

8. Compare the perspectives on violence in the selections by Mark Twain, Stephen Crane, and Shirley Jackson in this chapter. What insight into its causes or its workings does each author offer? Is there any common thread?

THE SCHOOL

Donald Barthelme

Humor has often been a last defense against disillusionment or despair. Many twentieth-century writers and artists have lost faith in traditional values or at least those who preach them. Some, like Donald Barthelme, have cultivated a madcap, zany kind of dark humor. Barthelme refuses to pay respect to time-honored institutions or middle-class notions of what is respectable. He often plays games with his task as writer: He turns upside down our expectations of what a short story should be or what would be a reasonable likeness of reality in fiction. He delights in parodying what critics and teachers conventionally say about literature. His stories often seem wildly improvisational, frustrating people with linear minds and delighting others by the free play of the author's imagination.

Barthelme started to write award-winning poems and stories while he was still in high school, and during the seventies and eighties he wrote fiction for the New Yorker *magazine. He developed a loyal following among readers looking for a "postmodern" style.*

Well, we had all these children out planting trees, see, because we figured that . . . that was part of their education, to see how, you know, the root systems . . . and also the sense of responsibility, taking care of things, being individually responsible. You know what I mean. And the trees all died. They were orange trees. I don't know why they died, they just died. Something wrong with the soil possibly or maybe the stuff we got from the nursery wasn't the best. We complained about it. So we've got thirty kids there, each kid had his or her own little tree to plant, and we've got these thirty dead trees. All these kids looking at these little brown sticks, it was depressing.

It wouldn't have been so bad except that just a couple of weeks before the thing with the trees, the snakes all died. But I think that the snakes— well, the reason that the snakes kicked off was that . . . you remember, the boiler was shut off for four days because of the strike, and that was explicable. It was something you could explain to the kids because of the strike. I mean, none of their parents would let them cross the picket line and they knew there was a strike going on and what it meant. So when things got started up again and we found the snakes they weren't too disturbed.

With the herb gardens it was probably a case of overwatering, and at least now they know not to overwater. The children were very conscientious with the herb gardens and some of them probably . . . you know, slipped them a little extra water when we weren't looking. Or maybe . . . well, I don't like to think about sabotage, although it did occur to us. I mean, it was something that crossed our minds. We were thinking that way probably because before that the gerbils had died, and the white mice had died, and the salamander . . . well, now they know not to carry them around in plastic bags.

Of course we *expected* the tropical fish to die, that was no surprise. Those numbers, you look at them crooked and they're belly-up on the surface. But the lesson plan called for a tropical-fish input at that point, there was nothing we could do, it happens every year, you just have to hurry past it.

We weren't even supposed to have a puppy.   5

We weren't even supposed to have one, it was just a puppy the Murdoch girl found under a Gristede's truck one day and she was afraid the truck would run over it when the driver had finished making his delivery, so she stuck it in her knapsack and brought it to school with her. So we had this puppy. As soon as I saw the puppy I thought, Oh Christ, I bet it will live for about two weeks and then . . . And that's what it did. It wasn't supposed to be in the classroom at all, there's some kind of regulation about it, but you can't tell them they can't have a puppy when the puppy is already there, right in front of them, running around on the floor and yap yap yapping. They named it Edgar—that is, they named it after me. They had a lot of fun running after it and yelling, "Here, Edgar! Nice Edgar!" Then they'd laugh like hell. They enjoyed the ambiguity. I enjoyed it myself. I don't mind being kidded. They made a little house for it in the supply closet and all that. I don't know what it died of. Distemper, I guess. It probably hadn't had any shots. I got it out of there before the kids got to school. I checked the supply closet each morning, routinely, because I knew what was going to happen. I gave it to the custodian.

And then there was this Korean orphan that the class adopted through the Help the Children program, all the kids brought in a quarter a month, that was the idea. It was an unfortunate thing, the kid's name was Kim and maybe we adopted him too late or something. The cause of death was not stated in the letter we got, they suggested we adopt another child instead and sent us some interesting case histories, but we didn't have the heart. The class took it pretty hard, they began (I think, nobody ever said anything to me directly) to feel that maybe there was something wrong with the school. But I don't think there's anything wrong with the school, particularly, I've seen better and I've seen worse. It was just a run of bad luck. We had an extraordinary number of parents passing away, for instance. There were I think two heart attacks and two suicides, one drowning, and four killed together in a car accident. One stroke. And we had the usual heavy mortality rate among the grandparents, or maybe it was heavier this year, it seemed so. And finally the tragedy.

The tragedy occurred when Matthew Wein and Tony Mavrogordo were playing over where they're excavating for the new federal office building. There were all these big wooden beams stacked, you know, at the edge of the excavation. There's a court case coming out of that, the parents are claiming that the beams were poorly stacked. I don't know what's true and what's not. It's been a strange year.

I forgot to mention Billy Brandt's father, who was knifed fatally when he grappled with a masked intruder in his home.

One day, we had a discussion in class. They asked me, where did they go? The trees, the salamander, the tropical fish, Edgar, the poppas and mommas, Matthew and Tony, where did they go? And I said, I don't know, I don't know. And they said, who knows? and I said, nobody knows. And they said, is death that which gives meaning to life? And I said, no, life is that which gives meaning to life. Then they said, but isn't death, considered as a fundamental datum, the means by which the taken-for-granted mundanity of the everyday may be transcended in the direction of—

I said, yes, maybe.

They said, we don't like it.

I said, that's sound.

They said, it's a bloody shame!

I said, it is.

They said, will you make love now with Helen (our teaching assistant) so that we can see how it is done? We know you like Helen.

I do like Helen but I said that I would not.

We've heard so much about it, they said, but we've never seen it.

I said I would be fired and that it was never, or almost never, done as a demonstration. Helen looked out of the window.

They said, please, please make love with Helen, we require an assertion of value, we are frightened.

I said that they shouldn't be frightened (although I am often frightened) and that there was value everywhere. Helen came and embraced me. I kissed her a few times on the brow. We held each other. The children were excited. Then there was a knock on the door, I opened the door, and the new gerbil walked in. The children cheered wildly.

The Responsive Reader

1. As the story unfolds, what details are deceptively normal or believable? What are striking zany or surreal touches? When do they first surface? The narrator keeps explaining the various events in reasonable, matter-of-fact terms. Why are these explanations funny?

2. How does the story develop? What for you is the turning point of the story? Where does it turn from comical to the mixture of the comical and the horrible that we call the grotesque? Death is normally the grimmest of subjects. Can you laugh at it in this story? Why or why not?

3. Could the concluding section of the story be a parody of sex education? Is there any connection between this part and the rest of the story?

4. Are the characters in this story in any way like a real teacher and real children?

Thinking, Talking, Writing

5. Can you relate to Barthelme's sense of humor? Why or why not? Does his story have an underlying serious point?
6. Does the reader have to be a pessimist to enjoy this story?
7. Does humor generally tend to imply a disillusioned attitude? Does it tend to have a disillusioning effect?

Thinking about Connections

8. Mark Twain and Donald Barthelme are both writers maintaining their sense of humor in a violent world. Compare and contrast the two as American humorists. (Features of American humor often identified include a deadpan style and the wild exaggeration of the tall tale. Do these or other familiar features play a role in the selections by these two writers?)

6

Black Identity: Let My People Go

Freedom now appeared, to disappear no more forever. It was heard in every sound and seen in everything. It was ever present to torment me with a sense of my wretched condition. I saw nothing without seeing it, and felt nothing without feeling it. It looked from every star, it smiled in every calm, breathed in every wind, and moved in every storm.

Frederick Douglass

If we do not now dare everything, the fulfillment of that prophecy, re-created from the Bible in song by a slave, is upon us: "God gave Noah the rainbow sign, No more water, the fire next time!"

James Baldwin

Our literature shows that humans can adjust to the unacceptable and yet still find a way to forgive.

Nikki Giovanni

LITERATURE IN CONTEXT

Slavery has been the great trauma of the American national experience. There were perhaps half a million African slaves in the country at the time of the American Revolution in 1776. Their number kept increasing as the slave trade revived at the end of the Revolutionary War, or War of Independence. According to one estimate, 80,000 people a year were carried out of Africa as slaves during the first few years after the war, many of them in American ships.

The first African voices that we hear in American literature spoke in a style copied from and approved of by their white masters. In 1761 Phillis Wheatley was carried away to America as an African slave at seven years old. She was taught English and Latin and became a celebrity as America's first black poet. She wrote, "Twas mercy brought me from my pagan land,/ Taught my benighted soul to understand/That there's a God, that there's a savior too." A hundred years later, the eloquent voices of escaped former slaves were indicting the institution that had forced conversion on Africans while allowing them to be bought and sold.

Frederick Douglass' *Autobiography* (1845) was a milestone in the tradition of black literature and oratory that extends through W.E.B. Du Bois' *The Souls of Black Folk* (1903) to the impassioned speeches of the Reverend Martin Luther King, Jr. The moral outrage triggered by accounts such as Douglass' helped fuel the abolitionist movement among white sympathizers, whose manifesto was Harriet Beecher Stowe's antislavery novel *Uncle Tom's Cabin* (1851). Protecting fugitive slaves from the police became for Northern liberals like Henry David Thoreau a test of their willingness to put conscience above an immoral law. The antislavery agitation eventually made slavery a central issue in national politics. North and South quarreled over the right of Southern states to extend slavery into the new Western territories and to have fugitive slaves returned to them from the North. This quarrel eventually led to the secession of the South and a bloody civil war between Yankees and Rebels. The result was the liberation of the slaves through the Fourteenth Amendment. The aftermath of the war was the period of "reconstruction" in the South and the century-long struggle to end officially sanctioned segregation in the South and de facto segregation in the North.

In the long march up from slavery, outstanding African American writers showed large audiences what it was like to be black in white America. The poet Langston Hughes for a time appeared in every anthology as the spokesperson for America's disenfranchised black citizens. Millions here and abroad read the novelists Richard Wright (*Native Son,* 1940 and *Black Boy,* 1945) and Ralph Ellison (*Invisible Man,* 1952). These searing books dramatized the realities of racism at home for a generation that had witnessed the horrors of racist genocide in Europe.

The sixties were the decade of black anger and black pride. Leroi Jones, who adopted the African name Amiri Baraka, in his provocative play *The Dutchman* turned white people's stereotypes upside down by showing a young black man teased, harassed, hounded, and finally killed by a white woman. James Baldwin was perhaps the most widely known and translated African American writer at the time. Although he came to be seen as an Uncle Tom by militants like the Black Muslims, Baldwin said, "Things are as bad as the Muslims say they are—in fact, they are worse." When the student nonviolent movement pitted moral force against the police dogs of redneck sheriffs, Baldwin said, "there is no reason that black men should be expected to be more patient, more forbearing, more farseeing than whites." Speaking of the legal battles fought by the NAACP on behalf of blacks, he said, "very few liberals have any notion of how long, how costly, and how heartbreaking a task it is to gather the evidence that one can carry into court, or how long such court battles take."

African American writers and artists today do not limit themselves to dealing with the black experience. However, the memory of slavery, the exploration of the colonial, imperialistic African past, the return to African roots, and the everyday reality of racial discrimination have been continuing themes. (Nicki Giovanni, one of the most widely anthologized black poets, describes how she attended an exhibit of African art in a Brooklyn museum and saw with her mind's eye superimposed on an artifact the burned village from which it was taken and its slain owners.)

At the same time, black writers have increasingly turned their attention to issues *within* the black community. Some of the most powerful and widely heard among them, from Alice Walker to Toni Morrison, have explored such issues as the abuse of black women by the macho male. Kay Lindsey, for instance, said about the inferior role assigned to women by militant black men:

> But now that the revolution needs numbers
> Motherhood got a new position
> Five steps behind manhood.
>
> And I thought sittin' in the back of the bus
> Went out with Martin Luther King.

For two centuries, the unfinished agenda of this nation has been to bring first the slaves and then the descendants of slaves into full participating citizenship. James Baldwin, whose powerful essays stirred the consciences of a generation of white liberals, voiced a prophetic warning in 1961: Unless the nation addressed the pervasive "unaccepted bitterness" of its black citizens, they were "very well placed indeed to precipitate chaos and ring down the curtain on the American dream."

SOMETIMES I FEEL LIKE AN EAGLE IN THE AIR

Nineteenth-Century Spiritual

Go down, Moses,
Way down in Egyptland
Tell old Pharaoh
Let my people go.
  Traditional Spiritual

> *The poet and anthologist Dudley Randall has called the folk poetry of slavery days "the root and inspiration" of later African American poetry. Generations of black Americans have found a special meaning in the themes of their traditional spirituals: the liberation of the Jews from captivity in Egypt, the triumph of the children of Israel over their enemies with the help of the Lord, the shedding of earthly burdens on the day of resurrection. As W.E.B. Du Bois, in* The Souls of Black Folk *(1903), said about the implied message in much of the traditional music and passionate oratory of black churches, "In song and exhortation swelled one refrain—Liberty!" The Reverend Martin Luther King Jr. concluded his "I Have a Dream" speech by looking forward to the day when all of God's children "will join hands and sing in the words of the old Negro spiritual, 'Free at last! free at last!' "*

Sometimes I feel like an eagle in the air
Some of these mornin's bright and fair
I'm goin' to lay down my heavy load,
Goin' to spread my wings and cleave the air.
You may bury me in the east,   5
You may bury me in the west,
But I'll hear the trumpet sound
in that mornin'.

The Responsive Reader

1. What makes the promise of resurrection a fitting symbol for the shedding of the burden of slavery? What made the Egyptian captivity and the escape from bondage of the children of Israel powerful symbols for American blacks?

Thinking, Talking, Writing

2. What other spirituals do you know? What kind of message do you think they had for an oppressed people?

Collaborative Projects

3. You may want to work with your classmates to organize a live reading/recital or a media presentation of traditional spirituals.

RUNAGATE, RUNAGATE

Robert Hayden

*During much of the nineteenth century, American political life was domi-
nated by the issue of slavery. Even in nonslavery states the issue was kept
before people's consciences by the arrival of runaway slaves—the "runagates"
of the following poem. The Fugitive Slave Law required Americans morally
opposed to slavery to extradite fugitive slaves to the South for return to their
former owners.*

*Robert Hayden, born in Detroit, studied at Wayne University and Uni-
versity of Michigan and taught at Fisk. He published collections of his poems
including* Heartshape in the Dust *(1940) and* A Ballad of Remembrance
*(1963). He wrote powerful poems about "the deep immortal human wish" for
freedom: about Cinquez, who led the rebellion on the slave ship Amistad;
about Nat Turner biding his time before the uprising; about Harriet Tubman
"alias The General, alias Moses, alias Stealer of Slaves"; about Frederick
Douglass, "exiled, visioning a world/where none is lonely, none hunted,
alien." In his more experimental poems, Hayden weaves a pattern from
thoughts and memories passing through the speaker's consciousness, including
snatches of hymns and quotations from speeches and documents.*

I.

Runs falls rises stumbles on from darkness into darkness   1
and the darkness thicketed with shapes of terror
and the hunters pursuing and the hounds pursuing
and the night cold and the night long and the river
to cross and the jack-muh-lanterns beckoning beckoning   5
and blackness ahead and when shall I reach that somewhere
morning and keep on going and never turn back and keep on going

    Runagate
        Runagate
            Runagate   10

Many thousands rise and go
many thousands crossing over

          O mythic North
        O star-shaped yonder Bible city

Some go weeping and some rejoicing   15
some in coffins and some in carriages
some in silks and some in shackles

      Rise and go or fare you well

No more auction block for me
no more driver's lash for me   *20*

    If you see my Pompey, 30 yrs of age,
    new breeches, plain stockings, negro shoes;
    if you see my Anna, likely young mulatto
    branded E on the right cheek, R on the left,
    catch them if you can and notify subscriber.   *25*
    Catch them if you can, but it won't be easy.
    They'll dart underground when you try to catch them,
    plunge into quicksand, whirlpools, mazes,
    turn into scorpions when you try to catch them.
    And before I'll be a slave   *30*
    I'll be buried in my grave

        North star and bonanza gold
        I'm bound for the freedom, freedom-bound
        and oh Susyanna don't you cry for me

                Runagate   *35*

                 Runagate

The Responsive Reader

1. How does the poem recreate the realities of the slave's life and of attempts at escape?
2. What is the effect on the reader of the contrast between the thoughts and emotions passing through the runaway's mind and the slaveowner's handbill or advertisement?

Thinking, Talking, Writing

3. African American writers and editors used to debate whether they were aiming at one audience or two—one black, one white—each bringing to a poem or fiction a different perspective and different assumptions. Do you think Hayden's poem reaches both audiences? Do you think the poem reaches white readers?

Collaborative Projects

4. Working with others, you may want to assign parts of this poem to different speakers for a choral reading.

BALLAD OF BIRMINGHAM
Dudley Randall

> *Much black writing of the sixties and seventies keeps alive the memory of the violence and repression encountered by the civil rights movement: the assassination of the leaders, the murder of civil rights workers, the abuse endured by black children sent to newly integrated schools. The following poem, published in 1966, is about the bombing of a black church in Birmingham, Alabama. Dudley Randall is a black poet who published his anthology* The Black Poets *in 1971. He aimed at including a new generation of black poets alienated from white society and turning away from white models and white values. He said, "When the poets saw the contorted faces of the mobs, saw officers of the law commit murder, and 'respectable' people scheme to break the law (there was no cry for law and order then), perhaps they asked themselves, Why should we seek to be integrated with such a society?"*

(On the bombing of a church in Birmingham, Alabama, 1963)

"Mother dear, may I go downtown   1
Instead of out to play,
And march the streets of Birmingham
In a Freedom March today?"

"No, baby, no, you may not go,   5
For the dogs are fierce and wild,
And clubs and hoses, guns and jails
Aren't good for a little child."

"But, mother, I won't be alone.
Other children will go with me,   10
And march the streets of Birmingham
To make our country free."

"No, baby, no, you may not go,
For I fear those guns will fire.
But you may go to church instead   15
And sing in the children's choir."

She has combed and brushed her night-dark hair,
And bathed rose petal sweet.
And drawn white gloves on her small brown hands,
And white shoes on her feet.   20

The mother smiled to know her child
Was in the sacred place,

But that smile was the last smile
To come upon her face.

For when she heard the explosion,   25
Her eyes grew wet and wild.
She raced through the streets of Birmingham
Calling for her child.

She clawed through bits of glass and brick,
Then lifted out a shoe.   30
"Oh, here's the shoe my baby wore,
But, baby, where are you?"

The Responsive Reader

1. The old folk ballads of England and Scotland often dealt with a terrible event by stripping it down to its essentials. Often the story would emerge from a dialogue between two principal participants in the event. Often the ballad would build to a climax through cumulative repetition: Key phrases or lines would be repeated, like a refrain, until the ballad reached its high point. Show how this poem uses the old ballad pattern.
2. What is the irony in the mother's role in the early stanzas of the poem?

Thinking, Talking, Writing

3. The ballad style excludes eloquent expressions of grief or passionate condemnations of injustice. Why do you think the poet chose it? Would the poem be more effective if the poet poured out his rage or indignation?
4. Do you think white people can share the outrage of the black community at the bombing of black churches? Regardless of what our group is, are we capable of feeling true compassion for or solidarity with someone who is "not one of us"?

I AM A BLACK WOMAN

Mari Evans

> Mari Evans says in one of her poems, "I/am the result of/President Lincoln/World War 1/and Paris/the/Red Ball Express/white drinking fountains/sitdowns and/sit-ins/Federal Troops/Marches on Washington/and/ prayer meetings . . ." Evans was writing at a time when the tone of black writing was changing "to one of pride and militancy," and when black writers started to speak "in bellicose voices to their brothers about the beauty of blackness and the necessity of resisting white cruelty with loaded guns and loaded words" that would "raise a nation of free black people" (Houston A. Baker Jr.). Evans' outspoken poetry moves between "raw-edged anguish" and bitter wit, between yearning for human warmth and disillusioned sarcasm. The following poem was published in the Negro Digest in 1969.

I am a black woman   1
the music of my song
some sweet arpeggio of tears
is written in a minor key
and I   5
can be heard humming in the night
Can be heard
    humming
in the night

I saw my mate leap screaming to the sea   10
and I/with these hands/cupped the lifebreath
from my issue in the canebrake
I lost Nat's swinging body in a rain of tears

and heard by son scream all the way from Anzio
for Peace he never knew . . . I   15
learned Da Nang and Pork Chop Hill
in anguish
Now my nostrils know the gas
and these trigger tire/d fingers
seek the softness in my warrior's beard   20

I
am a black woman
tall as a cypress
strong
beyond all definition still   25
defying place
and time

and circumstance
  assailed
    impervious
      indestructible   *30*

Look
  on me and be
renewed

The Responsive Reader

1. Why is the music early in the poem "in a minor key"? (What is an arpeggio? Where are people likely to hear it?)
2. Why does the poem mention Anzio in Italy, Pork Chop Hill in Korea, and Da Nang in Vietnam? Where would a black woman have seen her mate "leap screaming to the sea"? Why and when would she have "cupped the lifebreath" from her issue or offspring? How does the poem invoke the memory of Nat Turner, the leader of a slave revolt in Virginia in 1831?
3. How does this poem project the sense of black pride?

Thinking, Talking, Writing

4. The self-image of America's minorities has moved between the poles of being ashamed of one's heritage on the one hand and defiant self-assertion or pride on the other. Have you experienced or observed either or both?
5. Where have you been aware of music as part of people's lives and part of who they are?

WOMEN

Alice Walker

    A few black women during the nineteenth century emerged from anonymity to have their names recorded in history books: Sojourner Truth, an evangelist who was a freed former slave, preached abolition and women's rights and became famous for her "Ain't I a Woman" speech (1851); she helped gather supplies for black regiments fighting on the Union side during the Civil War. Harriet Tubman, an escaped former slave, returned to the South nineteen times to lead 300 of her people to freedom on the Underground Railroad. Alice Walker, author of The Color Purple *(1982), has paid tribute to the nameless black women of a later generation. Her widely read essay "In Search of Our Mothers' Garden" (1983) paid tribute to the creative ability that women like her mother, denied other outlets, channeled into their quilt-making and their gardens, "brilliant with colors," "magnificent with life and creativity."*

    For Walker, the heritage of black writers in the South includes "a compassion for the earth, a trust in humanity beyond the knowledge of evil, and an abiding love of justice." It also includes the responsibility to "give voice to centuries not only of silent bitterness and hate but also of neighborly kindness and sustaining love."

They were women then   *1*
My mamma's generation
Husky of voice—Stout of
Step
With fists as well as   *5*
Hands
How they battered down
Doors
And ironed
Starched white   *10*
Shirts
How they led
Armies
Headragged Generals
Across mined   *15*
Fields
Booby-trapped
Ditches
To discover books
Desks   *20*
A place for us
How they knew what we

Must know
Without knowing a page
Of it   *25*
Themselves.

The Responsive Reader

1. What stereotypes about womanhood does this poem challenge?
2. What kind of "mined fields" and "booby-trapped" ditches did the women in this poem have to contend with? (How or why were they "headragged generals"?)
3. A paradox is an apparent contradiction that makes sense on second thought. What is paradoxical about the conclusion of the poem?

Thinking, Talking, Writing

4. The vote or the ballot box has often been the symbol of emancipation for African Americans. Could you argue that books and desks are just as important?

Thinking about Connections

5. What images of black women do you see in the poems in this chapter?

THE INGRATE
Paul Laurence Dunbar

Paul Laurence Dunbar was one of the first black writers to reach white audiences after Emancipation. He wrote at a time when, as his colleague Charles Chesnutt said, "a literary work by an American of acknowledged color was a doubtful experiment, both for the writer and for the publisher."

Dunbar became famous as a dialect poet, handing on the folklore of the rural South, and seeming, in retrospect, to reinforce the stereotype of the Negro as minstrel and buffoon. Both his dialect poems and his short stories have been criticized for showing black people "as folksy, not-too-bright souls, all of whose concerns are minor" (Saunders Redding). When taken more seriously, Dunbar has been classed with contemporaries who shared Booker Washington's aim to show whites "how 'civilized' the Negro had become" and to prove that black people could be "responsible and respectable" (Melvin Drimmer). However, Dunbar also wrote stories that challenged racism with both solemn indignation and wry humor.

A familiar figure in African American folklore is the trickster depending for survival on his wits. For a time, it was illegal to teach slaves to read and write, since deep down the slaveholders sensed that education in the long run liberates people from the fetters of ignorance and oppression. In the following story, Dunbar turns the tables by having a literate slave outwit his skinflint master.

I

Mr. Leckler was a man of high principle. Indeed, he himself had admitted it at times to Mrs. Leckler. She was often called into counsel with him. He was one of those large-souled creatures with a hunger for unlimited advice, upon which he never acted. Mrs. Leckler knew this, but like the good, patient little wife that she was, she went on paying her poor tribute of advice and admiration. Today her husband's mind was particularly troubled— as usual, too, over a matter of principle. Mrs. Leckler came at his call.

"Mrs. Leckler," he said, "I am troubled in my mind. I—in fact, I am puzzled over a matter that involves either the maintaining or relinquishing of a principle."

"Well, Mr. Leckler?" said his wife interrogatively.

"If I had been a scheming, calculating Yankee, I should have been rich now; but all my life I have been too generous and confiding. I have always let principle stand between me and my interests." Mr. Leckler took himself all too seriously to be conscious of his pun, and went on: "Now this is a matter in which my duty and my principles seem to conflict. It stands thus: Josh has been doing a piece of plastering for Mr. Eckley over in Lexington,

1

and from what he says, I think that city rascal has misrepresented the amount of work to me and so cut down the pay for it. Now, of course, I should not care, the matter of a dollar or two being nothing to me; but it is a very different matter when we consider poor Josh." There was deep pathos in Mr. Leckler's tone. "You know Josh is anxious to buy his freedom, and I allow him a part of whatever he makes; so you see it's he that's affected. Every dollar that he is cheated out of cuts off just so much from his earnings, and puts further away his hope of emancipation."

If the thought occurred to Mrs. Leckler that, since Josh received only   5
about one tenth of what he earned, the advantage of just wages would be quite as much her husband's as the slave's, she did not betray it, but met the naïve reasoning with the question, "But where does the conflict come in, Mr. Leckler?"

"Just here. If Josh knew how to read and write and cipher—"

"Mr. Leckler, are you crazy!"

"Listen to me, my dear, and give me the benefit of your judgment. This is a very momentous question. As I was about to say, if Josh knew these things, he could protect himself from cheating when his work is at too great a distance for me to look after it for him."

"But teaching a slave—"

"Yes, that's just what is against my principles. I know how public opin-   10
ion and the law look at it. But my conscience rises up in rebellion every time I think of that poor black man being cheated out of his earnings. Really, Mrs. Leckler, I think I may trust to Josh's discretion and secretly give him such instructions as will permit him to protect himself."

"Well, of course, it's just as you think best," said his wife.

"I knew you would agree with me," he returned. "It's such a comfort to take counsel with you, my dear!" And the generous man walked out onto the veranda, very well satisfied with himself and his wife, and prospectively pleased with Josh. Once he murmured to himself, "I'll lay for Eckley next time."

Josh, the subject of Mr. Leckler's charitable solicitations, was the plantation plasterer. His master had given him his trade, in order that he might do whatever such work was needed about the place; but he became so proficient in his duties, having also no competition among the poor whites, that he had grown to be in great demand in the country thereabout. So Mr. Leckler found it profitable, instead of letting him do chores and field work in his idle time, to hire him out to neighboring farms and planters. Josh was a man of more than ordinary intelligence; and when he asked to be allowed to pay for himself by working overtime, his master readily agreed— for it promised more work to be done, for which he could allow the slave just what he pleased. Of course, he knew now that when the black man began to cipher this state of affairs would be changed; but it would mean such an increase of profit from the outside that he could afford to give up his own little peculations. Anyway, it would be many years before the slave could pay the two thousand dollars, which price he had set upon him. Should he approach that figure, Mr. Leckler felt it just possible that the market in slaves would take a sudden rise.

When Josh was told of his master's intention, his eyes gleamed with pleasure, and he went to his work with the zest of long hunger. He proved a remarkably apt pupil. He was indefatigable in doing the tasks assigned him. Even Mr. Leckler, who had great faith in his plasterer's ability, marveled at the speed which he had acquired the three R's. He did not know that on one of his many trips a free negro had given Josh the rudimentary tools of learning, and that ever since the slave had been adding to his store of learning by poring over signs and every bit of print that he could spell out. Neither was Josh so indiscreet as to intimate to his benefactor that he had been anticipated in his good intentions.

It was in this way, working and learning, that a year passed away, and   15 Mr. Leckler thought that his object had been accomplished. He could safely trust Josh to protect his own interests, and so he thought that it was quite time that his servant's education should cease.

"You know, Josh," he said, "I have already gone against my principles and against the law for your sake, and of course a man can't stretch his conscience too far, even to help another who's being cheated; but I reckon you can take care of yourself now."

"Oh, yes, suh, I reckon I kin," said Josh.

"And it wouldn't do for you to be seen with any books about you now."

"Oh, no, suh, su't'n'y not." He didn't intend to be seen with any books about him.

It was just now that Mr. Leckler saw the good results of all he had   20 done, and his heart was full of a great joy, for Eckley had been building some additions to his house and sent for Josh to do the plastering for him. The owner admonished his slave, took him over a few examples to freshen his memory, and sent him forth with glee. When the job was done, there was a discrepancy of two dollars in what Mr. Eckley offered for it and the price which accrued from Josh's measurements. To the employer's surprise, the black man went over the figures with him and convinced him of the incorrectness of the payment—and the additional two dollars were turned over.

"Some o' Leckler's work," said Eckley, "teaching a nigger to cipher! Close-fisted old reprobate—I've a mind to have the law on him."

Mr. Leckler heard the story with great glee. "I laid for him that time— the old fox." But to Mrs. Leckler he said, "You see, my dear wife, my rashness in teaching Josh to figure for himself is vindicated. See what he has saved for himself."

"What did he save?" asked the little woman indiscreetly.

Her husband blushed and stammered for a moment, and then replied, "Well, of course, it was only twenty cents saved to him, but to a man buying his freedom every cent counts; and after all, it is not the amount, Mrs. Leckler, it's the principle of the thing."

"Yes," said the lady meekly.   *25*

II

Unto the body it is easy for the master to say, "Thus far shalt thou go, and no farther." Gyves, chains, and fetters will enforce that command. But what master shall say unto the mind, "Here do I set the limit of your acquisition. Pass it not"? Who shall put gyves upon the intellect, or fetter the movement of thought? Joshua Leckler, as custom denominated him, had tasted of the forbidden fruit, and his appetite had grown by what it fed on. Night after night he crouched in his lonely cabin, by the blaze of a fat pine brand, poring over the few books that he had been able to secure and smuggle in. His fellow servants alternately laughed at him and wondered why he did not take a wife. But Joshua went on his way. He had no time for marrying or for love; other thoughts had taken possession of him. He was being swayed by ambitions other than the mere fathering of slaves for his master. To him his slavery was deep night. What wonder, then, that he should dream, and that through the ivory gate should come to him the forbidden vision of freedom? To own himself, to be master of his hands, feet, of his whole body—something would clutch at his heart as he thought of it, and the breath would come hard between his lips. But he met his master with an impassive face, always silent, always docile; and Mr. Leckler congratulated himself that so valuable and intelligent a slave should be at the same time so tractable. Usually intelligence in a slave meant discontent; but not so with Josh. Who more content than he? He remarked to his wife: "You see, my dear, this is what comes of treating even a nigger right."

Meanwhile the white hills of the North were beckoning to the chattel, and the north winds were whispering to him to be a chattel no longer. Often the eyes that looked away to where freedom lay were filled with a wistful longing that was tragic in its intensity, for they saw the hardships and the difficulties between the slave and his goal and, worst of all, an iniquitous law—liberty's compromise with bondage, that rose like a stone wall between him and hope—a law that degraded every free-thinking man to the level of a slave catcher. There it loomed up before him, formidable, impregnable, insurmountable. He measured it in all its terribleness, and paused. But on the other side there was liberty; and one day when he was away at work, a voice came out of the woods and whispered to him "Courage!"—and on that night the shadows beckoned him as the white hills had done, and the forest called to him, "Follow."

"It seems to me that Josh might have been able to get home tonight," said Mr. Leckler, walking up and down his veranda, "but I reckon it's just possible that he got through too late to catch a train." In the morning he said, "Well, he's not here yet; he must have had to do some extra work. If he doesn't get here by evening, I'll run up there."

In the evening, he did take the train for Joshua's place of employment, where he learned that his slave had left the night before. But where could he have gone? That no one knew, and for the first time it dawned upon his master that Josh had run away. He raged; he fumed; but nothing could be done until morning, and all the time Leckler knew that the most valuable slave on his plantation was working his way toward the North and freedom. He did not go back home, but paced the floor all night long. In the early dawn he hurried out, and the hounds were put on the fugitive's track. After some nosing around they set off toward a stretch of woods. In a few minutes they came yelping back, pawing their noses and rubbing their heads against the ground. They had found the trail, but Josh had played the old slave trick of filling his tracks with cayenne pepper. The dogs were soothed and taken deeper into the wood to find the trail. They soon took it up again, and dashed away with low bays. The scent led them directly to a little wayside station about six miles distant. Here it stopped. Burning with the chase, Mr. Leckler hastened to the station agent. Had he seen such a negro? Yes, he had taken the northbound train two nights before.

"But why did you let him go without a pass?" almost screamed the 30 owner.

"I didn't," replied the agent. "He had a written pass, signed James Leckler, and I let him go on it."

"Forged, forged!" yelled the master. "He wrote it himself."

"Humph!" said the agent. "How was I to know that? Our niggers round here don't know how to write."

Mr. Leckler suddenly bethought him to hold his peace. Josh was probably now in the arms of some northern abolitionist, and there was nothing to be done now but advertise; and the disgusted master spread his notices broadcast before starting for home. As soon as he arrived at his house, he sought his wife and poured out his griefs to her.

"You see, Mrs. Leckler, this is what comes of my goodness of heart. I 35 taught that nigger to read and write, so that he could protect himself—and look how he uses his knowledge. Oh, the ingrate, the ingrate! The very weapon which I give him to defend himself against others he turns upon me. Oh, it's awful—awful! I've always been too confiding. Here's the most valuable nigger on my plantation gone—gone, I tell you—and through my own kindness. It isn't his value, though, I'm thinking so much about. I could stand his loss, if it wasn't for the principle of the thing, the base ingratitude he has shown me. Oh, if I ever lay hands on him again!" Mr. Leckler closed his lips and clenched his fist with an eloquence that laughed at words.

Just at this time, in one of the underground railway stations, six miles north of the Ohio, an old Quaker was saying to Josh, "Lie still—thee'll be perfectly safe there. Here comes John Trader, our local slave catcher, but I will parley with him and send him away. Thee need not fear. None of thy

brethren who have come to us have ever been taken back to bondage.—
Good evening, Friend Trader!" and Josh heard the old Quaker's smooth voice
roll on, while he lay back half smothering in a bag, among other bags of
corn and potatoes.

It was after ten o'clock that night when he was thrown carelessly into
a wagon and driven away to the next station, twenty-five miles to the northward. And by such stages, hiding by day and traveling by night, helped by a
few of his own people who were blessed with freedom, and always by the
good Quakers wherever found, he made his way into Canada. And on one
never-to-be-forgotten morning he stood up, straightened himself, breathed
God's blessed air, and knew himself free!

III

To Joshua Leckler this life in Canada was all new and strange. It was a
new thing for him to feel himself a man and to have his manhood recognized
by the whites with whom he came into free contact. It was new, too, this
receiving the full measure of his worth in work. He went to his labor with a
zest that he had never known before, and he took a pleasure in the very
weariness it brought him. Ever and anon there came to his ears the cries of
his brethren in the South. Frequently he met fugitives who, like himself, had
escaped from bondage; and the harrowing tales that they told him made him
burn to do something for those whom he had left behind him. But these
fugitives and the papers he read told him other things. They said that the
spirit of freedom was working in the United States, and already men were
speaking out boldly in behalf of the manumission of the slaves; already there
was a growing army behind that noble vanguard, Sumner, Phillips, Douglass,
Garrison. He heard the names of Lucretia Mott and Harriet Beecher Stowe,
and his heart swelled, for on the dim horizon he saw the first faint streaks
of dawn.

So the years passed. Then from the surcharged clouds a flash of lightning broke, and there was the thunder of cannon and the rain of lead over
the land. From his home in the North he watched the storm as it raged and
wavered, now threatening the North with its awful power, now hanging dire
and dreadful over the South. Then suddenly from out the fray came a voice
like the trumpet tone of God to him: "Thou and thy brothers are free!" Free,
free, with the freedom not cherished by the few alone, but for all that had
been bound. Free, with the freedom not torn from the secret night, but open
to the light of heaven.

When the first call for colored soldiers came, Joshua Leckler hastened
down to Boston, and enrolled himself among those who were willing to
fight to maintain their freedom. On account of his ability to read and write
and his general intelligence, he was soon made an orderly sergeant. His
regiment had already taken part in an engagement before the public roster of
this band of Uncle Sam's niggers, as they were called, fell into Mr. Leckler's

hands. He ran his eye down the column of names. It stopped at that of Joshua Leckler, Sergeant, Company F. He handed the paper to Mrs. Leckler with his finger on the place.

"Mrs. Leckler," he said, "this is nothing less than a judgment on me for teaching a nigger to read and write. I disobeyed the law of my state and, as a result, not only lost my nigger, but furnished the Yankees with a smart officer to help them fight the South. Mrs. Leckler, I have sinned—and been punished. But I am content, Mrs. Leckler; it all came through my kindness of heart—and your mistaken advice. But, oh, that ingrate, that ingrate!"

The Responsive Reader

1. Does this story make a good trickster story?
2. What did you know about the "underground railroad"? What do you learn about it from this story?
3. Much of the literature of Dunbar's time was didactic—spelling out and preaching the moral values of the author. Where does this story get most overtly didactic? Do you find it eloquent or merely preachy?
4. According to historians of the post–Civil War period, the new black educated middle class aimed to advance its cause in alliance with liberal whites. How does the story and its treatment of whites reflect this tendency?

Thinking, Talking, Writing

5. The oppressed have often plotted against their masters while outwardly maintaining a submissive, obsequious Uncle Tom manner. How does this story mirror this pattern? Has this ploy outlived its usefulness—is it obsolete?

Collaborative Projects

6. Working with a group, you may want to study the Brer Rabbit stories and investigate recent controversies concerning this kind of dialect material.

1920

Toni Morrison

Every one of us could write a book about race. The text is already imprinted in our minds and evokes our moral character.

Andrew Hacker

Toni Morrison is the author of major novels that serve the reader as an initiation into the pervasive role of race in American life. They include The Bluest Eye *(1970),* Sula *(1973),* Song of Solomon *(1977),* Tar Baby *(1981), and* Jazz *(1992). Her spectacularly successful* Beloved *(1987) told the story of a mother, an escaped slave, who is haunted by the memory of the baby daughter she killed to keep her out of slave-catchers' hands. A reviewer called Morrison the quintessential black American writer, accomplishing the difficult feat of "being both academically and popularly canonized: her books claim a high place on college reading lists as well as on best-seller lists; she holds a prestigious professorship at Princeton University, and she is a prominent spokeswoman on racial questions, large and small" (Ann Hulbert). In 1993 Morrison was awarded the Nobel Prize for literature, the first American woman to win the award in fifty-five years.*

Morrison has been an aggressive critic of "whitemale" culture. Born near Cleveland, Ohio, as the child of sharecroppers, she has studied and taught at Howard University. For a time she worked as a senior editor for a New York publishing house. She has written critical essays on race as a challenge and an obsession in the work of white American writers. A book she edited probed the workings of sexism in the controversy swirling around charges of sexual harassment brought against Supreme Court nominee Clarence Thomas by another African American, Anita Hill.

The following self-contained narrative forms part of the novel Sula. *A black woman, "with heavy misgiving," takes the journey back home to the Old South that has become an almost archetypal experience in the work of African American writers. The time is two years after victory in World War I, when there are still uniformed veterans, black and white, on the trains. In New Orleans, people still know Creole, a local French dialect spoken by black people that goes back to French colonial times:* Vrai? *(Is that true?);* chère *(dear);* Comment t'appelle? *(What's your name);* oui *(yes); and* 'Voir *(short for* au revoir, *see you again). A "Frenchified shotgun house" is a colonial-French-style house with all rooms in line front to back. The "Elysian Fields," a street named after the fabled* Champs Elysées *in Paris, runs through the poor part of town.*

It had to be as far away from the Sundown House as possible. And her grandmother's middle-aged nephew who lived in a Northern town called

1

Medallion was the one chance she had to make sure it would be. The red shutters had haunted both Helene Sabat and her grandmother for sixteen years. Helene was born behind those shutters, daughter of a Creole whore who worked there. The grandmother took Helene away from the soft lights and flowered carpets of the Sundown House and raised her under the dolesome eyes of a multicolored Virgin Mary, counseling her to be constantly on guard for any sign of her mother's wild blood.

So when Wiley Wright came to visit his Great Aunt Cecile in New Orleans, his enchantment with the pretty Helene became a marriage proposal—under the pressure of both women. He was a seaman (or rather a lakeman, for he was a ship's cook on one of the Great Lakes lines), in port only three days out of every sixteen.

He took his bride to his home in Medallion and put her in a lovely house with a brick porch and real lace curtains at the window. His long absences were quite bearable for Helene Wright, especially when, after some nine years of marriage, her daughter was born.

Her daughter was more comfort and purpose than she had ever hoped to find in this life. She rose grandly to the occasion of motherhood—grateful, deep down in her heart, that the child had not inherited the great beauty that was hers: that her skin had dusk in it, that her lashes were substantial but not undignified in their length, that she had taken the broad flat nose of Wiley (although Helene expected to improve it somewhat) and his generous lips.

Under Helene's hand the girl became obedient and polite. Any enthusiasms that little Nel showed were calmed by the mother until she drove her daughter's imagination underground.   5

Helene Wright was an impressive woman, at least in Medallion she was. Heavy hair in a bun, dark eyes arched in a perpetual query about other people's manners. A woman who won all social battles with presence and a conviction of the legitimacy of her authority. Since there was no Catholic church in Medallion then, she joined the most conservative black church. And held sway. It was Helene who never turned her head in church when latecomers arrived; Helene who established the practice of seasonal altar flowers; Helene who introduced the giving of banquets of welcome to returning Negro veterans. She lost only one battle—the pronunciation of her name. The people in the Bottom refused to say Helene. They called her Helen Wright and left it at that.

All in all her life was a satisfactory one. She loved her house and enjoyed manipulating her daughter and her husband. She would sigh sometimes just before falling asleep, thinking that she had indeed come far enough away from the Sundown House.

So it was with extremely mixed emotions that she read a letter from Mr. Henri Martin describing the illness of her grandmother, and suggesting she come down right away. She didn't want to go, but could not bring herself to ignore the silent plea of the woman who had rescued her.

It was November. November, 1920. Even in Medallion there was a victorious swagger in the legs of white men and a dull-eyed excitement in the eyes of colored veterans.

Helene thought about the trip South with heavy misgiving but decided   *10* that she had the best protection: her manner and her bearing, to which she would add a beautiful dress. She bought some deep-brown wool and three-fourths of a yard of matching velvet. Out of this she made herself a heavy but elegant dress with velvet collar and pockets.

Nel watched her mother cutting the pattern from newspapers and moving her eyes rapidly from a magazine model to her own hands. She watched her turn up the kerosene lamp at sunset to sew far into the night.

The day they were ready, Helene cooked a smoked ham, left a note for her lake-bound husband, in case he docked early, and walked head high and arms stiff with luggage ahead of her daughter to the train depot.

It was a longer walk than she remembered, and they saw the train steaming up just as they turned the corner. They ran along the track looking for the coach pointed out to them by the colored porter. Even at that they made a mistake. Helene and her daughter entered a coach peopled by some twenty white men and women. Rather than go back and down the three wooden steps again, Helene decided to spare herself some embarrassment and walk on through to the colored car. She carried two pieces of luggage and a string purse; her daughter carried a covered basket of food.

As they opened the door marked COLORED ONLY, they saw a white conductor coming toward them. It was a chilly day but a light skim of sweat glistened on the woman's face as she and the little girl struggled to hold the door open, hang on to their luggage and enter all at once. The conductor let his eyes travel over the pale yellow woman and then stuck his little finger into his ear, jiggling it free of wax. "What you think you doin', gal?"

Helene looked up at him.   *15*

So soon. So soon. She hadn't even begun the trip back. Back to her grandmother's house in the city where the red shutters glowed, and already she had been called "gal." All the old vulnerabilities, all the old fears of being somehow flawed gathered in her stomach and made her hands tremble. She had heard only that one word; it dangled above her wide-brimmed hat, which had slipped, in her exertion, from its carefully leveled placement and was now tilted in a bit of a jaunt over her eye.

Thinking he wanted her tickets, she quickly dropped both the cowhide suitcase and the straw one in order to search for them in her purse. An eagerness to please and an apology for living met in her voice. "I have them. Right here somewhere, sir. . . ."

The conductor looked at the bit of wax his fingernail had retrieved. "What was you doin' back in there? What was you doin' in that coach yonder?"

Helene licked her lips. "Oh . . . I . . ." Her glance moved beyond the white man's face to the passengers seated behind him. Four or five black faces were watching, two belonging to soldiers still in their shit-colored uniforms and peaked caps. She saw their closed faces, their locked eyes, and turned for compassion to the gray eyes of the conductor.

"We made a mistake, sir. You see, there wasn't no sign. We just got in the wrong car, that's all. Sir." 20

"We don't 'low no mistakes on this train. Now git your butt on in there."

He stood there staring at her until she realized that he wanted her to move aside. Pulling Nel by the arm, she pressed herself and her daughter into the foot space in front of a wooden seat. Then, for no earthly reason, at least no reason that anybody could understand, certainly no reason that Nel understood then or later, she smiled. Like a street pup that wags its tail at the very doorjamb of the butcher shop he has been kicked away from only moments before, Helene smiled. Smiled dazzlingly and coquettishly at the salmon-colored face of the conductor.

Nel looked away from the flash of pretty teeth to the other passengers. The two black soldiers, who had been watching the scene with what appeared to be indifference, now looked stricken. Behind Nel was the bright and blazing light of her mother's smile; before her the midnight eyes of the soldiers. She saw the muscles of their faces tighten, a movement under the skin from blood to marble. No change in the expression of the eyes, but a hard wetness that veiled them as they looked at the stretch of her mother's foolish smile.

As the door slammed on the conductor's exit, Helene walked down the aisle to a seat. She looked about for a second to see whether any of the men would help her put the suitcases in the overhead rack. Not a man moved. Helene sat down, fussily, her back toward the men. Nel sat opposite, facing both her mother and the soldiers, neither of whom she could look at. She felt both pleased and ashamed to sense that these men, unlike her father, who worshiped his graceful, beautiful wife, were bubbling with a hatred for her mother that had not been there in the beginning but had been born with the dazzling smile. In the silence that preceded the train's heave, she looked deeply at the folds of her mother's dress. There in the fall of the heavy brown wool she held her eyes. She could not risk letting them travel upward for fear of seeing that the hooks and eyes in the placket of the dress had come undone and exposed the custard-colored skin underneath. She stared at the hem, wanting to believe in its weight but knowing that custard was all that it hid. If this tall, proud woman, this woman who was very particular about her friends, who slipped into church with unequaled elegance, who could quell a roustabout with a look, if *she* were really custard, then there was a chance that Nel was too.

It was on that train, shuffling toward Cincinnati, that she resolved to 25
be on guard—always. She wanted to make certain that no man ever looked at her that way. That no midnight eyes or marbled flesh would ever accost her and turn her into jelly.

For two days they rode; two days of watching sleet turn to rain, turn to purple sunsets, and one night knotted on the wooden seats (their heads on folded coats), trying not to hear the snoring soldiers. When they changed trains in Birmingham for the last leg of the trip, they discovered what luxury they had been in through Kentucky and Tennessee, where the rest stops had all had colored toilets. After Birmingham there were none. Helene's face was drawn with the need to relieve herself, and so intense was her distress she finally brought herself to speak about her problem to a black woman with four children who had got on in Tuscaloosa.

"Is there somewhere we can go to use the restroom?"

The woman looked up at her and seemed not to understand. "Ma'am?" Her eyes fastened on the thick velvet collar, the fair skin, the high-tone voice.

"The restroom," Helene repeated. Then, in a whisper, "The toilet."

The woman pointed out the window and said, "Yes, ma'am. Yonder."   30

Helene looked out of the window halfway expecting to see a comfort station in the distance; instead she saw gray-green trees leaning over tangled grass. "Where?"

"Yonder," the woman said. "Meridian. We be pullin' in direc'lin." Then she smiled sympathetically and asked, "Kin you make it?"

Helene nodded and went back to her seat trying to think of other things—for the surest way to have an accident would be to remember her full bladder.

At Meridian the women got out with their children. While Helene looked about the tiny stationhouse for a door that said COLORED WOMEN, the other woman stalked off to a field of high grass on the far side of the track. Some white men were leaning on the railing in front of the station-house. It was not only their tongues curling around toothpicks that kept Helene from asking information of them. She looked around for the other woman and, seeing just the top of her head rag in the grass, slowly realized where "yonder" was. All of them, the fat woman and her four children, three boys and a girl, Helene and her daughter, squatted there in the four o'clock Meridian sun. They did it again in Ellisville, again in Hattiesburg, and by the time they reached Slidell, not too far from Lake Pontchartrain, Helene could not only fold leaves as well as the fat woman, she never felt a stir as she passed the muddy eyes of the men who stood like wrecked Dorics under the station roofs of those towns.

The lift in spirit that such an accomplishment produced in her quickly   35
disappeared when the train finally pulled into New Orleans.

Cecile Sabat's house leaned between two others just like it on Elysian Fields. A Frenchified shotgun house, it sported a magnificent garden in the back and a tiny wrought-iron fence in the front. On the door hung a black crepe wreath with purple ribbon. They were too late. Helene reached up to touch the ribbon, hesitated, and knocked. A man in a collarless shirt opened the door. Helene identified herself and he said he was Henri Martin and that he was there for the settin'-up. They stepped into the house. The Virgin Mary clasped her hands in front of her neck three times in the front room and once in the bedroom where Cecile's body lay. The old woman had died without seeing or blessing her granddaughter.

No one other than Mr. Martin seemed to be in the house, but a sweet odor as of gardenias told them that someone else had been. Blotting her lashes with a white handkerchief, Helene walked through the kitchen to the back bedroom where she had slept for sixteen years. Nel trotted along behind, enchanted with the smell, the candles and the strangeness. When Helene bent to loosen the ribbons of Nel's hat, a woman in a yellow dress came out of the garden and onto the back porch that opened into the bedroom. The two women looked at each other. There was no recognition in the eyes of either. Then Helene said, "This is your . . . grandmother, Nel." Nel looked at her mother and then quickly back at the door they had just come out of.

"No. That was your great-grandmother. This is your grandmother. My mother . . ."

Before the child could think, her words were hanging in the gardenia air. "But she looks so young."

The woman in the canary-yellow dress laughed and said she was forty-eight, "an old forty-eight." ^{40}

Then it was she who carried the gardenia smell. This tiny woman with the softness and glare of a canary. In that somber house that held four Virgin Marys, where death sighed in every corner and candles sputtered, the gardenia smell and canary-yellow dress emphasized the funeral atmosphere surrounding them.

The woman smiled, glanced in the mirror and said, throwing her voice toward Helene, "That your only one?"

"Yes," said Helene.

"Pretty. A lot like you."

"Yes. Well. She's ten now." ^{45}

"Ten? Vrai? Small for her age, no?"

Helene shrugged and looked at her daughter's questioning eyes. The woman in the yellow dress leaned forward. "Come. Come, chère."

Helene interrupted. "We have to get cleaned up. We been three days on the train with no chance to wash or . . ."

"Comment t'appelle?"

"She doesn't talk Creole." ^{50}

"Then you ask her."

"She wants to know your name, honey."

With her head pressed into her mother's heavy brown dress, Nel told her and then asked, "What's yours?"

"Mine's Rochelle. Well. I must be going on." She moved closer to the mirror and stood there sweeping hair up from her neck back into its halolike roll, and wetting with spit the ringlets that fell over her ears. "I been here, you know, most of the day. She pass on yesterday. The funeral tomorrow. Henri takin' care." She struck a match, blew it out and darkened her eyebrows with the burnt head. All the while Helene and Nel watched her. The one in a rage at the folded leaves she had endured, the wooden benches she had slept on, all to miss seeing her grandmother and seeing instead that painted canary who never said a word of greeting or affection or . . .

Rochelle continued, "I don't know what happen to de house. Long time paid for. You be thinkin' on it? Oui?" Her newly darkened eyebrows queried Helene.

"Oui." Helene's voice was chilly. "I be thinkin' on it."

"Oh, well. Not for me to say . . ."

Suddenly she swept around and hugged Nel—a quick embrace tighter and harder than one would have imagined her thin soft arms capable of.

"'Voir! 'Voir!" and she was gone.

In the kitchen, being soaped head to toe by her mother, Nel ventured an observation. "She smelled so nice. And her skin was so soft."

Helene rinsed the cloth. "Much handled things are always soft."

"What does 'vwah' mean?"

"I don't know," her mother said. "I don't talk Creole." She gazed at her daughter's wet buttocks. "And neither do you."

When they got back to Medallion and into the quiet house they saw the note exactly where they had left it and the ham dried out in the icebox.

"Lord, I've never been so glad to see this place. But look at the dust. Get the rags, Nel. Oh, never mind. Let's breathe awhile first. Lord, I never thought I'd get back here safe and sound. Whoo. Well it's over. Good and over. Praise His name. Look at that. I told that old fool not to deliver any milk and there's the can curdled to beat all. What gets into people? I told him not to. Well, I got other things to worry 'bout. Got to get a fire started. I left it ready so I wouldn't have to do nothin' but light it. Lord, it's cold. Don't just sit there, honey. You could be pulling your nose . . ."

Nel sat on the red-velvet sofa listening to her mother but remembering the smell and the tight, tight hug of the woman in yellow who rubbed burned matches over her eyes.

Late that night after the fire was made, the cold supper eaten, the surface dust removed, Nel lay in bed thinking of her trip. She remembered clearly the urine running down and into her stockings until she learned how to squat properly; the disgust on the face of the dead woman and the sound of the funeral drums. It had been an exhilarating trip but a fearful one. She had been frightened of the soldiers' eyes on the train, the black wreath on the door, the custard pudding she believed lurked under her mother's heavy dress, the feel of unknown streets and unknown people. But she had gone on a real trip, and now she was different. She got out of bed and lit the lamp to look in the mirror. There was her face, plain brown eyes, three braids and the nose her mother hated. She looked for a long time and suddenly a shiver ran through her.

"I'm me," she whispered. "Me."

Nel didn't know quite what she meant, but on the other hand she knew exactly what she meant.

"I'm me. I'm not their daughter. I'm not Nel. I'm me. Me."   70

Each time she said the word *me* there was a gathering in her like power, like joy, like fear. Back in bed with her discovery, she stared out the window at the dark leaves of the horse chestnut.

"Me," she murmured. And then, sinking deeper into the quilts, "I want . . . I want to be . . . wonderful. Oh, Jesus, make me wonderful."

The many experiences of her trip crowded in on her. She slept. It was the last as well as the first time she was ever to leave Medallion.

For days afterward she imagined other trips she would take, alone though, to faraway places. Contemplating them was delicious. Leaving Medallion would be her goal. But that was before she met Sula, the girl she had seen for five years at Garfield Primary but never played with, never knew, because her mother said Sula's mother was sooty. The trip, perhaps, or her new found me-ness, gave her the strength to cultivate a friend in spite of her mother.

When Sula first visited the Wright house, Helene's curdled scorn   75 turned to butter. Her daughter's friend seemed to have none of the mother's slackness. Nel, who regarded the oppressive neatness of her home with dread, felt comfortable in it with Sula, who loved it and would sit on the red-velvet sofa for ten to twenty minutes at a time—still as dawn. As for Nel, she preferred Sula's woolly house, where a pot of something was always cooking on the stove; where the mother, Hannah, never scolded or gave directions; where all sorts of people dropped in; where newspapers were stacked in the hallway, and dirty dishes left for hours at a time in the sink, and where a one-legged grandmother named Eva handed you goobers from deep inside her pockets or read you a dream.

The Responsive Reader

1. What kind of central character does the author create for the reader early in the story? What is Helene Wright's life in the North? What are her memories of the South?

2. What does Helene mean when she says early during the trip South, "So soon"? How does the conductor play a central role as a representative of white society?

3. In fiction like Morrison's, small details often carry heavy symbolic weight. Why does the smile Helene gives the conductor at the end of their encounter become an issue in the story? Why does the restroom issue acquire major symbolic significance in this story?

4. "Nostalgia isn't what it used to be" was the title a widely admired French star of stage and screen gave to her autobiography. From the beginning, the central character in the story feels "extremely mixed emotions." What are her mixed, ambivalent feelings about the place and the people she revisits?

5. For Helene's daughter Nel, who seems to play a minor role during the trip, the experience nevertheless becomes a turning point in her life and outlook. How or why?

Thinking, Talking, Writing

6. Are the emotions and attitudes dramatized in this story a thing of the past?

7. In an antislavery novel published in 1852, one of the characters says, "The more low, brutal, and degraded a white man is, the more does he insist on the natural superiority of the white man, and the more he is shocked at the idea of allowing freedom to the 'niggers.'" Do you think something similar holds true today? To judge from your experience, observation, or reading, does racism correlate with lack of education or low social status?

8. Have you ever revisited a place or its people with a sense of "misgiving" or "mixed emotions"?

NOTES OF A NATIVE SON (PART I)

James Baldwin

I consider that I have many responsibilities, but none greater than this: to last, as Hemingway says, and get my work done. I want to be an honest man and a good writer.

James Baldwin

*James Baldwin was one of the most eloquent and influential American essayists of the twentieth century. He wrote novels (*Go Tell It on the Mountain, *1953;* Giovanni's Room, *1956) as well as a play (*Blues for Mister Charlie, *1964). However, he is best known for several collections of essays that dramatized and interpreted the psychology of American racism for a generation of readers. The lead essay in his* Notes of a Native Son *(1955) told the story of his struggle to emerge from the bleak poverty, violence, and paranoia of Harlem, where he for a time followed in the footsteps of his embittered father and preached as a Young Minister in a store-front church. He wrote of the rage that all black people in this country carried within them and that, if not faced or come to terms with, threatened to destroy them. In other essays Baldwin wrote about his experience as an expatriate American writer in Europe, where he lived off and on between 1948 and 1959, joining other black writers and artists.*

Baldwin's prophetic The Fire Next Time *(1963) warned of chaotic racial strife unless America faced up to the need to accept the black people in its midst and to grant them their "human reality" and their "human weight and complexity." In the sixties and seventies, Baldwin joined in the dialogue among black artists and intellectuals concerning the rediscovery of the African past, the rise of black militancy, and the validation of Black English. To the end, he was a voice of conscience for a country "unable to face why so many of the nonwhite are in prison, or on the needle, or standing, futureless, in the streets."*

Notes of a Native Son *centers on one of the great themes of classic autobiography: the alienated son in rebellion against the authoritarian father. The essay is driven by the son's need to understand his father and himself and to make his peace with the father's memory. However, father and son are at the same time players in a larger drama. Their experience is shaped in inescapable ways by what Baldwin calls the "weight of white people in the world."*

On the 29th of July, in 1943, my father died. On the same day, a few hours later, his last child was born. Over a month before this, while all our energies were concentrated in waiting for these events, there had been, in Detroit, one of the bloodiest race riots of the century. A few hours after my father's funeral, while he lay in state in the undertaker's chapel, a race riot

1

broke out in Harlem. On the morning of the 3rd of August, we drove my father to the graveyard through a wilderness of smashed plate glass.

The day of my father's funeral had also been my nineteenth birthday. As we drove him to the graveyard, the spoils of injustice, anarchy, discontent, and hatred were all around us. It seemed to me that God himself had devised, to mark my father's end, the most sustained and brutally dissonant of codas. And it seemed to me, too, that the violence which rose all about us as my father left the world had been devised as a corrective for the pride of his eldest son. I had declined to believe in that apocalypse which had been central to my father's vision; very well, life seemed to be saying, here is something that will certainly pass for an apocalypse until the real thing comes along. I had inclined to be contemptuous of my father for the conditions of his life, for the conditions of our lives. When his life had ended I began to wonder about that life and also, in a new way, to be apprehensive about my own.

I had not known my father very well. We had got on badly, partly because we shared, in our different fashions, the vice of stubborn pride. When he was dead I realized that I had hardly ever spoken to him. When he had been dead a long time I began to wish I had. It seems to be typical of life in America, where opportunities, real and fancied, are thicker than anywhere else on the globe, that the second generation has no time to talk to the first. No one, including my father, seems to have known exactly how old he was, but his mother had been born during slavery. He was of the first generation of free men. He, along with thousands of other Negroes, came North after 1919 and I was part of that generation which had never seen the landscape of what Negroes sometimes call the Old Country.

He had been born in New Orleans and had been a quite young man there during the time that Louis Armstrong, a boy, was running errands for the dives and honky-tonks of what was always presented to me as one of the most wicked of cities—to this day, whenever I think of New Orleans, I also helplessly think of Sodom and Gomorrah. My father never mentioned Louis Armstrong, except to forbid us to play his records; but there was a picture of him on our wall for a long time. One of my father's strong-willed female relatives had placed it there and forbade my father to take it down. He never did, but he eventually maneuvered her out of the house and when, some years later, she was in trouble and near death, he refused to do anything to help her.

He was, I think, very handsome. I gather this from photographs and ⟨5⟩ from my own memories of him, dressed in his Sunday best and on his way to preach a sermon somewhere, when I was little. Handsome, proud, and ingrown, "like a toe-nail," somebody said. But he looked to me, as I grew older, like pictures I had seen of African tribal chieftains: he really should have been naked, with war-paint on and barbaric mementos, standing among spears. He could be chilling in the pulpit and indescribably cruel in his personal life and he was certainly the most bitter man I have ever met; yet it must be said that there was something else in him, buried in him, which lent him his tremendous power and, even, a rather crushing charm. It had something to do with his blackness, I think—he was very black—with his blackness and his beauty, and with the fact that he knew that he was black but did not know that he was beautiful. He claimed to be proud of his blackness but it had also been the cause of much humiliation and it had fixed bleak boundaries to his life. He was not a young man when we were growing up and he had already suffered many kinds of ruin; in his outrageously demanding and protective way he loved his children, who were black like him and menaced, like him; and all these things sometimes showed in his face when he tried, never to my knowledge with any success, to establish contact with any of us. When he took one of his children on his knee to play, the child always became fretful and began to cry; when he tried to help one of us with our homework the absolutely unabating tension which emanated from him caused our minds and our tongues to become paralyzed, so that he, scarcely knowing why, flew into a rage and the child, not knowing why, was punished. If it ever entered his head to bring a surprise home for his children, it was, almost unfailingly, the wrong surprise and even the big watermelons he often brought home on his back in the summertime led to the most appalling scenes. I do not remember, in all those years, that one of his children was ever glad to see him come home. From what I was able to gather of his early life, it seemed that this inability to establish contact with other people had always marked him and had been one of the things which had driven him out of New Orleans. There was something in him, therefore, groping and tentative, which was never expressed and which was buried with him. One saw it most clearly when he was facing new people and hoping to impress them. But he never did, not for long. We went from church to smaller and more improbable church, he found himself in less and less demand as a minister, and by the time he died none of his friends had come to see him for a long time. He had lived and died in an intolerable bitterness of spirit and it frightened me, as we drove him to the graveyard through those unquiet, ruined streets, to see how powerful and overflowing this bitterness could be and to realize that this bitterness now was mine.

When he died I had been away from home for a little over a year. In that year I had had time to become aware of the meaning of all my father's bitter warnings, had discovered the secret of his proudly pursed lips and rigid carriage: I had discovered the weight of white people in the world. I saw that this had been for my ancestors and now would be for me an awful thing to live with and that the bitterness which had helped to kill my father could also kill me.

He had been ill a long time—in the mind, as we now realized, reliving instances of his fantastic intransigence in the new light of his affliction and endeavoring to feel a sorrow for him which never, quite, came true. We had not known that he was being eaten up by paranoia, and the discovery that his cruelty, to our bodies and our minds, had been one of the symptoms of his illness was not, then, enough to enable us to forgive him. The younger children felt, quite simply, relief that he would not be coming home anymore. My mother's observation that it was he, after all, who had kept them alive all these years meant nothing because the problems of keeping children alive are not real for children. The older children felt, with my father gone, that they could invite their friends to the house without fear that their friends would be insulted or, as had sometimes happened with me, being told that their friends were in league with the devil and intended to rob our family of everything we owned. (I didn't fail to wonder, and it made me hate him, what on earth we owned that anybody else would want.)

His illness was beyond all hope of healing before anyone realized that he was ill. He had always been so strange and had lived, like a prophet, in such unimaginably close communion with the Lord that his long silences which were punctuated by moans and hallelujahs and snatches of old songs while he sat at the living-room window never seemed odd to us. It was not until he refused to eat because, he said, his family was trying to poison him that my mother was forced to accept as a fact what had, until then, been only an unwilling suspicion. When he was committed, it was discovered that he had tuberculosis and, as it turned out, the disease of his mind allowed the disease of his body to destroy him. For the doctors could not force him to eat, either, and, though he was fed intravenously, it was clear from the beginning that there was no hope for him.

In my mind's eye I could see him, sitting at the window, locked up in his terrors; hating and fearing every living soul including his children who had betrayed him, too, by reaching towards the world which had despised him. There were nine of us. I began to wonder what it could have felt like for such a man to have had nine children whom he could barely feed. He used to make little jokes about our poverty, which never, of course, seemed very funny to us; they could not have seemed very funny to him, either, or else our all too feeble response to them would never have caused such rages. He spent great energy and achieved, to our chagrin, no small amount of success in keeping us away from the people who surrounded us, people who had all-night rent parties to which we listened when we should have been sleeping, people who cursed and drank and flashed razor blades on Lenox Avenue. He could not understand why, if they had so much energy to spare, they could not use it to make their lives better. He treated almost everybody on our block with a most uncharitable asperity and neither they, nor, of course, their children were slow to reciprocate.

The only white people who came to our house were welfare workers   *10* and bill collectors. It was almost always my mother who dealt with them, for my father's temper, which was at the mercy of his pride, was never to be trusted. It was clear that he felt their very presence in his home to be a violation: this was conveyed by his carriage, almost ludicrously stiff, and by his voice, harsh and vindictively polite. When I was around nine or ten I wrote a play which was directed by a young, white schoolteacher, a woman, who then took an interest in me, and gave me books to read and, in order to corroborate my theatrical bent, decided to take me to see what she somewhat tactlessly referred to as "real" plays. Theater-going was forbidden in our house, but, with the really cruel intuitiveness of a child, I suspected that the color of this woman's skin would carry the day for me. When, at school, she suggested taking me to the theater, I did not, as I might have done if she had been a Negro, find a way of discouraging her, but agreed that she should pick me up at my house one evening. I then, very cleverly, left all the rest to my mother, who suggested to my father, as I knew she would, that it would not be very nice to let such a kind woman make the trip for nothing. Also, since it was a schoolteacher, I imagine that my mother countered the idea of sin with the idea of "education," which word, even with my father, carried a kind of bitter weight.

Before the teacher came my father took me aside to ask *why* she was coming, what *interest* she could possibly have in our house, in a boy like me. I said I didn't know but I, too, suggested that it had something to do with education. And I understood that my father was waiting for me to say something—I didn't quite know what; perhaps that I wanted his protection against this teacher and her "education." I said none of these things and the teacher came and we went out. It was clear, during the brief interview in our living room, that my father was agreeing very much against his will and that he would have refused permission if he had dared. The fact that he did not dare caused me to despise him: I had no way of knowing that he was facing in that living room a wholly unprecedented and frightening situation.

Later, when my father had been laid off from his job, this woman became very important to us. She was really a very sweet and generous woman and went to a great deal of trouble to be of help to us, particularly during one awful winter. My mother called her by the highest name she knew: she said she was a "christian." My father could scarcely disagree but during the four or five years of our relatively close association he never trusted her and was always trying to surprise in her open, Midwestern face the genuine, cunningly hidden, and hideous motivation. In later years, particularly when it began to be clear that this "education" of mine was going to lead me to perdition, he became more explicit and warned me that my white friends in high school were not really my friends and that I would see, when I was older, how white people would do anything to keep a Negro down. Some of them could be nice, he admitted, but none of them were to be trusted and most of them were not even nice. The best thing was to have as little to do with them as possible. I did not feel this way and I was certain, in my innocence, that I never would.

But the year which preceded my father's death had made a great change in my life. I had been living in New Jersey, working in defense plants, working and living among southerners, white and black. I knew about the south, of course, and about how southerners treated Negroes and how they expected them to behave, but it had never entered my mind that anyone would look at me and expect *me* to behave that way. I learned in New Jersey that to be a Negro meant, precisely, that one was never looked at but was simply at the mercy of the reflexes the color of one's skin caused in other people. I acted in New Jersey as I had always acted, that is as though I thought a great deal of myself—I had to *act* that way—with results that were, simply, unbelievable. I had scarcely arrived before I had earned the enmity, which was extraordinarily ingenious, of all my superiors and nearly all my co-workers. In the beginning, to make matters worse, I simply did not know what was happening. I did not know what I had done, and I shortly began to wonder what *anyone* could possibly do, to bring about such unanimous, active, and unbearably vocal hostility. I knew about jim-crow but I had never experienced it. I went to the same self-service restaurant three times and stood with all the Princeton boys before the counter, waiting for a hamburger and coffee; it was always an extraordinarily long time before anything was set before me; but it was not until the fourth visit that I learned that, in fact, nothing had ever been set before me: I had simply picked something up. Negroes were not served there, I was told, and they had been waiting for me to realize that I was always the only Negro present. Once I was told this, I determined to go there all the time. But now they were ready for me and, though some dreadful scenes were subsequently enacted in that restaurant, I never ate there again.

It was the same story all over New Jersey, in bars, bowling alleys, diners, places to live. I was always being forced to leave, silently, or with mutual imprecations. I very shortly became notorious and children giggled behind me when I passed and their elders whispered or shouted—they really believed that I was mad. And it did begin to work on my mind, of course; I began to be afraid to go anywhere and to compensate for this I went places to which I really should not have gone and where, God knows, I had no desire to be. My reputation in town naturally enhanced my reputation at work and my working day became one long series of acrobatics designed to keep me out of trouble. I cannot say that these acrobatics succeeded. It began to seem that the machinery of the organization I worked for was turning over, day and night, with but one aim: to eject me. I was fired once, and contrived, with the aid of a friend from New York, to get back on the payroll; was fired again, and bounced back again. It took a while to fire me for the third time, but the third time took. There were no loopholes anywhere. There was not even any way of getting back inside the gates.

That year in New Jersey lives in my mind as though it were the year   *15* during which, having an unsuspected predilection for it, I first contracted some dread, chronic disease, the unfailing symptom of which is a kind of blind fever, a pounding in the skull and fire in the bowels. Once this disease is contracted, one can never be really carefree again, for the fever, without an instant's warning, can recur at any moment. It can wreck more important things than race relations. There is not a Negro alive who does not have this rage in his blood—one has the choice, merely, of living with it consciously or surrendering to it. As for me, this fever has recurred in me, and does, and will until the day I die.

My last night in New Jersey, a white friend from New York took me to the nearest big town, Trenton, to go to the movies and have a few drinks. As it turned out, he also saved me from, at the very least, a violent whipping. Almost every detail of that night stands out very clearly in my memory. I even remember the name of the movie we saw because its title impressed me as being so patly ironical. It was a movie about the German occupation of France, starring Maureen O'Hara and Charles Laughton and called *This Land Is Mine*. I remember the name of the diner we walked into when the movie ended: it was the "American Diner." When we walked in the counterman asked what we wanted and I remember answering with the casual sharpness which had become my habit: "We want a hamburger and a cup of coffee, what do you think we want?" I do not know why, after a year of such rebuffs, I so completely failed to anticipate his answer, which was, of course, "We don't serve Negroes here." This reply failed to discompose me, at least for the moment. I made some sardonic comment about the name of the diner and we walked out into the streets.

This was the time of what was called the "brown-out," when the lights in all American cities were very dim. When we re-entered the streets something happened to me which had the force of an optical illusion, or a nightmare. The streets were very crowded and I was facing north. People were moving in every direction but it seemed to me, in that instant, that all of the people I could see, and many more than that, were moving toward me, against me, and that everyone was white. I remember how their faces gleamed. And I felt, like a physical sensation, a *click* at the nape of my neck as though some interior string connecting my head to my body had been cut. I began to walk. I heard my friend call after me, but I ignored him. Heaven only knows what was going on in his mind, but he had the good sense not to touch me—I don't know what would have happened if he had—and to keep me in sight. I don't know what was going on in my mind, either; I certainly had no conscious plan. I wanted to do something to crush these white faces, which were crushing me. I walked for perhaps a block or two until I came to an enormous, glittering, and fashionable restaurant in which I knew not even the intercession of the Virgin would cause me to be served. I pushed through the doors and took the first vacant seat I saw, at a table for two, and waited.

I do not know how long I waited and I rather wonder, until today, what I could possibly have looked like. Whatever I looked like, I frightened the waitress who shortly appeared, and the moment she appeared all of my fury flowed towards her. I hated her for her white face, and for her great, astounded, frightened eyes. I felt that if she found a black man so frightening I would make her fright worth-while.

She did not ask me what I wanted, but repeated, as though she had learned it somewhere, "We don't serve Negroes here." She did not say it with the blunt, derisive hostility to which I had grown so accustomed, but, rather, with a note of apology in her voice, and fear. This made me colder and more murderous than ever. I felt I had to do something with my hands. I wanted her to come close enough for me to get her neck between my hands.

So I pretended not to have understood her, hoping to draw her closer. And she did step a very short step closer, with her pencil poised incongruously over her pad, and repeated the formula: ". . . don't serve Negroes here."

Somehow, with the repetition of that phrase, which was already ringing in my head like a thousand bells of a nightmare, I realized that she would never come any closer and that I would have to strike from a distance. There was nothing on the table but an ordinary water-mug half full of water, and I picked this up and hurled it with all my strength at her. She ducked and it missed her and shattered against the mirror behind the bar. And, with that sound, my frozen blood abruptly thawed, I returned from wherever I had been, I *saw,* for the first time, the restaurant, the people with their mouths open already, as it seemed to me, rising as one man, and I realized what I had done, and where I was, and I was frightened. I rose and began running for the door. A round, potbellied man grabbed me by the nape of the neck just as I reached the doors and began to beat me about the face. I kicked him and got loose and ran into the streets. My friend whispered, *"Run!"* and I ran.

My friend stayed outside the restaurant long enough to misdirect my pursuers and the police, who arrived, he told me, at once. I do not know what I said to him when he came to my room that night. I could not have said much. I felt, in the oddest, most awful way, that I had somehow betrayed him. I lived it over and over and over again, the way one relives an automobile accident after it has happened and one finds oneself alone and safe. I could not get over two facts, both equally difficult for the imagination to grasp, and one was that I could have been murdered. But the other was that I had been ready to commit murder. I saw nothing very clearly but I did see this: that my life, my *real* life, was in danger, and not from anything other people might do but from the hatred I carried in my own heart.

The Responsive Reader

1. What kind of person was Baldwin's father? What do you learn about the relationship between father and son? How does Baldwin try to make the reader understand the father's bitterness and cruelty? How would you sum up Baldwin's feelings about his father as the son looks back?

2. Baldwin was accused by young black militants of being a friend of whites. What is the role of white people in this story?

3. What does Baldwin say or show about the workings of Jim Crow? What was Baldwin's personal reaction to it?

4. The climactic final incident dramatizes the theme of black rage that pervades the work of many African American writers. What happened and why? Who or what was to blame? What for Baldwin was the lesson to be learned from it?

Thinking, Talking, Writing

5. Baldwin reached a large white audience. Why do you think he did? What in this essay is specific to the black experience? What is universal?

6. One collection of writing by African Americans was called *Anger and Beyond*. Do you think the pent-up anger of black Americans is diminishing or growing?

Thinking about Connections

7. What do you learn about racism from the selections by Dunbar, Morrison, and Baldwin in this chapter?

ROSELILY
Alice Walker

Alice Walker is a writer and feminist from Georgia who has written and lectured widely about race relations and male-female relationships and about the black woman writers who were her inspiration. As a student at Spelman College in Atlanta in the sixties, she was swept up in the rallies, sit-ins, and freedom marches of the civil rights movement, which, she said, "broke the pattern of black servitude in this country." Her novel The Color Purple *(1982) won the American Book Award and the Pulitzer Prize. Her novel* The Temple of My Familiar *was published in 1989.*

Like few other writers, Alice Walker has explored the true range of the African American experience. Her fiction is peopled, among others, by down-home people who have stayed close to their rural roots, by citified sophisticated middle-class blacks, and by black women trapped in relationships with abusive males. In the story that follows, we see a woman about to join the Black Muslims, embracing their creed of pride, austerity, and female modesty. We listen in on the thoughts going through the woman's mind as the minister performing the marriage service recites the familiar lines.

Dearly Beloved

She dreams; dragging herself across the world. A small girl in her mother's   1
white robe and veil, knee raised waist high through a bowl of quicksand soup. The man who stands beside her is against this standing on the front porch of her house, being married to the sound of cars whizzing by on highway 61.

we are gathered here

Like cotton to be weighed. Her fingers at the last minute busily removing dry leaves and twigs. Aware it is a superficial sweep. She knows he blames Mississippi for the respectful way the men turn their heads up in the yard, the women stand waiting and knowledgeable, their children held from mischief by teachings from the wrong God. He glares beyond them to the occupants of the cars, white faces glued to promises beyond a country wedding, noses thrust forward like dogs on a track. For him they usurp the wedding.

in the sight of God

Yes, open house. That is what country black folks like. She dreams she does not already have three children. A squeeze around the flowers in her hands chokes off three and four and five years of breath. Instantly she is ashamed and frightened in her superstition. She looks for the first time at the preacher, forces humility into her eyes, as if she believes he is, in fact, a man of God. She can imagine God, a small black boy, timidly pulling the preacher's coattail.

to join this man and this woman

She thinks of ropes, chains, handcuffs, his religion. His place of worship. Where she will be required to sit apart with covered head. In Chicago, a word she hears when thinking of smoke, from his description of what a cinder was, which they never had in Panther Burn. She sees hovering over the heads of the clean neighbors in her front yard black specks falling, clinging, from the sky. But in Chicago. Respect, a chance to build. Her children at last from underneath the detrimental wheel. A chance to be on top. What a relief, she thinks. What a vision, a view, from up so high.

in holy matrimony.

Her fourth child she gave away to the child's father who had some money.   5
Certainly a good job. Had gone to Harvard. Was a good man but weak because good language meant so much to him he could not live with Roselily. Could not abide TV in the living room, five beds in three rooms, no Bach except from four to six on Sunday afternoons. No chess at all. She does not forget to worry about her son among his father's people. She wonders if the New England climate will agree with him. If he will ever come down to Mississippi, as his father did, to try to right the country's wrongs. She wonders if he will be stronger than his father. His father cried off and on throughout her pregnancy. Went to skin and bones. Suffered nightmares, retching and falling out of bed. Tried to kill himself. Later told his wife he found the right baby through friends. Vouched for, the sterling qualities that would make up his character.

It is not her nature to blame. Still, she is not entirely thankful. She supposes New England, the North, to be quite different from what she knows. It seems right somehow to her that people who move there to live return home completely changed. She thinks of the air, the smoke, the cinders. Imagines cinders big as hailstones; heavy, weighing on the people. Wonders how this pressure finds it way into the veins, roping the springs of laughter.

If there's anybody here that knows a reason why

But of course they know no reason why beyond what they daily have come to know. She thinks of the man who will be her husband, feels shut away from him because of the stiff severity of his plain black suit. His religion. A lifetime of black and white. Of veils. Covered head. It is as if her children are already gone from her. Not dead, but exalted on a pedestal, a stalk that has no roots. She wonders how to make new roots. It is beyond her. She wonders what one does with memories in a brand-new life. This had seemed easy, until she thought of it. "The reasons why . . . the people who" . . . she thinks, and does not wonder where the thought is from.

these two should not be joined

She thinks of her mother, who is dead. Dead, but still her mother. Joined. This is confusing. Of her father. A gray old man who sold wild mink, rabbit, fox skins to Sears, Roebuck. He stands in the yard, like a man waiting for a train. Her young sisters stand behind her in smooth green dresses, with flowers in their hands and hair. They giggle, she feels, at the absurdity of the wedding. They are ready for something new. She thinks the man beside her should marry one of them. She feels old. Yoked. An arm seems to reach out from behind her and snatch her backward. She thinks of cemeteries and the long sleep of grandparents mingling in the dirt. She believes that she believes in ghosts. In the soil giving back what it takes.

together

In the city. He sees her in a new way. This she knows, and is grateful. But is it new enough? She cannot always be a bride and virgin, wearing robes and veil. Even now her body itches to be free of satin and voile, organdy and lily of the valley. Memories crash against her. Memories of being bare to the sun. She wonders what it will be like. Not to have to go to a job. Not to work in a sewing plant. Not to worry about learning to sew straight seams in workingmen's overalls, jeans, and dress pants. Her place will be in the home, he has said, repeatedly, promising her rest she had prayed for. But now she wonders. When she is rested, what will she do? They will make babies—she thinks practically about her fine brown body, his strong black one. They will be inevitable. Her hands will be full. Full of what? Babies. She is not comforted.

let him speak

She wishes she had asked him to explain more of what he meant. But she was impatient. Impatient to be done with sewing. With doing everything for three children, alone. Impatient to leave the girls she had known since child- hood, their children growing up, their husbands hanging around her, already old, seedy. Nothing about them that she wanted, or needed. The fathers of her children driving by, waving, not waving; reminders of times she would just as soon forget. Impatient to see the South Side, where they would live and build and be respectable and respected and free. Her husband would

10

free her. A romantic hush. Proposal. Promises. A new life! Respectable, re-claimed, renewed. Free! In robe and veil.

or forever hold

She does not even know if she loves him. She loves his sobriety. His refusal to sing just because he knows the tune. She loves his pride. His blackness and his gray car. She loves his understanding of her *condition.* She thinks she loves the effort he will make to redo her into what he truly wants. His love of her makes her completely conscious of how unloved she was before. This is something; though it makes her unbearably sad. Melancholy. She blinks her eyes. Remembers she is finally being married, like other girls. Like other girls, women? Something strains upward behind her eyes. She thinks of the something as a rat trapped, concerned, scurrying to and fro in her head, peering through the windows of her eyes. She wants to live for once. But doesn't know quite what that means. Wonders if she has ever done it. If she ever will. The preacher is odious to her. She wants to strike him out of the way, out of her light, with the back of her hand. It seems to her he has always been standing in front of her, barring her way.

his peace.

The rest she does not hear. She feels a kiss, passionate, rousing, within the general pandemonium. Cars drive up blowing their horns. Firecrackers go off. Dogs come from under the house and begin to yelp and bark. Her husband's hand is like the clasp of an iron gate. People congratulate. Her children press against her. They look with awe and distaste mixed with hope at their new father. He stands curiously apart, in spite of the people crowding about to grasp his free hand. He smiles at them all but his eyes are as if turned inward. He knows they cannot understand that he is not a Christian. He will not explain himself. He feels different, he looks it. The old women thought he was like one of their sons except that he had somehow got away from them. Still a son, not a son. Changed.

She thinks how it will be later in the night in the silvery gray car. How they will spin through the darkness of Mississippi and in the morning be in Chicago, Illinois. She thinks of Lincoln, the president. That is all she knows about the place. She feels ignorant, *wrong,* backward. She presses her worried fingers into his palm. He is standing in front of her. In the crush of well-wishing people, he does not look back.

The Responsive Reader

1. What kind of person is the intended husband? What do you learn in this story about him and his religion?

2. What kind of person is the woman getting married? What do you learn about her family history? What do you learn about her children and their fathers?

3. People often feel ambivalent about a planned marriage—they have mixed feelings. Why is Roselily ambivalent about the wedding? What were her motives for getting married? What does she see as her future? Why does she have misgivings?

4. Much modern fiction has explored the private thoughts and feelings that we normally keep from the world. This story takes us into the private thoughts and feelings of the main character. Do any of them strike you as the kind we are trained not to acknowledge or verbalize?

Thinking, Talking, Writing

5. Compare the woman's earlier relationship and her intended marriage. How are the two men in her life different? Do they have anything in common? Is there a pattern?

6. Do you think the woman in this story is making a mistake? Why or why not?

7. In her later writings, Walker has often examined critically the role of women, and especially black women, in our world. She has called herself a "womanist," an advocate of social change allowing black women a greater chance for self-expression and self-realization. Does this story as a whole make a statement about the role or status of women, and especially black women?

8. During a censorship controversy in California, this story was called "antireligious." Do you think it is?

Collaborative Projects

9. What are the history and current role of the Black Muslim movement in America? Your class may want to farm out different facets of this question to small groups.

toussaint

ntozake shange

ntozake shange's for colored girls who have considered suicide/when the rainbow is enuf *(1976) started as a series of poems read in a women's bar outside Berkeley, California. It developed into a Broadway play that, the author says, would be "enveloping almost 6000 people a week in the words of a young black girl's growing up, her triumphs & errors, our struggle to become all that is forbidden by our environment, all that is forfeited by our gender, all that we have forgotten."*

shange says that her "sense of the world" was shaped by a number of related influences: A women's studies program at Sonoma State College introduced her to an "articulated female heritage," including the work of Third World women writers. In the San Francisco setting, she discovered and worked with poets who promoted "the poetry and presence of women" in a traditional "male-poet's environment." As a dancer, she became immersed in the tradition of African dance and music. She became absorbed in dance and theater that helped audiences discover forgotten or misunderstood "women writers, painters, mothers, cowgirls, & union leaders of our pasts."

for colored girls grew out of individual poems; typically the poem was a monologue in which a black woman revealed her character or life history to the audience. In the finished play, these dramatic monologues and other pieces are interwoven to form a larger pattern. One of the twenty poems that form the larger play is reprinted here. The Toussaint L'Ouverture mentioned in this selection is the legendary leader of black revolutionary forces in Haiti. He defied the colonial armies of France, which at the time was first ruled by leaders like Robespierre and then by the emperor Napoleon. In the printed version of shange's play, the unusual spelling and punctuation create an effect similar to dialogue that includes echoes of the Black English or home dialect of the characters. Reviewers have admired shange's work for its fierce honesty and savage candor; one of them said that her poetry "has the power to move a body to tears, to rage, and to an ultimate rush of love" (Marilyn Stasio).

    lady in brown
de library waz right down from de trolly tracks   *1*
cross from de laundry-mat
thru de big shinin floors & granite pillars
ol st. louis is famous for
i found toussaint   *5*
but not til after months uv
cajun katie/pippi longstockin
christopher robin/eddie heyward & a pooh bear
in the children's room

only pioneer girls & magic rabbits   *10*
& big city white boys
i knew i waznt sposedta
but i ran inta the ADULT READING ROOM
       & came across

        TOUSSAINT   *15*

        my first blk man
(i never counted george washington carver
cuz i didnt like peanuts)
        still
TOUSSAINT waz a blk man a negro like my mama say   *20*
who refused to be a slave
& he spoke french
& didnt low no white man to tell him nothin
       not napolean
       not maximillien   *25*
       not robespierre

TOUSSAINT L'OUVERTURE
waz the beginnin uv reality for me
in the summer contest for
who colored child can read   *30*
15 books in three weeks
i won & raved abt TOUSSAINT L'OUVERTURE
at the afternoon ceremony
waz disqualified
       cuz Toussaint   *35*
        belonged in the ADULT READING ROOM
        & i cried
& carried dead Toussaint home in the book
he waz dead & livin to me
cuz TOUSSAINT & them   *40*
they held the citadel gainst the french
wid the spirits of ol dead africans from outta the ground
TOUSSAINT led they army of zombies
walkin cannon ball shootin spirits to free Haiti
& they waznt slaves no more   *45*

        TOUSSAINT L'OUVERTURE
became my secret lover at the age of 8
i entertained him in my bedroom
widda flashlight under my covers
way inta the night/we discussed strategies   *50*

how to remove white girls from my hopscotch games
& etc.
TOUSSAINT
waz layin in bed wit me next to raggedy ann
the night i decided to run away from my   *55*
    integrated home
      integrated street
       integrated school
1955 waz not a good year for lil blk girls

Toussaint said 'lets go to haiti'   *60*
i said 'awright'
& packed some very important things in a brown paper bag
so i wdnt haveta come back
then Toussaint & i took the hodiamont streetcar
to the river   *65*
last stop
only 15¢
cuz there waznt nobody cd see Toussaint cept me
& we walked all down thru north st. louis
where the french settlers usedta live   *70*
in tiny brick houses all huddled together
wit barely missin windows & shingles uneven
wit colored kids playin & women on low porches sippin beer

i cd talk to Toussaint down by the river
like this waz where we waz gonna stow away   *75*
on a boat for new orleans
& catch a creole fishin-rig for port-au-prince
then we waz just gonna read & talk all the time
& eat fried bananas
     we waz just walkin & skippin past ol drunk men   *80*
when dis ol young boy jumped out at me sayin
'HEY GIRL YA BETTAH COME OVAH HEAH N TALK TO ME'
well
i turned to TOUSSAINT (who waz furious)
& i shouted   *85*
'ya silly ol boy
ya bettah leave me alone
or TOUSSAINT'S gonna get yr ass'
de silly ol boy came round de corner laughin all in my face
'yellah gal   *90*
ya sure must be somebody to know my name so quick'
i waz disgusted
& wanted to get on to haiti

widout some tacky ol boy botherin me
still he kept standin there   95
kickin milk cartons & bits of brick
tryin to get all in my business
          i mumbled to L'OUVERTURE 'what shd I do'
finally
i asked this silly ol boy   100
'WELL WHO ARE YOU?'
he say
'MY NAME IS TOUSSAINT JONES'
well
i looked right at him   105
those skidded out cordoroy pants
a striped teashirt wid holes in both elbows
a new scab over his left eye
& i said
          'what's yr name again'   110
he say
'i'm toussaint jones'
'wow
i am on my way to see
TOUSSAINT L'OUVERTURE in HAITI   115
are ya any kin to him
he dont take no stuff from no white folks
& they gotta country all they own
& there aint no slaves'
that silly ol boy squinted his face all up   120
'looka heah girl
i am TOUSSAINT JONES
& i'm right heah lookin at ya
& i dont take no stuff from no white folks
ya dont see none round heah do ya?'   125
& he sorta pushed out his chest
then he say
'come on   lets go on down to the docks
& look at the boats'
i waz real puzzled goin down to the docks   130
wit my paper bag & my books
i felt TOUSSAINT L'OUVERTURE sorta leave me
& i waz sad
til i realized
TOUSSAINT JONES waznt too different   135
from TOUSSAINT L'OUVERTURE
cept the ol one waz in haiti
& this one wid me speakin english & eatin apples

yeah.
toussaint jones waz awright wit me   *140*
no tellin what all spirits we cd move
down by the river
st. louis 1955   hey wait.

The Responsive Reader

1. What kind of person is speaking to you in this monologue?
2. Education has often been advertised to young African Americans as the avenue to advancement. How do the girl's experiences with books and the library put this traditional advice in an ironic light?
3. Many African Americans of shange's generation rejected traditional role models like George Washington Carver. Why? What role does Toussaint play in the girl's fantasy life?
4. What is the relation between the girl's fantasy life and her real life?
5. Spoken English covers the full range from down-home dialect through the informal English of casual talk to the official English of school and office. What are key features of the language used in this monologue? How does the language affect you as the listener? Do you think the author should have written the scene in standard English?

Thinking, Talking, Writing

6. What role models are there in our society for young African Americans? Is it harder to find role models for young black males than for young black females?
7. People used to ridicule and put down speakers of social or regional dialects and of "immigrant English." What is the attitude toward language differences in our society today?

Collaborative Projects

8. You may want to work with your classmates to organize a reading or staging of this scene and perhaps of additional scenes from the original play.

Thinking About Connections

9. James Baldwin has written about anger or rage as part of the lot of every African American. What do you learn about black anger from the selections by Morrison, Baldwin, and shange?

7

Cityscapes: Contexts for Living

I was going to stay on the three million miles of bent and narrow rural American two-lane, the roads to Podunk and Toonerville. Into the sticks, the boondocks, the burgs, backwaters, jerkwaters, the wide-spots-in-the-road, the don't-blink-or-you'll-miss-it towns. Into those places where you say, "My God! What if you lived here!"

William Least Heat Moon

In the cities it cannot be so clear to one that he is a creature of the earth, feeling the soil between the toes, smelling the dust thrown up by the rain, loving the earth so much that one longs to taste it and sometimes does.

Alice Walker

LITERATURE IN CONTEXT

What makes us who we are? Many twentieth-century writers have taken a deterministic view of human beings as creatures of their environment. Who we are is determined by where we are born and where we live. Our view of the world, our ways of relating to others, our prejudices and fears—all are shaped by the setting in which we grow up. They come with the territory. A writer may show us people whose lives are shaped by the crowding, violence, and paranoia of the big city. Another writer may show us people caught up in the pettiness, boredom, and bigotry of a small town. The more deterministic a writer's world, the more the characters in a story or play remain trapped in the setting that limits their possibilities and their horizons. The less deterministic the writer's perspective, the better the chances for mavericks who test the boundaries, who challenge the limits of their world.

Some writers make us see the settings of people's lives through the lens of nostalgia. They know how to create a warm, comforting place that perhaps never was. In more innocent times, writers wrote about the glamor and

335

excitement of the big city as well as about the coziness of small-town life. Journalists and copywriters helped create a vision of an America of burgeoning cities linked by magnificent trains spanning the open spaces of a continent symbolizing opportunity. Thornton Wilder's play *Our Town* (which every high school student read) created an idyllic vision of a small-town world. It had kindly, caring parents, cranky gossipy neighbors, and trusting innocent youngsters. Incest, child abuse, serial killers, homelessness, drugs, and unchecked disease were not in the picture.

In the early twentieth century, a movement of social criticism had aimed at more unretouched pictures of the world in which Americans lived and worked. Worker safety and child labor laws first became realities when writers like Upton Sinclair (*The Jungle*) pilloried the contempt of laissez-faire tycoons for their workers' safety of life and limb. Sinclair Lewis in novels like *Main Street* satirized the boosterism and the the-dollar-is-god mentality of the brash new commercial centers of the Midwest.

In much contemporary fiction, the setting—city, suburb, or country—looms large. Minority writers like Toni Cade Bambara, Jamaica Kincaid, and Sandra Cisneros write about inner-city kids trying to maintain their pride and their faith in the future in a hostile environment. Joyce Carol Oates writes stories about adolescents wandering clueless in the spiritual waste land of suburbia. Science fiction writers project megacities of the future in which there is no room for individuality, loyalty, or compassion. Will future generations live in places that are fit for human habitation?

PENNSYLVANIA STATION
Langston Hughes

> *Langston Hughes was the first African American poet to appear in anthologies of American literature. As a young man, he came to New York City from Detroit and Cleveland. Instead of writing poems about songbirds and flowers in May, he wrote poems about black American citizens spending a lifetime of "yes, Sirring" affluent whites, about exasperated tenants landing in jail for standing up to slum landlords, or about white fathers disowning their mixed-race children. As an editor, he introduced American readers to the heritage of African myth and literature. He was the best-known writer of the Harlem Renaissance of the twenties and thirties.*

The Pennsylvania Station in New York   1
Is like some vast basilica of old
That towers above the terrors of the dark
As bulwark and protection to the soul.
Now people who are hurrying alone   5
And those who come in crowds from far away
Pass through this great concourse of steel and stone
To trains, or else from trains out into day.
And as in great basilicas of old
The search was ever for a dream of God,   10
So here the search is still within each soul
Some seed to find that sprouts a holy tree
To glorify the earth—and you—and me.

The Responsive Reader

1. In early industrial America, as in Europe, the great railroad stations were a hub of city life. Have you seen the kind of "vast" old-style railroad station that is at the center of this poem? What made it different from today's public transport stations?
2. A basilica was originally a place fit for a king, but it became the name for the early Christian cathedrals. How do you explain the religious references in this poem? What kind of "protection to the soul" can a building give? For the poet, what is the connection between architecture and the human search for God? (What for you is the key to the poet's religious feelings?)
3. For many people today, nature and technology are at odds. Is it strange or contradictory that the poet uses the metaphors of the seed and the tree in a poem about a triumph of human technology?

Thinking, Talking, Writing

4. Do you know buildings that would give people a glorious or glorified feeling? What kind of architecture excites or inspires you? What are key features? How would you try to make others share your enthusiasm?

Collaborative Projects

4. Does a city you know have different styles of architecture that represent cycles in its history? Different groups of classmates might each focus on one particular style or cycle and then pool their observations with the other groups.

PRAYERS OF STEEL *and* CHICAGO
Carl Sandburg

> *Carl Sandburg was a widely known poet of the people, who admired him for taking the side of the poor against the rich, and of the exploited against their exploiters. He wrote free-flowing, unrhymed "free verse" that mirrored the vigor and sweep of American life. He was the son of Swedish immigrants living in Illinois, and for a time he went from job to job in the Midwest. Far from being a booster in the style of chamber-of-commerce brochures, he yet shared in the romance of earlier generations with America's burgeoning cities and the new technology that built them.*

Prayers of Steel

Lay me on an anvil, O God.   1
Beat me and hammer me into a crowbar.
Let me pry loose old walls.
Let me lift and loosen old foundations.

Lay me on an anvil, O God.   5
Beat me and hammer me into a steel spike.
Drive me into the girders that hold a skyscraper together.

Take red-hot rivets and fasten me into the central girders.
Let me be the great nail holding a skyscraper through blue nights
into white stars.   10

Chicago

Hog Butcher for the World,   1
Tool maker, Stacker of Wheat,
Player with Railroads and the Nation's Freight
        Handler;
Stormy, husky, brawling,
City of the Big Shoulders: 5

They tell me you are wicked and I believe
        them, for I have seen your painted
        women under the gas lamps luring the
        farm boys.
And they tell me you are crooked and I answer:
        Yes, it is true I have seen the gunman   10
        kill and go free to kill again.
And they tell me you are brutal and my reply
        is: On the faces of women and children I
        have seen the marks of wanton hunger.

And having answered so I turn once more to
    those who sneer at this my city, and I
    give them back the sneer and say to
    them: 15
Come and show me another city with lifted
    head singing so proud to be alive and
    coarse and strong and cunning. 20
Flinging magnetic curses amid the toil of piling
    job on job, here is a tall bold slugger set
    vivid against the little soft cities;
Fierce as a dog with tongue lapping for action,
    cunning as a savage pitted against the 25
    wilderness,
        Bareheaded,
        Shoveling,
        Wrecking,
        Planning,
        Building, breaking, rebuilding, 30
Under the smoke, dust all over his mouth,
    laughing with white teeth,
Under the terrible burden of destiny laughing
    as a young man laughs,
Laughing even as an ignorant fighter laughs 35
    who has never lost a battle,
Bragging and laughing that under his wrist is
    the pulse, and under his ribs the heart of
    the people,
        Laughing!
Laughing the stormy, husky, brawling laughter 40
    of Youth, half-naked, sweating, proud to
    be Hog Butcher, Tool Maker, Stacker of
    Wheat, Player with Railroads and Freight
    Handler to the Nation.

The Responsive Reader

1. Many readers today have hostile attitudes or mixed feelings about modern technology. How is the basic attitude in "Prayers of Steel" different? Can you understand or sympathize with the poet's feelings? Have you ever experienced or observed similar emotions?

2. In "Chicago," how does the poet make it clear that he is not an uncritical booster or admirer of the city? What for you is the keynote in his praise of the city? What are striking details? Can you trace a network of words that all help project the same attitude or prevailing mood? What is a possible common denominator?

3. Sandburg's poems often have a chanting, hypnotic effect. What accounts for it? How should these poems sound when read aloud?

Thinking, Talking, Writing

4. Do you know Americans who feel strong pride in or love for their city? What do people mean when they say they feel love-hate for their city?
5. Write an indictment or defense of the American city as you know it.

Collaborative Projects

6. You may want to help set up a choral reading of the Hughes and Sandburg poems, allotting different parts to different voices.

THE BOY DIED IN MY ALLEY

Gwendolyn Brooks

Gwendolyn Brooks has written eloquent poems expressing her loyalty to people trapped in the web of poverty and racism. Her most widely reprinted poem, "We real cool," was a tribute to doomed, defiant youth lost in the jungle of the city. Brooks grew up in a home filled with poetry, story, and song. "No child abuse, no prostitution, no mafia membership," she later said about her close-knit, loving family. She came to Chicago from Kansas and became poet laureate of the state of Illinois. In 1950 she was the first African American woman to receive a Pulitzer Prize for poetry. In the sixties and seventies, she was a leader in the rediscovery of the black heritage and the African past.

Without my having known.   *1*
Policeman said, next morning,
"Apparently died Alone."
"You heard a shot?" Policeman said.
Shots I hear and Shots I hear.   *5*
I never see the dead.

The Shot that killed him yes I heard
as I heard the Thousand shots before;
careening tinnily down the nights
across my years and arteries.   *10*

Policeman pounded on my door.
"Who is it?" "POLICE!" Policeman yelled.
"A boy was dying in your alley.
A boy is dead, and in your alley.
And have you known this Boy before?"   *15*

I have known this Boy before.
I have known this Boy before, who
ornaments my alley.
I never saw his face at all.
I never saw his futurefall.   *20*
But I have known this Boy.

I have always heard him deal with death.
I have always heard the shout, the volley.
I have closed my heart-ears late and early.
And I have killed him ever.   *25*
I joined the Wild and killed him
with knowledgeable unknowing.

I saw where he was going.
I saw him Crossed. And seeing,
I did not take him down. 30

He cried not only "Father!"
but "Mother!
Sister!
Brother!"
The cry climbed up the alley. 35
It went up to the wind.
It hung upon the heaven
for a long
stretch-strain of Moment.

The red floor of my alley 40
is a special speech to me.

The Responsive Reader

1. What in this poem is literal? What is figurative or metaphorical? Did the speaker in the poem literally know the boy? Did the boy literally call "Father!" and also "Mother! Sister! Brother!"?
2. Why does the speaker in the poem say about the dead boy, "I have killed him ever"? How or why does she feel implicated in his death? What does she mean when she says "I saw him Crossed. And seeing,/ I did not take him down"?
3. In the end, what is the "special speech" that the blood-stained ground of the alley has for the poet? What is the poet's comment on violence in the city?

Thinking, Talking, Writing

4. Our society seems to be helpless in the face of escalating murderous violence in our cities. Why? (Why do we keep calling it "senseless violence"?)
5. Have you personally had a brush with violence? What was your experience? Was there anything to be learned from it?

Collaborative Projects

6. Homicide statistics speak a grim language. Is there anything to be learned from them? You may want to work with a group to compile, compare, and interpret available statistics.

THE MOUTH OF THE HUDSON
Robert Lowell

> *Robert Lowell was an East Coast poet who traced his family history back to colonial New England and who often placed his poems in a rural or small-town Massachusetts setting or on the Maine coast. Although he explored the religious fervors and spiritual agonies of the Puritan past in his poems, he converted to Roman Catholicism. He shared with other poets of his post–World War II generation the refusal to make the world seem superficially beautiful, and he shared their commitment to a tough-minded exploration of harsh reality.*

A single man stands like a bird-watcher,   *1*
and scuffles the pepper and salt snow
from a discarded, gray
Westinghouse Electric cable drum.
He cannot discover America by counting   *5*
the chains of condemned freight trains
from thirty states. They jolt and jar
and junk in the siding below him.
He has trouble with his balance.
His eyes drop,   *10*
and he drifts with the wild ice
ticking seaward down the Hudson,
like the blank sides of a jigsaw puzzle.

The ice ticks seaward like a clock.
A Negro toasts   *15*
Wheat seeds over the coke fumes
of a punctured barrel.
Chemical air
sweeps in from New Jersey,
and smells of coffee.   *20*

Across the river,
ledges of suburban factories tan
in the sulphur-yellow sun
of the unforgivable landscape.

The Responsive Reader

1. Pretend you have not yet read Lowell's poem. Jot down a few associations, images, or ideas that each of the following brings to mind: *bird-watcher, snow, discover America, air.* What feelings or expectations do normally cluster around these for you? How are your feelings or reac-

tions different when you encounter them in the context of the poem? How does this poem steer your reactions or change your perspective?

2. What for you is the key word in this poem and why? Look at half a dozen words in the poem that together build up a negative impression of the polluted landscape. What is the meaning, impact, or connotation of each?

3. Is there any hint in the poem of nature as it was prior to pollution?

Thinking, Talking, Writing

4. Americans have long carried on a love affair with the trains, cars, or airplanes that have been the symbols of our technological civilization. Is this infatuation on the wane?

Collaborative Projects

5. Are there any success stories in the battle against the pollution of our rivers, lakes, and oceans? Work with one of several groups investigating different parts of this question.

LIFE AND DEATH AMONG THE XEROX PEOPLE
Olga Cabral

> Olga Cabral was born in Port of Spain in Trinidad in what was then the British West Indies. After coming to New York City, she ran an art gallery, and she published juvenile fiction and several collections of poetry in the sixties and seventies. She has written haunting, provocative poems on subjects like world hunger: "black child/brown child/dying/on the naked roadsides of/ HUNGER/in the tin cities of/HUNGER."

It was the wrong office   1
    but I went in
not a soul knew me
    but they said: Sit Down
they showed me corridors of paper   5
    and said: Begin Here

They wheeled in a machine
    a miniature electric chair
sparks flew from the earplugs
    antennas sprang from my nostrils   10
they switched on the current
    the machine said: Marry Me

I had forgotten my numbers
    they said it could be serious
they showed me the paper cutter   15
    it sliced like a guillotine
my head fell bloodlessly
    into the waste basket

I mined my way through stockrooms
    I wrote urgent xxxxxxxxxx's every day   20
to faces flat as paper
    the telephones feared nothing human
the windows were mirages
    permanently nailed shut

They handed me a skin   25
    and said: Wear This
it was somebody else's life
    it didn't quite fit
so I left it lying there . . .
    that was a queer cemetery.   30

The Responsive Reader

1. What haunting images and imaginative comparisons project the poet's attitude toward the work environment she describes? Which are strongest or most striking? Which are strangest or most provocative?
2. Cabral's imagery often has a surreal, nightmarish quality. Does the office nevertheless seem like a real office to you? Why or why not?

Thinking, Talking, Writing

3. The poet starts by saying that "it was the wrong office" and "not a soul knew me," and she says toward the end, "it was somebody else's life." Have you ever experienced similar feelings at school or at work? Or have you had similar feelings in dealing with institutions?
4. Many critics charge that modern communications technology has depersonalized and dehumanized office work. (One student wrote, "Productivity was the paramount concern of the company; each and every second was counted, monitored, and evaluated by the master computer.") Are these concerns justified or exaggerated? What would you say in defense of today's automated, computerized workplace?

THE MAGIC BARREL

Bernard Malamud

> *Outstanding twentieth-century American novelists—Saul Bellow, Irwin Shaw, Philip Roth, Joseph Heller, Bernard Malamud—have drawn in their fiction on the rich cultural heritage of the American Jewish community. Malamud first reached a large audience with* The Assistant *(1956), the story of a struggling Jewish neighborhood grocer and the down-and-out young man he befriends.* The Fixer *(1966) told the story of a Jew accused of ritual murder in Czarist Russia. Malamud was born and went to school in Brooklyn; he went on to the City University of New York and Columbia University. He recreates in loving detail the Jewish life of the New York City setting. He captures a paradoxical combination of familiar qualities: One is the mournful tone of people used to being cast in the role of the victim (the hero of the following story reminds himself that he "is yet a Jew and that a Jew suffered"). However, the other is the zany, self-deprecating humor that was often his people's last best line of defense during centuries of persecution.*
>
> *The following story is an urban fairy-tale—with a naive, innocent hero; with trials and challenges on the journey to happiness; a fairy godmother (in the disguise of a traditional matchmaker); and a happy ending.*

Not long ago there lived in uptown New York, in a small, almost   *1*
meager room, though crowded with books, Leon Finkle, a rabbinical student in the Yeshivah University. Finkle, after six years of study, was to be ordained in June and had been advised by an acquaintance that he might find it easier to win himself a congregation if he were married. Since he had no present prospects of marriage, after two tormented days of turning it over in his mind, he called in Pinye Salzman, a marriage broker, whose two-line advertisement he had read in the *Forward*.

The matchmaker appeared one night out of the dark fourth-floor hallway of the graystone rooming house, grasping a black, strapped portfolio that had been worn thin with use. Salzman, who had been long in the business, was of slight but dignified build, wearing an old hat and an overcoat too short and tight for him. He smelled frankly of fish, which he loved to eat, and although he was missing a few teeth, his presence was not displeasing, because of an amiable manner curiously contrasted by mournful eyes. His voice, his lips, his wisp of beard, his bony fingers were animated, but give him a moment of repose, and his mild blue eyes soon revealed a depth of sadness, a characteristic that put Leo a little at ease although the situation, for him, was inherently tense.

He at once informed Salzman why he had asked him to come, explaining that his home was in Cleveland, and that but for his parents, who had married comparatively late in life, he was alone in the world. He had for six years devoted himself entirely to his studies, as a result of which, quite understandably, he had found himself without time for a social life and the company of young women. Therefore he thought it the better part of trial and error—of embarrassing fumbling—to call in an experienced person to advise him in these matters. He remarked in passing that the function of the marriage broker was ancient and honorable, highly approved in the Jewish community, because it made practical the necessary without hindering joy. Moreover, his own parents had been brought together by a matchmaker. They had made, if not a financially profitable marriage—since neither had possessed any worldly goods to speak of—at least a successful one in the sense of their everlasting devotion to one another. Salzman listened in embarrassed surprise, sensing a sort of apology. Later, however, he experienced a glow of pride in his work, an emotion that had left him years ago, and he heartily approved of Finkle.

The two men went to their business. Leo had led Salzman to the only clear place in the room, a table near a window that overlooked the lamplit city. He seated himself at the matchmaker's side but facing him, attempting by an act of will to suppress the unpleasant tickle in his throat. Salzman eagerly unstrapped his portfolio and removed a loose rubber band from a thin packet of much-handled cards. As he flipped through them, a gesture and sound that physically hurt Leo, the student pretended not to see and gazed steadfastly out the window. Although it was still February, winter was on its last legs, signs of which he had for the first time in years begun to notice. He now observed the round white moon, moving high in the sky through a cloud-menagerie, and watched with half-open mouth as it penetrated a huge hen and dropped out of her like an egg laying itself. Salzman, though pretending through eyeglasses he had just slipped on, to be engaged in scanning the writing on the cards, stole occasional glances at the young man's distinguished face, noting with pleasure the long, severe scholar's nose, brown eyes heavy with learning, sensitive yet ascetic lips, and a certain almost hollow quality of the dark cheeks. He gazed around at shelves upon shelves of books and let out a soft but happy sigh.

When Leo's eyes fell upon the cards, he counted six spread out in   5
Salzman's hand.

"So few?" he said in disappointment.

"You wouldn't believe me how much cards I got in my office," Salzman replied. "The drawers are already filled to the top, so I keep them now in a barrel, but is every girl good for a new rabbi?"

Leo blushed at this, regretting all he had revealed of himself in a curriculum vitae he had sent to Salzman. He had thought it best to acquaint him with his strict standards and specifications, but in having done so now felt he had told the marriage broker more than was absolutely necessary.

He hesitantly inquired, "Do you keep photographs of your clients on file?"

"First comes family, amount of dowry, also what kind promises," Salz- 10
man replied, unbuttoning his tight coat and settling himself in the chair.
"After comes pictures, rabbi."

"Call me Mr. Finkle. I'm not a rabbi yet."

Salzman said he would, but instead called him doctor, which he
changed to rabbi when Leo was not listening too attentively.

Salzman adjusted his horn-rimmed spectacles, gently cleared his throat
and read in an eager voice the contents of the top card:

"Sophie P. Twenty-four years. Widow for one year. No children. Educated high school and two years college. Father promises eight thousand
dollars. Has a wonderful wholesale business. Also real estate. On mother's
side comes teachers, also one actor. Well known on Second Avenue."

Leo gazed up in surprise. "Did you say a widow?" 15

"A widow don't mean spoiled, rabbi. She lived with her husband
maybe four months. He was a sick boy, she made a mistake to marry him."

"Marrying a widow has never entered my mind."

"This is because you have no experience. A widow, specially if she is
young and healthy like this girl, is a wonderful person to marry. She will be
thankful to you the rest of her life. Believe me, if I was looking now for a
bride, I would marry a widow."

Leo reflected, then shook his head.

Salzman hunched his shoulders in an almost imperceptible gesture of 20
disappointment. He placed the card down on the wooden table and began
to read another:

"Lily H. High-school teacher. Regular. Not a substitute. Has savings
and new Dodge car. Lived in Paris one year. Father is successful dentist
thirty-five years. Interested in professional man. Well Americanized family.
Wonderful opportunity.

"I know her personally," said Salzman. "I wish you could see this girl.
She is a doll. Also very intelligent. All day you could talk to her about books
and theater and what not. She also knows current events."

"I don't believe you mentioned her age?"

"Her age?" Salzman said, raising his brows in surprise. "Her age is
thirty-two years."

Leo said after a while, "I'm afraid that seems a little too old." 25

Salzman let out a laugh. "So how old are you, rabbi?"

"Twenty-seven."

"So what is the difference, tell me, between twenty-seven and thirty-
two? My own wife is seven years older than me. So what did I suffer?—
Nothing. If Rothschild's daughter wants to marry you, would you say on
account of her age, no?"

"Yes," Leo said dryly.

Salzman shook off the no in the yes. "Five years don't mean a thing. I 30
give you my word that when you will live with her for one week, you will

forget her age. What does it mean five years—that she lived more and knows more than somebody who is younger? On this girl, God bless her, years are not wasted. Each one that it comes makes better the bargain."

"What subject does she teach in high school?"

"Languages. If you heard the way she reads French, you will think it is music. I am in the business twenty-five years, and I recommend her with my whole heart. Believe me, I know what I'm talking, rabbi."

"What's on the next card?" Leo said abruptly.

Salzman reluctantly turned up the third card:

"Ruth K. Nineteen years. Honor student. Father offers thirteen thou-   35
sand dollars cash to the right bridegroom. He is a medical doctor. Stomach specialist with marvelous practice. Brother-in-law owns own garment business. Particular people."

Salzman looked up as if he had read his trump card.

"Did you say nineteen?" Leo asked with interest.

"On the dot."

"Is she attractive?" He blushed. "Pretty?"

Salzman kissed his fingertips. "A little doll. On this I give you my word.   40
Let me call the father tonight and you will see what means pretty."

But Leo was troubled. "You're sure she's that young?"

"This I am positive. The father will show you the birth certificate."

"Are you positive there isn't something wrong with her?" Leo insisted.

"Who says there is wrong?"

"I don't understand why an American girl her age should go to a   45
marriage broker."

A smile spread over Salzman's face.

"So for the same reason you went, she comes."

Leo flushed. "I am pressed for time."

Salzman, realizing he had been tactless, quickly explained. "The father came, not her. He wants she should have the best, so he looks around himself. When we will locate the right boy, he will introduce him and encourage. This makes a better marriage than if a young girl without experience takes for herself. I don't have to tell you this."

"But don't you think this young girl believes in love?" Leo spoke   50
uneasily.

Salzman was about to guffaw, but caught himself and said soberly, "Love comes with the right person, not before."

Leo parted dry lips but did not speak. Noticing that Salzman had snatched a quick glance at the next card, he cleverly asked, "How is her health?"

"Perfect," Salzman said, breathing with difficulty. "Of course, she is a little lame on her right foot from an auto accident that it happened to her when she was twelve years, but nobody notices on account she is so brilliant and also beautiful."

Leo got up heavily and went to the window. He felt curiously bitter and upbraided himself for having called in the marriage broker. Finally, he shook his head.

"Why not?" Salzman persisted, the pitch of his voice rising.   55

"Because I hate stomach specialists."

"So what do you care what is his business? After you marry her, do you need him? Who says he must come every Friday night to your house?"

Ashamed of the way the talk was going. Leo dismissed Salzman, who went home with melancholy eyes.

Though he had felt only relief at the marriage broker's departure, Leo was in low spirits the next day. He explained it as arising from Salzman's failure to produce a suitable bride for him. He did not care for his type of clientele. But when Leo found himself hesitating over whether to seek out another matchmaker, one more polished than Pinye, he wondered if it could be—his protestations to the contrary, and although he honored his father and mother—that he did not, in essence, care for the matchmaking institution? This thought he quickly put out of his mind yet found himself still upset. All day he ran around in a fog—missed an important appointment, forgot to give out his laundry, walked out of a Broadway cafeteria without paying and had to run back with the ticket in his hand; had even not recognized his landlady in the street when she passed with a friend and courteously called out, "A good evening to you, Doctor Finkle." By nightfall, however, he had regained sufficient calm to sink his nose into a book and there found peace from his thoughts.

Almost at once there came a knock on the door. Before Leo could say   60
enter, Salzman, commercial cupid, was standing in the room. His face was gray and meager, his expression hungry, and he looked as if he would expire on his feet. Yet the marriage broker managed, by some trick of the muscles, to display a broad smile.

"So good evening. I am invited?"

Leo nodded, disturbed to see him again, yet unwilling to ask him to leave.

Beaming still, Salzman laid his portfolio on the table. "Rabbi, I got for you tonight good news."

"I've asked you not to call me rabbi. I'm still a student."

"Your worries are finished. I have for you a first-class bride."   65

"Leave me in peace concerning this subject." Leo pretended lack of interest.

"The world will dance at your wedding."

"Please, Mr. Salzman, no more."

"But first must come back my strength," Salzman said weakly. He fumbled with the portfolio straps and took out of the leather case an oily paper bag, from which he extracted a hard seeded roll and a small smoked whitefish. With one motion of his hand he stripped the fish out of its skin and began ravenously to chew. "All day in a rush," he muttered.

Leo watched him eat.   70

"A sliced tomato you have maybe?" Salzman hesitantly inquired.

"No."

The marriage broker shut his eyes and ate. When he had finished, he carefully cleaned up the crumbs and rolled up the remains of the fish in the paper bag. His spectacled eyes roamed the room until he discovered, amid some piles of books, a one-burner gas stove. Lifting his hat, he humbly asked, "A glass of tea you got, rabbi?"

Conscience-stricken, Leo rose and brewed the tea. He served it with a chunk of lemon and two cubes of lump sugar, delighting Salzman.

After he had drunk his tea, Salzman's strength and good spirits were   75
restored.

"So tell me, rabbi," he said amiably, "you considered any more the three clients I mentioned yesterday?"

"There was no need to consider."

"Why not?"

"None of them suits me."

"What, then, suits you?"   80

Leo let it pass because he could give only a confused answer.

Without waiting for a reply, Salzman asked, "You remember this girl I talked to you—the high-school teacher?"

"Age thirty-two?"

But, surprisingly, Salzman's face lit in a smile. "Age twenty-nine."

Leo shot him a look. "Reduced from thirty-two?"   85

"A mistake," Salzman avowed. "I talked today with the dentist. He took me to his safety deposit box and showed me the birth certificate. She was twenty-nine last August. They made her a party in the mountains where she went for her vacation. When her father spoke to me the first time, I forgot to write the age and I told you thirty-two, but now I remember this was a different client, a widow."

"The same one you told me about? I thought she was twenty-four?"

"A different. Am I responsible that the world is filled with widows?"

"No, but I'm not interested in them, nor for that matter, in school-teachers."

Salzman passionately pulled his clasped hands to his breast. Looking   90
at the ceiling he exclaimed, "Jewish children, what can I say to somebody that he is not interested in high-school teachers? So what then you are interested?"

Leo flushed but controlled himself.

"In who else you will be interested," Salzman went on, "if you not interested in this fine girl that she speaks four languages and has personally in the bank ten thousand dollars? Also her father guarantees further twelve thousand. Also she has a new car, wonderful clothes, talks on all subjects, and she will give you a first-class home and children. How near do we come in our life to paradise?"

"If she's so wonderful, why wasn't she married ten years ago?"

"Why," said Salzman with a heavy laugh. "—Why? Because she is *partikler.* This is why. She wants only the *best.*"

Leo was silent, amused at how he had trapped himself. But Salzman   95
had aroused his interest in Lily H., and he began seriously to consider calling on her. When the marriage broker observed how intently Leo's mind was at work on the facts he had supplied, he felt positive they would soon come to an agreement.

Late Saturday afternoon, conscious of Salzman, Leo Finkle walked with Lily Hirschorn along Riverside Drive. He walked briskly and erectly, wearing with distinction the black fedora he had that morning taken with trepidation out of the dusty hatbox on his closet shelf, and the heavy black Saturday coat he had thoroughly whisked clean. Leo also owned a walking stick, a present from a distant relative, but had decided not to use it. Lily, petite and not unpretty, had on something signifying the approach of spring. She was *au courant,* animatedly, with all subjects, and he weighed her words and found her surprisingly sound—score another for Salzman, whom he uneasily sensed to be somewhere around, hiding perhaps high in a tree along the street, flashing the lady signals; or perhaps a cloven-hoofed Pan, piping nuptial ditties as he danced his invisible way before them, strewing wild buds on the walk and purple summer grapes in their path, symbolizing fruit of a union, of which there was yet none.

Lily startled Leo by remarking, "I was thinking of Mr. Salzman, a curious figure, wouldn't you say?"

Not certain what to answer, he nodded.

She bravely went on, blushing, "I for one am grateful for his introducing us. Aren't you?"

He courteously replied, "I am."   100

"I mean," she said with a little laugh—and it was all in good taste, or at least gave the effect of being not in bad—"do you mind that we came together so?"

He was not afraid of her honesty, recognizing that she meant to set the relationship aright, and understanding that it took a certain amount of experience in life, and courage, to want to do it quite that way. One had to have some sort of past to make that kind of beginning.

He said that he did not mind. Salzman's function was traditional and honorable—valuable for what it might achieve, which, he pointed out, was frequently nothing.

Lily agreed with a sigh. They walked on for a while, and she said after a long silence, again with a nervous laugh, "Would you mind if I asked you something a little bit personal? Frankly, I find the subject fascinating." Although Leo shrugged, she went on half embarrassedly, "How was it that you came to your calling? I mean, was it a sudden passionate inspiration?"

Leo, after a time, slowly replied, "I was always interested in the Law."   105

"You saw revealed in it the presence of the Highest?"

He nodded and changed the subject. "I understand you spent a little time in Paris, Miss Hirschorn?"

"Oh, did Mr. Salzman tell you, Rabbi Finkle?" Leo winced, but she went on, "It was ages and ages ago and almost forgotten. I remember I had to return for my sister's wedding."

But Lily would not be put off. "When," she asked in a trembly voice, "did you become enamored of God?"

He stared at her. Then it came to him that she was talking not about *110*
Leo Finkle, but a total stranger, some mystical figure, perhaps even passionate prophet that Salzman had conjured up for her—no relation to the living or dead. Leo trembled with rage and weakness. The trickster had obviously sold her a bill of goods, just as he had him, who'd expected to become acquainted with a young lady of twenty-nine, only to behold, the moment he laid eyes upon her strained and anxious face, a woman past thirty-five and aging very rapidly. Only his self-control, he thought, had kept him this long in her presence.

"I am not," he said gravely, "a talented religious person," and in seeking words to go on, found himself possessed by fear and shame. "I think," he said in a strained manner, "that I came to God not because I love Him, but because I did not."

This confession he spoke harshly because its unexpectedness shook him.

Lily wilted. Leo saw a profusion of loaves of bread sailing like ducks high over his head, not unlike the loaves by which he had counted himself to sleep last night. Mercifully, then, it snowed, which he would not put past Salzman's machinations.

He was infuriated with the marriage broker and swore he would throw him out of the room the moment he reappeared. But Salzman did not come that night, and when Leo's anger had subsided, an unaccountable despair grew in its place. At first he thought this was caused by his disappointment in Lily, but before long it became evident that he had involved himself with Salzman without a true knowledge of his own intent. He gradually realized—with an emptiness that seized him with six hands—that he had called in the broker to find him a bride because he was incapable of doing it himself. This terrifying insight he had derived as a result of his meeting and conversation with Lily Hirschorn. Her probing questions had somehow irritated him into revealing—to himself more than her—the true nature of his relationship with God, and from that it had come upon him, with shocking force, that apart from his parents, he had never loved anyone. Or perhaps it went the other way, that he did not love God so well as he might, because he had not loved man. It seemed to Leo that his whole life stood starkly revealed and he saw himself, for the first time, as he truly was—unloved and loveless. This bitter but somehow not fully unexpected revelation brought him to a point of panic controlled only by extraordinary effort. He covered his face with his hands and wept.

The week that followed was the worst of his life. He did not eat, and lost weight. His beard darkened and grew ragged. He stopped attending lectures and seminars and almost never opened a book. He seriously considered leaving the Yeshivah, although he was deeply troubled at the thought of the loss of all his years of study—saw them like pages from a book strewn over the city—and at the devastating effect of this decision upon his parents. But he had lived without knowledge of himself, and never in the Five Books and all the Commentaries—*mea culpa*—had the truth been revealed to him. He did not know where to turn, and in all this desolating loneliness there was no *to whom*, although he often thought of Lily but not once could bring himself to go downstairs and make the call. He became touchy and irritable, especially with his landlady, who asked him all manner of questions; on the other hand, sensing his own disagreeableness, he waylaid her on the stairs and apologized abjectly, until mortified, she ran from him. Out of this, however, he drew the consolation that he was yet a Jew and that a Jew suffered. But gradually, as the long and terrible week drew to a close, he regained his composure and some idea of purpose in life: to go on as planned. Although he was imperfect, the ideal was not. As for his quest of a bride, the thought of continuing afflicted him with anxiety and heartburn, yet perhaps with this new knowledge of himself he would be more successful than in the past. Perhaps love would now come to him and a bride to that love. And for this sanctified seeking who needed a Salzman?

The marriage broker, a skeleton with haunted eyes, returned that very night. He looked, withal, the picture of frustrated expectancy—as if he had steadfastly waited the week at Miss Lily Hirschorn's side for a telephone call that never came.

Casually coughing, Salzman came immediately to the point: "So how did you like her?"

Leo's anger rose and he could not refrain from chiding the matchmaker: "Why did you lie to me, Salzman?"

Salzman's pale face went dead white, as if the world had snowed on him.

"Did you not state that she was twenty-nine?" Leo insisted.

"I give you my word—"

"She was thirty-five. At *least* thirty-five."

"Of this I would not be too sure. Her father told me—"

"Never mind. The worst of it was that you lied to her."

"How did I lie to her, tell me?"

"You told her things about me that weren't true. You made me out to be more, consequently less than I am. She had in mind a totally different person, a sort of semimystical Wonder Rabbi."

"All I said, you was a religious man."

"I can imagine."

Salzman sighed. "This is my weakness that I have," he confessed. "My wife says to me I shouldn't be a salesman, but when I have two fine people that they would be wonderful to be married, I am so happy that I talk too much." He smiled wanly. "This is why Salzman is a poor man."

Leo's anger went. "Well, Salzman, I'm afraid that's all." 130

The marriage broker fastened hungry eyes on him.

"You don't want any more a bride?"

"I do," said Leo, "but I have decided to seek her in a different way. I am no longer interested in an arranged marriage. To be frank, I now admit the necessity of premarital love. That is, I want to be in love with the one I marry."

"Love?" said Salzman, astounded. After a moment he said, "For us, our love is our life, not for the ladies. In the ghetto they—"

"I know, I know," said Leo. "I've thought of it often. Love, I have said 135 to myself, should be a by-product of living and worship rather than its own end. Yet for myself I find it necessary to establish the level of my need and to fulfill it."

Salzman shrugged but answered, "Listen, rabbi, if you want love, this I can find for you also. I have such beautiful clients that you will love them the minute your eyes will see them."

Leo smiled unhappily. "I'm afraid you don't understand."

But Salzman hastily unstrapped his portfolio and withdrew a manila packet from it.

"Pictures," he said, quickly laying the envelope on the table.

Leo called after him to take the pictures away, but as if on the wings of 140 the wind, Salzman had disappeared.

March came. Leo had returned to his regular routine. Although he felt not quite himself yet—lacked energy—he was making plans for a more active social life. Of course it would cost something, but he was an expert in cutting corners; and when there were no corners left he could make circles rounder. All the while Salzman's pictures had lain on the table, gathering dust. Occasionally as Leo sat studying, or enjoying a cup of tea, his eyes fell on the manila envelope, but he never opened it.

The days went by, and no social life to speak of developed with a member of the opposite sex—it was difficult, given the circumstances of his situation. One morning Leo toiled up the stairs to his room and stared out the window at the city. Although the day was bright, his view of it was dark. For some time he watched the people in the street below hurrying along and then turned with a heavy heart to his little room. On the table was the packet. With a sudden relentless gesture he tore it open. For a half-hour he stood there, in a state of excitement, examining the photographs of the ladies Salzman had included. Finally, with a deep sigh he put them down. There were six, of varying degrees of attractiveness, but look at them long enough and they all became Lily Hirschorn: all past their prime, all starved behind bright smiles, not a true personality in the lot. Life, despite their anguished struggles and frantic yoohooings, had passed them by; they were photographs in a briefcase that stank of fish. After a while, however, as Leo attempted to return the pictures into the envelope, he found another in it, a small snapshot of the type taken by a machine for a quarter. He gazed at it a moment and let out a cry.

Her face deeply moved him. Why, he could at first not say. It gave him the impression of youth—all spring flowers—yet age—a sense of having been used to the bone, wasted; this all came from the eyes, which were hauntingly familiar, yet absolutely strange. He had a strong impression that he had met her before, but try as he might he could not place her, although he could almost recall her name, as if he had read it written in her own handwriting. No, this couldn't be; he would have remembered her. It was not, he affirmed, that she had an extraordinary beauty—no, although her face was attractive enough; it was that *something* about her moved him. Feature for feature, even some of the ladies of the photographs could do better; but she leaped forth to the heart—had lived, or wanted to—more than just wanted, perhaps regretted it—had somehow deeply suffered: it could be seen in the depths of those reluctant eyes, and from the way the light enclosed and shone from her, and within her, opening whole realms of possibility: this was her own. Her he desired. His head ached and eyes narrowed with the intensity of his gazing, then, as if a black fog had blown up in the mind, he experienced fear of her and was aware that he had received an impression, somehow, of filth. He shuddered, saying softly, it is thus with us all. Leo brewed some tea in a small pot and sat sipping it, without sugar, to calm himself. But before he had finished drinking, again with excitement he examined the face and found it good: good for him. Only such a one could truly understand Leo Finkle and help him to seek whatever he was seeking. How she had come to be among the discards in Salzman's barrel he could never guess, but he knew he must urgently go find her.

Leo rushed downstairs, grabbed up the Bronx telephone book, and searched for Salzman's home address. He was not listed, nor was his office. Neither was he in the Manhattan book. But Leo remembered having written down the address on a slip of paper after he had read Salzman's advertisement in the "personals" column of the *Forward*. He ran up to his room and tore through his papers, without luck. It was exasperating. Just when he needed the matchmaker he was nowhere to be found. Fortunately Leo remembered to look in his wallet. There on a card he found his name written and a Bronx address. No phone number was listed, which, Leo now recalled, was the reason he had originally communicated with Salzman by letter. He got on his coat, put a hat on over his skull cap and hurried to the subway station. All the way to the far end of the Bronx he sat on the edge of his seat. He was more than once tempted to take out the picture and see if the girl's face was as he remembered it, but he refrained, allowing the snapshot to remain in his inside coat pocket, content to have her so close. When the train pulled into the station, he was waiting at the door and bolted out. He quickly located the street Salzman had advertised.

The building he sought was less than a block from the subway, but it   *145* was not an office building, nor even a loft, nor a store in which one could rent office space. It was an old and grimy tenement. Leo found Salzman's name in pencil on a soiled tag under the bell and climbed three dark flights to his apartment. When he knocked, the door was opened by a thin, asthmatic, gray-haired woman, in felt slippers.

"Yes?" she said, expecting nothing. She listened without listening. He could have sworn he had seen her somewhere before but knew it was illusion.

"Salzman—does he live here? Pinye Salzman," he said, "the matchmaker?"

She stared at him a long time. "Of course."

He felt embarrassed. "Is he in?"

"No." Her mouth was open, but she offered nothing more.   150

"This is urgent. Can you tell me where his office is?"

"In the air." She pointed upward.

"You mean he has no office?" Leo said.

"In his socks."

He peered into the apartment. It was sunless and dingy, one large room   155
divided by a half-open curtain, beyond which he could see a sagging metal bed. The nearer side of the room was crowded with rickety chairs, old bureaus, a three-legged table, racks of cooking utensils, and all the apparatus of a kitchen. But there was no sign of Salzman or his magic barrel, probably also a figment of his imagination. An odor of frying fish made Leo weak to the knees.

"Where is he?" he insisted. "I've got to see your husband."

At length she answered, "So who knows where he is? Every time he thinks a new thought he runs to a different place. Go home, he will find you."

"Tell him Leo Finkle."

She gave no sign that she had heard.

He went downstairs, deeply depressed.   160

But Salzman, breathless, stood waiting at his door.

Leo was overjoyed and astounded. "How did you get here before me?"

"I rushed."

"Come inside."

They entered. Leo fixed tea and a sardine sandwich for Salzman.   165

As they were drinking, he reached behind him for the packet of pictures and handed them to the marriage broker.

Salzman put down his glass and said expectantly. "You found maybe somebody you like?"

"Not among these."

The marriage broker turned sad eyes away.

"Here's the one I like." Leo held forth the snapshot.   170

Salzman slipped on his glasses and took the picture into his trembling hand. He turned ghastly and let out a miserable groan.

"What's the matter?" cried Leo.

"Excuse me. Was an accident this picture. She is not for you."

Salzman frantically shoved the manila packet into his portfolio. He thrust the snapshot into his pocket and fled down the stairs.

Leo, after momentary paralysis, gave chase and cornered the marriage   175
broker in the vestibule. The landlady made hysterical outcries, but neither of them listened.

"Give me back the picture, Salzman."

"No." The pain in his eyes was terrible.

"Tell me where she is then."

"This I can't tell you. Excuse me."

He made to depart, but Leo, forgetting himself, seized the matchmaker   180
by his tight coat and shook him frenziedly.

"Please," sighed Salzman. "*Please.*"

Leo ashamedly let him go. "Tell me who she is," he begged. "It's very important for me to know."

"She is not for you. She is a wild one—wild, without shame. This is not a bride for a rabbi."

"What do you mean wild?"

"Like an animal. Like a dog. For her to be poor was a sin. This is why   185
she is dead now."

"In God's name, what do you mean?"

"Her I can't introduce to you," Salzman cried.

"Why are you so excited?"

"Why he asks," Salzman said, bursting into tears. "This is my baby, my Stella, she should burn in hell."

Leo hurried up to bed and hid under the covers. Under the covers he   190
thought his whole life through. Although he soon fell asleep he could not sleep her out of his mind. He woke, beating his breast. Though he prayed to be rid of her, his prayers went unanswered. Through days of torment he struggled endlessly not to love her; fearing success, he escaped it. He then concluded to convert her to goodness, himself to God. The idea alternately nauseated and exalted him.

He perhaps did not know that he had come to a final decision until he encountered Salzman in a Broadway cafeteria. He was sitting alone at a rear table sucking the bony remains of a fish. The marriage broker appeared haggard, and transparent to the point of vanishing.

Salzman looked up at first without recognizing him. Leo had grown a pointed beard, and his eyes were weighted with wisdom.

"Salzman," he said, "love has at last come to my heart."

"Who can love from a picture?" mocked the marriage broker.

"It is not impossible."   195

"If you can love her, then you can love anybody. Let me show you some new clients that they just sent me their photographs. One is a little doll."

"Just her I want," Leo murmured.

"Don't be a fool, doctor. Don't bother with her."

"Put me in touch with her, Salzman," Leo said humbly. "Perhaps I can do her a service."

Salzman had stopped chewing, and Leo understood with emotion that   200
it was now arranged.

Leaving the cafeteria, he was, however, afflicted by a tormenting suspicion that Salzman had planned it all to happen this way.

Leo was informed by letter that she would meet him on a certain corner, and she was there one spring night, waiting under a street lamp. He appeared, carrying a small bouquet of violets and rosebuds. Stella stood by the lamppost, smoking. She wore white with red shoes, which fitted his expectations, although in a troubled moment he had imagined the dress red, and only the shoes white. She waited uneasily and shyly. From afar he saw that her eyes—clearly her father's—were filled with desperate innocence. He pictured, in hers, his own redemption. Violins and lit candles revolved in the sky. Leo ran forward with the flowers outthrust.

Around the corner, Salzman, leaning against a wall, chanted prayers for the dead.

The Responsive Reader

1. How does Malamud recreate the setting in which his characters live? What kind of life does Finkle live? What kind of life does Salzman live? What are revealing sad and funny touches?
2. How Jewish are Malamud's characters? (Are there echoes of Yiddish in the way they talk?) How do they feel about being Jewish? Does Malamud share the mixed emotions that some Americans have about their ethnic heritage?
3. What happens in this story? How essential is Salzman's role in the story? Is there a recurrent pattern in Finkle's dealing with the matchmaker? Did the ending catch you by surprise? (At the end, do you share Finkle's suspicion that "Salzman had planned it all to happen this way"?)

Thinking, Talking, Writing

4. How much in this story is fairy-tale? How much is reality?
5. Is Leo's story a story of rebellion against the Jewish tradition? Or is his story an affirmation of it?
6. Is this a story about love? What kind of love story is it? Is the attitude toward romance in this story obsolete in our current state of changing awareness of sex roles?

Collaborative Projects

7. Working with a group, explore the influence of Yiddish on American English.

Thinking about Connections

8. Students often complain that to read a love story they have to turn to lightweight popular fiction. Compare Mary Robison's "Yours" and Bernard Malamud's "The Magic Barrel" as modern love stories.

A BOTTLE OF MILK FOR MOTHER
Nelson Algren

Nelson Algren knew at first hand the life of the large cities of the midcontinent. He was born in 1909 in Detroit and lived most of his life in or near Chicago. He graduated from a school of journalism during the Great Depression of the thirties, and much of his fiction is set in the crowded, slum-ridden residential areas of big cities with large white ethnic—Polish, Italian, Lithuanian—populations. Algren became famous with his novel The Man with the Golden Arm *in 1949. He said, "living in a very dense area, you're conscious of how the people underneath live, and you have a certain feeling toward them—so much so that you'd rather live among them than with the business classes . . . you write out of—well, I wouldn't call it indignation, but a kind of irritability that these people on top should be so contented, so absolutely unaware of these other people, and so sure that their values are the right ones."*

The following story takes us to the mean streets of the big city where young street toughs from immigrant backgrounds live in a world without a future. What is behind their swagger and bravado?

I feel I am of them—
I belong to those convicts and prostitutes myself,
And henceforth I will not deny them—
For how can I deny myself?

        WHITMAN

Two months after the Polish Warriors S.A.C. had had their heads shaved, Bruno Lefty Bicek got into his final difficulty with the Racine Street police. The arresting officers and a reporter from the *Dziennik Chicagoski* were grouped about the captain's desk when the boy was urged forward into the room by Sergeant Adamovitch, with two fingers wrapped about the boy's broad belt: a full-bodied boy wearing a worn and sleeveless blue work shirt grown too tight across the shoulders; and the shoulders themselves with a loose swing to them. His skull and face were shining from a recent scrubbing, so that the little bridgeless nose glistened between the protective points of the cheekbones. Behind the desk sat Kozak, eleven years on the force and brother to an alderman. The reporter stuck a cigarette behind one ear like a pencil.

"We spotted him followin' the drunk down Chicago—" Sergeant Comiskey began.

Captain Kozak interrupted. "Let the jackroller tell us how he done it hisself."

"I ain't no jackroller."

"What you doin' here, then?"

Bicek folded his naked arms.

"Answer me. If you ain't here for jackrollin' it must be for strong-arm robb'ry—'r you one of them Chicago Av'noo moll-buzzers?"

"I ain't that neither."

"C'mon, c'mon, I seen you in here before—what were you up to, followin' that poor old man?"

"I ain't been in here before." 10

Neither Sergeant Milano, Comiskey, nor old Adamovitch moved an inch; yet the boy felt the semicircle about him drawing closer. Out of the corner of his eye he watched the reporter undoing the top button of his mangy raccoon coat, as though the barren little query room were already growing too warm for him.

"What were you doin' on Chicago Av'noo in the first place when you live up around Division? Ain't your own ward big enough you have to come down here to get in trouble? What do you *think* you're here for?"

"Well, I was just walkin' down Chicago like I said, to get a bottle of milk for Mother, when the officers jumped me. I didn't even see 'em drive up, they wouldn't let me say a word, I got no idea what I'm here for. I was just doin' a errand for Mother 'n—"

"All right, son, you want us to book you as a pickup 'n hold you overnight, is that it?"

"Yes sir." 15

"What about this, then?"

Kozak flipped a spring-blade knife with a five-inch blade onto the police blotter; the boy resisted an impulse to lean forward and take it. His own double-edged double-jointed spring-blade cuts-all genuine Filipino twisty-handled all-American gut-ripper.

"Is it yours or ain't it?"

"Never seen it before, Captain."

Kozak pulled a billy out of his belt, spread the blade across the bend of 20 the blotter before him, and with one blow clubbed the blade off two inches from the handle. The boy winced as though he himself had received the blow. Kozak threw the broken blade into a basket and the knife into a drawer.

"Know why I did that, son?"

"Yes sir."

"Tell me."

"'Cause it's three inches to the heart."

"No. 'Cause it's against the law to carry more than three inches of 25 knife. C'mon, Lefty, tell us about it. 'N it better be good."

The boy began slowly, secretly gratified that Kozak appeared to know he was the Warriors' first-string left-hander: maybe he'd been out at that game against the Knothole Wonders the Sunday he'd finished his own game and then had relieved Dropkick Kodadek in the sixth in the second. Why hadn't anyone called him "Iron-Man Bicek" or "Fireball Bruno" for that one?

"Everythin' you say can be used against you," Kozak warned him earnestly. "Don't talk unless you want to." His lips formed each syllable precisely.

Then he added absently, as though talking to someone unseen, "We'll just hold you on an open charge till you do."

And his lips hadn't moved at all.

The boy licked his own lips, feeling a dryness coming into his throat 30 and a tightening in his stomach. "We seen this boobatch with his collar turned inside out cash'n his check by Konstanty Stachula's Tonsorial Palace of Art on Division. So I followed him a way, that was all. Just break'n the old monotony was all. Just a notion, you might say, that come over me. I'm just a neighborhood kid, Captain."

He stopped as though he had finished the story. Kozak glanced over the boy's shoulder at the arresting officers and Lefty began again hurriedly.

"Ever' once in a while he'd pull a little single-shot of Scotch out of his pocket, stop a second t' toss it down, 'n toss the bottle at the car tracks. I picked up a bottle that didn't bust but there wasn't a spider left in 'er, the boobatch'd drunk her dry. 'N do you know, he had his pockets *full* of them little bottles? 'Stead of buyin' hisself a fifth in the first place. Can't understand a man who'll buy liquor that way. Right before the corner of Walton 'n Noble he popped into a hallway. That was Chiney-Eye-the-Princinct-Captain's hallway, so I popped right in after him. Me 'n Chiney-Eye 'r just like that." The boy crossed two fingers of his left hand and asked innocently, "Has the alderman been in to straighten this out, Captain?"

"What time was all this, Lefty?"

"Well, some of the street lamps was lit awready 'n I didn't see nobody either way down Noble. It'd just started spitt'n a little snow 'n I couldn't see clear down Walton account of Wojciechowski's Tavern bein' in the way. He was a old guy, a dino you. He couldn't speak a word of English. But he started in cryin' about how every time he gets a little drunk the same old thing happens to him 'n he's gettin' fed up, he lost his last three checks in the very same hallway 'n it's gettin' so his family don't believe him no more . . ."

Lefty paused, realizing that his tongue was going faster than his brain. 35 He unfolded his arms and shoved them down his pants pockets; the pants were turned up at the cuffs and the cuffs were frayed. He drew a colorless cap off his hip pocket and stood clutching it in his left hand.

"I didn't take him them other times, Captain," he anticipated Kozak.

"Who did?"

Silence.

"What's Benkowski doin' for a livin' these days, Lefty?"

"Just nutsin' around." 40

"What's Nowogrodski up to?"

"Goes wolfin' on roller skates by Riverview. The rink's open all year round."

"Does he have much luck?"

"Never turns up a hair. They go by too fast."

"What's that evil-eye up to?"   45
Silence.
"You know who I mean. Idzikowski."
"The Finger?"
"You know who I mean. Don't stall."
"He's hexin' fights, I heard."   50
"Seen Kodadek lately?"
"I guess. A week 'r two 'r a month ago."
"What was *he* up to?"
"Sir?"
"What was Kodadek doin' the last time you seen him?"   55
"You mean Dropkick? He was nutsin' around."
"Does he nuts around drunks in hallways?"
Somewhere in the room a small clock or wrist watch began ticking
distinctly.
"Nutsin' around ain't jackrollin'."
"You mean Dropkick ain't a jackroller but you are."   60
The boy's blond lashes shuttered his eyes.
"All right, get ahead with your lyin' a little faster."
Kozak's head came down almost neckless onto his shoulders, and his
face was molded like a flatiron, the temples narrow and the jaws rounded.
Between the jaws and the open collar, against the graying hair of the chest,
hung a tiny crucifix, slender and golden, a shade lighter than his tunic's
golden buttons.
"I told him I wasn't gonna take his check, I just needed a little change,
I'd pay it back someday. But maybe he didn't understand. He kept hollerin'
how he lost his last check, please to let him keep this one. 'Why you drink'n
it all up, then,' I put it to him, 'if you're that anxious to hold onto it?' He
gimme a foxy grin then 'n pulls out four of them little bottles from four
different pockets, 'n each one was a different kind of liquor. I could have
one, he tells me in Polish, which do I want, 'n I slapped all four out of his
hands. All four. I don't like to see no full-grown man drinkin' that way. A
Polak hillbilly he was, 'n certain'y no citizen.
" 'Now let me have that change,' I asked him, 'n that wasn't so much t'   65
ask. I don't go around just lookin' fer trouble, Captain. 'N my feet was
slopfull of water 'n snow. I'm just a neighborhood fella. But he acted like I
was gonna kill him 'r somethin'. I got one hand over his mouth 'n a half
nelson behind him 'n talked polite-like in Polish in his ear, 'n he begun
sweatin' 'n tryin' t' wrench away on me. 'Take it easy,' I asked him. 'Be
reas'nable, we're both in this up to our necks now.' 'N he wasn't drunk no
more then, 'n he was plenty t' hold onto. You wouldn't think a old boobatch
like that'd have so much stren'th left in him, boozin' down Division night
after night, year after year, like he didn't have no home to go to. He pulled
my hand off his mouth 'n started hollerin', '*Mlody bandyta! Mlody bandyta!*' 'n
I could feel him slippin'. He was just too strong fer a kid like me to hold—"

"Because you were reach'n for his wallet with the other hand?"

"Oh no. The reason I couldn't hold him was my right hand had the nelson 'n I'm not so strong there like in my left 'n even my left ain't what it was before I thrun it out pitchin' that double-header."

"So you kept the rod in your left hand?"

The boy hesitated. Then: "Yes sir." And felt a single drop of sweat slide down his side from under his armpit. Stop and slide again down to the belt.

"What did you get off him?"   70

"I tell you, I had my hands too full to get *anythin'*—that's just what I been tryin' to tell you. I didn't get so much as one of them little single-shots for all my trouble."

"How many slugs did you fire?"

"Just one, Captain. That was all there was in 'er. I didn't really fire, though. Just at his feet. T' scare him so's he wouldn't jump me. I fired in self-defense. I just wanted to get out of there." He glanced helplessly around at Comiskey and Adamovitch. "You do crazy things sometimes, fellas—well, that's all I was doin'."

The boy caught his tongue and stood mute. In the silence of the query room there was only the scraping of the reporter's pencil and the unseen wrist watch. "I'll ask Chiney-Eye if it's legal, a reporter takin' down a confession, that's my out," the boy thought desperately, and added aloud, before he could stop himself: " 'N beside I had to show him—"

"Show him what, son?"   75

Silence.

"Show him what, Left-hander?"

"That I wasn't just another greenhorn sprout like he thought."

"Did he say you were just a sprout?"

"No. But I c'd tell. Lot of people think I'm just a green kid. I show   80
'em. I guess I showed 'em now all right." He felt he should be apologizing for something and couldn't tell whether it was for strong-arming a man or for failing to strong-arm him.

"I'm just a neighborhood kid. I belonged to the Keep-Our-City-Clean Club at St. John Catn'us. I told him polite-like, like a Polish-American citizen, this was Chiney-Eye-a-Friend-of-Mine's hallway. 'No more after this one,' I told him. 'This is your last time gettin' rolled, old man. After this I'm pertectin' you, I'm seein' to it nobody touches you—but the people who live here don't like this sort of thing goin' on any more'n you 'r I do. There's gotta to be a stop to it, old man—'n we all gotta live, don't we?' That's what I told him in Polish."

Kozak exchanged glances with the prim-faced reporter from the *Chicagoski*, who began cleaning his black tortoise-shell spectacles hurriedly yet delicately, with the fringed tip of his cravat. They depended from a black ribbon; he snapped them back onto his beak.

"You shot him in the groin, Lefty. He's dead."

The reporter leaned slightly forward, but perceived no special reaction and so relaxed. A pretty comfy old chair for a dirty old police station, he thought lifelessly. Kozak shaded his eyes with his gloved hand and looked down at his charge sheet. The night lamp on the desk was still lit, as though he had been working all night; as the morning grew lighter behind him lines came out below his eyes, black as though packed with soot, and a curious droop came to the St. Bernard mouth.

"You shot him through the groin—zip." Kozak's voice came, flat and unemphatic, reading from the charge sheet as though without understanding. "Five children. Stella, Mary, Grosha, Wanda, Vincent. Thirteen, ten, six, six, and one two months. Mother invalided since last birth, name of Rose. WPA fifty-five dollars. You told the truth about *that,* at least." 85

Lefty's voice came in a shout: "You know *what?* That bullet must of bounced, that's what!"

"Who was along?"

"I was singlin'. Lone-wolf stuff." His voice possessed the first faint touch of fear.

"You said, 'We seen the man.' Was he a big man? How big a man was he?"

"I'd judge two hunerd twenty pounds," Comiskey offered, "at least. Fifty pounds heavier 'n this boy, just about. 'N half a head taller." 90

"Who's 'we,' Left-hander?"

"Captain, I said, 'We seen.' Lots of people, fellas, seen him is all I meant, cashin' his check by Stachula's when the place was crowded. Konstanty cashes checks if he knows you. Say, I even know the project that old man was on, far as that goes, because my old lady wanted we should give up the store so's I c'd get on it. But it was just me done it, Captain."

The raccoon coat readjusted his glasses. He would say something under a by-line like "This correspondent has never seen a colder gray than that in the eye of the wanton killer who arrogantly styles himself the *lone wolf of Potomac Street.*" He shifted uncomfortably, wanting to get farther from the wall radiator but disliking to rise and push the heavy chair.

"Where was that bald-headed pal of yours all this time?"

"Don't know the fella, Captain. Nobody got hair any more around the neighborhood, it seems. The whole damn Triangle went 'n got army haircuts by Stachula's." 95

"Just you 'n Benkowski, I mean. Don't be afraid, son—we're not tryin' to ring in anythin' you done afore this. Just this one you were out cowboyin' with Benkowski on; were you help'n him 'r was he help'n you? Did you 'r him have the rod?"

Lefty heard a Ford V-8 pull into the rear of the station, and a moment later the splash of the gas as the officers refueled. Behind him he could hear Milano's heavy breathing. He looked down at his shoes, carefully buttoned all the way up and tied with a double bowknot. He'd have to have new laces mighty soon or else start tying them with a single bow.

"That Benkowski's sort of a toothless monkey used to go on at the City Garden at around a hundred an' eighteen pounds, ain't he?"

"Don't know the fella well enough t' say."

"Just from seein' him fight once 'r twice is all. 'N he wore a mouth- *100* piece, I couldn't tell about his teeth. Seems to me he came in about one thirty-three, if he's the same fella you're thinkin' of, Captain."

"I guess you fought at the City Garden once 'r twice yourself, ain't you?"

"Oh, once 'r twice."

"How'd you make out, Left'?"

"Won 'em both on K.O.s. Stopped both fights in the first. One was against that boogie from the Savoy. If he woulda got up I woulda killed him fer life. Fer Christ I would. I didn't know I could hit like I can."

"With Benkowski in your corner both times?" *105*

"Oh no, sir."

"That's a bloodsuck'n lie. I seen him in your corner with my own eyes the time you won off Cooney from the C.Y.O. He's your manager, jack-roller."

"I didn't say he wasn't."

"You said he wasn't secondin' you."

"He don't." *110*

"Who does?"

"The Finger."

"You told me the Finger was your hex-man. Make up your mind."

"He does both, Captain. He handles the bucket 'n sponge 'n in be-tween he fingers the guy I'm fightin', 'n if it's close he fingers the ref 'n judges. Finger, he never losed a fight. He waited for the boogie outside the dressing room 'n pointed him clear to the ring. He win that one for me awright." The boy spun the frayed greenish cap in his hand in a concentric circle about his index finger, remembering a time when the cap was new and had earlaps. The bright checks were all faded now, to the color of worn pavement, and the earlaps were tatters.

"What possessed your mob to get their heads shaved, Lefty?" *115*

"I strong-armed him myself, I'm rugged as a bull." The boy began to swell his chest imperceptibly; when his lungs were quite full he shut his eyes, like swimming under water at the Oak Street beach, and let his breath out slowly, ounce by ounce.

"I didn't ask you that. I asked you what happened to your hair."

Lefty's capricious mind returned abruptly to the word "possessed" that Kozak had employed. That had a randy ring, sort of: "What possessed you boys?"

"I forgot what you just asked me."

"I asked you why you didn't realize it'd be easier for us to catch up *120* with your mob when all of you had your heads shaved."

"I guess we figured there'd be so many guys with heads shaved it'd be harder to catch a finger than if we all had hair. But that was some accident all the same. A fella was gonna lend Ma a barber chair 'n go fifty-fifty with her shavin' all the Polaks on P'tom'c Street right back of the store, for relief tickets. So she started on me, just to show the fellas, but the hair made her sicker 'n ever 'n back of the store's the only place she got to lie down 'n I hadda finish the job myself.

"The fellas begun giv'n me a Christ-awful razzin' then, ever' day. God oh God, wherever I went around the Triangle, all the neighborhood fellas 'n little niducks 'n old-time hoods by the Broken Knuckle, whenever they seen me they was pointin' 'n laughin' 'n sayin', 'Hi, Baldy Bicek!' So I went home 'n got the clippers 'n the first guy I seen was Bibleback Watrobinski, you wouldn't know him. I jumps him 'n pushes the clip right through the middle of his hair—he ain't had a haircut since the alderman got indicted you—'n then he took one look at what I done in the drugstore window 'n we both bust out laughin' 'n laughin', 'n fin'lly Bible says I better finish what I started. So he set down on the curb 'n I finished him. When I got all I could off that way I took him back to the store 'n heated water 'n shaved him close 'n Ma couldn't see the point at all.

"Me 'n Bible prowled around a couple days 'n here come Catfoot Nowogrodski from Fry Street you, out of Stachula's with a spanty-new side-burner haircut 'n a green tie. I grabbed his arms 'n let Bible run it through the middle just like I done him. Then it was Catfoot's turn, 'n we caught Chester Chekhovka fer *him,* 'n fer Chester we got Cowboy Okulanis from by the Nort'western Viaduct you, 'n fer him we got Mustang, 'n fer Mustang we got John from the Joint, 'n fer John we got Snake Baranowski, 'n we kep' right on goin' that way till we was doin' guys we never seen before even, Wallios 'n Greeks 'n a Flip from Clark Street he musta been, walkin' with a white girl we done it to. 'N fin'lly all the sprouts in the Triangle start comin' around with their heads shaved, they want to join up with the Baldheads A.C., they called it. They thought it was a club you.

"It got so a kid with his head shaved could beat up on a bigger kid because the big one'd be a-scared to fight back hard, he thought the Baldheads'd get him. So that's why we changed our name then, that's why we're not the Warriors any more, we're the Baldhead True American Social 'n Athletic Club.

"I played first for the Warriors when I wasn't on the mound," he added   125 cautiously, "'n I'm enterin' the Gold'n Gloves next year 'less I go to collitch instead. I went to St. John Cant'us all the way through. Eight' grade, that is. If I keep on gainin' weight I'll be a hunerd ninety-eight this time next year 'n be five-foot-ten—I'm a fair-size light-heavy right this minute. That's what in England they call a cruiser weight you."

He shuffled a step and made as though to unbotton his shirt to show his proportions. But Adamovitch put one hand on his shoulders and slapped the boy's hand down. He didn't like this kid. This was a low-class Polak. He himself was a high-class Polak because his name was Adamovitch and not

Adamowski. This sort of kid kept spoiling things for the high-class Polaks by always showing off instead of just being good citizens like the Irish. That was why the Irish ran the City Hall and Police Department and the Board of Education and the Post Office while the Polaks stayed on relief and got drunk and never got anywhere and had everybody down on them. All they could do like the Irish, old Adamovitch reflected bitterly, was to fight under Irish names to get their ears knocked off at the City Garden.

"That's why I want to get out of this jam," this one was saying beside him. "So's it don't ruin my career in the rope' arena. I'm goin' straight. This has sure been one good lesson fer me. Now I'll go to a big-ten collitch 'n make good you."

Now, if the college-coat asked him, "What big-ten college?" he'd answer something screwy like "The Boozological Stoodent-Collitch." That ought to set Kozak back awhile, they might even send him to a bug doc. He'd have to be careful—not *too* screwy. Just screwy enough to get by without involving Benkowski.

He scuffed his shoes and there was no sound in the close little room save his uneasy scuffling; square-toed boy's shoes, laced with a button-hook. He wanted to look more closely at the reporter but every time he caught the glint of the fellow's glasses he felt awed and would have to drop his eyes; he'd never seen glasses on a string like that before and would have given a great deal to wear them a moment. He took to looking steadily out of the barred window behind Kozak's head, where the January sun was glowing sullenly, like a flame held steadily in a fog. Heard an empty truck clattering east on Chicago, sounding like either a '38 Chevvie or a '37 Ford dragging its safety chain against the car tracks; closed his eyes and imagined sparks flashing from the tracks as the iron struck, bounced, and struck again. The bullet had bounced too. Wow.

"What do you think we ought to do with a man like you, Bicek?"   130

The boy heard the change from the familiar "Lefty" to "Bicek" with a pang; and the dryness began in his throat again.

"One to fourteen is all I can catch fer manslaughter." He appraised Kozak as coolly as he could.

"You like farm work the next fourteen years? Is that okay with you?"

"I said that's all I could get, at the most. This is a first offense 'n self-defense too. I'll plead the unwritten law."

"Who give you *that* idea?"   135

"Thought of it myself. Just now. You ain't got a chance to send me over the road 'n you know it."

"We can send you to St. Charles, Bicek. 'N transfer you when you come of age. Unless we can make it first-degree murder."

The boy ignored the latter possibility.

"Why, a few years on a farm'd true me up fine. I planned t' cut out cigarettes 'n whisky anyhow before I turn pro—a farm'd be just the place to do that."

"By the time you're released you'll be thirty-two, Bicek—too late to   *140*
turn pro then, ain't it?"

"I wouldn't wait that long. Hungry Piontek-from-by-the-Warehouse
you, he lammed twice from that St. Charles farm. 'N Hungry don't have all
his marbles even. He ain't even a citizen."

"Then let's talk about somethin' you couldn't lam out of so fast 'n easy.
Like the chair. Did you know that Bogatski from Noble Street, Bicek? The
boy that burned last summer, I mean."

A plain-clothes man stuck his head in the door and called confidently:
"That's the man, Captain. That's the man."

Bicek forced himself to grin good-naturedly. He was getting pretty
good, these last couple days, at grinning under pressure. When a fellow got
sore he couldn't think straight, he reflected anxiously. And so he yawned in
Kozak's face with deliberateness, stretching himself as effortlessly as a cat.

"Captain, I ain't been in serious trouble like this before . . ." he ac-   *145*
knowledged, and paused dramatically. He'd let them have it straight from the
shoulder now: "So I'm mighty glad to be so close to the alderman. Even if
he is indicted."

There. Now they knew. He'd told them.

"You talkin' about my brother, Bicek?"

The boy nodded solemnly. Now they knew who they had hold of
at last.

The reporter took the cigarette off his ear and hung it on his lower lip.
And Adamovitch guffawed.

The boy jerked toward the officer: Adamovitch was laughing openly at   *150*
him. Then they were all laughing openly at him. He heard their derision,
and a red rain danced one moment before his eyes; when the red rain was
past, Kozak was sitting back easily, regarding him with the expression of a
man who has just been swung at and missed and plans to use the provocation
without undue haste. The captain didn't look like the sort who'd swing back
wildly or hurriedly. He didn't look like the sort who missed. His compla-
cency for a moment was as unbearable to the boy as Adamovitch's guffaw
had been. He heard his tongue going, trying to regain his lost composure by
provoking them all.

"Hey, Stingywhiskers!" He turned on the reporter. "Get your Ever-
sharp goin' there, write down I plugged the old rumpot, write down Bicek
carries a rod night 'n day 'n don't care where he points it. You, I go around
slappin' the crap out of whoever I feel like—"

But they all remained mild, calm, and unmoved: for a moment he
feared Adamovitch was going to pat him on the head and say something
fatherly in Polish.

"Take it easy, lad," Adamovitch suggested. "You're in the query room.
We're here to help you, boy. We want to see you through this thing so's you
can get back to pugging. You just ain't letting us help you, son."

Kozak blew his nose as though that were an achievement in itself, and spoke with the false friendliness of the insurance man urging a fleeced customer toward the door.

"Want to tell us where you got that rod now, Lefty?"   *155*

"I don't want to tell you anything." His mind was setting hard now, against them all. Against them all in here and all like them outside. And the harder it set, the more things seemed to be all right with Kozak: he dropped his eyes to his charge sheet now and everything was all right with everybody. The reporter shoved his notebook into his pocket and buttoned the top button of his coat as though the questioning were over.

It was all too easy. They weren't going to ask him anything more, and he stood wanting them to. He stood wishing them to threaten, to shake their heads ominously, wheedle and cajole and promise him mercy if he'd just talk about the rod.

"I ain't mad, Captain. I don't blame you men either. It's your job, it's your bread 'n butter to talk tough to us neighborhood fellas—ever'body got to have a racket, 'n yours is talkin' tough." He directed this last at the captain, for Comiskey and Milano had left quietly. But Kozak was studying the charge sheet as though Bruno Lefty Bicek were no longer in the room. Nor anywhere at all.

"I'm still here," the boy said wryly, his lip twisting into a dry and bitter grin.

Kozak looked up, his big, wind-beaten, impassive face looking sud-   *160* denly to the boy like an autographed pitcher's mitt he had once owned. His glance went past the boy and no light of recognition came into his eyes. Lefty Bicek felt a panic rising in him: a desperate fear that they weren't going to press him about the rod, about the old man, about his feelings. "Don't look at me like I ain't nowheres," he asked. And his voice was struck flat by fear.

Something else! The time he and Dropkick had broken into a slot machine! The time he and Casey had played the attention racket and made four dollars! Something! Anything else!

The reporter lit his cigarette.

"Your case is well disposed of," Kozak said, and his eyes dropped to the charge sheet forever.

"I'm born in this country. I'm educated here—"

But no one was listening to Bruno Lefty Bicek any more.   *165*

He watched the reporter leaving with regret—at least the guy could have offered him a drag—and stood waiting for someone to tell him to go somewhere now, shifting uneasily from one foot to the other. Then he started slowly, backward, toward the door: he'd make Kozak tell Adamovitch to grab him. Halfway to the door he turned his back on Kozak.

There was no voice behind him. Was this what "well disposed of" meant? He turned the knob and stepped confidently into the corridor; at the end of the corridor he saw the door that opened into the courtroom, and his heart began shaking his whole body with the impulse to make a run for it. He glanced back and Adamovitch was five yards behind, coming up catfooted like only an old man who has been a citizen-dress man can come up catfooted, just far enough behind and just casual enough to make it appear unimportant whether the boy made a run for it or not.

The Lone Wolf of Potomac Street waited miserably, in the long unlovely corridor, for the sergeant to thrust two fingers through the back of his belt. Didn't they realize that he might have Dropkick and Catfoot and Benkowski with a sub-machine gun in a streamlined cream-colored roadster right down front, that he'd zigzag through the courtroom onto the courtroom fire escape and—swish—down off the courtroom roof three stories with the copper still under his arm and through the car's roof and into the driver's seat? Like that George Raft did that time he was innocent at the Chopin, and cops like Adamovitch had better start ducking when Lefty Bicek began making a run for it. He felt the fingers thrust overfamiliarly between his shirt and his belt.

A cold draft came down the corridor when the door at the far end opened; with the opening of the door came the smell of disinfectant from the basement cells. Outside, far overhead, the bells of St. John Cantius were beginning. The boy felt the winding steel of the staircase to the basement beneath his feet and heard the whining screech of a Chicago Avenue streetcar as it paused on Ogden for the traffic lights and then screeched on again, as though a cat were caught beneath its back wheels. Would it be snowing out there still? he wondered, seeing the whitewashed basement walls.

"Feel all right, son?" Adamovitch asked in his most fatherly voice, *170* closing the cell door while thinking to himself: "The kid don't *feel* guilty is the whole trouble. You got to make them *feel* guilty or they'll never go to church at all. A man who goes to church without feeling guilty for *something* is wasting his time, I say." Inside the cell he saw the boy pause and go down on his knees in the cell's gray light. The boy's head turned slowly toward him, a pious oval in the dimness. Old Adamovitch took off his hat.

"This place'll rot down 'n mold over before Lefty Bicek starts prayin', boobatch. Prays, squeals, 'r bawls. So run along 'n I'll see you in hell with yer back broke. I'm lookin' for my cap I dropped is all."

Adamovitch watched him crawling forward on all fours, groping for the pavement-colored cap; when he saw Bicek find it he put his own hat back on and left feeling vaguely dissatisfied.

He did not stay to see the boy, still on his knees, put his hands across his mouth and stare at the shadowed wall.

Shadows were there within shadows.

"I knew I'd never get to be twenty-one anyhow," Lefty told himself *175* softly at last.

The Responsive Reader

1. How does Algren create the setting? In what kind of a world does Bicek live? What glimpses of the city environment do we get in this story?
2. How did the robbery become a homicide? What were the boy's motives? What went on in his mind? What goes on in Bicek's mind during the interrogation?
3. In recent years, there has been much criticism of the police. What is Algren's attitude toward the police officers in this story? Who are they? How do they treat the boy? How do they feel about the boy?
4. Why is the newspaper correspondent in the story? Does Algren intend a comment on the way the media treat juvenile crime?

Thinking, Talking, Writing

5. Is Algren taking sides in this story? With whom or with what? How?
6. Is Bicek's world a thing of the past? Is there any connection between Bicek's story and what you know or hear about today's young criminals?
7. Liberal sociologists place much of the blame for juvenile crime on social conditions and parental neglect. Do you agree with them?

Collaborative Projects

8. Working with a group, what can you learn by interviewing counselors, lawyers, or law enforcement officers working with juvenile crime?

RAYMOND'S RUN

Toni Cade Bambara

Toni Cade Bambara has an ear for the tough street talk and quick wit of kids from the other side of the tracks. She grew up in New York City and has degrees from Queens and City College. She started writing in the activist political climate of the sixties and has published two collections of short stories, Gorilla, My Love *(1972) and* The Sea Birds Are Still Alive *(1977). Her novel* The Salt Eaters *was published in 1980.*

In Bambara's best-known story, "The Lesson," a well-intentioned teacher takes a group of uptown kinds downtown into Manhattan for an educational field trip. The excursion turns into an object lesson in the conspicuous consumption and ostentatious display of the affluent upper strata of American society, oblivious to the poverty and despair that surrounds them. The following story takes place in Harlem, where street kids play the dozens, a fast-moving verbal game in which the participants try to outdo one another in improvising insults, and where the Police Athletic League (PAL) sponsors athletic events for children. What is the persona, or assumed identity, of the narrator in the story?

I don't have much work to do around the house like some girls. My mother does that. And I don't have to earn my pocket money by hustling; George runs errands for the big boys and sells Christmas cards. And anything else that's got to get done, my father does. All I have to do in life is mind my brother Raymond, which is enough.

Sometimes I slip and say my little brother Raymond. But as any fool can see he's much bigger and he's older too. But a lot of people call him my little brother cause he needs looking after cause he's not quite right. And a lot of smart mouths got lots to say about that too, especially when George was minding him. But now, if anybody has anything to say to Raymond, anything to say about his big head, they have to come by me. And I don't play the dozens or believe in standing around with somebody in my face doing a lot of talking. I much rather just knock you down and take my chances even if I am a little girl with skinny arms and a squeaky voice, which is how I got the name Squeaky. And if things get too rough, I run. And as anybody can tell you, I'm the fastest thing on two feet.

There is no track meet that I don't win the first-place medal. I used to win the twenty-yard dash when I was a little kid in kindergarten. Nowadays, it's the fifty-yard dash. And tomorrow I'm subject to run the quarter-meter relay all by myself and come in first, second, and third. The big kids call me Mercury cause I'm the swiftest thing in the neighborhood. Everybody knows that—except two people who know better, my father and me. He can beat me to Amsterdam Avenue with me having a two-fire-hydrant head start and him running with his hands in his pockets and whistling. But that's private information. Cause can you imagine some thirty-five-year-old man stuffing himself into PAL shorts to race little kids? So as far as everyone's concerned, I'm the fastest and that goes for Gretchen, too, who has put out the tale that she is going to win the first-place medal this year. Ridiculous. In the second place, she's got short legs. In the third place, she's got freckles. In the first place, no one can beat me and that's all there is to it.

I'm standing on the corner admiring the weather and about to take a stroll down Broadway so I can practice my breathing exercises, and I've got Raymond walking on the inside close to the buildings, cause he's subject to fits of fantasy and starts thinking he's a circus performer and that the curb is a tightrope strung high in the air. And sometimes after a rain he likes to step down off his tightrope right into the gutter and slosh around getting his shoes and cuffs wet. Then I get hit when I get home. Or sometimes if you don't watch him he'll dash across traffic to the island in the middle of Broadway and give the pigeons a fit. Then I have to go behind him apologizing to all the old people sitting around trying to get some sun and getting all upset with the pigeons fluttering around them, scattering their newspapers and upsetting the wax paper lunches in their laps. So I keep Raymond on the inside of me, and he plays like he's driving a stagecoach which is O.K. by me so long as he doesn't run me over or interrupt my breathing exercises, which I have to do on account of I'm serious about my running, and I don't care who knows it.

Now some people like to act like things come easy to them, won't let   5
on that they practice. Not me, I'll high-prance down 34th Street like a rodeo pony to keep my knees strong even if it does get my mother uptight so that she walks ahead like she's not with me, don't know me, is all by herself on a shopping trip, and I am somebody else's crazy child. Now you take Cynthia Procter for instance. She's just the opposite. If there's a test tomorrow, she'll say something like, "Oh, I guess I'll play handball this afternoon and watch television tonight," just to let you know she ain't thinking about the test. Or like last week when she won the spelling bee for the millionth time. "A good thing you got 'receive,' Squeaky, cause I would have got it wrong. I com-pletely forgot about the spelling bee." And she'll clutch the lace on her blouse like it was a narrow escape. Oh, brother. But of course when I pass her house on my early morning trots around the block, she is practicing the scales on the piano over and over and over and over. Then in music class she always lets herself get bumped around so she falls accidently on purpose onto the piano stool and is so surprised to find herself sitting there that she decides just for fun to try out the ole keys. And what do you know—Chopin's waltzes just spring out of her fingertips and she's the most surprised thing in the world. A regular prodigy. I could kill people like that. I stay up all night studying the words for the spelling bee. And you can see me any time of day practicing running. I never walk if I can trot, and shame on Raymond if he can't keep up. But of course he does, cause if he hangs back someone's

liable to walk up to him and get smart, or take his allowance from him, or ask him where he got that great big pumpkin head. People are so stupid sometimes.

So I'm strolling down Broadway breathing out and breathing in on counts of seven, which is my lucky number, and here comes Gretchen and her sidekicks: Mary Louise, who used to be a friend of mine when she first moved to Harlem from Baltimore and got beat up by everybody till I took up for her on account of her mother and my mother used to sing in the same choir when they were young girls, but people ain't grateful, so now she hangs out with the new girl Gretchen and talks about me like a dog; and Rosie, who is as fat as I am skinny and has a big mouth where Raymond is concerned and is too stupid to know that there is not a big deal of difference between herself and Raymond and that she can't afford to throw stones. So they are steady coming up Broadway and I see right away that it's going to be one of those Dodge City scenes cause the street ain't that big and they're close to the buildings just as we are. First I think I'll step into the candy store and look over the new comics and let them pass. But that's chicken and I've got a reputation to consider. So then I think I'll just walk straight on through them or even over them if necessary. But as they get to me, they slow down. I'm ready to fight, cause like I said I don't feature a whole lot of chitchat. I much prefer to just knock you down right from the jump and save everybody a lotta precious time.

"You signing up for the May Day races?" smiles Mary Louise, only it's not a smile at all. A dumb question like that doesn't deserve an answer. Besides, there's just me and Gretchen standing there really, so no use wasting my breath talking to shadows.

"I don't think you're going to win this time," says Rosie, trying to signify with her hands on her hips all salty, completely forgetting that I have whupped her behind many times for less salt than that.

"I always win cause I'm the best," I say straight at Gretchen who is, as far as I'm concerned, the only one talking in this ventriloquist-dummy routine. Gretchen smiles, but it's not a smile, and I'm thinking that girls never really smile at each other because they don't know how and don't want to know how and there's probably no one to teach us how, cause grownup girls don't know either. Then they all look at Raymond who has just brought his mule team to a standstill. And they're about to see what trouble they can get into through him.

"What grade you in now, Raymond?" 10

"You got anything to say to my brother, you say it to me, Mary Louise Williams of Raggedy Town, Baltimore."

"What are you, his mother?" sasses Rosie.

"That's right, Fatso. And the next word out of anybody and I'll be *their* mother too." So they just stand there and Gretchen shifts from one leg to the other and so do they. Then Gretchen puts her hands on her hips and is about to say something with her freckle-face self but doesn't. Then she walks around me looking me up and down but keeps walking up Broadway, and her sidekicks follow her. So me and Raymond smile at each other and he says, "Giddyap" to his team and I continue with my breathing exercises, strolling down Broadway toward the ice man on 145th with not a care in the world cause I am Miss Quicksilver herself.

I take my time getting to the park on May Day because the track meet is the last thing on the program. The biggest thing on the program is the Maypole dancing, which I can do without, thank you, even if my mother thinks it's a shame I don't take part and act like a girl for a change. You'd think my mother'd be grateful not to have to make me a white organdy dress with a big satin sash and buy me new white baby-doll shoes that can't be taken out of the box till the big day. You'd think she'd be glad her daughter ain't out there prancing around a Maypole getting the new clothes all dirty and sweaty and trying to act like a fairy or a flower or whatever you're supposed to be when you should be trying to be yourself, whatever that is, which is, as far as I am concerned, a poor black girl who really can't afford to buy shoes and a new dress you only wear once a lifetime cause it won't fit next year.

I was once a strawberry in a Hansel and Gretel pageant when I was in   *15* nursery school and didn't have no better sense than to dance on tiptoe with my arms in a circle over my head doing umbrella steps and being a perfect fool just so my mother and father could come dressed up and clap. You'd think they'd know better than to encourage that kind of nonsense. I am not a strawberry. I do not dance on my toes. I run. That is what I am all about. So I always come late to the May Day program, just in time to get my number pinned on and lay in the grass till they announce the fifty-yard dash.

I put Raymond in the little swings, which is a tight squeeze this year and will be impossible next year. Then I look around for Mr. Pearson, who pins the numbers on. I'm really looking for Gretchen if you want to know the truth, but she's not around. The park is jam-packed. Parents in hats and corsages and breastpocket handkerchiefs peeking up. Kids in white dresses and light blue suits. The parkees unfolding chairs and chasing the rowdy kids from Lenox as if they had no right to be there. The big guys with their caps on backwards, leaning against the fence swirling the basketballs on the tips of their fingers, waiting for all these crazy people to clear out the park so they can play. Most of the kids in my class are carrying bass drums and glockenspiels and flutes. You'd think they'd put in a few bongos or something for real like that.

Then here comes Mr. Pearson with his clipboard and his cards and pencils and whistles and safety pins and fifty million other things he's always dropping all over the place with his clumsy self. He sticks out in a crowd because he's on stilts. We used to call him Jack and the Beanstalk to get him mad. But I'm the only one that can outrun him and get away, and I'm too grown for that silliness now.

"Well, Squeaky," he says, checking my name off the list and handing me number seven and two pins. And I'm thinking he's got no right to call me Squeaky, if I can't call him Beanstalk.

"Hazel Elizabeth Deborah Parker," I correct him and tell him to write it down on his board.

"Well, Hazel Elizabeth Deborah Parker, going to give someone else a break this year?" I squint at him real hard to see if he is seriously thinking I should lose the race on purpose just to give someone else a break. "Only six girls running this time," he continues, shaking his head sadly like it's my fault all of New York didn't turn out in sneakers. "That new girl should give you a run for your money." He looks around the park for Gretchen like a periscope in a submarine movie. "Wouldn't it be a nice gesture if you were . . . to ahhh . . ."   20

I give him such a look he couldn't finish putting that idea into words. Grownups got a lot of nerve sometimes. I pin number seven to myself and stomp away, I'm so burnt. And I go straight for the track and stretch out on the grass while the band winds up with "Oh, the Monkey Wrapped His Tail Around the Flagpole," which my teacher calls by some other name. The man on the loudspeaker is calling everyone over to the track and I'm on my back looking at the sky, trying to pretend I'm in the country, but I can't, because even grass in the city feels hard as sidewalk, and there's just no pretending you are anywhere but in a "concrete jungle" as my grandfather says.

The twenty-yard dash takes all of two minutes cause most of the little kids don't know no better than to run off the track or run the wrong way or run smack into the fence and fall down and cry. One little kid, though, has got the good sense to run straight for the white ribbon up ahead so he wins. Then the second-graders line up for the thirty-yard dash and I don't even bother to turn my head to watch cause Raphael Perez always wins. He wins before he even begins by psyching the runners, telling them they're going to trip on their shoelaces and fall on their faces or lose their shorts or something, which he doesn't really have to do since he is very fast, almost as fast as I am. After that is the forty-yard dash which I use to run when I was in first grade. Raymond is hollering from the swings cause he knows I'm about to do my thing cause the man on the loudspeaker has just announced the fifty-yard dash, although he might just as well be giving a recipe for angel food cake cause you can hardly make out what he's saying for the static. I get up and slip off my sweat pants and then I see Gretchen standing at the starting line, kicking her legs out like a pro. Then as I get into place I see that ole Raymond is on line on the other side of the fence, bending down with his fingers on the ground just like he knew what he was doing. I was going to yell at him but then I didn't. It burns up your energy to holler.

Every time, just before I take off in a race, I always feel like I'm in a dream, the kind of dream you have when you're sick with fever and feel all hot and weightless. I dream I'm flying over a sandy beach in the early morning sun, kissing the leaves of the trees as I fly by. And there's always the smell of apples, just like in the country when I was little and used to think I was a choo-choo train, running through the fields of corn and chugging up the hill to the orchard. And all the time I'm dreaming this, I get lighter and lighter until I'm flying over the beach again, getting blown through the sky like a feather that weighs nothing at all. But once I spread my fingers in the dirt and crouch over the Get on Your Mark, the dream goes and I am solid again and am telling myself, Squeaky you must win, you must win, you are the fastest thing in the world, you can even beat your father up Amsterdam if you really try. And then I feel my weight coming back just behind my knees then down to my feet then into the earth and the pistol shot explodes in my blood and I am off and weightless again, flying past the other runners, my arms pumping up and down and the whole world is quiet except for the crunch as I zoom over the gravel in the track. I glance to my left and there is no one. To the right, a blurred Gretchen, who's got her chin jutting out as if it would win the race all by itself. And on the other side of the fence is Raymond with his arms down to his side and the palms tucked up behind him, running in his very own style, and it's the first time I ever saw that and I almost stop to watch my brother Raymond on his first run. But the white ribbon is bouncing toward me and I tear past it, racing into the distance till my feet with a mind of their own start digging up footfuls of dirt and brake me short. Then all the kids standing on the side pile on me, banging me on the back and slapping my head with their May Day programs, for I have won again and everybody on 151st Street can walk tall for another year.

"In first place . . ." the man on the loudspeaker is clear as a bell now, but then he pauses and the loudspeaker starts to whine. Then static. And I lean down to catch my breath and here comes Gretchen walking back, for she's overshot the finish line too, huffing and puffing with her hands on her hips taking it slow, breathing in steady time like a real pro and I sort of like her a little for the first time. "In first place . . ." and then three or four voices get all mixed up on the loudspeaker and I dig my sneaker into the grass and stare at Gretchen who's staring back, we both wondering just who did win. I can hear old Beanstalk arguing with the man on the loudspeaker and then a few others running their mouths about what the stopwatches say. Then I hear Raymond yanking at the fence to call me and I wave to shush him, but he keeps rattling the fence like a gorilla in a cage like in them gorilla movies, but then like a dancer or something he starts climbing up nice and easy but very fast. And it occurs to me, watching how smoothly he climbs hand over hand and remembering how he looked running with his arms down to his side and with the wind pulling his mouth back and his teeth showing and all, it occurred to me that Raymond would make a very fine runner. Doesn't he always keep up with me on my trots? And he surely knows how to breathe in counts of seven cause he's always doing it at the dinner table, which drives my brother George up the wall. And I'm smiling to beat the band cause if

I've lost this race, or if me and Gretchen tied, or even if I've won. I can always retire as a runner and begin a whole new career as a coach with Raymond as my champion. After all, with a little more study I can beat Cynthia and her phony self at the spelling bee. And if I bugged my mother, I could get piano lessons and become a star. And I have a big rep as the baddest thing around. And I've got a roomful of ribbons and medals and awards. But what has Raymond got to call his own?

So I stand there with my new plans, laughing out loud by this time as Raymond jumps down from the fence and runs over with his teeth showing and his arms down to the side, which no one before him has quite mastered as a running style, and by the time he comes over I'm jumping up and down so glad to see him—my brother Raymond, a great runner in the family tradition. But of course everyone thinks I'm jumping up and down because the men on the loudspeaker have finally gotten themselves together and compared notes and are announcing "In first place—Miss Hazel Elizabeth Deborah Parker." (Dig that.) "In second place—Miss Gretchen P. Lewis." And I look at Gretchen wondering what the "P" stands for. And I smile. Cause she's good, no doubt about it. Maybe she'd like to help me coach Raymond; she obviously is serious about running, as any fool can see. And she nods to congratulate me and then she smiles. And I smile. We stand there with this big smile of respect between us. It's about as real a smile as girls can do for each other, considering we don't practice real smiling every day, you know, cause maybe we too busy being flowers or fairies or strawberries instead of something honest and worthy of respect . . . you know . . . like being people.

The Responsive Reader

1. What is the narrator's relationship with the other girls? Are the girls hostile or "catty" toward one another?
2. What kind of person is telling the story? The narrator's philosophy is that "you should be trying to be yourself, whatever that is." In what ways does she try to be herself? What are some of the things that for her are not "for real?"
3. Do Raymond and his running have a symbolic significance in this story? What do they symbolize?
4. How much is the language used by the narrator part of her persona? What are some typical examples of her style of talking? Bambara has been praised for her use of "uncondescending, witty, poetic Black English." What makes expressions like "maybe we too busy being flowers" Black English? What other touches of Black English can you find in the story? What features of the informal English the narrator uses sound to you like street English or neighborhood English not limited to black neighborhoods?

Thinking, Talking, Writing

5. Does this story challenge or modify stereotypes about inner-city youth? Does it in any way confirm them?
6. What is the etiquette for the use of first names or nicknames? Why does the narrator object to Mr. Pearson's calling her Squeaky?
7. Do the author's "sexual politics" play a role in this story?

Collaborative Projects

8. Working in small groups, your class may want to explore questions like the following: What is a dialect? Some students of language object to Black English being called a dialect. Why? Some claim that all language is dialect. What do they mean? Dialect used to be widely used for comic effect. Why do many now consider this practice offensive?

Thinking about Connections

9. How important is ethnicity in the stories by Malamud, Algren, and Bambara? How much in these stories is Jewish, Polish, or African American? How much is universal or generally human?

THE PEDESTRIAN

Ray Bradbury

Science fiction takes us to a sphere different from a fantasy world peopled by dwarves, magicians, and monsters acting out the irrational fears shaping our nightmares. The best science fiction asks rational questions and tries to answer them imaginatively.

Ray Bradbury is one of the great masters of fiction that asks intelligent people to imagine the future. Although the planet Mars now seems inhospitable to life, who is to say that future colonists might not encounter haunting hints of a now vanished civilization? (The Martian Chronicles, *1950.*) *Since high-tech entertainment has blurred the line between game and reality, who is to say that youngsters would not call up wild animals in a multimedia theme park and egg them on to devour nagging parents?* (The Veldt, *1951.*) *With book-burners cropping up here and abroad, why would it be illogical to imagine a future society where books are banned and where books illegally hidden—and the people who read them—are put to the torch?* (Fahrenheit 451, *1953.*)

Bradbury has long been a believer in the power of fantasy to illuminate reality. He once said that people who are unaware of the way their own civilization works can be "enlightened and refocused by a journey through some foreign country such as Mexico" *where they see their* "own customs through the Looking Glass, brought into an astonishing clarity so they suddenly become ridiculous or understandable or both." *So passengers* "through the land of fantasy should return, freshened and clear of eye," *to their normal existence.*

In the following story, how believable is Bradbury's vision of the automated, robotized city of the future? As is already the case in many American cities, anyone going for a walk after dark will be under suspicion. Anyone talking back to law enforcement is in serious trouble.

To enter out into that silence that was the city at eight o'clock of a misty evening in November, to put your feet upon that buckling concrete walk, to step over grassy seams and make your way, hands in pockets, through the silences, that was what Mr. Leonard Mead most dearly loved to do. He would stand upon the corner of an intersection and peer down long moonlit avenues of sidewalk in four directions, deciding which way to go, but it really made no difference; he was alone in this world of A.D. 2131, or as good as alone, and with a final decision made, a path selected, he would stride off sending patterns of frosty air before him like the smoke of a cigar.

Sometimes he would walk for hours and miles and return only at midnight to his house. And on his way he would see the cottages and homes with their dark windows, and it was not unequal to walking through a graveyard, because only the faintest glimmers of firefly light appeared in flickers behind the windows. Sudden gray phantoms seemed to manifest themselves upon inner room walls where a curtain was still undrawn against the night, or there were whisperings and murmurs where a window in a tomblike building was still open.

Mr. Leonard Mead would pause, cock his head, listen, look, and march on, his feet making no noise on the lumpy walk. For a long while now the sidewalks had been vanishing under flowers and grass. In ten years of walking by night or day, for thousands of miles, he had never met another person walking, not one in all that time.

He now wore sneakers when strolling at night, because the dogs in intermittent squads would parallel his journey with barkings if he wore hard heels, and lights might click on and faces appear, and an entire street be startled by the passing of a lone figure, himself, in the early November evening.

On this particular evening he began his journey in a westerly direction, toward the hidden sea. There was a good crystal frost in the air; it cut the nose going in and made the lungs blaze like a Christmas tree inside; you could feel the cold light going on and off, all the branches filled with invisible snow. He listened to the faint push of his soft shoes through autumn leaves with satisfaction, and whistled a cold quiet whistle between his teeth, occasionally picking up a leaf as he passed, examining its skeletal pattern in the infrequent lamplights as he went on, smelling its rusty smell.

"Hello, in there," he whispered to every house on every side as he moved. "What's up tonight on Channel 4, Channel 7, Channel 9? Where are the cowboys rushing, and do I see the United States Cavalry over the next hill to the rescue?"

The street was silent and long and empty, with only his shadow moving like the shadow of a hawk in mid-country. If he closed his eyes and stood very still, frozen, he imagined himself upon the center of a plain, a wintry windless Arizona country with no house in a thousand miles, and only dry riverbeds, the streets, for company.

"What is it now?" he asked the houses, noticing his wristwatch. "Eight-thirty P.M. Time for a dozen assorted murders? A quiz? A revue? A comedian falling off the stage?"

Was that a murmur of laughter from within a moon-white house? He hesitated, but went on when nothing more happened. He stumbled over a particularly uneven section of walk as he came to a cloverleaf intersection which stood silent where two main highways crossed the town. During the day it was a thunderous surge of cars, the gas stations open, a great insect rustling and ceaseless jockeying for position as the scarab beetles, a faint incense puttering from their exhausts, skimmed homeward to the far horizons. But now these highways too were like streams in a dry season, all stone and bed and moon radiance.

He turned back on a side street, circling around toward his home. He   *10*
was within a block of his destination when the lone car turned a corner quite
suddenly and flashed a fierce white cone of light upon him. He stood entranced, not unlike a night moth, stunned by the illumination and then
drawn toward it.

A metallic voice called to him:

"Stand still. Stay where you are! Don't move!"

He halted.

"Put up your hands."

"But—" he said.   *15*

"Your hands up! Or we'll shoot!"

The police, of course, but what a rare, incredible thing; in a city of
three million, there was only one police car left. Ever since a year ago, 2130,
the election year, the force had been cut down from three cars to one. Crime
was ebbing; there was no need now for the police, save for this one lone car
wandering and wandering the empty streets.

"Your name?" said the police car in a metallic whisper. He couldn't see
the men in it for the bright light in his eyes.

"Leonard Mead," he said.

"Speak up!"   *20*

"Leonard Mead!"

"Business or profession?"

"I guess you'd call me a writer."

"No profession," said the police car, as if talking to itself. The light held
him fixed like a museum specimen, needle thrust through chest.

"You might say that," said Mr. Mead. He hadn't written in years. Mag-   *25*
azines and books didn't sell any more. Everything went on in the tomblike
houses at night now, he thought, continuing his fancy. The tombs, ill-lit by
television light, where the people sat like the dead, the gray or multi-colored
lights touching their expressionless faces but never really touching *them*.

"No profession," said the phonograph voice, hissing. "What are you
doing out?"

"Walking," said Leonard Mead.

"Walking!"

"Just walking," he said, simply, but his face felt cold.

"Walking, just walking, walking?"   *30*

"Yes, sir."

"Walking where? For what?"

"Walking for air. Walking to *see*."

"Your address!"

"Eleven South St. James Street."   *35*

"And there is air *in* your house, you have an air-*conditioner*, Mr. Mead?"

"Yes."

"And you have a viewing screen in your house to see with?"

"No."

"No?" There was a crackling quiet that in itself was an accusation. *40*
"Are you married, Mr. Mead?"

"No."

"Not married," said the police voice behind the fiery beam. The moon was high and clear among the stars and the houses were gray and silent.

"Nobody wanted me," said Leonard Mead, with a smile.

"Don't speak unless you're spoken to!" *45*

Leonard Mead waited in the cold night.

"Just walking, Mr. Mead?"

"Yes."

"But you haven't explained for what purpose."

"I explained: for air and to see, and just to walk." *50*

"Have you done this often?"

"Every night for years."

The police car sat in the center of the street with its radio throat faintly humming.

"Well, Mr. Mead," it said.

"Is that all?" he asked politely. *55*

"Yes," said the voice. "Here." There was a sigh, a pop. The back door of the police car sprang wide. "Get in."

"Wait a minute, I haven't done anything!"

"Get in."

"I protest!"

"Mr. Mead." *60*

He walked like a man suddenly drunk. As he passed the front window of the car he looked in. As he had expected, there was no one in the front seat, no one in the car at all.

"Get in."

He put his hand to the door and peered into the back seat, which was a little cell, a little black jail with bars. It smelled of riveted steel. It smelled of harsh antiseptic; it smelled too clean and hard and metallic. There was nothing soft there.

"Now if you had a wife to give you an alibi," said the iron voice. "But—"

"Where are you taking me?" *65*

The car hesitated, or rather gave a faint whirring click, as if information, somewhere, was dropping card by punch-slotted card under electric eyes. "To the Psychiatric Center for Research on Regressive Tendencies."

He got in. The door shut with a soft thud. The police car rolled through the night avenues, flashing its dim lights ahead.

They passed one house on one street a moment later, one house in an entire city of houses that were dark, but this one particular house had all its electric lights brightly lit, every window a loud yellow illumination, square and warm in the cool darkness.

"That's *my* house," said Leonard Mead.

No one answered him.   70

The car moved down the empty river bed streets and off away, leaving the empty streets with the empty sidewalks, and no sound and no motion all the rest of the chill November night.

The Responsive Reader

1. How does Bradbury try to make you understand the motives and attitudes that make the central character somewhat of a freak in his society? Is Bradbury successful? (Would Mead be somewhat of a freak in your own neighborhood?)
2. Is Bradbury's satirical portrait of a couch-potato society a hilarious exaggeration? Or is it merely a logical extension of current trends?
3. Does the driverless police car seem fantastic to you? Does it seem fantastic to you that law enforcement could be as automated, impersonal, or robotized as in this story?

Thinking, Talking, Writing

4. Has automation begun to depersonalize your own life?
5. Does our society frown on "regressive tendencies"?
6. Do you have nightmares—sleeping or waking—about the future?

Collaborative Projects

7. Bradbury's stories have often been dramatized—turned into plays or movies. Working with a group, you may want to help draft a script for a trial of Mead for regressive tendencies or for a scene in the psychiatric ward of the future where he was taken.

Thinking About Connections

8. Thoreau, LeGuin (in Chapter 4), and Bradbury each envision a future different from their present. Compare their visions of a better or worse tomorrow.

8

Desperate Glory: War and Its Aftermath

God must love the music of military bands, because he has arranged so many occasions for the playing of it.

Leszek Kolakowski

War is evil, and it is often the lesser evil.
George Orwell

LITERATURE IN CONTEXT

Thomas Hobbes, a British philosopher who is often misquoted, said that *in times of war* life is "nasty, brutish, and short." He blamed humanity's failure to live in peace on powerful motives: The first is the lust for power, which impels human beings to lord it over others, to seize their territory, and to plunder their wealth. The second motive is fear, which makes human beings want to crush others whom they consider evil, whom they consider a threat to their safety and well-being. The third is pride, which makes them wage war because their wounded vanity or national honor will not let them admit that an enemy has bested them in a fight.

War has been a subtext in American history from the beginnings. In the earliest colonial times, England and France imported their imperial quarrels to the New World, using Native American tribes as pawns in the power struggles of Old World nations. The new American nation found its identity in the War of Independence, fought by the colonists to overthrow British colonial rule and the tyranny of George III. "These are the times that try men's souls," said Tom Paine in the fiery patriotic pamphlets he published between 1776 and 1783. "The summer soldier and the sunshine patriot will, in this crisis, shrink from the service of his country; but he that stands it NOW deserves the love and thanks of man and woman. Tyranny, like hell, is not easily conquered; yet we have this consolation with us that the harder the conflict, the more glorious the triumph."

The bloodiest war in American history was fought to prevent the South from seceding from the Union over the issue of slavery. The Civil War, or the War between the States, has been called the first modern war, fought with the murderous firepower made possible by advances in military weaponry. An estimated 618,000 Americans died, more than in any other war in this country's history. Like other civil wars, it pitted against one another people speaking the same language, claiming the same ancestry, invoking the same ideals, and quoting the same Bible. The war made President Lincoln and generals like Sherman and Grant on the Northern and Lee on the Southern side into towering figures in the national mythology. It left behind a legacy of smouldering resentment, racial prejudice, and economic dislocation.

In the twentieth century, American armies twice crossed the oceans to join their British and French allies after years of reluctance to become embroiled in foreign wars. American military and industrial strength made the difference in the fight against the imperial armies of the Kaiser—the German emperor Wilhelm—in World War I (1914–1918). American military might again tipped the balance in the struggle against the genocidal war machines of Nazi Germany and Imperial Japan in World War II (1939–1945).

In both world wars, a large coordinated propaganda effort rallied public opinion behind the fight to "make the world safe for democracy." However, after the defeat of Germany and Japan in World War II, America underwent a crisis of conscience when its leaders called on a new generation to sacrifice their lives in wars fought in Korea and Vietnam to contain the spread of Communism in Asia. During the Vietnam War, television brought into America's living rooms close-ups of a nation trying to emerge from colonialism and martyred in a relentless guerilla war. Years of antiwar protest and political turmoil at home ended with the withdrawal of a demoralized American force and the return of traumatized veterans who felt they had been lied to by their leaders. While the South was still harboring memories of defeat in a much earlier conflict, most Americans for the first time experienced the bitterness, guilt feelings, and mutual recriminations of a lost war.

Writers and artists have seldom shared the rah-rah patriotism of the official media. Stephen Crane's Civil War novel *The Red Badge of Courage* is the classic tribute to the memory of a generation sacrificed on the altar of war. Writers like Ernest Hemingway came back from the carnage of World War I disillusioned not only with official war aims but also with the professed ideals of Western civilization. Hemingway's contemporary, the American poet Ezra Pound, said:

> There died a myriad
> And of the best, among them,
> For a bitch long in the teeth,
> For a botched civilization,

Charm, smiling at the good mouth,
Quick eyes gone under earth's lid,
For two gross of broken statues,
For a few thousand battered books.

The antiwar literature triggered by the Vietnam War ranges from Denise Levertov's tribute to the civilian victims to Luis Valdez' play *Soldado Razo,* about a Chicano GI sent to die in Vietnam. Today, with the resurgence of nationalism and tribalism, war remains the great unsolved problem of contemporary civilization. What have we learned from the wars fought by this nation?

A SIGHT IN CAMP IN THE DAYBREAK GRAY AND DIM

Walt Whitman

> *Walt Whitman more than others had the imaginative writer's gift for identifying with other people. During the Civil War, he spent time in military hospitals close to the front in Virginia and Washington, helping tend the wounded and bury the dead. He recorded the experience in diary entries in* Specimen Days *and in poems collected in a volume called* Drum Taps *(1865). He wrote not about "hard-fought engagements or sieges tremendous" but about the wounded and dying, "Where they lie on the ground after the battle brought in,/Where their priceless blood reddens the grass, the ground."*

A sight in camp in the daybreak gray and dim,   1
As from my tent I emerge so early sleepless,
As slow I walk in the cool fresh air, the path near by the hospital tent,
Three forms I see on stretchers lying, brought out there untended lying,
Over each the blanket spread, ample brownish woolen blanket,   5
Gray and heavy blanket, folding, covering all.

Curious I halt and silent stand,
Then with light fingers I from the face of the nearest the first just lift the
    blanket.
Who are you elderly man so gaunt and grim, with well-gray'd hair, and
    flesh all sunken about the eyes?
Who are you my dear comrade?   10

Then to the second I step—and who are you my child and darling?
Who are you sweet boy with cheeks yet blooming?

Then to the third—a face nor child nor old, very calm, as of beautiful
    yellow-white ivory,
Young man I think I know you—I think this face is the face of the Christ
    himself.
Dead and divine and brother of all, and here again he lies.   15

The Responsive Reader

1. How do the six lines of the first stanza set the scene? What about them
   could have a special impact on the reader?
2. Why did the poet select these three among the many victims to write
   about? What effect on the reader has the order in which they are
   presented?

3. Why does the poet keep asking "Who are you?" How does the poet use the Christ metaphor at the end of the poem? Do you think the poet's use of the comparison with Christ is appropriate or justified?

Thinking, Talking, Writing

4. Are the war dead too soon forgotten?

ON A FIELD TRIP AT FREDERICKSBURG

Dave Smith

> *More than a century later, tourists are still going on pilgrimage to the battlefields—Shiloh, Gettysburg —of the Civil War. Countless books, movies, and television series reenact the turning points in the "great purging experience of the American people, their shame and their pride" (Denis Brogan). The following poem records the poet's mixed emotions on a field trip to Fredericksburg in Virginia, site of a Confederate victory in 1862. Dave Smith became known in the seventies and eighties for poems rooted, in the words of one editor, "in the southern soil." Smith grew up in Virginia, West Virginia, and Maryland, and he came to know well land that had been fought over in the Civil War. The Brady mentioned in the poem was a pioneering photographer who recorded many scenes of the war.*

The big steel tourist shield says maybe   1
fifteen thousand got it here. No word
of either Whitman or one uncle
I barely remember in the smoke
that filled his tiny mountain house.   5

If each finger were a thousand of them
I could clap my hands and be dead
up to my wrists. It was quick
though not so fast as we can do it
now, one bomb, atomic or worse,   10
the tiny pod slung on wingtip,
high up, an egg cradled
by some rapacious mockingbird.

Hiroshima canned nine times their number
in a flash. Few had the time   15
to moan or feel the feeling
ooze back in the groin.

In a ditch I stand
above Marye's Heights, the book-
bred faces of Brady's fifteen-year-old   20
drummers, before battle, rigid
as August's dandelions
all the way to the Potomac
rolling in my skull.

If Audubon came here, the names   25
of birds would gush, the marvel

single feathers make
evoke a cloud, a nation,
a gray blur preserved
on a blue horizon, but   *30*
there is only a wandering child,
one dark stalk snapped off
in her hand. Hopeless teacher,
I take it, try to help her
hold its obscure syllables   *35*
one instant in her mouth,
like a drift of wind
at the forehead, the front door,
the black, numb fingernails.

The Responsive Reader

1. What is irreverent about the language of the poem? How does the poet's language contrast with a more hushed or solemn style? Why do you think the poet is using irreverent language? Is he irreverent or disrespectful toward the dead?

2. What are striking examples of the poet's ability to bring his subject to life by wildly imaginative images? What effect do the poet's imaginative leaps to the bombing of Hiroshima or to the naturalist Audubon's paintings of birds have on you as the reader? How are these two passages related to the rest of the poem?

3. What is the role of the child in the poem? Why do you think the speaker in the poem calls himself "hopeless teacher"?

Thinking, Talking, Writing

4. Why have there been heated arguments about the nature and style of war memorials? For instance, what is the difference in style between the Vietnam memorial wall in Washington, DC, and a more recent memorial for American women who died in Vietnam?

APOSTROPHE TO MAN

Edna St. Vincent Millay

> *In the period between the two murderous World Wars (1918–1939), antiwar sentiment, antiwar art, and antiwar literature flourished in Europe and America. The German writer Erich Maria Remarque published his classic* All Quiet on the Western Front; *the French playwright Jean Giraudoux wrote* The Trojan War Will Not Take Place; *a British playwright wrote* Journey's End. *In the thirties, however, many voices warned that the warmongers were again gearing up for armed conflict. ("In the nightmare of the dark, all the dogs of Europe bark," wrote W. H. Auden in "September 1, 1939.") Edna St. Vincent Millay had been writing poems that were too frank and rebellious for tight-laced contemporaries but that appealed to readers attuned to her direct and frankly emotional style. She wrote the following angry indictment when the lights were about to go out in Europe.*

(on reflecting that the world is ready to go to war again)

Detestable race, continue to expunge yourself, die out.   1
Breed faster, crowd, encroach, sing hymns, build bombing airplanes;
Make speeches, unveil statues, issue bonds, parade;
Convert again into explosives the bewildered ammonia and
    the distracted cellulose;
Convert again into putrescent matter drawing flies   5
The hopeful bodies of the young; exhort,
Pray, pull long faces, be earnest, be all but overcome,
    be photographed;
Confer, perfect your formulae, commercialize
Bacteria harmful to human tissue,
Put death on the market;   10
Breed, crowd, encroach, expand, expunge yourself, die out,
Homo called *sapiens.*

The Responsive Reader

1. An apostrophe traditionally was a solemn speech or poem addressed to a godlike being or personified ideal, like Liberty or Justice. Why do you think the poet called this poem "Apostrophe to Man"?
2. A basic strategy of much antiwar literature between the wars was to juxtapose the uplifting language and solemn rituals glorifying war with the ghastly realities. How does the poem follow this pattern? What about war weighed particularly on the poet's mind?

3. What have ammonia and cellulose to do with war? Literally, these substances are inert, so why does the poet call them "bewildered" and "distracted"? Why does the poet remind us that the species *homo* is only called *sapiens?*

Thinking, Talking, Writing

4. Do you think this poet truly detested the human race?
5. At times in the nation's history, antiwar sentiment has been vocal and widespread. Have Americans become apathetic or cynical about war?

Collaborative Projects

6. What antiwar literature have you and your classmates read? What antiwar art do they know? Compare your exposure to or involvement with antiwar literature and art with that of your classmates.

PIANO AFTER WAR

Gwendolyn Brooks

Even if you are not ready for day
It cannot always be night.
                 Gwendolyn Brooks

*Gwendolyn Brooks wrote many of her poems about people in her imaginary
black community of Bronzeville, writing with special empathy and affection
about the elderly, the disabled, and children born into poverty. She published
increasingly politically committed poetry in the years of black militancy and
rebellion in the sixties and seventies. She gave writing workshops for members
of a street gang in Chicago. She wrote poems about the Emmett Till murders
and about race riots, starting the title poem of her collection Riot (1968) with
a quotation from Martin Luther King: "A riot is the language of the unheard."
She wrote the following poem in 1945, with the memory of those killed in
World War II fresh in her mind. The poem follows the pattern of the traditional
sonnet: fourteen lines divided into two sets of four (quatrains) and a concluding
set of six (sestet). The traditional sonnet has an interlaced rhyme scheme; here
the rhymes are only half-rhymes (fingers/hungers; pink/thank).*

On a snug evening I shall watch her fingers,   1
Cleverly ringed, declining to clever pink,
Beg glory from the willing keys. Old hungers
Will break their coffins, rise to eat and thank.
And music, warily, like the golden rose   5
That sometimes after sunset warms the west,
Will warm that room, persuasively suffuse
That room and me, rejuvenate a past.
But suddenly, across my climbing fever
Of proud delight—a multiplying cry.   10
A cry of bitter dead men who will never
Attend a gentle maker of musical joy.
Then my thawed eye will go again to ice.
And stone will shove the softness from my face.

The Responsive Reader

1. In the opening description of the woman playing the piano, are there
   any strange touches or false notes?
2. What "old hungers" rise from their coffins in this poem? What from
   the past is rejuvenated or brought back to life? What feelings and
   memories cluster around the piano recital for the poet?

3. Where is the turning point in this poem? What makes the poet's softened eyes "go again to ice"? What explains the bitterness in this poem?

Thinking, Talking, Writing

4. Many of Brooks' poems are harsh or bitter in tone. Do you think she is by temperament a bitter person?
5. Some believe that in times of war the pursuit of traditional culture (Bach, Beethoven, Mozart, Van Gogh, Picasso) becomes frivolous. It enables people to evade the true challenge of the times. Their retreat into traditional culture shows their indifference to human suffering. Others claim that in times of war culture is more necessary than ever to help people keep their faith in the human spirit. Music and art are needed to remind us of the human capacity for good. Which side are you inclined to take and why?

Thinking about Connections

6. Gwendolyn Brooks wrote the following poem as a companion poem to "Piano after War." How are the two poems related? What is similar and what is different about the way they treat the same theme?

mentors

For I am rightful fellow of their band.
My best allegiances are to the dead.
I swear to keep the dead upon my mind,
Disdain for all time to be overglad.
Among spring flowers, under summer trees,
By chilling autumn waters, in the frosts
Of supercilious winter—all my days
I'll have as mentors those reproving ghosts.
And at that cry, at that remotest whisper,
I'll stop my casual business. Leave the banquet.
Or leave the ball—reluctant to unclasp her
Who may be fragrant as the flower she wears,
Make gallant bows and dim excuses, then quit
Light for the midnight that is mine and theirs.

WHAT WERE THEY LIKE?

Denise Levertov

Denise Levertov writes passionate, provocative poems that challenge the reader to become emotionally involved. She writes in a tough-minded modern vein about the pain of living and the failure of human beings to live up to ideal standards. Levertov was born in England of Welsh and Jewish parentage. Her parents' house was visited by "Jewish booksellers, German theologians, Russian priests from Paris, and Viennese opera singers"; during World War II, it became a center for the support of Jewish refugees. After she married an American and moved to the United States, she became active in the Free Speech Movement at Berkeley and in the protest against the war in Vietnam. She has published many collections of her poetry and prose, including Jacob's Ladder *(1961),* O Taste and See *(1964),* Freeing of the Dust *(1975), and* Breathing the Water *(1987). The poem that follows is one of the most widely anthologized poems about the Vietnam War.*

1) Did the people of Vietnam   *1*
    use lanterns of stone?
2) Did they hold ceremonies
    to reverence the opening of buds?
3) Were they inclined to quiet laughter?   *5*
4) Did they use bone and ivory,
    jade and silver, for ornament?
5) Had they an epic poem?
6) Did they distinguish between speech and singing?

1) Sir, their light hearts turned to stone.   *10*
    It is not remembered whether in gardens
    stone lanterns illumined pleasant ways.
2) Perhaps they gathered once to delight in blossom,
    but after the children were killed
    there were no more buds.   *15*
3) Sir, laughter is bitter to the burned mouth.
4) A dream ago, perhaps. Ornament is for joy.
    All the bones were charred.
5) It is not remembered. Remember,
    most were peasants; their life   *20*
    was in rice and bamboo.
    When peaceful clouds were reflected in the paddies
    and the water buffalo stepped surely along terraces,
    maybe fathers told their sons old tales.
    When bombs smashed those mirrors   *25*
    there was time only to scream.

6) There is an echo yet
of their speech which was like a song.
It was reported their singing resembled
the flight of moths in moonlight.   *30*
Who can say? It is silent now.

The Responsive Reader

1. Why does the poem start with a series of questions? What kind of person is asking them?
2. What kind of person is answering the questions? What kind of answers does the second speaker give? What is the tone of the answers? Why is the poem written in a question-and-answer format?
3. How does the poem as a whole answer the question it asks in the title? What picture of the people emerges from the poem? What perspective on the war emerges from the poem?

Thinking, Talking, Writing

4. What do you know about the Vietnam War, and from what sources? What made it different from other wars in this nation's past?

Thinking about Connections

5. Is there a common thread in the antiwar poems by Millay, Brooks, and Levertov? How do they differ in focus or perspective? Which of them is for you most eloquent or persuasive, and why?

GETTYSBURG ADDRESS *and* SECOND INAUGURAL ADDRESS

Abraham Lincoln

I believe this government cannot endure permanently half slave and half free.

Abraham Lincoln

More has been written about President Lincoln than perhaps about anyone except Christ. Historians probing his role in American history have said that the country won its independence in the Revolutionary War, but that it was in the Civil War, eighty years later, that America was defined as a nation. The war became the nation's morality play, in which a mythical, larger-than-life leader "shoulders the nation's burdens and dies for its sins"—assassinated at the moment of victory on Good Friday of 1865 (Michael Skube).

As the self-educated son of a backwoods pioneer family, Abraham Lincoln became the embodiment of the American log cabin myth. He made his way as hired hand, rail splitter, storekeeper, postmaster, military officer, lawyer, and politician. Elected to Congress, he opposed the extension of slavery to new territories. As an unsuccessful candidate for senator for the newly formed Republican party, he engaged in a series of debates with Douglas, his Democratic opponent, that established his reputation as a formidable speaker and debater. In a speech launching his senatorial campaign, he accused the proslavery faction of perverting the right of self-government to mean "that if any one man choose to enslave another, no third man shall be allowed to object." He won the presidency on the Republican ticket in 1860, at a time when the South was preparing for secession. He became the legendary leader of the North in the war precipitated by the quarrel over the slavery issue.

The Battle of Gettysburg, fought during three days in July 1863, was a turning point in the middle of a war that was to claim more casualties than all other American wars together. The battlefield near the small Pennsylvania town of Gettysburg was covered with the rotting flesh and bones of men and boys. The state of Pennsylvania and other northern states organized a burial ceremony with much solemn oratory. Lincoln spoke for a few minutes after a long speech by one of the leading orators of the era. At a time when the outcome of an unpopular war was still in doubt, Lincoln's carefully phrased address summed up the purpose of the war and of the American nation in words quoted and remembered ever since.

At the time of Lincoln's inauguration for his second term in March 1865, victory in the war was at hand. On April 9, General Lee surrendered the Army of Virginia to Grant at Appomattox. On the night of April 14, Lincoln was assassinated by John Wilkes Booth while the president was attending a performance in Ford's Theater in the nation's capital.

Address at the Dedication of the Gettysburg National Cemetery

Four score and seven years ago our fathers brought forth on this continent, a new nation, conceived in Liberty, and dedicated to the proposition that all men are created equal.

Now we are engaged in a great civil war; testing whether that nation, or any nation so conceived and so dedicated, can long endure. We are met on a great battlefield of that war. We have come to dedicate a portion of that field as a final resting-place for those who here gave their lives that that nation might live. It is altogether fitting and proper that we should do this.

But, in a larger sense, we cannot dedicate—we cannot consecrate—we cannot hallow—this ground. The brave men, living and dead, who struggled here have consecrated it, far above our poor power to add or detract. The world will little note, nor long remember, what we say here, but it can never forget what they did here. It is for us the living, rather, to be dedicated here to the unfinished work which they who fought here have thus far so nobly advanced. It is rather for us to be here dedicated to the great task remaining before us—that from these honored dead we take increased devotion to that cause for which they gave the last full measure of devotion; that we here highly resolve that these dead shall not have died in vain; that this nation, under God, shall have a new birth of freedom; and that government of the people, by the people, for the people, shall not perish from the earth.

Second Inaugural Address

At this second appearing to take the oath of the presidential office, there is less occasion for an extended address than there was at the first. Then a statement, somewhat in detail, of a course to be pursued, seemed fitting and proper. Now, at the expiration of four years, during which public declarations have been constantly called forth on every point and phase of the great contest which still absorbs the attention and engrosses the energies of the nation, little that is new could be presented. The progress of our arms, upon which all else chiefly depends, is as well known to the public as to myself; and it is, I trust, reasonably satisfactory and encouraging to all. With high hope for the future, no prediction in regard to it is ventured.

On the occasion corresponding to this four years ago, all thoughts were anxiously directed to an impending civil war. All dreaded it—all sought to avert it. While the inaugural address was being delivered from this place, devoted altogether to saving the Union without war, insurgent agents were in the city seeking to destroy it without war—seeking to dissolve the Union, and divide effects, by negotiation. Both parties deprecated war; but one of them would make war rather than let the nation survive; and the other would accept war rather than let it perish. And the war came.

One-eighth of the whole population were colored slaves, not distributed generally over the Union, but localized in the Southern part of it. These slaves constituted a peculiar and powerful interest. All knew that this interest was, somehow, the cause of the war. To strengthen, perpetuate, and extend this interest was the object for which the insurgents would rend the Union, even by war; while the government claimed no right to do more than to restrict the territorial enlargement of it.

Neither party expected for the war the magnitude or the duration which it has already attained. Neither anticipated that the cause of the conflict might cease with, or even before, the conflict itself should cease. Each looked for an easier triumph, and a result less fundamental and astounding. Both read the same Bible, and pray to the same God; and each invokes his aid against the other. It may seem strange that any men should dare to ask a just God's assistance in wringing their bread from the sweat of other men's faces; but let us judge not, that we be not judged. The prayers of both could not be answered—that of neither has been answered fully.

The Almighty has his own purposes. "Woe unto the world because of offences! for it must needs be that offences come; but woe to that man by whom the offence cometh." If we shall suppose that American slavery is one of those offences which, in the providence of God, must needs come, but which, having continued through His appointed time, He now wills to remove, and that He gives to both North and South this terrible war, as the woe due to those by whom the offence came, shall we discern therein any departure from those divine attributes which the believers in a Living God always ascribe to Him? Fondly do we hope—fervently do we pray—that this mighty scourge of war may speedily pass away. Yet, if God wills that it continue until all the wealth piled by the bondman's two hundred and fifty years of unrequited toil shall be sunk, and until every drop of blood drawn with the lash shall be paid by another drawn with the sword, as was said three thousand years ago, so still it must be said, "The judgments of the Lord are true and righteous altogether."

With malice toward none; with charity for all; with firmness in the right, as God gives us to see the right, let us strive on to finish the work we are in; to bind up the nation's wounds; to care for him who shall have borne the battle, and for his widow, and his orphan—to do all which may achieve and cherish a just and lasting peace, among ourselves, and with all nations.

The Responsive Reader

1. A recent biographer of Lincoln says that the Gettysburg address "called up a new nation out of the blood and trauma" (Garry Wills). What key phrases in the speech sum up, in the words of one reader, "the way Americans conceive of themselves as a people"? What to you are the full implications of these key passages or key phrases? Are they still meaningful for the blasé modern reader today?

2. Lincoln delivered his second inaugural address in 1865, when victory over the remaining Confederate forces was in sight. The abolition of slavery had not been one of the original war aims of the Union.

According to this address, what *had* been the original objective of the Union? What key phrase in this speech sums up the Union's original stand on slavery?

3. Two years before Lincoln made this speech, he had published the Emancipation Proclamation freeing the slaves (January 1, 1863). Where and how does he express his condemnation of slavery in the inaugural address? Where and how does he express his feeling that the war might have been the retribution of an angry God for the offense of slavery?

4. Many listeners and readers have seen the second inaugural address as conciliatory, designed to heal the divisions caused by the war. What evidence in the speech can you cite in support of this view?

Thinking, Talking, Writing

5. Do Americans today have a chance to hear the side of the South? How or where?

6. African slaves were brought to this country as cheap exploited labor, but they were denied the rights of citizenship. Immigrants often perform menial labor today. Is there a parallel between our use of slave labor in the past and immigrant labor in the present? What is similar or what is different about the two situations?

Collaborative Projects

7. Ken Burns' public television series on the Civil War has attracted large audiences. Your class may want to farm out to small groups questions like the following: What does the series emphasize? What light does it shed on the causes of the war? What is its general perspective on the war? How does it treat the Southern side in the war? How does it treat the issue of slavery?

AN OCCURRENCE AT OWL CREEK BRIDGE

Ambrose Bierce

Like Mark Twain and Bret Harte—widely read storytellers of nineteenth-century America—Ambrose Bierce made a living as a journalist. He knew how to write the kind of story that appealed to the popular audience of his time. Although a story might contain some shrewd insights into human nature, it tended to emphasize plot rather than character. The story was likely to have melodramatic flourishes: Characters might act gallant or imperturbable ("cool") in the face of death. The author might stage tear-jerking separations from or reunions with loved ones. At the same time, the writer was likely to use a caustic, hard-nosed wit to show readers that he was nobody's fool. Readers loved the kind of twist that gave a story a surprise ending.

Bierce enlisted in the Union army as a drummer boy in the Indiana Infantry during the Civil War. He rose through the ranks, became a staff officer, and was wounded twice. He witnessed the battle at Shiloh and General Sherman's march to the sea. The war experience reinforced his pessimistic outlook on life, which explains his nickname, "Bitter Bierce." The Civil War story that follows was part of a collection of his stories published in 1891. It takes place after the Confederate army lost Corinth in Mississippi in 1862.

I

A man stood upon a railroad bridge in Northern Alabama, looking down into the swift waters twenty feet below. The man's hands were behind his back, the wrists bound with a cord. A rope loosely encircled his neck. It was attached to a stout cross-timber above his head, and the slack fell to the level of his knees. Some loose boards laid upon the sleepers supporting the metals of the railway supplied a footing for him and his executioners—two private soldiers of the Federal army, directed by a sergeant, who in civil life may have been a deputy sheriff. At a short remove upon the same temporary platform was an officer in the uniform of his rank, armed. He was a captain. A sentinel at each end of the bridge stood with his rifle in the position known as "support," that is to say, vertical in front of the left shoulder, the hammer resting on the forearm thrown straight across the chest—a formal and unnatural position, enforcing an erect carriage of the body. It did not appear to be the duty of these two men to know what was occurring at the centre of the bridge; they merely blockaded the two ends of the foot plank which traversed it.

Beyond one of the sentinels nobody was in sight; the railroad ran straight away into a forest for a hundred yards, then, curving, was lost to view. Doubtless there was an outpost further along. The other bank of the stream was open ground—a gentle acclivity crowned with a stockade of vertical tree trunks, loop-holed for rifles, with a single embrasure through which protruded the muzzle of a brass cannon commanding the bridge. Midway of the slope between bridge and fort were the spectators—a single company of infantry in line, at "parade rest," the butts of the rifles on the ground, the barrels inclining slightly backward against the right shoulder, the hands crossed upon the stock. A lieutenant stood at the right of the line, the point of his sword upon the ground, his left hand resting upon his right. Excepting the group of four at the centre of the bridge not a man moved. The company faced the bridge, staring stonily, motionless. The sentinels, facing the banks of the stream, might have been statues to adorn the bridge. The captain stood with folded arms, silent, observing the work of his subordinates but making no sign. Death is a dignitary who, when he comes announced, is to be received with formal manifestations of respect, even by those most familiar with him. In the code of military etiquette silence and fixity are forms of deference.

The man who was engaged in being hanged was apparently about thirty-five years of age. He was a civilian, if one might judge from his dress, which was that of a planter. His features were good—a straight nose, firm mouth, broad forehead, from which his long, dark hair was combed straight back, falling behind his ears to the collar of his well-fitting frock coat. He wore a moustache and pointed beard, but no whiskers; his eyes were large and dark grey and had a kindly expression which one would hardly have expected in one whose neck was in the hemp. Evidently this was no vulgar assassin. The liberal military code makes provision for hanging many kinds of people, and gentlemen are not excluded.

The preparations being complete, the two private soldiers stepped aside and each drew away the plank upon which he had been standing. The sergeant turned to the captain, saluted and placed himself immediately behind that officer, who in turn moved apart one pace. These movements left the condemned man and the sergeant standing on the two ends of the same plank, which spanned three of the cross-ties of the bridge. The end upon which the civilian stood almost, but not quite, reached a fourth. This plank had been held in place by the weight of the captain; it was now held by that of the sergeant. At a signal from the former, the latter would step aside, the plank would tilt and the condemned man go down between two ties. The arrangement commended itself to his judgment as simple and effective. His face had not been covered nor his eyes bandaged. He looked a moment at his "unsteadfast footing," then let his gaze wander to the swirling water of the stream racing madly beneath his feet. A piece of dancing driftwood caught his attention and his eyes followed it down the current. How slowly it appeared to move! What a sluggish stream!

He closed his eyes in order to fix his last thoughts upon his wife and children. The water, touched to gold by the early sun, the brooding mists under the banks at some distance down the stream, the fort, the soldiers, the 5 piece of drift—all had distracted him. And now he became conscious of a new disturbance. Striking through the thought of his dear ones was a sound which he could neither ignore nor understand, a sharp, distinct, metallic percussion like the stroke of a blacksmith's hammer upon the anvil; it had the same ringing quality. He wondered what it was, and whether immeasurably distant or near by—it seemed both. Its recurrence was regular, but as slow as the tolling of a death knell. He awaited each stroke with impatience and—he knew not why—apprehension. The intervals of silence grew progressively longer, the delays became maddening. With their greater infrequency the sounds increased in strength and sharpness. They hurt his ear like the thrust of a knife; he feared he would shriek. What he heard was the ticking of his watch.

He unclosed his eyes and saw again the water below him. "If I could free my hands," he thought, "I might throw off the noose and spring into the stream. By diving I could evade the bullets, and, swimming vigorously, reach the bank, take to the woods, and get away home. My home, thank God, is as yet outside their lines; my wife and little ones are still beyond the invader's farthest advance."

As these thoughts, which have here to be set down in words, were flashed into the doomed man's brain rather than evolved from it, the captain nodded to the sergeant. The sergeant stepped aside.

II

Peyton Farquhar was a well-to-do planter, of an old and highly-respected Alabama family. Being a slave owner, and, like other slave owners, a politician, he was naturally an original secessionist and ardently devoted to the Southern cause. Circumstances of an imperious nature which it is unnecessary to relate here, had prevented him from taking service with the gallant army which had fought the disastrous campaigns ending with the fall of Corinth, and he chafed under the inglorious restraint, longing for the release of his energies, the larger life of the soldier, the opportunity for distinction. That opportunity, he felt, would come, as it comes to all in war time. Meanwhile he did what he could. No service was too humble for him to perform in aid of the South, no adventure too perilous for him to undertake if consistent with the character of a civilian who was at heart a soldier, and who in good faith and without too much qualification assented to at least a part of the frankly villainous dictum that all is fair in love and war.

One evening while Farquhar and his wife were sitting on a rustic bench near the entrance to his grounds, a grey-clad soldier rode up to the gate and asked for a drink of water. Mrs. Farquhar was only too happy to serve him with her own white hands. While she was gone to fetch the water, her husband approached the dusty horseman and inquired eagerly for news from the front.

"The Yanks are repairing the railroads," said the man, "and are getting *10* ready for another advance. They have reached the Owl Creek bridge, put it in order, and built a stockade on the other bank. The commandant has issued an order, which is posted everywhere, declaring that any civilian caught interfering with the railroad, its bridges, tunnels, or trains, will be summarily hanged. I saw the order."

"How far is it to the Owl Creek bridge?" Farquhar asked.

"About thirty miles."

"Is there no force on this side the creek?"

"Only a picket post half a mile out, on the railroad, and a single sentinel at this end of the bridge."

"Suppose a man—a civilian and student of hanging—should elude the picket post and perhaps get the better of the sentinel," said Farquhar, smiling, "what could he accomplish?"   *15*

The soldier reflected. "I was there a month ago," he replied. "I observed that the flood of last winter had lodged a great quantity of driftwood against the wooden pier at this end of the bridge. It is now dry and would burn like tow."

The lady had now brought the water, which the soldier drank. He thanked her ceremoniously, bowed to her husband, and rode away. An hour later, after nightfall, he repassed the plantation, going northward in the direction from which he had come. He was a Federal scout.

III

As Peyton Farquhar fell straight downward through the bridge, he lost consciousness and was as one already dead. From this state he was awakened—ages later, it seemed to him—by the pain of a sharp pressure upon his throat, followed by a sense of suffocation. Keen, poignant agonies seemed to shoot from his neck downward through every fibre of his body and limbs. These pains appeared to flash along well-defined lines of ramification, and to beat with an inconceivably rapid periodicity. They seemed like streams of pulsating fire heating him to an intolerable temperature. As to his head, he was conscious of nothing but a feeling of fullness—of congestion. These sensations were unaccompanied by thought. The intellectual part of his nature was already effaced; he had power only to feel, and feeling was torment. He was conscious of motion. Encompassed in a luminous cloud, of which he was now merely the fiery heart, without material substance, he swung through unthinkable arcs of oscillation, like a vast pendulum. Then all at once, with terrible suddenness, the light about him shot upward with the noise of a loud plash; a frightful roaring was in his ears, and all was cold and dark. The power of thought was restored; he knew that the rope had broken and he had fallen into the stream. There was no additional strangulation; the noose about his neck was already suffocating him, and kept the water from his lungs. To die of hanging at the bottom of a river!—the idea seemed to him ludicrous. He opened his eyes in the blackness and saw above him a gleam of light, but how distant, how inaccessible! He was still sinking, for the light became fainter and fainter until it was a mere glimmer. Then it began to grow and brighten, and he knew that he was rising toward the surface—knew it with reluctance, for he was now very comfortable. "To be hanged and drowned," he thought, "that is not so bad; but I do not wish to be shot. No; I will not be shot; that is not fair."

He was not conscious of an effort, but a sharp pain in his wrist apprised him that he was trying to free his hands. He gave the struggle his attention, as an idler might observe the feat of a juggler, without interest in the outcome. What splendid effort!—what magnificent, what superhuman strength! Ah, that was a fine endeavour! Bravo! The cord fell away; his arms parted and floated upward, the hands dimly seen on each side in the growing light. He watched them with a new interest as first one and then the other pounced upon the noose at his neck. They tore it away and thrust it fiercely aside, its undulations resembling those of a water-snake. "Put it back, put it back!" He thought he shouted these words to his hands, for the undoing of the noose had been succeeded by the direst pang which he had yet experienced. His neck ached horribly; his brain was on fire; his heart, which had been fluttering faintly, gave a great leap, trying to force itself out at his mouth. His whole body was racked and wrenched with an insupportable anguish! But his disobedient hands gave no heed to the command. They beat the water vigorously with quick, downward strokes, forcing him to the surface. He felt his head emerge; his eyes were blinded by the sunlight; his chest expanded convulsively, and with a supreme and crowning agony his lungs engulfed a great draught of air, which instantly he expelled in a shriek!

He was now in full possession of his physical senses. They were, indeed, preternaturally keen and alert. Something in the awful disturbance of his organic system had so exalted and refined them that they made record of things never before perceived. He felt the ripples upon his face and heard their separate sounds as they struck. He looked at the forest on the bank of the stream, saw the individual trees, the leaves and the veining of each leaf— the very insects upon them, the locusts, the brilliant-bodied flies, the grey spiders stretching their webs from twig to twig. He noted the prismatic colors in all the dewdrops upon a million blades of grass. The humming of the gnats that danced above the eddies of the stream, the beating of the dragon flies' wings, the strokes of the water spiders' legs, like oars which had lifted their boat—all these made audible music. A fish slid along beneath his eyes and he heard the rush of its body parting the water. 20

He had come to the surface facing down the stream; in a moment the visible world seemed to wheel slowly round, himself the pivotal point, and he saw the bridge, the fort, the soldiers upon the bridge, the captain, the sergeant, the two privates, his executioners. They were in silhouette against the blue sky. They shouted and gesticulated, pointing at him; the captain had drawn his pistol, but did not fire; the others were unarmed. Their movements were grotesque and horrible, their forms gigantic.

Suddenly he heard a sharp report and something struck the water smartly within a few inches of his head, spattering his face with spray. He heard a second report, and saw one of the sentinels with his rifle at his shoulder, a light cloud of blue smoke rising from the muzzle. The man in the water saw the eye of the man on the bridge gazing into his own through the sights of the rifle. He observed that it was a grey eye, and remembered having read that grey eyes were keenest and that all famous marksmen had them. Nevertheless, this one had missed.

A counter swirl had caught Farquhar and turned him half round; he was again looking into the forest on the bank opposite the fort. The sound of a clear, high voice in a monotonous singsong now rang out behind him and came across the water with a distinctness that pierced and subdued all other sounds, even the beating of the ripples in his ears. Although no soldier, he had frequented camps enough to know the dread significance of that deliberate, drawling, aspirated chant; the lieutenant on shore was taking a part in the morning's work. How coldly and pitilessly—with what an even, calm intonation, presaging and enforcing tranquility in the men—with what accurately-measured intervals fell those cruel words:

"Attention, company. . . . Shoulder arms. . . . Ready. . . . Aim. . . . Fire."

Farquhar dived—dived as deeply as he could. The water roared in his ears like the voice of Niagara, yet he heard the dulled thunder of the volley, and rising again toward the surface, met shining bits of metal, singularly flattened, oscillating slowly downward. Some of them touched him on the face and hands, then fell away, continuing their descent. One lodged between his collar and neck; it was uncomfortably warm, and he snatched it out.

As he rose to the surface, gasping for breath, he saw that he had been a long time under water; he was perceptibly farther down stream—nearer to safety. The soldiers had almost finished reloading; the metal ramrods flashed all at once in the sunshine as they were drawn from the barrels, turned in the air, and thrust into their sockets. The two sentinels fired again, independently and ineffectually.

The hunted man saw all this over his shoulder; he was now swimming vigorously with the current. His brain was as energetic as his arms and legs; he thought with the rapidity of lightning.

"The officer," he reasoned, "will not make that martinet's error a second time. It is as easy to dodge a volley as a single shot. He has probably already given the command to fire at will. God help me, I cannot dodge them all!"

An appalling plash within two yards of him, followed by a loud rushing sound, *diminuendo,* which seemed to travel back through the air to the fort and died in an explosion which stirred the very river to its deeps! A rising sheet of water, which curved over him, fell down upon him, blinded him, strangled him! The cannon had taken a hand in the game. As he shook his head free from the commotion of the smitten water, he heard the deflected

25

shot humming through the air ahead, and in an instant it was cracking and smashing the branches in the forest beyond.

"They will not do that again," he thought; "the next time they will use *30* a charge of grape. I must keep my eye upon the gun; the smoke will apprise me—the report arrives too late; it lags behind the missile. It is a good gun."

Suddenly he felt himself whirled round and round—spinning like a top. The water, the banks, the forest, the now distant bridge, fort and men—all were commingled and blurred. Objects were represented by their colors only; circular horizontal streaks of color—that was all he saw. He had been caught in a vortex and was being whirled on with a velocity of advance and gyration which made him giddy and sick. In a few moments he was flung upon the gravel at the foot of the left bank of the stream—the southern bank—and behind a projecting point which concealed him from his enemies. The sudden arrest of his motion, the abrasion of one of his hands on the gravel, restored him and he wept with delight. He dug his fingers into the sand, threw it over himself in handfuls and audibly blessed it. It looked like gold, like diamonds, rubies, emeralds; he could think of nothing beautiful which it did not resemble. The trees upon the bank were giant garden plants; he noted a definite order in their arrangement, inhaled the fragrance of their blooms. A strange, roseate light shone through the spaces among their trunks, and the wind made in their branches the music of æolian harps. He had no wish to perfect his escape, was content to remain in that enchanting spot until retaken.

A whizz and rattle of grapeshot among the branches high above his head roused him from his dream. The baffled cannoneer had fired him a random farewell. He sprang to his feet, rushed up the sloping bank, and plunged into the forest.

All that day he travelled, laying his course by the rounding sun. The forest seemed interminable; nowhere did he discover a break in it, not even a woodman's road. He had not known that he lived in so wild a region. There was something uncanny in the revelation.

By nightfall he was fatigued, footsore, famishing. The thought of his wife and children urged him on. At last he found a road which led him in what he knew to be the right direction. It was as wide and straight as a city street, yet it seemed untravelled. No fields bordered it, no dwelling anywhere. Not so much as the barking of a dog suggested human habitation. The black bodies of the great trees formed a straight wall on both sides, terminating on the horizon in a point, like a diagram in a lesson in perspective. Overhead, as he looked up through this rift in the wood, shone great golden stars looking unfamiliar and grouped in strange constellations. He was sure they were arranged in some order which had a secret and malign significance. The wood on either side was full of singular noises, among which— once, twice, and again—he distinctly heard whispers in an unknown tongue.

His neck was in pain, and, lifting his hand to it, he found it horribly *35* swollen. He knew that it had a circle of black where the rope had bruised it.

His eyes felt congested; he could no longer close them. His tongue was swollen with thirst; he relieved its fever by thrusting it forward from between his teeth into the cool air. How softly the turf had carpeted the untravelled avenue! He could no longer feel the roadway beneath his feet!

Doubtless, despite his suffering, he fell asleep while walking, for now he sees another scene—perhaps he has merely recovered from a delirium. He stands at the gate of his own home. All is as he left it, and all bright and beautiful in the morning sunshine. He must have travelled the entire night. As he pushes open the gate and passes up the wide white walk, he sees a flutter of female garments; his wife, looking fresh and cool and sweet, steps down from the verandah to meet him. At the bottom of the steps she stands waiting, with a smile of ineffable joy, an attitude of matchless grace and dignity. Ah, how beautiful she is! He springs forward with extended arms. As he is about to clasp her, he feels a stunning blow upon the back of the neck; a blinding white light blazes all about him, with a sound like the shock of a cannon—then all is darkness and silence!

Peyton Farquhar was dead; his body, with a broken neck, swung gently from side to side beneath the timbers of the Owl Creek bridge.

The Responsive Reader

1. Bierce tells us that Farquhar was no "vulgar assassin"—he was not low-class or uneducated. What else do we learn about him? What kind of portrait of the condemned man does the author paint? Is it hostile, sympathetic, indifferent?
2. What picture do we get of the executioners? Why is the author so pedantically accurate about the details of the arrangements? Does the story imply a judgment on the officers and soldiers carrying out the execution? What do you think is the author's attitude toward the military?
3. Did you allow yourself to be carried away by the excitement of the apparent escape by the doomed man? Why or why not?
4. Why did the author delay his revelation of the truth till the very last moment?
5. Bierce was known for his bitter sense of irony and his sardonic wit. Do they show in this story?

Thinking, Talking, Writing

6. Bierce fought on the Union or Federal side. Is it paradoxical that the central character in his story is a Southerner—one of the original supporters of secession from the Union and "ardently devoted to the Southern cause"?
7. Does this story make a statement about war? Or is it masterfully concocted entertainment?

8. The British writer George Orwell once said that even antiwar books are at some deeper level pro-war. They stimulate the atavistic, primitive instincts of aggression and fear. They make us experience the sick thrill of bloodletting and violence. What attitudes toward war were acted out in war movies you have seen?

IN ANOTHER COUNTRY
Ernest Hemingway

Ernest Hemingway may be, after Mark Twain, the most widely read and admired American around the world. He was for a long time a giant among writers of twentieth century fiction, until he was stereotyped as perpetuating a macho pose and his reputation waned.

Hemingway was part of a post–World War I generation radically disillusioned with and distrustful of language. Like others of his time, he had come to hate high-flown language used to justify the death and maiming in an insane war between nations whose aristocratic, militaristic traditions were very much alike. He had taken part in World War I as an American volunteer serving on the side of the Allies. He served as an ambulance driver in Italy, where the following story takes place. The experience left him with an abiding disgust with corrupt patriotic rhetoric. (War propaganda, said George Orwell, a fellow truth teller, "makes thinking people sympathize with the enemy.") The characters in Hemingway's novels and short stories often kept silent—not because they were inarticulate, but because they were sickened by "all that talking."

One way Hemingway tried to serve the truth was his loving attention to concrete details that do not lie. He was a master at recreating the way things look and feel and smell. He was a shrewd observer of the little gestures that reveal what people think or feel. Even so, he was always looking for a way courage, loyalty, and human solidarity could survive in a world that had lost faith in these and other abstractions. His books, read by millions around the world, include The Sun Also Rises *(1926),* A Farewell to Arms *(1929),* For Whom the Bell Tolls *(1940), and* The Old Man and the Sea *(1953). Hemingway cultivated the image of the hunter, the bullfight aficionado, and the deep-sea fisherman, and he killed himself with a shotgun blast to the head. He has been accused of cultivating a superficial macho mystique. However, some of his best stories are about men struggling to assert their sense of manhood and the women who have to put up with them. Some think that as a writer of the modern short story Hemingway remains unsurpassed.*

In the fall the war was always there, but we did not go to it any more. *1*
It was cold in the fall in Milan and the dark came very early. Then the electric lights came on, and it was pleasant along the streets looking in the windows. There was much game hanging outside the shops, and the snow powdered in the fur of the foxes and the wind blew their tails. The deer hung stiff and heavy and empty, and small birds blew in the wind and the wind turned their feathers. It was a cold fall and the wind came down from the mountains.

We were all at the hospital every afternoon, and there were different ways of walking across the town through the dusk to the hospital. Two of the ways were alongside canals, but they were long. Always, though, you crossed a bridge across a canal to enter the hospital. There was a choice of three bridges. On one of them a woman sold roasted chestnuts. It was warm, standing in front of her charcoal fire, and the chestnuts were warm afterward in your pocket. The hospital was very old and very beautiful, and you entered through a gate and walked across a courtyard and out a gate on the other side. There were usually funerals starting from the courtyard. Beyond the old hospital were the new brick pavilions, and there we met every afternoon and were all very polite and interested in what was the matter, and sat in the machines that were to make so much difference.

The doctor came up to the machine where I was sitting and said: "What did you like best to do before the war? Did you practice a sport?"

I said: "Yes, football."

"Good," he said. "You will be able to play football again better than ever."   5

My knee did not bend and the leg dropped straight from the knee to the ankle without a calf, and the machine was to bend the knee and make it move as in riding a tricycle. But it did not bend yet, and instead the machine lurched when it came to the bending part. The doctor said: "That will all pass. You are a fortunate young man. You will play football again like a champion."

In the next machine was a major who had a little hand like a baby's. He winked at me when the doctor examined his hand, which was between two leather straps that bounced up and down and flapped the stiff fingers, and said: "And will I too play football, captain-doctor?" He had been a very great fencer, and before the war the greatest fencer in Italy.

The doctor went to his office in a back room and brought a photograph which showed a hand that had been withered almost as small as the major's, before it had taken a machine course, and after was a little larger. The major held the photograph with his good hand and looked at it very carefully. "A wound?" he asked.

"An industrial accident," the doctor said.

"Very interesting, very interesting," the major said, and handed it back   10
to the doctor.

"You have confidence?"

"No," said the major.

There were three boys who came each day who were about the same age I was. They were all three from Milan, and one of them was to be a lawyer, and one was to be a painter, and one had intended to be a soldier, and after we were finished with the machines, sometimes we walked back together to the Café Cova, which was next door to the Scala. We walked the short way through the communist quarter because we were four together. The people hated us because we were officers, and from a wine-shop some one would call out, "A basso gli ufficiali!" as we passed. Another boy who walked with us sometimes and made us five wore a black silk handkerchief across his face because he had no nose then and his face was to be rebuilt. He had gone out to the front from the military academy and been wounded within an hour after he had gone into the front line for the first time. They rebuilt his face, but he came from a very old family and they could never get the nose exactly right. He went to South America and worked in a bank. But this was a long time ago, and then we did not any of us know how it was going to be afterward. We only knew then that there was always the war, but that we were not going to it any more.

We all had the same medals, except the boy with the black silk bandage across his face, and he had not been at the front long enough to get any medals. The tall boy with a very pale face who was to be a lawyer had been a lieutenant of Arditi and had three medals of the sort we each had only one of. He had lived a very long time with death and was a little detached. We were all a little detached, and there was nothing that held us together except that we met every afternoon at the hospital. Although, as we walked to the Cova through the tough part of town, walking in the dark, with light and singing coming out of the wine-shops, and sometimes having to walk into the street when the men and women would crowd together on the sidewalk so that we would have had to jostle them to get by, we felt held together by there being something that had happened that they, the people who disliked us, did not understand.

We ourselves all understood the Cova, where it was rich and warm and not too brightly lighted, and noisy and smoky at certain hours, and there were always girls at the tables and the illustrated papers on a rack on the wall. The girls at the Cova were very patriotic, and I found that the most patriotic people in Italy were the café girls—and I believe they are still patriotic.   *15*

The boys at first were very polite about my medals and asked me what I had done to get them. I showed them the papers, which were written in very beautiful language and full of *fratellanza* and *abnegazione,* but which really said, with the adjectives removed, that I had been given the medals because I was an American. After that their manner changed a little toward me, although I was their friend against outsiders. I was a friend, but I was never really one of them after they had read the citations, because it had been different with them and they had done very different things to get their medals. I had been wounded, it was true; but we all knew that being wounded, after all, was really an accident. I was never ashamed of the ribbons, though, and sometimes, after the cocktail hour, I would imagine myself having done all the things they had done to get their medals; but walking home at night through the empty streets with the cold wind and all the shops closed, trying to keep near the street lights, I knew that I would never have done such things, and I was very much afraid to die, and often lay in bed at night by myself, afraid to die and wondering how I would be when I went back to the front again.

The three with the medals were like hunting-hawks; and I was not a hawk, although I might seem a hawk to those who had never hunted; they, the three, knew better and so we drifted apart. But I stayed good friends with the boy who had been wounded his first day at the front, because he would never know now how he would have turned out; so he could never be accepted either, and I liked him because I thought perhaps he would not have turned out to be a hawk either.

The major, who had been the great fencer, did not believe in bravery, and spent much time while we sat in the machines correcting my grammar. He had complimented me on how I spoke Italian, and we talked together very easily. One day I had said that Italian seemed such an easy language to me that I could not take a great interest in it; everything was so easy to say. "Ah, yes," the major said. "Why, then, do you not take up the use of grammar?" So we took up the use of grammar, and soon Italian was such a difficult language that I was afraid to talk to him until I had the grammar straight in my mind.

The major came very regularly to the hospital. I do not think he ever missed a day, although I am sure he did not believe in the machines. There was a time when none of us believed in the machines, and one day the major said it was all nonsense. The machines were new then and it was we who were to prove them. It was an idiotic idea, he said, "a theory, like another." I had not learned my grammar, and he said I was a stupid impossible disgrace, and he was a fool to have bothered with me. He was a small man and he sat straight up in his chair with his right hand thrust into the machine and looked straight ahead at the wall while the straps thumped up and down with his fingers in them.

"What will you do when the war is over if it is over?" he asked me.   20
"Speak grammatically!"

"I will go to the States."

"Are you married?"

"No, but I hope to be."

"The more of a fool you are," he said. He seemed very angry. "A man must not marry."

"Why, Signor Maggiore?"   25

"Don't call me 'Signor Maggiore.' "

"Why must not a man marry?"

"He cannot marry. He cannot marry," he said angrily. "If he is to lose everything, he should not place himself in a position to lose that. He should not place himself in a position to lose. He should find things he cannot lose."

He spoke very angrily and bitterly, and looked straight ahead while he talked.

"But why should he necessarily lose it?"   30

"He'll lose it," the major said. He was looking at the wall. Then he looked down at the machine and jerked his little hand out from between the straps and slapped it hard against his thigh. "He'll lose it," he almost shouted.

"Don't argue with me!" Then he called to the attendant who ran the machines. "Come and turn this damned thing off."

He went back into the other room for the light treatment and the massage. Then I heard him ask the doctor if he might use his telephone and he shut the door. When he came back into the room, I was sitting in another machine. He was wearing his cape and had his cap on, and he came directly toward my machine and put his arm on my shoulder.

"I am so sorry," he said, and patted me on the shoulder with his good hand. "I would not be rude. My wife has just died. You must forgive me."

"Oh—" I said, feeling sick for him. "I am *so* sorry."

He stood there biting his lower lip. "It is very difficult," he said. "I   35
cannot resign myself."

He looked straight past me and out through the window. Then he began to cry. "I am utterly unable to resign myself," he said and choked. And then crying, his head up looking at nothing, carrying himself straight and soldierly, with tears on both his cheeks and biting his lips, he walked past the machines and out the door.

The doctor told me that the major's wife, who was very young and whom he had not married until he was definitely invalided out of the war, had died of pneumonia. She had been sick only a few days. No one expected her to die. The major did not come to the hospital for three days. Then he came at the usual hour, wearing a black band on the sleeve of his uniform. When he came back, there were large framed photographs around the wall, of all sorts of wounds before and after they had been cured by the machines. In front of the machine the major used were three photographs of hands like his that were completely restored. I do not know where the doctor got them. I always understood we were the first to use the machines. The photographs did not make much difference to the major because he only looked out of the window.

The Responsive Reader

1. Hemingway often recreates the setting of his stories in loving detail. What details help bring the city and the institution to life for you? Is there a connecting thread or prevailing mood?
2. Who is telling the story? What kind of person is he? What clues does the story provide to his history and situation?
3. Irony often exploits the contrast between ideal and reality, or between wishful thinking and the harsh facts. Can you show that this kind of irony pervades the story? What are outstanding examples?
4. What role does the major play in the story? What kind of foil does he provide for the narrator—what kind of revealing contrast that makes features of the central character stand out? What are the storyteller's feelings toward the major? How do you think the author expects you as the reader to feel toward him?

Thinking, Talking, Writing

5. As in other Hemingway stories, much of what the characters think and feel remains unsaid. Write a monologue in which the young American would pour out his feelings about the war, about the hospital, about the therapy, and about his fellow patients.
6. Do you feel that people tend to be too tongue-tied when it comes to expressing their true feelings? Or do you feel that people tend to be too gushy and sentimental?
7. World War I meant for many writers and artists the kind of trauma that the Vietnam War meant for a later generation. What do you know about the First World War, and how did you learn about it? How is the role the war plays in this story different from the way it is often treated or described?

INTERNMENT CAMP HAIKU

Violet Kazue Matsuda

World War II started with the German invasion of Poland in 1939. It developed into a worldwide conflagration in which an estimated 55 million died. There is no way to take a count of the people maimed, the families destroyed, the cities reduced to rubble, and human hopes reduced to ashes. The United States entered the war with the bombing of Pearl Harbor by the Japanese in 1941. It stayed in the war until the surrender of Nazi Germany after the Red Army took Berlin and finally of Imperial Japan after atomic bombs leveled Hiroshima and Nagasaki in 1945.

An enduring symbol of the World War II era and its aftermath was the camp. Hitler's Germany built concentration camps to "reeducate" communists, socialists, intellectuals, artists, homosexuals, and "antisocial elements." It built the death camps to which an army of henchmen, informers, and bureaucratic paper pushers sent more than five million Jewish men, women, and children. Millions of captured Russian and German soldiers died in prisoner-of-war camps. Japanese prisoner-of-war camps became a byword for malnutrition and abuse. Russian prisoners of war who survived the conflict were accused of having collaborated with the Nazis and disappeared into the camps of Stalin's Gulag Archipelago.

After the outbreak of the war in the Pacific, the US government evacuated more than 120,000 persons of Japanese ancestry to detention camps, removing them forcibly from their communities, businesses, and schools. (Many were drafted from the camps into the American army.) In her "poetic reflections" on life in the camps, Violet Kazue Matsuda recreates for today's reader the sense of injustice and hopelessness felt by the inmates of the "relocation camps," many of whom were American-born and American citizens. Born in Hawaii, Matsuda had her first five years of schooling in Japan and then attended high school and college in California. During the war, her husband and son were both classified as "enemy aliens," and after the war she was "expatriated" to Japan. Her Japanese husband had never registered his American marriage in Japan and was thus legally free to abandon her and take a Japanese wife. She remarried and made her way back to the United States.

She called her poems about camp life free-form haiku. They do not follow the elaborate rules of the traditional haiku, which alternates lines of five, seven, and five syllables for a total of seventeen syllables. However, like the traditional haiku, these poems capture a moment in time. They leave the reader with a memorable, thought-provoking image. The following are the poet's own rendering into English prose of the original Japanese poems.

Dandelions

The Tule Lake "Segregation Center" was built on volcanic ashes in the   *1*
desolate lava beds of northern California, near the Oregon border. During
the spring and summer it was very dry and dusty, and in the winter it was a
muddy swamp, making it impossible for the internees to walk to the mess
hall and to the communal washroom and toilet facilities. This condition
made it necessary for the internees to build wooden catwalks connecting the
barracks and the facilities serving them.

After the long and harsh winter dandelions sprang up between the
wooden planks of the catwalks only to be stepped on by passers-by. One day,
as if by a miracle, I found just one perfect dandelion among the many which
had been crushed—as the down-trodden internees had been trampled underfoot by circumstances. As each day was a reminder of the humiliating and
oppressive existence we were forced to endure, this one perfectly blooming
dandelion was a symbol which inspired and fortified me. The pleasure I
derived from this one blossom filled me with determination to endure the
harsh conditions of camp life and to overcome all obstacles and difficulties.

Sun Rays

The arrival of spring and summer is typically late in the high plains of
Tule Lake, the largest of the ten internment camps built to house more than
eighteen thousand detainees on about six square miles of black volcanic ash.

After the long, gloomy winter days the intense glare of summer creates
a strong contrast and makes the low, dark, tar-papered barracks seem even
more dismal and disheartening for the internees.

Brother's Imprisonment

The November 4, 1943, warehouse incident, caused by reports of thefts   *5*
of food for the internees by War Relocation Authority (WRA) personnel,
resulted in confrontations and disturbances at Tule Lake.

Brother Tokio, an innocent bystander, had been asked to help restore
order among the agitators. As he was about to do so, he was arrested by
WRA Internal Security personnel and accused of taking part in the disorder.
During a night of brutal interrogation he was cruelly beaten and, not only
was he denied medical treatment for his injuries, but he was imprisoned in
the "Bull Pen" of the camp stockade—a place of maximum punishment for
serious offenders.

Following the occurrence army troops took over control of the camp
and martial law was declared at Tule Lake.

Then came spring, the snow melted and the Tule reeds sprouted and
grew. By July the reeds even had blossoms. Brother Tokio was still confined
in the "Bull Pen," after nine months of imprisonment without trial or a
hearing. Fall was about to come again and, under those conditions of dark

uncertainty and desperation, everything was measured in terms of the growth and death of the Tule reeds.

Harsh Summer

After a short spring, the severe summer heat of the high plateau reflected from the black volcanic ash became unbearable, especially to one allergic to the wild grasses, weeds, and to the abundant dust to Tule Lake.

Every day was one of emotional and physical illness, of inner struggle, and of resignation.   *10*

Visitor

A priest friend was finally transferred to Tule Lake after being incarcerated in several isolation camps as a result of reports by WRA informers, including some of the so-called community analysts and researchers.

His visit to me brought happiness and tranquility, but also the realization that the summertime ground was still monotonously flat—that nothing had really changed.

Bare Feet

I frequently walked the lonely path leading to the hospital area to visit my dying mother-in-law terminally ill with cancer.

One day, while kicking the black volcanic ash off my sandals, I noticed for the first time my bare white feet. With aching heart, and challenging the war and the elements, I realized the monotony and the futility of our existence.

Autumn Sky/War

Fall comes early to the lava beds of Tule Lake and by September the   *15* weather turns blustery, with sudden storms blanketing the area. The dismal autumn sky relates to my thoughts about the war and I become aware that it is the war our lives depend on. What is happening to the war? How many tears must I shed until it ends? What is befalling my parents in Hiroshima City?

Spider Web

My baby is taking a nap and soon I shall leave for the camp hospital to see my dying mother-in-law, who is still waiting to hear from her only son interned in the Santa Fe camp. Letters to my husband and his letters to me, and to his mother, are censored and news is scanty. What shall I tell her today?

This is the third year the Tule Lake Segregation Center has been in operation and even the spider webs have turned black. What a long confinement it has been in our barren room where even a spider web focuses my attention!

Cosmos Flowers

One autumn day, on my way to the hospital, I saw an elderly man tending his flower garden. He was picking and discarding the wilting cosmos flowers, wrenching them out at times but with no visible signs of emotion. Ojisan probably had only the flowers for solace, as many of us did during the four years of confinement. I watched him awhile then walked away without saying anything to him, but a sense of compassion and affinity permeated me as I left him in his own world of nature.

Shape of the Mountain

Castle Rock Mountain, the last battleground of the Modoc Indians, was my inspiration during my Tule Lake days. The Castle Rock area was also the location of the WRA Administration Office, the camp hospital, the military police, and the infamous "Bull Pen" of the stockade.

It was in the "Bull Pen" that my brother Tokio was imprisoned for ten months, without due process of law, in the most severe and degrading conditions, after being falsely accused of inciting the November fourth food riots.

I made numerous visits to this area to appeal to the camp authorities for the release of my brother from the "Bull Pen," to plead that my husband, who was being detained in the Santa Fe camp, be permitted to visit his dying mother, and later, that he be allowed to attend her funeral. All to no avail because the authorities were insensitive and indifferent to our plight and branded me a trouble-maker for my pains.

How abandoned I felt! How I longed to have the authorities heed my pleas for justice and humane treatment! How I ached for my relatives caught in the web of man's inhumanity to man! And always my vision and my thoughts were drawn to Castle Rock, comparing our fate to the Modoc Indians' last stand in their Lava Bed Campaign of 1872–73.

Forced to Be Here

Forced to be in Tule Lake for two summers. I have already gathered the seeds of this year's flowers. How many more years must I keep doing this?

Autumn Grass

It is not yet autumn by the calendar yet the fall weather is here. The stunted Tule reeds already have tassels and we are heading for another long and gloomy winter of confinement and uncertainty. Fall comes too soon in captivity. Where do I turn to lament my fate?

Autumn Day

Brother Tokio, a U.S. citizen by birth, and many of his companions,   *25*
are being sent to the Justice Department camp for enemy aliens in Santa Fe,
New Mexico.

After much pleading with U.S. government agencies and with the
Spanish consulate, the neutral protective power for enemy aliens, my kindly
mother-in-law was finally sent to the hospital in Oregon for radium treatment—escorted by two armed soldiers with rifles and fixed bayonets. On
the train one sat beside her and the other on the opposite seat. They stood
guard over her when she used the train lavatory, and outside her hospital
room. What danger did she pose to U.S. security?

Having been treated so shabbily by the government, was it a crime that
she had requested repatriation to Japan so she could die in her native country
and be buried by her family?

How do I express my feelings of repugnance, except to talk to my
flowers? How do I suppress my pride? For whom do I shed my tears?

Flowers Are Good

How am I to endure these hardships? My young children and I are
constantly ill. Yesterday's "friends" have become informers for the WRA and
other government agencies. The constant harassment by WRA Internal Security personnel are creating "disloyals" to justify their tactics of "divide and
conquer."

Again, I turn to my flowers for solace so I can endure the indignity,   *30*
inhumanity, and injustice.

My lovely flowers—I love you!

Death

Many tragedies happened during my four years of internment, but one
of the most cruel was the suicide of my haiku pal following her relocation to
the Midwest. She was to have been the "prize" for her husband's gambling
debts so she took her own life instead.

Hatsujo had helped me during my child-bearing days in Fresno, and
later, in caring for my young children in the Jerome Internment Center. She
was an exceptional Kibei and there was a remarkable perception in the things
she saw and the elegance of the haiku she wrote.

When news of Hatsujo's suicide reached me in Tule Lake, I sank
into an uncontrollable depression, unable to rationalize her death although,
deep in my heart, I felt it was the result of the harsh realities of the internment.

Then I realized we must all die sooner or later, whether today, tomor-   *35*
row, or later on, and peace came to my tormented soul as I dedicated this
haiku to her memory.

The Responsive Reader

1. In the poet's mind, sights she sees often start a train of thoughts and feelings, and often things she observes take on symbolic significance. What are striking examples?
2. What do you gather from these poems about the legal status of the internees, their treatment by the authorities, the internees' grievances, or their ties with Japan?
3. Is there a strong sense of solidarity among the internees? Is there evidence of mixed feelings about fellow Japanese?

Thinking, Talking, Writing

4. What do you think would be the worst part of being interned in a camp like the one described in these poems?
5. Americans of German or Italian descent were not interned during World War II, although this country was at war with Germany and Italy as well as Japan. Why do you think Japanese Americans were singled out? Is there a way of defending the government's action?

Thinking about Connections

6. Look back over the selections by Bierce, Hemingway, and Matsuda. Compare the different perspectives they offer on the victims of war.

GOING AFTER CACCIATO
Tim O'Brien

Some thought the war was proper and others didn't and most didn't care.

Tim O'Brien

The Vietnam War divided the American nation. After World War II, the French had fought a disastrous losing war to reestablish colonial rule over the Indochinese territories they had lost. After partition, an uneasy truce existed for a time between communist North Vietnam and the Western-sponsored govern-ment of South Vietnam. Since the independence movement in Indochina was dominated by the communist Vietminh in Vietnam and the communist Kmer Rouge in Cambodia, the Americans declared the Western-sponsored successor governments to French colonial rule part of the "free world" and committed to defend them against communist aggression. The resulting war turned into a quagmire, with ever-growing American involvement and with an increasingly radicalized antiwar movement at home. The Vietcong, the southern arm of the Vietnamese communist movement, fought a classic guerilla war of ambush and harassment, with the conventionally trained American army, like the blinded giant in the story of Ulysses, striking out at the civilian population in which the enemy, in the words of Chairman Mao, "swam like the fish in the sea." None of these political and military considerations are mentioned in the following story about American GIs in Vietnam. (Why not?)

Tim O'Brien was in college in 1968 when he received his draft notice. He went to Vietnam convinced that the war was wrong, "wrongly conceived and poorly justified." Returning to tell the story of those sent to die in Vietnam, he published magazine pieces that became part of his autobiographical If I Die in a Combat Zone Box Me Up and Ship me Home *(1973) and of his novel* Going after Cacciato *(1976). A few expressions in the following story are GI slang, some fairly obvious, like* arty *for artillery, or* illum *for illumination (*Willie Peter *stands for white phosphorus). A* click *is a measure of distance determined by the elevation of a gunsight. An MIA is a soldier missing in action.*

It was a bad time. Billy Boy Watkins was dead, and so was Frenchie *1*
Tucker. Billy Boy had died of fright, scared to death on the field of battle, and Frenchie Tucker had been shot through the neck. Lieutenants Sidney Martin and Walter Gleason had died in tunnels. Pederson was dead and Bernie Lynn was dead. Buff was dead. They were all among the dead. The war was always the same, and the rain was part of the war. The rain fed fungus that grew in the men's socks and boots, and their socks rotted, and their feet turned white and soft so that the skin could be scraped off with a fingernail, and Stink Harris woke up screaming one night with a leech on

his tongue. When it was not raining, a low mist moved like sleep across the paddies, blending the elements into a single gray element, and the war was cold and pasty and rotten. Lieutenant Corson, who came to replace Lieutenant Martin, contracted the dysentery. The tripflares were useless. The ammunition corroded and the foxholes filled with mud and water during the nights and in the mornings there was always the next village and the war was always the same. In early September Vaught caught an infection. He'd been showing Oscar Johnson the sharp edge on his bayonet, drawing it swiftly along his forearm and peeling off a layer of mushy skin. "Like a Gillette Blueblade." Vaught had grinned. It did not bleed, but in a few days the bacteria soaked in and the arm turned yellow, and Vaught was carried aboard a Huey that dipped perpendicular, blades clutching at granite air, rising in its own wet wind and taking Vaught away. He never returned to the war. Later they had a letter from him that described Japan as smoky and full of bedbugs, but in the enclosed snapshot Vaught looked happy enough, posing with two sightly nurses, a long-stemmed bottle of wine rising from between his thighs. It was a shock to learn that he'd lost the arm. Soon afterward Ben Nystrom shot himself in the foot, but he did not die, and he wrote no letters. These were all things to talk about. The rain, too. Oscar said it made him think of Detroit in the month of May. "Not the rain," he liked to say. "Just the dark and gloom. It's Number One weather for rape and looting. The fact is, I do ninety-eight percent of my total rape and looting in weather just like this." Then somebody would say that Oscar had a pretty decent imagination for a nigger.

That was one of the jokes. There was a joke about Oscar. There were many jokes about Billy Boy Watkins, the way he'd collapsed in fright on the field of glorious battle. Another joke was about the lieutenant's dysentery, and another was about Paul Berlin's purple boils. Some of the jokes were about Cacciato, who was as dumb, Stink said, as a bullet, or, Harold Murphy said, as an oyster fart.

In October, at the end of the month, in the rain, Cacciato left the war.

"He's gone away," said Doc Peret. "Split for parts unknown."

The lieutenant didn't seem to hear. He was too old to be a lieutenant, anyway. The veins in his nose and cheeks were shattered by booze. Once he had been a captain on the way to being a major, but whiskey and the fourteen dull years between Korea and Vietnam had ended all that, and now he was just an old lieutenant with the dysentery. He lay on his back in the pagoda, naked except for green socks and green undershorts.

"Cacciato," Doc Peret repeated. "He's gone away. Split, departed."

The lieutenant did not sit up. He held his belly with both hands as if to contain the disease.

"He's gone to Paris," Doc said. "That's what he tells Paul Berlin, anyhow, and Paul Berlin tells me, so I'm telling you. He's gone, packed up and gone."

"Paree," the lieutenant said softly. "In France, Paree? *Gay* Paree?"

"Yes, sir. That's what he says. That's what he told Paul Berlin, and that's   *10*
what I'm telling you. You ought to cover up, sir."

The lieutenant sighed. He pushed himself up, breathing loud, then sat
stiffly before a can of Sterno. He lit the Sterno and cupped his hands around
the flame and bent down, drawing in the heat. Outside, the rain was steady.
"Paree," he said wearily. "You're saying Cacciato's left for gay Paree, is that
right?"

"That's what he said, sir. I'm just relaying what he told to Paul Berlin.
Hey, really, you better cover yourself up."

"Who's Paul Berlin?"

"Right here, sir. This is Paul Berlin."

The lieutenant looked up. His eyes were bright blue, oddly out of place   *15*
in the sallow face. "You Paul Berlin?"

"Yes, sir," said Paul Berlin. He pretended to smile.

"Geez, I thought you were Vaught."

"Vaught's the one who cut himself, sir."

"I thought that was you. How do you like that?"

"Fine, sir."   *20*

The lieutenant sighed and shook his head sadly. He held a boot to dry
over the burning Sterno. Behind him in the shadows sat the crosslegged,
roundfaced Buddha, smiling benignly from its elevated perch. The pagoda
was cold. Dank and soggy from a month of rain, the place smelled of clays
and silicates and old incense. It was a single square room, built like a pillbox,
with a flat ceiling that forced the soldiers to stoop and kneel. Once it might
have been an elegant house of worship, neatly tiled and painted and clean,
candles burning in holders at the Buddha's feet, but now it was bombed-out
junk. Sandbags blocked the windows. Bits of broken pottery lay under
chipped pedestals. The Buddha's right arm was missing and his fat groin was
gouged with shrapnel. Still, the smile was intact. Head cocked, he seemed
interested in the lieutenant's long sigh. "So, Cacciato's gone away, is that it?"

"There it is," Doc Peret said. "You've got it now."

Paul Berlin smiled and nodded.

"To gay Paree," the lieutenant said. "Old Cacciato's going to Paree in
France." He giggled, then shook his head gravely. "Still raining?"

"A bitch, sir."   *25*

"You ever seen rain like this? I mean, ever?"

"No, sir," Paul Berlin said.

"You Cacciato's buddy, I suppose?"

"No, sir," Paul Berlin said. "Sometimes he'd tag along, but not really."

"Who's his buddy?"   *30*

"Vaught, sir. I guess Vaught was, sometime."

"Well," the lieutenant said, dropping his nose inside the boot to smell
the sweaty leather, "well, I guess we should just get Mister Vaught in here."

"Vaught's gone, sir. He's the one who cut himself—gangrene, remember?"

"Mother of Mercy."

Doc Peret draped a poncho over the lieutenant's shoulders. The rain   *35*
was steady and thunderless and undramatic. Though it was mid-morning,
the feeling was of endless dusk.

"Paree," the lieutenant murmured. "Cacciato's going to gay Paree—
pretty girls and bare ass and Frogs everywhere. What's wrong with him?"

"Just dumb, sir. He's just awful dumb, that's all."

"And he's walking? He says he's walking to gay Paree?"

"That's what he says, sir, but you know how Cacciato can be."

"Does he know how far it is?"   *40*

"Six thousand eight hundred statute miles, sir. That's what he told
me—six thousand eight hundred miles on the nose. He had it down pretty
well. He had a compass and fresh water and maps and stuff."

"Maps," the lieutenant said. "Maps, flaps, schnaps. I guess those maps
will help him cross the oceans, right? I guess he can just rig up a canoe out
of those maps, no problem."

"Well, no," said Paul Berlin. He looked at Doc Peret, who shrugged.
"No, sir. He showed me on the maps. See, he says he's going through Laos,
then into Thailand and Burma, and then India, and then some other country,
I forget, and then into Iran and Iraq, and then Turkey, and then Greece, and
the rest is easy. That's exactly what he said. The rest is easy, he said. He had
it all doped out."

"In other words," the lieutenant said, lying back, "in other words,
fuckin AWOL."

"There it is," said Doc Peret. "There it is."   *45*

The lieutenant rubbed his eyes. His face was sallow and he needed a
shave. For a time he lay very still, listening to the rain, hands on his belly,
then he giggled and shook his head and laughed. "What for? Tell me—what
the fuck for?"

"Easy," Doc said. "Really, you got to stay covered up, sir. I told
you that."

"What for? I mean, what for?"

"Shhhhhhh, he's just dumb, that's all."

The lieutenant's face was yellow. He laughed, rolling onto his side and   *50*
dropping the boot. "I mean, why? What sort of shit is this—walking to
fucking gay Paree? What kind of bloody war is this, tell me, what's wrong
with you people? Tell me—what's *wrong* with you?"

"Shhhhhh," Doc purred, covering him up and putting a hand on his
forehead. "Easy does it."

"Angel of Mercy, Mother of Virgins, what's wrong with you guys?
Walking to gay Paree, what's *wrong?*"

"Nothing, sir. It's just Cacciato. You know how Cacciato can be when
he puts his head to it. Relax now and it'll be all fine. Fine. It's just that
rockhead, Cacciato."

The lieutenant giggled. Without rising, he pulled on his pants and boots and a shirt, then rocked miserably before the blue Sterno flame. The pagoda smelled like the earth, and the rain was unending. "Shoot." The lieutenant sighed. He kept shaking his head, grinning, then looked at Paul Berlin. "What squad you in?"

"Third, sir."

"That's Cacciato's squad?"

"Yes, sir."

"Who else?"

"Me and Doc and Eddie Lazzutti and Stink and Oscar Johnson and Harold Murphy. That's all, except for Cacciato."

"What about Pederson and Buff?"

"They're the dead ones, sir."

"Shoot." The lieutenant rocked before the flame. He did not look well. "Okay." He sighed, getting up. "Third Squads goes after Cacciato."

Leading to the mountains were four clicks of level paddy. The mountains jerked straight out of the rice, and beyond those mountains and other mountains was Paris.

The tops of the mountains could not be seen for the mist and clouds. The rain was glue that stuck the sky to the land.

The squad spent the night camped at the base of the first mountain, then in the morning they began the ascent. At midday Paul Berlin spotted Cacciato. He was half a mile up, bent low and moving patiently, steadily. He was not wearing a helmet—surprising, because Cacciato always took great care to cover the pink bald spot at the crown of his skull. Paul Berlin spotted him, but it was Stink Harris who spoke up.

Lieutenant Corson took out the binoculars.

"Him, sir?"

The lieutenant watched while Cacciato climbed toward the clouds.

"That him?"

"It's him. Bald as an eagle's ass."

Stink giggled. "Bald as Friar Tuck—it's Cacciato, all right. Dumb as a dink."

They watched until Cacciato was swallowed in the rain and clouds.

"Dumb-dumb." Stink giggled.

They walked fast, staying in a loose column. First the lieutenant, then Oscar Johnson, then Stink, then Eddie Lazzutti, then Harold Murphy, then Doc, then, at the rear, Paul Berlin. Who walked slowly, head down. He had nothing against Cacciato. The whole episode was silly, of course, a dumb and immature thing typical of Cacciato, but even so he had nothing special against him. It was just too bad. A waste of time in the midst of infinitely wider waste.

Climbing, he tried to picture Cacciato's face. The image came out fuzzed and amorphous and bland—entirely compatible with the boy's personality. Doc Peret, an acute observer of such things, hypothesized that

Cacciato had missed Mongolian idiocy by the breadth of a single, wispy genetic hair. "Could have gone either way," Doc had said confidentially. "You see the slanting eyes? The pasty flesh, just like jelly, right? The odd-shaped head? I mean, hey, let's face it—the guy's fucking ugly. It's only a theory, mind you, but I'd wager big money that old Cacciato has more than a smidgen of the Mongol in him."

There may have been truth to it. Cacciato looked curiously unfinished, 75 as though nature had struggled long and heroically but finally jettisoned him as a hopeless cause, not worth the diminishing returns. Open-faced, round, naive, plump, tender-complected, and boyish, Cacciato lacked the fine detail, the refinements and final touches that maturity ordinarily marks on a boy of seventeen years. All this, the men concluded, added up to a case of simple gross stupidity. He wasn't positively disliked—except perhaps by Stink Harris, who took instant displeasure with anything vaguely his inferior—but at the same time Cacciato was no one's friend. Vaught, maybe. But Vaught was dumb, too, and he was gone from the war. At best, Cacciato was tolerated. The way men will sometimes tolerate a pesky dog.

It was just too bad. Walking to Paris; it was one of those ridiculous things Cacciato would do. Like winning the Bronze Star for shooting a dink in the face. Dumb. The way he was forever whistling. Too blunt-headed to know better, blind to the bodily and spiritual dangers of human combat. In some ways this made him a good soldier. He walked point like a boy at his first county fair. He didn't mind the tunnel work. And his smile, more decoration than an expression of emotion, stayed with him in the most lethal of moments—when Billy Boy turned his last card, when Pederson floated face-up in a summer day's paddy, when Buff's helmet overflowed with an excess of red and gray fluids.

It was sad, a real pity.

Climbing the mountain, Paul Berlin felt an odd affection for the kid. Not friendship, exactly, but—real pity.

Not friendship. Not exactly. Pity, pity plus wonder. It was all silly, walking away in the rain, but it was something to think about.

They did not reach the summit of the mountain until midafternoon. 80 The climb was hard, the rain sweeping down, the mountain oozing from beneath their feet. Below, the clouds were expansive, hiding the paddies and the war. Above, in more clouds, were more mountains.

Oscar Johnson found where Cacciato had spent the first night, a rock formation with an outcropping ledge as a roof, a can of burned-out Sterno, a chocolate wrapper, and a partly burned map. On the map, traced in red ink, was a dotted line that ran through the paddyland and up the first small mountain of the Annamese Cordillera. The dotted line ended there, apparently to be continued on another map.

"He's serious," the lieutenant said softly. "The blockhead's serious." He held the map as if it had a bad smell.

Stink and Oscar and Eddie Lazzutti nodded.

They rested in Cacciato's snug rock nest. Tucked away, looking out on the slate rain toward the next mountain, the men were quiet. Paul Berlin laid out a game of solitaire. Harold Murphy rolled a joint, inhaled, then passed it along, and they smoked and watched the rain and clouds and wilderness. It was peaceful. The rain was nice.

No one spoke until the ritual was complete.   85

Then, in a hush, all the lieutenant could say was, "Mercy."

"Shit," was what Stink Harris said.

The rain was unending.

"We could just go back," Doc Peret finally said. "You know, sir? Just head on back and forget him."

Stink Harris giggled.   90

"Seriously," Doc kept on, "we could just let the poor kid go. Make him M.I.A., strayed in battle, the lost lamb. Sooner or later he'll wake up, you know, and he'll see how insane it is and he'll come back."

The lieutenant stared into the rain. His face was yellow except for the network of broken veins.

"So what say you, sir? Let him go?"

"Dumber than a rock." Stink giggled.

"And smarter than Stink Harris."   95

"You know *what*, Doc."

"Pickle it."

"Who's saying to pickle it?"

"Just pickle it," said Doc Peret. "That's what."

Stink giggled but he shut up.   100

"What do you say, sir? Turn back?"

The lieutenant was quiet. At last he shivered and went into the rain with a wad of toilet paper. Paul Berlin sat alone, playing solitaire in the style of Las Vegas. Pretending, of course. Pretending to pay thirty thousand dollars for the deck, pretending ways to spend his earnings.

When the lieutenant returned he told the men to saddle up.

"We turning back?" Doc asked.

The lieutenant shook his head. He looked sick.   105

"I knew it!" Stink crowed. "Damn straight, I knew it! Can't hump away from a war, isn't that right, sir? The dummy has got to learn you can't just hump your way out of a war." Stink grinned and flicked his eyebrows at Doc Peret. "I knew it. By golly, I knew it!"

Cacciato had reached the top of the second mountain. Standing bareheaded, hands loosely at his sides, he was looking down on them through a blur of rain. Lieutenant Corson had the binoculars on him.

"Maybe he don't see us," Oscar said. "Maybe he's lost."

"Oh, he sees us. He sees us fine. Sees us real fine. And he's not lost. Believe me, he's not."

"Throw out smoke, sir?"   110

"Why not?" the lieutenant said. "Sure, why not throw out pretty smoke, why not?" He watched Cacciato through the glasses while Oscar threw out the smoke. It fizzled for a time and then puffed up in a heavy cloud of lavender. "Oh, he sees us," the lieutenant whispered. "He sees us fine."

"The bastard's *waving!*"

"I can see that, thank you. Mother of Saints."

As if stricken, the lieutenant suddenly sat down in a puddle, put his head in his hands and began to rock as the lavender smoke drifted up the face of the mountain. Cacciato was waving both arms. Not quite waving. The arms were flapping. Paul Berlin watched through the glasses. Cacciato's head was huge, floating like a balloon in the high fog, and he did not look at all frightened. He looked young and stupid. His face was shiny. He was smiling, and he looked happy.

"I'm sick," the lieutenant said. He kept rocking. "I tell you, I'm a sick, 115 sick man."

"Should I shout up to him?"

"Sick." The lieutenant moaned. "Sick, sick. It wasn't this way on Pusan, I'll tell you that. Sure, call up to him—I'm sick."

Oscar Johnson cupped his hands and hollered, and Paul Berlin watched through the glasses. For a moment Cacciato stopped waving. He spread his arms wide, as if to show them empty, slowly spreading them out like wings, palms up. Then his mouth opened wide, and in the mountains there was thunder.

"What'd he say?" The lieutenant rocked on his haunches. He was clutching himself and shivering. "Tell me what he said."

"Can't hear, sir. Oscar—?" 120

There was more thunder, long-lasting thunder that came in waves from deep in the mountains. It rolled down and moved the trees and grasses.

"Shut the shit up!" The lieutenant was rocking and shouting at the rain and wind and thunder. "What'd the dumb fucker say?"

Paul Berlin watched through the glasses, and Cacciato's mouth opened and closed and opened, but there was only more thunder. Then his arms began flapping again. Flying, Paul Berlin suddenly realized. The poor kid was perched up there, arms flapping, trying to fly. Fly! Incredibly, the flapping motion was smooth and practiced and graceful.

"A chicken!" Stink squealed. "Look it! A squawking chicken!"

"Mother of Children." 125

"Look it!"

"A miserable chicken, you see that? A chicken!"

The thunder came again, breaking like Elephant Feet across the mountains, and the lieutenant rocked and held himself.

"For Christ sake." He moaned. "What'd he say? Tell me."

Paul Berlin could not hear. But he saw Cacciato's lips move, and the 130 happy smile.

"Tell me."

So Paul Berlin, watching Cacciato fly, repeated it. "He said goodbye."

In the night the rain hardened into fog, and the fog was cold. They camped in the fog, near the top of the mountains, and the thunder stayed through the night. The lieutenant vomited. Then he radioed that he was in pursuit of the enemy.

"Gunships, Papa Two-Niner?" came the answer from far away.

"Negative," said the old lieutenant.   *135*

"Arty? Tell you what. You got a real sweet voice, Papa Two-Niner. No shit, a lovely voice." The radio voice paused. "So, here's what I'll do, I'll give you a bargain on the arty—two for the price of one, no strings and a warranty to boot. How's that? See, we got this terrific batch of new one–fifty-five in, first-class ordinance, I promise you, and what we do, what we do is this. What we do is we go heavy on volume here, you know? Keeps the prices low."

"Negative," the lieutenant said.

"Well, geez. Hard to please, right? Maybe some nice illum, then? Willie Peter, real boomers with some genuine sparkles mixed in. We're having this close-out sale, one time only."

"Negative. Negative, negative, negative."

"You'll be missing out on some fine shit."   *140*

"Negative, you monster."

"Okay," the radio voice said, disappointed-sounding, "but you'll wish . . . No offense, Papa Two-Niner. Have some happy hunting."

"Mercy," said the lieutenant into a blaze of static.

The night fog was worse than the rain, colder and more saddening. They lay under a sagging lean-to that seemed to catch and hold the fog like a net. Oscar and Harold Murphy and Stink and Eddie Lazzutti slept anyway, curled around one another like lovers. They could sleep and sleep.

"I hope he's moving," Paul Berlin whispered to Doc Peret. "I just hope *145* he keeps moving. He does that, we'll never get him."

"Then they'll chase him with choppers. Or planes or something."

"Not if he gets himself lost," Paul Berlin said. "Not if he hides."

"What time is it?"

"Don't know."

"What time you got, sir?"   *150*

"Very lousy late," said the lieutenant from the bushes.

"Come on."

"Four o'clock. O-four-hundred, which is to say A.M. Got it?"

"Thanks."

"Charmed." His ass, hanging six inches from the earth, made a soft *155* warm glow in the dark.

"You okay, sir?"

"I'm wonderful. Can't you see how wonderful I am?"

"I just hope Cacciato keeps moving," Paul Berlin whispered. "That's all I hope—I hope he uses his head and keeps moving."

"It won't get him anywhere."

"Get him to Paris maybe." 160

"Maybe." Doc sighed, turning onto his side. "And where is he then?"

"In Paris."

"No way. I like adventure, too, but, see, you can't walk to Paris from here. You just can't."

"He's smarter than you think," Paul Berlin said, not quite believing it. "He's not all that dumb."

"I know," the lieutenant said. He came from the bushes. "I know all 165 about that."

"Impossible. None of the roads go to Paris."

"Can we light a Sterno, sir?"

"No," the lieutenant said, crawling under the lean-to and lying flat on his back. His breath came hard. "No, you can't light a fucking Sterno, and no, you can't go out to play without your mufflers and galoshes, and no, kiddies and combatants, no, you can't have chocolate sauce on your broccoli. No."

"All right."

"No!" 170

"You saying no, sir?"

"No." The lieutenant sighed with doom. "It's still a war, isn't it?"

"I guess."

"There you have it. It's still a war."

The rain resumed. It started with thunder, then lightning lighted the 175 valley deep below in green and mystery, then more thunder, then it was just the rain. They lay quietly and listened. Paul Berlin, who considered himself abnormally sane, uncluttered by high ideas or lofty ambitions or philosophy, was suddenly struck between the eyes by a vision of murder. Butchery, no less. Cacciato's right temple caving inward, a moment of black silence, then the enormous explosion of outward-going brains. It was no metaphor; he didn't think in metaphors. No, it was a simple scary vision. He tried to reconstruct the thoughts that had led to it, but there was nothing to be found—the rain, the discomfort of mushy flesh. Nothing to justify such a bloody image, no origins. Just Cacciato's round head suddenly exploding like a pricked bag of helium: boom.

Where, he thought, was all this taking him, and where would it end? Murder was the logical circuit-stopper, of course; it was Cacciato's rightful, maybe inevitable due. Nobody can get away with stupidity forever, and in war the final price for it is always paid in purely biological currency, hunks of toe or pieces of femur or bits of exploded brain. And it *was* still a war, wasn't it?

Pitying Cacciato with wee-hour tenderness, and pitying himself for the affliction that produced such visions, Paul Berlin hoped for a miracle. He was tired of murder. Not scared by it—not at that particular moment—and not awed by it, just fatigued.

"He did some awfully brave things," he whispered. Then realized that Doc was listening. "He did. The time he dragged that dink out of his bunker, remember that."

"Yeah."

"The time he shot the kid in the kisser."   180

"I remember."

"At least you can't call him a coward, can you? You can't say he ran away because he was scared."

"You can say a lot of other shit, though."

"True. But you can't say he wasn't brave. You can't say that."

"Fair enough," Doc said. He sounded sleepy.   185

"I wonder if he talks French."

"You kidding, partner?"

"Just wondering. You think it's hard to learn French, Doc?"

"Cacciato?"

"Yeah, I guess not. It's a neat thing to think about, though, old Cac-   190
ciato walking to Paris."

"Go to sleep," Doc Peret advised. "Remember, pal, you got your own health to think of."

They were in the high country.

It was country far from the war, high and peaceful country with trees and thick grass, no people and no dogs and no lowland drudgery. Real wilderness, through which a single trail, liquid and shiny, kept taking them up.

The men walked with their heads down. Stink at point, then Eddie Lazzutti and Oscar, next Harold Murphy with the machine gun, then Doc, then the lieutenant, and last Paul Berlin.

They were tired and did not talk. Their thoughts were in their legs   195
and feet, and their legs and feet were heavy with blood, for they'd been on the march many hours and the day was soggy with the endless rain. There was nothing symbolic, or melancholy, about the rain. It was simple rain, everywhere.

They camped that night beside the trail, then in the morning continued the climb. Though there were no signs of Cacciato, the mountain had only one trail and they were on it, the only way west.

Paul Berlin marched mechanically. At his sides, balancing him evenly and keeping him upright, two canteens of Kool-Aid lifted and fell with his hips, and the hips rolled in their ball-and-socket joints. He respired and sweated. His heart hard, his back strong, up the high country.

They did not see Cacciato, and for a time Paul Berlin thought they might have lost him forever. It made him feel better, and he climbed the trail and enjoyed the scenery and the sensations of being high and far from the real war, and then Oscar found the second map.

The red dotted line crossed the border into Laos.

Farther ahead they found Cacciato's helmet and armored vest, then his dogtags, then his entrenching tool and knife.

"Dummy just keeps to the trail." The lieutenant moaned. "Tell me why? Why doesn't he leave the trail?"

"It's the only way to Paris," Paul Berlin said.

"A rockhead," said Stink Harris. "That's why."

Liquid and shiny, a mix of rain and red clay, the trail took them higher.

Cacciato eluded them but he left behind the wastes of his march— empty tins, bits of bread, a belt of golden ammo dangling from a dwarf pine, a leaking canteen, candy wrappers, and worn rope. Clues that kept them going. Tantalizing them on, one step then the next—a glimpse of his bald head, the hot ash of a breakfast fire, a handkerchief dropped coyly along the path.

So they kept after him, following the trails that linked one to the next westward in a simple linear direction without deception. It was deep, jagged, complex country, dark with the elements of the season, and ahead was the frontier.

"He makes it that far," Doc Peret said, pointing to the next line of mountains, "and we can't touch him."

"How now?"

"The border," Doc said. The trail had leveled out and the march was easier. "He makes it to the border and it's bye-bye Cacciato."

"How far?"

"Two clicks maybe. Not far."

"Then he's made it," whispered Paul Berlin.

"Maybe so."

"By God!"

"Maybe so," Doc said.

"Boy, lunch at Tour d'Argent! A night at the old opera!"

"Maybe so."

The trail narrowed, then climbed, and a half hour later they saw him.

He stood at the top of a small grassy hill, two hundred meters ahead. Loose and at ease, smiling, Cacciato already looked like a civilian. His hands were in his pockets and he was not trying to hide himself. He might have been waiting for a bus, patient and serene and not at all frightened.

"Got him!" Stink yelped. "I knew it! Now we got him!"

The lieutenant came forward with the glasses.

"I knew it," Stink crowed, pressed forward. "The blockhead's finally giving it up—giving up the old ghost, I knew it!"

"What do we do, sir?"

The lieutenant shrugged and stared through the glasses.

"Fire a shot?" Stink held his rifle up and before the lieutenant could   225
speak he squeezed off two quick rounds, one a tracer that turned like a
corkscrew through the mist. Cacciato smiled and waved.

"Look at him," Oscar Johnson said. "I do think we got ourselves a
predicament. Truly a predicament."

"There it is," Eddie said, and they both laughed, and Cacciato kept
smiling and waving.

"A true predicament."

Stink Harris took the point, walking fast and chattering, and Cacciato
stopped waving and watched him come, arms folded and his big head cocked
as if listening for something. He looked amused.

There was no avoiding it.   230

Stink saw the wire as he tripped it, but there was no avoiding it.

The first sound was that of a zipper suddenly yanked up; next, a popping noise, the spoon releasing and primer detonating; then the sound of the
grenade dropping; then the fizzling sound. The sounds came separately but
quickly.

Stink knew it as it happened. With the next step, in one fuzzed motion,
he flung himself down and away, rolling, covering his skull, mouth open,
yelping a funny, trivial little yelp.

They all knew it.

Eddie and Oscar and Doc Peret dropped flat, and Harold Murphy bent   235
double and did an oddly graceful jackknife for a man of his size, and the
lieutenant coughed and collapsed, and Paul Berlin, seeing purple, closed his
eyes and fists and mouth, brought his knees to his belly, coiling, and let
himself fall.

Count, he thought, but the numbers came in a tangle without sequence.

His belly hurt. That was where it started. First the belly, a release of
fluids in the bowels next, a shitting feeling, a draining of all the pretensions
and silly hopes for himself, and he was back where he started, writhing. The
lieutenant was beside him. The air was windless—just the misty rain. His
teeth hurt. Count, he thought, but his teeth hurt and no numbers came. I
don't want to die, he thought lucidly, with hurting teeth.

There was no explosion. His teeth kept hurting and his belly was
floating in funny ways.

He was ready, steeled. His lungs hurt now. He was ready, but there was
no explosion. Then came a fragile pop. Smoke, he thought without thinking,
smoke.

"Smoke." The lieutenant moaned, then repeated it. "Fucking smoke."   240

Paul Berlin smelled it. He imagined its velvet color, purple, but he could
not open his eyes. He tried, but he could not open his eyes or unclench his
fists or uncoil his legs, and the heavy fluids in his stomach were holding him
down, and he could not wiggle or run to escape. There was no explosion.

"Smoke," Doc said softly. "Just smoke."

It was red smoke, and the message seemed clear. It was all over them. Brilliant red, thick, acid-tasting. It spread out over the earth like paint, then began to climb against gravity in a lazy red spiral.

"Smoke," Doc said. "Smoke."

Stink Harris was crying. He was on his hands and knees, chin against his throat, bawling and bawling. Oscar and Eddie had not moved.

"He had us," the lieutenant whispered. His voice was hollowed out, senile-sounding, almost a reminiscence. "He could've had all of us."

"Just smoke," Doc said. "Lousy smoke is all."

"The dumb fucker could've had us."

Paul Berlin could not move. He felt entirely conscious, a little embarrassed but not yet humiliated, and he heard their voices, heard Stink weeping and saw him beside the trail on his hands and knees, and he saw the red smoke everywhere, but he could not move.

"He won't come," said Oscar Johnson, returning under a white flag. "Believe me, I tried, but the dude just won't play her cool."

It was dusk and the seven soldiers sat in pow-wow.

"I told him all the right stuff, but he won't give it up. Told him it was crazy as shit and he'd probably end up dead, and I told him how he'd end up court-martialed at the best, and I told him how his old man would shit when he heard about it. Told him maybe things wouldn't go so hard if he just gave up and came back right now. I went through the whole spiel, top to bottom. The dude just don't listen."

The lieutenant was lying prone, Doc's thermometer in his mouth, sick-looking. It wasn't his war. The skin on his arms and neck was loose around deteriorating muscle.

"I told him—I told him all that good shit. Told him it's ridiculous, dig? I told him it won't work, no matter what, and I told him we're fed up. Fed up."

"You tell him we're out of rations?"

"Shit, yes, I told him that. And I told him he's gonna starve his own ass if he keeps going, and I told him we'd have to call in gunships if it came to it."

"You tell him he can't walk to France?"

Oscar grinned. He was black enough to be indistinct in the dusk. "Maybe I forgot to tell him that."

"You should've told him."

The lieutenant slid a hand behind his neck and pushed against it as if to relieve some spinal pressure. "What else?" he asked. "What else did he say?"

"Nothing, sir. He said he's doing okay. Said he was sorry to scare us with the smoke."

"The bastard." Stink kept rubbing his hands against the black stock of his rifle.

"What else?"

"Nothing. You know how he is, sir. Just a lot of smiles and stupid stuff. He asked how everybody was, so I said we're fine, except for the scare with the smoke boobytrap, and then he said he was sorry about that, so I told him it was okay. What can you say to a dude like that?"

The lieutenant nodded, pushing against his neck. He was quiet a while. *265* He seemed to be making up his mind. "All right." He finally sighed. "What'd he have with him?"

"Sir?"

"Musketry," the lieutenant said. "What kind of weapons?"

"His rifle. That's all, his rifle and some bullets. I didn't get much of a look.

"Claymores?"

Oscar shook his head. "I didn't see none. Maybe so."   *270*

"Grenades?"

"I don't know. Maybe a couple."

"Beautiful recon job, Oscar. Real pretty."

"Sorry, sir. He had his stuff tight, though."

"I'm sick."   *275*

"Yes, sir."

"Dysentery's going through me like coffee. What you got for me, Doc?"

Doc Peret shook his head. "Nothing, sir. Rest."

"That's it," the lieutenant said. "What I need is rest."

"Why not let him go, sir?"   *280*

"Rest," the lieutenant said, "is what I need."

Paul Berlin did not sleep. Instead he watched Cacciato's small hill and tried to imagine a proper ending.

There were only a few possibilities remaining, and after what had happened it was hard to see a happy end to it. Not impossible, of course. It could still be done. With skill and boldness, Cacciato might slip away and cross the frontier mountains and be gone. He tried to picture it. Many new places. Villages at night with barking dogs, people whose eyes and skins would change in slow evolution and counterevolution as Cacciato moved westward with whole continents before him and the war far behind him and all the trails connecting and leading toward Paris. It could be done. He imagined the many dangers of Cacciato's march, treachery and deceit at every turn, but he also imagined the many good times ahead, the stinging feel of aloneness, and new leanness and knowledge of strange places. The rains would end and the trails would go dry and be baked to dust, and there would be changing foliage and great expanses of silence and songs and pretty girls in straw huts and, finally, Paris.

It could be done. The odds were like poison, but it could be done.

Later, as if a mask had been peeled off, the rain ended and the sky *285* cleared and Paul Berlin woke to see the stars.

They were in their familiar places. It wasn't so cold. He lay on his back and counted the stars and named those that he knew, named the constellations and the valleys of the moon. It was just too bad. Crazy, but still sad. He should've kept going—left the trails and waded through streams to rinse away the scent, buried his feces, swung from the trees branch to branch; he should've slept through the days and ran through the nights. It might have been done.

Toward dawn he saw Cacciato's breakfast fire. He heard Stink playing with the safety catch on his M-16, a clicking noise like a slow morning cricket. The sky lit itself in patches.

"Let's do it," the lieutenant whispered.

Eddie Lazzutti and Oscar and Harold Murphy crept away toward the south. Doc and the lieutenant waited a time then began to circle west to block a retreat. Stink Harris and Paul Berlin were to continue up the trail.

Waiting, trying to imagine a rightful and still happy ending, Paul Berlin   290
found himself pretending, in a vague sort of way, that before long the war would reach a climax beyond which everything else would become completely commonplace. At that point he would stop being afraid. All the bad things, the painful and grotesque things, would be in the past, and the things ahead, if not lovely, would at least be tolerable. He pretended he had crossed that threshold.

When the sky was half-light, Doc and the lieutenant fired a red flare that streaked high over Cacciato's grassy hill, hung there, then exploded in a fanning starburst like the start of a celebration. Cacciato Day, it might have been called. October something, in the year 1968, the Year of the Pig.

In the trees at the southern slope of the hill Oscar and Eddie and Harold Murphy each fired red flares to signal their advance.

Stink went into the weeds and hurried back, zipping up his trousers. He was very excited and happy. Deftly, he released the bolt on his weapon and it slammed hard into place.

"Fire the flare," he said, "and let's go."

Paul Berlin took a long time opening his pack.   295

But he found the flare, unscrewed its lid, laid the firing pin against the primer, then jammed it in.

The flare jumped away from him. It went high and fast, rocketing upward and taking a smooth arc that followed the course of the trail, leaving behind a dirty wake of smoke.

At its apex, with barely a sound, the flare exploded in a green dazzle over Cacciato's hill. It was a fine, brilliant shade of green.

"Go," whispered Paul Berlin. It did not seem enough. "Go," he said, and then he shouted, "Go."

The Responsive Reader

1. At the beginning, the narrator keeps saying, "the war was always the same." What was the same about it? How does the story of Vaught help set the tone for the story?
2. Where in this story are the people and the culture of Vietnam? What does it contribute to the story that the group of GIs is headquartered in a pagoda?
3. Why do the lieutenant and his men go after Cacciato? What is going on in the lieutenant's mind? What are the feelings or attitudes of the men? What will happen to Cacciato? (Is there any foreshadowing of the outcome earlier in the story?)
4. Cacciato's leaving his unit is at the heart of this story. Is he out of his mind? Do you understand his thinking or his motives? Does Cacciato's story have a symbolic meaning? What do you think it says about the author's attitude toward the war?

Thinking, Talking, Writing

5. What kind of people are the American GIs in this story? What is their ethnic or social mix? (Does it matter?) What role does their humor play in the story? (Are they cynics? Are they racists?) What has the war done to them?
6. Who is the enemy in this story?

Thinking about Connections

7. Traditional war monuments and traditional war literature commemorate the heroism of those who fought or died for their country. Would you call any of the characters in the war literature in this chapter heroes? Why or why not? Is there a common denominator for those who fall short?

9

Inner Quest: The Searching Self

O mother, mother, where is happiness?
Gwendolyn Brooks, "The Sonnet-Ballad"

I went to a masquerade
Disguised as myself.
Bob Kaufman, "Heavy Water Blues"

There are both outer space and inner space to be explored.
Nikki Giovanni

LITERATURE IN CONTEXT

Much thinking about how to improve people's lives focuses on the social conditions and political structures that favor or hinder their advancement. In periods of heightened political awareness, many writers see social criticism and social change as the necessary preconditions for human happiness. However, during other cycles, poets, writers of fiction, and dramatists turn inward. They set out in search of the true self thwarted by convention. The need for educating the emotions, the need for finding one's true identity, the need for developing a worthy self-image or self-esteem then loom large among the themes explored by writers and artists.

A recurrent note in American literature, like the tolling of a bell, has been the lack of emotional fulfillment. Writers and artists have often found themselves in an environment hostile to passion, to love, or to flights of the imagination. In poem, story, or play, we encounter characters who have never realized their true selves or whose capacity for emotion has been stunted. They may once have had a capacity for joy or love, but they find themselves leading joyless lives. They find it difficult to form lasting human bonds. For a hundred years, perhaps the most widely read American short story has been Herman Melville's "Bartleby the Scrivener," about an office worker who has no ties, no social life, no emotional outlet, no fantasy life, and no sex life—in short, no life.

For a time, observers traced the emotional barrenness of much American life to the Puritan past. No matter how emancipated from the dogma of their Puritan forebears, many Americans were said to carry with them the legacy of a world view focused on human depravity and original sin. The suspicion of sin lurking under a beguiling surface left people incapacitated for the innocent enjoyment of frivolity. It made them frown on dancing, drinking, and merrymaking—let alone smoking, nudity, or immorality. Although historians insisted that the Puritans were not as austere as they were painted—they were hearty eaters, for instance—there seemed to be some truth to the stereotype of Puritan New England as a place where "Joy shivers in the corner as she knits/And Conscience always has the rocking chair" (E. A. Robinson).

In the twenties and thirties, American writers came under the spell of the Freudian psychology. Sigmund Freud, the Viennese father of psychoanalysis, had linked the maladjustments and neuroses of modern civilization to people's failure to come to terms with their repressed instinctual selves. People denied healthy outlets or normal growth in their emotional lives became twisted, neurotic adults. Writers like Sherwood Anderson chronicled small-town life in the Midwest, with characters unable to find fulfilling human contacts, let alone realize their heart's desire. In a later cycle and in a more passionate vein, the Southerner Tennessee Williams (*The Glass Menagerie, A Streetcar Named Desire, Cat on a Hot Tin Roof*) put on his stage characters whose basic emotional needs were thwarted and who were driven to violence and despair. A major theme of women writers from Kate Chopin to Alice Walker has been the barriers to emotional fulfillment that women encounter in a male-dominated, patriarchal society.

In much recent writing, women have probed barriers in the way of self-realization. They have written about confining sex roles, identity crises, or failed relationships. They have written about the need for self-assertion and self-discovery. At the same time, much current fiction by both women and men explores the fear of emotional commitment—the fear of being used, the fear of being hurt. What are barriers to self-realization in our society? Can they be overcome?

WOMAN

Nikki Giovanni

it's intellectual devastation
of everybody
to avoid emotional commitment
Nikki Giovanni, "Woman Poem"

> Nikki Giovanni started to publish at the time of the civil rights movement
> and of changing awareness of the role race plays in American life. She became
> known for personal, outspoken, and often funny or sarcastic poems about grow-
> ing up as a young black woman in changing times. Born in Tennessee, Giovanni
> graduated from Fisk University in Nashville and did graduate work at the
> University of Pennsylvania and Columbia. Her first volume of poems, Black
> Feeling, Black Talk, appeared in 1968.

she wanted to be a blade   1
of grass amid the fields
but he wouldn't agree
to be the dandelion

she wanted to be a robin singing   5
through the leaves
but he refused to be
her tree

she spun herself into a web
    and looking for a place to rest   10
turned to him
but he stood straight
declining to be her corner

she tried to be a book
but he wouldn't read   15
she turned herself into a bulb
but he wouldn't let her grow

she decided to become
a woman
and though he still refused   20
to be a man
she decided it was all
right

The Responsive Reader

1. The woman speaking in this poem gives voice to her desires or needs in a series of changing metaphors. Which of these imaginative comparisons seem humorous; which seem serious? What need or desire does each of them project? Are they related? What do they have in common?
2. What definition does this poem imply of what it means to be a woman and what it means to be a man?

Thinking, Talking, Writing

3. Does this poem echo or reinforce familiar current complaints made by women about men? Or does it put male-female relationships in a new perspective?
4. Suppose you were to write a poem or paragraph about what an imaginary man wanted from a woman. What do you say? What do you include?

AFTER WORK
Gary Snyder

Gary Snyder has been called "one of the most successful of the poets of the Pacific Northwest." His early poems date back to the world of the Beat poets of the fifties—dropouts from an exploitative, materialistic civilization who were searching for an alternative lifestyle inspired by Zen Buddhism and the Native American past. Snyder's interest in Buddhism and in Chinese and Japanese culture led him to Japan, where he has lived much of the time since the midfifties. In his later poems, we see the poet "making a new world of ourselves" in a setting where there are "Navajo turquoise beads over the bed" that has a Japanese badger pelt for a mattress, with the poet engaged in fashioning an axe handle or making bread.

The shack and a few trees   1
float in the blowing fog

I pull out your blouse,
warm my cold hands
            on your breasts.   5
you laugh and shudder
peeling garlic by the
            hot iron stove.
bring in the axe, the rake,
the wood   10

we'll lean on the wall
against each other
stew simmering on the fire
as it grows dark
            drinking wine.   15

The Responsive Reader

1. Do you think this poem represents a daydream or the memory of an actual incident?
2. Would you call this poem a male fantasy? Is it written exclusively for a male audience?

Thinking, Talking, Writing

3. If you were the editor of a student magazine and the poet were a student submitting this poem, would you ask him to edit out the reference to the woman's breasts?

4. In our modern world, is the idea of a life of simple pleasures in a shack among trees a mirage?
5. You may want to try your hand at rewriting this poem from the woman's point of view.

AUNT JENNIFER'S TIGERS
Adrienne Rich

In widely read poems and eloquent essays, Adrienne Rich has written about women searching for self-fulfillment. In a rereading of Charlotte Bronte's great nineteenth-century novel Jane Eyre, *Rich asked the modern reader to see Jane's life story as an archetypal journey in search of full womanhood: Jane struggles with the threat of poverty as an underpaid governess; she avoids the trap of Romantic love with a glamorous aristocratic married man; she rejects the alternative of self-abnegating service as the helpmate of a humanitarian, idealistic male; and she finally enters into a marriage in which she can be a full partner and which is a true union of body and soul. A prize-winning poet, Rich has published more than half a dozen volumes of poetry, including* Diving into the Wreck *(1973),* The Dream of a Common Language *(1978), and* The Fact of a Doorframe *(1984). She has been an inspiration to feminist and lesbian poets.*

Aunt Jennifer's tigers prance across a screen,   *1*
Bright topaz denizens of a world of green.
They do not fear the men beneath the tree;
They pace in sleek chivalric certainty.

Aunt Jennifer's fingers fluttering through her wool   *5*
Find even the ivory needle hard to pull.
The massive weight of Uncle's wedding band
Sits heavily upon Aunt Jennifer's hand.

When Aunt is dead, her terrified hands will lie
Still ringed with ordeals she was mastered by.   *10*
The tigers in the panel that she made
Will go on prancing, proud and unafraid.

The Responsive Reader

1. The image of the tigers dominates the poem. What role do they play in it? How do they fit into the overall pattern of the poem? (What is the meaning of *topaz* and *chivalric*, and what associations do these words bring into the poem? What network of other related words rounds out your impression of the animals? Why do they "prance"—why not "slide" or "slink"?)
2. What were the ordeals the aunt "was mastered by"? What serves as the symbol for them in the poem?

Thinking, Talking, Writing

3. This poem plays off dramatically opposed central symbols. For you, do they make good symbols of freedom and constraint? What symbols would you choose for these two opposite poles?
4. In your own mental universe, is there a clash between the world of reality and the world of the imagination?

THE MUTES
Denise Levertov

> *Although Denise Levertov grew up in England as the daughter of Welsh and Russian Jewish parents, she has been called "paradoxically . . . one of the most American of writers." Her passionate and explicit poems have paid homage to Ishtar, the Babylonian earth goddess of love and fertility; they have frankly explored women's sensuality; they have rebelled against the constraints of marriage when defined as being locked into "wedlock" rather than as the encounter and communion of free beings.*

Those groans men use   1
passing a woman on the street
or on the steps of the subway
to tell her she is a female
and their flesh knows it,   5

are they a sort of tune,
an ugly enough song, sung
by a bird with a slit tongue

but meant for music?

Or are they the muffled roaring   10
of deafmutes trapped in a building that is
slowly filling with smoke?

Perhaps both.

Such men most often
look as if groan were all they could do,   15
yet a woman, in spite of herself,

knows it's a tribute:
if she were lacking all grace
they'd pass her in silence:

so it's not only to say she's   20
a warm hole. It's a word

in grief-language, nothing to do with
primitive, not an ur-language;°   *earliest human language*
language stricken, sickened, cast down

in decrepitude.° She wants to   *decay*   25
throw the tribute away, dis-
gusted, and can't,

it goes on buzzing in her ear,
it changes the pace of her walk,
the torn posters in echoing corridors   30

spell it out, it
quakes and gnashes as the train comes in.
Her pulse sullenly

had picked up speed,
but the cars slow down and   35
jar to a stop while her understanding

keeps on translating:
"Life after life after life goes by
without poetry
without seemliness   40
without love."

The Responsive Reader

1. What is the view of male sexuality that underlies this poem? What do
   the bird metaphor, the deafmute metaphor, and the sickness metaphor
   each in turn contribute to the poem? Is the subway setting incidental,
   or is it especially suitable?
2. What are the mixed emotions or contradictory feelings that the woman
   in the poem experiences "in spite of herself"?
3. Who has the last word, and how would you put it into your own
   words?

Thinking, Talking, Writing

4. Is the poet hostile toward men in general? Is Levertov guilty of lumping
   all men together in order to judge and condemn them as a species?
5. Do you believe that men's and women's attitudes toward love and sex
   are generically different?

Thinking about Connections

6. Has the traditional "war between the sexes" become exacerbated in
   recent times, and have relationships between the sexes become more
   adversarial? What light do the poems by Giovanni, Rich, and Levertov
   throw upon this question? Is there a common strand or a recurrent
   theme?

LESBIANS LOVE TO DANCE
Judy Grahn

Some say a host of cavalry, others of infantry, and others of ships, is the most beautiful thing on the black earth, but I say it is whatsoever a person loves.

Sappho

In the eighties, Judy Grahn became a positive, affirmative voice for women who no longer wanted to be someone else's property, helpmate, gofer, plaything, or punching bag but instead wanted to be themselves. Like other feminist poets, she has explored in her poetry the echoes of an early stage of culture centered on the worship of the earth goddess or of a life-giving, life-preserving feminine principle. She has written much about Sappho, the woman whom many ancient Greeks considered their greatest lyric poet. Sappho is said to have run a school for women on the island of Lesbos, and gay women still call themselves lesbians in her honor. Grahn has paid tribute to the lives of ordinary women in her poems in The Work of a Common Woman *(1978). More recently she has been working on a cycle of poems about Helen of Troy seen as a goddess of beauty and love, of the womb and the source of life. The following poem is from* The Queen of Swords.

Lesbians love to dance   *1*
outside in the rain
with lightning darting
all around them. Lesbians
love to dance together   *5*
in the pouring rain, in
summer.
Lesbians love to dance
inside the thunder,
sheets of water   *10*
washing over their whole bodies
and the dark clouds
boiling and roiling like a
giant voice calling.
Lesbians love to answer   *15*
voices calling like that.
Lesbians love to
dance without their clothing
in thunderstorms with
lightning as their partner.   *20*
Screaming, holding hands
and turning soaking faces

skyward in tumultuous noise and yearning. Lesbians
love to see each other
learning to completely   *25*
rejoice. Lesbians love
to feel the power
and the glory they can dance
inside of, in a storm
of their communal choice.   *30*

The Responsive Reader

1. Does this poem have any relation to ideas or assumptions you have about lesbians? Do you think lesbians and readers who are not lesbians will react to this poem differently?

Thinking, Talking, Writing

2. Grahn has written about the "terrible division we have been taught to make between the physical and the spiritual, between the body and the mind, between the sexual and the sacred, between beauty and the beast." Do you think this poem can help readers overcome that division?

3. Most of Sappho's poetry became the victim of book burners of later ages. What would you say to people who want to censor or ban Grahn's poem?

Collaborative Projects

4. Grahn says that many of her readers and friends were saved from floundering in alienation by discovering sources of bonding through poetry, poetry readings, and bookshops. Does a bookstore or do bookstores in your area serve similar functions? Do they cater to special groups of readers?

THE STORY OF AN HOUR
Kate Chopin

Kate Chopin came from a wealthy St. Louis family. Her mother was from a French Louisiana, or Creole, background, as was the man Chopin married. She moved south with him, and her popular early stories were about New Orleans or about life on a cotton plantation. She read much contemporary fiction and polemical literature that challenged traditional religious and moral conventions. Darwin's theory of evolution was causing traditionalists and moderns to choose sides in heated controversies. Feminists were championing the "new woman," asking for economic equality and political representation.

In her novel The Awakening *(1899) and other fiction, Chopin explored topics that were becoming major themes of feminist or profeminist literature in Europe and America: a woman's right to rebel against a stifling marriage; a woman's right to recognize her own sensual nature and emotional needs; a woman's right to have the same freedom to act upon her erotic desires that men were taking for granted. The heroine of* The Awakening, *who is destroyed by the conventions of a sexually repressed society, rejects the traditional ideal that a woman should be willing to "sacrifice herself for her children" and should let husband and children "possess her, body and soul." Chopin's plea for the emotional and sexual emancipation of women scandalized respectable society. Her work was treated with condescension by the literary establishment, and she was nearly forgotten until today's feminist editors and critics championed her as an early rebel against what she called "the soul's slavery."*

Knowing that Mrs. Mallard was afflicted with a heart trouble, great care was taken to break to her as gently as possible the news of her husband's death.

It was her sister Josephine who told her, in broken sentences, veiled hints that revealed in half concealing. Her husband's friend Richards was there, too, near her. It was he who had been in the newspaper office when intelligence of the railroad disaster was received, with Brently Mallard's name leading the list of "killed." He had only taken the time to assure himself of its truth by a second telegram, and had hastened to forestall any less careful, less tender friend in bearing the sad message.

She did not hear the story as many women have heard the same, with a paralyzed inability to accept its significance. She wept at once, with sudden, wild abandonment, in her sister's arms. When the storm of grief had spent itself she went away to her room alone. She would have no one follow her.

There stood, facing the open window, a comfortable, roomy armchair. Into this she sank, pressed down by a physical exhaustion that haunted her body and seemed to reach into her soul.

She could see in the open square before her house the tops of trees that   *5*
were all aquiver with the new spring life. The delicious breath of rain was in
the air. In the street below a peddler was crying his wares. The notes of a
distant song which some one was singing reached her faintly, and countless
sparrows were twittering in the eaves.

There were patches of blue sky showing here and there through the
clouds that had met and piled above the other in the west facing her window.

She sat with her head thrown back upon the cushion of the chair quite
motionless, except when a sob came up into her throat and shook her, as a
child who has cried itself to sleep continues to sob in its dreams.

She was young, with a fair, calm face, whose lines bespoke repression
and even a certain strength. But now there was a dull stare in her eyes, whose
gaze was fixed away off yonder on one of those patches of blue sky. It was
not a glance of reflection, but rather indicated a suspension of intelligent
thought.

There was something coming to her and she was waiting for it, fearfully. What was it? She did not know; it was too subtle and elusive to name.
But she felt it, creeping out of the sky, reaching toward her through the
sounds, the scents, the color that filled the air.

Now her bosom rose and fell tumultuously. She was beginning to   *10*
recognize this thing that was approaching to possess her, and she was striving
to beat it back with her will—as powerless as her two white slender hands
would have been.

When she abandoned herself a little whispered word escaped her
slightly parted lips. She said it over and over under her breath: "Free, free,
free!" The vacant stare and the look of terror that had followed it went from
her eyes. They stayed keen and bright. Her pulses beat fast, and the coursing
blood warmed and relaxed every inch of her body.

She did not stop to ask if it were not a monstrous joy that held her.
A clear and exalted perception enabled her to dismiss the suggestion as
trivial.

She knew that she would weep again when she saw the kind, tender
hands folded in death; the face that had never looked save with love upon
her, fixed and gray and dead. But she saw beyond that bitter moment a long
procession of years to come that would belong to her absolutely. And she
opened and spread her arms out to them in welcome.

There would be no one to live for during those coming years; she
would live for herself. There would be no powerful will bending her in that
blind persistence with which men and women believe they have a right to
impose a private will upon a fellow creature. A kind intention or a cruel
intention made the act seem no less a crime as she looked upon it in that
brief moment of illumination.

And yet she had loved him—sometimes. Often she had not. What did   *15*
it matter! What could love, the unsolved mystery, count for in face of this

possession of self-assertion which she suddenly recognized as the strongest impulse of her being.

"Free! Body and soul free!" she kept whispering.

Josephine was kneeling before the closed door with her lips to the keyhole, imploring for admission. "Louise, open the door! I beg; open the door—you will make yourself ill. What are you doing, Louise? For heaven's sake open the door."

"Go away. I am not making myself ill." No; she was drinking in a very elixir of life through that open window.

Her fancy was running riot along those days ahead of her. Spring days, and summer days, and all sorts of days that would be her own. She breathed a quick prayer that life might be long. It was only yesterday she had thought with a shudder that life might be long.

She arose at length and opened the door to her sister's importunities.   20 There was a feverish triumph in her eyes, and she carried herself unwittingly like a goddess of Victory. She clasped her sister's waist, and together they descended the stairs. Richard stood waiting for them at the bottom.

Some one was opening the front door with a latchkey. It was Brently Mallard who entered, a little travel-stained, composedly carrying his grip-sack and umbrella. He had been far from the scene of accident, and did not even know there had been one. He stood amazed at Josephine's piercing cry; at Richards' quick motion to screen him from the view of his wife.

But Richards was too late.

When the doctors came they said she had died of heart disease—of joy that kills.

The Responsive Reader

1. Had Mrs. Mallard's been a loveless marriage? What do you learn in the story about her relationship with her husband? How did she feel about the marriage?
2. How might you expect the familiar themes of liberation and self-assertion to be treated in a story? How are they treated here? What makes this story different? What may have made it shocking or provocative to Chopin's contemporary readers?
3. Chopin was a pioneer in exploring women's unacknowledged and unexpressed desires and emotions. Which of the central character's emotions and thoughts do you find easy to understand or explain? Which are hard for you to understand?
4. Readers of Chopin's time liked trick endings—sudden reversals or marvelous coincidences that give a story an ironic twist. Does the ending of this story seem contrived, or does it serve the central theme of the story?

Thinking, Talking, Writing

5. Much has been written in recent years about people locked into situations of repression or dependency. Have you ever experienced strong feelings of rebellion or defiance? Have you ever experienced moments of strong self-assertion?
6. What attitudes and behaviors does our society expect of the bereaved? Have you or others ever disappointed these expectations?

THE CHRYSANTHEMUMS

John Steinbeck

John Steinbeck became famous in the thirties and forties as a voice for the dispossessed. He first became known for bittersweet stories about loners, drifters, and eccentrics—of white, Mexican, and Native American ancestry—who lived on the fringes of respectable society. He found large audiences for books like Tortilla Flat *(1935),* Of Mice and Men *(1937), and* Cannery Row *(1945). Millions of readers here and abroad came to know Steinbeck country— the Salinas valley and Monterey Bay in California where farms grew lettuce and artichokes and where sardine canneries lined the Monterey waterfront. Steinbeck's great American classic was* The Grapes of Wrath *(1939), which chronicled the odyssey of Midwesterners driven from their farms by the dust storms, economic blight, and foreclosed mortgages of the Great Depression. The novel and the movie classic based on it had a powerful message for those who still had property and jobs and who looked on the homeless unemployed as tramps and parasites: These "Okies" (because many of them had trekked to California from Oklahoma in search of jobs as migrant workers) were fellow human beings just like them, forced into poverty and despair by a soulless, bankrupt economic system. In his novel* In Dubious Battle *(1936), Steinbeck used the story of a fruit-pickers' strike to dramatize his political commitments and his experience with the Communists who were trying to organize the proletariat for action.*

At a time when feminist critics question the ability of male authors to provide a convincing, unblinkered view of women, they have credited Steinbeck with more insight into his female characters than they would expect from a male writer. Do you agree with them?

The high grey-flannel fog of winter closed off the Salinas Valley from the sky and from all the rest of the world. On every side it sat like a lid on the mountains and made of the great valley a closed pot. On the broad, level land floor the gang plows bit deep and left the black earth shining like metal where the shares had cut. On the foothill ranches across the Salinas River, the yellow stubble fields seemed to be bathed in pale cold sunshine, but there was no sunshine in the valley now in December. The thick willow scrub along the river flamed with sharp and positive yellow leaves.   *1*

It was a time of quiet and of waiting. The air was cold and tender. A light wind blew up from the southwest so that the farmers were mildly hopeful of a good rain before long; but fog and rain do not go together.

Across the river, on Henry Allen's foothill ranch there was little work to be done, for the hay was cut and stored and the orchards were plowed up to receive the rain deeply when it should come. The cattle on the higher slopes were becoming shaggy and rough-coated.

Elisa Allen, working in her flower garden, looked down across the yard and saw Henry, her husband, talking to two men in business suits. The three of them stood by the tractor shed, each man with one foot on the side of the little Fordson. They smoked cigarettes and studied the machine as they talked.

Elisa watched them for a moment and then went back to her work. She was thirty-five. Her face was lean and strong and her eyes were as clear as water. Her figure looked blocked and heavy in her gardening costume, a man's black hat pulled low down over her eyes, clodhopper shoes, a figured print dress almost completely covered by a big corduroy apron with four big pockets to hold the snips, the trowel and scratcher, the seeds and the knife she worked with. She wore heavy leather gloves to protect her hands while she worked. 5

She was cutting down the old year's chrysanthemum stalks with a pair of short and powerful scissors. She looked down toward the men by the tractor shed now and then. Her face was eager and mature and handsome; even her work with the scissors was over-eager, over-powerful. The chrysanthemum stems seemed too small and easy for her energy.

She brushed a cloud of hair out of her eyes with the back of her glove, and left a smudge of earth on her cheek in doing it. Behind her stood the neat white farm house with red geraniums close-banked around it as high as the windows. It was a hard-swept looking little house, with hard-polished windows, and a clean mud-mat on the front steps.

Elisa cast another glance toward the tractor shed. The strangers were getting into their Ford coupe. She took off a glove and put her strong fingers down into the forest of new green chrysanthemum sprouts that were growing around the old roots. She spread the leaves and looked down among the close-growing stems. No aphids were there, no sowbugs or snails or cutworms. Her terrier fingers destroyed such pests before they could get started.

Elisa started at the sound of her husband's voice. He had come near quietly, and he leaned over the wire fence that protected her flower garden from cattle and dogs and chickens.

"At it again," he said. "You've got a strong new crop coming." 10

Elisa straightened her back and pulled on the gardening glove again. "Yes. They'll be strong this coming year." In her tone and on her face there was a little smugness.

"You've got a gift with things," Henry observed. "Some of those yellow chrysanthemums you had this year were ten inches across. I wish you'd work out in the orchard and raise some apples that big."

Her eyes sharpened. "Maybe I could do it, too. I've a gift with things, all right. My mother had it. She could stick anything in the ground and make it grow. She said it was having planters' hands that knew how to do it."

"Well, it sure works with flowers," he said.

"Henry, who were those men you were talking to?" 15

"Why, sure, that's what I came to tell you. They were from the Western Meat Company. I sold those thirty head of three-year-old steers. Got nearly my own price, too."

"Good," she said. "Good for you."

"And I thought," he continued, "I thought how it's Saturday afternoon, and we might go into Salinas for dinner at a restaurant, and then to a picture show—to celebrate, you see."

"Good," she repeated. "Oh, yes. That will be good."

Henry put on his joking tone. "There's fights tonight. How'd you like to go to the fights?" *20*

"Oh, no," she said breathlessly. "No, I wouldn't like fights."

"Just fooling, Elisa. We'll go to a movie. Let's see. It's two now. I'm going to take Scotty and bring down those steers from the hill. It'll take us maybe two hours. We'll go in town about five and have dinner at the Cominos Hotel. Like that?"

"Of course I'll like it. It's good to eat away from home."

"All right, then. I'll go get up a couple of horses."

She said, "I'll have plenty of time to transplant some of these sets, I guess." *25*

She heard her husband calling Scotty down by the barn. And a little later she saw the two men ride up the pale yellow hillside in search of the steers.

There was a little square sandy bed kept for rooting the chrysanthemums. With her trowel she turned the soil over and over, and smoothed it and patted it firm. Then she dug ten parallel trenches to receive the sets. Back at the chrysanthemum bed she pulled out the little crisp shoots, trimmed off the leaves of each one with her scissors and laid it on a small orderly pile.

A squeak of wheels and plod of hoofs came from the road. Elisa looked up. The country road ran along the dense bank of willows and cottonwoods that bordered the river, and up this road came a curious vehicle, curiously drawn. It was an old spring-wagon, with a round canvas top on it like the cover of a prairie schooner. It was drawn by an old bay horse and a little grey-and-white burro. A big stubble-bearded man sat between the cover flaps and drove the crawling team. Underneath the wagon, between the hind wheels, a lean and rangy mongrel dog walked sedately. Words were painted on the canvas, in clumsy, crooked letters. "Pots, pans, knives, sisors, lawn mores, Fixed." Two rows of articles, and the triumphantly definitive "Fixed" below. The black paint had run down in little sharp points beneath each letter.

Elisa, squatting on the ground, watched to see the crazy, loose-jointed wagon pass by. But it didn't pass. It turned into the farm road in front of her house, crooked old wheels skirling and squeaking. The rangy dog darted from between the wheels and ran ahead. Instantly the two ranch shepherds flew out at him. Then all three stopped, and with stiff and quivering tails, with taut straight legs, with ambassadorial dignity, they slowly circled, sniffing daintily. The caravan pulled up to Elisa's wire fence and stopped. Now the newcomer dog, feeling out-numbered, lowered his tail and retired under the wagon with raised hackles and bared teeth.

The man on the wagon seat called out, "That's a bad dog in a fight when he gets started." 30

Elisa laughed. "I see he is. How soon does he generally get started?"

The man caught up her laughter and echoed it heartily. "Sometimes not for weeks and weeks," he said. He climbed stiffly down, over the wheel. The horse and the donkey drooped like unwatered flowers.

Elisa saw that he was a very big man. Although his hair and beard were greying, he did not look old. His worn black suit was wrinkled and spotted with grease. The laughter had disappeared from his face and eyes the moment his laughing voice ceased. His eyes were dark, and they were full of the brooding that gets in the eyes of teamsters and of sailors. The calloused hands he rested on the wire fence were cracked, and every crack was a black line. He took off his battered hat.

"I'm off my general road, ma'am," he said. "Does this dirt road cut over across the river to the Los Angeles highway?"

Elisa stood up and shoved the thick scissors in her apron pocket. "Well, yes, it does, but it winds around and then fords the river. I don't think your team could pull through the sand." 35

He replied with some asperity, "It might surprise you what them beasts can pull through."

"When they get started?" she asked.

He smiled for a second. "Yes. When they get started."

"Well," said Elisa, "I think you'll save time if you go back to the Salinas road and pick up the highway there."

He drew a big finger down the chicken wire and made it sing. "I ain't in any hurry, ma'am. I go from Seattle to San Diego and back every year. Takes all my time. About six months each way. I aim to follow nice weather." 40

Elisa took off her gloves and stuffed them in the apron pocket with the scissors. She touched the under edge of her man's hat, searching for fugitive hairs. "That sounds like a nice kind of a way to live," she said.

He leaned confidentially over the fence. "Maybe you noticed the writing on my wagon. I mend pots and sharpen knives and scissors. You got any of them things to do?"

"Oh, no," she said quickly. "Nothing like that." Her eyes hardened with resistance.

"Scissors is the worst thing," he explained. "Most people just ruin scissors trying to sharpen 'em, but I know how. I got a special tool. It's a little bobbit kind of thing, and patented. But it sure does the trick."

"No. My scissors are all sharp." 45

"All right, then. Take a pot," he continued earnestly, "a bent pot, or a pot with a hole. I can make it like new so you don't have to buy no new ones. That's a saving for you."

"No," she said shortly. "I tell you I have nothing like that for you to do."

His face fell to an exaggerated sadness. His voice took on a whining undertone. "I ain't had a thing to do today. Maybe I won't have no supper tonight. You see I'm off my regular road. I know folks on the highway clear from Seattle to San Diego. They save their things for me to sharpen up because they know I do it so good and save them money."

"I'm sorry," Elisa said irritably. "I haven't anything for you to do."

His eyes left her face and fell to searching the ground. They roamed about until they came to the chrysanthemum bed where she had been working. "What's them plants, ma'am?" 50

The irritation and resistance melted from Elisa's face. "Oh, those are chrysanthemums, giant whites and yellows. I raise them every year, bigger than anybody around here."

"Kind of a long-stemmed flower? Looks like a quick puff of colored smoke?" he asked.

"That's it. What a nice way to describe them."

"They smell kind of nasty till you get used to them," he said.

"It's a good bitter smell," she retorted, "not nasty at all." 55

He changed his tone quickly. "I like the smell myself."

"I had ten-inch blooms this year," she said.

The man leaned farther over the fence. "Look. I know a lady down the road a piece, has got the nicest garden you ever seen. Got nearly every kind of flower but no chrysanthemums. Last time I was mending a copper-bottom washtub for her (that's a hard job but I do it good), she said to me, 'If you ever run acrost some nice chrysantheums I wish you'd try to get me a few seeds.' That's what she told me."

Elisa's eyes grew alert and eager. "She couldn't have known much about chrysanthemums. You *can* raise them from seed, but it's much easier to root the little sprouts you see there."

"Oh," he said. "I s'pose I can't take none to her, then." 60

"Why yes you can," Elisa cried. "I can put some in damp sand, and you can carry them right along with you. They'll take root in the pot if you keep them damp. And then she can transplant them."

"She'd sure like to have some, ma'am. You say they're nice ones?"

"Beautiful," she said. "Oh, beautiful." Her eyes shone. She tore off the battered hat and shook out her dark pretty hair. "I'll put them in a flower pot, and you can take them right with you. Come into the yard."

While the man came through the picket gate Elisa ran excitedly along the geranium-bordered path to the back of the house. And she returned carrying a big red flower pot. The gloves were forgotten now. She kneeled on the ground by the starting bed and dug up the sandy soil with her fingers and scooped it into the bright new flower pot. Then she picked up the little pile of shoots she had prepared. With her strong fingers she pressed them into the sand and tamped around them with her knuckles. The man stood over her. "I'll tell you what to do," she said. "You remember so you can tell the lady."

"Yes, I'll try to remember."   65

"Well, look. These will take root in about a month. Then she must set them out, about a foot apart in good rich earth like this, see?" She lifted a handful of dark soil for him to look at. "They'll grow fast and tall. Now remember this: In July tell her to cut them down, about eight inches from the ground."

"Before they bloom?" he asked.

"Yes, before they bloom." Her face was tight with eagerness. "They'll grow right up again. About the last of September the buds will start."

She stopped and seemed perplexed. "It's the budding that takes the most care," she said hesitantly. "I don't know how to tell you." She looked deep into his eyes, searchingly. Her mouth opened a little, and she seemed to be listening. "I'll try to tell you," she said. "Did you ever hear of planting hands?"

"Can't say I have, ma'am."   70

"Well, I can only tell you what it feels like. It's when you're picking off the buds you don't want. Everything goes right down into your fingertips. You watch your fingers work. They do it themselves. You can feel how it is. They pick and pick the buds. They never make a mistake. They're with the plant. Do you see? Your fingers and the plant. You can feel that, right up your arm. They know. They never make a mistake. You can feel it. When you're like that you can't do anything wrong. Do you see that? Can you understand that?"

She was kneeling on the ground looking up at him. Her breast swelled passionately.

The man's eyes narrowed. He looked away self-consciously. "Maybe I know," he said. "Sometimes in the night in the wagon there—"

Elisa's voice grew husky. She broke in on him, "I've never lived as you do, but I know what you mean. When the night is dark—why, the stars are sharp-pointed, and there's quiet. Why, you rise up and up! Every pointed star gets driven into your body. It's like that. Hot and sharp and—lovely."

Kneeling there, her hand went out toward his legs in the greasy black   75
trousers. Her hesitant fingers almost touched the cloth. Then her hand dropped to the ground. She crouched low like a fawning dog.

He said, "It's nice, just like you say. Only when you don't have no dinner, it ain't."

She stood up then, very straight, and her face was ashamed. She held the flower pot out to him and placed it gently in his arms. "Here. Put it in your wagon, on the seat, where you can watch it. Maybe I can find something for you to do."

At the back of the house she dug in the can pile and found two old and battered aluminum saucepans. She carried them back and gave them to him. "Here, maybe you can fix these."

His manner changed. He became professional. "Good as new I can fix them." At the back of his wagon he set a little anvil, and out of an oily tool box dug a small machine hammer. Elisa came through the gate to watch him while he pounded out the dents in the kettles. His mouth grew sure and knowing. At a difficult part of the work he sucked his under-lip.

"You sleep right in the wagon?" Elisa asked.   80

"Right in the wagon, ma'am. Rain or shine I'm dry as a cow in there."

"It must be nice," she said. "It must be very nice. I wish women could do such things."

"It ain't the right kind of a life for a woman."

Her upper lip raised a little, showing her teeth. "How do you know? How can you tell?" she said.

"I don't know, ma'am," he protested. "Of course I don't know. Now   85 here's your kettles, done. You don't have to buy no new ones."

"How much?"

"Oh, fifty cents'll do. I keep my prices down and my work good. That's why I have all them satisfied customers up and down the highway."

Elisa brought him a fifty-cent piece from the house and dropped it in his hand. "You might be surprised to have a rival some time. I can sharpen scissors, too. And I can beat the dents out of little pots. I could show you what a woman might do."

He put his hammer back in the oily box and shoved the little anvil out of sight. "It would be a lonely life for a woman, ma'am, and a scarey life, too, with animals creeping under the wagon all night." He climbed over the singletree, steadying himself with a hand on the burro's white rump. He settled himself in the seat, picked up the lines. "Thank you kindly, ma'am," he said. "I'll do like you told me; I'll go back and catch the Salinas road."

"Mind," she called, "if you're long in getting there, keep the sand   90 damp."

"Sand, ma'am? . . . Sand? Oh, sure. You mean around the chrysanthemums. Sure I will." He clucked his tongue. The beasts leaned luxuriously into their collars. The mongrel dog took his place between the back wheels. The wagon turned and crawled out the entrance road and back the way it had come, along the river.

Elisa stood in front of her wire fence watching the slow progress of the caravan. Her shoulders were straight, her head thrown back, her eyes half-closed, so that the scene came vaguely into them. Her lips moved silently, forming the words "Good-bye—good-bye." Then she whispered, "That's a bright direction. There's a glowing there." The sound of her whisper startled her. She shook herself free and looked about to see whether anyone had been listening. Only the dogs had heard. They lifted their heads toward her from their sleeping in the dust, and then stretched out their chins and settled asleep again. Elisa turned and ran hurriedly into the house.

In the kitchen she reached behind the stove and felt the water tank. It was full of hot water from the noonday cooking. In the bathroom she tore off her soiled clothes and flung them into the corner. And then she scrubbed herself with a little block of pumice, legs and thighs, loins and chest and arms, until her skin was scratched and red. When she had dried herself she stood in front of a mirror in her bedroom and looked at her body. She tightened her stomach and threw out her chest. She turned and looked over her shoulder at her back.

After a while she began to dress, slowly. She put on her newest under-clothing and her nicest stockings and the dress which was the symbol of her prettiness. She worked carefully on her hair, penciled her eyebrows and rouged her lips.

Before she was finished she heard the little thunder of hoofs and the   95
shouts of Henry and his helper as they drove the red steers into the corral. She heard the gate bang shut and set herself for Henry's arrival.

His step sounded on the porch. He entered the house calling, "Elisa, where are you?"

"In my room, dressing. I'm not ready. There's hot water for your bath. Hurry up. It's getting late."

When she heard him splashing in the tub, Elisa laid his dark suit on the bed, and shirt and socks and tie beside it. She stood his polished shoes on the floor beside the bed. Then she went to the porch and sat primly and stiffly down. She looked toward the river road where the willow-line was still yellow with frosted leaves so that under the high grey fog they seemed a thin band of sunshine. This was the only color in the grey afternoon. She sat unmoving for a long time. Her eyes blinked rarely.

Henry came banging out of the door, shoving his tie inside his vest as he came. Elisa stiffened and her face grew tight. Henry stopped short and looked at her. "Why—why, Elisa. You look so nice!"

"Nice? You think I look nice? What do you mean by 'nice'?"   100

Henry blundered on. "I don't know. I mean you look different, strong and happy."

"I am strong? Yes, strong. What do you mean 'strong'?"

He looked bewildered. "You're playing some kind of a game," he said helplessly. "It's a kind of a play. You look strong enough to break a calf over your knee, happy enough to eat it like a watermelon."

For a second she lost her rigidity. "Henry! Don't talk like that. You didn't know what you said." She grew complete again. "I'm strong," she boasted. "I never knew before how strong."

Henry looked down toward the tractor shed, and when he brought his   105
eyes back to her, they were his own again. "I'll get out the car. You can put on your coat while I'm starting."

Elisa went into the house. She heard him drive to the gate and idle down his motor, and then she took a long time to put on her hat. She pulled it here and pressed it there. When Henry turned the motor off she slipped into her coat and went out.

The little roadster bounced along on the dirt road by the river, raising the birds and driving the rabbits into the brush. Two cranes flapped heavily over the willow-line and dropped into the river-bed.

Far ahead on the road Elisa saw a dark speck. She knew.

She tried not to look as they passed it, but her eyes would not obey. She whispered to herself sadly, "He might have thrown them off the road. That wouldn't have been much trouble, not very much. But he kept the pot," she explained. "He had to keep the pot. That's why he couldn't get them off the road."

The roadster turned a bend and she saw the caravan ahead. She swung *110* full around toward her husband so she could not see the little covered wagon and the mismatched team as the car passed them.

In a moment it was over. The thing was done. She did not look back.

She said loudly, to be heard above the motor, "It will be good, tonight, a good dinner."

"Now you're changed again," Henry complained. He took one hand from the wheel and patted her knee. "I ought to take you in to dinner oftener. It would be good for both of us. We get so heavy out on the ranch."

"Henry," she asked, "could we have wine at dinner?"

"Sure we could. Say! That will be fine." *115*

She was silent for a while; then she said, "Henry, those prize fights, do the men hurt each other very much?"

"Sometimes a little, not often. Why?"

"Well, I've read how they break noses, and blood runs down their chests. I've read how the fighting gloves get heavy and soggy with blood."

He looked around at her. "What's the matter, Elisa? I didn't know you read things like that." He brought the car to a stop, then turned to the right over the Salinas River bridge.

"Do any women ever go to the fights?" she asked. *120*

"Oh, sure, some. What's the matter, Elisa? Do you want to go? I don't think you'd like it, but I'll take you if you really want to go."

She relaxed limply in the seat. "Oh, no. No. I don't want to go. I'm sure I don't." Her face was turned away from him. "It will be enough if we can have wine. It will be plenty." She turned up her coat collar so he could not see that she was crying weakly—like an old woman.

The Responsive Reader

1. What kind of person is Elisa? What portrait of her does Steinbeck give his readers at the beginning of the story? What details to you seem especially significant? What do we learn about her from Steinbeck's description of her work in the garden?

2. What is the role of the tinker in the story? What is significant in the author's original description of him? What is the nature of the

attraction he exerts on Elisa? Do you at some point begin to be disillusioned with him? (Or were you on to him from the beginning?)

3. What kind of person is the husband? What are his strengths, and what are his weaknesses? What contrast does Steinbeck set up between the husband and the itinerant tinker?

4. What is the role of traditional sex roles in this story? What assumptions about men and women or about masculine and feminine traits play a role in the story? (Does Steinbeck seem to endorse them or to question them?)

5. What is the role of the chrysanthemums in the story as a whole? What makes them a central symbol in the story? Would you call their reappearance toward the end the climax or high point of the story?

Thinking, Talking, Writing

5. Critics have explored the role of "strong women" in Steinbeck's fiction. Would you call Elisa a strong or a weak person?

6. Critics have seen this story as suffused with sexual imagery, sexual symbols, and hints of sexual energy. What is Steinbeck's perspective on sex in this story? Does his treatment of sex seem outdated to you?

7. How might this story have been different if it had been written by a woman?

Collaborative Projects

8. Working alone or with your classmates, you might want to try your hand at doing a rewrite or writing a sequel that would update the story. You might want to have Elisa tell *her* side of the story.

SHILOH

Bobbie Ann Mason

Bobbie Ann Mason writes about the New South, where the war against the Yankees is ancient history and where Civil War battlefields like Shiloh are mere tourist attractions. The stories in her collection Shiloh and Other Stories *(1982) take place in rural Kentucky, where she grew up. Her characters are truck drivers, sales clerks, and community college students who bake casseroles from potatoes and mushroom soup and who in their spare time build model log cabins from Lincoln logs or make wall hangings of an Arizona sunset. They live in world of shopping malls, talk shows, and made-for-TV movies. The secret of Mason's fiction is that she does not look down on her ordinary characters but patiently chronicles their efforts to find meaning and direction in their ordinary lives. She writes about unraveling relationships, confining marriages, and tongue-tied, uncommunicative men. Often her people have a vague sense of having missed out on something important, of having at some point missed an important turn in the road.*

Mason makes the people in her stories real not by staging great dramatic confrontations but by tracing patiently revealing little things they do and say. She is a fanatic for apparently trivial detail that in retrospect tells us something important about people and their lives.

Leroy Moffitt's wife, Norma Jean, is working on her pectorals. She lifts three-pound dumbbells to warm up, then progresses to a twenty-pound barbell. Standing with her legs apart, she reminds Leroy of Wonder Woman.

"I'd give anything if I could just get these muscles to where they're real hard," says Norma Jean. "Feel this arm. It's not as hard as the other one."

"That's 'cause you're right-handed," says Leroy, dodging as she swings the barbell in an arc.

"Do you think so?"

"Sure."

Leroy is a truckdriver. He injured his leg in a highway accident four months ago, and his physical therapy, which involves weights and a pulley, prompted Norma Jean to try building herself up. Now she is attending a body-building class. Leroy has been collecting temporary disability since his tractor-trailer jackknifed in Missouri, badly twisting his left leg in its socket. He has a steel pin in his hip. He will probably not be able to drive his rig again. It sits in the backyard, like a gigantic bird that has flown home to roost. Leroy has been home in Kentucky for three months, and his leg is almost healed, but the accident frightened him and he does not want to drive any more long hauls. He is not sure what to do next. In the meantime, he makes things from craft kits. He started by building a miniature log cabin from notched Popsicle sticks. He varnished it and placed it on the TV set, where it remains. It reminds him of a rustic Nativity scene. Then he tried string art (sailing ships on black velvet), a macramé owl kit, a snap-together B-17 Flying Fortress, and a lamp made out of a model truck, with a light fixture screwed in the top of the cab. At first the kits were diversions, something to kill time, but now he is thinking about building a full-scale log house from a kit. It would be considerably cheaper than building a regular house, and besides, Leroy has grown to appreciate how things are put together. He has begun to realize that in all the years he was on the road he never took time to examine anything. He was always flying past scenery.

"They won't let you build a log cabin in any of the new subdivisions," Norma Jean tells him.

"They will if I tell them it's for you," he says, teasing her. Ever since they were married, he has promised Norma Jean he would build her a new home one day. They have always rented, and the house they live in is small and nondescript. It does not even feel like a home, Leroy realizes now.

Norma Jean works at the Rexall drugstore, and she has acquired an amazing amount of information about cosmetics. When she explains to Leroy the three stages of complexion care, involving creams, toners, and moisturizers, he thinks happily of other petroleum products—axle grease, diesel fuel. This is a connection between him and Norma Jean. Since he has been home, he has felt unusually tender about his wife and guilty over his long absences. But he can't tell what she feels about him. Norma Jean has never complained about his traveling; she has never made hurt remarks, like calling his truck a "widow-maker." He is reasonably certain she has been faithful to him, but he wishes she would celebrate his permanent homecoming more happily. Norma Jean is often startled to find Leroy at home, and he thinks she seems a little disappointed about it. Perhaps he reminds her too much of the early days of their marriage, before he went on the road. They had a child who died as an infant, years ago. They never speak about their memories of Randy, which have almost faded, but now that Leroy is home all the time, they sometimes feel awkward around each other, and Leroy wonders if one of them should mention the child. He has the feeling that they are waking up out of a dream together—that they must create a new marriage, start afresh. They are lucky they are still married. Leroy has read that for most people losing a child destroys the marriage—or else he heard this on *Donahue*. He can't always remember where he learns things anymore.

At Christmas, Leroy bought an electric organ for Norma Jean. She   10
used to play the piano when she was in high school. "It don't leave you," she told him once. "It's like riding a bicycle."

The new instrument had so many keys and buttons that she was bewildered by it at first. She touched the keys tentatively, pushed some buttons, then pecked out "Chopsticks." It came out in an amplified fox-trot rhythm, with marimba sounds.

"It's an orchestra!" she cried.

The organ had a pecan-look finish and eighteen preset chords, with optional flute, violin, trumpet, clarinet, and banjo accompaniments. Norma Jean mastered the organ almost immediately. At first she played Christmas songs. Then she bought *The Sixties Songbook* and learned every tune in it, adding variations to each with the rows of brightly colored buttons.

"I didn't like these old songs back then," she said. "But I have this crazy feeling I missed something."

"You didn't miss a thing," said Leroy.   *15*

Leroy likes to lie on the couch and smoke a joint and listen to Norma Jean play "Can't Take My Eyes Off You" and "I'll Be Back." He is back again. After fifteen years on the road, he is finally settling down with the woman he loves. She is still pretty. Her skin is flawless. Her frosted curls resemble pencil trimmings.

Now that Leroy has come home to stay, he notices how much the town has changed. Subdivisions are spreading across western Kentucky like an oil slick. The sign at the edge of town says "Pop: 11,500"—only seven hundred more than it said twenty years before. Leroy can't figure out who is living in all the new houses. The farmers who used to gather around the courthouse square on Saturday afternoons to play checkers and spit tobacco juice have gone. It has been years since Leroy has thought about the farmers, and they have disappeared without his noticing.

Leroy meets a kid named Stevie Hamilton in the parking lot at the new shopping center. While they pretend to be strangers meeting over a stalled car, Stevie tosses an ounce of marijuana under the front seat of Leroy's car. Stevie is wearing orange jogging shoes and a T-shirt that says CHATTAHOO-CHEE SUPER-RAT. His father is a prominent doctor who lives in one of the expensive subdivisions in a new white-columned brick house that looks like a funeral parlor. In the phone book under his name there is a separate number, with the listing "Teenagers."

"Where do you get this stuff?" asks Leroy. "From your pappy?"

"That's for me to know and you to find out," Stevie says. He is slit-   *20* eyed and skinny.

"What else you got?"

"What you interested in?"

"Nothing special. Just wondered."

Leroy used to take speed on the road. Now he has to go slowly. He needs to be mellow. He leans back against the car and says, "I'm aiming to build me a log house, soon as I get time. My wife, though, I don't think she likes the idea."

"Well, let me know when you want me again," Stevie says. He has a   *25* cigarette in his cupped palm, as though sheltering it from the wind. He takes a long drag, then stomps it on the asphalt and slouches away.

Stevie's father was two years ahead of Leroy in high school. Leroy is thirty-four. He married Norma Jean when they were both eighteen, and their child Randy was born a few months later, but he died at the age of four months and three days. He would be about Stevie's age now. Norma Jean and Leroy were at the drive-in, watching a double feature (*Dr. Strangelove* and *Lover Come Back*), and the baby was sleeping in the back seat. When the first movie ended, the baby was dead. It was the sudden infant death syndrome. Leroy remembers handing Randy to a nurse at the emergency room, as though he were offering her a large doll as a present. A dead baby feels like a sack of flour. "It just happens sometimes," said the doctor, in what Leroy always recalls as a nonchalant tone. Leroy can hardly remember the child anymore, but he still sees vividly a scene from *Dr. Strangelove* in which the President of the United States was talking in a folksy voice on the hot line to the Soviet premier about the bomber accidentally headed toward Russia. He was in the War Room, and the world map was lit up. Leroy remembers Norma Jean standing catatonically beside him in the hospital and himself thinking: Who is this strange girl? He had forgotten who she was. Now scientists are saying that crib death is caused by a virus. Nobody knows anything, Leroy thinks. The answers are always changing.

When Leroy gets home from the shopping center, Norma Jean's mother, Mabel Beasley, is there. Until this year, Leroy has not realized how much time she spends with Norma Jean. When she visits, she inspects the closets and then the plants, informing Norma Jean when a plant is droopy or yellow. Mabel calls the plants "flowers," although there are never any blooms. She always notices if Norma Jean's laundry is piling up. Mabel is a short, overweight woman whose tight, brown-dyed curls looked more like a wig than the actual wig she sometimes wears. Today she has brought Norma Jean an off-white dust ruffle she made for the bed; Mabel works in a custom-upholstery shop.

"This is the tenth one I made this year," Mabel says. "I got started and couldn't stop."

"It's real pretty," says Norma Jean.

"Now we can hide things under the bed," says Leroy, who gets along   30
with his mother-in-law primarily by joking with her. Mabel has never really forgiven him for disgracing her by getting Norma Jean pregnant. When the baby died, she said that fate was mocking her.

"What's that thing?" Mabel says to Leroy in a loud voice, pointing to a tangle of yarn on a piece of canvas.

Leroy holds it up for Mabel to see. "It's my needlepoint," he explains. "This is a *Star Trek* pillow cover."

"That's what a woman would do," says Mabel. "Great day in the morning!"

"All the big football players on TV do it," he says.

"Why, Leroy, you're always trying to fool me. I don't believe you for   35
one minute. You don't know what to do with yourself—that's the whole trouble. Sewing!"

"I'm aiming to build a log house," says Leroy. "Soon as my plans come."

"Like *heck* you are," says Norma Jean. She takes Leroy's needlepoint and shoves it into a drawer. "You have to find a job first. Nobody can afford to build now anyway."

Mabel straightens her girdle and says, "I still think before you get tied down y'all ought to take a little run to Shiloh."

"One of these days, Mama," Norma Jean says impatiently.

Mabel is talking about Shiloh, Tennessee. For the past few years, she has been urging Leroy and Norma Jean to visit the Civil War battleground there. Mabel went there on her honeymoon—the only real trip she ever took. Her husband died of a perforated ulcer when Norma Jean was ten, but Mabel, who was accepted into the United Daughters of the Confederacy in 1975, is still preoccupied with going back to Shiloh.

"I've been to kingdom come and back in that truck out yonder," Leroy says to Mabel, "but we never yet set foot in that battleground. Ain't that something? How did I miss it?"

"It's not even that far," Mabel says.

After Mabel leaves, Norma Jean reads to Leroy from a list she has made. "Things you could do," she announces. "You could get a job as a guard at Union Carbide, where they'd let you set on a stool. You could get on at the lumberyard. You could do a little carpenter work, if you want to build so bad. You could—"

"I can't do something where I'd have to stand up all day."

"You ought to try standing up all day behind a cosmetics counter. It's amazing that I have strong feet, coming from two parents that never had strong feet at all." At the moment Norma Jean is holding on to the kitchen counter, raising her knees one at a time as she talks. She is wearing two-pound ankle weights.

"Don't worry," says Leroy. "I'll do something."

"You could truck calves to slaughter for somebody. You wouldn't have to drive any big old truck for that."

"I'm going to build you this house," says Leroy. "I want to make you a real home."

"I don't want to live in any log cabin."

"It's not a cabin. It's a house."

"I don't care. It looks like a cabin."

"You and me together could lift those logs. It's just like lifting weights."

Norma Jean doesn't answer. Under her breath, she is counting. Now she is marching through the kitchen. She is doing goose steps.

Before his accident, when Leroy came home he used to stay in the house with Norma Jean, watching TV in bed and playing cards. She would cook fried chicken, picnic ham, chocolate pie—all his favorites. Now he is home alone much of the time. In the mornings, Norma Jean disappears, leaving a cooling place in the bed. She eats a cereal called Body Buddies, and she leaves the bowl on the table, with the soggy tan balls floating in a milk puddle. He sees things about Norma Jean that he never realized before. When she chops onions, she stares off into a corner, as if she can't bear to look. She puts on her house slippers almost precisely at nine o'clock every evening and nudges her jogging shoes under the couch. She saves bread heels for the birds. Leroy watches the birds at the feeder. He notices the peculiar way goldfinches fly past the window. They close their wings, then fall, then spread their wings to catch and lift themselves. He wonders if they close their eyes when they fall. Norma Jean closes her eyes when they are in bed. She wants the lights turned out. Even then, he is sure she closes her eyes.

He goes for long drives around town. He tends to drive a car rather   55 carelessly. Power steering and an automatic shift make a car feel so small and inconsequential that his body is hardly involved in the driving process. His injured leg stretches out comfortably. Once or twice he has almost hit something, but even the prospect of an accident seems minor in a car. He cruises the new subdivisions, feeling like a criminal rehearsing for a robbery. Norma Jean is probably right about a log house being inappropriate here in the new subdivisions. All the houses look grand and complicated. They depress him.

One day when Leroy comes home from a drive he finds Norma Jean in tears. She is in the kitchen making a potato and mushroom-soup casserole, with grated-cheese topping. She is crying because her mother caught her smoking.

"I didn't hear her coming. I was standing here puffing away pretty as you please," Norma Jean says, wiping her eyes.

"I knew it would happen sooner or later," says Leroy, putting his arm around her.

"She don't know the meaning of the word 'knock,'" says Norma Jean. "It's a wonder she hadn't caught me years ago."

"Think of it this way," Leroy says. "What if she caught me with a   60 joint?"

"You better not let her!" Norma Jean shrieks. "I'm warning you, Leroy Moffitt!"

"I'm just kidding. Here, play me a tune. That'll help you relax."

Norma Jean puts the casserole in the oven and sets the timer. Then she plays a ragtime tune, with horns and banjo, as Leroy lights up a joint and lies on the couch, laughing to himself about Mabel's catching him at it. He thinks of Stevie Hamilton—a doctor's son pushing grass. Everything is funny. The whole town seems crazy and small. He is reminded of Virgil Mathis, a boastful policeman Leroy used to shoot pool with. Virgil recently led a drug bust in a back room at a bowling alley, where he seized ten thousand dollars' worth of marijuana. The newspaper had a picture of him holding up the bags of grass and grinning widely. Right now, Leroy can imagine Virgil breaking down the door and arresting him with a lungful of smoke. Virgil would probably have been alerted to the scene because of all the racket Norma Jean is making. Now she sounds like a hard-rock band. Norma Jean is terrific. When she switches to a Latin-rhythm version of "Sunshine

Superman," Leroy hums along. Norma Jean's foot goes up and down, up and down.

"Well, what do you think?" Leroy says, when Norma Jean pauses to search through her music.

"What do I think about what?"   65

His mind has gone blank. Then he says, "I'll sell my rig and build a house." That wasn't what he wanted to say. He wanted to know what she thought—what she *really* thought—about them.

"Don't start in on that again," says Norma Jean. She begins playing "Who'll Be the Next in Line?"

Leroy used to tell hitchhikers his whole life story—about his travels, his hometown, the baby. He would end with a question: "Well, what do you think?" It was just a rhetorical question. In time, he had the feeling that he'd been telling the same story over and over to the same hitchhikers. He quit talking to hitchhikers when he realized how his voice sounded—whining and self-pitying, like some teenage-tragedy song. Now Leroy has the sudden impulse to tell Norma Jean about himself, as if he had just met her. They have known each other so long they have forgotten a lot about each other. They could become reacquainted. But when the oven timer goes off and she runs to the kitchen, he forgets why he wants to do this.

The next day, Mabel drops by. It is Saturday and Norma Jean is cleaning. Leroy is studying the plans of his log house, which have finally come in the mail. He has them spread out on the table—big sheets of stiff blue paper, with diagrams and numbers printed in white. While Norma Jean runs the vacuum, Mabel drinks coffee. She sets her coffee cup on a blueprint.

"I'm just waiting for time to pass," she says to Leroy, drumming her   70 fingers on the table.

As soon as Norma Jean switches off the vacuum, Mabel says in a loud voice, "Did you hear about the datsun dog that killed the baby?"

Norma Jean says, "The word is 'dachshund.'"

"They put the dog on trial. It chewed the baby's legs off. The mother was in the next room all the time." She raises her voice. "They thought it was neglect."

Norma Jean is holding her ears. Leroy manages to open the refrigerator and get some Diet Pepsi to offer Mabel. Mabel still has some coffee and she waves away the Pepsi.

"Datsuns are like that," Mabel says. "They're jealous dogs. They'll tear   75 a place to pieces if you don't keep an eye on them."

"You better watch out what you're saying, Mabel," says Leroy.

"Well, facts is facts."

Leroy looks out the window at his rig. It is like a huge piece of furniture gathering dust in the backyard. Pretty soon it will be an antique. He hears the vacuum cleaner. Norma Jean seems to be cleaning the living room rug again.

Later, she says to Leroy, "She just said that about the baby because she caught me smoking. She's trying to pay me back."

"What are you talking about?" Leroy says, nervously shuffling blueprints.   *80*

"You know good and well," Norma Jean says. She is sitting in a kitchen chair with her feet up and her arms wrapped around her knees. She looks small and helpless. She says, "The very idea, her bringing up a subject like that! Saying it was neglect."

"She didn't mean that," Leroy says.

"She might not have *thought* she meant it. She always says things like that. You don't know how she goes on."

"But she didn't really mean it. She was just talking."

Leroy opens a king-sized bottle of beer and pours it into two glasses,   *85* dividing it carefully. He hands a glass to Norma Jean and she takes it from him mechanically. For a long time, they sit by the kitchen window watching the birds at the feeder.

Something is happening. Norma Jean is going to night school. She has graduated from her six-week body-building course and now she is taking an adult-education course in composition at Paducah Community College. She spends her evenings outlining paragraphs.

"First you have a topic sentence," she explains to Leroy. "Then you divide it up. Your secondary topic has to be connected to your primary topic."

To Leroy, this sounds intimidating. "I never was any good in English," he says.

"It makes a lot of sense."

"What are you doing this for, anyhow?"   *90*

She shrugs. "It's something to do." She stands up and lifts her dumbbells a few times.

"Driving a rig, nobody cared about my English."

"I'm not criticizing your English."

Norma Jean used to say, "If I lose ten minutes' sleep, I just drag all day." Now she stays up late, writing compositions. She got a B on her first paper— a how-to theme on soup-based casseroles. Recently Norma Jean has been cooking unusual foods—tacos, lasagna, Bombay chicken. She doesn't play the organ anymore, though her second paper was called "Why Music Is Important to Me." She sits at the kitchen table, concentrating on her outlines, while Leroy plays with his log house plans, practicing with a set of Lincoln Logs. The thought of getting a truckload of notched, numbered logs scares him, and he wants to be prepared. As he and Norma Jean work together at the kitchen table, Leroy has the hopeful thought that they are sharing something, but he knows he is a fool to think this. Norma Jean is miles away. He knows he is going to lose her. Like Mabel, he is just waiting for time to pass.

One day, Mabel is there before Norma Jean gets home from work, and   *95* Leroy finds himself confiding in her. Mabel, he realizes, must know Norma Jean better than he does.

"I don't know what's got into that girl," Mabel says. "She used to go to bed with the chickens. Now you say she's up all hours. Plus her a-smoking. I like to died."

"I want to make her this beautiful home," Leroy says, indicating the Lincoln Logs. "I don't thinks she even wants it. Maybe she was happier with me gone."

"She don't know what to make of you, coming home like this."

"Is that it?"

Mabel takes the roof off his Lincoln Log cabin. "You couldn't get *me*   100
in a log cabin," she says. "I was raised in one. It's no picnic, let me tell you."

"They're different now," says Leroy.

"I tell you what," Mabel says, smiling oddly at Leroy.

"What?"

"Take her on down to Shiloh. Y'all need to get out together, stir a little. Her brain's all balled up over them books."

Leroy can see traces of Norma Jean's features in her mother's face.   105
Mabel's worn face has the texture of crinkled cotton, but suddenly she looks pretty. It occurs to Leroy that Mabel has been hinting all along that she wants them to take her with them to Shiloh.

"Let's all go to Shiloh," he says. "You and me and her. Some Sunday."

Mabel throws up her hands in protest. "Oh, no, not me. Young folks want to be by theirselves."

When Norma Jean comes in with groceries, Leroy says excitedly, "Your mama here's been dying to go to Shiloh for forty-five years. It's about time we went, don't you think?"

"I'm not going to butt in on anybody's second honeymoon," Mabel says.

"Who's going on a honeymoon, for Christ's sake?" Norma Jean says   110
loudly.

"I never raised no daughter of mine to talk that-a-way," Mabel says.

"You ain't seen nothing yet," says Norma Jean. She starts putting away boxes and cans, slamming cabinet doors.

"There's a log cabin at Shiloh," Mabel says. "It was there during the battle. There's bullet holes in it."

"When are you going to *shut up* about Shiloh, Mama?" asks Norma Jean.

"I always thought Shiloh was the prettiest place, so full of history," 115
Mabel goes on. "I just hoped y'all could see it once before I die, so you could tell me about it." Later, she whispers to Leroy, "You do what I said. A little change is what she needs."

"Your name means 'the king,'" Norma Jean says to Leroy that evening. He is trying to get her to go to Shiloh, and she is reading a book about another century.

"Well, I reckon I ought to be right proud."

"I guess so."

"Am I still king around here?"

Norma Jean flexes her biceps and feels them for hardness. "I'm not   *120*
fooling around with anybody, if that's what you mean," she says.

"Would you tell me if you were?"

"I don't know."

"What does *your* name mean?"

"It was Marilyn Monroe's real name."

"No kidding!"   *125*

"Norma comes from the Normans. They were invaders," she says. She
closes her book and looks hard at Leroy. "I'll go to Shiloh with you if you'll
stop staring at me."

On Sunday, Norma Jean packs a picnic and they go to Shiloh. To
Leroy's relief, Mabel says she does not want to come with them. Norma Jean
drives, and Leroy, sitting beside her, feels like some boring hitchhiker she has
picked up. He tries some conversation, but she answers him in monosyllables.
At Shiloh, she drives aimlessly through the park, past bluffs and trails and
steep ravines. Shiloh is an immense place, and Leroy cannot see it as a
battleground. It is not what he expected. He thought it would look like a
golf course. Monuments are everywhere, showing through the thick clusters
of trees. Norma Jean passes the log cabin Mabel mentioned. It is surrounded
by tourists looking for bullet holes.

"That's not the kind of log house I've got in mind," says Leroy
apologetically.

"I know *that*."

"This is a pretty place. Your mama was right."   *130*

"It's O.K.," says Norma Jean. "Well, we've seen it. I hope she's satisfied."

They burst out laughing together.

At the park museum, a movie on Shiloh is shown every half hour, but
they decide that they don't want to see it. They buy a souvenir Confederate
flag for Mabel, and then they find a picnic spot near the cemetery. Norma
Jean has brought a picnic cooler, with pimiento sandwiches, soft drinks, and
Yodels. Leroy eats a sandwich and then smokes a joint, hiding it behind the
picnic cooler. Norma Jean has quit smoking altogether. She is picking cake
crumbs from the cellophane wrapper, like a fussy bird.

Leroy says, "So the boys in gray ended up in Corinth. The Union
soldiers zapped 'em finally, April 7, 1862."

They both know that he doesn't know any history. He is just talking   *135*
about some of the historical plaques they have read. He feels awkward, like
a boy on a date with an older girl. They are still just making conversation.

"Corinth is where Mama eloped to," says Norma Jean.

They sit in silence and stare at the cemetery for the Union dead and,
beyond, at a tall cluster of trees. Campers are parked nearby, bumper to
bumper, and small children in bright clothing are cavorting and squealing.
Norma Jean wads up the cake wrapper and squeezes it tightly in her hand.
Without looking at Leroy, she says, "I want to leave you."

Leroy takes a bottle of Coke out of the cooler and flips off the cap. He holds the bottle poised near his mouth but cannot remember to take a drink. Finally he says, "No, you don't."

"Yes, I do."

"I won't let you."   140

"You can't stop me."

"Don't do me that way."

Leroy knows Norma Jean will have her own way. "Didn't I promise to be home from now on?" he says.

"In some ways, a woman prefers a man who wanders," says Norma Jean. "That sounds crazy, I know."

"You're not crazy."   145

Leroy remembers to drink from his Coke. Then he says, "Yes, you *are* crazy. You and me could start all over again. Right back at the beginning."

"We *have* started all over again," says Norma Jean. "And this is how it turned out."

"What did I do wrong?"

"Nothing."

"Is this one of those women's lib things?" Leroy asks.   150

"Don't be funny."

The cemetery, a green slope dotted with white markers, looks like a subdivision site. Leroy is trying to comprehend that his marriage is breaking up, but for some reason he is wondering about white slabs in a graveyard.

"Everything was fine till Mama caught me smoking," says Norma Jean, standing up. "That set something off."

"What are you talking about?"

"She won't leave me alone—*you* won't leave me alone." Norma Jean   155 seems to be crying, but she is looking away from him. "I feel eighteen again. I can't face that all over again." She starts walking away. "No, it *wasn't* fine. I don't know what I'm saying. Forget it."

Leroy takes a lungful of smoke and closes his eyes as Norma Jean's words sink in. He tries to focus on the fact that thirty-five hundred soldiers died on the grounds around him. He can only think of that war as a board game with plastic soldiers. Leroy almost smiles, as he compares the Confederates' daring attack on the Union camps and Virgil Mathis's raid on the bowling alley. General Grant, drunk and furious, shoved the Southerners back to Corinth, where Mabel and Jet Beasley were married years later, when Mabel was still thin and good-looking. The next day, Mabel and Jet visited the battleground, and then Norma Jean was born, and then she married Leroy and they had a baby, which they lost, and now Leroy and Norma Jean are here at the same battleground. Leroy knows he is leaving out a lot. He is leaving out the insides of history. History was always just names and dates to him. It occurs to him that building a house out of logs is similarly empty—too simple. And the real inner workings of a marriage, like most of history, have escaped him. Now he sees that building a log house is the dumbest idea he could have had. It was clumsy of him to think Norma Jean would want a log house. It was a crazy idea. He'll have to think of something else, quickly. He will wad the blueprints into tight balls and fling them into the lake. Then he'll get moving again. He opens his eyes. Norma Jean has moved away and is walking through the cemetery, following a serpentine brick path.

Leroy gets up to follow his wife, but his good leg is asleep and his bad leg still hurts him. Norma Jean is far away, walking rapidly toward the bluff by the river, and he tries to hobble toward her. Some children run past him, screaming noisily. Norma Jean has reached the bluff, and she is looking out over the Tennessee River. Now she turns toward Leroy and waves her arms. Is she beckoning to him? She seems to be doing an exercise for her chest muscles. The sky is unusually pale—the color of the dust ruffle Mabel made for their bed.

The Responsive Reader

1. What kind of person is the husband in this story? What is Leroy's situation? What is his attitude toward his wife? His life? The future?
2. What kind of person is Norma Jean? When do you begin to see that she and her husband are heading in different directions? What is at the bottom of their differences? What is wrong with their relationship?
3. What is the possible symbolic significance in this story of Leroy's rig, of his injury, and of the log cabin model he assembles? Are there other details that for you seem to play a symbolic role? What details in Norma Jean's life might have a symbolic meaning?
4. What is the role of the mother-in-law in the story? Is her role to provide comic relief—to lighten the seriousness of the story by providing a humorous counterpoint? Or does she also contribute something more serious to the story?
5. Where are the two principal characters headed at the end of the story? What lies ahead for them?

Thinking, Talking, Writing

6. Do you read the story as the history of two individuals with their own special problems? Or do they seem representative of larger patterns? Is their relationship in some ways typical or representative? How?
7. Much has been written in recent years about the need for self-awareness or self-understanding. Do the characters in this story understand what is happening to them?
8. If you were a marriage counselor or other concerned person, what would you tell the two main characters in this story?

Thinking about Connections

9. Compare the two women who are central characters in Steinbeck's "The Chrysanthemums" and Mason's "Shiloh." What do they have in common; what sets them apart? Would you call Steinbeck's story the more pessimistic and Mason's the more optimistic of the two?

QUILTING ON THE REBOUND

Terry McMillan

Terry McMillan was born in Michigan, studied at Berkeley, and went to live in California. Her first novel, Mama, *was published in 1987 and was followed by* Disappearing Acts *and* Waiting To Exhale. *Because of her honest account of tensions in black male-female relationships, she has been accused of "male-bashing" (as have other African American women authors writing today). One of her many enthusiastic readers answered such charges by writing in* Ebony *magazine, "African-American females have been and remain to this day strong with and without their men. Too many brothers, however, have given up their duties and obligations to love, respect, protect and honor the Black woman. Our men have become weakened by a system which was designed to systematically weaken and destroy them mentally; a system which divides and separates the love and efforts of men and women" (Shirley G. Perry).*

Five years ago, I did something I swore I'd never do—went out with someone I worked with. We worked for a large insurance company in L.A. Richard was a senior examiner and I was a chief underwriter. The first year, we kept it a secret, and not because we were afraid of jeopardizing our jobs. Richard was twenty-six and I was thirty-four. By the second year, everybody knew it anyway and nobody seemed to care. We'd been going out for three years when I realized that this relationship was going nowhere. I probably could've dated him for the rest of my life and he'd have been satisfied. Richard had had a long reputation for being a Don Juan of sorts, until he met me. I cooled his heels. His name was also rather ironic, because he looked like a black Richard Gere. The fact that I was older than he was made him feel powerful in a sense, and he believed that he could do for me what men my own age apparently couldn't. But that wasn't true. He was a challenge. I wanted to see if I could make his head and heart turn 360 degrees, and I did. I blew his young mind in bed, but he also charmed me into loving him until I didn't care how old he was.

Richard thought I was exotic because I have slanted eyes, high cheekbones, and full lips. Even though my mother is Japanese and my dad is black, I inherited most of his traits. My complexion is dark, my hair is nappy, and I'm five-six. I explained to Richard that I was proud of both of my heritages, but he has insisted on thinking of me as being mostly Japanese. Why, I don't know. I grew up in a black neighborhood in L.A., went to Dorsey High School—which was predominantly black, Asian, and Hispanic—and most of my friends are black. I've never even considered going out with anyone other than black men.

1

My mother, I'm glad to say, is not the stereotypical passive Japanese wife either. She's been the head nurse in Kaiser's cardiovascular unit for over twenty years, and my dad has his own landscaping business, even though he should've retired years ago. My mother liked Richard and his age didn't bother her, but she believed that if a man loved you he should marry you. Simple as that. On the other hand, my dad didn't care who I married just as long as it was soon. I'll be the first to admit that I was a spoiled-rotten brat because my mother had had three miscarriages before she finally had me and I was used to getting everything I wanted. Richard was no exception. "Give him the ultimatum," my mother had said, if he didn't propose by my thirty-eighth birthday.

But I didn't have to. I got pregnant.

We were having dinner at an Italian restaurant when I told him. "You   5 want to get married, don't you?" he'd said.

"Do you?" I asked.

He was picking through his salad and then he jabbed his fork into a tomato. "Why not, we were headed in that direction anyway, weren't we?" He did not eat his tomato but laid his fork down on the side of the plate.

I swallowed a spoonful of my clam chowder, then asked, "Were we?"

"You know the answer to that. But hell, now's as good a time as any. We're both making good money, and sometimes all a man needs is a little incentive." He didn't look at me when he said this, and his voice was strained. "Look," he said, "I've had a pretty shitty day, haggling with one of the adjusters, so forgive me if I don't appear to be boiling over with excitement. I am happy about this. Believe me, I am," he said, and picked up a single piece of lettuce with a different fork and put it into his mouth.

My parents were thrilled when I told them, but my mother was nev-   10 ertheless suspicious. "Funny how this baby pop up, isn't it?" she'd said.

"What do you mean?"

"You know exactly what I mean. I hope baby doesn't backfire."

I ignored what she'd just said. "Will you help me make my dress?" I asked.

"Yes," she said. "But we must hurry."

My parents—who are far from well off—went all out for this wedding.   15 My mother didn't want anyone to know I was pregnant, and to be honest, I didn't either. The age difference was enough to handle as it was. Close to three hundred people had been invited, and my parents had spent an astronomical amount of money to rent a country club in Marina Del Rey. "At your age," my dad had said, "I hope you'll only be doing this once." Richard's parents insisted on taking care of the caterer and the liquor, and my parents didn't object. I paid for the cake.

About a month before the Big Day, I was meeting Richard at the jeweler because he'd picked out my ring and wanted to make sure I liked it.

He was so excited, he sounded like a little boy. It was beautiful, but I told him he didn't have to spend four thousand dollars on my wedding ring. "You're worth it," he'd said and kissed me on the cheek. When we got to the parking lot, he opened my door and stood there staring at me. "Four more weeks," he said, "and you'll be my wife." He didn't smile when he said it, but closed the door and walked around to the driver's side and got in. He'd driven four whole blocks without saying a word and his knuckles were almost white because of how tight he was holding the steering wheel.

"Is something wrong, Richard?" I asked him.

"What would make you think that?" he said. Then he laid on the horn because someone in front of us hadn't moved and the light had just barely turned green.

"Richard, we don't have to go through with this, you know."

"I know we don't *have* to, but it's the right thing to do, and I'm going   20
to do it. So don't worry, we'll be happy."

But I *was* worried.

I'd been doing some shopping at the Beverly Center when I started getting these stomach cramps while I was going up the escalator, so I decided to sit down. I walked over to one of the little outside cafés and I felt something lock inside my stomach, so I pulled out a chair. Moments later my skirt felt like it was wet. I got up and looked at the chair and saw a small red puddle. I sat back down and started crying. I didn't know what to do. Then a punkish-looking girl came over and asked if I was okay. "I'm pregnant, and I've just bled all over this chair," I said.

"Can I do something for you? Do you want me to call an ambulance?" She was popping chewing gum and I wanted to snatch it out of her mouth.

By this time at least four other women had gathered around me. The punkish-looking girl told them about my condition. One of the women said, "Look, let's get her to the rest room. She's probably having a miscarriage."

Two of the women helped me up and all four of them formed a circle   25
around me, then slowly led me to the ladies' room. I told them that I wasn't in any pain, but they were still worried. I closed the stall door, pulled down two toilet seat covers, and sat down. I felt as if I had to go, so I pushed. Something plopped out of me and it made a splash. I was afraid to get up but I got up and looked at this large dark mass that looked like liver. I put my hand over my mouth because I knew that was my baby.

"Are you okay in there?"

I went to open my mouth, but the joint in my jawbone clicked and my mouth wouldn't move.

"Are you okay in there, miss?"

I wanted to answer, but I couldn't.

"Miss." I heard her banging on the door.   30

I felt my mouth loosen. "It's gone," I said. "It's gone."

"Honey, open the door," someone said, but I couldn't move. Then I heard myself say, "I think I need a sanitary pad." I was staring into the toilet bowl when I felt a hand hit my leg. "Here, are you sure you're okay in there?"

"Yes," I said. Then I flushed the toilet with my foot and watched my future disappear. I put the pad on and reached inside my shopping bag, pulled out a Raiders sweatshirt I'd bought for Richard, and tied it around my waist. When I came out, all of the women were waiting for me. "Would you like us to call your husband? Where are you parked? Do you feel light-headed, dizzy?"

"No, I'm fine, really, and thank you so much for your concern. I appreciate it, but I feel okay."

I drove home in a daze and when I opened the door to my condo, I   35
was glad I lived alone. I sat on the couch from one o'clock to four o'clock without moving. When I finally got up, it felt as if I'd only been there for five minutes.

I didn't tell Richard. I didn't tell anybody. I bled for three days before I went to see my doctor. He scolded me because I'd gotten some kind of an infection and had to be prescribed antibiotics, then he sent me to the out-patient clinic, where I had to have a D & C.

Two weeks later, I had a surprise shower and got enough gifts to fill the housewares department at Bullock's. One of my old girlfriends, Gloria, came all the way from Phoenix, and I hadn't seen her in three years. I hardly recognized her, she was as big as a house. "You don't know how lucky you are, girl," she'd said to me. "I wish I could be here for the wedding but Tarik is having his sixteenth birthday party and I am not leaving a bunch of teen-agers alone in my house. Besides, I'd probably have a heart attack watching you or anybody else walk down an aisle in white. Come to think of it, I can't even remember the last time I went to a wedding."

"Me either," I said.

"I know you're gonna try to get pregnant in a hurry, right?" she asked, holding out her wrist with the watch on it.

I tried to smile. "I'm going to work on it," I said.   40

"Well, who knows?" Gloria said, laughing. "Maybe one day you'll be coming to my wedding. We may both be in wheelchairs, but you never know."

"I'll be there," I said.

All Richard said when he saw the gifts was, "What are we going to do with all this stuff? Where are we going to put it?"

"It depends on where we're going to live," I said, which we hadn't even talked about. My condo was big enough and so was his apartment.

"It doesn't matter to me, but I think we should wait a while before   45 buying a house. A house is a big investment, you know. Thirty years." He gave me a quick look.

"Are you getting cold feet?" I blurted out.

"No, I'm not getting cold feet. It's just that in two weeks we're going to be man and wife, and it takes a little getting used to the idea, that's all."

"Are you having doubts about the idea of it?"

"No."

"Are you sure?"   50

"I'm sure," he said.

I didn't stop bleeding, so I took some vacation time to relax and finish my dress. I worked on it day and night and was doing all the beadwork by hand. My mother was spending all her free time at my place trying to make sure everything was happening on schedule. A week before the Big Day I was trying on my gown for the hundredth time when the phone rang. I thought it might be Richard, since he hadn't called me in almost forty-eight hours, and when I finally called him and left a message, he still hadn't returned my call. My father said this was normal.

"Hello," I said.

"I think you should talk to Richard." It was his mother.

"About what?" I asked.   55

"He's not feeling very well," was all she said.

"What's wrong with him?"

"I don't know for sure. I think it's his stomach."

"Is he sick?"

"I don't know. Call him."   60

"I did call him but he hasn't returned my call."

"Keep trying," she said.

So I called him at work, but his secretary said he wasn't there. I called him at home and he wasn't there either, so I left another message and for the next three hours I was a wreck, waiting to hear from him. I knew something was wrong.

I gave myself a facial, a manicure, and a pedicure and watched Oprah Winfrey while I waited by the phone. It didn't ring. My mother was downstairs hemming one of the bridesmaid's dresses. I went down to get myself a glass of wine. "How you feeling, Marilyn Monroe?" she asked.

"What do you mean, how am I feeling? I'm feeling fine."   65

"All I meant was you awful lucky with no morning sickness or anything, but I must say, hormones changing because you getting awfully irritating."

"I'm sorry, Ma."

"It's okay. I had jitters too."

I went back upstairs and closed my bedroom door, then went into my bathroom. I put the wineglass on the side of the bathtub and decided to take a bubble bath in spite of the bleeding. I must have poured half a bottle of

Secreti in. The water was too hot but I got in anyway. Call, dammit, call. Just then the phone rang and scared me half to death. I was hyperventilating and couldn't say much except, "Hold on a minute," while I caught my breath.

"Marilyn?" Richard was saying. "Marilyn?" But before I had a chance 70 to answer he blurted out what must have been on his mind all along. "Please don't be mad at me, but I can't do this. I'm not ready. I wanted to do the right thing, but I'm only twenty-nine years old. I've got my whole life ahead of me. I'm not ready to be a father yet. I'm not ready to be anybody's husband either, and I'm scared. Everything is happening too fast. I know you think I'm being a coward, and you're probably right. But I've been having nightmares, Marilyn. Do you hear me, nightmares about being imprisoned. I haven't been able to sleep through the night. I doze off and wake up dripping wet. And my stomach. It's in knots. Believe me, Marilyn, it's not that I don't love you because I do. It's not that I don't care about the baby, because I do. I just can't do this right now. I can't make this kind of commitment right now. I'm sorry. Marilyn? Marilyn, are you still there?"

I dropped the portable phone in the bathtub and got out.

My mother heard me screaming and came tearing into the room. "What happened?"

I was dripping wet and ripping the pearls off my dress but somehow I managed to tell her.

"He come to his senses," she said. "This happen a lot. He just got cold feet, but give him day or two. He not mean it."

Three days went by and he didn't call. My mother stayed with me and 75 did everything she could to console me, but by that time I'd already flushed the ring down the toilet.

"I hope you don't lose baby behind this," she said.

"I've already lost the baby," I said.

"What?"

"A month ago."

Her mouth was wide open. She found the sofa with her hand and sat 80 down. "Marilyn," she said and let out an exasperated sigh.

"I couldn't tell anybody."

"Why not tell somebody? Why not me, your mother?"

"Because I was too scared."

"Scared of what?"

"That Richard might change his mind."   85

"Man love you, dead baby not change his mind."

"I was going to tell him after we got married."

"I not raise you to be dishonest."

"I know."

"No man in world worth lying about something like this. How could 90 you?"

"I don't know."
"I told you it backfire, didn't I?"

For weeks I couldn't eat or sleep. At first, all I did was think about what was wrong with me. I was too old. For him. No. He didn't care about my age. It was the gap in my teeth, or my slight overbite, from all those years I used to suck my thumb. But he never mentioned anything about it and I was really the only one who seemed to notice. I was flat-chested. I had cellulite. My ass was square instead of round. I wasn't exciting as I used to be in bed. No. I was still good in bed, that much I did know. I couldn't cook. I was a terrible housekeeper. That was it. If you couldn't cook and keep a clean house, what kind of wife would you make?

I had to make myself stop thinking about my infinite flaws, so I started quilting again. I was astonished at how radiant the colors were that I was choosing, how unconventional and wild the patterns were. Without even realizing it, I was fusing Japanese and African motifs and was quite excited by the results. My mother was worried about me, even though I had actually stopped bleeding for two whole weeks. Under the circumstances, she thought that my obsession with quilting was not normal, so she forced me to go to the doctor. He gave me some kind of an antidepressant, which I refused to take. I told him I was not depressed, I was simply hurt. Besides, a pill wasn't any antidote or consolation for heartache.

I began to patronize just about every fabric store in downtown Los Angeles, and while I listened to the humming of my machine, and concentrated on designs that I couldn't believe I was creating, it occurred to me that I wasn't suffering from heartache at all. I actually felt this incredible sense of relief. As if I didn't have to anticipate anything else happening that was outside of my control. And when I did grieve, it was always because I had lost a child, not a future husband.

I also heard my mother all day long on my phone, lying about some tragedy that had happened and apologizing for any inconvenience it may have caused. And I watched her, bent over at the dining room table, writing hundreds of thank-you notes to the people she was returning gifts to. She even signed my name. My father wanted to kill Richard. "He was too young, and he wasn't good enough for you anyway," he said. "This is really a blessing in disguise."

I took a leave of absence from my job because there was no way in hell I could face those people, and the thought of looking at Richard infuriated me. I was not angry at him for not marrying me, I was angry at him for not being honest, for the way he handled it all. He even had the nerve to come over without calling. I had opened the door but wouldn't let him inside. He was nothing but a little pipsqueak. A handsome, five-foot-seven-inch pipsqueak.

"Marilyn, look, we need to talk."

"About what?"

"Us. The baby."

"There is no baby."

"What do you mean, there's no baby?"

"It died."

"You mean you got rid of it?"

"No, I lost it."

"I'm sorry, Marilyn," he said and put his head down. How touching, I thought. "This is all my fault."

"It's not your fault, Richard."

"Look. Can I come in?"

"For what?"

"I want to talk. I need to talk to you."

"About what?"

"About us."

"Us?"

"Yes, us. I don't want it to be over between us. I just need more time, that's all."

"Time for what?"

"To make sure this is what I want to do."

"Take all the time you need," I said and slammed the door in his face. He rang the buzzer again, but I just told him to get lost and leave me alone.

I went upstairs and sat at my sewing machine. I turned the light on, then picked up a piece of purple and terra-cotta cloth. I slid it under the pressure foot and dropped it. I pressed down on the pedal and watched the needle zigzag. The stitches were too loose so I tightened the tension. Richard is going to be the last in a series of mistakes I've made when it comes to picking a man. I've picked the wrong one too many times, like a bad habit that's too hard to break. I haven't had the best of luck when it comes to keeping them either, and to be honest, Richard was the one who lasted the longest.

When I got to the end of the fabric, I pulled the top and bobbin threads together and cut them on the thread cutter. Then I bent down and picked up two different pieces. They were black and purple. I always want what I can't have or what I'm not supposed to have. So what did I do? Created a pattern of choosing men that I knew would be a challenge. Richard's was his age. But the others—all of them from Alex to William— were all afraid of something: namely, committing to one woman. All I wanted to do was seduce them hard enough—emotionally, mentally, and physically—so they wouldn't even be aware that they were committing to anything. I just wanted them to crave me, and no one else but me. I wanted to be their healthiest addiction. But it was a lot harder to do than I thought. What I found out was that men are a hard nut to crack.

But some of them weren't. When I was in my late twenties, early thir- ties—before I got serious and realized I wanted a long-term relationship—

I'd had at least twenty different men fall in love with me, but of course these were the ones I didn't want. They were the ones who after a few dates or one rousing night in bed, ordained themselves my "man" or were too quick to want to marry me, and even some considered me their "property." When it was clear that I was dealing with a different species of man, a hungry element, before I got in too deep, I'd tell them almost immediately that I hope they wouldn't mind my being bisexual or my being unfaithful because I was in no hurry to settle down with one man, or that I had a tendency of always falling for my man's friends. Could they tolerate that? I even went so far as to tell them that I hoped having herpes wouldn't cause a problem, that I wasn't really all that trustworthy because I was a habitual liar, and that if they wanted the whole truth they should find themselves another woman. I told them that I didn't even think I was good enough for them, and they should do themselves a favor, find a woman who's truly worthy of having such a terrific man.

I had it down to a science, but by the time I met Richard, I was tired of lying and conniving. I was sick of the games. I was whipped, really, and allowed myself to relax and be vulnerable because I knew I was getting old.

When Gloria called to see how my honeymoon went, I told her the truth about everything. She couldn't believe it. "Well, I thought I'd heard 'em all, but this one takes the cake. How you holding up?"

"I'm hanging in there."

"This is what makes you want to castrate a man."

"Not really, Gloria."   125

"I know. But you know what I mean. Some of them have a lot of nerve, I swear they do. But really, Marilyn, how are you feeling for real, baby?"

"I'm getting my period every other week, but I'm quilting again, which is a good sign."

"First of all, take your behind back to that doctor and find out why you're still bleeding like this. And, honey, making quilts is no consolation for a broken heart. It sounds like you could use some R and R. Why don't you come visit me for a few days?"

I looked around my room, which had piles and piles of cloth and half-sewn quilts, from where I'd changed my mind. Hundreds of different-colored threads were all over the carpet, and the satin stitch I was trying out wasn't giving me the effect I thought it would. I could use a break, I thought. I could. "You know what?" I said. "I think I will."

"Good, and bring me one of those tacky quilts. I don't have anything   130 to snuggle up with in the winter, and contrary to popular belief, it does get cold here come December."

I liked Phoenix and Tempe, but I fell in love with Scottsdale. Not only was it beautiful but I couldn't believe how inexpensive it was to live in the entire area, which was all referred to as the Valley. I have to thank Gloria for being such a lifesaver. She took me to her beauty salon and gave me a whole new look. She chopped off my hair, and one of the guys in her shop showed me how to put on my makeup in a way that would further enhance what assets he insisted I had.

We drove to Tucson, to Canyon Ranch for what started out as a simple Spa Renewal Day. But we ended up spending three glorious days and had the works. I had an herbal wrap, where they wrapped my entire body in hot thin linen that had been steamed. Then they rolled me up in flannel blankets and put a cold washcloth on my forehead. I sweated in the dark for a half hour. Gloria didn't do this because she said she was claustrophobic and didn't want to be wrapped up in anything where she couldn't move. I had a deep-muscle and shiatsu massage on two different days. We steamed. We Jacuzzied. We both had a mud facial, and then this thing called aromatherapy—where they put distilled essences from flowers and herbs on your face and you look like a different person when they finish. On the last day, we got this Persian Body Polish where they actually buffed our skin with crushed pearl creams, sprayed us with some kind of herbal spray, then used an electric brush to make us tingle. We had our hands and feet moisturized and put in heated gloves and booties, and by the time we left, we couldn't believe we were the same women.

In Phoenix, Gloria took me to yet another resort where we listened to live music. We went to see a stupid movie and I actually laughed. Then we went on a two-day shopping spree and I charged whatever I felt like. I even bought her son a pair of eighty-dollar sneakers, and I'd only seen him twice in my life.

I felt like I'd gotten my spirit back, so when I got home, I told my parents I'd had it with the smog, the traffic, the gangs, and L.A. in general. My mother said, "You cannot run from heartache," but I told her I wasn't running from anything. I put my condo on the market, and in less than a month it sold for four times what I paid for it. I moved in with my mother and father, asked for a job transfer for health reasons, and when it came through, three months later, I moved to Scottsdale.

The town house I bought feels like a house. It's twice the size of the one I had and cost less than half of what I originally spent. My complex is *135* pretty standard for Scottsdale. It has two pools and four tennis courts. It also has vaulted ceilings, wall-to-wall carpet, two fireplaces, and a garden bathtub with a Jacuzzi in it. The kitchen has an island in the center and I've got a 180-degree view of Phoenix and mountains. It also has three bedrooms. One I sleep in, one I use for sewing, and the other is for guests.

I made close to forty thousand dollars after I sold my condo, so I sent four to my parents because the money they'd put down for the wedding was nonrefundable. They really couldn't afford that kind of loss. The rest I put in an IRA and CDs until I could figure out something better to do with it.

I hated my new job. I had to accept a lower-level position and less money, which didn't bother me all that much at first. The office, however, was much smaller and full of rednecks who couldn't stand the thought of a black woman working over them. I was combing the classifieds, looking for a comparable job, but the job market in Phoenix is nothing close to what it is in L.A.

But thank God Gloria's got a big mouth. She'd been boasting to all of her clients about my quilts, had even hung the one I'd given her on the wall at the shop, and the next thing I know I'm getting so many orders I couldn't keep up with them. That's when she asked me why didn't I consider opening my own shop? That never would've occurred to me, but what did I have to lose?

She introduced me to Bernadine, a friend of hers who was an accountant. Bernadine in turn introduced me to a good lawyer, and he helped me draw up all the papers. Over the next four months, she helped me devise what turned out to be a strong marketing and advertising plan. I rented an 800-square-foot space in the same shopping center where Gloria's shop is, and opened Quilt-works, Etc.

It wasn't long before I realized I needed to get some help, so I hired 140 two seamstresses. They took a lot of the strain off of me, and I was able to take some jewelry-making classes and even started selling small pieces in the shop. Gloria gave me this tacky T-shirt for my thirty-ninth birthday, which gave me the idea to experiment with making them. Because I go overboard in everything I do, I went out and spent a fortune on every color of metallic and acrylic fabric paint they made. I bought one hundred 100-percent cotton heavy-duty men's T-shirts and discovered other uses for sponges, plastic, spray bottles, rolling pins, lace, and even old envelopes. I was having a great time because I'd never felt this kind of excitement and gratification doing anything until now.

I'd been living here a year when I found out that Richard had married another woman who worked in our office. I wanted to hate him, but I didn't. I wanted to be angry, but I wasn't. I didn't feel anything toward him, but I sent him a quilt and a wedding card to congratulate him, just because.

To be honest, I've been so busy with my shop, I haven't even thought about men. I don't even miss having sex unless I really just *think* about it. My libido must be evaporating, because when I *do* think about it, I just make quilts or jewelry or paint T-shirts and the feeling goes away. Some of my best ideas come at these moments.

Basically, I'm doing everything I can to make Marilyn feel good. And at thirty-nine years old my body needs tightening, so I joined a health club and started working out three to four times a week. Once in a while, I babysit for Bernadine, and it breaks my heart when I think about the fact that I don't have a child of my own. Sometimes, Gloria and I go out to hear some music. I frequent most of the major art galleries, go to just about every football and basketball game at Arizona State, and see at *least* one movie a week.

I am rarely bored. Which is why I've decided that at this point in my life, I really don't care if I ever get married. I've learned that I don't need a man in order to survive, that a man is nothing but an intrusion, and they require too much energy. I don't think they're worth it. Besides, they have too much power, and from what I've seen, they always seem to abuse it. The one thing I *do* have is power over my own life. I like it this way, and I'm not about to give it up for something that may not last.

The one thing I do want is to have a baby. Someone I could love who   *145* would love me back with no strings attached. But at thirty-nine, I know my days are numbered. I'd be willing to do it alone, if that's the only way I can have one. But right now, my life is almost full. It's fun, it's secure, and it's safe. About the only thing I'm concerned about these days is whether or not it's time to branch out into leather.

The Responsive Reader

1. What do you think made the narrator conclude "that this relationship was going nowhere"? What were the two different personalities involved in the relationship? What separated them, and what kept them together?
2. Can you see Richard's point of view? What do you think of him? Do you think the narrator's account is biased against him? Is she guilty of "male-bashing"?
3. What is the mother's role in the story? What is the relationship between mother and daughter? Is there a "generation gap" between them? What is Gloria's role? Does she serve as a foil—offering a revealing contrast?
4. The title is a play on words. What words? African American writers like Alice Walker have written about quilt-making as an outlet for the creative abilities of black women denied other opportunities. What role does quilting play in the story?
5. By the end of the story, the narrator seems to be thinking about having a child and raising it on her own as a single mother. Do you sympathize? If asked, would you favor or advise against the idea?

Thinking, Talking, Writing

6. To what extent or in what ways do the two lovers seem representative of their generation? Does this story make you think of Richard as a typical young male? Does it at any point make you say about the woman "just like a woman"?
7. What does this short story say about the options open to the woman telling her story? How much control does she have over her life? Could or should she have done something different? What and why?
8. Does race matter in this story?

Thinking about Connections

9. Much has been written in recent years about the difficulties of communication between the sexes. Explore the treatment of this theme in the stories by Steinbeck, Mason, and McMillan.

JING-MEI WOO: TWO KINDS
Amy Tan

Amy Tan, who has been called one of the "prime storytellers writing fiction today," has introduced millions of readers to the world of California's immigrant Chinese. She was born in Oakland, California, and did graduate work at San Jose State University. In 1993 the movie based on Tan's The Joy Luck Club *introduced a nationwide audience to the interlocking stories of four mothers and their daughters, each trying to find her identity, charting her course between the memories of the Chinese past and the challenges of the American present. In several vignettes, or self-contained parts of her story, Amy Tan chronicles in turn the spiritual journey of each young woman in search of herself. Each is trying to find a way of being neither a dutiful obedient daughter in the Chinese tradition nor an imitation of the media image of American womanhood but a person in her own right. In her novel* The Kitchen God's Wife, *Tan continued her exploration of the ties of American Chinese with the mainland culture and of family relations, family myths, and family secrets.*

My mother believed you could be anything you wanted to be in Amer-   1
ica. You could open a restaurant. You could work for the government and get good retirement. You could buy a house with almost no money down. You could become rich. You could become instantly famous.

"Of course you can be prodigy, too," my mother told me when I was nine. "You can be best anything. What does Auntie Lindo know? Her daughter, she is only best tricky."

America was where all my mother's hopes lay. She had come here in 1949 after losing everything in China: her mother and father, her family home, her first husband, and two daughters, twin baby girls. But she never looked back with regret. There were so many ways for things to get better.

We didn't immediately pick the right kind of prodigy. At first my mother thought I could be a Chinese Shirley Temple. We'd watch Shirley's old movies on TV as though they were training films. My mother would poke my arm and say, *"Ni kan"*—You watch. And I would see Shirley tapping her feet, or singing a sailor song, or pursing her lips into a very round O while saying, "Oh my goodness."

"Ni kan," said my mother as Shirley's eyes flooded with tears. "You   5
already know how. Don't need talent for crying!"

Soon after my mother got this idea about Shirley Temple, she took me to a beauty training school in the Mission district and put me in the hands of a student who could barely hold the scissors without shaking. Instead of getting big fat curls, I emerged with an uneven mass of crinkly black fuzz. My mother dragged me off to the bathroom and tried to wet down my hair.

"You look like Negro Chinese," she lamented, as if I had done this on purpose.

The instructor of the beauty training school had to lop off these soggy clumps to make my hair even again. "Peter Pan is very popular these days," the instructor assured my mother. I now had hair the length of a boy's, with straight-across bangs that hung at a slant two inches above my eyebrows. I like the haircut and it made me actually look forward to my future fame.

In fact, in the beginning, I was just as excited as my mother, maybe even more so. I pictured this prodigy part of me as many different images, trying each one on for size. I was a dainty ballerina girl standing by the curtains, waiting to hear the right music that would send me floating on my tiptoes. I was like the Christ child lifted out of the straw manger, crying with holy indignity. I was Cinderella stepping from her pumpkin carriage with sparkly cartoon music filling the air.

In all of my imaginings, I was filled with a sense that I would soon become *perfect*. My mother and father would adore me. I would be beyond reproach. I would never feel the need to sulk for anything.

But sometimes the prodigy in me became impatient. "If you don't hurry up and get me out of here, I'm disappearing for good," it warned. "And then you'll always be nothing."

Every night after dinner, my mother and I would sit at the Formica kitchen table. She would present new tests, taking her examples from stories of amazing children she had read in *Ripley's Believe It or Not,* or *Good House-keeping, Reader's Digest,* and a dozen other magazines she kept in a pile in our bathroom. My mother got these magazines from people whose houses she cleaned. And since she cleaned many houses each week, we had a great assortment. She would look through them all, searching for stories about remarkable children.

The first night she brought out a story about a three-year-old boy who knew the capitals of all the states and even most of the European countries. A teacher was quoted as saying the little boy could also pronounce the names of the foreign cities correctly.

"What's the capital of Finland?" my mother asked me, looking at the magazine story.

All I knew was the capital of California, because Sacramento was the name of the street we lived on in Chinatown. "Nairobi!" I guessed, saying the most foreign word I could think of. She checked to see if that was possibly one way to pronounce "Helsinki" before showing me the answer.

The tests got harder—multiplying numbers in my head, finding the queen of hearts in a deck of cards, trying to stand on my head without using my hands, predicting the daily temperatures in Los Angeles, New York, and London.

One night I had to look at a page from the Bible for three minutes and then report everything I could remember. "Now Jehoshaphat had riches and honor in abundance and . . . that's all I remember, Ma," I said.

And after seeing my mother's disappointed face once again, something inside of me began to die. I hated the tests, the raised hopes and failed expectations. Before going to bed that night, I looked in the mirror above the bathroom sink and when I saw only my face staring back—and that it would always be this ordinary face—I began to cry. Such a sad, ugly girl! I made high-pitched noises like a crazed animal, trying to scratch out the face in the mirror.

And then I saw what seemed to be the prodigy side of me—because I had never seen that face before. I looked at my reflection, blinking so I could see more clearly. The girl staring back at me was angry, powerful. This girl and I were the same. I had new thoughts, willful thoughts, or rather thoughts filled with lots of won'ts. I won't let her change me, I promised myself. I won't be what I'm not.

So now on nights when my mother presented her tests, I performed   *20* listlessly, my head propped on one arm. I pretended to be bored. And I was. I got so bored I started counting the bellows of the foghorns out on the bay while my mother drilled me in other areas. The sound was comforting and reminded me of the cow jumping over the moon. And the next day, I played a game with myself, seeing if my mother would give up on me before eight bellows. After a while I usually counted only one, maybe two bellows at most. At last she was beginning to give up hope.

Two or three months had gone by without any mention of my being a prodigy again. And then one day my mother was watching *The Ed Sullivan Show* on TV. The TV was old and the sound kept shorting out. Every time my mother got halfway up from the sofa to adjust the set, the sound would go back on and Ed would be talking. As soon as she sat down, Ed would go silent again. She got up, the TV broke into loud piano music. She sat down. Silence. Up and down, back and forth, quiet and loud. It was like a stiff embraceless dance between her and the TV set. Finally she stood by the set with her hand on the sound dial.

She seemed entranced by the music, a little frenzied piano piece with this mesmerizing quality, sort of quick passages and then teasing lilting ones before it returned to the quick playful parts.

"*Ni kan,*" my mother said, calling me over with hurried hand gestures. "Look here."

I could see why my mother was fascinated by the music. It was being pounded out by a little Chinese girl, about nine years old, with a Peter Pan haircut. The girl had the sauciness of a Shirley Temple. She was proudly modest like a proper Chinese child. And she also did this fancy sweep of a curtsy, so that the fluffy skirt of her white dress cascaded slowly to the floor like the petals of a large carnation.

In spite of these warning signs, I wasn't worried. Our family had no 25 piano and we couldn't afford to buy one, let alone reams of sheet music and piano lessons. So I could be generous in my comments when my mother bad-mouthed the little girl on TV.

"Play note right, but doesn't sound good! No singing sound," complained my mother.

"What are you picking on her for?" I said carelessly. "She's pretty good. Maybe she's not the best, but she's trying hard." I knew almost immediately I would be sorry I said that.

"Just like you," she said. "Not the best. Because you not trying." She gave a little huff as she let go of the sound dial and sat down on the sofa.

The little Chinese girl sat down also to play an encore of "Anitra's 30 Dance" by Grieg. I remember the song, because later on I had to learn how to play it.

Three days after watching *The Ed Sullivan Show,* my mother told me what my schedule would be for piano lessons and piano practice. She had talked to Mr. Chong, who lived on the first floor of our apartment building. Mr. Chong was a retired piano teacher and my mother had traded house-cleaning services for weekly lessons and a piano for me to practice on every day, two hours a day, from four until six.

When my mother told me this, I felt as though I had been sent to hell. I whined and then kicked my foot a little when I couldn't stand it anymore.

"Why don't you like me the way I am? I'm *not* a genius! I can't play the piano. And even if I could, I wouldn't go on TV if you paid me a million dollars!" I cried.

My mother slapped me. "Who ask you be genius?" she shouted. "Only ask you be your best. For you sake. You think I want you be genius? Hnnh! What for! Who ask you!"

"So ungrateful," I heard her mutter in Chinese. "If she had as much 35 talent as she has temper, she would be famous now."

Mr. Chong, whom I secretly nicknamed Old Chong, was very strange, always tapping his fingers to the silent music of an invisible orchestra. He looked ancient in my eyes. He had lost most of the hair on top of his head and he wore thick glasses and had eyes that always looked tired and sleepy. But he must have been younger than I thought, since he lived with his mother and was not yet married.

I met Old Lady Chong once and that was enough. She had this peculiar smell like a baby that had done something in its pants. And her fingers felt like a dead person's, like an old peach I once found in the back of the refrigerator; the skin just slid off the meat when I picked it up.

I soon found out why Old Chong had retired from teaching piano. He was deaf. "Like Beethoven!" he shouted to me. "We're both listening only in our head!" And he would start to conduct his frantic silent sonatas.

Our lessons went like this. He would open the book and point to different things, explaining their purpose: "Key! Treble! Bass! No sharps or flats! So this is C major! Listen now and play after me!"

And then he would play the C scale a few times, a simple chord, and then, as if inspired by an old, unreachable itch, he gradually added more notes and running trills and a pounding bass until the music was really something quite grand.

I would play after him, the simple scale, the simple chord, and then I just played some nonsense that sounded like a cat running up and down on top of garbage cans. Old Chong smiled and applauded and then said, "Very good! But now you must learn to keep time!"

So that's how I discovered that Old Chong's eyes were too slow to keep up with the wrong notes I was playing. He went through the motions in half-time. To help me keep rhythm, he stood behind me, pushing down on my right shoulder for every beat. He balanced pennies on top of my wrists so I would keep them still as I slowly played scales and arpeggios. He had me curve my hand around an apple and keep that shape when playing chords. He marched stiffly to show me how to make each finger dance up and down, staccato like an obedient little soldier.

He taught me all these things, and that was how I also learned I could be lazy and get away with mistakes, lots of mistakes. If I hit the wrong notes because I hadn't practiced enough, I never corrected myself. I just kept playing in rhythm. And Old Chong kept conducting his own private reverie.

So maybe I never really gave myself a fair chance. I did pick up the basics pretty quickly, and I might have become a good pianist at that young age. But I was so determined not to try, not to be anybody different that I learned to play only the most ear-splitting preludes, the most discordant hymns.

Over the next year, I practiced like this, dutifully in my own way. And then one day I heard my mother and her friend Lindo Jong both talking in a loud bragging tone of voice so others could hear. It was after church, and I was leaning against the brick wall wearing a dress with stiff white petticoats. Auntie Lindo's daughter, Waverly, who was about my age, was standing farther down the wall about five feet away. We had grown up together and shared all the closeness of two sisters squabbling over crayons and dolls. In other words, for the most part, we hated each other. I thought she was snotty. Waverly Jong had gained a certain amount of fame as "Chinatown's Littlest Chinese Chess Champion."

"She bring home too many trophy," lamented Auntie Lindo that Sunday. "All day she play chess. All day I have no time do nothing but dust off her winnings." She threw a scolding look at Waverly, who pretended not to see her.

"You lucky you don't have this problem," said Auntie Lindo with a sigh to my mother.

And my mother squared her shoulders and bragged: "Our problem worser than yours. If we ask Jing-mei wash dish, she hear nothing but music. It's like you can't stop this natural talent."

And right then, I was determined to put a stop to her foolish pride.

A few weeks later, Old Chong and my mother conspired to have me play in a talent show which would be held in the church hall. By then, my parents had saved up enough to buy me a secondhand piano, a black Wurlitzer spinet with a scarred bench. It was the showpiece of our living room.

For the talent show, I was to play a piece called "Pleading Child" from Schumann's *Scenes from Childhood*. It was a simple, moody piece that sounded more difficult than it was. I was supposed to memorize the whole thing, playing the repeat parts twice to make the piece sound longer. But I dawdled over it, playing a few bars and then cheating, looking up to see what notes followed. I never really listened to what I was playing. I daydreamed about being somewhere else, about being someone else.

The part I liked to practice best was the fancy curtsy: right foot out, touch the rose on the carpet with a pointed foot, sweep to the side, left leg bends, look up and smile.

My parents invited all the couples from the Joy Luck Club to witness my debut. Auntie Lindo and Uncle Tin were there. Waverly and her two older brothers had also come. The first two rows were filled with children both younger and older than I was. The littlest ones got to go first. They recited simple nursery rhymes, squawked out tunes on miniature violins, twirled Hula Hoops, pranced in pink ballet tutus, and when they bowed or curtsied, the audience would sigh in unison, "Awww," and then clap enthusiastically.

When my turn came, I was very confident. I remember my childish excitement. It was as if I knew, without a doubt, that the prodigy side of me really did exist. I had no fear whatsoever, no nervousness. I remember thinking to myself, This is it! This is it! I looked out over the audience, at my mother's blank face, my father's yawn, Auntie Lindo's stiff-lipped smile, Waverly's sulky expression. I had on a white dress layered with sheets of lace, and a pink bow in my Peter Pan haircut. As I sat down I envisioned people jumping to their feet and Ed Sullivan rushing up to introduce me to everyone on TV.

And I started to play. It was so beautiful. I was so caught up in how lovely I looked that at first I didn't worry how I would sound: So it was a surprise to me when I hit the first wrong note and I realized something didn't sound quite right. And then I hit another and another followed that. A chill started at the top of my head and began to trickle down. Yet I couldn't stop playing, as though my hands were bewitched. I kept thinking my fingers would adjust themselves back, like a train switching to the right track. I played this strange jumble through two repeats, the sour notes staying with me all the way to the end.

When I stood up, I discovered my legs were shaking. Maybe I had just been nervous and the audience, like Old Chong, had seen me go through the right motions and had not heard anything wrong at all. I swept my right foot out, went down on my knee, looked up and smiled. The room was quiet, except for Old Chong, who was beaming and shouting, "Bravo! Bravo! Well done!" But then I saw my mother's face, her stricken face. The audience clapped weakly, and as I walked back to my chair, with my whole face quivering as I tried not to cry, I heard a little boy whisper loudly to his mother, "That was awful," and the mother whispered back, "Well, she certainly tried."

And now I realized how many people were in the audience, the whole world it seemed. I was aware of eyes burning into my back. I felt the shame of my mother and father as they sat stiffly throughout the rest of the show.

We could have escaped during intermission. Pride and some strange sense of honor must have anchored my parents to their chairs. And so we watched it all: the eighteen-year-old boy with a fake mustache who did a magic show and juggled flaming hoops while riding a unicycle. The breasted girl with white makeup who sang from *Madama Butterfly* and got honorable mention. And the eleven-year-old boy who won first prize playing a tricky violin song that sounded like a busy bee.

After the show, the Hsus, the Jongs, and the St. Clairs from the Joy Luck Club came up to my mother and father.

"Lots of talented kids," Auntie Lindo said vaguely, smiling broadly.   60

"That was somethin' else," said my father, and I wondered if he was referring to me in a humorous way, or whether he even remembered what I had done.

Waverly looked at me and shrugged her shoulders. "You aren't a genius like me," she said matter-of-factly. And if I hadn't felt so bad, I would have pulled her braids and punched her stomach.

But my mother's expression was what devastated me: a quiet, blank look that said she had lost everything. I felt the same way, and it seemed as if everybody were now coming up, like gawkers at the scene of an accident, to see what parts were actually missing. When we got on the bus to go home, my father was humming the busy-bee tune and my mother was silent. I kept thinking she wanted to wait until we got home before shouting at me. But when my father unlocked the door to our apartment, my mother walked in and then went to the back, into the bedroom. No accusations. No blame. And in a way, I felt disappointed. I had been waiting for her to start shouting, so I could shout back and cry and blame her for all my misery.

I assumed my talent-show fiasco meant I never had to play the piano again. But two days later, after school, my mother came out of the kitchen and saw me watching TV.

"Four clock," she reminded me as if it were any other day. I was   65 stunned, as though she were asking me to go through the talent-show torture again. I wedged myself more tightly in front of the TV.

"Turn off TV," she called from the kitchen five minutes later.

I didn't budge. And then I decided. I didn't have to do what my mother said anymore. I wasn't her slave. This wasn't China. I had listened to her before and look what happened. She was the stupid one.

She came out from the kitchen and stood in the arched entryway of the living room. "Four clock," she said once again, louder.

"I'm not going to play anymore," I said nonchalantly. "Why should I? I'm not a genius."

She walked over and stood in front of the TV. I saw her chest was   70
heaving up and down in an angry way.

"No!" I said, and I now felt stronger, as if my true self had finally emerged. So this was what had been inside me all along.

"No! I won't!" I screamed.

She yanked me by the arm, pulled me off the floor, snapped off the TV. She was frighteningly strong, half pulling, half carrying me toward the piano as I kicked the throw rugs under my feet. She lifted me up and onto the hard bench. I was sobbing by now, looking at her bitterly. Her chest was heaving even more and her mouth was open, smiling crazily as if she were pleased I was crying.

"You want me to be someone that I'm not!" I sobbed. "I'll never be the kind of daughter you want me to be!"

"Only two kinds of daughters," she shouted in Chinese. "Those who   75
are obedient and those who follow their own mind! Only one kind of daughter can live in this house. Obedient daughter!"

"Then I wish I wasn't your daughter. I wish you weren't my mother," I shouted. As I said these things I got scared. I felt like worms and toads and slimy things were crawling out of my chest, but it also felt good, as if this awful side of me had surfaced, at last.

"Too late change this," said my mother shrilly.

And I could sense her anger rising to its breaking point. I wanted to see it spill over. And that's when I remembered the babies she had lost in China, the ones we never talked about. "Then I wish I'd never been born!" I shouted. "I wish I were dead! Like them."

It was as if I had said the magic words. Alakazam!—and her face went blank, her mouth closed, her arms went slack, and she backed out of the room, stunned, as if she were blowing away like a small brown leaf, thin, brittle, lifeless.

It was not the only disappointment my mother felt in me. In the years   80
that followed, I failed her so many times, each time asserting my own will, my right to fall short of expectations. I didn't get straight As. I didn't become class president. I didn't get into Stanford. I dropped out of college.

For unlike my mother, I did not believe I could be anything I wanted to be. I could only be me.

And for all those years, we never talked about the disaster at the recital or my terrible accusations afterward at the piano bench. All that remained unchecked, like a betrayal that was now unspeakable. So I never found a way to ask her why she had hoped for something so large that failure was inevitable.

And even worse, I never asked her what frightened me the most: Why had she given up hope?

For after our struggle at the piano, she never mentioned my playing again. The lessons stopped. The lid to the piano was closed, shutting out the dust, my misery, and her dreams.

So she surprised me. A few years ago, she offered to give me the piano,   *85* for my thirtieth birthday. I had not played in all those years. I saw the offer as a sign of forgiveness, a tremendous burden removed.

"Are you sure?" I asked shyly. "I mean, won't you and Dad miss it?"

"No, this your piano," she said firmly. "Always your piano. You only one can play."

"Well, I probably can't play anymore," I said. "It's been years."

"You pick up fast," said my mother, as if she knew this was certain. "You have natural talent. You could been genius if you want to."

"No I couldn't."   *90*

"You just not trying," said my mother. And she was neither angry nor sad. She said it as if to announce a fact that could never be disproved. "Take it," she said.

But I didn't at first. It was enough that she had offered it to me. And after that, every time I saw it in my parents' living room, standing in front of the bay windows, it made me feel proud, as if it were a shiny trophy I had won back.

Last week I sent a tuner over to my parents' apartment and had the piano reconditioned, for purely sentimental reasons. My mother had died a few months before and I had been getting things in order for my father, a little bit at a time. I put the jewelry in special silk pouches. The sweaters she had knitted in yellow, pink, bright orange—all the colors I hated—I put those in moth-proof boxes. I found some old Chinese silk dresses, the kind with little slits up the sides. I rubbed the old silk against my skin, then wrapped them in tissue and decided to take them home with me.

After I had the piano tuned, I opened the lid and touched the keys. It sounded even richer than I remembered. Really, it was a very good piano. Inside the bench were the same exercise notes with handwritten scales, the same secondhand music books with their covers held together with yellow tape.

I opened up the Schumann book to the dark little piece I had played   *95* at the recital. It was on the left-hand side of the page, "Pleading Child." It looked more difficult than I remembered. I played a few bars, surprised at how easily the notes came back to me.

And for the first time, or so it seemed, I noticed the piece on the right-hand side. It was called "Perfectly Contented." I tried to play this one as well. It had a lighter melody but the same flowing rhythm and turned out to be quite easy. "Pleading Child" was shorter but slower; "Perfectly Contented" was longer but faster. And after I played them both a few times, I realized they were two halves of the same song.

The Responsive Reader

1. What is the role in this story of the traditional lure of America as the land of promise?
2. What is serious and what is funny in Tan's story of the mother's ambition for her child? What makes the mother act the way she does? What makes the daughter react the way she does?
3. How does the contest of wills between the two play itself out? What makes the climactic confrontation between the two frightening or traumatic?
4. Stories of parent-child conflict sometimes end on a note of reconciliation. Does this one?

Thinking, Talking, Writing

5. Is the confrontation in this story the result of the child having immigrant parents? Or does the story play out a scenario of conflict and defiance that in similar form you have seen acted out elsewhere? (Is this kind of conflict an inevitable part of growing up?)
6. Do you think that in this story the daughter is entirely right and the mother entirely wrong?
7. Have you ever said to yourself, "I won't be what I'm not"? If asked to opt for a personal credo, would you choose "I can be anything I want to be" or "I can only be me"?

Collaborative Projects

8. Psychologists stress the role that traumatic experiences in early childhood play in shaping the personality of the adult. You and your classmates may want to collaborate on a mosaic of early childhood experiences, happy or unhappy, recounted by members of the group.

10

American Mosaic:
Multicultural America

We can become a place where the cultures of the worlds crisscross. . . .
The world is here.

Ishmael Reed

Now that I live in the southwest, I'm even more appalled by the absence
of brown people in mainstream literature and more committed than ever
to populating the Texas literary landscape, the American literary land-
scape, with stories about mexicanos, *Chicanos, and Latinos.*

Sandra Cisneros

In the last two decades, millions of new immigrants have come to North
America from Eastern Europe and the former Soviet republics, China,
Southeast and South Asia, Central and South America, the Middle
East and the Caribbean. Undoubtedly these recent world-wide migra-
tions—the result of complex, often violent geopolitical and economic
forces—have literally changed the face of North America.

Alan Soldofsky

LITERATURE IN CONTEXT

For centuries, the melting pot was the symbol for the promise of America. Many immigrants became Americanized in one generation. Parents might settle in Little Italy or Chinatown, and they might do their shopping and their cooking in the old-country style. However, their children went to schools where English was the language not only of the classroom but also of the playground. Peer pressure and peer models, more than educational theories or government programs, made children who knew no English on the first day of school into Americans who wisecracked, ate hot dogs, and played sandlot baseball. Lithuanians or Armenians who had walked from the port to the factory towns for lack of bus fare saw their children graduate from high school, go to college, and become accountants, teachers, or physicians.

Although much questioned in recent years, the melting-pot metaphor still works to some extent: Koreans, still treated as foreigners in Japan after several generations, come to America and run small businesses. They join the local chamber of commerce, buy guns to protect their stores, and vote for the candidates of their choice. Ethiopians and Russians who are refugees from failed socialist experiments drive cabs in New York or Los Angeles and, like the natives, complain about taxes, bureaucracy, and congested traffic.

The question many Americans ask today is: Are we reaching the limits of assimilation? Has Americanization always worked best for European immigrants in a Eurocentric nation? Then what about the millions of Chinese, Vietnamese, Laotians, Filipinos, Pakistanis, or Arabs who have come into the country in recent years? Will the barrio or the immigrant ghetto prove for many of them not a waystation but a trap? Mexican Americans who supported leaders like Cesar Chavez in the struggle for a decent living standard for migrant workers see their efforts defeated by Anglo growers and Anglo politicians. After decades of civil rights legislation and affirmative action, more young black Americans are in jail than in college. Politicians stoke anti-immigrant sentiment.

Many who believe in a pluralistic America have traded in the idea of the melting pot for the idea of the American mosaic. A mosaic is an overall picture made up of many small, different-colored pieces of stone. Each part contributes to the whole without losing its own identity. Some of the most vigorous, thought-provoking writing published today is by bilingual or bicultural Americans. Asian American writers like Amy Tan or Maxine Hong Kingston and Mexican American writers like Richard Rodriguez or Luis Valdez have reached millions of readers. They help other Americans understand and value the experience of people who literally live or work next door. As millions of Americans do every day, these writers may practice what language scholars call code-switching—shifting to a first language when the context demands it or when their second language does not have the right words.

Are we learning to honor diversity without losing sight of the common center? Can a multicultural America have a common culture—that through its popular culture and lifestyle is in fact a dominant influence around the globe? During the last two or three decades, many widely read ethnic authors have written eloquently about Americans who live between two worlds—who consider themselves American but are considered different by mainstream Anglo society. As one reviewer said about José Antonio Villareal's *Pocho* (1959), one of the first widely read novels about today's ethnic Americans:

> Villareal writes with gusto and sureness of the *pochos,* the population born of Mexican parents, who retain some of the cultural characteristics of their Mexican ancestry: the love of Mexican food, the customs of the old country, the acceptance of the patriarchal family pattern, and

something of the Spanish language. But pochos can no longer be Mexican, if only because they saw the light of day in the United States, but more importantly because their way of life eventually develops into a concoction of Mexican and American customs, traditions, and aspirations. (Ramón Eduardo Ruiz)

LOST SISTER
Cathy Song

He thinks when we die we'll go to China.
Cathy Song

> Cathy Song was born in Honolulu and grew up in a small town on the
> island of Oahu. Her grandmother had come to Hawaii from Korea as a "picture
> bride" to marry a man she had never seen. Song has written about the Chinese
> laborers who came to "Gold Mountain" to build the Western railroad and many
> of whom "had always meant to go back." Her poems recreate the world of
> Chinatowns that "all look alike," with their odors of ethnic food and spices and
> with old men telling stories on street corners. She has a special empathy for a
> younger generation trying to emerge from the "steamy cauldron" of the tradition-
> bound world of their elders. Her poems have been collected in Picture Bride
> (1983) and Frameless Window, Squares of Light (1988).

1

In China,   1
even the peasants
named their first daughters
Jade—
the stone that in the far fields   5
could moisten the dry season,
could make men move mountains
for the healing green of the inner hills
glistening like slices of winter melon.

And the daughters were grateful: 10
They never left home.
To move freely was a luxury
stolen from them at birth.
Instead, they gathered patience;
learning to walk in shoes   15
the size of teacups,
without breaking—
the arc of their movements
as dormant as the rooted willow,
as redundant as the farmyard hens.   20

But they traveled far
in surviving,
learning to stretch the family rice,
to quiet the demons,
the noisy stomachs.   25

2

There is a sister
across the ocean,
who relinquished her name,
diluting jade green
with the blue of the Pacific.   30
Rising with a tide of locusts,
she swarmed with others
to inundate another shore.
In America,
there are many roads   35
and women can stride along with men.

But in another wilderness,
the possibilities,
the loneliness,
can strangulate like jungle veins.   40
The meager provisions and sentiments
of once belonging—
fermented roots, Mah-Jong° tiles and firecrackers—set but   *Asian game*
a flimsy household
in a forest of nightless cities.   45
A giant snake rattles above,
spewing black clouds into your kitchen.
Dough-faced landlords
slip in and out of your keyholes,
making claims you don't understand,   50
tapping into your communication systems
of laundry lines and restaurant chains.

You find you need China:
your one fragile identification,
a jade link   55
handcuffed to your wrist.
You remember your mother
who walked for centuries,
footless—
and like her,   60
you have left no footprints,
but only because
there is an ocean in between,
the unremitting space of your rebellion.

The Responsive Reader

1. What is the central opposition or dilemma at the heart of this poem?

2. Why has the hobbled gait resulting from the tradition of foot-binding become for feminists a symbol of centuries-old oppression? What role does this tradition play in this poem? How does the poem try to make you rethink the role of women in traditional Chinese culture?

3. What explains the ambivalent or mixed feelings in this poem about the other sister who traveled "across the ocean"? What did she gain? What did she lose? Where does she live? (Is the giant snake an elevated train rattling past people's windows?)

4. How or why does the person addressed in this poem "need China"? How is she like and unlike her mother?

Thinking, Talking, Writing

5. What lies behind the tourist image of an American Chinatown, Little Saigon, Little Italy, or other ethnic neighborhood?

6. Is there something to be said in favor or in defense of immigrants clustering together in their own ethnic neighborhoods?

ORANGES

Gary Soto

> *Gary Soto is an award-winning, widely published Chicano poet who grew up in a Mexican American neighborhood in Fresno, California. He has said about his childhood home that it had only two books in it: the Bible and a medical manual. He went on from there to study at Fresno State and at the University of California at Irvine and to become a professor on the Berkeley campus. His poems often tell bittersweet stories of childhood and adolescence. He says that literature "reshapes experience—both real and invented—to help us see ourselves—our foibles, failures, potential, beauty, pettiness."*

The first time I walked 1
With a girl, I was twelve,
Cold, and weighted down
With two oranges in my jacket.
December. Frost cracking 5
Beneath my steps, my breath
Before me, then gone,
As I walked toward
Her house, the one whose
Porch light burned yellow 10
Night and day, in any weather.
A dog barked at me, until
She came out pulling
At her gloves, face bright
With rouge. I smiled, 15
Touched her shoulder, and led
Her down the street, across
A used car lot and a line
Of newly planted trees,
Until we were breathing 20
Before a drugstore. We
Entered, the tiny bell
Bringing a saleslady
Down a narrow aisle of goods.
I turned to the candies 25
Tiered like bleachers
And asked what she wanted—
Light in her eyes, a smile
Starting at the corners
Of her mouth. I fingered 30
A nickel in my pocket,
And when she lifted a chocolate

That cost a dime,
I didn't say anything.
I took the nickel from   35
My pocket, then an orange,
And set them quietly on
The counter. When I looked up,
The lady's eyes met mine,
And held them, knowing   40
Very well what it was all
About.

    Outside;
A few cars hissing past;
Fog hanging like old   45
Coats between the trees.
I took my girl's hand
In mine for two blocks,
Then released it to let
Her unwrap the chocolate.   50
I peeled my orange
That was so bright against
The grey of December
That, from some distance,
Someone might have thought
I was making a fire in my hands.   55

The Responsive Reader

1. How does this poem show Soto's patient, loving observation of everyday details?
2. Why was this incident important to the poet? What did it mean to
   him? Do you think it was important enough to write a poem about?
3. Why does it make a difference to the impact of this poem that the
   events happen in the "gray of December"?

Thinking, Talking, Writing

4. Are young people today too prematurely experienced, too blasé, to
   share in the poet's emotions?

Collaborative Projects

5. You may want to help your class set up groups exploring and presenting to the class the work of current bilingual American poets.

INCANTATION

Czeslaw Milosz

In the second half of the twentieth century, many immigrants have been refugees from central and eastern Europe who were leaving behind a totalitarian past. The essence of totalitarianism is to make all aspects of life, including especially art and education, serve the political purposes of those in power. Nazism and Stalinism, the two great totalitarian ideologies, had strung barbed wire across much of Europe. They had sent millions to perish in concentration camps and labor camps, and they had brutalized intellectuals and artists who would not follow the party line.

For dissidents like the Polish poet Czeslaw Milosz, one of the great crimes of totalitarianism was its abuse of language. Oppression was glorified as part of a heroic struggle for justice. People who knew the truth were reviled or driven into exile. Books with ideas considered dangerous were shredded or reduced to pulp, while party hacks were rewarded with luxuries for writing drivel in praise of the authorities. As a young writer, Milosz was part of the Polish resistance during the Nazi occupation of Poland in World War II. He served with the postwar communist government in Poland, but he defected to the West when his conscience would no longer allow him to collaborate with the new leaders. He came to California to teach at Berkeley and won the Nobel Prize for literature in 1980.

Human reason is beautiful and invincible.   *1*
No bars, no barbed wire, no pulping of books,
No sentence of banishment can prevail against it.
It establishes the universal ideas in language,
And guides our hand so we write Truth and Justice   *5*
With capital letters, lie and oppression with small.
It puts what should be above things as they are,
Is an enemy of despair and a friend of hope.
It does not know Jew from Greek or slave from master,
Giving us the estate of the world to manage.   *10*
It saves austere and transparent phrases
From the filthy discord of tortured words.
It says that everything is new under the sun,
Opens the congealed fist of the past.
Beautiful and very young are Philo-Sophia   *15*
And poetry, her ally in the service of the good.
As late as yesterday Nature celebrated their birth,
The news was brought to the mountains by a unicorn and an echo.
Their friendship will be glorious; their time has no limit.
Their enemies have delivered themselves to destruction.   *20*

The Responsive Reader

1. Does this poem imply any kind of political program or political philosophy?
2. Why does the poet write "Truth and Justice/with capital letters, lie and oppression with small"?
3. The spelling *Philo-Sophia* reminds us of the original meaning of *philosophy:* "the love of wisdom." Do you think philosophy and poetry have anything to do with politics or with political truth?
4. What are symbolic uses or symbolic meanings of the human hand? What is the symbolic meaning of reason opening "the congealed fist of the past"? What does this phrase make you see or imagine? What does it make you feel? What does it make you think?

Thinking, Talking, Writing

5. Are you cynical about the language of politics? Do you believe anything political leaders say? The word *austere* means "bare, stripped down" but by the same token also "pure, uncorrupted." Do you think the language of politics could ever consist of "austere and transparent phrases"?
6. What's a unicorn? What is it doing in this poem?

INDIAN MOVIE, NEW JERSEY

Chitra Divakaruni

Born in Calcutta in India, Chitra Banerjee Divakaruni has a doctorate in English literature from the University of California at Berkeley and is becoming a widely published American poet. She has been fascinated with the "rich cosmopolitan mix" of contemporary America and with the way not only race but also economics, sex, and gender shape our multicultural society. She has published three books of poetry, including Black Candle, and teaches at Foothill College in the San Francisco Bay Area. One of her colleagues there described her collection of multicultural readings, Multitude (1993), as "a new kind of anthology altogether, with a virtual multitude of converging, creative possibilities and perspectives" (Scott Lankford). Her first collection of stories, Arranged Marriage, was scheduled for publication in 1995.

Divakaruni's poems often center on the problems of adjustment faced by immigrants from Asian Third World countries.

Not like the white filmstars, all rib   1
and gaunt cheekbone, the Indian sex-goddess
smiles plumply from behind a flowery
branch. Below her brief red skirt, her thighs
are satisfying-solid, redeeming   5
as tree trunks. She swings her hips
and the men-viewers whistle. The lover-hero
dances in to a song, his lip-sync
a little off, but no matter, we
know the words already and sing along.   10
It is safe here, the day
golden and cool so no one sweats,
roses on every bush and the Dal Lake
clean again.
        The sex-goddess switches   15
to thickened English to emphasize
a joke. We laugh and clap. Here
we need not be embarrassed by words
dropping like lead pellets into foreign ears.
The flickering movie-light   20
wipes from our faces years of America, sons
who want mohawks and refuse to run
the family store, daughters who date
on the sly.

When at the end the hero   25
dies for his friend who also
loves the sex-goddess and now can marry her,
we weep, understanding. Even the men
clear their throats to say, "What *qurbani!*°   *sacrifice*
What *dosti!*"° After, we mill around   *friendship*   30
unwilling to leave, exchange greetings
and good news: a new gold chain, a trip
to India. We do not speak
of motel raids, cancelled permits, stones
thrown through glass windows, daughters and sons   35
raped by Dotbusters.
        In this dim foyer,
we can pull around us the faint, comforting smell
of incense and *pakoras,*° can arrange   *ethnic food*
our children's marriages with hometown boys and girls,   40
open a franchise, win a million
in the mail. We can retire
in India, a yellow two-storeyed house
with wrought-iron gates, our own
Ambassador car. Or at least   45
move to a rich white suburb, Summerfield
or Fort Lee, with neighbors that will
talk to us. Here while the film-songs still echo
in the corridors and restrooms, we can trust
in movie truths: sacrifice, success, love and luck,   50
the America that was supposed to be.

The Responsive Reader

1. What hints, scattered in the poem, does the poet give at of the realities
   of immigrant life from which the movie provides an escape? (Who are
   the "Dotbusters," and why are they given that name? What role do
   language difficulties play in the immigrants' lives?)
2. What comment does the poem offer on the vision of America that
   brought the immigrants here?
3. We are often told today that ideals of beauty are relative—they are
   culturally conditioned. How does the poem support this view?

Thinking, Talking, Writing

4. What ideals of beauty—female and male—do the mass media pro-
   mote? Is it true, as many feminists claim, that our ideal of female beauty

is damaging to women? (Is something similar true of the image of the handsome male created by the media?)

5. What kind of fantasy world created by the media is your own favorite retreat from reality?

Thinking about Connections

6. A widely read memoir by a Mexican American author was called *Hunger of Memory*. With some immigrant poets or poets of immigrant descent, the echoes of an earlier history or memories of an old-country past are especially strong. What role do such memories play in the poems by Song, Milosz, and Divakaruni?

THE PILGRIM

Estela Portillo

> *Like many Americans of Mexican descent, Estele Portillo was born and has lived all her life in Texas. She was born in the border town of El Paso and has an MA in English and American literature from the University of Texas campus there. She taught school, was a radio talk show host, and staged some of her own plays at the local community college. In the seventies, she started to publish her poetry, short fiction, and drama in El Grito, published at the University of California in Berkeley and devoted to the writings of Mexican American authors. She has taken a special interest in promoting the role of Chicanas, or Mexican American women, in literature and art.*
>
> *The following story is from Portillo's* Rain of Scorpion, *which she published as the expanded and revised version of an earlier collection in 1991. In this story, the Rio Grande, the great river dividing El Paso from the city of Juarez on the Mexican side, becomes the symbolic dividing line between the affluent North and the impoverished South. Many of the place names in this part of the country—San Antonio, Santa Fe, El Paso—are Spanish, as are the names of churches like el Sagrado Corazón—the church of the Sacred Heart—that plays a role in this story. The job of* la migra, *the immigration service, is to stem the tide of illegal immigration faced everywhere by the wealthy countries of the industrialized North.*
>
> *Does this story make you empathize with the "wetback" battling* la migra?

Trini walked with stumbling feet behind La Chaparra. They had fol- [1] lowed a network of alleys through El Barrio de la Bola overlooking the western bank of the Río Grande. The adobe choza on top of the sandhill gaped empty, roofless, without windows or door. A gaunt cat sitting on a pile of adobe stared at them with the frugal blank eyes of starvation. It was unusual to see a cat in this barrio. They were usually eaten by the starving people who lived in the makeshift cardboard and tin huts scattered along the hill. La Chaparra, her back against the wall, slid down to the ground, out of breath. The barrio ended on top of a hill that overlooked the smelter across the river on the United States side. Trini, tired, brooding, followed the path that led to the river with her eyes, shading them against the harsh sun. La Chaparra had brought her to the easiest crossing. The boundary between Juárez and Smeltertown in El Paso was no more than a series of charcos extending about fifty feet.

"You sure you want to do it?" La Chaparra's voice was skeptical. She muttered under her breath, "You're crazy, no money, having a baby in a strange land—you're crazy."

Trini turned to reassure the seasoned wetback, though her body was feeling the strain of the climb. "Everything will be fine, now that I know the way, thanks to you." She would wait for the pains of birth, then her pilgrimage would begin to the Virgin across the river. Somewhere in El Paso was a church, el Sagrado Corazón. She would be led. Things had been taken care of haphazardly. Tonio had sent her forty American dollars which she promptly gave to Elia for Linda's keep. This time, Linda, she promised, this time will be the last time I shall leave you behind. I will find land, and there we'll stay. The dream stifled her guilt. For her, destiny was an intuitive pull, a plan with a dream, sometimes without practical considerations. But practical considerations were luxuries in life. She could not afford to think of the dangers ahead, the suffering. She must just go. Pull, pull through a dark hole, Perla had said.

On the way back home, La Chaparra cautioned her of the dangers— watch out for la migra, stay away from the highway. If they catch you, you might have the baby in jail if they don't process you back soon enough. Day crossings were easier through El Barrio de la Bola. La Chaparra wished her well and left her at the entrance to El Arroyo Colorado.

The birth pains came before dawn a few days later, a soft, late autumn dawn that wove its mysteries for her between pains. She took a streetcar at six that left her on the edge of El Barrio de la Bola. From there she walked all the way down the sandhill through the arrabales leading to the river. The river was not a threat. Most of the water had been banked upstream into irrigation ditches that followed new-found fields converted into farmland from the desert.

This was the point of safe crossing, safe from deep water, if not completely safe from the border patrols who made their morning rounds on the highway that followed the river. Still, her chances were good. Her pains were coming with regularity, but at distant intervals. From the Juárez side of the river she could see the small, humble homes scattered in the hills of Smeltertown. She rested under a tree on the edge of the river, her pores feeling the chill of the coming winter. She leaned her head against the tree, a lilac tree, of all things, in the middle of nowhere! For an instant, she seemed to feel a force from the earth, from her hold on the tree. She laughed, then pain cut sharply through her body. It sharpened and focused her instinct. Failure was impossible.

She took off her shoes and waded across a shallow area until she came to a place where the water was flowing uniformly downstream. She made her way carefully, looking for sure footing, her toes clutching at cold sand. Brown mimosa seeds floated on the surface of the water. Then, without warning, she felt herself slipping into the river. As she fell, a pain broke crimson, a red pain that mixed and swirled with the mud water that was up to her breasts now. She had lost the shoes she was carrying. Her feet sank into the deep soft sand, and she kicked forward to free herself. The steady flow of water helped pull her toward a dry section of riverbed. She was but a few feet away from the American side. Then, she was across.

Shoeless, drenched through and through, holding a wet rebozo around her, she made her way, breathless and cold, to a dirt road leading to the main highway. She looked both ways for any sign of a patrol car, but saw none. She sighed with relief, searching around for a place to rest. Ahead, she saw an abandoned gas station with a rusty broken-down car by its side. She could hide there until a bus arrived. She sat behind the car with the highway before her; looming across the highway was a mountain carved by the machinery of the smelter, contoured by time, veined with the colors of a past life. Its granite silence gave her comfort. She understood mountains. Like trees and the earth, they bound her, gave her their strength. Pain again. It consumed her as she clutched the edge of a fender, the metal cutting into her palm.

While the pain still wavered, she saw a bus approaching far away along the stretch of highway. She wiped the perspiration from her face with the wet rebozo, her body shivering, her vision hazed as she fixed her eyes on the moving, yellow hope that came toward her. Her blood was singing birth, a fading and then a sharpening of her senses. She felt weak as she raised her heavy, tortured body and made her way to the edge of the highway. She stood, feet firm, arms waving. Oh, Sweet Virgin, make it stop! She waited, eyes closed, until she heard the grinding stop. Thank you, Sweet Mother. She opened her eyes to see the door of the bus swing open. When she got on, she saw the driver's eyes questioning. Words came out of her mouth; the clearness of her voice surprised her. "I have no money, but I must get to a church."

For a second, the bus driver stared at the pregnant woman, muddied   10 and unkempt, standing her ground. He simply nodded, and the bus went on its way. She saw that the people on the bus were mostly Mexican like herself. Their eyes were frankly and curiously staring. A woman came up and helped her to a seat. She asked with concern, "Is there anything I can do?"

Trini looked at her with pleading eyes. "Where is the church?" She was breathing hard against the coming of another pain.

"A Catholic church?"

Trini nodded. The pain came in purple streaks. She bent her head, her face perspiring freely.

"It's your time," the woman whispered. "There's a hospital near."

"No, no, no, the church." Trini's plea swirled with the pain. She whis-   15 pered, "The Virgin told me."

"¡Jesucristo!"

It seemed that the bus driver was going faster without making his usual stops. No one protested. The church was the destination now. Trini leaned her head against the window, hardly conscious of buildings interlacing light and sounds. At a distance, a church steeple rose south of the maze of city buildings. Someone said, "Over there, El Sagrado Corazón."

Joy danced on the brink of Trini's pain. El Sagrado Corazón! She had been led. She had been helped. She was certain now that her child was meant to be born in the church. The pain pierced, bounced, and dispersed. Then she breathed freely. The bus had stopped. The driver was pointing out directions. "Just go all the way down the street, then turn left."

The woman helped Trini off the bus as voices called out words of sympathy and good luck. As the bus took off again, Trini's legs gave way. She fell on bended knee on the sidewalk. The pains were almost constant now. She looked up at the woman with pleading eyes as the woman cleansed her brow, encouraging, "Just a little way now, pobrecita."

"I have to find the Virgin . . ." The words were dry in her throat.   20

"The rectory . . ."

"No, the church." Trini shook her head in desperation, breathing hard. "The Virgin."

The woman said no more, bracing herself to hold Trini's weight. Through a wave of nausea, Trini saw the church before her. Ave María, Madre de Dios, bendita seas entre todas las mujeres. The prayer came like a flowing relief. They were climbing the steps slowly. Happy moans broke from Trini's throat as her legs wavered and her body shook in pain. She could feel herself leaning heavily on the woman. The woman opened the door of the church, and they walked into its silence. Before them were the long aisles leading up to the altar, a long, quiet, shadowy path. The woman whispered, "Can you make it?"

Trini looked up and saw what seemed like miles before her, but in front of the altar to the right was the Virgin Mary holding out her arms to her. The same smile on Her face as when she had looked down at Trini in the Juárez church. The pain was now one thing tightrope made of colored ribbons that went round and round, swirls of red and black. Reflections from the stained glass windows pulsed their colors, hues of mystery, creation. Colors wavered and swam before her eyes, the Virgin's heartbeat. Yes, she would make it. She stretched out her hand, feeling for the side of a pew to support herself. There was peace now in spite of the pain. The candles flickered, dancing a happiness before the Virgin. But now her body made its own demand, one drumming blow of pain. She fell back in a faint, and the woman broke her fall to the floor as two priests ran down the aisle to see what the matter was. Yes, the Virgin had been right all along . . .

Trini held the piece of paper in her shaking hand. It was in English so   25
the words meant little to her, but the name Ricardo Esconde written in black ink stood out bold and strong. Her eyes, radiant in her triumph, looked for a second into the unconcerned eyes of the clerk, then flickered away. "Gracias."

Thank you, God—thank you, clerk—it was all over. Her son's birth had been registered. She walked away unsteadily, the weight of the baby in her arms, the paper held tightly in her hand. She made her way to a chair in the corner of the office, a queasiness commanding, stomach churning, the taste of vomit in her mouth. She let herself fall into the chair as she tightened her hold on the baby. Her breath came in spurts. She raised her head, throwing it back, mouth half-open to draw in air, her body withstanding many things—fear, hunger, fatigue. She had run away from the priests. Her mind retraced the time of her escape as her shaking hands carefully folded the birth certificate.

It was now in the pocket of her skirt. She had run away, not because the priests had been unkind. They had helped with the birth on the floor of the church, angry questions lost among sympathetic murmurings. After that, sleep overtook the pain. When she awoke, the priests placed a son in her arms, clean, wrapped in a kitchen towel. She had smiled her gratitude and had gone back to sleep. Later, she eagerly drank the hot soup and ate the bread they offered her, the baby close and warm by her side. But then the priest who spoke Spanish told her that the immigration people had to be notified. It was the law. The woman had told them that she had crossed the river.

When they had left her alone, she had simply taken the baby and walked away, out of a side door into an empty street in the early afternoon. She had walked south. When she could walk no more, she sat on a corner bench to rest. A Mexican woman sat next to her, waiting for a bus. She looked at Trini and the baby with interested eyes but said nothing until Trini asked, "Where do I register my baby as a citizen?"

Instantly, the woman understood. She shook her head as if to push away the futility of things, but answered, "City-county building." The woman was pointing north. "It's closed now."

"How far?" 30

"About twelve, thirteen blocks north, on San Antonio Street." The woman's eyes were troubled. "Just walk up, then turn left, but watch out for la migra. You look like you just came out of the river."

The bus stopped before them, and the woman disappeared behind its doors. Trini looked around and saw warehouses with closed doors, parking lots yawning their emptiness. She had the urge to cry, to give up, but the sun was falling in the west, and the baby in her arms told her differently. She sat numb, without plan, without thought as buses came and went, loading and unloading passengers. She sat on the bench until dark, putting the baby to her breast before she set out again. How insatiable was her drowsy, grey fatigue. She set one foot before the other without direction as gauze clouds were swallowed by the night. The night had swallowed her and the baby too. She made her way to an alley, away from the wind, and there in a corner slept, the baby clasped tightly in her arms.

That had been yesterday. Now it was all over. She had found the building—the baby was registered. A thought came to her like the climbing of a mountain, steep and harsh. What now? What now? She caught the stare of a woman waiting for the clerk. Then Trini noticed the clerk's eyes on the baby. The man was clasping his hands, then unclasping them, then tapping his fingers on the counter as if he were deciding to call the authorities.

Wan and pale, Trini drew the baby closely to her and made her way to the door marked "Vital Statistics." Her hands were trembling out of weakness and fear. The baby began to cry as Trini made her way out of the building, shouldering her way through people, avoiding eyes. She was a curious sight, a muddied, barefoot woman with wild hair and feverish eyes, holding a baby, running for dear life. She ran along the streets that took her away from tall buildings, from uniforms, from American people. She was going south again. Her mouth felt dry and raw, and the towel the baby was wrapped in was soaking wet. Oh, my baby, I have to change you, feed you, her heart cried. But still, she ran until she could run no more, standing against the wall of a building to catch her breath, avoiding the curious stares of people. Before her was a street sign. The words were distended images, visions of hope: "Santa Fe."

Holy Faith! The name of the street was Holy Faith! An omen—a *35* guiding force—a new decision. The hope was as feverish as her body. She would follow the street to its very end. She started on her way again, feet heavy, body numb, the baby now crying lustily in her arms. People had been left behind. Only one man passed her, unconcerned. Before her was a railroad yard, across the street a bar, beyond that an old familiar bridge, El Puente Negro! Strange, the circle of her life. The end of Santa Fe had brought her to a dead end. She did not want to cross the bridge. She did not want to go back. She had to find a place nearby to rest, to look after the baby's needs.

Behind a warehouse was a lumberyard fenced off with sagging, rusty wire. She made her way through one section where the fence had sagged to the ground, her feet stepping over a desiccated piece of lumber, half-buried in dry mud. She sat down against the wall of the building and hushed her baby with soft tones of love. The baby had to be changed. She raised her skirt and jerked at the cotton slip underneath. It did not give. The baby lay on the ground crying harder. She pulled at a shoulder strap, tearing it, repeating the process until both straps gave. She pulled the garment from the knees, stepped out of it, then tore it in pieces to make a diaper. With quick fingers she unpinned the wet towel, flinging it over a pile of lumber. Afterwards she placed the dry pieces of cloth on the ground and lifted the baby onto them. He was whimpering in tired, spasmodic little sobs. Her breasts were hard and sore in their fullness. Now she rested against the building, picking up the baby and turning him tenderly toward her. The nipple touched his lips. He took it eagerly, drops of milk forming on the sides of his little mouth. Then she dozed with the baby at her breast.

After a while she awoke with a start, aware of the greyness of the day. She sat quite still, the baby fast asleep. Her arms felt cramped and stiff, so she laid the child low on her lap and stretched out her legs.

Through half-closed lids she saw El Puente Negro at a great distance, like a blot against the greyness of the day. Her mind was a greyness too, things not yet clear or distinct. Thoughts ran: a world in circles, a black bridge standing, pulling through a dark hole, Santa Fe—faith, faith and the burning of a fire, a plan. Perhaps it was all useless, this trying. She felt as if she were a blot lost in space. All she wanted was a chance, a way to stay in the United States, to find a piece of land, to have the family together.

It had taken Celestina fifteen years to buy a thirsty, ungiving piece of land in Mexico—fifteen years! No, there was a better way in the United States where the poor and hungry did not have to stay poor and hungry. Something had pulled her to this country of miracles. It was all still shapeless, meaningless, beyond her. But things would take shape. She would give them shape. A blot in space was the beginning of many things in all directions. She looked down at the sleeping child, Sabochi's child, a son, Rico.

The Responsive Reader

1. At the beginning of the story, how does Portillo sketch out conditions south of the border that impel many to look for a "miracle" in the North?
2. What is the future mother's plan for overcoming the immigration barriers? What are the obstacles to her carrying it out? What is in her favor?
3. Do you think that in the long run the woman's plan will work?
4. States like California and Texas have large Spanish-speaking populations. How familiar to you are Spanish terms like *barrio, arroyo,* or *rebozo?* What can you do with some of the other Spanish phrases in this story—for instance, the woman's prayer? Where or how much do you come into contact with Spanish as a major minority language in the United States?

Thinking, Talking, Writing

5. How does Portillo show her sympathy for the central character in this story? What side are you on in this story and why?
6. How aware are you of illegal immigration as a hot political issue? Where do you take your stand on this issue?

TWISTERS AND SHOUTERS
Maxine Hong Kingston

In exploring her dual Chinese and American heritage, Maxine Hong Kingston weaves a fascinating web of sharp-eyed realism, traditional lore, far-ranging fantasy, and madcap humor. She does not romanticize her ethnic origins, nor does she forgive a history of racial prejudice and exclusion. She grew up as the daughter of Chinese immigrants running a laundry in Stockton, California. Her autobiographical The Woman Warrior: Memoirs of a Childhood Among Ghosts *won the National Book Critics' Circle award for nonfiction in 1976. In this intensely personal account, she wrote about growing up within the narrow boundaries set for women by the traditional patriarchal Chinese culture. She told the story of relatives who had stayed behind in China and were destroyed in the turmoil of the Communist revolution. She recorded her own struggles with racism and sexism in the land of the "Gold Mountain." In* China Men *(1980), Kingston chronicled the barriers and humiliations nineteenth-century Chinese immigrants, imported as cheap labor, experienced in America.*

In 1989, Kingston published Tripmaster Monkey: His Fake Book, *from which the following excerpt is taken. As in* Woman Warrior *or* ChinaMen, *the characters in Kingston's new novel are wanderers between two worlds, people in search of a new identity. Kingston's fiction is at the opposite pole from plodding literal-minded realism. Quizzical observation of haunting everyday reality blends with the fruits of a freely roaming imagination. At any point, the reader may encounter snatches of Shakespeare, Disney cartoon characters, or allusions to a writer of the beat generation or to a German poet (like the poet who wrote about Malte Laurids Brigge).*

In the Tenderloin, depressed and unemployed, the jobless Wittman Ah Sing felt a kind of bad freedom. Agoraphobic on Market Street, ha ha. There was nowhere he had to be, and nobody waiting to hear what happened to him today. Fired. Aware of Emptiness now. Ha ha. A storm will blow from the ocean or down from the mountains, and knock the set of the City down. If you dart quick enough behind the stores, you'll see that they are stage flats propped up. On the other side of them is ocean forever, and the great Valley between the Coast Range and the Sierras. Is that snow on Mt. Shasta?

And what for had they set up Market Street? To light up the dark jut of land into the dark sea. To bisect the City diagonally with a swath of lights. We are visible. See us? We're here. Here we are.

What else this street is for is to give suggestions as to what to do with oneself. What to do. What to buy. How to make a living. What to eat. Unappetizing. The street was full of schemes: FIRE SALE. LOANS. OLD GOLD. GUNS NEW AND USED. BOUGHT AND SOLD. GOING OUT OF BUSINESS.

OUR PAIN YOUR GAIN. Food. Fast-food joints. Buy raw, sell cooked. If he got a-hold of food, he'd just eat it, not sell it. But we're supposed to sell that food in order to buy, cook, and eat omnivorously. If you're the more imaginative type, go to the mud flats, collect driftwood, build yourself a cart or a stand, sell umbrellas on rainy and foggy days, sell flowers, sell fast portable hot dogs, tacos, caramel corn, ice-cream sandwiches, hamburgers. Daedalate the line-up from cow to mouth, and fill up your life. If a human being did not have to eat every day, three times a day, ninety percent of life would be solved.

Clothes are no problem. He'd found his Wembley tie on a branch of a potted plant in front of the Durant Hotel, and an Eastern school tie hanging on a bush on Nob Hill. Coats are left on fences and wristwatches inside of shoes at the beach.

Musicians have a hard time of it. Sax players and guitarists and a bass   5 player have left their instruments in pawnshops; they're away perhaps forever, trying to make money, and to eat. A lot of hocked jewelry sits in the windows overnight; the real diamonds, they keep in the twirling-lock safe. These cellos and jewels belonged to people who for a while appreciated more than food. The nature of human beings is also that they buy t.v.s, coffee tables, nightstands, sofas, daddy armchairs for dressing the set of their life dramas.

Market Street is not an avenue or a boulevard or a champs that sweeps through arches of triumph. Tangles of cables on the ground and in the air, open manholes, construction for years. Buses and cars trying to get around one another, not falling into trenches, and not catching tires in or sliding on tracks, lanes taken up by double and triple parking. Pedestrians stranded on traffic islands. How am I to be a boulevardier on Market Street? I am not a boulevardier; I am a bum-how, I am a fleaman.

Now what? Where does a fleaman go for the rest of the evening, the rest of his adult life? The sets haven't started at the Black Hawk, but no more spending extravagant money on music. Music should be overflowing everywhere. It's time to find out how much free music there is. And no hanging out at the Albatross anymore, taken over by scary Spades. To feel the green earth underfoot, he could walk on the green Marina, look at the moon over the sea, and perhaps a second moon in the sea. Keep track of moonphases; are you going through changes in sync with werewolves? But something about that nightlight on the grass that looked sick, like the Green Eye Hospital. *I saw: Hospitals.* No walk in the Palace of the Legion of Honor either, not to be by himself in that huge dark; better to have a companion, and impress her at high noon, Wittman Ah Sing as Hercules chained to the columns and pulling them down, while shouting Shakespeare. If he went to Playland at the Beach, he would get freaked out by Sal, The Laughing Lady setting off the laughing gulls. Haaw. Haaaw. Haaaaw. He had yet to walk across the Golden Gate at night, but did not just then feel like being suspended in the open cold above the Bay; the breath of the cars would not be warm enough. Continue, then, along Market.

No boulevardiers here. Who's here? Who are my familiars? Here I am among my familiars, yeah, like we're Kerouac's people, tripping along the street.

> Soldiers, sailors,
> the panhandlers and drifters,
> [no] zoot suiters, the hoodlums,
> the young men who washed dishes in cafeterias
>   from coast to coast,
> the hitchhikers, the hustlers, the drunks,
> the battered lonely young Negroes,
> the twinkling little Chinese,
> the dark Puerto Ricans [and braceros and pachucos]
> and the varieties of dungareed Young Americans
>   in leather jackets
>   who were seamen and mechanics and garagemen everywhere . . .
> The same girls who walked in rhythmic pairs,
> the occasional whore in purple pumps and red raincoat
>   whose passage down these sidewalks was always so sensational,
> the sudden garish sight of some incredible homosexual
>   flouncing by with an effeminate shriek of general greeting to every-
>   one, anyone:
>   "I'm just so knocked out and you all know it,
>   you mad things!"
>   —and vanishing in a flaunt of hips . . .

Well, no such red-and-purple whore or resplendent homosexual. Might as well expect a taxi door to open and out step a geisha in autumn kimono, her face painted white with tippy red lips and smudge-moth eyebrows, white tabi feet winking her out of sight on an assignation in the floating demi-monde.

Shit. The "twinkling little Chinese" must be none other than himself. "Twinkling"?! "Little"?! Shit. Bumkicked again. If King Kerouac, King of the Beats, were walking here tonight, he'd see Wittman and think, "Twinkling little Chinese." Refute "little." Gainsay "twinkling." A man does not twinkle. A man with balls is not little. As a matter of fact, Kerouac didn't get "Chinese" right either. Big football player white all-American jock Kerouac. Jock Kerouac. I call into question your naming of me. I trust your sight no more. You tell people by their jobs. And by their race. And the wrong race at that. If Ah Sing were to run into Kerouac—grab him by the lapels of his lumberjack shirt. Pull him up on his toes. Listen here, you twinkling little Canuck. What do you know, Kerouac? What do you know? You don't know shit. I'm the American here. I'm the American walking here. Fuck Kerouac and his American road anyway. Et tu, Kerouac. Aiya, even you. Just for that, I showed you, I grew to six feet. May still be growing.

10

Like headlines, the movie marquees seemed to give titles to what was going down—MONDO CANE, THE TRIAL, LORD OF THE FLIES, DR. NO, MANCHURIAN CANDIDATE, HOW THE WEST WAS WON. Now, if there is one thing that makes life bearable, it's the movies. Let them show a movie once a week, and Wittman can take anything, live anywhere—jail, a totalitarian socialist country, the Army. Not educational films but big-bucks full-production-values American glitz movies. WEST SIDE STORY. The biggest reddest block caps told him to go see *West Side Story,* which had returned from the sixth International Film Festival at Cannes. The girl in the ornate ticket booth said that he was on time, so he bought a ticket and went into the Fox. Inhaling the smell of the popcorn and the carpet, he felt happy. In the middle seat a screen-and-a-half's width away from the front, he continued happy. In the breast pocket of his Brooks Brothers suit, on a page margin, Malte Laurids Brigge: *This which towered before me, with its shadows ordered in the semblance of a face, with the darkness gathered in the mouth of its centre, bounded, up there, by the symmetrically curling hairdos of the cornice; this was the strong, all-covering antique mask, behind which the world condensed into a face. Here, in this great incurved amphitheatre of seats, there reigned a life of expectancy, void, absorbent: all happening was yonder: gods and destiny; and thence (when one looks, up high) came lightly, over the wall's rim: the eternal entry of the heavens.* Then a thunder-clapping pleasure—the movie started with simultaneous blasts of Technicolor and horns.

"When you're a Jet, you're a Jet all the way from your first cigarette to your last dying day." Oh, yes, that's me, that's me, a-crouching and a-leaping, fight-dancing through the city, fingers snapping, tricky feet attacking and backing up and attacking, the gang altogether turning and pouncing—monkey kung fu. "You got brothers around . . . You're never disconnected . . . You're well protected."

Oh, yes, all the dances in all the wide and lonely gyms of our adolescence should have been like this. Us guys against one wall and you girls across the basketball court and along the opposite wall ought to have come bursting out at one another in two co-operating teams. The girls, led by Rita Moreno, high-kicking and lifting their skirts and many petticoats. "I like to be in America. Everything free in America."

And Tony meets Natalie Wood, and asks her to dance, and falls in love at first sight with her. Me too. "I just met a girl named Maria." And I'm in love with her too. Though her brother and her boyfriend belong to the Sharks, I love her like a religion.

In this world without balconies, climb a fire escape to court the city   *15* girl. And no sooner kiss her but have to part. "There's a place for us." Our monkey finds himself crying. Stop it. Look, identify with Chino, the reject. "Stick to your own kind." What kind of people are Tony and Maria anyway, both with black wavy hair, and looking more like each other than anybody else on or off the screen? They are on the same mafioso side, Natalie Wood as dark as a star can be. "Make of our hands one hand, make of our hearts one heart, make of our lives one life, day after day, one life." (Wittman had been to a wedding, he was best man, where his college friends had sung that song as part of the ceremony. The bride was Protestant and the groom was agnostic.)

The Jets are an Italian gang? But what about jet black? Like the Fillmore, the Western Addition. Black. Only they don't hire and cast Blacks, so Russ Tamblyn, as Riff the gangleader with kinky hair, indicates Blackness, right? (Like Leslie Caron with her wide mouth as Mardou Fox in *The Subterraneans* is supposed to be Black. George Peppard as Jack Kerouac, also as Holly Golightly's boyfriend in *Breakfast at Tiffany's.* Mickey Rooney with an eye job and glasses as Holly's jap landlord, speaking snuffling bucktoof patois.) The leader of the Sharks is Bernardo, Maria's brother, played by George Chakiris. Greek Danish Puerto Ricans of the East Coast. This is Back East, where they worry about Puerto Rican gangs, who are Black and white and blond. Don't the rest of the audience get Sharks and Jets mixed up in the fight-dancing? They should have hired dark actors for one side or the other. But not a face up there was darker than Pancake #11. Come on. Since when? A white-boy gang? Two white-boy gangs. White boys don't need a gang because they own the country. They go about the country individually and confidently, and not on the lookout for whom to ally with. "You got brothers around; you're a family man . . . We're gonna beat every last buggin gang on the whole buggin street." They mean they can beat kung fu tongs, who invented fight-dancing, and they can beat the dancing Black boxers, who fight solo.

Wittman got up and moved to a seat two rows forward, on the aisle, near the exit, but entered the movie no deeper, looking up at the squished faces. Can't get sucked in anymore. He went up to the balcony, smoked, nobody telling him to put out his smoke, and watched Tony talk to Doc, this lovable old *Jewish* candy-store guy—get it?—this movie is not prejudiced. Some of the Italians are good guys, Tony is reformed, and some are bad guys; the bad guys, see, are bad for reasons other than innateness. Wittman got up again and climbed to the back of the balcony. He would walk out except that he was too cheap to leave in the middle of movies. There weren't very many people in the audience, and they were spread out singly with rows of empty seats around each one, alone at the movies on Friday night with no place else to go. "The world is just an address. . . ." So, white guys, lonely also, borrow movie stars' faces, movie stars having inhabitable faces, and pretend to be out with Natalie, and to have a gang.

Chino does not disappear de-balled from the picture. He hunts Tony down and shoots him dead. Maria/Natalie kneels beside his body, and sings with tears in her eyes. "One hand, one heart, only death will part us now." Gangboys look on through the cyclone fence. She throws away the gun, which hits the cement but doesn't go off. "Te adoro, Anton," she says foreignly. Some Sharks, some Jets, biersmen, in rue, bear the dead away. The end.

Where are you, Bugs Bunny? We need you, Mr. Wabbit in Wed.

Wittman came out of the theater to the natural world that moves at a   *20*
medium rate with no jump cuts to the interesting parts. Headache. Bad for
the head to dream at the wrong time of day. The day gone. Should have cut
out—the only human being in the world to walk out on *West Side Story*—
too late. He'd stayed, and let the goddamn movies ruin his life.

Well, here was First Street, and the Terminal. The end of the City. The
end of the week. Maws—gaps and gapes—continuing to open. But Wittman
did too have a place to go, he'd been invited to a party, which he'd meant to
turn down. He entered the Terminal, which is surrounded by a concrete
whirlpool for the buses to turn around on spirals of ramps. Not earth dirt
but like cement dirt covered everything, rush-hour feet scuffing up lime,
noses and mouths inhaling lime rubbings. A last flower stand by the main
entrance—chrysanthemums. And a bake shop with birthday cakes. A couple
of people were eating creampuffs as they hurried along. People eat here, with
the smell of urinal cakes issuing from johns. They buy hot dogs at one end
of the Terminal and finish eating on their way through. They buy gifts at the
last moment. Wittman bought two packs of Pall Malls in preparation for the
rest of the weekend. No loiterers doing anything freaky. Keep it moving.
Everybody's got a place to go tonight. Wittman bought a ticket for the
Oakland-Berkeley border, and rode up the escalator to the lanes of buses.
The people on traffic islands waited along safety railings. Birds beak-dived
from the steel rafters to land precisely at a crumb between grill bars. The
pigeons and sparrows were greyish and the cheeks of men were also grey.
Pigeon dust. Pigeons fan our breathing air with pigeon dander.

Wittman was one of the first passengers to board, and chose the aisle
seat behind the driver. He threw his coat on the window seat to discourage
company, stuck his long legs out diagonally, and put on his metaphor glasses
and looked out the window.

Up into the bus clambered this very plain girl, who lifted her leg in
such an ungainly manner that anybody could see up her skirt to thighs, but
who'd be interested in looking? She was carrying string bags of books and
greasy butcher-paper bundles and pastry boxes. He wished she weren't Chinese, the kind who works hard and doesn't fix herself up. She, of course,
stood beside him until he moved his coat and let her bump her bags across
him and sit herself down to ride. This girl and her roast duck will ride beside
him all the way across the San Francisco-Oakland Bay Bridge. She must have
figured he was saving this seat for her, fellow ethnick.

The bus went up the turnaround ramp and over a feeder ramp, this girl
working away at opening her window—got it open when they passed the
Hills Brothers factory, where the long tall Hindu in the white turban and
yellow gown stood quaffing his coffee. The smell of the roasting coffee made
promises of comfort. Then they were on the bridge, not the bridge for
suicides, and journeying through the dark. The eastbound traffic takes the
bottom deck, which may as well be a tunnel. You can see lights between the

railings and the top deck, and thereby identify the shores, the hills, islands, highways, the other bridge.

"Going to Oakland?" asked the girl. She said "Oak Lun."   25

"Haw," he grunted, a tough old China Man. If he were Japanese, he could have said, "Ee, chotto." Like "Thataway for a spell." Not impolite. None of your business, ma'am.

"I'm in the City Fridays to work," she said. "Tuesdays and Thursdays, I'm taking a night course at Cal Extension, over by the metal overpass on Laguna Street. There's the bar and the traffic light on the corner? Nobody goes into or comes out of that bar. I stand there at that corner all by myself, obeying the traffic light. There aren't any cars. It's sort of lonely going to college. What for you go City?" He didn't answer. Does she notice that he isn't the forthcoming outgoing type? "On business, huh?" Suggesting an answer for him.

"Yeah. Business."

"I signed up for psychology," she said, as if he'd conversably asked. "But I looked up love in tables of contents and indexes, and do you know love isn't in psychology books? So I signed up for philosophy, but I'm getting disappointed. I thought we were going to learn about good and evil, human nature, how to be good. You know. What God is like. You know. How to live. But we're learning about P plus Q arrows R or S. What's that, haw? I work all day, and commute for two hours, and what do I get? P plus Q arrows R."

She ought to be interesting, going right to what's important. The trou-   30
ble with most people is that they don't think about the meaning of life. And here's this girl trying for heart truth. She may even have important new information. So how come she's boring? She's annoying him. Because she's presumptuous. Nosiness must be a Chinese racial trait. She was supposing, in the first place, that he was Chinese, and therefore, he has to hear her out. Care how she's getting along. She's reporting to him as to how one of our kind is faring. And she has a subtext: I am intelligent. I am educated. Why don't you ask me out? He took a side-eye look at her flat profile. She would look worse with her glasses off. Her mouse-brown hair was pulled tight against her head and up into a flat knot on top, hairpins showing, crisscross-ing. (Do Jews look down on men who use bobby pins to hold their yarmul-kes on?) A person has to have a perfect profile to wear her hair like that. She was wearing a short brownish jacket and her bony wrists stuck out of the sleeves. A thin springtime skirt. She's poor. Loafers with striped socks. Flat shoes, flat chest, flat hair, flat face, flat color. A smell like hot restaurant air that blows into alleys must be coming off her. Char sui? Fire duck? Traveling with food, unto this generation. Yeah, the lot of us riding the Greyhound out of Fresno and Watsonville and Gardena and Lompoc to college—even Stanford—guys *named* Stanford—with mama food and grandma food in the overhead rack and under the seat. Pretending the smell was coming off some-body else's luggage. And here was this girl, a night-school girl, a Continuing

Ed girl, crossing the Bay, bringing a fire duck weekend treat from Big City Chinatown to her aging parents.

"Do you know my cousin Annette Ah Tye?" she asked. "She's from Oak Lun."

"No," he said.

"How about Susan Lew? Oh, come on. Susie Lew. Robert Lew. Do you know Fanny them? Fanny, Bobby, Chance Ong, Uncle Louis. I'm related to Fanny them."

"No, I don't know them," said Wittman, who would not be badgered into saying, "Oh, yeah, Susan them. I'm related by marriage to her cousin from Walnut Creek."

"I'm thinking of dropping philosophy," she said. "Or do you think the prof is working up to the best part?" 35

"I don't know what you say," said Wittman. *Know* like *no*, like *brain*. "I major in engineer."

"Where do you study engineering?"

"Ha-ah." He made a noise like a samurai doing a me-ay, or an old Chinese guy who smokes too much.

"You ought to develop yourself," she said. "Not only mentally but physically, spiritually, and socially." What nerve. Chinese have a lot of nerve. Going to extension classes was her college adventure. Let's us who wear intellectual's glasses talk smart to each other. "You may be developing yourself mentally," she said. "But you know what's wrong with Chinese boys? All you do is study, but there's more to life than that. You need to be well rounded. Go out for sports. Go out on dates. Those are just two suggestions. You have to think up other activities on your own. You can't go by rote and succeed, as in engineering school. You want a deep life, don't you? That's what's wrong with Chinese boys. Shallow lives."

What Wittman ought to say at this point was, "Just because none of us 40 asks you out doesn't mean we don't go out with girls." Instead, to be kind, he said, "I not Chinese. I Japanese boy. I hate being taken for a chinaman. Now, which of my features is it that you find peculiarly Chinese? Go on. I'm interested."

"Don't say chinaman," she said.

Oh, god. O Central Casting, who do you have for me now? And what is this role that is mine? Confederates who have an interest in race: the Ku Klux Klan, Lester Maddox, fraternity guys, Governor Faubus, Governor Wallace, Nazis—stupid people on his level. The dumb part of himself that eats Fritos and goes to movies was avidly interested in race, a topic unworthy of a great mind. Low-karma shit. Babytalk. Stuck at A,B,C. Can't get to Q. Crybaby. Race—a stupid soul-narrowing topic, like women's rights, like sociology, easy for low-I.Q. people to feel like they're thinking. Stunted and runted at a low level of inquiry, stuck at worm. All right, then, his grade-point average was low (because of doing too many life things), he's the only Chinese American of his generation not in grad school, he'll shovel shit.

"It's the nose, isn't it, that's a chinaman nose?" he asked this flat-nosed girl. "Or my big Shinajin eyes? Oh, I know. I know. Legs. You noticed my Chinese legs." He started to pull up a pants leg. "I'm lean in the calf. Most Japanese are meaty in the calf by nature, made for wading in rice paddies. Or it's just girls who have daikon legs? How about you? You got daikon legs?"

She was holding her skirt down, moving her legs aside, not much room among her packages. Giggling. Too bad she was not offended. Modern youth in flirtation. "You Japanese know how to have a social life much better than Chinese," she said. "At least you Japanese boys take your girls out. You have a social life."

Oh, come on. Don't say "your girls." Don't say "social life." Don't say   *45* "boys." Or "prof." Those Continuing Ed teachers are on a non-tenure, non-promotional track. Below lecturers. Don't say "Chinese." Don't say "Japanese."

"You know why Chinese boys don't go out?" she asked, confiding some more. Why? What's the punchline? He ought to kill her with his bare hands, but waited to hear just why Chinese boys stay home studying and masturbating. You could hear her telling on us to some infatuated sinophile. Here it comes, the real skinny. "Because no matter how dumb-soo, every last short boy unable to get a date in high school or at college can go to Hong Kong and bring back a beautiful woman. Chinese boys don't bother to learn how to socialize. It's not fair. Can you imagine a girl going to China looking for a husband? What would they say about her? Have you ever heard of a Japanese girl sending for a picture groom?"

"No," he said.

"And if Chinese boys don't learn to date, and there are millions of wives waiting to be picked out, then what becomes of girls like me, haw?"

Oh, no, never to be married but to a girl like this one. Montgomery Clift married to Shelley Winters in *A Place in the Sun*. Never Elizabeth Taylor.

"You shouldn't go to China to pick up a guy anyway," he said. "Don't   *50* truck with foreigners. They'll marry you for your American money, and a green card. They'll say and do anything for a green card and money. Don't be fooled. They'll dump you once they get over here."

Another plan for her or for anybody might be to go to a country where your type is their ideal of physical beauty. For example, he himself would go over big in Scandinavia. But where would her type look good? Probably the U.S.A. is already her best bet. There's always white guys from Minnesota and Michigan looking for geisha girls.

"No, they won't," she said. "They'd be grateful. They're grateful and faithful forever. I'm not going to China. People can't just go to China. I was talking hypothetically." Oh, sure, she's so attractive.

"Last weekend, I went to a church dance," she said, letting him know she's with it. "I went with my girlfriends. We go to dances without a date for to meet new boys. All the people who attended the dance were Chinese.

How is that? I mean, it's not even an all-Chinese church. The same thing happens at college dances. Posters on campuses say 'Spring Formal,' but everyone knows it's a Chinese-only dance. How do they know? Okay, Chinese know. They know. But how does everybody else know not to come? Is it like that with you Japanese?"

"I don't go to dances." Don't say "they."

"You ought to socialize. I guess the church gave the dance so we could   55 meet one another. It's a church maneuver, see?, to give us something beneficial. We'd come to their buildings for English lessons, dances, pot luck, and pretty soon, we're staying for the services. Anyway, there was a chaperone at this dance who was a white acquaintance of mine from high school. We're the same age, but he was acting like an adult supervisor of children. We used to talk with each other at school, but at this dance, of course, he wouldn't ask me to dance."

"What for you want to dance with him? Oh. Oh, I get it. I know you. I know who you are. You're Pocahontas. That's who you are. Aren't you? Pocahontas. I should have recognized you from your long crane neck."

"No, my name is Judy. Judy Louis." She continued telling him more stuff about her life. On and on. Hadn't recognized her for a talker until too late. Strange moving lights, maybe airplanes, maybe satellites, were traveling through the air. The high stationary lights were warnings, the tops of hills. It seemed a long ride; this voice kept going on beside his ear. He looked at the girl again, and she looked blue-black in the dark. He blinked, and saw sitting beside him a blue boar. Yes, glints of light on bluish dagger tusks. Little shining eyes. Not an illusion because the details were very sharp. Straight black bristly eyelashes. A trick of the dark? But it was lasting. Eyes and ivory tusks gleaming black and silver. Like black ocean with star plankton and black sky with stars. And the mouth moving, opening and closing in speech, and a blue-red tongue showing between silver teeth, and two ivory sword tusks. He leaned back in his seat, tried forward, and she remained a blue boar. (You might make a joke about it, you know. "Boar" and "bore.") He couldn't see where her face left off from her hair and the dark. He made no ado about this hallucination, acted as if she were a normal girl. Concentrated hard to hear what she was saying. "You're putting me on, aren't you?" she was saying.

"What you mean?"

"You're not really Japanese. You're *Chinese*. Japanese have good manners." Her piggy eyes squinted at him. He wanted to touch her, but she would think he was making a pass. But, surely, he could try touching a tusk, because the tusks can't actually be there. "And you look Chinese. Big bones. Long face. Sort of messy."

"Listen here. I'm not going to ask you out, so quit hinting around,   60 okay?"

"What?! Me go out with you? I not hinting around. I wouldn't go out with you if you ask me. You not my type. Haw."

"What type is that? Missionaries? Missionaries your type? You know where you ought to go for your type? I know the place for you. In New York, there's a nightclub for haoles and orientals to pick each other up. It's like a gay bar, that is, not your average straight thing. Sick. Girls such as yourself go there looking for an all-American boy to assimilate with, and vice versa. You can play Madame Butterfly or the Dragon Lady and find yourself a vet who's remembering Seoul or Pearl Harbor or Pusan or Occupied Japan. All kinds of Somerset Maugham combinations you hardly want to know about. Pseudo psycho lesbo sappho weirdo hetero homo combos."

"You the one sick. Look who's sick. Don't call me sick. You sick." The blue boar had eyebrows, and they were screwed together in perplexity. "*If* you are a Japanese, you shouldn't go out with a Chinese girl anyway, and I wouldn't go out with you. Japanese males work too hard. Chinese males dream too much, and fly up in the air. The Chinese female is down-to-earth, and makes her man work. When a Japanese man marries a Chinese woman, which does not happen often, it's tragic. They would never relax and have fun. A Japanese man needs a girl who will help him loosen up, and a Chinese man needs a girl who will help him settle down. Chinese man, Chinese woman stay together. I'm going to do a study of that if I go into psych."

"Don't say 'tragic.' You want the address of that place where keto hakujin meet shinajin and nihonjin? Look, I'm just helping you out with your social life."

His talking to her, and her speaking, did not dispel her blueness or her   *65*
boarness. The lips moved, the tusks flashed. He wanted her to talk some more so he could look closely at her. What was causing this effect? The other people on the bus had not turned into animals.

"Help *yourself* out with your *own* social life. Why *don't* you ask me out on a date? Haw?" The boar lips parted smiling. "Because you are scared." "Sked," she pronounced it. "You been thinking about it this whole trip, but you sked." Don't say "date."

"No, I'm not." You're homely. He can't say that. She functions like she's as good-looking as the next person, and he's not going to be the one to disabuse her.

This guise, though, in not plain. A magnificent creature. The voice that was coming out of it was the plain girl's. She must be sitting next to him engulfed in a mirage.

He touched her on a tusk, and it was there, all right. It did not fade into a strip of metal that was the window frame. The narrow eyes looked at him in surprise. "Hey, cut it out," she said, pushing his hand away from her mouth with a gentle cloven hoof. She giggled, and he backed away as far over by the aisle as he could back. What he had touched was harder than flesh. Bony. Solid. Therefore, real, huh? She giggled again. It is pretty funny to have somebody touching you on the teeth. Warm teeth.

"What was that for? Why did you do that?" she said. "Why you touch   70
my teeth? That isn't the way to ask for a date."

"I'm not asking you for a date. I do not want to date you."

"Well, I understand. You don't like aggressive girls. Most guys can't
take aggressive girls. I'm very aggressive." She'll never admit to homeliness.
"Aggressive girls are especially bad for Japanese boys."

"Lay off my race," he said. "Cool it." Which was what he should have
said in the first place. She went quiet. Sat there. But did not change back.
The bus went on for a long time in the dark. And whenever he glanced her
way, there beside him was the blue-black boar. Gleaming.

"Hey," he said, tapping her on the shoulder. Boar skin feels like
corduroy. She cocked a flap of silky ear toward him. "See these people
on the bus? They all look human, don't they? They look like humans but
they're not."

"They are too," she said.   75

"Let me warn you." He looked behind him, and behind her. "Some
of them only appear to be human." What he was saying even sent shivers
up his own back. "There are non-humans in disguise as men and women
amongst us."

"Do you see them everywhere, or only on this bus?"

"On this bus, maybe a few other places. I'm surprised you haven't
noticed. Well, some of them have gotten the disguise down very well. But
there's usually a slip-up that gives them away. Do you want me to tell you
some signs to watch out for?"

The boar's great blue-black head nodded.

"You've seen 'The Twilight Zone' on t.v., haven't you? Have you no-   80
ticed that Rod Serling doesn't have an upper lip?" He demonstrated, pressing
his upper lip against his teeth. "That's a characteristic sign of the werewolf."
The glittery eyes of the boar opened wider, surprised. "Their hands are
different from ours. They wear gloves. Walt Disney draws them accurately.
And Walter Lantz does too. Goofy wears gloves, but not Pluto. Goofy is a
dog, and Pluto is a dog, but Pluto is a real dog. Mickey and Minnie, Donald
and the nephews, Unca Scrooge—and Yosemite Sam—never take their
gloves off. Minnie and Daisy wash dishes with their gloves on. You see
women in church with those same little white gloves, huh? They are often
going to church. There are more of these werewomen in San Francisco than
in other cities."

"What do they want? What are they doing here?"

"You tell me. I think they're here because they belong here. That's just
the way the world is. There's all kinds. There are cataclysms and luck that
they probably manipulate. But there's different kinds of them too, you know;
they don't get along with one another. It's not like they're all together in a
conspiracy against our kind."

"Aiya-a-ah, nay gum sai nay, a-a-ah," said the creature—the Pig

Woman—beside him. "Mo gum sai nay, la ma-a-ah." Such a kind voice, such a loving-kind voice, so soothing, so sorry for him, telling him to let go of the old superstitious ways.

At last, the bus shot out of the tunnel-like bridge. Under the bright lights, she turned back into a tan-and-grey drab of a girl again. Wittman got himself to his feet, rode standing up, and the bus reached the intersection of College and Alcatraz. Here's where I get off.

"Goodbye," she said. "Let's talk again. It will make our commute more interesting." She was not admitting to having weirdly become Pig Woman.

He said, "Huh." Samurai.

The Responsive Reader

1. The story is set in San Francisco, the city of the beat poets and the Kerouac generation. Kerouac, author of *On the Road,* wrote about people who dropped out of the bourgeois rat race to fraternize with the down and out and dispossessed. What is Wittman's paradoxical relation to this tradition? How does Wittman seem a descendant of the Kerouac generation? Why does he react negatively to the Kerouac passage he quotes?

2. Wittman tells us that "if there is one thing that makes life bearable, it's the movies." He does not mean "educational films but big-bucks full-production-values American glitz movies." What role do the movies play in his fantasy life or in his mental universe? What are striking or revealing details in his running commentary on the film *West Side Story*—a much ballyhooed adaptation of Shakespeare's *Romeo and Juliet* in a musical about Puerto Rican gangs in New York City?

3. Does the narrator, or person telling the story seem hypersensitive to references to race or ethnicity? What are striking examples of his heightened awareness of racial or ethnic origins, overtones, or implications? Can you put your finger on his overall attitude?

4. What does Wittman's encounter with the Chinese fellow passenger tell us about him and his relation to his Chinese origins? Why is there so much talk about whether or not he is Japanese? What stereotypes or ideas about ethnicity are touched on in the young woman's conversation? Would you call Wittman's attitude or behavior toward her sexist?

5. The narrator, or person telling the story, loves word play and puns. His fellow passenger reminds him of a boar (a male pig), but she is also a bore. He is "agoraphobic on Market Street"; that is, he suffers from fear of crowded public places—"market anxiety"—on Market Street. What other examples of word play can you find in the story? What other examples of his zany humor can you find?

Thinking, Talking, Writing

6. What is the proportion of all–American and ethnic ingredients in the cultural mix of Wittman's thinking and imagination? How Americanized does he seem to you? How ethnic is he?

7. What role does humor play in the story as a whole?

8. We are often told that young people not only in this country but around the world absorb much of their way of thinking, feeling, talking, dressing, and behaving from American movies and television. How do you think movies and television have shaped your own ways of thinking and feeling? How have they influenced your view of the world?

Thinking about Connections

9. Compare and contrast Wittman with one or more of the city dwellers in the stories by Malamud, Algren, and Bambara.

A LETTER TO HARVEY MILK

Lesléa Newman

I remember too much; the pen is like a knife twisting in my heart.

Lesléa Newman

> *Survivors of the Holocaust brought to this country memories of persecution and genocide hard or impossible to put into words but also impossible to repress or forget. Millions of European Jews were murdered in the Nazi death camps, as were gypsies, homosexuals, and other "undesirables." In the following story, memories of the concentration camps intermesh with memories of the more recent past: the murder of Harvey Milk, the Jewish homosexual supervisor in San Francisco, by Dan White, which made Milk a martyr for the gay cause.*
>
> *The story that follows was included in* Women on Women *(1990), a collection designed to introduce new lesbian writers to the public at large and to "give voice to the variety of experience rising out of ethnic, race, class, and generational differences." In the words of the editors, in this story "a widowed elderly Jewish man relives painful but intensely alive memories as he does writing exercises for his young lesbian writing teacher, for whom he has almost become family." Both teacher and student are Jewish, with the younger woman trying to understand and appropriate a heritage that the older man tries in vain to leave behind.*
>
> *The narrator's language, like that of many immigrants, is colored by the language of his youth. He uses many Yiddish words and expressions, such as* stetl *for the small Jewish communities of Eastern Europe,* meshuge *for crazy,* shanda *for shame,* mensh *for a true human being.*

for Harvey Milk 1930–1978

I.

The teacher says we should write about our life, everything that happened today. So *nu*, what's there to tell? Why should today be different than any other day? May 5, 1986. I get up, I have myself a coffee, a little cottage cheese, half an English muffin. I get dressed. I straighten up the house a little, nobody should drop by and see I'm such a slob. I go down to the Senior Center and see what's doing. I play a little cards. I have some lunch, a bagel with cheese. I read a sign in the cafeteria. Writing Class 2:00. I think to myself, why not, something to pass the time. So at two o'clock I go in. The teacher says we should write about our life.

Listen, I want to say to this teacher, I. B. Singer I'm not. You think anybody cares what I did all day? Even my own children, may they live and be well, don't call. You think the whole world is waiting to see what Harry Weinberg had for breakfast?

The teacher is young and nice. She says everybody has something important to say. Yeah, sure, when you're young you believe things like that. She has short brown hair and big eyes, a nice figure, *zaftig* like my poor Fannie, may she rest in peace. She's wearing a Star of David around her neck, hanging from a purple string, that's nice. She gave us all notebooks and told us we're gonna write something every day, and if we want we can even write at home. Who'd a thunk it, me—Harry Weinberg, seventy-seven-years old— scribbling in a notebook like a schoolgirl. Why not, it passes the time.

So after the class I go to the store. I pick myself up a little orange juice, a few bagels, a nice piece of chicken. I shouldn't starve to death. I go up, I put on the slippers, I eat the chicken, I watch a little TV, I write in this notebook, I get ready for bed. *Nu,* for this somebody should give me a Pulitzer Prize?

II.

Today the teacher tells us something about herself. She's a Jew, this we   5 know from the *Mogen David* she wears around her neck. She tells us she wants to collect stories from old Jewish people, to preserve our history. *Oy,* such stories that I could tell her, shouldn't be preserved by nobody. She tells us she's learning Yiddish. For what, I wonder. I can't figure this teacher out. She's young, she's pretty, she shouldn't be with the old people so much. I wonder is she married. She doesn't wear a ring. Her grandparents won't tell her stories, she says, and she's worried that the Jews her age won't know nothing about the culture, about life in the *shtetls.* Believe me, life in the *shtetl* is nothing worth knowing about. Hunger and more hunger. Better off we're here in America, the past is past.

Then she gives us our homework, the homework we write in the class, it's a little *meshugeh,* but alright. She wants us to write a letter to somebody from our past, somebody who's no longer with us. She reads us a letter a child wrote to Abraham Lincoln, like an example. Right away I see everybody's getting nervous. So I raise my hand. "Teacher," I say, "you can tell me maybe how to address such a letter? There's a few things I've wanted to ask my wife for a long time." Everybody laughs. Then they start to write.

I sit for a few minutes, thinking about Fannie, thinking about my sister Frieda, my mother, my father, may they all rest in peace. But it's the strangest thing, the one I really want to write to is Harvey.

> *Dear Harvey:*
>
> You had to go get yourself killed for being a *faygeleh?* You couldn't let somebody else have such a great honor? Alright, alright, so you liked the boys, I wasn't wild about the idea. But I got used to it. I never said you wasn't welcome in my house, did I?

Nu, Harvey, you couldn't leave well enough alone? You had your own camera store, your own business, what's bad? You couldn't keep still about the boys, you weren't satisfied until the whole world knew? Harvey Milk, with the big ears and the big ideas, had to go make himself something, a big politician. I know, I know, I said, "Harvey, make something of yourself, don't be an old *shmegeggie* like me, Harry the butcher." So now I'm eating my words, and they stick like a chicken bone in my old throat.

It's a rotten world, Harvey, and rottener still without you in it. You 10 know what happened to that *momzer,* Dan White? They let him out of jail, and he goes and kills himself so nobody else should have the pleasure. Now you know me, Harvey, I'm not a violent man. But this was too much, even for me. In the old country, I saw things you shouldn't know from, things you couldn't imagine one person could do to another. But here in America, a man climbs through the window, kills the Mayor of San Francisco, kills Harvey Milk, and a couple years later he's walking around on the street? This I never thought I'd see in my whole life. But from a country that kills the Rosenbergs, I should expect something different?

Harvey, you should be glad you weren't around for the trial. I read about it in the papers. The lawyer, that son of a bitch, said Dan White ate too many Twinkies the night before he killed you, so his brain wasn't working right. Twinkies, *nu,* I ask you. My kids ate Twinkies when they were little, did they grow up to be murderers, God forbid? And now, do they take the Twinkies down from the shelf, somebody else shouldn't go a little crazy, climb through a window, and shoot somebody? No, they leave them right there next to the cupcakes and the donuts, to torture me every time I go to the store to pick up a few things, I shouldn't starve to death.

Harvey, I think I'm losing my mind. You know what I do every week? Every week I go to the store, I buy a bag of jelly beans for you, you should have something to *nosh* on, I remember what a sweet tooth you have. I put them in a jar on the table, in case you should come in with another crazy petition for me to sign. Sometimes I think you're gonna just walk through my door and tell me it was another *meshugeh* publicity stunt.

Harvey, now I'm gonna tell you something. The night you died the whole city of San Francisco cried for you. Thirty thousand people marched in the street, I saw it on TV. Me, I didn't go down. I'm an old man, I don't walk so good, they said there might be riots. But no, there were no riots. Just people walking in the street, quiet, each one with a candle, until the street looked like the sky all lit up with a million stars. Old people, young people, black people, white people, Chinese people. You name it, they were there. I remember thinking, Harvey must be so proud, and then I remembered you were dead and such a lump rose in my throat, like a grapefruit it was, and then the tears ran down my face like rain. Can you imagine, Harvey, an old man like me, sitting alone in his apartment, crying and carrying on like a baby? But it's the God's truth. Never did I carry on so in all my life.

And then all of a sudden I got mad. I yelled at the people on TV: for getting shot you made him into such a hero? You couldn't march for him when he was alive, he couldn't *shep* a little *naches?*

But *nu,* what good does getting mad do, it only makes my pressure 15 go up. So I took myself a pill, calmed myself down.

Then they made speeches for you, Harvey. The same people who called you a *shmuck* when you were alive, now you were dead, they were calling you a *mensh.* You were a *mensh,* Harvey, a *mensh* with a heart of gold. You were too good for this rotten world. They just weren't ready for you.

> *Oy Harveleh, alav ha-sholom,*
> *Harry*

III.

Today the teacher asks me to stay for a minute after class. *Oy,* what did I do wrong now, I wonder. Maybe she didn't like my letter to Harvey? Who knows?

After the class she comes and sits down next to me. She's wearing purple pants and a white T-shirt. "*Feh,*" I can just hear Fannie say. "God forbid she should wear a skirt? Show off her figure a little? The girls today dressing like boys and the boys dressing like girls—this I don't understand."

"Mr. Weinberg," the teacher says.

"Call me Harry," I says. 20

"O.K., Harry," she says. "I really liked the letter you wrote to Harvey Milk. It was terrific, really. It meant a lot to me. It even made me cry."

I can't even believe my own ears. My letter to Harvey Milk made the teacher cry?

"You see, Harry," she says, "I'm gay, too. And there aren't many Jewish people your age that are so open-minded. At least that I know. So your letter gave me lots of hope. In fact, I was wondering if you'd consider publishing it."

Publishing my letter? Again I couldn't believe my own ears. Who would want to read a letter from Harry Weinberg to Harvey Milk? No, I tell her. I'm too old for fame and glory. I like the writing class, it passes the time. But what I write is my own business. The teacher looks sad for a moment, like a cloud passes over her eyes. Then she says, "Tell me about Harvey Milk. How did you meet him? What was he like?" *Nu,* Harvey, you were a pain in the ass when you were alive, you're still a pain in the ass now that you're dead. Everybody wants to hear about Harvey.

So I tell her. I tell her how I came into the camera shop one day with 25 a roll of film from when I went to visit the grandchildren. How we started talking, and I said, "Milk, that's not such a common name. Are you related to the Milks in Woodmere?" And so we found out we were practically neighbors forty years ago, when the children were young, before we moved out here. Gracie was almost the same age as Harvey, a couple years older, maybe, but they went to different schools. Still, Harvey leans across the counter and gives me such a hug, like I'm his own father.

I tell her more about Harvey, how he didn't believe there was a good *kosher* butcher in San Francisco, how he came to my store just to see. But all the time I'm talking I'm thinking to myself, no, it can't be true. Such a gorgeous girl like this goes with the girls, not with the boys? Such a *shanda.* Didn't God in His wisdom make a girl a girl and a boy a boy—boom they should meet, boom they should get married, boom they should have babies, and that's the way it is? Harvey I loved like my own son, but this I never could understand. And *nu,* why was the teacher telling me this, it's my business who she sleeps with? She has some sadness in her eyes, this teacher. Believe me I've known such sadness in my life, I can recognize it a hundred miles away. Maybe she's lonely. Maybe after class one day I'll take her out for a coffee, we'll talk a little bit, I'll find out.

IV.

It's 3:00 in the morning, I can't sleep. So *nu,* here I am with this crazy notebook. Who am I kidding, maybe I think I'm Yitzhak Peretz? What would the children think, to see their old father sitting up in his bathrobe with a cup of tea, scribbling in his notebook? *Oy, meyn kinder,* they should only live and be well and call their old father once in a while.

Fannie used to keep up with them. She could be such a *nudge,* my Fannie. "What's the matter, you're too good to call your old mother once in a while?" she'd yell into the phone. Then there'd be a pause. "Busy-shmusy," she'd yell even louder. "Was I too busy to change your diapers? Was I too busy to put food into your mouth?" *Oy,* I haven't got the strength, but Fannie could she yell and carry on.

You know sometimes, in the middle of the night, I'll reach across the bed for Fannie's hand. Without even thinking, like my hand got a mind of its own, it creeps across the bed, looking for Fannie's hand. After all this time, fourteen years she's been dead, but still, a man gets used to a few things. Forty-two years, the body doesn't forget. And my little *Faigl* had such hands, little *hentelehs,* tiny like a child's. But strong. Strong from kneading *challah,* from scrubbing clothes, from rubbing the children's backs to put them to sleep. My Fannie, she was so ashamed from those hands. After thirty-five years of marriage when finally, I could afford to buy her a diamond ring, she said no. She said it was too late already, she'd be ashamed. A girl needs nice hands to show off a diamond, her hands were already ruined, better yet buy a new stove.

Ruined? *Feh.* To me her hands were beautiful. Small, with veins *30* running through them like rivers, and cracks in the skin like the desert. A hundred times I've kicked myself for not buying Fannie that ring.

V.

Today in the writing class the teacher read my notebook. Then she says I should make a poem about Fannie. "A poem," I says to her, "now Shakespeare you want I should be?" She says I have a good eye for detail. I says to her, "Excuse me, Teacher, you live with a woman for forty-two years, you start to notice a few things."

She helps me. We do it together, we write a poem called "Fannie's Hands":

Fannie's hands are two little birds
that fly into her lap.
Her veins are like rivers.
Her skin is cracked like the desert.
Her strong little hands
baked *challah,* scrubbed clothes,
rubbed the children's backs.
Her strong little hands
and my big clumsy hands
fit together in the night
like pieces of a jigsaw puzzle
made in Heaven, by God.

So *nu,* who says you can't teach an old dog new tricks? I read it to the class and such a fuss they made. "A regular Romeo," one of them says. "If only my husband, may he live and be well, would write such a poem for me," says another. I wish Fannie was still alive, I could read it to her. Even the teacher was happy, I could tell, but still, there was a ring of sadness around her eyes.

After the class I waited till everybody left, they shouldn't get the wrong idea, and I asked the teacher would she like to go get a coffee. "*Nu,* it's enough writing already," I said. "Come, let's have a little treat." 35

So we take a walk, it's a nice day. We find a diner, nothing fancy, but clean and quiet. I try to buy her a piece of cake, a sandwich maybe, but no, all she wants is coffee.

So we sit and talk a little. She wants to know about my childhood in the old country, she wants to know about the boat ride to America, she wants to know did my parents speak Yiddish to me when I was growing up. "Harry," she says to me, "when I hear old people talking Yiddish, it's like a love letter blowing in the wind. I try to run after them, and sometimes I catch a phrase that makes me cry or a word that makes me laugh. Even if I don't understand, it always touches my heart."

Oy, this teacher has some strange ideas. "Why do you want to speak Jewish?" I ask her. "Here in America, everybody speaks English. You don't need it. What's done is done, what's past is past. You shouldn't go with the old people so much. You should go out, make friends, have a good time. You got some troubles you want to talk about? Maybe I shouldn't pry," I say, "but you shouldn't look so sad, a young girl like you. When you're old you got plenty to be sad. You shouldn't think about the old days so much, let the dead rest in peace. What's done is done."

I took a swallow of my coffee, to calm down my nerves. I was getting a little too excited.

"Harry, listen to me," the teacher says. "I'm thirty years old and no one   40
in my family will talk to me because I'm gay. It's all Harvey Milk's fault. He made such an impression on me. You know, when he died, what he said, 'If a bullet enters my brain, let that bullet destroy every closet door.' So when he died, I came out to everyone—the people at work, my parents. I felt it was my duty, so the Dan Whites of the world wouldn't be able to get away with it. I mean, if every single gay person came out—just think of it!— everyone would see they had a gay friend or a gay brother or a gay cousin or a gay teacher. Then they couldn't say things like 'Those gays should be shot.' Because they'd be saying you should shoot my neighbor or my sister or my daughter's best friend."

I never saw the teacher get so excited before. Maybe a politician she should be. She reminded me a little bit of Harvey.

"So *nu,* what's the problem?" I ask.

"The problem is my parents," she says with a sigh, and such a sigh I never heard from a young person before. "My parents haven't spoken to me since I told them I was gay. 'How could you do this to us?' they said. I wasn't doing anything to them. I tried to explain I couldn't help being gay, like I couldn't help being a Jew, but that they didn't want to hear. So I haven't spoken to them in eight years."

"Eight years, *Gottenyu,*" I say to her. This I never heard in my whole life. A father and a mother cut off their own daughter like that. Better they should cut off their own hand. I thought about Gracie, a perfect daughter she's not, but your child is your child. When she married the *Goy,* Fannie threatened to put her head in the oven, but she got over it. Not to see your own daughter for eight years, and such a smart, gorgeous girl, such a good teacher, what a *shanda.*

So what can I do, I ask. Does she want me to talk to them, a letter   45
maybe I could write. Does she want I should adopt her, the hell with them, I make a little joke. She smiles. "Just talking to you makes me feel better," she says. So *nu,* now I'm Harry the social worker. She says that's why she wants the old people's stories so much, she doesn't know nothing from her own family history. She wants to know about her own people, maybe write a book. But it's hard to get the people to talk to her, she says, she doesn't understand.

"Listen, Teacher," I tell her. "These old people have stories you shouldn't know from. What's there to tell? Hunger and more hunger.

Suffering and more suffering. I buried my sister over twenty years ago, my mother, my father—all dead. You think I could just start talking about them like I just saw them yesterday? You think I don't think about them every day? Right here I keep them," I say, pointing to my heart. "I try to forget them, I should live in peace, the dead are gone. Talking about them won't bring them back. You want stories, go talk to somebody else. I ain't got no stories."

I sat down then, I didn't even know I was standing up, I got so excited. Everybody in the diner was looking at me, a crazy man shouting at a young girl.

Oy, and now the teacher was cryin. "I'm sorry," I says to her. "You want another coffee?"

"No thanks, Harry," she says. "I'm sorry, too."

"Forget it. We can just pretend it never happened," I say, and then   50 we go.

VI.

All this crazy writing has shaken me up inside a little bit. Yesterday I was walking home from the diner, I thought I saw Harvey walking in front of me. No, it can't be, I says to myself, and my heart started to pound so, I got afraid I shouldn't drop dead in the street from a heart attack. But then the man turned around and it wasn't Harvey. It didn't even look like him at all.

I got myself upstairs and took myself a pill, I could feel my pressure was going up. All this talk about the past—Fannie, Harvey, Frieda, my mother, my father—what good does it do? This teacher and her crazy ideas. Did I ever ask my mother, my father, what their childhood was like? What nonsense. Better I shouldn't know.

So today is Saturday, no writing class, but still I'm writing in this crazy notebook. I ask myself, Harry, what can I do to make you feel a little better? And I answer myself, make me a nice chicken soup.

You think an old man like me can't make chicken soup? Let me tell you, on all the holidays it was Harry that made the soup. Every *Pesach* it was Harry skimming the *shmaltz* from the top of the pot, it was Harry making the *kreplach.* I ask you, where is it written that a man shouldn't know from chicken soup?

So I take myself down to the store, I buy myself a nice chicken, some   55 carrots, some celery, some parsley—onions I already got, parsnips I can do without. I'm afraid I shouldn't have a heart attack *shlepping* all that food up the steps, but thank God, I make it alright.

I put up the pot with water, throw everything in one-two-three, and soon the whole house smells from chicken soup.

I remember the time Harvey came to visit and there I was with my apron on, skimming the *shmaltz* from the soup. Did he kid me about that!

The only way I could get him to keep still was to invite him to dinner. "Listen, Harvey," I says to him. "Whether you're a man or a woman, it doesn't matter. You gotta learn to cook. When you're old, nobody cares. Nobody will do for you. You gotta learn to do for yourself."

"I won't live past fifty, Har," he says, smearing a piece of rye bread with *shmaltz*.

"Nobody wants to grow old, believe me, I know," I says to him. "But listen, it's not so terrible. What's the alternative? Nobody wants to die young, either." I take off my apron and sit down with him.

"No, I mean it Harry," he says to me with his mouth full. "I won't   60 make it to fifty. I've always known it. I'm a politician. A gay politician. Someone's gonna take a pot shot at me. It's a risk you gotta take."

The way he said it, I tell you, a chill ran down my back like I never felt before. He was forty-seven at the time, just a year before he died.

VII.

Today after the writing class, the teacher tells us she's going away for two days. Everyone makes a big fuss, the class they like so much already. She tells us she's sorry, something came up she has to do. She says we can come have class without her, the room will be open, we can read to each other what we write in our notebooks. Someone asks her what we should write about.

"Write me a letter," she says. "Write a story called 'What I Never Told Anyone.'"

So, after everyone leaves, I ask her does she want to go out, have a coffee, but she says no, she has to go home and pack.

I tell her wherever she's going she should have a good time.   65

"Thanks, Harry," she says. "You'll be here when I get back?"

"Sure," I tell her. "I like this crazy writing. It passes the time."

She swings a big black bookbag onto her shoulder, a regular Hercules this teacher is, and she smiles at me. "I gotta run, Harry. Have a good week." She turns and walks away and something on her bookbag catches my eye. A big shiny pin that spells out her name all fancy-shmancy in rhinestones: Barbara. And under that, right away I see sewn onto her bookbag an upside-down pink triangle.

I stop in my tracks, stunned. No, it can't be, I says to myself. Maybe it's just a design? Maybe she doesn't know from this? My heart is beating fast now, I know I should go home, take myself a pill, my pressure, I can feel it going up.

But I just stand there. And then I get mad. What, she thinks maybe   70 I'm blind as well as old. I can't see what's right in front of my nose? Or maybe we don't remember such things? What right does she have to walk in here with that, that thing on her bag, to remind us of what we been through? Haven't we seen enough?

Stories she wants. She wants we should cut our hearts open and give her stories so she could write a book. Well, alright, now I'll tell her a story.

This is what I never told anyone. One day, maybe seven, eight years ago—no, maybe longer, I think Harvey was still alive—one day Izzie comes knocking on my door. I open the door and there's Izzie, standing there, his face white as a sheet. I bring him inside, I make him a coffee. "Izzie, what is it," I says to him. "Something happened to the children, to the grandchildren, God forbid?"

He sits down, he doesn't drink his coffee. He looks through me like I'm not even there. Then he says, "Harry, I'm walking down the street, you know I had a little lunch at the Center, and then I come outside, I see a young man, maybe twenty-five, a good-looking guy, walking toward me. He's wearing black pants, a white shirt, and on his shirt he's got a pink triangle."

"So," I says. "A pink triangle, a purple triangle, they wear all kinds of crazy things these days."

"*Heshel,*" he tells me, "don't you understand? The gays are wearing   75 pink triangles just like the war, just like in the camps."

No, this I can't believe. Why would they do a thing like that? But if Izzie says it, it must be true. Who would make up such a thing?

"He looked a little bit like *Yussl,*" Izzie says, and then he begins to cry, and such a cry like I never heard. Like a baby he was, with the tears streaming down his cheeks and his shoulders shaking with great big sobs. Such moans and groans I never heard from a grown man in all my life. I thought maybe he was gonna have a heart attack the way he was carrying on. I didn't know what to do. I was afraid the neighbors would hear, they shouldn't call the police, such sounds he was making. Fifty-eight years old he was, but he looked like a little boy sitting there, sniffling. And who was *Yussl?* Thirty years we'd been friends, and I never heard from *Yussl.*

So finally, I put my arms around him, and I held him, I didn't know what else to do. His body was shaking so, I thought his bones would crack from knocking against each other. Soon his body got quiet, but then all of sudden his mouth got noisy.

"Listen, *Heshel,* I got to tell you something, something I never told nobody in my whole life. I was young in the camps, nineteen, maybe twenty when they took us away." The words poured from his mouth like a flood. "*Yussl* was my best friend in the camps. Already I saw my mother, my father, my Hannah marched off to the ovens. *Yussl* was the only one I had to hold on to.

"One morning, during the selection, they pointed me to the right,   80 *Yussl* to the left. I went a little crazy, I ran after him. 'No, he stays with me, they made a mistake,' I said, and I grabbed him by the hand and dragged him back in line. Why the guard didn't kill us right then, I couldn't tell you. Nothing made sense in that place.

"*Yussl* and I slept together on a wooden bench. That night I couldn't sleep. It happened pretty often in that place. I would close my eyes and see such things that would make me scream in the night, and for that I could get shot. I don't know what was worse, asleep or awake. All I saw was suffering.

"On this night, *Yussl* was awake, too. He didn't move a muscle, but I could tell. Finally he said my name, just a whisper, but something broke in me and I began to cry. He put his arms around me and we cried together, such a close call we'd had.

"And then he began to kiss me. 'You saved my life,' he whispered, and he kissed my eyes, my cheeks, my lips. And Harry, I kissed him back. Harry, I never told nobody this before. I, we . . . we, you know, that was such a place that hell, I couldn't help it. The warmth of his body was just too much for me and Hannah was dead already and we would soon be dead too, probably, so what did it matter?"

He looked up at me then, the tears streaming from his eyes. "It's O.K., Izzie," I said. "Maybe I would have done the same."

"There's more, Harry," he says, and I got him a tissue, he should blow   85
his nose. What more could there be?

"This went on for a couple of months maybe, just every once in a while when we couldn't sleep. He'd whisper my name and I'd answer with his, and then we'd, you know, we'd touch each other. We were very, very quiet, but who knows, maybe some other boys in the barracks were doing the same.

"To this day I don't know how it happened, but somehow someone found out. One day *Yussl* didn't come back to the barracks at night. I went almost crazy, you can imagine, all the things that went through my mind, the things they might have done to him, those lousy Nazis. I looked everywhere, I asked everyone, three days he was gone. And then on the third day, they lined us up after supper and there they had *Yussl*. I almost collapsed on the ground when I saw him. They had him on his knees with his hands tied behind his back. His face was swollen so, you couldn't even see his eyes. His clothes were stained with blood. And on his uniform they had sewn a pink triangle, big, twice the size of our yellow stars.

"*Oy*, did they beat him but good. 'Who's your friend?' they yelled at him. 'Tell us and we'll let you live.' But no, he wouldn't tell. He knew they were lying, he knew they'd kill us both. They asked him again and again, 'Who's your friend? Tell us which one he is.' And every time he said no, they'd crack him with a whip until the blood ran from him like a river. Such a sight he was, like I've never seen. How he remained conscious I'll never know.

"Everything inside me was broken after that. I wanted to run to his side, but I didn't dare, so afraid I was. At one point he looked at me, right in the eye, as though he was saying, *Izzie, save yourself. Me, I'm finished, but you, you got a chance to live through this and tell the world our story.*

"Right after he looked at me, he collapsed, and they shot him, Harry,   90
right there in front of us. Even after he was dead they kicked him in the head a little bit. They left his body out there for two days, as a warning to

us. They whipped us all that night, and from then on we had to sleep with all the lights on and with our hands on top of the blankets. Anyone caught with their hands under the blankets would be shot.

"He died for me, Harry, they killed him for that, was it such a terrible thing? *Oy*, I haven't thought about *Yussl* for twenty-five years maybe, but when I saw that kid on the street today, it was too much." And then he started crying again, and he clung to me like a child.

So what could I do? I was afraid he shouldn't have a heart attack, maybe he was having a nervous breakdown, maybe I should get the doctor. *Vay iss mir,* I never saw anybody so upset in my whole life. And such a story, *Gottenyu.*

"Izzie, come lie down," I says, and I took him by the hand to the bed. I laid him down, I took off his shoes, and still he was crying. So what could I do? I lay down with him, I held him tight. I told him he was safe, he was in America. I don't know what else I said, I don't think he heard me, still he kept crying.

I stroked his head, I held him tight. "Izzie, it's alright," I said. "Izzie, Izzie, *Izzaleh.*" I said his name over and over, like a lullaby, until his crying got quiet. He said my name once softly, *Heshel,* or maybe he said *Yussl,* I don't remember, but thank God he finally fell asleep. I tried to get up from the bed, but Izzie held onto me tight. So what could I do? Izzie was my friend for thirty years, for him I would do anything. So I held him all night long, and he slept like a baby.

And this is what I never told nobody, not even Harvey. That there in   *95*
that bed, where Fannie and I slept together for forty-two years, me and Izzie spent the night. Me, I didn't sleep a wink, such a lump in my throat I had, like the night Harvey died.

Izzie passed on a couple months after that. I saw him a few more times, and he seemed different somehow. How, I couldn't say. We never talked about that night. But now that he had told someone his deepest secret, he was ready to go, he could die in peace. Maybe now that I told, I can die in peace, too?

VIII.

Dear Teacher:

You said write what you never told nobody, and write you a letter. I always did all my homework, such a student I was. So *nu,* I got to tell you something. I can't write in this notebook no more, I can't come no more to the class. I don't want you should take offense, you're a good teacher and a nice girl. But me, I'm an old man, I don't sleep so good at night, these stories are like a knife in my heart. Harvey, Fannie, Izzie, *Yussl,* my father, my mother, let them all rest in peace. The dead are gone. Better to live for today. What good does remembering do, it doesn't bring back the dead. Let them rest in peace.

But Teacher, I want you should have my notebook. It doesn't have nice stories in it, no love letters, no happy endings for a nice girl like you. A bestseller it ain't, I guarantee. Maybe you'll put it in a book someday, the world shouldn't forget.

Meanwhile, good luck to you, Teacher. May you live and be well and not get shot in the head like poor Harvey, may he rest in peace. Maybe someday we'll go out, have a coffee again, who knows? But me, I'm too old for this crazy writing. I remember too much, the pen is like a knife twisting in my heart.

One more thing, Teacher. Between parents and children, it's not so easy. Believe me, I know. Don't give up on them. One father, one mother, it's all you got. If you were my *tochter,* I'd be proud of you.

Harry

The Responsive Reader

1. What is Jewish about the teacher and the student in this story? What customs, references, or features of language do you recognize?
2. What kind of person is the narrator? What did Harvey Milk mean to him? Why do you think the lesbian author made the narrator deplore the fact that the teacher is lesbian? What is the narrator's attitude toward gays?
3. What kind of person is the teacher in the story? What did Harvey Milk and his death mean to her? What is her relation to her family?
4. Why do you think the concentration camp memories do not appear till very late in the story? Do they confirm or change what you know or have read about the camps?
5. What role does the dead wife play in the story?

Thinking, Talking, Writing

6. For the author of this story, what is the connection between the concentration camp memories and Harvey Milk?
7. Have you encountered any explanations for or theories about the causes of the unspeakable brutalities of the Nazi camps?
8. Are you aware of stereotypes or prejudices concerning Jews? Does this story in any way comment on them or counteract them?

Collaborative Projects

9. You may want to collaborate on a report on the Holocaust Museum in Washington, DC.

A WIFE'S STORY
Bharati Mukherjee

> Bharati Mukherjee was born in India but has lived for many years in Canada and then in the United States, where she became a professor at Berkeley. She became known for her collection The Middleman and Other Stories (1988) and for novels including The Tiger's Daughter and Jasmine. Her fiction is populated by a new wave of immigrants from Asia and other parts of the Third World, who often find the clash of cultures and the difficulties of assimilation more formidable than did the mostly European immigrants of earlier times. Some enter the world of illegal aliens and are exploited as menial labor. Others enter a world of artists and intellectuals critical of the contradictions in both the culture they left behind and in their new world.
>
> Mukherjee's stories typically take place in a "postcolonial" period in history, where countries that were once part of the British or French colonial empires have achieved independence but continue to show the European influence in language, education, and politics. She often writes about immigrants from India, who may be in the process of Americanizing their names and their ways but also still practice old-country customs like entering into arranged marriages.

Imre says forget it, but I'm going to write David Mamet. So Patels are 1 hard to sell real estate to. You buy them a beer, whisper Glengarry Glen Ross, and they smell swamp instead of sun and surf. They work hard, eat cheap, live ten to a room, stash their savings under futons in Queens, and before you know it they own half of Hoboken. You say, where's the sweet gullibility that made this nation great?

Polish jokes, Patel jokes: that's not why I want to write Mamet:

Seen their women?

Everybody laughs. Imre laughs. The dozing fat man with the Barnes & Noble sack between his legs, the woman next to him, the usher, everybody. The theater isn't so dark that they can't see me. In my red silk sari I'm conspicuous. Plump, gold paisleys sparkle on my chest.

The actor is just warming up. *Seen their women?* He plays a salesman, 5 he's had a bad day and now he's in a Chinese restaurant trying to loosen up. His face is pink. His wool-blend slacks are creased at the crotch. We bought our tickets at half-price, we're sitting in the front row, but at the edge, and we see things we shouldn't be seeing. At least I do, or think I do. Spittle, actors goosing each other, little winks, streaks of makeup.

Maybe they're improvising dialogue too. Maybe Mamet's provided them with insult kits, Thursdays for Chinese, Wednesdays for Hispanics, today for Indians. Maybe they get together before curtain time, see an Indian woman settling in the front row off to the side, and say to each other: "Hey, forget Friday. Let's get *her* today. See if she cries. See if she walks out." Maybe, like the salesmen they play, they have a little bet on.

Maybe I shouldn't feel betrayed.

Their women, he goes again. *They look like they've just been fucked by a dead cat.*

The fat man hoots so hard he nudges my elbow off our shared armrest.

"Imre. I'm going home." But Imre's hunched so far forward he doesn't   10
hear. English isn't his best language. A refugee from Budapest, he has to listen hard. "I didn't pay eighteen dollars to be insulted."

I don't hate Mamet. It's the tyranny of the American dream that scares me. First, you don't exist. Then you're invisible. Then you're funny. Then you're disgusting. Insult, my American friends will tell me, is a kind of acceptance. No instant dignity here. A play like this, back home, would cause riots. Communal, racist, and antisocial. The actors wouldn't make it off stage. This play, and all these awful feelings, would be safely locked up.

I long, at times, for clear-cut answers. Offer me instant dignity, today, and I'll take it.

"What?" Imre moves toward me without taking his eyes off the actor. "Come again?"

Tears come. I want to stand, scream, make an awful scene. I long for ugly, nasty rage.

The actor is ranting, flinging spittle. *Give me a chance. I'm not finished, I*   15
can get back on the board. I tell that asshole, give me a real lead. And what does that asshole give me? Patels. Nothing but Patels.

This time Imre works an arm around my shoulders. "Panna, what is Patel? Why are you taking it all so personally?"

I shrink from his touch, but I don't walk out. Expensive girls' schools in Lausanne and Bombay have trained me to behave well. My manners are exquisite, my feelings are delicate, my gestures refined, my moods undetectable. They have seen me through riots, uprootings, separation, my son's death.

"I'm not taking it personally."

The fat man looks at us. The woman looks too, and shushes.

I stare back at the two of them. Then I stare, mean and cool, at the   20
man's elbow. Under the bright blue polyester Hawaiian shirt sleeve, the elbow looks soft and runny. "Excuse me," I say. My voice has the effortless meanness of well-bred displaced Third World women, though my rhetoric has been learned elsewhere. "You're exploiting my space."

Startled, the man snatches his arm away from me. He cradles it against his breast. By the time he's ready with comebacks, I've turned my back on him. I've probably ruined the first act for him. I know I've ruined it for Imre.

It's not my fault; it's the *situation.* Old colonies wear down. Patels—the new pioneers—have to be suspicious. Idi Amin's lesson is permanent. AT&T

wires move good advice from continent to continent. Keep all assets liquid. Get into 7-11s, get out of condos and motels. I know how both sides feel, that's the trouble. The Patel sniffing out scams, the sad salesmen on the stage: postcolonialism has made me their referee. It's hate I long for; simple, brutish, partisan hate.

After the show Imre and I make our way toward Broadway. Sometimes he holds my hand; it doesn't mean anything more than that crazies and drunks are crouched in doorways. Imre's been here over two years, but he's stayed very old-world, very courtly, openly protective of women. I met him in a seminar on special ed. last semester. His wife is a nurse somewhere in the Hungarian countryside. There are two sons, and miles of petitions for their emigration. My husband manages a mill two hundred miles north of Bombay. There are no children.

"You make things tough on yourself," Imre says. He assumed Patel was a Jewish name or maybe Hispanic; everything makes equal sense to him. He found the play tasteless, he worried about the effect of vulgar language on my sensitive ears. "You have to let go a bit." And as though to show me how to let go, he breaks away from me, bounds ahead with his head ducked tight, then dances on amazingly jerky legs. He's a Magyar, he often tells me, and deep down, he's an Asian too. I catch glimpses of it, knife-blade Attila cheekbones, despite the blondish hair. In his faded jeans and leather jacket, he's a rock video star. I watch MTV for hours in the apartment when Charity's working the evening shift at Macy's. I listen to WPLJ on Charity's earphones. Why should I be ashamed? Television in India is so uplifting.

Imre stops as suddenly as he'd started. People walk around us. The   *25* summer sidewalk is full of theatergoers in seersucker suits; Imre's year-round jacket is out of place. European. Cops in twos and threes huddle, lightly tap their thighs with night sticks and smile at me with benevolence. I want to wink at them, get us all in trouble, tell them the crazy dancing man is from the Warsaw Pact. I'm too shy to break into dance on Broadway. So I hug Imre instead.

The hug takes him by surprise. He wants me to let go, but he doesn't really expect me to let go. He staggers, though I weigh no more than 104 pounds, and with him, I pitch forward slightly. Then he catches me, and we walk arm in arm to the bus stop. My husband would never dance or hug a woman on Broadway. Nor would my brothers. They aren't stuffy people, but they went to Anglican boarding schools and they have a well-developed sense of what's silly.

"Imre." I squeeze his big, rough hand. "I'm sorry I ruined the evening for you."

"You did nothing of the kind." He sounds tired. "Let's not wait for the bus. Let's splurge and take a cab instead."

Imre always has unexpected funds. The Network, he calls it, Class of '56.

In the back of the cab, without even trying, I feel light, almost free.   *30*

Memories of Indian destitutes mix with the hordes of New York street people, and they float free, like astronauts, inside my head. I've made it. I'm making something of my life. I've left home, my husband, to get a Ph.D. in special ed. I have a multiple-entry visa and a small scholarship for two years. After that, we'll see. My mother was beaten by her mother-in-law, my grandmother, when she'd registered for French lessons at the Alliance Française. My grandmother, the eldest daughter of a rich zamindar, was illiterate.

Imre and the cabdriver talk away in Russian. I keep my eyes closed. That way I can feel the floaters better. I'll write Mamet tonight. I feel strong, reckless. Maybe I'll write Steven Spielberg too; tell him that Indians don't eat monkey brains.

We've made it. Patels must have made it. Mamet, Spielberg: they're not condescending to us. Maybe they're a little bit afraid.

Charity Chin, my roommate, is sitting on the floor drinking Chablis out of a plastic wineglass. She is five foot six, three inches taller than me, but weighs a kilo and a half less than I do. She is a "hands" model. Orientals are supposed to have a monopoly in the hands-modelling business, she says. She had her eyes fixed eight or nine months ago and out of gratitude sleeps with her plastic surgeon every third Wednesday.

"Oh, good," Charity says. "I'm glad you're back early. I need to talk."

She's been writing checks. MCI, Con Ed, Bonwit Teller. Envelopes, 35 already stamped and sealed, form a pyramid between her shapely, knee-socked legs. The checkbook's cover is brown plastic, grained to look like cowhide. Each time Charity flips back the cover, white geese fly over sky-colored checks. She makes good money, but she's extravagant. The difference adds up to this shared, rent-controlled Chelsea one-bedroom.

"All right. Talk."

When I first moved in, she was seeing an analyst. Now she sees a nutritionist.

"Eric called. From Oregon."

"What did he want?"

"He wants me to pay half the rent on his loft for last spring. He asked 40 me to move back, remember? He *begged* me."

Eric is Charity's estranged husband.

"What does your nutritionist say?" Eric now wears a red jumpsuit and tills the soil in Rajneeshpuram.

"You think Phil's a creep too, don't you? What else can he be when creeps are all I attract?"

Phil is a flutist with thinning hair. He's very touchy on the subject of *flautists* versus *flutists*. He's touchy on every subject, from music to books to foods to clothes. He teaches at a small college upstate, and Charity bought a used blue Datsun ("Nissan," Phil insists) last month so she could spend weekends with him. She returns every Sunday night, exhausted and exasperated. Phil and I don't have much to say to each other—he's the only musician I know; the men in my family are lawyers, engineers, or in business—but I like him. Around me, he loosens up. When he visits, he bakes us loaves of pumpernickel bread. He waxes our kitchen floor. Like many men in this country, he seems to me a displaced child, or even a woman, looking for something that passed him by, or for something that he can never have. If he thinks I'm not looking, he sneaks his hands under Charity's sweater, but there isn't too much there. Here, she's a model with high ambitions. In India, she'd be a flat-chested old maid.

I'm shy in front of the lovers. A darkness comes over me when I see   45
them horsing around.

"It isn't the money," Charity says. Oh? I think. "He says he still loves me. Then he turns around and asks me for five hundred."

What's so strange about that, I want to ask. She still loves Eric, and Eric, red jump suit and all, is smart enough to know it. Love is a commodity, hoarded like any other. Mamet knows. But I say, "I'm not the person to ask about love." Charity knows that mine was a traditional Hindu marriage. My parents, with the help of a marriage broker, who was my mother's cousin, picked out a groom. All I had to do was get to know his taste in food.

It'll be a long evening, I'm afraid. Charity likes to confess. I unpleat my silk sari—it no longer looks too showy—wrap it in muslin cloth and put it away in a dresser drawer. Saris are hard to have laundered in Manhattan, though there's a good man in Jackson Heights. My next step will be to brew us a pot of chrysanthemum tea. It's a very special tea from the mainland. Charity's uncle gave it to us. I like him. He's a humpbacked, awkward, terrified man. He runs a gift store on Mott Street, and though he doesn't speak much English, he seems to have done well. Once upon a time he worked for the railways in Chengdu, Szechwan Province, and during the Wuchang Uprising, he was shot at. When I'm down, when I'm lonely for my husband, when I think of our son, or when I need to be held, I think of Charity's uncle. If I hadn't left home, I'd never have heard of the Wuchang Uprising. I've broadened my horizons.

Very late that night my husband calls me from Ahmadabad, a town of textile mills north of Bombay. My husband is a vice president at Lakshmi Cotton Mills. Lakshmi is the goddess of wealth, but LCM (Priv.), Ltd., is doing poorly. Lockouts, strikes, rock-throwings. My husband lives on digitalis, which he calls the food for our *yuga* of discontent.

"We had a bad mishap at the mill today." Then he says nothing for   50
seconds.

The operator comes on. "Do you have the right party, sir? We're trying to reach Mrs. Butt."

"Bhatt," I insist. "*B* for Bombay, *H* for Haryana, *A* for Ahmadabad, double *T* for Tamil Nadu." It's a litany. "This is she."

"One of our lorries was firebombed today. Resulting in three deaths. The driver, old Karamchand, and his two children."

I know how my husband's eyes look this minute, how the eye rims sag and the yellow corneas shine and bulge with pain. He is not an emotional man—the Ahmadabad Institute of Management has trained him to cut losses, to look on the bright side of economic catastrophes—but tonight he's feeling low. I try to remember a driver named Karamchand, but can't. That part of my life is over, the way *trucks* have replaced *lorries* in my vocabulary, the way Charity Chin and her lurid love life have replaced inherited notions of marital duty. Tomorrow he'll come out of it. Soon he'll be eating again. He'll sleep like a baby. He's been trained to believe in turnovers. Every morning he rubs his scalp with cantharidine oil so his hair will grow back again.

"It could be your car next." Affection, love. Who can tell the difference 55
in a traditional marriage in which a wife still doesn't call her husband by his first name?

"No. They know I'm a flunky, just like them. Well paid, maybe. No need for undue anxiety, please."

Then his voice breaks. He says he needs me, he misses me, he wants me to come to him damp from my evening shower, smelling of sandalwood soap, my braid decorated with jasmines.

"I need you too."

"Not to worry, please," he says. "I am coming in a fortnight's time. I have already made arrangements."

Outside my window, fire trucks whine, up Eighth Avenue. I wonder if 60
he can hear them, what he thinks of a life like mine, led amid disorder.

"I am thinking it'll be like a honeymoon. More or less."

When I was in college, waiting to be married, I imagined honeymoons were only for the more fashionable girls, the girls who came from slightly racy families, smoked Sobranies in the dorm lavatories and put up posters of Kabir Bedi, who was supposed to have made it as a big star in the West. My husband wants us to go to Niagara. I'm not to worry about foreign exchange. He's arranged for extra dollars through the Gujarati Network, with a cousin in San Jose. And he's bought four hundred more on the black market. "Tell me you need me. Panna, please tell me again."

I change out of the cotton pants and shirt I've been wearing all day and put on a sari to meet my husband at JFK. I don't forget the jewelry; the marriage necklace of *mangalsutra,* gold drop earrings, heavy gold bangles. I don't wear them every day. In this borough of vice and greed, who knows when, or whom, desire will overwhelm.

My husband spots me in the crowd and waves. He has lost weight, and changed his glasses. The arm, uplifted in a cheery wave, is bony, frail, almost opalescent.

In the Carey Coach, we hold hands. He strokes my fingers one by one. 65
"How come you aren't wearing my mother's ring?"

"Because muggers know about Indian women," I say. They know with us it's 24-karat. His mother's ring is showy, in ghastly taste anywhere but

India: a blood-red Burma ruby set in a gold frame of floral sprays. My mother-in-law got her guru to bless the ring before I left for the States.

He looks disconcerted. He's used to a different role. He's the knowing, suspicious one in the family. He seems to be sulking, and finally he comes out with it. "You've said nothing about my new glasses." I compliment him on the glasses, how chic and Western-executive they make him look. But I can't help the other things, necessities until he learns the ropes. I handle the money, buy the tickets. I don't know if this makes me unhappy.

Charity drives her Nissan upstate, so for two weeks we are to have the apartment to ourselves. This is more privacy than we ever had in India. No parents, no servants, to keep us modest. We play at housekeeping. Imre has lent us a hibachi, and I grill saffron chicken breasts. My husband marvels at the size of the Perdue hens. "They're big like peacocks, no? These Americans, they're really something!" He tries out pizzas, burgers, McNuggets. He chews. He explores. He judges. He loves it all, fears nothing, feels at home in the summer odors, the clutter of Manhattan streets. Since he thinks that the American palate is bland, he carries a bottle of red peppers in his pocket. I wheel a shopping cart down the aisles of the neighborhood Grand Union, and he follows, swiftly, greedily. He picks up hair rinses and high-protein diet powders. There's so much I already take for granted.

One night, Imre stops by. He wants us to go with him to a movie. In his work shirt and red leather tie, he looks arty or strung out. It's only been a week, but I feel as though I am really seeing him for the first time. The yellow hair worn very short at the sides, the wide, narrow lips. He's a good-looking man, but self-conscious, almost arrogant. He's picked the movie we should see. He always tells me what to see, what to read. He buys the *Voice*. He's a natural avant-gardist. For tonight he's chosen *Numéro Deux*.

"Is it a musical?" my husband asks. The Radio City Music Hall is on   70
his list of sights to see. He's read up on the history of the Rockettes. He doesn't catch Imre's sympathetic wink.

Guilt, shame, loyalty. I long to be ungracious, not ingratiate myself with both men.

That night my husband calculates in rupees the money we've wasted on Godard. "That refugee fellow, Nagy, must have a screw loose in his head. I paid very steep price for dollars on the black market."

Some afternoons we go shopping. Back home we hated shopping, but now it is a lovers' project. My husband's shopping list startles me. I feel I am just getting to know him. Maybe, like Imre, freed from the dignities of old-world culture, he too could get drunk and squirt Cheez Whiz on a guest. I watch him dart into stores in his gleaming leather shoes. Jockey shorts on sale in outdoor bins on Broadway entrance him. White tube socks with different bands of color delight him. He looks for microcassettes, for anything small and electronic and smuggleable. He needs a garment bag. He calls it a "wardrobe," and I have to translate.

"All of New York is having sales, no?"

My heart speeds watching him this happy. It's the third week in August, *75*
almost the end of summer, and the city smells ripe, it cannot bear more heat,
more money, more energy.

"This is so smashing! The prices are so excellent!" Recklessly, my pru-
dent husband signs away traveller's checks. How he intends to smuggle it all
back I don't dare ask. With a microwave, he calculates, we could get rid of
our cook.

This has to be love, I think. Charity, Eric, Phil: they may be experts
on sex. My husband doesn't chase me around the sofa, but he pushes me
down on Charity's battered cushions, and the man who has never entered
the kitchen of our Ahmadabad house now comes toward me with a dish tub
of steamy water to massage away the pavement heat.

Ten days into his vacation my husband checks out brochures for sightseeing tours. Shortline, Grayline, Crossroads: his new vinyl briefcase is full of
schedules and pamphlets. While I make pancakes out of a mix, he compari-
son-shops. Tour number one costs $10.95 and will give us the World Trade
Center, Chinatown, and the United Nations. Tour number three would take
us both *uptown and* downtown for $14.95, but my husband is absolutely sure
he doesn't want to see Harlem. We settle for tour number four: Downtown
and the Dame. It's offered by a new tour company with a small, dirty office
at Eighth and Forty-eighth.

The sidewalk outside the office is colorful with tourists. My husband
sends me in to buy the tickets because he has come to feel Americans don't
understand his accent.

The dark man, Lebanese probably, behind the counter comes on too *80*
friendly. "Come on, doll, make my day!" He won't say which tour is his.
"Number four? Honey, no! Look, you've wrecked me! Say you'll change
your mind." He takes two twenties and gives back change. He holds the
tickets, forcing me to pull. He leans closer. "I'm off after lunch."

My husband must have been watching me from the sidewalk. "What
was the chap saying?" he demands. "I told you not to wear pants. He thinks
you are Puerto Rican. He thinks he can treat you with disrespect."

The bus is crowded and we have to sit across the aisle from each other.
The tour guide begins his patter on Forty-sixth. He looks like an actor, his
hair bleached and blow-dried. Up close he must look middle-aged, but from
where I sit his skin is smooth and his cheeks faintly red.

"Welcome to the Big Apple, folks." The guide uses a microphone. "Big
Apple. That's what we native Manhattan degenerates call our city. Today we
have guests from fifteen foreign countries and six states from this U.S. of A.
That makes the Tourist Bureau real happy. And let me assure you that while
we may be the richest city in the richest country in the world, it's okay to
tip your charming and talented attendant." He laughs. Then he swings his
hip out into the aisle and sings a song.

"And it's might fancy on old Delancey Street, you know. . . ."

My husband looks irritable. The guide is, as expected, a good singer. 85 "The bloody man should be giving us histories of buildings we are passing, no?" I pat his hand, the mood passes. He cranes his neck. Our window seats have both gone to Japanese. It's the tour of his life. Next to this, the quick business trips to Manchester and Glasgow pale.

"And tell me what street compares to Mott Street, in July. . . ."

The guide wants applause. He manages a derisive laugh from the Americans up front. He's working the aisles now. "I coulda been somebody, right? I coulda been a star!" Two or three of us smile, those of us who recognize the parody. He catches my smile. The sun is on his harsh, bleached hair. "Right, your highness? Look, we gotta maharani with us! Couldn't I have been a star?"

"Right!" I say, my voice coming out a squeal. I've been trained to adapt; what else can I say?

We drive through traffic past landmark office buildings and churches. The guide flips his hands. "Art deco," he keeps saying. I hear him confide to one of the Americans: "Beats me. I went to a cheap guide's school." My husband wants to know more about this Art Deco, but the guide sings another song.

"We made a foolish choice," my husband grumbles. "We are sitting in 90 the bus only. We're not going into famous buildings." He scrutinizes the pamphlets in his jacket pocket. I think, at least it's air-conditioned in here. I could sit here in the cool shadows of the city forever.

Only five of us appear to have opted for the "Downtown and the Dame" tour. The others will ride back uptown past the United Nations after we've been dropped off at the pier for the ferry to the Statue of Liberty.

An elderly European pulls a camera out of his wife's designer tote bag. He takes pictures of the boats in the harbor, the Japanese in kimonos eating popcorn, scavenging pigeons, me. Then, pushing his wife ahead of him, he climbs back on the bus and waves to us. For a second I feel terribly lost. I wish we were on the bus going back to the apartment. I know I'll not be able to describe any of this to Charity, or to Imre. I'm too proud to admit I went on a guided tour.

The view of the city from the Circle Line ferry is seductive, unreal. The skyline wavers out of reach, but never quite vanishes. The summer sun pushes through fluffy clouds and dapples the glass of office towers. My husband looks thrilled, even more than he had on the shopping trips down Broadway. Tourists and dreamers, we have spent our life's savings to see this skyline, this statue.

"Quick, take a picture of me!" my husband yells as he moves toward a gap of railings. A Japanese matron has given up her position in order to change film. "Before the Twin Towers disappear!"

I focus, I wait for a large Oriental family to walk out of my range. My 95 husband holds his pose tight against the railing. He wants to look relaxed, an international businessman at home in all the financial markets.

A bearded man slides across the bench toward me. "Like this," he says and helps me get my husband in focus. "You want me to take the photo for you?" His name, he says, is Goran. He is Goran from Yugoslavia, as though that were enough for tracking him down. Imre from Hungary. Panna from India. He pulls the old Leica out of my hand, signaling the Orientals to beat it, and clicks away. "I'm a photographer," he says. He could have been a camera thief. That's what my husband would have assumed. Somehow, I trusted. "Get you a beer?" he asks.

"I don't. Drink, I mean. Thank you very much." I say those last words very loud, for everyone's benefit. The odd bottles of Soave with Imre don't count.

"Too bad." Goran gives back the camera.

"Take one more!" my husband shouts from the railing. "Just to be sure!"

The island itself disappoints. The Lady has brutal scaffolding holding   100
her in. The museum is closed. The snack bar is dirty and expensive. My husband reads out the prices to me. He orders two french fries and two Cokes. We sit at picnic tables and wait for the ferry to take us back.

"What was that hippie chap saying?"

As if I could say. A day-care center has brought its kids, at least forty of them, to the island for the day. The kids, all wearing name tags, run around us. I can't help noticing how many are Indian. Even a Patel, probably a Bhatt if I looked hard enough. They toss hamburger bits at pigeons. They kick styrofoam cups. The pigeons are slow, greedy, persistent. I have to shoo one off the table top. I don't think my husband thinks about our son.

"What hippie?"

"The one on the boat. With the beard and the hair."

My husband doesn't look at me. He shakes out his paper napkin and   105
tries to protect his french fries from pigeon feathers.

"Oh, him. He said he was from Dubrovnik." It isn't true, but I don't want trouble.

"What did he say about Dubrovnik?"

I know enough about Dubrovnik to get by. Imre's told me about it. And about Mostar and Zagreb. In Mostar white Muslims sing the call to prayer. I would like to see that before I die: white Muslims. Whole peoples have moved before me; they've adapted. The night Imre told me about Mostar was also the night I saw my first snow in Manhattan. We'd walked down to Chelsea from Columbia. We'd walked and talked and I hadn't felt tired at all.

"You're too innocent," my husband says. He reaches for my hand. "Panna," he cries with pain in his voice, and I am brought back from perfect, floating memories of snow, "I've come to take you back. I have seen how men watch you."

"What?"   110

"Come back, now. I have tickets. We have all the things we will ever need. I can't live without you."

A little girl with wiry braids kicks a bottle cap at his shoes. The pigeons wheel and scuttle around us. My husband covers his fries with spread-out fingers. "No kicking," he tells the girl. Her name, Beulah, is printed in green ink on a heart-shaped name tag. He forces a smile, and Beulah smiles back. Then she starts to flap her arms. She flaps, she hops. The pigeons go crazy for fries and scraps.

"Special ed. course is two years," I remind him. "I can't go back."

My husband picks up our trays and throws them into the garbage before I can stop him. He's carried disposability a little too far. "We've been taken," he says, moving toward the dock, though the ferry will not arrive for another twenty minutes. "The ferry costs only two dollars round-trip per person. We should have chosen tour number one for $10.95 instead of tour number four for $14.95."

With my Lebanese friend, I think. "But this way we don't have to   115
worry about cabs. The bus will pick us up at the pier and take us back to midtown. Then we can walk home."

"New York is full of cheats and whatnot. Just like Bombay." He is not accusing me of infidelity. I feel dread all the same.

That night, after we've gone to bed, the phone rings. My husband listens, then hands the phone to me. "What is this woman saying?" He turns on the pink Macy's lamp by the bed. "I am not understanding these Negro people's accents."

The operator repeats the message. It's a cable from one of the directors of Lakshmi Cotton Mills. "Massive violent labor confrontation anticipated. Stop. Return posthaste. Stop. Cable flight details. Signed Kantilal Shah."

"It's not your factory," I say. "You're supposed to be on vacation."

"So, you are worrying about me? Yes? You reject my heartfelt wishes   120
but you worry about me?" He pulls me close, slips the straps of my nightdress off my shoulder. "Wait a minute."

I wait, unclothed, for my husband to come back to me. The water is running in the bathroom. In the ten days he has been here he has learned American rites: deodorants, fragrances. Tomorrow morning he'll call Air India; tomorrow evening he'll be on his way back to Bombay. Tonight I should make up to him for my years away, the gutted trucks, the degree I'll never use in India. I want to pretend with him that nothing has changed.

In the mirror that hangs on the bathroom door, I watch my naked body turn, the breasts, the thighs glow. The body's beauty amazes. I stand here shameless, in ways he has never seen me. I am free, afloat, watching somebody else.

The Responsive Reader

1. What kind of person is the narrator? What clues in the story remind you that she is from an affluent upper-class background in India?

What has she kept of the lifestyle or customs of her native country? What signs show that she is becoming Americanized?

2. Why does the narrator take the Mamet play so personally? What is her theory about the stages new immigrants (like the "Patels," or immigrants from India, in this story) go through as Americans become aware of them? Are her American friends right when they tell her that in this country insult "is a kind of acceptance?"

3. What role do minor characters play in the story? What role does the narrator's Hungarian friend play? Does it matter that he is also an immigrant? What role does the narrator's Chinese roommate play?

4. What is the narrator's relationship with her husband? How did they get married? How and why did she become estranged from him? Does she feel guilty? Should she?

5. During the sightseeing tour and at other points in the story, does the narrator seem to you exceptionally aware of people's ethnicity and of their culturally conditioned behavior? Or is the range of ethnically diverse people in this story only natural in the New York City setting?

Thinking, Talking, Writing

6. How American do you think the narrator has become? What are the major conflicts between her ethnic past and her new American identity? How is she reconciling them?

7. Why do people tell ethnic jokes? What role do they play in perpetuating prejudice? Is ethnic humor always hostile?

8. Is it true that insults and rudeness have become a standard feature of American entertainment? Is it true that some of the most successful media celebrities deliberately use insults and rude language? If so, why? Why are viewers or spectators attracted to this kind of entertainment? Does American popular culture merely mirror the increased rudeness and hostility of American life?

Collaborative Projects

9. Working in small groups, your class may want to research the nature and effect of recent immigration from Asia in your area. How is this country changing the immigrants? How are the immigrants changing America?

Thinking about Connections

10. Terry McMillan and Bhjarati Mukherjee are among writers in this volume who patiently chronicle problems and tensions in male-female relationships. How close do they seem to life or to psychological truth? Is there a common thread in their stories?

LOS VENDIDOS

Luis Valdez

Luis Valdez is the founder of the Teatro Campesino, *the political theater voicing the aspirations and grievances of the migrant Mexican American farm workers of California. Valdez himself was working in the fields at age six, receiving the often-interrupted schooling of the children of America's migrant workers. He accepted a scholarship at San Jose State University and after graduating in 1964 started the field workers' theater that at first performed its* actos—*short, one-act plays—in community centers, church halls, and the fields. Valdez worked as a union organizer in the movement led by Cesar Chavez, which used strikes and boycotts to force California growers and agribusiness to grant their workers a living wage and living conditions fit for human beings.*

Valdez' plays include Soldado Razo *(The Buck Private, 1971) and* The Shrunken Head of Pancho Villa *(1982). He wrote and directed the movie* La Bamba *(1987), about the Chicano rock 'n' roll singer Ritchie Valens. His public television production of* Corridos: Tales of Passion and Revolution, *with Linda Ronstadt, won the Peabody Award. His play* Los Vendidos *(Those Who Sold Out, 1967) satirizes white politicians who use token representatives of minorities to mask their indifference to groups denied their place in the sun.*

The Chicano (Mexican American) characters in the play are bilingual, switching easily from the English of the white power structure to the Spanish that gives voice to their aspirations. They use terms like la raza, *the word used by political activists for the Mexican American community, or* huelga, *the word for strike. The play ends with a call to join in the struggle: VAMOS LEVANTADO ARMAS PARA LIBERARNOS DE ESTOS DE-GRACIADOS GABACHOS QUE NOS EXPLOTAN! (take up arms to liberate ourselves from the bloodsucking whites); ESTA GRAND HU-MANIDAD HA DICHO BASTA! (This mass of humanity says enough is enough); VIVA LA CAUSA! (long live our cause).*

Characters

HONEST SANCHO

SECRETARY

FARM WORKER

JOHNNY

REVOLUCIONARIO

MEXICAN-AMERICAN

Scene HONEST SANCHO'S *Used Mexican Lot and Mexican Curio Shop. Three models are on display in* HONEST SANCHO*'s shop: to the right, there is a*

REVOLUCIONARIO, *complete with sombrero, carrilleras, and carabina 30-30.*
At center, on the floor, there is the FARM WORKER, *under a broad straw som-*
brero. At stage left is the PACHUCO, *filero in hand.*

(HONEST SANCHO *is moving among his models, dusting them off and preparing*
for another day of business.)

SANCHO: Bueno, bueno, mis monos, vamos a ver a quien vendemos ahora,
¿no? (*To audience.*) ¡Quihubo! I'm Honest Sancho and this is my shop.
Antes fui contratista pero ahora longré tener mi negocito. All I need
now is a customer. (*A bell rings offstage.*) Ay, a customer!

SECRETARY: (*Entering*) Good morning, I'm Miss Jiménez from—

SANCHO: ¡Ah, una chicana! Welcome, welcome Señorita Jiménez.

SECRETARY: (*Anglo pronunciation*) JIM-enez.

SANCHO: ¿Qué?

SECRETARY: My name is Miss JIM-enez. Don't you speak English?
What's wrong with you?

SANCHO: Oh, nothing, Señorita JIM-enez. I'm here to help you.

SECRETARY: That's better. As I was starting to say, I'm a secretary from
Governor Reagan's office, and we're looking for a Mexican type for the
administration.

SANCHO: Well, you come to the right place, lady. This is Honest Sancho's
Used Mexican lot, and we got all types here. Any particular type you
want?

SECRETARY: Yes, we were looking for somebody suave—

SANCHO: Suave.

SECRETARY: Debonair.

SANCHO: De buen aire.

SECRETARY: Dark.

SANCHO: Prieto.

SECRETARY: But of course not too dark.

SANCHO: No muy prieto.

SECRETARY: Perhaps, beige.

SANCHO: Beige, just the tone. Así como cafecito con leche, ¿no?

SECRETARY: One more thing. He must be hard-working.

SANCHO: That could only be one model. Step right over here to the
center of the shop, lady. (*They cross to the* FARM WORKER.) This is
our standard farm worker model. As you can see, in the words of our
beloved Senator George Murphy, he is "built close to the ground."
Also take special notice of his four-ply Goodyear huaraches, made from
the rain tire. This wide-brimmed sombrero is an extra added feature—
keeps off the sun, rain, and dust.

SECRETARY: Yes, it does look durable.

SANCHO: And our farm worker model is friendly. Muy amable. Watch.
(*Snaps his fingers.*)

FARM WORKER: (*Lifts up head*) Buenos días, señorita. (*His head drops.*)

SECRETARY: My, he's friendly.

SANCHO: Didn't I tell you? Loves his patrones! But his most attractive feature is that he's hard-working. Let me show you. (*Snaps fingers.* FARM WORKER *stands.*)

FARM WORKER: ¡El jale! (*He begins to work.*)

SANCHO: As you can see, he is cutting grapes.

SECRETARY: Oh, I wouldn't know.

SANCHO: He also picks cotton. (*Snap.* FARM WORKER *begins to pick cotton.*)

SECRETARY: Versatile isn't he?

SANCHO: He also picks melons. (*Snap.* FARM WORKER *picks melons.*) That's his slow speed for late in the season. Here's his fast speed. (*Snap.* FARM WORKER *picks faster.*)

SECRETARY: ¡Chihuahua! . . . I mean, goodness, he sure is a hard worker.

SANCHO: (*Pulls the* FARM WORKER *to his feet*) And that isn't the half of it. Do you see these little holes on his arms that appear to be pores? During those hot sluggish days in the field, when the vines or the branches get so entangled, it's almost impossible to move; these holes emit a certain grease that allow our model to slip and slide right through the crop with no trouble at all.

SECRETARY: Wonderful. But is he economical?

SANCHO: Economical? Señorita, you are looking at the Volkswagen of Mexicans. Pennies a day is all it takes. One plate of beans and tortillas will keep him going all day. That, and chile. Plenty of chile. Chile jalapenos, chile verde, chile colorado. But, of course, if you do give him chile (*Snap.* FARM WORKER *turns left face.* *Snap.* FARM WORKER *bends over.*) then you have to change his oil filter once a week.

SECRETARY: What about storage?

SANCHO: No problem. You know these new farm labor camps our Honorable Governor Reagan has built out by Parlier or Raisin City? They were designed with our model in mind. Five, six, seven, even ten in one of those shacks will give you no trouble at all. You can also put him in old barns, old cars, river banks. You can even leave him out in the field overnight with no worry!

SECRETARY: Remarkable.

SANCHO: And here's an added feature: Every year at the end of the season, this model goes back to Mexico and doesn't return, automatically, until next Spring.

SECRETARY: How about that. But tell me: does he speak English?

SANCHO: Another outstanding feature is that last year this model was programmed to go out on STRIKE! (*Snap.*)

FARM WORKER: ¡HUELGA! ¡HUELGA! Hermanos, sálganse de esos files. (*Snap. He stops.*)

SECRETARY: No! Oh no, we can't strike in the State Capitol.

SANCHO: Well, he also scabs. (*Snap.*)

FARM WORKER: Me vendo barato, ¿y qué? (*Snap.*)

SECRETARY: That's much better, but you didn't answer my question. Does he speak English?

SANCHO: Bueno . . . no pero he has other—

SECRETARY: No.

SANCHO: Other features.

SECRETARY: NO! He just won't do!

SANCHO: Okay, okay pues. We have other models.

SECRETARY: I hope so. What we need is something a little more sophisticated.

SANCHO: Sophisti—¿qué?

SECRETARY: An urban model.

SANCHO: Ah, from the city! Step right back. Over here in this corner of the shop is exactly what you're looking for. Introducing our new 1969 JOHNNY PACHUCO model! This is our fast-back model. Streamlined. Built for speed, low-riding, city life. Take a look at some of these features. Mag shoes, dual exhausts, green chartreuse paint-job, dark-tint windshield, a little poof on top. Let me just turn him on. (*Snap.* JOHNNY *walks to stage center with a pachuco bounce.*)

SECRETARY: What was that?

SANCHO: That, señorita, was the Chicano shuffle.

SECRETARY: Okay, what does he do?

SANCHO: Anything and everything necessary for city life. For instance, survival: He knife fights. (*Snap.* JOHNNY *pulls out switch blade and swings at* SECRETARY.)

(SECRETARY *screams.*)

SANCHO: He dances. (*Snap.*)

JOHNNY: (*Singing*) "Angel Baby, my Angel Baby . . ." (*Snap.*)

SANCHO: And here's a feature no city model can be without. He gets arrested, but not without resisting, of course. (*Snap.*)

JOHNNY: ¡En la madre, la placa! I didn't do it! I didn't do it! (JOHNNY *turns and stands up against an imaginary wall, legs spread out, arms behind his back.*)

SECRETARY: Oh no, we can't have arrests! We must maintain law and order.

SANCHO: But he's bilingual!

SECRETARY: Bilingual?

SANCHO: Simón que yes. He speaks English! Johnny, give us some English. (*Snap.*)

JOHNNY: (*Comes downstage.*) Fuck-you!

SECRETARY: (*Gasps*) Oh! I've never been so insulted in my whole life!

SANCHO: Well, he learned it in your school.

SECRETARY: I don't care where he learned it.

SANCHO: But he's economical!

SECRETARY: Economical?

SANCHO: Nickels and dimes. You can keep Johnny running on hamburgers, Taco Bell tacos, Lucky Lager beer, Thunderbird wine, yesca—

SECRETARY: Yesca?

SANCHO: Mota.

SECRETARY: Mota?

SANCHO: Leños . . . Marijuana. (*Snap;* JOHNNY *inhales on an imaginary joint.*)

SECRETARY: That's against the law!

JOHNNY: (*Big smile, holding his breath*) Yeah.

SANCHO: He also sniffs glue. (*Snap.* JOHNNY *inhales glue, big smile.*)

JOHNNY: Tha's too much man, ése.

SECRETARY: No, Mr. Sancho, I don't think this—

SANCHO: Wait a minute, he has other qualities I know you'll love. For example, an inferiority complex. (*Snap.*)

JOHNNY: (*To* SANCHO) You think you're better than me, huh ése? (*Swings switch blade.*)

SANCHO: He can also be beaten and he bruises, cut him and he bleeds; kick him and he— (*He beats, bruises and kicks* PACHUCO.) would you like to try it?

SECRETARY: Oh, I couldn't.

SANCHO: Be my guest. He's a great scapegoat.

SECRETARY: No, really.

SANCHO: Please.

SECRETARY: Well, all right. Just once. (*She kicks* PACHUCO.) Oh, he's so soft.

SANCHO: Wasn't that good? Try again.

SECRETARY: (*Kicks* PACHUCO) Oh, he's so wonderful! (*She kicks him again.*)

SANCHO: Okay, that's enough, lady. You ruin the merchandise. Yes, our Johnny Pachuco model can give you many hours of pleasure. Why, the L.A.P.D. just bought twenty of these to train their rookie cops on. And talk about maintenance. Señorita, you are looking at an entirely self-supporting machine. You're never going to find our Johnny Pachuco model on the relief rolls. No, sir, this model knows how to liberate.

SECRETARY: Liberate?

SANCHO: He steals. (*Snap.* JOHNNY *rushes the* SECRETARY *and steals her purse.*)

JOHNNY: ¡Dame esa bolsa, vieja! (*He grabs the purse and runs. Snap by* SANCHO. *He stops.*)

(SECRETARY *runs after* JOHNNY *and grabs purse away from him, kicking him as she goes.*)

SECRETARY: No, no, no! We can't have any *more* thieves in the State Administration. Put him back.

SANCHO: Okay, we still got other models. Come on, Johnny, we'll sell you to some old lady. (SANCHO *takes* JOHNNY *back to his place.*)

SECRETARY: Mr. Sancho, I don't think you quite understand what we need. What we need is something that will attract the women voters. Something more traditional, more romantic.

SANCHO: Ah, a lover. (*He smiles meaningfully.*) Step right over here, señorita. Introducing our standard Revolucionario and/or Early California Bandit type. As you can see he is well-built, sturdy, durable. This is the International Harvester of Mexicans.

SECRETARY: What does he do?

SANCHO: You name it, he does it. He rides horses, stays in the mountains, crosses deserts, plains, rivers, leads revolutions, follows revolutions, kills, can be killed, serves as a martyr, hero, movie star—did I say movie star? Did you ever see *Viva Zapata? Viva Villa? Villa Rides? Pancho Villa Returns? Pancho Villa Goes Back? Pancho Villa Meets Abbot and Costello*—

SECRETARY: I've never seen any of those.

SANCHO: Well, he was in all of them. Listen to this. (*Snap.*)

REVOLUCIONARIO: (*Scream.*) ¡VIVA VILLAAAAA!

SECRETARY: That's awfully loud.

SANCHO: He has a volume control. (*He adjusts volume. Snap.*)

REVOLUCIONARIO: (*Mousey voice*) ¡Viva Villa!

SECRETARY: That's better.

SANCHO: And even if you didn't see him in the movies, perhaps you saw him on TV. He makes commercials. (*Snap.*)

REVOLUCIONARIO: Is there a Frito Bandito in your house?

SECRETARY: Oh yes, I've seen that one!

SANCHO: Another feature about this one is that he is economical. He runs on raw horsemeat and tequila!

SECRETARY: Isn't that rather savage?

SANCHO: Al contrario, it makes him a lover. (*Snap.*)

REVOLUCIONARIO: (*To* SECRETARY) ¡Ay, mamasota, cochota, ven pa'ca! (*He grabs* SECRETARY *and folds her back—Latin-lover style.*)

SANCHO: (*Snap.* REVOLUCIONARIO *goes back upright.*) Now wasn't that nice?

SECRETARY: Well, it was rather nice.

SANCHO: And finally, there is one outstanding feature about this model I KNOW the ladies are going to love: He's a GENUINE antique! He was made in Mexico in 1910!

SECRETARY: Made in Mexico?

SANCHO: That's right. Once in Tijuana, twice in Guadalajara, three times in Cuernavaca.

SECRETARY: Mr. Sancho, I thought he was an American product.

SANCHO: No, but—

SECRETARY: No, I'm sorry. We can't buy anything but American-made products. He just won't do.

SANCHO: But he's an antique!

SECRETARY: I don't care. You still don't understand what we need. It's true we need Mexican models such as these, but it's more important that he be *American*.

SANCHO: American?

SECRETARY: That's right, and judging from what you've shown me, I don't think you have what we want. Well, my lunch hour's almost over; I better—

SANCHO: Wait a minute! Mexican but American?

SECRETARY: That's correct.

SANCHO: Mexican but . . . (*A sudden flash.*) AMERICAN! Yeah, I think we've got exactly what you want. He just came in today! Give me a minute. (*He exits. Talks from backstage.*) Here he is in the shop. Let me just get some papers off. There. Introducing our new 1970 Mexican-American! Ta-ra-ra-ra-ra-ra-RA-RAAA!

(SANCHO *brings out the* MEXICAN-AMERICAN *model, a clean-shaven middle-class type in business suit, with glasses.*)

SECRETARY: (*Impressed*) Where have you been hiding this one?

SANCHO: He just came in this morning. Ain't he a beauty? Feast your eyes on him! Sturdy US STEEL frame, streamlined, modern. As a matter of fact, he is built exactly like our Anglo models except that he comes in a variety of darker shades: naugahyde, leather, or leatherette.

SECRETARY: Naugahyde.

SANCHO: Well, we'll just write that down. Yes, señorita, this model represents the apex of American engineering! He is bilingual, college educated, ambitious! Say the word "acculturate" and he accelerates. He is intelligent, well-mannered, clean—did I say clean? (*Snap.* MEXICAN-AMERICAN *raises his arm.*) Smell.

SECRETARY: (*Smells*) Old Sobaco, my favorite.

SANCHO: (*Snap.* MEXICAN-AMERICAN *turns toward* SANCHO.) Eric! (*To* SECRETARY.) We call him Eric Garcia. (*To* ERIC.) I want you to meet Miss JIM-enez, Eric.

MEXICAN-AMERICAN: Miss JIM-enez, I am delighted to make your acquaintance. (*He kisses her hand.*)

SECRETARY: Oh, my, how charming!

SANCHO: Did you feel the suction? He has seven especially engineered suction cups right behind his lips. He's a charmer all right!

SECRETARY: How about boards? Does he function on boards?

SANCHO: You name them, he is on them. Parole boards, draft boards, school boards, taco quality control boards, surf boards, two-by-fours.

SECRETARY: Does he function in politics?

SANCHO: Señorita, you are looking at a political MACHINE. Have you ever heard of the OEO, EOC, COD, WAR ON POVERTY? That's our model! Not only that, he makes political speeches.

SECRETARY: May I hear one?

SANCHO: With pleasure. (*Snap.*) Eric, give us a speech.

MEXICAN-AMERICAN: Mr. Congressman, Mr. Chairman, members of the board, honored guests, ladies and gentlemen. (SANCHO *and* SECRETARY *applaud.*) Please, please, I come before you as a Mexican-American to tell you about the problems of the Mexican. The problems of the Mexican stem from one thing and one thing alone: He's stupid. He's uneducated. He needs to stay in school. He needs to be ambitious, forward-looking, harder-working. He needs to think American, American, American, AMERICAN, AMERICAN, AMERICAN. GOD BLESS AMERICA! GOD BLESS AMERICA!! (*He goes out of control.*)

(SANCHO *snaps frantically and the* MEXICAN-AMERICAN *finally slumps forward, bending at the waist.*)

SECRETARY: Oh my, he's patriotic too!

SANCHO: Sí, señorita, he loves his country. Let me just make a little adjustment here. (*Stands* MEXICAN-AMERICAN *up.*)

SECRETARY: What about upkeep? Is he economical?

SANCHO: Well, no, I won't lie to you. The Mexican-American costs a little bit more, but you get what you pay for. He's worth every extra cent. You can keep him running on dry martinis, Langendorf bread.

SECRETARY: Apple pie?

SANCHO: Only Mom's. Of course, he's also programmed to eat Mexican food on ceremonial functions, but I must warn you: an overdose of beans will plug up his exhaust.

SECRETARY: Fine! There's just one more question: HOW MUCH DO YOU WANT FOR HIM?

SANCHO: Well, I tell you what I'm gonna do. Today and today only, because you've been so sweet, I'm gonna let you steal this model from me! I'm gonna let you drive him off the lot for the simple price of—let's see taxes and license included—$15,000.

SECRETARY: Fifteen thousand DOLLARS? For a MEXICAN!

SANCHO: Mexican? What are you talking, lady? This is a Mexican-AMERICAN! We had to melt down two pachucos, a farm worker and three gabachos to make this model! You want quality, but you gotta pay for it! This is no cheap run-about. He's got class!

SECRETARY: Okay, I'll take him.

SANCHO: You will?

SECRETARY: Here's your money.

SANCHO: You mind if I count it?

SECRETARY: Go right ahead.

SANCHO: Well, you'll get your pink slip in the mail. Oh, do you want me to wrap him up for you? We have a box in the back.

SECRETARY: No, thank you. The Governor is having a luncheon this afternoon, and we need a brown face in the crowd. How do I drive him?

SANCHO: Just snap your fingers. He'll do anything you want.

(SECRETARY *snaps.* MEXICAN-AMERICAN *steps forward.*)

MEXICAN-AMERICAN: RAZA QUERIDA, ¡VAMOS LEVANTANDO ARMAS PARA LIBERARNOS DE ESTOS DESGRACIADOS GABACHOS QUE NOS EXPLOTAN! VAMOS.

SECRETARY: What did he say?

SANCHO: Something about lifting arms, killing white people, etc.

SECRETARY: But he's not supposed to say that!

SANCHO: Look, lady, don't blame me for bugs from the factory. He's your Mexican-American; you bought him, now drive him off the lot!

SECRETARY: But he's broken!

SANCHO: Try snapping another finger.

(SECRETARY *snaps.* MEXICAN-AMERICAN comes to life again.)

MEXICAN-AMERICAN: ¡ESTA GRAN HUMANIDAD HA DICHO BASTA! Y SE HA PUESTO EN MARCHA! ¡BASTA! ¡BASTA! ¡VIVA LA RAZA! ¡VIVA LA CAUSA! ¡VIVA LA HUELGA! ¡VIVAN LOS BROWN BERETS! ¡VIVAN LOS ESTUDIANTES! ¡CHICANO POWER!

(*The* MEXICAN-AMERICAN *turns toward the* SECRETARY, *who gasps and backs up. He keeps turning toward the* PACHUCO, FARM WORKER, *and* REVOLUCIONARIO, *snapping his fingers and turning each of them on, one by one.*)

PACHUCO: (*Snap. To* SECRETARY) I'm going to get you, baby! ¡Viva La Raza!

FARM WORKER: (*Snap. To* SECRETARY) ¡Viva la huelga! ¡Viva la Huelga! ¡VIVA LA HUELGA!

REVOLUCIONARIO: (*Snap. To* SECRETARY) ¡Viva la revolución! ¡VIVA LA REVOLUCIÓN!

REVOLUCIONARIO: (*Snap. To* SECRETARY) ¡Viva la revolución! ¡VIVA LA REVOLUCIÓN!

(*The three models join together and advance toward the* SECRETARY *who backs up and runs out of the shop screaming.* SANCHO *is at the other end of the shop holding his money in his hand. All freeze. After a few seconds of silence, the* PACHUCO *moves and stretches, shaking his arms and loosening up. The* FARM WORKER *and* REVOLUCIONARIO *do the same.* SANCHO *stays where he is, frozen to his spot.*)

JOHNNY: Man, that was a long one, ése. (*Others agree with him.*)

FARM WORKER: How did we do?

JOHNNY: Perty good, look all that lana, man! (*He goes over to* SANCHO *and removes the money from his hand.* SANCHO *stays where he is.*)

REVOLUCIONARIO: En la madre, look at all the money.

JOHNNY: We keep this up, we're going to be rich.

FARM WORKER: They think we're machines.

REVOLUCIONARIO: Burros.

JOHNNY: Puppets.

MEXICAN-AMERICAN: The only thing I don't like is—how come I always got to play the goddamn Mexican-American?

JOHNNY: That's what you get for finishing high school.

FARM WORKER: How about our wages, ése?

JOHNNY: Here it comes right now. $3,000 for you, $3,000 for you, $3,000 for you, and $3,000 for me. The rest we put back into the business.

MEXICAN-AMERICAN: Too much, man. Heh, where you vatos going tonight?

FARM WORKER: I'm going over to Concha's. There's a party.

JOHNNY: Wait a minute, vatos. What about our salesman? I think he needs an oil job.

REVOLUCIONARIO: Leave him to me.

(*The* PACHUCO, FARM WORKER, *and* MEXICAN-AMERICAN *exit, talking loudly about their plans for the night. The* REVOLUCIONARIO *goes over to* SANCHO, *removes his derby hat and cigar, lifts him up and throws him over his shoulder.* SANCHO *hangs loose, lifeless.*)

REVOLUCIONARIO: (*To audience*) He's the best model we got! ¡Ajua! (*Exit.*)

The Responsive Reader

1. What about the way Miss Jimenez talks and acts shows that she has assimilated (although maybe not 100 percent) to the ruling strata of society? What is her errand?

2. What telling features does Honest Sancho include in his sales spiel for the Farm Worker? What are some bitter satirical touches? Why does Miss Jimenez look for someone the color of *cafecito con leche*—coffee with milk?

3. What does Sancho include in his description of the young Mexican who has moved from the migrant camps into the city—the *pachuco?* What makes this portrait brutally frank? Why do you think the playwright did not choose to idealize the pachuco type or to treat him more sympathetically? What role does the pachuco character play in the larger white society?

4. How does Sancho's introduction of the *revolucionario* parody media stereotypes about Mexicans?
5. What, in Sancho's portrait of him, are telltale features of the "acculturated" Mexican American? What role does he play in white society?
6. Did the turn the play takes at the end catch you unawares? How effective is the conclusion as a political statement?

Thinking, Talking, Writing

7. Which of the satirical barbs in this play hit targets that you recognize? What in the play was new or unexpected? Did anything in the play strike you as misleading or unfair?

Collaborative Projects

8. Could you and your classmates assemble a similar cast of types and stereotypes for a play about another group you know as an insider? What would you include in character portraits for three or four key players?

Thinking about Connections

9. The issue of Americanization—of assimilation or acculturation—is explored from a variety of perspectives in the stories by Portillo, Kingston, Newman, and Mukherjee, and in the play by Valdez. Is there a central recurrent theme? Are there key contrasts? Are there major unresolved questions?

11

Invisible Walls: The Untapped Potential

Bring me your fallen fledgling, your bummer lamb,
lead the abused, the starvelings, into my barn.
                    Maxine Kumin, "Nurture"

The true crime is waste—the waste of potential, the withering of hopes,
the bud that did not open.

                    Anonymous

LITERATURE IN CONTEXT

Many people who came to America were down and out, and sympathy for the underdog has often been claimed as an American national trait. Besting the bully was long a favorite theme in American popular entertainment. The high point in movies from Hollywood's golden age is a sensitive, soft-spoken Jimmy Stewart type causing the demise of the sneering, loud-mouthed villain.

This sympathy for the underdog has often extended to those battered by fate or defeated by the system. Americans have often taken a special interest in those held back by poverty and disability or defeated by social taboos. Visitors from more jaded societies have marveled at such crusades as the March of Dimes campaign against child-crippling polio or the movement to provide wheelchair access to public buildings and transportation. The story of Helen Keller triumphing over adversity is part of American folklore. Special Olympics for the disabled, special education for dyslexics, computers helping the blind read and write—even in times of official callousness and neglect, such causes stir the imagination of media audiences. We are learning to think of the deaf or the blind not so much as people with handicaps but as fellow citizens with different abilities and challenges.

How much of this is true empathy? Is some of it sentimentality, which allows us to bask in a warm glow of love for those bested by life while we do little to get at the root causes of poverty or deprivation? Empathy makes us share in the feelings and needs of the less fortunate. It should cause us to take concrete steps to help them realize their potential or preserve their dignity.

Imaginative literature makes us walk a mile in someone else's shoes. It can help us look at the world through the eyes of someone whom in real life we might try to avoid or ignore. It can make us care instead of walking by on the other side of the street.

RINGING THE BELLS
Anne Sexton

> *Anne Sexton wrestled with the demons of mental illness in the dark ages of mental health care, before revolutionary medications led experts to trace mental disorders to malfunctions in the biochemistry of the brain (rather than to childhood traumas or the stress of failed relationships). After a first episode at age twenty-eight, Sexton embarked on a familiar odyssey of revolving-door hospitalizations, futile therapies like those described in the following poem, and botched suicide attempts. For a time, her writing provided a bulwark and defense against her illness. She published eight books of poetry; her* Live or Die *won the Pulitzer Prize in 1967. She finally succeeded in taking her own life in 1974. She was the object of fierce loyalty and admiration on the part of fellow writers and fellow poets.*

And this is the way they ring   *1*
the bells in Bedlam
and this is the bell-lady
who comes each Tuesday morning
to give us a music lesson   *5*
and because the attendants make you go
and because we mind by instinct,
like bees caught in the wrong hive,
we are the circle of the crazy ladies
who sit in the lounge of the mental house   *10*
and smile at the smiling woman
who passes us each a bell,
who points at my hand
that holds my bell, E flat,
and this is the gray dress next to me   *15*
who grumbles as if it were special
to be old, to be old,
and this is the small hunched squirrel girl
on the other side of me
who picks at the hair over her lip,   *20*
who picks at the hair over her lip all day,
and this is how the bells really sound,
as untroubled and clean
as a workable kitchen,
and this is always my bell responding   *25*
to my hand that responds to the lady
who points at me, E flat;
and although we are no better for it,
they tell you to go. And you do.

The Responsive Reader

1. In this poem, everything seems to run together without end punctuation, and there is much repetition of phrases or parts of sentences. Why? What are striking examples?
2. How are the patients "like bees caught in the wrong hive"? What is ironic about the bells sounding "untroubled and clean"? To people who know mental hospitals, what is likely to be sad about the reference to a "workable kitchen"?

Thinking, Talking, Writing

3. We often assume that mental patients are "out of it" and don't know what is going on. Does this poem make you reexamine that assumption?
4. Can you identify with or relate to any of the people in this poem? Why or why not?
5. Bedlam was a notorious British insane asylum where people came to gawk at the antics of the mentally ill. What does the word *bedlam* usually mean today? The poet refers to herself and the other patients as "the crazy ladies." Today, we are often admonished not to use such language—because it is insulting, condescending, or demeaning. Why does the poet use these terms anyway?

Collaborative Projects

6. The way we talk about people who face serious physical or mental problems has changed—for instance, from *crippled* to *handicapped* to *disabled* to *differently abled*. Why? Working with a group, investigate current issues in how we refer to (and therefore think of) groups facing special physical or mental challenges.

SISTER OUTSIDER
Audre Lorde

Audre Lorde was a black lesbian feminist poet who fought racism and sexism and championed the forces that make for positive change. Her poetry chronicled "her unyielding struggle for the human rights of all people" (Claudia Tate). Lorde called love "a source of tremendous power" and spoke "of the erotic as the deepest life force, a force which moves us toward living in a fundamental way." Born in New York City of West Indian parents, she studied and taught at Hunter College. She admired African writers from Chinua Achebe and Amos Tutuola to Ama Ata Aidoo and was fascinated by the matriarchal traditions and goddesses of West Africa and the West Indies. She wrote about her losing struggle with breast cancer in The Cancer Journals *(1980).*

We were born in a poor time   *1*
never touching
each other's hunger
never
sharing our crusts   *5*
in fear
the bread became enemy.

Now we raise our children
to respect themselves
as well as each other.   *10*

Now you have made loneliness
holy and useful
and no longer needed
now
your light shines very brightly   *15*
but I want you
to know
your darkness also
rich
and beyond fear.   *20*

The Responsive Reader

1. What is the metaphorical meaning of bread and hunger in this poem? To judge from the rest of the poem, why were the earlier days "a poor time"? Why do you think the speaker felt fear that "the bread became enemy"?

2. What do you think is the symbolic meaning of light and darkness in this poem?

Thinking, Talking, Writing

3. Self-respect or self-esteem and respect for others have become watch-words in much recent discussion. Why? Where and by whom are they used? Why do they seem so central or important to many? What special meaning do these terms have today?
4. Is this poem likely to change preconceptions or stereotypes about lesbians?

A GATHERING OF DEAFS

John Heaviside

Many of us have in recent years been asked to rethink our attitudes toward the disabled—the blind, the deaf, or wheelchair users. People speaking for the deaf community have challenged traditional attitudes of false pity and exclusion. They have described the sign language used by many of the hearing-impaired as a rich and human medium of communication and the key to a shared culture. John Heaviside wrote the following poem as a student for the Olivetree Review, *a publication devoted to student work at Hunter College of the City University of New York.*

By the turnstiles   1
in the station
where the L train greets
the downtown six there was
a congregation of deafs   5
passing forth
a jive wild
and purely physical
in a world dislocated
from the subway howling   10
hard sole shoe stampede
punk rock blasted radio
screaming, pounding, honking
they gather in community
lively and serene, engaging   15
in a dexterous conversation

An old woman
of her dead husband tells
caressing the air
with wrinkled fingers that demonstrate the story with   20
delicate, mellifluous motion
she places gentle configurations before the faces of the group

A young Puerto Rican
describes a fight with his mother emphasizing each word
with abrupt, staccato movements jerking his elbows   25
and twisting his wrists
teeth clenched and lips pressed
he concluded the story
by pounding his fist
into his palm   30

By the newsstand
two lovers express emotion
caressing the air
with syllables
graceful and slow   35
joining their thoughts
by the flow of fingertips

The Responsive Reader

1. How does the noisy world of sound acquire negative connotations in
   this poem? How does it set the scene for the contrasting world of the
   deaf?
2. What is the meaning of *serene, dexterous, mellifluous, staccato?* How do
   these words and their connotations or associations counteract stereotypes about the deaf? What picture does the poet create of the sign
   language used by this "congregation"?
3. Why or how did the poet select the "speakers" that we are asked to
   focus on in this poem?

Thinking, Talking, Writing

4. What has been your own experience with disability or the disabled?

THE 1ST

Lucille Clifton

when they ask you
why is your mama so funny
say
she is a poet
she don't have no sense
Lucille Clifton, "Admonitions"

> *Lucille Clifton is a black poet who has prided herself on her refusal to be awed by white people and white ways. Her poetry, with its echoes of downhome black dialect, has been called daring, feisty, and exuberant. The mother of six children, she often writes about everyday people and everyday lives, including the lives of people for whom poverty or economic hardship is part of everyday reality. She was born in Depew, New York, and attended Howard University. She has published several volumes of her poetry and many books for children. She was named the state poet, or poet laureate, of Maryland in 1979.*

What I remember about that day   1
is boxes stacked across the walk
and couch springs curling through the air
and drawers and tables balanced on the curb
and us, hollering,   5
leaping up and around
happy to have a playground,

nothing about the emptied rooms
nothing about the emptied family

The Responsive Reader

1. What is the situation in this poem? What is happening? Why do you think the poet says nothing about what caused the events or who is responsible?
2. How do the emptied rooms become a symbol in this poem?

Thinking, Talking, Writing

3. Has our society tired of the "war on poverty"? Are we losing the war?
4. In spite of the democratic commitment to equality, Americans often seem to be more tolerant of a drastic gap between rich and poor than other societies. What do you think explains this attitude?

5. What has been your personal observation of poverty? Where have you observed or experienced what poverty does to shape people's lives and personalities?

THE RAKE: SCENES FROM
MY CHILDHOOD

David Mamet

Popular literature and art have often pictured childhood as an idyllic time. They have painted childhood as a sheltered time of innocence and play before the young adult begins to confront the challenges of the real world. More recently, however, the media have conditioned us to a different picture of the child's world. Instead of happy childhood memories, we encounter the testimony of young people with severe emotional traumas that are the legacy of broken homes, abusive parents, and loveless marriages. Do the childhood memories in the following selection strike you as the story of a family with very severe special problems? Or do they tell a story that is more common than we care to think?

David Mamet is an American playwright and screenwriter who made his mark with aggressive, hostility-charged plays, from American Buffalo *(1975) to* Oleanna *(1992). He sees drama as speaking to our subconscious, and he has put on his stage people acting out rituals of bonding and rejection, people at odds trying to fulfill their frustrated sexuality, people close to the seamy underside of American life. His plays have been called "in turn hilarious and chilling," taking a pitiless look at fallible and corrupt humanity. In 1992 his play* Glengarry Glen Ross *was made into a movie—with Al Pacino, Jack Lemmon, and Alan Arkin—that painted a corrosive picture of huckstering and sleaze in a society in decline.*

There was the incident of the rake and there was the incident of the school play, and it seems to me that they both took place at the round kitchen table.

The table was not in the kitchen proper but in an area called "the nook," which held its claim to that small measure of charm by dint of a waist-high wall separating it from an adjacent area known as the living room.

All family meals were eaten in the nook. There was a dining room to the right, but, as in most rooms of that name at that time and in those surroundings, it was never used.

The round table was of wrought iron and topped with glass; it was noteworthy for that glass, for it was more than once and rather more than several times, I am inclined to think, that my stepfather would grow so angry as to bring some object down on the glass top, shattering it, thus giving us to know how we had forced him out of control.

And it seems that most times when he would shatter the table, as often as that might have been, he would cut some portion of himself on the glass, or that he or his wife, our mother, would cut their hands on picking up the glass afterward, and that we children were to understand, and did understand, that these wounds were our fault.

So the table was associated in our minds with the notion of blood.

The house was in a brand-new housing development in the southern suburbs. The new community was built upon, and now bordered, the remains of what had once been a cornfield. When our new family moved in, there were but a few homes in the development completed, and a few more under construction. Most streets were mud, and boasted a house here or there, and many empty lots marked out by white stakes.

The house we lived in was the development's Model Home. The first time we had seen it, it had signs plastered on the front and throughout the interior telling of the various conveniences it contained. And it had a lawn, and was one of the only homes in the new community that did.

My stepfather was fond of the lawn, and he detailed me and my sister to care for it, and one fall afternoon we found ourselves assigned to rake the leaves.

Why this chore should have been so hated I cannot say, except that we children, and I especially, felt ourselves less than full members of this new, cobbled-together family, and disliked being assigned to the beautification of a home that we found unbeautiful in all respects, and for which we had neither natural affection nor a sense of proprietary interest. *10*

We went to the new high school. We walked the mile down the open two-lane road on one side of which was the just-begun suburban community and on the other side of which was the cornfield.

The school was as new as the community, and still under construction for the first three years of its occupancy. One of its innovations was the notion that honesty would be engendered by the absence of security, and so the lockers were designed and built both without locks and without the possibility of attaching locks. And there was the corresponding rash of thievery and many lectures about the same from the school administration, but it was difficult to point with pride to any scholastic or community tradition supporting the suggestion that we, the students, pull together in this new, utopian way. We were, in school, in an uncompleted building in the midst of a mud field in the midst of a cornfield. Our various sports teams were called The Spartans; and I played on those teams, which were of a wretchedness consistent with their novelty.

Meanwhile my sister interested herself in the drama society. The year after I had left the school she obtained the lead in the school play. It called for acting and singing, both of which she had talent for, and it looked to be a signal triumph for her in her otherwise unremarkable and unenjoyed school career.

On the night of the play's opening she sat down to dinner with our mother and our stepfather. It may be that they ate a trifle early to allow her to get to the school to enjoy the excitement of the opening night. But however it was, my sister had no appetite, and she nibbled a bit at her food, and then she got up from the table to carry her plate back to scrape it in the sink, when my mother suggested that she sit down, as she had not finished her food. My sister said she really had no appetite, but my mother insisted that, as the meal had been prepared, it would be good form to sit and eat it.

My sister sat down with the plate and pecked at her food and she tried   *15* to eat a bit, and told my mother that, no, really, she possessed no appetite whatever, and that was due, no doubt, not to the food, but to her nervousness and excitement at the prospect of opening night.

My mother, again, said that, as the food had been cooked, it had to be eaten, and my sister tried and said that she could not; at which my mother nodded. She then got up from the table and went to the telephone and looked the number up and called the school and got the drama teacher and identified herself and told him that her daughter wouldn't be coming to school that night, that, no, she was not ill, but that she would not be coming in. Yes, yes, she said, she knew that her daughter had the lead in the play, and, yes, she was aware that many children and teachers had worked hard for it, et cetera, and so my sister did not play the lead in her school play. But I was long gone, out of the house by that time, and well out of it. I heard that story, and others like it, at the distance of twenty-five years.

In the model house our rooms were separated from their room, the master bedroom, by a bathroom and a study. On some weekends I would go alone to visit my father in the city and my sister would stay and sometimes grow frightened or lonely in her part of the house. And once, in the period when my grandfather, then in his sixties, was living with us, she became alarmed at a noise she had heard in the night; or perhaps she just became lonely, and she went out of her room and down the hall, calling for my mother, or my stepfather, or my grandfather, but the house was dark, and no one answered.

And, as she went farther down the hall, toward the living room, she heard voices, and she turned the corner, and saw a light coming from under the closed door in the master bedroom, and heard my stepfather crying, and the sound of my mother weeping. So my sister went up to the door, and she heard my stepfather talking to my grandfather and saying, "Jack. Say the words. Just say the words . . ." And my grandfather, in his Eastern European accent, saying, with obvious pain and difficulty, "No. No. I can't. Why are you making me do this? Why?" And the sound of my mother crying convulsively.

My sister opened the door, and she saw my grandfather sitting on the bed, and my stepfather standing by the closet and gesturing. On the floor of the closet she saw my mother, curled in a fetal position, moaning and crying and hugging herself. My stepfather was saying, "Say the words. Just say the words." And my grandfather was breathing fast and repeating, "I can't. She knows how I feel about her. I can't." And my stepfather said, "Say the words, Jack. Please. Just say you love her." At which my mother would moan louder. And my grandfather said, "I can't."

My sister pushed the door open farther and said—I don't know what she said, but she asked, I'm sure, for some reassurance, or some explanation, and my stepfather turned around and saw her and picked up a hairbrush from a dresser that he passed as he walked toward her, and he hit her in the face and slammed the door on her. And she continued to hear "Jack, say the words." 20

She told me that on weekends when I was gone my stepfather ended every Sunday evening by hitting or beating her for some reason or other. He would come home from depositing his own kids back at their mother's house after their weekend visitation, and would settle down tired and angry, and, as a regular matter on those evenings, would find out some intolerable behavior on my sister's part and slap or hit or beat her.

Years later, at my mother's funeral, my sister spoke to our aunt, my mother's sister, who gave a footnote to this behavior. She said when they were young, my mother and my aunt, they and their parents lived in a small flat on the West Side. My grandfather was a salesman on the road from dawn on Monday until Friday night. Their family had a fiction, and that fiction, that article of faith, was that my mother was a naughty child. And each Friday, when he came home, his first question as he climbed the stairs was, "What has she done this week . . . ?" At which my grandmother would tell him the terrible things that my mother had done, after which she, my mother, was beaten.

This was general knowledge in my family. The footnote concerned my grandfather's behavior later in the night. My aunt had a room of her own, and it adjoined her parents' room. And she related that each Friday, when the house had gone to bed, she, through the thin wall, heard my grandfather pleading for sex. "Cookie, please." And my grandmother responding, "No, Jack." "Cookie, please." "No, Jack." "Cookie, please."

And once, my grandfather came home and asked, "What has she done this week?" and I do not know, but I imagine that the response was not completed, and perhaps hardly begun; in any case, he reached and grabbed my mother by the back of the neck and hurled her down the stairs.

And once, in our house in the suburbs there had been an outburst by my stepfather directed at my sister. And she had, somehow, prevailed. It was, I think, that he had the facts of the case wrong, and had accused her of the commission of something for which she had demonstrably had no opportunity, and she pointed this out to him with what I can imagine, given the circumstances, was an understandable, and, given my prejudice, a commendable degree of freedom. Thinking the incident closed she went back to her room to study, and, a few moments later, saw him throw open her door, bat the book out of her hands, and pick her up and throw her against the far wall, where she struck the back of her neck on a shelf. 25

She was told, the next morning, that her pain, real or pretended, held no weight, and that she would have to go to school. She protested that she could not walk, or, if at all, only with the greatest of difficulty and in great pain; but she was dressed and did walk to school, where she fainted, and was brought home. For years she suffered various headaches; an X ray taken twenty years later for an unrelated problem revealed that when he threw her against the shelf he had cracked her vertebrae.

When we left the house we left in good spirits. When we went out to dinner, it was an adventure, which was strange to me, looking back, because many of these dinners ended with my sister or myself being banished, sullen or in tears, from the restaurant, and told to wait in the car, as we were in disgrace.

These were the excursions that had ended, due to her or my intolerable arrogance, as it was then explained to us.

The happy trips were celebrated and capped with a joke. Here is the joke: My stepfather, my mother, my sister, and I would exit the restaurant, my stepfather and mother would walk to the car, telling us that they would pick us up. We children would stand by the restaurant entrance. They would drive up in the car, open the passenger door, and wait until my sister and I had started to get in. They would then drive away.

They would drive ten or fifteen feet, and open the door again, and we would walk up again, and they would drive away again. They sometimes would drive around the block. But they would always come back, and by that time the four of us would be laughing in camaraderie and appreciation of what, I believe, was our only family joke.

We were raking the lawn, my sister and I. I was raking, and she was stuffing the leaves into a bag. I loathed the job, and my muscles and my mind rebelled, and I was viciously angry, and my sister said something, and I turned and threw the rake at her and it hit her in the face.

The rake was split bamboo and metal, and a piece of metal caught her lip and cut her badly.

We were both terrified, and I was sick with guilt, and we ran into the house, my sister holding her hand to her mouth, and her mouth and her hand and the front of her dress covered in blood.

We ran into the kitchen where my mother was cooking dinner, and my mother asked what happened.

Neither of us, myself out of guilt, of course, and my sister out of a desire to avert the terrible punishment she knew I would receive, neither of us would say what occurred.

My mother pressed us, and neither of us would answer. She said that until one or the other answered, we would not go to the hospital; and so the family sat down to dinner where my sister clutched a napkin to her face and the blood soaked the napkin and ran down onto her food, which she had to eat; and I also ate my food and we cleared the table and went to the hospital.

I remember the walks home from school in the frigid winter, along the cornfield that was, for all its proximity to the city, part of the prairie. The winters were viciously cold. From the remove of years, I can see how the area might and may have been beautiful. One could have walked in the stubble of the cornfields, or hunted birds, or enjoyed any of a number of pleasures naturally occurring.

The Responsive Reader

1. What about the setting or the context of these memories strikes you as fairly normal? What were ordinary circumstances in these people's lives? Why is it ironic that the family lived in the housing development's Model Home?
2. How does the glass-topped table become a weighty symbol early in the story?
3. Tell the story of some of the traumatic incidents that provide the meat of the story. How does Mamet make these nightmare situations real? What are striking, haunting details?
4. Do you understand the notions of discipline that cause ghastly incidents in the children's lives? Do you understand the psychology at work? Have teachers and parents left it behind?
5. What is the scene the sister came upon in the parents' bedroom all about? What makes people unable to say "the words"?

Thinking, Talking, Writing

6. What is basically wrong with this family? Is there any central clue to what is amiss? Are their problems passed on from generation to generation? How?
7. A family history like Mamet's was often kept secret. Why? Why do you think people have become much more open about stories like Mamet's?
8. Who or what could have helped these people? What is the answer to spousal abuse? What is the answer to child abuse?

Collaborative Projects

9. In your community, what is done to raise consciousness about domestic violence, battered women, or child abuse? You may want to work with a small group exploring one area of the larger problem.

SPEECH

Richard Umans

Recent years have seen a growing awareness of the gay lifestyle. Gays and the police, gays and the military, gays and the Boy Scouts of America—these have been topics of controversy in the national media. Gay communities in New York, San Francisco, or Los Angeles have attracted media attention, ranging from sensation-mongering to honest explorations of gay life. In popular entertainment, homosexual jokes have been replaced by plot twists in which the revelation of someone's sexual orientation provides a comic touch or dramatic angle. Gay authors like Gore Vidal, James Baldwin, or Tennessee Williams have long been widely known and widely read.

Earlier fiction by or about gays often focused on the furtive lives led by people forced to hide their sexual orientation because of the prejudices of society. Some of the most successful or widely read writers have focused on the conflict between gay people and their parents. As gays have openly declared their sexual preference, writers have become more explicit in the description of gay sexual needs, practices, and customs. In the words of one editor of gay fiction, recent gay and lesbian writers have "effectively moved the focus of gay literature away from the lonely homosexual figure doomed to unhappiness toward the elaboration of a world in which homosexuality was no longer an exclusively psychological issue shrouded in secrecy and guilt but a social reality" (George Stambolian).

The following story first appeared in The James White Review, *a journal published in the Midwest. One editor saw the story as focused on the difficulty of finding a language for feelings and behavior not recognized by society. How do people communicate about what the society around them considers taboo?*

Danny Murray and I were best friends for years, through elementary school all the way into junior high. We never had to ask if we'd be spending Saturday together, just what we'd be doing. Weather permitting, we'd usually ride bikes. Danny and I were great bikers.

Our Saturday afternoon expeditions took us not over country roads but into city streets, far from the calm predictability of our boring suburb. We explored much of the city on our bicycles, sailing freely through unfamiliar neighborhoods, walking our bikes past the exotic window displays downtown. We imagined ourselves tough city kids, looking for a gang to join. In fact, without knowing it, we were practicing for times to come, when this city or its like would provide the setting for our high school dating, our college adventures, our adult careers.

We were not without safe havens, even downtown. My uncle had a shoe store on Clarendon Street. He would sometimes take us for sandwiches or at least treat us to ice cream. But the real excitement lay all the way in the downtown shopping center, on Washington Street, where Danny's father's store stood. My uncle's little shoe shop paled by comparison.

I. J. Murray occupied its own six-story building. The first three floors were retail space, selling women's clothing, especially furs. Danny and I, unlike mere customers, were allowed to ride the service elevator to the top three floors, where the furs were stored, cut, and stitched into coats. We would visit Danny's father's grand fourth-floor office and be treated to lunch. And we had the run of the place.

The most absorbing area was the fifth-floor cutting rooms. Here the furs would be laid out, backed, and cut to shape by skilled craftsmen. The process remained forever magical to me, and two factors gave it special meaning. First, a single mistake could cost hundreds, even thousands, of dollars. Second, one of the cutters was Danny's Uncle Leo.

Leo Murray was dashingly handsome. Even in a long grey work apron, his fine slacks and pure white shirt set him worlds apart from the other cutters. His hair gleamed with sleek blackness, one curl sometimes tumbling Gene Vincent-like over the crest of his forehead. His large black eyes gazed with sensitive alertness, and his jaw stood square and firm, framing thick, straight lips. Altogether, he reminded me of Superman, barely disguised as Clark Kent.

When Danny and I entered the cutting room, Uncle Leo stopped whatever he was doing. He gave Danny a long, powerful hug, his face brilliant with delight, and they would talk. Uncle Leo's voice would soar and whoop, and Danny's mouth would silently form big, emphatic words. I never learned to understand more than a little of Uncle Leo's strange speech, and Danny told me that most people had the same problem. But Danny, his deaf uncle's favorite, had grown up hearing that speech and understood it with ease.

Danny's sharing of a secret language with this intriguing adult, who would drop everything to hurry over and chat, seemed to me the height of special friendship. In my school, some of the girls had trained themselves to speak a variation of Pig Latin, at lightning speed, in order to confound the boys and undermine the teachers. Since I'd long ago learned to decipher my parents' use of spelled words when they wished to disguise their meaning from me, nothing had so excluded me as the girls' annoying gobbledygook. Miffed, I'd taught myself through lonely practice to understand it, though speaking it in public was beneath masculine dignity.

Danny's conversations with Uncle Leo remained impenetrable to me, however. Far more than schoolgirls' nonsense talk, the excited exchanges of my best friend and his dazzling uncle thrilled me with a sense of witnessing a rare intimacy, a bond between man and boy that crossed social boundaries. It was the kind of buddyhood common on television, where heroes often had a young sidekick—the Range Rider and Dick West, The Rifleman and Mark, even Tarzan and Boy. But real life held few openings for sidekicks. My friends and I all had harried, overworked fathers, well-meaning but locked within their own worlds. Other male grownups—gym teachers, camp counselors—managed us where necessary, but always from the unbridgeable distance of their adulthood.

Only Danny Murray, of all the boys I knew, seemed able to enter the   *10* private world of an adult male—not only adult, but moviestar glamorous, and appealingly set off from the rest of the world by his mysterious speech. Danny had a rare and precious access, and I watched enviously as Danny communicated with his uncle with far greater ease than even Mr. Murray, Danny's father, who was Uncle Leo's brother and boss.

Only Ernie, Uncle Leo's elderly co-worker, seemed able to understand him as well as Danny did. Ernie, Danny said, had trained Leo Murray as a fur-cutter when the youth had come out of a prestigious school for the deaf with few skills in lipreading or speech and little academic training of any kind. Uncle Leo had always been a rebel, Danny confided. He'd been thrown out of school several times, and only his father's wealth and position had gotten him back in. Crusty old I. J. Murray had intended for young Leo to "overcome" his deafness and become an executive like his older brother. Instead, Leo had taken avidly to the craftsmanship of cutting fur, married a deaf woman from school, fathered three hearing children, and moved into a lesser neighborhood of the same suburb where Danny and I lived.

Sometimes Uncle Leo would pull Danny and me over to his work table to show us what he was working on or lead us to the storage vaults to show us a new shipment of gleaming pelts. His voice would swoop like a crazed sparrow, his hands and face signaling most of his intent. I would smile and nod along, imagining I understood. Then Danny and his uncle, and sometimes old Ernie as well, would explode into laughter at a remark of Leo's, a remark I could no more distinguish from the cascade of his vocalizing than a particular quart of water from a gushing torrent. Danny would translate for me, and I would laugh energetically, glad to be part of the interchange once more, even if emptily, and too late.

One summer afternoon, on a trip home in my late twenties, I chanced to visit a small country club in a suburb near the one in which I'd grown up. The country club had no golf course, only a pool and clubhouse, and it failed to hold its own against clubs that offered golf and tennis. Some gay entrepreneurs had bought it, and now it was prospering as a gay pool club.

The poolside atmosphere was pleasant and low-pressure, with people who had moved to the suburbs for many of the same reasons as my parents. The men lounged and chatted, and the women horsed around. A few show-offs practiced diving or swam self-conscious laps in the pool. Here and there sat pairs of recent lovers, with eyes for no one but each other.

A tall, handsome man in his early forties strode past. Shocked, I deter-   *15* mined to listen for the voice, but the black, sympathetic eyes were the give-away. At once I fell to smoothing my hair and sucking in my stomach. Then

I realized that I had with any luck changed far too much in fifteen years for Leo Murray to recognize me now.

He still looked fine. His body was thicker, but not fat, and his hair was wavy and dark, greying slightly at the temples. I watched him cross to his lounge chair and sit beside a tall, skinny blond, with whom he began to talk comfortably. His eyes still flashed with lively humor.

Screwing up my courage, I approached Leo Murray and his companion and introduced myself as Danny Murray's boyhood chum. Leo's face enlivened instantly, just the way I remembered, though his friend's held some residual suspicion. As I asked for details of Danny's recent years, however, Carl had to repeat most of Leo's answers for me, and he began to warm to his role as go-between.

I quickly satisfied myself regarding Danny's progress and pressed on about Leo himself. He obliged me with the information that he was divorced, his kids grown, and he still worked for I. J. Murray, though the firm was much reduced by declines in the fur market. He lived, he said, with his sister. Carl, though obviously close, was apparently not Leo's lover.

I listened greedily. Leo Murray's voice still darted wildly up and down, detached from the meaning of his words. But reading the constant flicker of emotion across his face, I felt the remembered impression of comprehending his message without actually making out his words. It was as pleasing a sensation now as then, a kind of private, prelingual communication, full of intimacy even in blazing sunlight beside a crowded pool. I sat talking long after there was anything left to say.

Returning to my own friends at their lounges, I found myself making   20
disparaging remarks—not about Leo, whom I simply described as an acquaintance from childhood, but about Carl. Cattily I described his skinny body, his pockmarked face, his lisping, pretentious speech. Slowly it dawned on me that I was jealous. Once again I had had to speak to Leo Murray through an intermediary. Once again he had chosen another to be his intimate. Why not me? Why was I again, unfairly, too late?

Several years later, on another pass through town, I was left with two hours to kill before my train left. It was an awkward space of time, not enough to call friends, too much to spend comfortably in a train station. I rented a locker for my suitcase and went for a walk.

The train station stood alongside the financial district, and at early evening the sidewalks were already nearly empty. There was only one movie theater in this end of town, and my timing would be unlikely to permit me a full feature. At this theater, however, it mattered little at what point you walked in. I paid the high admission fee and went in to watch the grainy, scratched film with its mismatched soundtrack.

When I entered, all eyes turned to survey the new arrival. The audience was all male, as I knew it would be. Men were seated at odd intervals throughout the small theater, occasionally in pairs. There was a cluster standing behind the back row of seats. A steady stream of individuals trooped back and forth from the lounges located at the very front of the theater, behind the screen.

I watched the film for a few minutes, and the crowd. Then I took a walk through the lounge area. It was dimly lit. There were men standing within and outside both bathrooms. Some of the stall doors stood ajar. No one spoke. The shadowy figures passed in and out in silence, sometimes lingering, blending into deeper shadows. Back in the theater, the flickering light of the movie made the spectators' closed faces superficially alive.

On my second pass through the lounge area, I spotted Leo Murray. He   25 was cruising the same way I was, moving slowly through the hallway, which was lined with slouched figures. He looked me full in the face, but I couldn't tell whether he recognized me or not. His eyes were already wide, engorged with perception, before he caught sight of me.

I carefully passed him two or three more times, doing everything possible within the conventions of this place to alert him to my presence. Reluctantly I refrained from planting myself in front of him, tapping him on the shoulder, or signaling him directly. I slowed to a crawl each time he approached; I eyed him sullenly. He simply moved past like a figure in a dream, at ease in this silent world, his black eyes glinting, bottomless. We each glided along like the others, stopping sometimes to cling to a wall, otherwise floating past each other in the purgatory murk. Different stall doors stood ajar.

At length I drifted back out to the theater. I took a seat as far as possible from everyone else and applied myself to the unwatchable movie. Some minutes later a figure joined me in my row. It was Leo Murray, watching the screen with a gentle, beatific smile illuminating his face. I moved over two seats and sat beside him. Like a spotlight on a pivot, he turned and flooded me with his smile. His eyes glowed, black and wet.

I placed a daring hand on his knee. The fabric of the slacks was thick, luxurious, elegant. His own hand danced across my thigh, and he turned toward me further. Then he spoke to me, only to me, and I dropped my head back and listened.

The Responsive Reader

1. How does this story challenge or confirm assumptions that you or the society around you have about gays? Does the story break down stereotypes?
2. What subjects do you know for which our society has no language and that as a result remain unspoken and unheard? Have you seen evidence of things now being verbalized that used to be unspoken?

Thinking, Talking, Writing

3. Some readers object to explicit discussions of the gay lifestyle. Others ask that the large gay and lesbian communities receive more than token recognition in the media and in education. Where do you stand on this issue and why?

A SMALL, GOOD THING

Raymond Carver

Raymond Carver had a special empathy, or fellow feeling, for characters whom Fate had thrown a curve ball. He himself was from a working class background, where unemployment, alcoholism, or a failed marriage was always just around the corner. One of his best-known stories, "The Third Thing That Killed My Father Off," is about a retarded man who is the target of stupid pranks by his fellow workers and who finally destroys himself when his stubborn attempt to gain some measure of dignity fails. Carver became a writer by taking courses at California state colleges (Humboldt and Chico) while working the night shift or doing odd jobs. His first major work was published by the English Club at Sacramento State College. Appointments at prestige universities and a Guggenheim fellowship came later.

Carver's fiction takes us into a world where there are no pretty-boy leading men, no glamorous phonies, no smug celebrities, and no ballplayers on million-dollar contracts. His characters are often what one of his editors called "under-educated," and they struggle to make a living. Carver's great contribution is that he makes his readers feel that, although his people do not have a trust fund or a degree from an elite school, "these are human lives that matter" (George Perkins). The following story appears in a collection published in 1983.

Saturday afternoon she drove to the bakery in the shopping center. After looking through a loose-leaf binder with photographs of cakes taped onto the pages, she ordered chocolate, the child's favorite. The cake she chose was decorated with a space ship and launching pad under a sprinkling of white stars, and a planet made of red frosting at the other end. His name, SCOTTY, would be in green letters beneath the planet. The baker, who was an older man with a thick neck, listened without saying anything when she told him the child would be eight years old next Monday. The baker wore a white apron that looked like a smock. Straps cut under his arms, went around in back and then to the front again, where they were secured under his heavy waist. He wiped his hands on his apron as he listened to her. He kept his eyes down on the photographs and let her talk. He let her take her time. He'd just come to work and he'd be there all night, baking, and he was in no real hurry.

She gave the baker her name, Ann Weiss, and her telephone number. The cake would be ready on Monday morning, just out of the oven, in plenty of time for the child's party that afternoon. The baker was not jolly. There were no pleasantries between them, just the minimum exchange of words, the necessary information. He made her feel uncomfortable, and she didn't like that. While he was bent over the counter with the pencil in his hand, she studied his coarse features and wondered if he'd ever done anything else with his life besides be a baker. She was a mother and thirty-three years old, and it seemed to her that everyone, especially someone the baker's age— a man old enough to be her father—must have children who'd gone through this special time of cakes and birthday parties. There must be that between them, she thought. But he was abrupt with her—not rude, just abrupt. She gave up trying to make friends with him. She looked into the back of the bakery and could see a long, heavy wooden table with aluminum pie pans stacked at one end; and beside the table a metal container filled with empty racks. There was an enormous oven. A radio was playing country-Western music.

The baker finished printing the information on the special order card and closed up the binder. He looked at her and said, "Monday morning." She thanked him and drove home.

On Monday morning, the birthday boy was walking to school with another boy. They were passing a bag of potato chips back and forth and the birthday boy was trying to find out what his friend intended to give him for his birthday that afternoon. Without looking, the birthday boy stepped off the curb at an intersection and was immediately knocked down by a car. He fell on his side with his head in the gutter and his legs out in the road. His eyes were closed, but his legs moved back and forth as if he were trying to climb over something. His friend dropped the potato chips and started to cry. The car had gone a hundred feet or so and stopped in the middle of the road. The man in the driver's seat looked back over his shoulder. He waited until the boy got unsteadily to his feet. The boy wobbled a little. He looked dazed, but okay. The driver put the car into gear and drove away.

The birthday boy didn't cry, but he didn't have anything to say about   5 anything either. He wouldn't answer when his friend asked him what it felt like to be hit by a car. He walked home, and his friend went on to school. But after the birthday boy was inside his house and was telling his mother about it—she sitting beside him on the sofa, holding his hands in her lap, saying, "Scotty, honey, are you sure you feel all right, baby?" thinking she would call the doctor anyway—he suddenly lay back on the sofa, closed his eyes, and went limp. When she couldn't wake him up, she hurried to the telephone and called her husband at work. Howard told her to remain calm, remain calm, and then he called an ambulance for the child and left for the hospital himself.

Of course, the birthday party was canceled. The child was in the hospital with a mild concussion and suffering from shock. There'd been vomiting, and his lungs had taken in fluid which needed pumping out that afternoon. Now he simply seemed to be in a very deep sleep—but no coma, Dr. Francis had emphasized, no coma, when he saw the alarm in the parents' eyes. At eleven o'clock that night, when the boy seemed to be resting comfortably enough after the many X-rays and the lab work, and it was just a matter of his waking up and coming around, Howard left the hospital. He and Ann had been at the hospital with the child since that afternoon, and he was going home for a short while to bathe and change clothes. "I'll be back in an hour," he said. She nodded. "It's fine," she said. "I'll be right here." He kissed her on the forehead, and they touched hands. She sat in the chair beside the bed and looked at the child. She was waiting for him to wake up and be all right. Then she could begin to relax.

Howard drove home from the hospital. He took the wet, dark streets very fast, then caught himself and slowed down. Until now, his life had gone smoothly and to his satisfaction—college, marriage, another year of college for the advanced degree in business, a junior partnership in an investment firm. Fatherhood. He was happy and, so far, lucky—he knew that. His parents were still living, his brothers and his sister were established, his friends from college had gone out to take their places in the world. So far, he had kept away from any real harm, from those forces he knew existed and that could cripple or bring down a man if the luck went bad, if things suddenly turned. He pulled into the driveway and parked. His left leg began to tremble. He sat in the car for a minute and tried to deal with the present situation in a rational manner. Scotty had been hit by a car and was in the hospital, but he was going to be all right. Howard closed his eyes and ran his hand over his face. He got out of the car and went up to the front door. The dog was barking inside the house. The telephone rang and rang while he unlocked the door and fumbled for the light switch. He shouldn't have left the hospital, he shouldn't have. "Goddamn it!" he said. He picked up the receiver and said, "I just walked in the door!"

"There's a cake here that wasn't picked up," the voice on the other end of the line said.

"What are you saying?" Howard asked.

"A cake," the voice said. "A sixteen-dollar cake." *10*

Howard held the receiver against his ear, trying to understand. "I don't know anything about a cake," he said. "Jesus, what are you talking about?"

"Don't hand me that," the voice said.

Howard hung up the telephone. He went into the kitchen and poured himself some whiskey. He called the hospital. But the child's condition remained the same; he was still sleeping and nothing had changed there. While water poured into the tub, Howard lathered his face and shaved. He'd just stretched out in the tub and closed his eyes when the telephone rang again. He hauled himself out, grabbed a towel, and hurried through the house, saying, "Stupid, stupid," for having left the hospital. But when he picked up the receiver and shouted, "Hello!" there was no sound at the other end of the line. Then the caller hung up.

He arrived back at the hospital a little after midnight. Ann still sat in the chair beside the bed. She looked up at Howard, and then she looked back at the child. The child's eyes stayed closed, the head was still wrapped in bandages. His breathing was quiet and regular. From an apparatus over the bed hung a bottle of glucose with a tube running from the bottle to the boy's arm.

"How is he?" Howard said. "What's all this?" waving at the glucose and the tube.

"Dr. Francis's orders," she said. "He needs nourishment. He needs to keep up his strength. Why doesn't he wake up, Howard? I don't understand, if he's all right."

Howard put his hand against the back of her head. He ran his fingers through her hair. "He's going to be all right. He'll wake up in a little while. Dr. Francis knows what's what."

After a time, he said, "Maybe you should go home and get some rest. I'll stay here. Just don't put up with this creep who keeps calling. Hang up right away."

"Who's calling?" she asked.

"I don't know who, just somebody with nothing better to do than call up people. You go on now."

She shook her head. "No," she said, "I'm fine."

"Really," he said. "Go home for a while, and then come back and spell me in the morning. It'll be all right. What did Dr. Francis say? He said Scotty's going to be all right. We don't have to worry. He's just sleeping now, that's all."

A nurse pushed the door open. She nodded at them as she went to the bedside. She took the left arm out from under the covers and put her fingers on the wrist, found the pulse, then consulted her watch. In a little while, she put the arm back under the covers and moved to the foot of the bed, where she wrote something on a clipboard attached to the bed.

"How is he?" Ann said. Howard's hand was a weight on her shoulder. She was aware of the pressure from his fingers.

"He's stable," the nurse said. Then she said, "Doctor will be in again shortly. Doctor's back in the hospital. He's making rounds right now."

"I was saying maybe she'd want to go home and get a little rest," Howard said. "After the doctor comes," he said.

"She could do that," the nurse said. "I think you should both feel free to do that, if you wish." The nurse was a big Scandinavian woman with blond hair. There was the trace of an accent in her speech.

"We'll see what the doctor says," Ann said. "I want to talk to the doctor. I don't think he should keep sleeping like this. I don't think that's a good sign." She brought her hand up to her eyes and let her head come forward a little. Howard's grip tightened on her shoulder, and then his hand moved up to her neck, where his fingers began to knead the muscles there.

"Dr. Francis will be here in a few minutes," the nurse said. Then she left the room.

Howard gazed at his son for a time, the small chest quietly rising and falling under the covers. For the first time since the terrible minutes after

Ann's telephone call to him at his office, he felt a genuine fear starting in his limbs. He began shaking his head. Scotty was fine, but instead of sleeping at home in his own bed, he was in a hospital bed with bandages around his head and a tube in his arm. But this help was what he needed right now.

Dr. Francis came in and shook hands with Howard, though they'd just seen each other a few hours before. Ann got up from the chair. "Doctor?"

"Ann," he said and nodded. "Let's just first see how he's doing," the doctor said. He moved to the side of the bed and took the boy's pulse. He peeled back one eyelid and then the other. Howard and Ann stood beside the doctor and watched. Then the doctor turned back the covers and listened to the boy's heart and lungs with his stethoscope. He pressed his fingers here and there on the abdomen. When he was finished, he went to the end of the bed and studied the chart. He noted the time, scribbled something on the chart, and then looked at Howard and Ann.

"Doctor, how is he?" Howard said. "What's the matter with him exactly?"

"Why doesn't he wake up?" Ann said.

The doctor was a handsome, big-shouldered man with a tanned face.   *35* He wore a three-piece blue suit, a striped tie, and ivory cufflinks. His gray hair was combed along the sides of his head, and he looked as if he had just come from a concert. "He's all right," the doctor said. "Nothing to shout about, he could be better, I think. But he's all right. Still, I wish he'd wake up. He should wake up pretty soon." The doctor looked at the boy again. "We'll know some more in a couple of hours, after the results of a few more tests are in. But he's all right, believe me, except for the hairline fracture of the skull. He does have that."

"Oh, no," Ann said.

"And a bit of a concussion, as I said before. Of course, you know he's in shock," the doctor said. "Sometimes you see this in shock cases. This sleeping."

"But he's out of any real danger?" Howard said. "You said before he's not in a coma. You wouldn't call this a coma, then—would you, doctor?" Howard waited. He looked at the doctor.

"No, I don't want to call it a coma," the doctor said and glanced over at the boy once more. "He's just in a very deep sleep. It's a restorative measure the body is taking on its own. He's out of any real danger, I'd say that for certain, yes. But we'll know more when he wakes up and the other tests are in," the doctor said.

"It's a coma," Ann said. "Of sorts."   *40*

"It's not a coma yet, not exactly," the doctor said. "I wouldn't want to call it coma. Not yet, anyway. He's suffered shock. In shock cases, this kind of reaction is common enough; it's a temporary reaction to bodily trauma. Coma. Well, coma is a deep, prolonged unconsciousness, something that could go on for days, or weeks even. Scotty's not in that area, not as far as we can tell. I'm certain his condition will show improvement by morning. I'm betting that it will. We'll know more when he wakes up, which shouldn't be long now. Of course, you may do as you like, stay here or go home for a time. But by all means feel free to leave the hospital for a while if you want. This is not easy, I know." The doctor gazed at the boy again, watching him, and then he turned to Ann and said, "You try not to worry, little mother. Believe me, we're doing all that can be done. It's just a question of a little more time now." He nodded at her, shook hands with Howard again, and then he left the room.

Ann put her hand over the child's forehead. "At least he doesn't have a fever," she said. Then she said, "My God, he feels so cold, though. Howard? Is he supposed to feel like this? Feel his head."

Howard touched the child's temples. His own breathing had slowed. "I think he's supposed to feel this way right now," he said. "He's in shock, remember? That's what the doctor said. The doctor was just in here. He would have said something if Scotty wasn't okay."

Ann stood there a while longer, working her lip with her teeth. Then she moved over to her chair and sat down.

Howard sat in the chair next to her chair. They looked at each other.   45 He wanted to say something else and reassure her, but he was afraid, too. He took her hand and put it in his lap, and this made him feel better, her hand being there. He picked up her hand and squeezed it. Then he just held her hand. They sat like that for a while, watching the boy and not talking. From time to time, he squeezed her hand. Finally, she took her hand away.

"I've been praying," she said.

He nodded.

She said, "I almost thought I'd forgotten how, but it came back to me. All I had to do was close my eyes and say, 'Please God, help us—help Scotty,' and then the rest was easy. The words were right there. Maybe if you prayed, too," she said to him.

"I've already prayed," he said. "I prayed this afternoon—yesterday afternoon, I mean—after you called, while I was driving to the hospital. I've been praying," he said.

"That's good," she said. For the first time, she felt they were together   50 in it, this trouble. She realized with a start that, until now, it had only been happening to her and to Scotty. She hadn't let Howard into it, though he was there and needed all along. She felt glad to be his wife.

The same nurse came in and took the boy's pulse again and checked the flow from the bottle hanging above the bed.

In an hour, another doctor came in. He said his name was Parsons, from Radiology. He had a bushy mustache. He was wearing loafers, a Western shirt, and a pair of jeans.

"We're going to take him downstairs for more pictures," he told them. "We need to do some more pictures, and we want to do a scan."

"What's that?" Ann said. "A scan?" She stood between this new doctor and the bed. "I thought you'd already taken all your X-rays."

"I'm afraid we need some more," he said. "Nothing to be alarmed   55
about. We just need some more pictures, and we want to do a brain scan
on him."

"My God," Ann said.

"It's perfectly normal procedure in cases like this," this new doctor said.
"We just need to find out for sure why he isn't back awake yet. It's normal
medical procedure, and nothing to be alarmed about. We'll be taking him
down in a few minutes," this doctor said.

In a little while, two orderlies came into the room with a gurney. They
were black-haired, dark-complexioned men in white uniforms, and they said
a few words to each other in a foreign tongue as they unhooked the boy
from the tube and moved him from his bed to the gurney. Then they
wheeled him from the room. Howard and Ann got on the same elevator.
Ann gazed at the child. She closed her eyes as the elevator began its descent.
The orderlies stood at either end of the gurney without saying anything,
though once one of the men made a comment to the other in their own
language, and the other man nodded slowly in response.

Later that morning, just as the sun was beginning to lighten the windows in the waiting room outside the X-ray department, they brought the
boy out and moved him back up to his room. Howard and Ann rode up on
the elevator with him once more, and once more they took up their places
beside the bed.

They waited all day, but still the boy did not wake up. Occasionally,   60
one of them would leave the room to go downstairs to the cafeteria to drink
coffee and then, as if suddenly remembering and feeling guilty, get up from
the table and hurry back to the room. Dr. Francis came again that afternoon
and examined the boy once more and then left after telling them he was
coming along and could wake up at any minute now. Nurses, different nurses
from the night before, came in from time to time. Then a young woman
from the lab knocked and entered the room. She wore white slacks and a
white blouse and carried a little tray of things which she put on the stand
beside the bed. Without a word to them, she took blood from the boy's arm.
Howard closed his eyes as the woman found the right place on the boy's arm
and pushed the needle in.

"I don't understand this," Ann said to the woman.

"Doctor's orders," the young woman said. "I do what I'm told. They
say draw that one, I draw. What's wrong with him, anyway?" she said. "He's
a sweetie."

"He was hit by a car," Howard said. "A hit-and-run."

The young woman shook her head and looked again at the boy. Then
she took her tray and left the room.

"Why won't he wake up?" Ann said. "Howard? I want some answers   65
from these people."

Howard didn't say anything. He sat down again in the chair and crossed one leg over the other. He rubbed his face. He looked at his son and then he settled back in the chair, closed his eyes, and went to sleep.

Ann walked to the window and looked out at the parking lot. It was night, and cars were driving into and out of the parking lot with their lights on. She stood at the window with her hands gripping the sill, and knew in her heart that they were into something now, something hard. She was afraid, and her teeth began to chatter until she tightened her jaws. She saw a big car stop in front of the hospital and someone, a woman in a long coat, get into the car. She wished she were that woman and somebody, anybody, was driving her away from here to somewhere else, a place where she would find Scotty waiting for her when she stepped out of the car, ready to say *Mom* and let her gather him in her arms.

In a little while, Howard woke up. He looked at the boy again. Then he got up from the chair, stretched, and went over to stand beside her at the window. They both stared out at the parking lot. They didn't say anything. But they seemed to feel each other's insides now, as though the worry had made them transparent in a perfectly natural way.

The door opened and Dr. Francis came in. He was wearing a different suit and tie this time. His gray hair was combed along the sides of his head, and he looked as if he had just shaved. He went straight to the bed and examined the boy. "He ought to have come around by now. There's just no good reason for this," he said. "But I can tell you we're all convinced he's out of any danger. We'll just feel better when he wakes up. There's no reason, absolutely none, why he shouldn't come around. Very soon. Oh, he'll have himself a dilly of a headache when he does, you can count on that. But all of his signs are fine. They're as normal as can be."

"It is a coma, then?" Ann said. 70

The doctor rubbed his smooth cheek. "We'll call it that for the time being, until he wakes up. But you must be worn out. This is hard. I know this is hard. Feel free to go out for a bite," he said. "It would do you good. I'll put a nurse in here while you're gone if you'll feel better about going. Go and have yourselves something to eat."

"I couldn't eat anything," Ann said.

"Do what you need to do, of course," the doctor said. "Anyway, I wanted to tell you that all the signs are good, the tests are negative, nothing showed up at all, and just as soon as he wakes up he'll be over the hill."

"Thank you, doctor," Howard said. He shook hands with the doctor again. The doctor patted Howard's shoulder and went out.

"I suppose one of us should go home and check on things," Howard 75 said. "Slug needs to be fed, for one thing."

"Call one of the neighbors," Ann said. "Call the Morgans. Anyone will feed a dog if you ask them to."

"All right," Howard said. After a while, he said, "Honey, why don't *you* do it? Why don't you go home and check on things, and then come back?

It'll do you good. I'll be right here with him. Seriously," he said. "We need to keep up our strength on this. We'll want to be here for a while even after he wakes up."

"Why don't *you* go?" she said. "Feed Slug. Feed yourself."

"I already went," he said. "I was gone for exactly an hour and fifteen minutes. You go home for an hour and freshen up. Then come back."

She tried to think about it, but she was too tired. She closed her eyes   *80* and tried to think about it again. After a time, she said, "Maybe I *will* go home for a few minutes. Maybe if I'm not just sitting right here watching him every second, he'll wake up and be all right. You know? Maybe he'll wake up if I'm not here. I'll go home and take a bath and put on clean clothes. I'll feed Slug. Then I'll come back."

"I'll be right here," he said. "You go on home, honey. I'll keep an eye on things here." His eyes were bloodshot and small, as if he'd been drinking for a long time. His clothes were rumpled. His beard had come out again. She touched his face, and then she took her hand back. She understood he wanted to be by himself for a while, not have to talk or share his worry for a time. She picked her purse up from the nightstand, and he helped her into her coat.

"I won't be gone long," she said.

"Just sit and rest for a little while when you get home," he said. "Eat something. Take a bath. After you get out of the bath, just sit for a while and rest. It'll do you a world of good, you'll see. Then come back," he said. "Let's try not to worry. You heard what Dr. Francis said."

She stood in her coat for a minute trying to recall the doctor's exact words, looking for any nuances, any hint of something behind his words other than what he had said. She tried to remember if his expression had changed any when he bent over to examine the child. She remembered the way his features had composed themselves as he rolled back the child's eyelids and then listened to his breathing.

She went to the door, where she turned and looked back. She looked   *85* at the child, and then she looked at the father. Howard nodded. She stepped out of the room and pulled the door closed behind her.

She went past the nurses' station and down to the end of the corridor, looking for the elevator. At the end of the corridor, she turned to her right and entered a little waiting room where a Negro family sat in wicker chairs. There was a middle-aged man in a khaki shirt and pants, a baseball cap pushed back on his head. A large woman wearing a housedress and slippers was slumped in one of the chairs. A teenaged girl in jeans, hair done in dozens of little braids, lay stretched out in one of the chairs smoking a cigarette, her legs crossed at the ankles. The family swung their eyes to Ann as she entered the room. The little table was littered with hamburger wrappers and Styrofoam cups.

"Franklin," the large woman said as she roused herself. "Is it about Franklin?" Her eyes widened. "Tell me now, lady," the woman said. "Is it about Franklin?" She was trying to rise from her chair, but the man had closed his hand over her arm.

"Here, here," he said. "Evelyn."

"I'm sorry," Ann said. "I'm looking for the elevator. My son is in the hospital, and now I can't find the elevator."

"Elevator is down that way, turn left," the man said as he aimed a finger.   90

The girl drew on her cigarette and stared at Ann. Her eyes were narrowed to slits, and her broad lips parted slowly as she let the smoke escape. The Negro woman let her head fall on her shoulder and looked away from Ann, no longer interested.

"My son was hit by a car," Ann said to the man. She seemed to need to explain herself. "He has a concussion and a little skull fracture, but he's going to be all right. He's in shock now, but it might be some kind of coma, too. That's what really worries us, the coma part. I'm going out for a little while, but my husband is with him. Maybe he'll wake up while I'm gone."

"That's too bad," the man said and shifted in the chair. He shook his head. He looked down at the table, and then he looked back at Ann. She was still standing there. He said, "Our Franklin, he's on the operating table. Somebody cut him. Tried to kill him. There was a fight where he was at. At this party. They say he was just standing and watching. Not bothering nobody. But that don't mean nothing these days. Now he's on the operating table. We're just hoping and praying, that's all we can do now." He gazed at her steadily.

Ann looked at the girl again, who was still watching her, and at the older woman, who kept her head down, but whose eyes were now closed. Ann saw the lips moving silently, making words. She had an urge to ask what those words were. She wanted to talk more with these people who were in the same kind of waiting she was in. She was afraid, and they were afraid. They had that in common. She would have liked to have said something else about the accident, told them more about Scotty, that it had happened on the day of his birthday, Monday, and that he was still unconscious. Yet she didn't know how to begin. She stood looking at them without saying anything more.

She went down the corridor the man had indicated and found the   95 elevator. She waited a minute in front of the closed doors, still wondering if she was doing the right thing. Then she put out her finger and touched the button.

She pulled into the driveway and cut the engine. She closed her eyes and leaned her head against the wheel for a minute. She listened to the ticking sounds the engine made as it began to cool. Then she got out of the car. She could hear the dog barking inside the house. She went to the front door, which was unlocked. She went inside and turned on lights and put on a kettle of water for tea. She opened some dogfood and fed Slug on the back porch. The dog ate in hungry little smacks. It kept running into the kitchen to see that she was going to stay. As she sat down on the sofa with her tea, the telephone rang.

"Yes!" she said as she answered. "Hello!"

"Mrs. Weiss," a man's voice said. It was five o'clock in the morning, and she thought she could hear machinery or equipment of some kind in the background.

"Yes, yes! What is it?" she said. "This is Mrs. Weiss. This is she. What is it, please?" She listened to whatever it was in the background. "Is it Scotty, for Christ's sake?"

"Scotty," the man's voice said. "It's about Scotty, yes. It has to do with Scotty, that problem. Have you forgotten about Scotty?" the man said. Then he hung up.

She dialed the hospital's number and asked for the third floor. She demanded information about her son from the nurse who answered the telephone. Then she asked to speak to her husband. It was, she said, an emergency.

She waited, turning the telephone cord in her fingers. She closed her eyes and felt sick at her stomach. She would have to make herself eat. Slug came in from the back porch and lay down near her feet. He wagged his tail. She pulled at his ear while he licked her fingers. Howard was on the line.

"Somebody just called here," she said. She twisted the telephone cord. "He said it was about Scotty," she cried.

"Scotty's fine," Howard told her. "I mean, he's still sleeping. There's been no change. The nurse has been in twice since you've been gone. A nurse or else a doctor. He's all right."

"This man called. He said it was about Scotty," she told him.

"Honey, you rest for a little while, you need the rest. It must be that same caller I had. Just forget it. Come back down here after you've rested. Then we'll have breakfast or something."

"Breakfast," she said. "I don't want any breakfast."

"You know what I mean," he said. "Juice, something. I don't know. I don't know anything, Ann. Jesus, I'm not hungry, either. Ann, it's hard to talk now. I'm standing here at the desk. Dr. Francis is coming again at eight o'clock this morning. He's going to have something to tell us then, something more definite. That's what one of the nurses said. She didn't know any more than that. Ann? Honey, maybe we'll know something more then. At eight o'clock. Come back here before eight. Meanwhile, I'm right here and Scotty's all right. He's still the same," he added.

"I was drinking a cup of tea," she said, "when the telephone rang. They said it was about Scotty. There was a noise in the background. Was there a noise in the background on that call you had, Howard?"

"I don't remember," he said. "Maybe the driver of the car, maybe he's a psychopath and found out about Scotty somehow. But I'm here with him. Just rest like you were going to do. Take a bath and come back by seven or so, and we'll talk to the doctor together when he gets here. It's going to be all right, honey. I'm here, and there are doctors and nurses around. They say his condition is stable."

"I'm scared to death," she said.

She ran water, undressed, and got into the tub. She washed and dried quickly, not taking the time to wash her hair. She put on clean underwear, wool slacks, and a sweater. She went into the living room, where the dog looked up at her and let its tail thump once against the floor. It was just starting to get light outside when she went out to the car.

She drove into the parking lot of the hospital and found a space close to the front door. She felt she was in some obscure way responsible for what had happened to the child. She let her thoughts move to the Negro family. She remembered the name Franklin and the table that was covered with hamburger papers, and the teenaged girl staring at her as she drew on her cigarette. "Don't have children," she told the girl's image as she entered the front door of the hospital. "For God's sake, don't."

She took the elevator up to the third floor with two nurses who were just going on duty. It was Wednesday morning, a few minutes before seven. There was a page for a Dr. Madison as the elevator doors slid open on the third floor. She got off behind the nurses, who turned in the other direction and continued the conversation she had interrupted when she'd gotten into the elevator. She walked down the corridor to the little alcove where the Negro family had been waiting. They were gone now, but the chairs were scattered in such a way that it looked as if people had just jumped up from them the minute before. The tabletop was cluttered with the same cups and papers, the ashtray was filled with cigarette butts.

She stopped at the nurses' station. A nurse was standing behind the counter, brushing her hair and yawning. 115

"There was a Negro boy in surgery last night," Ann said. "Franklin was his name. His family was in the waiting room. I'd like to inquire about his condition."

A nurse who was sitting at a desk behind the counter looked up from a chart in front of her. The telephone buzzed and she picked up the receiver, but she kept her eyes on Ann.

"He passed away," said the nurse at the counter. The nurse held the hairbrush and kept looking at her. "Are you a friend of the family or what?"

"I met the family last night," Ann said. "My own son is in the hospital. I guess he's in shock. We don't know for sure what's wrong. I just wondered about Franklin, that's all. Thank you." She moved down the corridor. Elevator doors the same color as the walls slid open and a gaunt, bald man in white pants and white canvas shoes pulled a heavy cart off the elevator. She hadn't noticed these doors last night. The man wheeled the cart out into the corridor and stopped in front of the room nearest the elevator and consulted a clipboard. Then he reached down and slid a tray out of the cart. He rapped lightly on the door and entered the room. She could smell the unpleasant odors of warm food as she passed the cart. She hurried on without looking at any of the nurses and pushed open the door to the child's room.

Howard was standing at the window with his hands behind his back.   *120* He turned around as she came in.

"How is he?" she said. She went over to the bed. She dropped her purse on the floor beside the nightstand. It seemed to her she had been gone a long time. She touched the child's face. "Howard?"

"Dr. Francis was here a little while ago," Howard said. She looked at him closely and thought his shoulders were bunched a little.

"I thought he wasn't coming until eight o'clock this morning," she said quickly.

"There was another doctor with him. A neurologist."

"A neurologist," she said.   *125*

Howard nodded. His shoulders were bunching, she could see that. "What'd they say, Howard? For Christ's sake, what'd they say? What is it?"

"They said they're going to take him down and run more tests on him, Ann. They think they're going to operate, honey. Honey, they *are* going to operate. They can't figure out why he won't wake up. It's more than just shock or concussion, they know that much now. It's in his skull, the fracture, it has something, something to do with that, they think. So they're going to operate. I tried to call you, but I guess you'd already left the house."

"Oh, God," she said. "Oh, please, Howard, please," she said, taking his arms.

"Look!" Howard said. "Scotty! Look, Ann!" He turned her toward the bed.

The boy had opened his eyes, then closed them. He opened them again   *130* now. The eyes stared straight ahead for a minute, then moved slowly in his head until they rested on Howard and Ann, then traveled away again.

"Scotty," his mother said, moving to the bed.

"Hey, Scott," his father said. "Hey, son."

They leaned over the bed. Howard took the child's hand in his hands and began to pat and squeeze the hand. Ann bent over the boy and kissed his forehead again and again. She put her hands on either side of his face. "Scotty, honey, it's Mommy and Daddy," she said. "Scotty?"

The boy looked at them, but without any sign of recognition. Then his mouth opened, his eyes scrunched closed, and he howled until he had no more air in his lungs. His face seemed to relax and soften then. His lips parted as his last breath was puffed through his throat and exhaled gently through the clenched teeth.

The doctors called it a hidden occlusion and said it was a one-in-a-   *135* million circumstance. Maybe if it could have been detected somehow and surgery undertaken immediately, they could have saved him. But more than likely not. In any case, what would they have been looking for? Nothing had shown up in the tests or in the X-rays.

Dr. Francis was shaken. "I can't tell you how badly I feel. I'm so very sorry, I can't tell you," he said as he led them into the doctors' lounge. There was a doctor sitting in a chair with his legs hooked over the back of another chair, watching an early-morning TV show. He was wearing a green delivery-room outfit, loose green pants and green blouse, and a green cap that covered his hair. He looked at Howard and Ann and then looked at Dr. Francis. He got to his feet and turned off the set and went out of the room. Dr. Francis guided Ann to the sofa, sat down beside her, and began to talk in a low, consoling voice. At one point, he leaned over and embraced her. She could feel his chest rising and falling evenly against her shoulder. She kept her eyes open and let him hold her. Howard went into the bathroom, but he left the door open. After a violent fit of weeping, he ran water and washed his face. Then he came out and sat down at the little table that held a telephone. He looked at the telephone as though deciding what to do first. He made some calls. After a time, Dr. Francis used the telephone.

"Is there anything else I can do for the moment?" he asked them.

Howard shook his head. Ann stared at Dr. Francis as if unable to comprehend his words.

The doctor walked them to the hospital's front door. People were entering and leaving the hospital. It was eleven o'clock in the morning. Ann was aware of how slowly, almost reluctantly, she moved her feet. It seemed to her that Dr. Francis was making them leave when she felt they should stay, when it would be more the right thing to do to stay. She gazed out into the parking lot and then turned around and looked back at the front of the hospital. She began shaking her head. "No, no," she said. "I can't leave him here, no." She heard herself say that and thought how unfair it was that the only words that came out were the sort of words used on TV shows where people were stunned by violent or sudden deaths. She wanted her words to be her own. "No," she said, and for some reason the memory of the Negro woman's head lolling on the woman's shoulder came to her. "No," she said again.

"I'll be talking to you later in the day," the doctor was saying to How- 140
ard. "There are still some things that have to be done, things that have to be cleared up to our satisfaction. Some things that need explaining."

"An autopsy," Howard said.

Dr. Francis nodded.

"I understand," Howard said. Then he said, "Oh, Jesus. No, I don't understand, doctor. I can't, I can't. I just can't."

Dr. Francis put his arm around Howard's shoulders. "I'm sorry. God, how I'm sorry." He let go of Howard's shoulders and held out his hand. Howard looked at the hand, and then he took it. Dr. Francis put his arms around Ann once more. He seemed full of some goodness she didn't understand. She let her head rest on his shoulder, but her eyes stayed open. She kept looking at the hospital. As they drove out of the parking lot, she looked back at the hospital.

At home, she sat on the sofa with her hands in her coat pockets. *145*
Howard closed the door to the child's room. He got the coffee-maker going
and then he found an empty box. He had thought to pick up some of the
child's things that were scattered around the living room. But instead he sat
down beside her on the sofa, pushed the box to one side, and leaned forward,
arms between his knees. He began to weep. She pulled his head over into
her lap and patted his shoulder. "He's gone," she said. She kept patting his
shoulder. Over his sobs, she could hear the coffee-maker hissing in the
kitchen. "There, there," she said tenderly. "Howard, he's gone. He's gone
and now we'll have to get used to that. To being alone."

In a little while, Howard got up and began moving aimlessly around
the room with the box, not putting anything into it, but collecting some
things together on the floor at one end of the sofa. She continued to sit with
her hands in her coat pockets. Howard put the box down and brought coffee
into the living room. Later, Ann made calls to relatives. After each call had
been placed and the party had answered, Ann would blurt out a few words
and cry for a minute. Then she would quietly explain, in a measured voice,
what had happened and tell them about arrangements. Howard took the box
out to the garage, where he saw the child's bicycle. He dropped the box and
sat down on the pavement beside the bicycle. He took hold of the bicycle
awkwardly so that it leaned against his chest. He held it, the rubber pedal
sticking into his chest. He gave the wheel a turn.

Ann hung up the telephone after talking to her sister. She was looking up another number when the telephone rang. She picked it up on the
first ring.

"Hello," she said, and she heard something in the background, a humming noise. "Hello!" she said. "For God's sake," she said. "Who is this? What
is it you want?"

"Your Scotty, I got him ready for you," the man's voice said. "Did you
forget him?"

"You evil bastard!" she shouted into the receiver. "How can you do *150*
this, you evil son of a bitch?"

"Scotty," the man said. "Have you forgotten about Scotty?" Then the
man hung up on her.

Howard heard the shouting and came in to find her with her head on
her arms over the table, weeping. He picked up the receiver and listened to
the dial tone.

Much later, just before midnight, after they had dealt with many things,
the telephone rang again.

"You answer it," she said. "Howard, it's him, I know." They were sitting
at the kitchen table with coffee in front of them. Howard had a small glass
of whiskey beside his cup. He answered on the third ring.

"Hello," he said. "Who is this? Hello! Hello!" The line went dead. "He *155*
hung up," Howard said. "Whoever it was."

"It was him," she said. "That bastard. I'd like to kill him," she said. "I'd like to shoot him and watch him kick," she said.

"Ann, my God," he said.

"Could you hear anything?" she said. "In the background? A noise, machinery, something humming?"

"Nothing, really. Nothing like that," he said. "There wasn't much time. I think there was some radio music. Yes, there was a radio going, that's all I could tell. I don't know what in God's name is going on," he said.

She shook her head. "If I could, could get my hands on him." It came to her then. She knew who it was. Scotty, the cake, the telephone number. She pushed the chair away from the table and got up. "Drive me down to the shopping center," she said. "Howard." *160*

"What are you saying?"

"The shopping center. I know who it is who's calling. I know who it is. It's the baker, the son-of-a-bitching baker, Howard. I had him bake a cake for Scotty's birthday. That's who's calling. That's who has the number and keeps calling us. To harass us about that cake. The baker, that bastard."

They drove down to the shopping center. The sky was clear and stars were out. It was cold, and they ran the heater in the car. They parked in front of the bakery. All of the shops and stores were closed, but there were cars at the far end of the lot in front of the movie theater. The bakery windows were dark, but when they looked through the glass they could see a light in the back room and, now and then, a big man in an apron moving in and out of the white, even light. Through the glass, she could see the display cases and some little tables with chairs. She tried the door. She rapped on the glass. But if the baker heard them, he gave no sign. He didn't look in their direction.

They drove around behind the bakery and parked. They got out of the car. There was a lighted window too high up for them to see inside. A sign near the back door said THE PANTRY BAKERY, SPECIAL ORDERS. She could hear faintly a radio playing inside and something creak—an oven door as it was pulled down? She knocked on the door and waited. Then she knocked again, louder. The radio was turned down and there was a scraping sound now, the distinct sound of something, a drawer, being pulled open and then closed.

Someone unlocked the door and opened it. The baker stood in the light and peered out at them. "I'm closed for business," he said. "What do you want at this hour? It's midnight. Are you drunk or something?" *165*

She stepped into the light that fell through the open door. He blinked his heavy eyelids as he recognized her. "It's you," he said.

"It's me," she said. "Scotty's mother. This is Scotty's father. We'd like to come in."

The baker said, "I'm busy now. I have work to do."

She had stepped inside the doorway anyway. Howard came in behind her. The baker moved back. "It smells like a bakery in here. Doesn't it smell like a bakery in here, Howard?"

"What do you want?" the baker said. "Maybe you want your cake? *170* That's it, you decided you want your cake. You ordered a cake, didn't you?"

"You're pretty smart for a baker," she said. "Howard, this is the man who's been calling us." She clenched her fists. She stared at him fiercely. There was a deep burning inside her, an anger that made her feel larger than herself, larger than either of these men.

"Just a minute here," the baker said. "You want to pick up your three-day-old cake? That it? I don't want to argue with you, lady. There it sits over there, getting stale. I'll give it to you for half of what I quoted you. No. You want it? You can have it. It's no good to me, no good to anyone now. It cost me time and money to make that cake. If you want it, okay, if you don't that's okay, too. I have to get back to work." He looked at them and rolled his tongue behind his teeth.

"More cakes," she said. She knew she was in control of it, of what was increasing in her. She was calm.

"Lady, I work sixteen hours a day in this place to earn a living," the baker said. He wiped his hands on his apron. "I work night and day in here, trying to make ends meet." A look crossed Ann's face that made the baker move back and say, "No trouble, now." He reached to the counter and picked up a rolling pin with his right hand and began to tap it against the palm of his other hand. "You want the cake or not? I have to get back to work. Bakers work at night," he said again. His eyes were small, mean-looking, she thought, nearly lost in the bristly flesh around his cheeks. His neck was thick with fat.

"I know bakers work at night," Ann said. "They make phone calls at *175* night, too. You bastard," she said.

The baker continued to tap the rolling pin against his hand. He glanced at Howard. "Careful, careful," he said to Howard.

"My son's dead," she said with a cold, even finality. "He was hit by a car Monday morning. We've been waiting with him until he died. But, of course, you couldn't be expected to know that, could you? Bakers can't know everything—can they, Mr. Baker? But he's dead. He's dead, you bastard!" Just as suddenly as it had welled in her, the anger dwindled, gave way to something else, a dizzy feeling of nausea. She leaned against the wooden table that was sprinkled with flour, put her hands over her face, and began to cry, her shoulders rocking back and forth. "It isn't fair," she said. "It isn't, isn't fair."

Howard put his hand at the small of her back and looked at the baker. "Shame on you," Howard said to him. "Shame."

The baker put the rolling pin back on the counter. He undid his apron and threw it on the counter. He looked at them, and then he shook his head slowly. He pulled a chair out from under the card table that held papers and receipts, an adding machine, and a telephone directory. "Please sit down," he said. "Let me get you a chair," he said to Howard. "Sit down now, please." The baker went into the front of the shop and returned with two little wrought-iron chairs. "Please sit down, you people."

Ann wiped her eyes and looked at the baker. "I wanted to kill you," *180* she said. "I wanted you dead."

The baker had cleared a space for them at the table. He shoved the adding machine to one side, along with the stacks of notepaper and receipts. He pushed the telephone directory onto the floor, where it landed with a thud. Howard and Ann sat down and pulled their chairs up to the table. The baker sat down, too.

"Let me say how sorry I am," the baker said, putting his elbows on the table. "God alone knows how sorry. Listen to me. I'm just a baker. I don't claim to be anything else. Maybe once, maybe years ago, I was a different kind of human being. I've forgotten, I don't know for sure. But I'm not any longer, if I ever was. Now I'm just a baker. That don't excuse my doing what I did, I know. But I'm deeply sorry. I'm sorry for your son, and sorry for my part in this," the baker said. He spread his hands out on the table and turned them over to reveal his palms. "I don't have any children myself, so I can only imagine what you must be feeling. All I can say to you now is that I'm sorry. Forgive me, if you can," the baker said. "I'm not an evil man, I don't think. Not evil, like you said on the phone. You got to understand what it comes down to is I don't know how to act anymore, it would seem. Please," the man said, "let me ask you if you can find it in your hearts to forgive me?"

It was warm inside the bakery. Howard stood up from the table and took off his coat. He helped Ann from her coat. The baker looked at them for a minute and then nodded and got up from the table. He went to the oven and turned off some switches. He found cups and poured coffee from an electric coffee-maker. He put a carton of cream on the table, and a bowl of sugar.

"You probably need to eat something," the baker said. "I hope you'll eat some of my hot rolls. You have to eat and keep going. Eating is a small, good thing in a time like this," he said.

He served them warm cinnamon rolls just out of the oven, the icing *185* still runny. He put butter on the table and knives to spread the butter. Then the baker sat down at the table with them. He waited. He waited until they each took a roll from the platter and began to eat. "It's good to eat something," he said, watching them. "There's more. Eat up. Eat all you want. There's all the rolls in the world in here."

They ate rolls and drank coffee. Ann was suddenly hungry, and the rolls were warm and sweet. She ate three of them, which pleased the baker. Then he began to talk. They listened carefully. Although they were tired and in anguish, they listened to what the baker had to say. They nodded when the baker began to speak of loneliness, and of the sense of doubt and limitation that had come to him in his middle years. He told them what it was like to be childless all these years. To repeat the days with the ovens endlessly full and endlessly empty. The party food, the celebrations he'd worked over. Icing knuckle-deep. The tiny wedding couples stuck into cakes. Hundreds of them, no, thousands by now. Birthdays. Just imagine all those candles burning. He had a necessary trade. He was a baker. He was glad he wasn't a florist. It was better to be feeding people. This was a better smell anytime than flowers.

"Smell this," the baker said, breaking open a dark loaf. "It's a heavy bread, but rich." They smelled it, then he had them taste it. It had the taste of molasses and coarse grains. They listened to him. They ate what they could. They swallowed the dark bread. It was like daylight under the fluorescent trays of light. They talked on into the early morning, the high, pale cast of light in the windows, and they did not think of leaving.

The Responsive Reader

1. How does Carver describe the accident? Does it seem like an ordinary event that could happen any time? How do the parents react? Do they seem like ordinary normal people?
2. Many people have negative feelings about hospitals. In much modern writing, they are described as cold, hostile, impersonal institutions. How do you normally feel about hospitals? How does Carver make you feel about the hospital and its personnel in this story?
3. What is the role in the story of the boy that was knifed and of his family?
4. What kind of person is the baker? What is his role in the story? How would you normally feel about someone like him? How does this story make you feel about him?

Thinking, Talking, Writing

5. Do you think that what the baker did at the end of the story did any good? How much good are expressions of sympathy in situations like the one in this story? What difference does it make to the story that the man is a baker?
6. What is the meaning of the title?
7. The cake plays a major role in the story. Do you think it is a symbol? What could be its symbolic meaning?
8. Carver says that at the end of the story the couple "listened carefully" to the baker. How good a listener are you in similar situations? Have you ever in time of need encountered someone who is a good listener?

Collaborative Projects

9. What information or research is available on childhood accidents?

THE YELLOW WALLPAPER

Charlotte Perkins Gilman

The following story was first published in 1892, and readers at one time read it as a nineteenth-century horror story. The woman narrator traces in agonizing detail her struggle against and her final descent into madness. We watch with growing horror as we see the surreal events of the story unfold and we begin to understand what is happening.

However, the author was a leading early feminist, from a family of suffragists—women fighting for the right to vote. One of her great-aunts was Harriett Beecher Stowe, the abolitionist author of Uncle Tom's Cabin. *Gilman's story early raised a question that many feminists have asked since: How much of what was called mental illness in women was induced by a repressive society? How many of women's "emotional problems" were caused or made worse by misguided treatment by insensitive males like the doctor-husband in this story? The story was autobiographical in part. Gilman had suffered from a severe postpartum depression after the birth of a daughter in 1884. The Weir Mitchell mentioned as the expert in the story prescribed a rest cure with bed rest and no physical exertion or intellectual stimulation. Gilman later said that this therapy drove her "so near the borderline of mental ruin" that she "could see over."*

It is very seldom that mere ordinary people like John and myself secure   *1*
ancestral halls for the summer.

A colonial mansion, a hereditary estate, I would say a haunted house, and reach the height of romantic felicity—but that would be asking too much of fate!

Still I will proudly declare that there is something queer about it.

Else, why should it be let so cheaply? And why have stood so long untenanted?

John laughs at me, of course, but one expects that in marriage.   *5*

John is practical in the extreme. He has no patience with faith, an intense horror of superstition, and he scoffs openly at any talk of things not to be felt and seen and put down in figures.

John is a physician, and *perhaps*—(I would not say it to a living soul, of course, but this is dead paper and a great relief to my mind—) *perhaps* that is one reason I do not get well faster.

You see he does not believe I am sick!

And what can one do?

If a physician of high standing, and one's own husband, assures friends   *10*
and relatives that there is really nothing the matter with one but temporary nervous depression—a slight hysterical tendency—what is one to do?

My brother is also a physician, and also of high standing, and he says the same thing.

So I take phosphates or phosphites—whichever it is, and tonics, and journeys, and air, and exercise, and am absolutely forbidden to "work" until I am well again.

Personally, I disagree with their ideas.

Personally, I believe that congenial work, with excitement and change, would do me good.

But what is one to do?   15

I did write for a while in spite of them; but it *does* exhaust me a good deal—having to be so sly about it, or else meet with heavy opposition.

I sometimes fancy that in my condition if I had less opposition and more society and stimulus—but John says the very worst thing I can do is to think about my condition, and I confess it always makes me feel bad.

So I will let it alone and talk about the house.

The most beautiful place! It is quite alone, standing well back from the road, quite three miles from the village. It makes me think of English places that you read about, for there are hedges and walls and gates that lock, and lots of separate little houses for the gardeners and people.

There is a *delicious* garden! I never saw such a garden—large and shady,   20
full of box-bordered paths, and lined with long grape-covered arbors with seats under them.

There were greenhouses, too, but they are all broken now.

There was some legal trouble, I believe, something about the heirs and coheirs; anyhow, the place has been empty for years.

That spoils my ghostliness, I am afraid, but I don't care—there is something strange about the house—I can feel it.

I even said so to John one moonlight evening, but he said what I felt was a *draught,* and shut the window.

I get unreasonably angry with John sometimes. I'm sure I never used   25
to be so sensitive. I think it is due to this nervous condition.

But John says if I feel so, I shall neglect proper self-control; so I take pains to control myself—before him, at least, and that makes me very tired.

I don't like our room a bit. I wanted one downstairs that opened on the piazza and had roses all over the window, and such pretty old-fashioned chintz hangings! but John would not hear of it.

He said there was only one window and not room for two beds, and no near room for him if he took another.

He is very careful and loving, and hardly lets me stir without special direction.

I have a schedule prescription for each hour in the day; he takes all care   30
from me, and so I feel basely ungrateful not to value it more.

He said we came here solely on my account, that I was to have perfect rest and all the air I could get. "Your exercise depends on your strength, my dear," said he, "and your food somewhat on your appetite; but air you can absorb all the time." So we took the nursery at the top of the house.

It is a big, airy room, the whole floor nearly, with windows that look all ways, and air and sunshine galore. It was nursery first and then playroom and gymnasium, I should judge; for the windows are barred for little children, and there are rings and things in the walls.

The paint and paper look as if a boys' school had used it. It is stripped off—the paper—in great patches all around the head of my bed, about as far as I can reach, and in a great place on the other side of the room low down. I never saw a worse paper in my life.

One of those sprawling flamboyant patterns committing every artistic sin.

It is dull enough to confuse the eye in following, pronounced enough 35 to constantly irritate and provoke study, and when you follow the lame uncertain curves for a little distance they suddenly commit suicide—plunge off at outrageous angles, destroy themselves in unheard of contradictions.

The color is repellent, almost revolting; a smouldering unclean yellow, strangely faded by the slow-turning sunlight.

It is a dull yet lurid orange in some places, a sickly sulphur tint in others.

No wonder the children hated it! I should hate it myself if I had to live in this room long.

There comes John, and I must put this away,—he hates to have me write a word.

I

We have been here two weeks, and I haven't felt like writing before, 40 since that first day.

I am sitting by the window now, up in this atrocious nursery, and there is nothing to hinder my writing as much as I please, save lack of strength.

John is away all day, and even some nights when his cases are serious.

I am glad my case is not serious!

But these nervous troubles are dreadfully depressing.

John does not know how much I really suffer. He knows there is no 45 *reason* to suffer, and that satisfies him.

Of course it is only nervousness. It does weigh on me so not to do my duty in any way!

I meant to be such a help to John, such a real rest and comfort, and here I am a comparative burden already!

Nobody would believe what an effort it is to do what little I am able,— to dress and entertain, and order things.

It is fortunate Mary is so good with the baby. Such a dear baby!

And yet I *cannot* be with him, it makes me so nervous. 50

I suppose John never was nervous in his life. He laughs at me so about this wallpaper!

At first he meant to repaper the room, but afterwards he said that I was letting it get the better of me, and that nothing was worse for a nervous patient than to give way to such fancies.

He said that after the wallpaper was changed it would be the heavy bedstead, and then the barred windows, and then that gate at the head of the stairs, and so on.

"You know the place is doing you good," he said, "and really, dear, I don't care to renovate the house just for a three months' rental."

"Then do let us go downstairs," I said, "there are such pretty rooms   55 there."

Then he took me in his arms and called me a blessed little goose, and said he would go down cellar, if I wished, and have it whitewashed into the bargain.

But he is right enough about the beds and windows and things.

It is as airy and comfortable room as any one need wish, and, of course, I would not be so silly as to make him uncomfortable just for a whim.

I'm really getting quite fond of the big room, all but that horrid paper.

Out of one window I can see the garden, those mysterious deep-shaded   60 arbors, the riotous old-fashioned flowers, and bushes and gnarly trees.

Out of another I get a lovely view of the bay and a little private wharf belonging to the estate. There is a beautiful shaded lane that runs down there from the house. I always fancy I see people walking in these numerous paths and arbors, but John has cautioned me not to give way to fancy in the least. He says that with my imaginative power and habit of story-making, a nervous weakness like mine is sure to lead to all manner of excited fancies, and that I ought to use my will and good sense to check the tendency. So I try.

I think sometimes that if I were only well enough to write a little it would relieve the press of ideas and rest me.

But I find I get pretty tired when I try.

It is so discouraging not to have any advice and companionship about my work. When I get really well, John says we will ask Cousin Henry and Julia down for a long visit; but he says he would as soon put fireworks in my pillow-case as to let me have those stimulating people about now.

I wish I could get well faster.   65

But I must not think about that. This paper looks to me as if it *knew* what a vicious influence it had!

There is a recurrent spot where the pattern lolls like a broken neck and two bulbous eyes stare at you upside down.

I get positively angry with the impertinence of it and the everlastingness. Up and down and sideways they crawl, and those absurd, unblinking eyes are everywhere. There is one place where two breadths didn't match, and the eyes go all up and down the line, one a little higher than the other.

I never saw so much expression in an inanimate thing before, and we all know how much expression they have! I used to lie awake as a child and get more entertainment and terror out of blank walls and plain furniture than most children could find in a toy-store.

I remember what a kindly wink the knobs of our big, old bureau used to have, and there was one chair that always seemed like a strong friend.

I used to feel that if any of the other things looked too fierce I could always hop into that chair and be safe.

The furniture in this room is no worse than inharmonious, however, for we had to bring it all from downstairs. I suppose when this was used as a playroom they had to take the nursery things out, and no wonder! I never saw such ravages as the children have made here.

The wallpaper, as I said before, is torn off in spots, and it sticketh closer than a brother—they must have had perseverance as well as hatred.

Then the floor is scratched and gouged and splintered, the plaster itself is dug out here and there, and this great heavy bed which is all we found in the room, looks as if it had been through the wars.

But I don't mind it a bit—only the paper.

There comes John's sister. Such a dear girl as she is, and so careful of me! I must not let her find me writing.

She is a perfect and enthusiastic housekeeper, and hopes for no better profession. I verily believe she thinks it is the writing which made me sick!

But I can write when she is out, and see her a long way off from these windows.

There is one that commands the road, a lovely shaded winding road, and one that just looks off over the country. A lovely country, too, full of great elms and velvet meadows.

This wallpaper has a kind of subpattern in a different shade, a particularly irritating one, for you can only see it in certain lights, and not clearly then.

But in the places where it isn't faded and where the sun is just so—I can see a strange, provoking, formless sort of figure, that seems to skulk about behind that silly and conspicuous front design.

There's sister on the stairs!

II

Well, the Fourth of July is over! The people are all gone and I am tired out. John thought it might do me good to see a little company, so we just had mother and Nellie and the children down for a week.

Of course I didn't do a thing. Jennie sees to everything now.

But it tired me all the same.

John says if I don't pick up faster he shall send me to Weir Mitchell in the fall.

But I don't want to go there at all. I had a friend who was in his hands once, and she says he is just like John and my brother, only more so!

Besides, it is such an undertaking to go so far.

I don't feel as if it was worth while to turn my hand over for anything, and I'm getting dreadfully fretful and querulous.

I cry at nothing, and cry most of the time.   *90*

Of course I don't when John is here, or anybody else, but when I am alone.

And I am alone a good deal just now. John is kept in town very often by serious cases, and Jennie is good and lets me alone when I want her to.

So I walk a little in the garden or down that lovely lane, sit on the porch under the roses, and lie down up here a good deal.

I'm getting really fond of the room in spite of the wallpaper. Perhaps *because* of the wallpaper.

It dwells in my mind so!   *95*

I lie here on this great immovable bed—it is nailed down, I believe— and follow that pattern about by the hour. It is as good as gymnastics, I assure you. I start, we'll say, at the bottom, down in the corner over there where it has not been touched, and I determine for the thousandth time that I *will* follow that pointless pattern to some sort of a conclusion.

I know a little of the principle of design, and I know this thing was not arranged on any laws of radiation, or alternation, or repetition, or symmetry, or anything else that I ever heard of.

It is repeated, of course, by the breadths, but not otherwise.

Looked at in one way each breadth stands alone, the bloated curves and flourishes—a kind of "debased Romanesque" with *delirium tremens* go wad- dling up and down in isolated columns of fatuity.

But, on the other hand, they connect diagonally, and the sprawling   *100* outlines run off in great slanting waves of optic horror, like a lot of wallowing seaweeds in full chase.

The whole thing goes horizontally, too, at least it seems so, and I exhaust myself in trying to distinguish the order of its going in that direction.

They have used a horizontal breadth for a frieze, and that adds won- derfully to the confusion.

There is one end of the room where it is almost intact, and there, when the crosslights fade and the low sun shines directly upon it, I can almost fancy radiation after all,—the interminable grotesques seem to form around a com- mon center and rush off in headlong plunges of equal distraction.

It makes me tired to follow it. I will take a nap I guess.

III

I don't know why I should write this.   *105*

I don't want to.

I don't feel able.

And I know John would think it absurd. But I *must* say what I feel and think in some way—it is such a relief!

But the effort is getting to be greater than the relief.

Half the time now I am awfully lazy, and lie down ever so much.   *110*

John says I mustn't lose my strength, and has me take cod liver oil and lots of tonics and things, to say nothing of ale and wine and rare meat.

Dear John! He loves me very dearly, and hates to have me sick. I tried to have a real earnest reasonable talk with him the other day, and tell him how I wish he would let me go and make a visit to Cousin Henry and Julia.

But he said I wasn't able to go, nor able to stand it after I got there; and I did not make out a very good case for myself, for I was crying before I had finished.

It is getting to be a great effort for me to think straight. Just this nervous weakness I suppose.

And dear John gathered me up in his arms, and just carried me upstairs *115* and laid me on the bed, and sat by me and read to me till it tired my head.

He said I was his darling and his comfort and all he had, and that I must take care of myself for his sake, and keep well.

He says no one but myself can help me out of it, that I must use my will and self-control and not let any silly fancies run away with me.

There's one comfort, the baby is well and happy, and does not have to occupy this nursery with the horrid wallpaper.

If we had not used it, that blessed child would have! What a fortunate escape! Why, I wouldn't have a child of mine, an impressionable little thing, live in such a room for worlds.

I never thought of it before, but it is lucky that John kept me here after *120* all, I can stand it so much easier than a baby, you see.

Of course I never mention it to them any more—I am too wise,—but I keep watch of it all the same.

There are things in that paper that nobody knows but me, or ever will.

Behind that outside pattern the dim shapes get clearer every day.

It is always the same shape, only very numerous.

And it is like a woman stooping down and creeping about behind that *125* pattern. I don't like it a bit. I wonder—I begin to think—I wish John would take me away from here!

IV

It is so hard to talk with John about my case, because he is so wise, and because he loves me so.

But I tried it last night.

It was moonlight. The moon shines in all around just as the sun does.

I hate to see it sometimes, it creeps so slowly, and always comes in by one window or another.

John was asleep and I hated to waken him, so I kept still and watched *130* the moonlight on that undulating wallpaper till I felt creepy.

The faint figure behind seemed to shake the pattern, just as if she wanted to get out.

I got up softly and went to feel and see if the paper *did* move, and when I came back John was awake.

"What is it, little girl?" he said. "Don't go walking about like that—you'll get cold."

I thought it was a good time to talk, so I told him that I really was not gaining here, and that I wished he would take me away.

"Why, darling!" said he, "our lease will be up in three weeks, and I   *135* can't see how to leave before.

"The repairs are not done at home, and I cannot possibly leave town just now. Of course if you were in any danger, I could and would, but you really are better, dear, whether you can see it or not. I am a doctor, dear, and I know. You are gaining flesh and color, your appetite is better, I feel really much easier about you."

"I don't weigh a bit more," said I, "nor as much; and my appetite may be better in the evening when you are here, but it is worse in the morning when you are away!"

"Bless her little heart!" said he with a big hug, "she shall be as sick as she pleases! But now let's improve the shining hours by going to sleep, and talk about it in the morning!"

"And you won't go away?" I asked gloomily.

"Why, how can I, dear? It is only three weeks more and then we will   *140* take a nice little trip of a few days while Jennie is getting the house ready. Really dear you are better!"

"Better in body perhaps—" I began, and stopped short, for he sat up straight and looked at me with such a stern, reproachful look that I could not say another word.

"My darling," said he, "I beg of you, for my sake and for our child's sake, as well as for your own, that you will never for one instant let that idea enter your mind! There is nothing so dangerous, so fascinating, to a temperament like yours. It is a false and foolish fancy. Can you not trust me as a physician when I tell you so?"

So of course I said no more on that score, and we went to sleep before long. He thought I was asleep first, but I wasn't, and lay there for hours trying to decide whether that front pattern and the back pattern really did move together or separately.

V

On a pattern like this, by daylight, there is a lack of sequence, a defiance of law, that is a constant irritant to a normal mind.

The color is hideous enough, and unreliable enough, and infuriating   *145* enough, but the pattern is torturing.

You think you have mastered it, but just as you get well underway in following, it turns a back-somersault and there you are. It slaps you in the face, knocks you down, and tramples upon you. It is like a bad dream.

The outside pattern is a florid arabesque, reminding one of a fungus. If you can imagine a toadstool in joints, an interminable string of toadstools, budding and sprouting in endless convolutions—why, that is something like it.

That is, sometimes!

There is one marked peculiarity about this paper, a thing nobody seems to notice but myself, and that is that it changes as the light changes.

When the sun shoots in through the east window—I always watch for that first long, straight ray—it changes so quickly that I never can quite believe it.

That is why I watch it always.

By moonlight—the moon shines in all night when there is a moon—I wouldn't know it was the same paper.

At night in any kind of light, in twilight, candlelight, lamplight, and worst of all by moonlight, it becomes bars! The outside pattern I mean, and the woman behind it is as plain as can be.

I didn't realize for a long time what the thing was that showed behind, that dim subpattern, but now I am quite sure it is a woman.

By daylight she is subdued, quiet. I fancy it is the pattern that keeps her so still. It is so puzzling. It keeps me quiet by the hour.

I lie down ever so much now. John says it is good for me, and to sleep all I can.

Indeed he started the habit by making me lie down for an hour after each meal.

It is a very bad habit I am convinced, for you see I don't sleep.

And that cultivates deceit, for I don't tell them I'm awake—O no!

The fact is I am getting a little afraid of John.

He seems very queer sometimes, and even Jennie has an inexplicable look.

It strikes me occasionally, just as a scientific hypothesis,—that perhaps it is the paper!

I have watched John when he did not know I was looking, and come into the room suddenly on the most innocent excuses, and I've caught him several times *looking at the paper!* And Jennie too. I caught Jennie with her hand on it once.

She didn't know I was in the room, and when I asked her in a quiet, a very quiet voice, with the most restrained manner possible, what she was doing with the paper—she turned around as if she had been caught stealing, and looked quite angry—asked me why I should frighten her so!

Then she said that the paper stained everything it touched, that she had found yellow smooches on all my clothes and John's, and she wished we would be more careful!

Did not that sound innocent? But I know she was studying that pattern, and I am determined that nobody shall find it out but myself!

VI

Life is very much more exciting now than it used to be. You see I have something more to expect, to look forward to, to watch. I really do eat better, and am more quiet than I was.

John is so pleased to see me improve! He laughed a little the other day, and said I seemed to be flourishing in spite of my wallpaper.

I turned it off with a laugh. I had no intention of telling him it was *because* of the wallpaper—he would make fun of me. He might even want to take me away.

I don't want to leave now until I have found it out. There is a week   *170* more, and I think that will be enough.

VII

I'm feeling ever so much better! I don't sleep much at night, for it is so interesting to watch developments; but I sleep a good deal in the daytime.

In the daytime it is tiresome and perplexing.

There are always new shoots on the fungus, and new shades of yellow all over it. I cannot keep count of them, though I have tried conscientiously.

It is the strangest yellow, that wallpaper! It makes me think of all the yellow things I ever saw—not beautiful ones like buttercups, but old foul, bad yellow things.

But there is something else about that paper—the smell! I noticed it   *175* the moment we came into the room, but with so much air and sun it was not bad. Now we have had a week of fog and rain, and whether the windows are open or not, the smell is here.

It creeps all over the house.

I find it hovering in the dining-room, skulking in the parlor, hiding in the hall, lying in wait for me on the stairs.

It gets into my hair.

Even when I go to ride, if I turn my head suddenly and surprise it— there is that smell!

Such a peculiar odor, too! I have spent hours in trying to analyze it, to   *180* find what it smelled like.

It is not bad—at first, and very gentle, but quite the subtlest, most enduring odor I ever met.

In this damp weather it is awful, I wake up in the night and find it hanging over me.

It used to disturb me at first. I thought seriously of burning the house—to reach the smell.

But now I am used to it. The only thing I can think of that it is like is the *color* of the paper! A yellow smell.

There is a very funny mark on this wall, low down, near the mopboard.   *185*

A streak that runs round the room. It goes behind every piece of furniture, except the bed, a long, straight, even *smooch,* as if it had been rubbed over and over.

I wonder how it was done and who did it, and what they did it for. Round and round and round—round and round and round!—it makes me *dizzy!*

VIII

I really have discovered something at last.

Through watching so much at night, when it changes so, I have finally found out.

The front pattern *does* move—and no wonder! The woman behind shakes it!

Sometimes I think there are a great many women behind, and some-   *190*
times only one, and she crawls around fast, and her crawling shakes it all over.

Then in the very bright spots she keeps still, and in the very shady spots she just takes hold of the bars and shakes them hard.

And she is all the time trying to climb through. But nobody could climb through that pattern—it strangles so; I think that is why it has so many heads.

They get through, and then the pattern strangles them off and turns them upside down, and makes their eyes white!

If those heads were covered or taken off it would not be half so bad.

IX

I think that woman gets out in the daytime!   *195*

And I'll tell you why—privately—I've seen her!

I can see her out of every one of my windows!

It is the same woman, I know, for she is always creeping, and most women do not creep by daylight.

I see her in that long shaded lane, creeping up and down. I see her in those dark grape arbors, creeping all around the garden.

I see her on that long road under the trees, creeping along, and when   *200*
a carriage comes she hides under the blackberry vines.

I don't blame her a bit. It must be very humiliating to be caught creeping by daylight!

I always lock the door when I creep by daylight. I can't do it at night, for I know John would suspect something at once.

And John is so queer now, that I don't want to irritate him. I wish he would take another room! Besides, I don't want anybody to get that woman out at night but myself.

I often wonder if I could see her out of all the windows at once.

But, turn as fast as I can, I can only see out of one at one time.   *205*

And though I always see her, she *may* be able to creep faster than I can turn!

I have watched her sometimes away off in the open country, creeping as fast as a cloud shadow in a high wind.

X

If only that top pattern could be gotten off from the under one! I mean to try it, little by little.

I have found out another funny thing, but I shan't tell it this time! It does not do to trust people too much.

There are only two more days to get this paper off, and I believe John *210* is beginning to notice. I don't like the look in his eyes.

And I heard him ask Jennie a lot of professional questions about me. She had a very good report to give.

She said I slept a good deal in the daytime.

John knows I don't sleep very well at night, for all I'm so quiet!

He asked me all sorts of questions, too, and pretended to be very loving and kind.

As if I couldn't see through him! *215*

Still, I don't wonder he acts so, sleeping under this paper for three months.

It only interests me, but I feel sure John and Jennie are secretly affected by it.

XI

Hurrah! This is the last day, but it is enough. John to stay in town over night, and won't be out until this evening.

Jennie wanted to sleep with me—the sly thing! but I told her I should undoubtedly rest better for a night all alone.

That was clever, for really I wasn't alone a bit! As soon as it was moon- *220* light and that poor thing began to crawl and shake the pattern, I got up and ran to help her.

I pulled and she shook, I shook and she pulled, and before morning we had peeled off yards of that paper.

A strip about as high as my head and half around the room.

And then when the sun came and that awful pattern began to laugh at me, I declared I would finish it today!

We go away tomorrow, and they are moving all my furniture down again to leave things as they were before.

Jennie looked at the wall in amazement, but I told her merrily that I *225* did it out of pure spite at the vicious thing.

She laughed and said she wouldn't mind doing it herself, but I must not get tired.

How she betrayed herself that time!

But I am here, and no person touches this paper but me,—not *alive!*

She tried to get me out of the room—it was too patent! But I said it was so quiet and empty and clean now that I believed I would lie down again and sleep all I could; and not to wake me even for dinner—I would call when I woke.

So now she is gone, and the servants are gone, and the things are gone, 230 and there is nothing left but that great bedstead nailed down, with the canvas mattress we found on it.

We shall sleep downstairs tonight, and take the boat home tomorrow.

I quite enjoy the room, now it is bare again.

How those children did tear about here!

This bedstead is fairly gnawed!

But I must get to work. 235

I have locked the door and thrown the key down into the front path.

I don't want to go out, and I don't want to have anybody come in, till John comes.

I want to astonish him.

I've got a rope up here that even Jennie did not find. If that woman does get out, and tries to get away, I can tie her!

But I forgot I could not reach far without anything to stand on! 240

This bed will *not* move!

I tried to lift and push it until I was lame, and then I got so angry I bit off a little piece at one corner—but it hurt my teeth.

Then I peeled off all the paper I could reach standing on the floor. It sticks horribly and the pattern just enjoys it! All those strangled heads and bulbous eyes and waddling fungus growths just shriek with derision!

I am getting angry enough to do something desperate. To jump out of the window would be admirable exercise, but the bars are too strong even to try.

Besides I wouldn't do it. Of course not. I know well enough that a 245 step like that is improper and might be misconstrued.

I don't like to *look* out of the windows even—there are so many of those creeping women, and they creep so fast.

I wonder if they all come out of that wallpaper as I did?

But I am securely fastened now by my well-hidden rope—you don't get *me* out in the road there!

I suppose I shall have to get back behind the pattern when it comes night, and that is hard!

It is so pleasant to be out in this great room and creep around as I 250 please!

I don't want to go outside. I won't, even if Jennie asks me to.

For outside you have to creep on the ground, and everything is green instead of yellow.

But here I can creep smoothly on the floor, and my shoulder just fits in that long smooch around the wall, so I cannot lose my way.

Why there's John at the door!

It is no use, young man, you can't open it! *255*

How he does call and pound!

Now he's crying for an axe.

It would be a shame to break down that beautiful door!

"John dear!" said I in the gentlest voice, "the key is down by the front steps, under a plaintain leaf!"

That silenced him for a few moments. *260*

Then he said—very quietly indeed, "Open the door, my darling!"

"I can't," said I. "The key is down by the front door under a plaintain leaf!"

And then I said it again, several times, very gently and slowly, and said it so often that he had to go and see, and he got it of course, and came in. He stopped short by the door.

"What is the matter?" he cried. "For God's sake, what are you doing!"

I kept on creeping just the same, but I looked at him over my shoulder. *265*

"I've got out at last," said I, "in spite of you and Jennie! And I've pulled off most of the paper, so you can't put me back!"

Now why should that man have fainted? But he did, and right across my path by the wall, so that I had to creep over him every time!

The Responsive Reader

1. How does the very first page of the story bring the central issue into focus? Why and how do the narrator and her physician-husband disagree about her condition?

2. When do you first become aware that the wallpaper is becoming a central symbol in the story? How does the narrator's perception of it change and develop? Who is the woman behind the wallpaper? What does the wallpaper symbolize?

3. What role does the contrast between the garden and the locked room play in the story? (Why does the narrator herself throw the key away?)

4. Feminist critics have found special meaning in the narrator's being a writer. Why? What role does the woman's writing play in the story?

Thinking, Talking, Writing

5. We usually look at mentally ill people from the outside. What difference does it make to the story that we see everything in it from the point of view of the patient? Can you identify with the woman telling the story?

6. Severe emotional problems or mental illness have in the past often been kept under wraps, with patients and their families hiding the patient's condition as far as possible from the outside world. What has been your own observation of or experience with severe emotional, nervous, or mental disorders?

7. The treatment of mental illness in the past has often been called barbaric. What assumptions about or attitudes toward mental illness are reflected in the media today?

Collaborative Projects

8. What is the fate of the mentally ill in our society today? Working with a group, what answers to this question can you obtain from patients, doctors, technicians, patients' families, and concerned organizations?

TRIFLES

Susan Glaspell

Susan Glaspell is an early twentieth-century playwright who has been praised by today's feminist critics for creating a "woman's version" of events. Like her British contemporary Virginia Woolf, she has become an inspiration to women whose goal is "control over their own bodies and a voice with which to speak about it" (Susan Rubin Suleiman). While male playwrights like the Norwegian Henrik Ibsen and the Irish Bernard Shaw had begun to put women at the center of the stage, Glaspell was one of the first writers to realize that "women would have to exist in a world tailored to their persons and speak a language not borrowed from men" (Enoch Brater).

Born in Iowa, Glaspell attended Drake University in Des Moines and the University of Chicago. Although she did most of her work in the East, she said, "almost everything I write has its roots in the Middle West; I suppose because my own are there." Many of her characters struggle against "fixity and stagnation," trying to move, as their pioneer forebears did, "into a new sphere, if not of place then of spirit" (Enoch Brater). Glaspell was a cofounder of the Provincetown Players, who performed many of her plays as well as early plays by Eugene O'Neill, who was to become one of America's best-known dramatists. Glaspell acted and directed; in 1930 she won the Pulitzer Prize for Alison's House, a play based on the life story of Emily Dickinson. As director of the Chicago office of the Federal Theater Project, she reviewed hundreds of plays and helped in the production of important works by black playwrights.

Glaspell's Trifles (1916) is a play about the different worlds in which men and women live. As the playwright unravels the motives in a murder mystery, the perceptions and interpretations of the male and female characters diverge. The men who represent law enforcement or the legal establishment miss the vital clues that can be read by the women in the play, who are attuned to the ways of thinking and feeling of one of their own. To the men, the central clues to what happened to the murder victim are mere "trifles."

Characters

GEORGE HENDERSON, *County Attorney*
HENRY PETERS, *Sheriff*
LEWIS HALE, *A Neighboring Farmer*
MRS. PETERS
MRS. HALE

THE SETTING *The kitchen in the now abandoned farmhouse of* JOHN WRIGHT

SCENE: *The kitchen in the now abandoned farmhouse of John Wright, a gloomy kitchen, and left without having been put in order—unwashed pans under the sink, a loaf of bread outside the breadbox, a dish towel on the table—other signs of incompleted work. At the rear the outer door opens and the* SHERIFF *comes in followed by the* COUNTY ATTORNEY *and* HALE. *The* SHERIFF *and* HALE *are men in middle life, the* COUNTY ATTORNEY *is a young man; all are much bundled up and go at once to the stove. They are followed by the two women—the* SHERIFF'S *wife first; she is a slight wiry woman, a thin nervous face.* MRS. HALE *is larger and would ordinarily be called more comfortable looking, but she is disturbed now and looks fearfully about as she enters. The women have come in slowly, and stand close together near the door.*

COUNTY ATTORNEY: (*Rubbing his hands*) This feels good. Come up to the fire, ladies.

MRS. PETERS: (*After taking a step forward*) I'm not—cold.

SHERIFF: (*Unbuttoning his overcoat and stepping away from the stove as if to mark the beginning of official business*) Now, Mr. Hale, before we move things about, you explain to Mr. Henderson just what you saw when you came here yesterday morning.

COUNTY ATTORNEY: By the way, has anything been moved? Are things just as you left them yesterday?

SHERIFF: (*Looking about*) It's just the same. When it dropped below zero last night I thought I'd better send Frank out this morning to make a fire for us—no use getting pneumonia with a big case on, but I told him not to touch anything except the stove—and you know Frank.

COUNTY ATTORNEY: Somebody should have been left here yesterday.

SHERIFF: Oh—yesterday. When I had to send Frank to Morris Center for that man who went crazy—I want you to know I had my hands full yesterday, I knew you could get back from Omaha by today and as long as I went over everything here myself—

COUNTY ATTORNEY: Well, Mr. Hale, tell just what happened when you came here yesterday morning.

HALE: Harry and I had started to town with a load of potatoes. We came along the road from my place and as I got here I said, "I'm going to see if I can't get John Wright to go in with me on a party telephone." I spoke to Wright about it once before and he put me off, saying folks talked too much anyway, and all he asked was peace and quiet—I guess you know about how much he talked himself; but I thought maybe if I went to the house and talked about it before his wife, though I said to Harry that I didn't know as what his wife wanted made much difference to John—

COUNTY ATTORNEY: Let's talk about that later, Mr. Hale. I do want to talk about that, but tell now just what happened when you got to the house.

HALE: I didn't hear or see anything; I knocked at the door, and still it was all quiet inside. I knew they must be up, it was past eight o'clock. So I knocked again, and I thought I heard somebody say, "Come in." I wasn't sure, I'm not sure yet, but I opened the door—this door (*indicating the door by which the two women are still standing*) and there in that rocker—(*pointing to it*) sat Mrs. Wright.

(*They all look at the rocker.*)

COUNTY ATTORNEY: What—was she doing?

HALE: She was rockin' back and forth. She had her apron in her hand and was kind of—pleating it.

COUNTY ATTORNEY: And how did she—look?

HALE: Well, she looked queer.

COUNTY ATTORNEY: How do you mean—queer?

HALE: Well, as if she didn't know what she was going to do next. And kind of done up.

COUNTY ATTORNEY: How did she seem to feel about your coming?

HALE: Why, I don't think she minded—one way or other. She didn't pay much attention. I said, "How do, Mrs. Wright, it's cold, ain't it?" And she said, "Is it?"—and went on kind of pleating at her apron. Well, I was surprised; she didn't ask me to come up to the stove, or to set down, but just sat there, not even looking at me, so I said, "I want to see John." And then she—laughed. I guess you would call it a laugh. I thought of Harry and the team outside, so I said a little sharp: "Can't I see John?" "No," she says, kind o'dull like. "Ain't he home?" says I. "Yes," says she, "he's home." "Then why can't I see him?" I asked her, out of patience. "'Cause he's dead," says she. *"Dead?"* says I. She just nodded her head, not getting a bit excited, but rockin' back and forth. "Why—where is he?" says I, not knowing what to say. She just pointed upstairs—like that (*Himself pointing to the room above.*) I got up, with the idea of going up there. I walked from there to here—then I says, "Why, what did he die of?" "He died of a rope round his neck," says she, and just went on pleatin' at her apron. Well, I went out and called Harry. I thought I might—need help. We went upstairs and there he was lyin'—

COUNTY ATTORNEY: I think I'd rather have you go into that upstairs, where you can point it all out. Just go on now with the rest of the story.

HALE: Well, my first thought was to get that rope off. It looked . . . (*Stops, his face twitches*) . . . but Harry, he went up to him, and he said, "No, he's dead all right, and we'd better not touch anything." So we went back down stairs. She was still sitting that same way. "Has anybody been notified?" I asked. "No," says she, unconcerned. "Who did this, Mrs. Wright?" said Harry. He said it businesslike—and she stopped pleatin' of her apron. "I don't know," she says. "You don't *know?"* says

Harry. "No," says she. "Weren't you sleepin' in the bed with him?" says Harry. "Yes," says she, "but I was on the inside." "Somebody slipped a rope round his neck and strangled him and you didn't wake up?" says Harry. "I didn't wake up," she said after him. We must 'a looked as if we didn't see how that could be, for after a minute she said. "I sleep sound." Harry was going to ask her more questions but I said maybe we ought to let her tell her story first to the coroner, or the sheriff, so Harry went fast as he could to Rivers' place, where there's a telephone.

COUNTY ATTORNEY: And what did Mrs. Wright do when she knew that you had gone for the coroner?

HALE: She moved from that chair to this one over here (*Pointing to a small chair in the corner*) and just sat there with her hands held together and looking down. I got a feeling that I ought to make some conversation, so I said I had come in to see if John wanted to put in a telephone, and at that she started to laugh, and then she stopped and looked at me— scared. (*The* COUNTY ATTORNEY, *who has had his notebook out, makes a note.*) I dunno, maybe it wasn't scared. I wouldn't like to say it was. Soon Harry got back, and then Dr. Lloyd came, and you, Mr. Peters, and so I guess that's all I know that you don't.

COUNTY ATTORNEY: (*Looking around*) I guess we'll go upstairs first— and then out to the barn and around there. (*To the* SHERIFF) You're convinced that there was nothing important here—nothing that would point to any motive.

SHERIFF: Nothing here but kitchen things.

(*The* COUNTY ATTORNEY *after again looking around the kitchen, opens the door of a cupboard closet. He gets up on a chair and looks on a shelf. Pulls his hand away, sticky.*)

COUNTY ATTORNEY: Here's a nice mess.

(*The women draw nearer.*)

MRS. PETERS: (*To the other woman*) Oh, her fruit; it did freeze. (*To the* COUNTY ATTORNEY) She worried about that when it turned so cold. She said the fire'd go out and her jars would break.

SHERIFF: Well, can you beat the women! Held for murder and worryin' about her preserves.

COUNTY ATTORNEY: I guess before we're through she may have something more serious than preserves to worry about.

HALE: Well, women are used to worrying over trifles.

(*The two women move a little closer together.*)

COUNTY ATTORNEY: (*With the gallantry of a young politician*) And yet, for all their worries, what would we do without the ladies? (*The women do not unbend. He goes to the sink, takes a dipperful of water from the pail and pouring it into a basin, washes his hands. Starts to wipe them on the roller towel, turns it for a cleaner place*) Dirty towels! (*Kicks his foot against the pans under the sink*) Not much of a housekeeper, would you say, ladies?

MRS. HALE: (*Stiffly*) There's a great deal of work to be done on a farm.

COUNTY ATTORNEY: To be sure. And yet (*With a little bow to her*) I know there are some Dickson county farmhouses which do not have such roller towels.

(*He gives it a pull to expose its full length again.*)

MRS. HALE: Those towels get dirty awful quick. Men's hands aren't always as clean as they might be.

COUNTY ATTORNEY: Ah, loyal to your sex, I see. But you and Mrs. Wright were neighbors. I suppose you were friends, too.

MRS. HALE: (*Shaking her head*) I've not seen much of her of late years. I've not been in this house—it's more than a year.

COUNTY ATTORNEY: And why was that? You didn't like her?

MRS. HALE: I liked her all well enough. Farmers' wives have their hands full, Mr. Henderson. And then—

COUNTY ATTORNEY: Yes—?

MRS. HALE: (*Looking about*) It never seemed a very cheerful place.

COUNTY ATTORNEY: No—it's not cheerful. I shouldn't say she had the homemaking instinct.

MRS. HALE: Well, I don't know as Wright had, either.

COUNTY ATTORNEY: You mean that they didn't get on very well?

MRS. HALE: No, I don't mean anything. But I don't think a place'd be any cheerfuller for John Wright's being in it.

COUNTY ATTORNEY: I'd like to talk more of that a little later. I want to get the lay of things upstairs now.

(*He goes to the left, where three steps lead to a stair door.*)

SHERIFF: I suppose anything Mrs. Peters does'll be all right. She was to take in some clothes for her, you know, and a few little things. We left in such a hurry yesterday.

COUNTY ATTORNEY: Yes, but I would like to see what you take, Mrs. Peters, and keep an eye out for anything that might be of use to us.

MRS. PETERS: Yes, Mr. Henderson.

(*The women listen to the men's steps on the stairs, then look about the kitchen.*)

MRS. HALE: I'd hate to have men coming into my kitchen, snooping around and criticising.

(*She arranges the pans under sink which the COUNTY ATTORNEY had shoved out of place.*)

MRS. PETERS: Of course it's no more than their duty.

MRS. HALE: Duty's all right, but I guess that deputy sheriff that came out to make the fire might have got a little of this on. (*Gives the roller towel a pull*) Wish I'd thought of that sooner. Seems mean to talk about her for not having things slicked up when she had to come away in such a hurry.

MRS. PETERS: (*Who has gone to a small table in the left rear corner of the room, and lifted one end of a towel that covers a pan*) She had bread set.

(*Stands still*)

MRS. HALE: (*Eyes fixed on a loaf of bread beside the breadbox, which is on a low shelf at the other side of the room. Moves slowly toward it*) She was going to put this in there. (*Picks up loaf, then abruptly drops it. In a manner of returning to familiar things*) It's a shame about her fruit. I wonder if it's all gone. (*Gets up on the chair and looks*) I think there's some here that's all right, Mrs. Peters. Yes—here; (*Holding it toward the window*) this is cherries, too. (*Looking again*) I declare I believe that's the only one. (*Gets down, bottle in her hand. Goes to the sink and wipes it off on the outside*) She'll feel awful bad after all her hard work in the hot weather. I remember the afternoon I put up my cherries last summer.

(*She puts the bottle on the big kitchen table, center of the room. With a sigh, is about to sit down in the rocking-chair. Before she is seated realizes what chair it is; with a slow look at it, steps back. The chair which she has touched rocks back and forth.*)

MRS. PETERS: Well, I must get those things from the front room closet. (*She goes to the door at the right, but after looking into the other room, steps back.*) You coming with me, Mrs. Hale? You could help me carry them.

(*They go in the other room; reappear,* MRS. PETERS *carrying a dress and skirt,* MRS. HALE *following with a pair of shoes.*)

MRS. PETERS: My, it's cold in there.

(*She puts the clothes on the big table, and hurries to the stove.*)

MRS. HALE: (*Examining the skirt*) Wright was close. I think maybe that's why she kept so much to herself. She didn't even belong to the Ladies Aid. I suppose she felt she couldn't do her part, and then you don't enjoy things when you feel shabby. She used to wear pretty clothes and be lively, when she was Minnie Foster, one of the town girls singing in the choir. But that—oh, that was thirty years ago. This all you was to take in?

MRS. PETERS: She said she wanted an apron. Funny thing to want, for there isn't much to get you dirty in jail, goodness knows. But I suppose just to make her feel more natural. She said they was in the top drawer in this cupboard. Yes, here. And then her little shawl that always hung behind the door. (*Opens stair door and looks*) Yes, here it is.

(*Quickly shuts door leading upstairs*)

MRS. HALE: (*Abruptly moving toward her*) Mrs. Peters?

MRS. PETERS: Yes, Mrs. Hale?

MRS. HALE: Do you think she did it?

MRS. PETERS: (*In a frightened voice*) Oh, I don't know.

MRS. HALE: Well, I don't think she did. Asking for an apron and her little shawl. Worrying about her fruit.

MRS. PETERS: (*Starts to speak, glances up, where footsteps are heard in the room above. In a low voice*) Mr. Peters says it looks bad for her. Mr. Henderson is awful sarcastic in a speech and he'll make fun of her sayin' she didn't wake up.

MRS. HALE: Well, I guess John Wright didn't wake when they was slipping that rope under his neck.

MRS. PETERS: No, it's strange. It must have been done awful crafty and still. They say it was such a—funny way to kill a man, rigging it all up like that.

MRS. HALE: That's just what Mr. Hale said. There was a gun in the house. He says that's what he can't understand.

MRS. PETERS: Mr. Henderson said coming out that what was needed for the case was a motive; something to show anger, or—sudden feeling.

MRS. HALE: (*Who is standing by the table*) Well, I don't see any signs of anger around here. (*She puts her hand on the dish towel which lies on the table, stands looking down at table, one half of which is clean, the other half messy.*) It's wiped to here. (*Makes a move as if to finish work, then turns and looks at loaf of bread outside the breadbox. Drops towel. In that voice of coming back to familiar things*) Wonder how they are finding things upstairs. I hope she had it a little more red-up up there. You know, it seems kind of *sneaking.* Locking her up in town and then coming out here and trying to get her own house to turn against her!

MRS. PETERS: But Mrs. Hale, the law is the law.

MRS. HALE: I s'pose 'tis. (*Unbuttoning her coat*) Better loosen up your things, Mrs. Peters. You won't feel them when you go out.

(MRS. PETERS *takes off her fur tippet, goes to hang it on hook at back of room, stands looking at the under part of the small corner table.*)

MRS. PETERS: She was piecing a quilt.

(*She brings the large sewing basket and they look at the bright pieces.*)

MRS. HALE: It's log cabin pattern. Pretty, isn't it? I wonder if she was goin' to quilt it or just knot it?

(*Footsteps have been heard coming down the stairs. The* SHERIFF *enters followed by* HALE *and the* COUNTY ATTORNEY.)

SHERIFF: They wonder if she was going to quilt it or just knot it!

(*The men laugh; the women look abashed.*)

COUNTY ATTORNEY: (*Rubbing his hands over the stove*) Frank's fire didn't do much up there, did it? Well, let's go out to the barn and get that cleared up.

(*The men go outside.*)

MRS. HALE: (*Resentfully*) I don't know as there's anything so strange, our takin' up our time with little things while we're waiting for them to get the evidence. (*She sits down at the big table smoothing out a block with decision.*) I don't see as it's anything to laugh about.

MRS. PETERS: (*Apologetically*) Of course they've got awful important things on their minds.

(*Pulls up a chair and joins* MRS. HALE *at the table*)

MRS. HALE: (*Examining another block*) Mrs. Peters, look at this one. Here, this is the one she was working on, and look at that sewing! All the rest of it has been so nice and even. And look at this! It's all over the place! Why, it looks as if she didn't know what she was about!

(*After she has said this they look at each other, then start to glance back at the door. After an instant* MRS. HALE *has pulled at a knot and ripped the sewing.*)

MRS. PETERS: Oh, what are you doing, Mrs. Hale?

MRS. HALE: (*Mildly*) Just pulling out a stitch or two that's not sewed very good. (*Threading a needle*) Bad sewing always made me fidgety.

MRS. PETERS: (*Nervously*) I don't think we ought to touch things.

MRS. HALE: I'll just finish up this end. (*Suddenly stopping and leaning forward*) Mrs. Peters?

MRS. PETERS: Yes, Mrs. Hale?

MRS. HALE: What do you suppose she was so nervous about?

MRS. PETERS: Oh—I don't know. I don't know as she was nervous. I sometimes sew awful queer when I'm just tired. (MRS. HALE *starts to say something, looks at* MRS. PETERS, *then goes on sewing.*) Well, I must get these things wrapped up. They may be through sooner than we think. (*Putting apron and other things together*) I wonder where I can find a piece of paper, and string.

MRS. HALE: In that cupboard, maybe.

MRS. PETERS: (*Looking in cupboard*) Why, here's a birdcage. (*Holds it up*) Did she have a bird, Mrs. Hale?

MRS. HALE: Why, I don't know whether she did or not—I've not been here for so long. There was a man around last year selling canaries cheap, but I don't know as she took one; maybe she did. She used to sing real pretty herself.

MRS. PETERS: (*Glancing around*) Seems funny to think of a bird here. But she must have had one, or why would she have a cage? I wonder what happened to it.

MRS. HALE: I s'pose maybe the cat got it.

MRS. PETERS: No, she didn't have a cat. She's got that feeling some people have about cats—being afraid of them. My cat got in her room and she was real upset and asked me to take it out.

MRS. HALE: My sister Bessie was like that. Queer, ain't it?

MRS. PETERS: (*Examining the cage*) Why, look at this door. It's broke. One hinge is pulled apart.

MRS. HALE: (*Looking too*) Looks as if someone must have been rough with it.

MRS. PETERS: Why, yes.

(*She brings the cage forward and puts it on the table.*)

MRS. HALE: I wish if they're going to find any evidence they'd be about it. I don't like this place.

MRS. PETERS: But I'm awful glad you came with me, Mrs. Hale. It would be lonesome for me sitting here alone.

MRS. HALE: It would, wouldn't it? (*Dropping her sewing*) But I tell you what I do wish, Mrs. Peters. I wish I had come over sometimes when *she* was here. I—(*Looking around the room*)—wish I had.

MRS. PETERS: But of course you were awful busy, Mrs. Hale—your house and your children.

MRS. HALE: I could've come. I stayed away because it weren't cheerful—and that's why I ought to have come. I—I've never liked this place. Maybe because it's down in a hollow and you don't see the road. I dunno what it is, but it's a lonesome place and always was. I wish I had come over to see Minnie Foster sometimes. I can see now—

(*Shakes her head*)

MRS. PETERS: Well you mustn't reproach yourself, Mrs. Hale. Somehow we just don't see how it is with other folks until—something comes up.

MRS. HALE: Not having children makes less work—but it makes a quiet house, and Wright out to work all day, and no company when he did come in. Did you know John Wright, Mrs. Peters?

MRS. PETERS: Not to know him; I've seen him in town. They say he was a good man.

MRS. HALE: Yes—good; he didn't drink, and kept his word as well as most, I guess, and paid his debts. But he was a hard man, Mrs. Peters. Just to pass the time of day with him—(*Shivers*) Like a raw wind that gets to the bone. (*Pauses, her eye falling on the cage*) I should think she would 'a wanted a bird. But what do you suppose went with it?

MRS. PETERS: I don't know, unless it got sick and died.

(*She reaches over and swings the broken door, swings it again. Both women watch it.*)

MRS. HALE: You weren't raised round here, were you? (MRS. PETERS *shakes her head.*) You didn't know—her?

MRS. PETERS: Not till they brought her yesterday.

MRS. HALE: She—come to think of it, she was kind of like a bird herself—real sweet and pretty, but kind of timid and—fluttery. How—she—did—change. (*Silence; then as if struck by a happy thought and relieved to get back to every day things*) Tell you what, Mrs. Peters, why don't you take the quilt in with you? It might take up her mind.

MRS. PETERS: Why, I think that's a real nice idea, Mrs. Hale. There couldn't possibly be any objection to it, could there? Now, just what would I take? I wonder if her patches are in here—and her things.

(*They look in the sewing basket.*)

MRS. HALE: Here's some red. I expect this has got sewing things in it. (*Brings out a fancy box*) What a pretty box. Looks like something somebody would give you. Maybe her scissors are in here. (*Opens box. Suddenly puts her hand to her nose*) Why—(MRS. PETERS *bends nearer, then turns her face away.*) There's something wrapped up in this piece of silk.

MRS. PETERS: Why, this isn't her scissors.

MRS. HALE: (*Lifting the silk*) Oh, Mrs. Peters—its—

(MRS. PETERS *bends closer.*)

MRS. PETERS: It's the bird.

MRS. HALE: (*Jumping up*) But, Mrs. Peters—look at it! Its neck! Look at its neck! It's all—other side *to.*

MRS. PETERS: Somebody—wrung—its—neck.

(*Their eyes meet. A look of growing comprehension, of horror. Steps are heard outside.* MRS. HALE *slips box under quilt pieces, and sinks into her chair. Enter* SHERIFF *and* COUNTY ATTORNEY. MRS. PETERS *rises.*)

COUNTY ATTORNEY: (*As one turning from serious things to little pleasantries*) Well, ladies, have you decided whether she was going to quilt it or knot it?

MRS. PETERS: We think she was going to —knot it.

COUNTY ATTORNEY: Well, that's interesting, I'm sure. (*Seeing the birdcage*) Has the bird flown?

MRS. HALE: (*Putting more quilt pieces over the box*) We think the—cat got it.

COUNTY ATTORNEY: (*Preoccupied*) Is there a cat?

(MRS. HALE *glances in a quick covert way at* MRS. PETERS.)

MRS. PETERS: Well, not *now.* They're superstitious, you know. They leave.

COUNTY ATTORNEY: (*To* SHERIFF PETERS *continuing an interrupted conversation*) No sign at all of anyone having come from the outside.

Their own rope. Now let's go up again and go over it piece by piece. (*They start upstairs.*) It would have to have been someone who knew just the—

(MRS. PETERS *sits down. The two women sit there not looking at one another, but as if peering into something and at the same time holding back. When they talk now it is in the manner of feeling their way over strange ground, as if afraid of what they are saying, but as if they cannot help saying it.*)

MRS. HALE: She liked the bird. She was going to bury it in that pretty box.

MRS. PETERS: (*In a whisper*) When I was a girl—my kitten—there was a boy took a hatchet, and before my eyes—and before I could get there—(*Covers her face an instant*) If they hadn't held me back I would have—(*Catches herself, looks upstairs where steps are heard, falters weakly*)— hurt him.

MRS. HALE: (*With a slow look around her*) I wonder how it would seem never to have had any children around. (*Pause*) No, Wright wouldn't like the bird—a thing that sang. She used to sing. He killed that, too.

MRS. PETERS: (*Moving uneasily*) We don't know who killed the bird.

MRS. HALE: I knew John Wright.

MRS. PETERS: It was an awful thing was done in this house that night, Mrs. Hale. Killing a man while he slept, slipping a rope around his neck that choked the life out of him.

MRS. HALE: His neck. Choked the life out of him.

(*Her hand goes out and rests on the birdcage.*)

MRS. PETERS: (*With rising voice*) We don't know who killed him. We don't know.

MRS. HALE: (*Her own feeling not interrupted*) If there'd been years and years of nothing, then a bird to sing to you, it would be awful—still, after the bird was still.

MRS. PETERS: (*Something within her speaking*) I know what stillness is. When we homesteaded in Dakota, and my first baby died—after he was two years old, and me with no other then—

MRS. HALE: (*Moving*) How soon do you suppose they'll be through, look-ing for the evidence?

MRS. PETERS: I know what stillness is. (*Pulling herself back*) The law has got to punish crime, Mrs. Hale.

MRS. HALE: (*Not as if answering that*) I wish you'd seen Minnie Foster when she wore a white dress with blue ribbons and stood up there in the choir and sang. (*A look around the room*) Oh, I wish I'd come over here once in a while! That was a crime! That was a crime! Who's going to punish that?

MRS. PETERS: (*Looking upstairs*) We mustn't—take on.

MRS. HALE: I might have known she needed help! I know how things can be—for women. I tell you, it's queer, Mrs. Peters. We live close to-gether and we live far apart. We all go through the same things—it's all just a different kind of the same thing. (*Brushes her eyes; noticing the bottle of fruit, reaches out for it*) If I was you I wouldn't tell her her fruit was gone. Tell her it *ain't*. Tell her it's all right. Take this in to prove it to her. She—she may never know whether it was broke or not.

MRS. PETERS: (*Takes the bottle, looks about for something to wrap it in, takes petticoat from the clothes brought from the other room, very nervously begins winding this around the bottle. In a false voice*) My, it's a good thing the men couldn't hear us. Wouldn't they just laugh! Getting all stirred up over a little thing like a—dead canary. As if that could have anything to do with—with—wouldn't they *laugh!*

(*The men are heard coming down stairs.*)

MRS. HALE: (*Under her breath*) Maybe they would—maybe they wouldn't.

COUNTY ATTORNEY: No, Peters, it's all perfectly clear except a reason for doing it. But you know juries when it comes to women. If there was some definite thing. Something to show—something to make a story about—a thing that would connect up with this strange way of doing it—

(*The women's eyes meet for an instant. Enter* HALE *from outer door.*)

HALE: Well, I've got the team around. Pretty cold out there.

COUNTY ATTORNEY: I'm going to stay here a while by myself. (*To the* SHERIFF) You can send Frank out for me, can't you? I want to go over everything. I'm not satisfied that we can't do better.

SHERIFF: Do you want to see what Mrs. Peters is going to take in?

(*The* COUNTY ATTORNEY *goes to the table, picks up the apron, laughs.*)

COUNTY ATTORNEY: Oh, I guess they're not very dangerous things the ladies have picked out. (*Moves a few things about, disturbing the quilt pieces which cover the box. Steps back*) No, Mrs. Peters doesn't need supervising. For that matter, a sheriff's wife is married to the law. Ever think of it that way, Mrs. Peters?

MRS. PETERS: Not—just that way.

SHERIFF: (*Chuckling*) Married to the law. (*Moves toward the other room*) I just want you to come in here a minute, George. We ought to take a look at these windows.

COUNTY ATTORNEY: (*Scoffingly*) Oh, windows!

SHERIFF: We'll be right out, Mr. Hale.

(HALE *goes outside. The* SHERIFF *follows the* COUNTY ATTORNEY *into the other room. Then* MRS. HALE *rises, hands tight together, looking*

intensely at MRS. PETERS, *whose eyes make a slow turn, finally meeting*
MRS. HALE*'s. A moment* MRS. HALE *holds her, then her own eyes point
the way to where the box is concealed. Suddenly* MRS. PETERS *throws back
quilt pieces and tries to put the box in the bag she is wearing. It is too big. She
opens box, starts to take bird out, cannot touch it, goes to pieces, stands there
helpless. Sound of a knob turning in the other room.* MRS. HALE *snatches
the box and puts it in the pocket of her big coat. Enter* COUNTY ATTOR-
NEY *and* SHERIFF.)

COUNTY ATTORNEY: (*Facetiously*) Well, Henry, at least we found out
that she was not going to quilt it. She was going to—what is it you call
it, ladies?

MRS. HALE: (*her hand against her pocket*) We call it—knot it, Mr. Henderson.

The Responsive Reader

1. Hale, the neighbor, strikes the keynote of the play when he says, "Well,
   women are used to worrying over trifles." What are the trifles that
   gradually assume a major role in the play? Which of the "little things"
   are least important, which most? How do they help you piece together
   the true story of what happened to John Wright?
2. Early in the first scene, Hale says in passing "I didn't know as what his
   wife wanted made much difference to John." What else do you learn
   about John Wright, and how? What picture of John Wright's character
   emerges as the women talk mostly about other things? What is ironic
   about his being called "a good man"?
3. Mrs. Hale says, "I know how things can be for women." How does
   Mrs. Hale show that she does not share the men's views but instead
   feels solidarity with Mrs. Wright? How does this play make you look
   at things from the women's point of view?
4. What is ironic about Mrs. Peters' being "married to the law"? She says,
   "The law has got to punish crime." What answer does the play as a
   whole give to this statement?
5. What makes the bird a central symbol in this play?

Thinking, Talking, Writing

6. Is there a common failing or shortcoming that both the dead man and
   the living men in this play are guilty of? What is it?
7. In recent surveys, up to 51 percent of the women questioned called
   murder or mayhem committed by women against abusive partners justified. Are you surprised by this figure? Why or why not? Where do
   you stand on this issue?

Collaborative Projects

8. You and your classmates may want to study recent media reports of retaliatory justice administered by abused women to abusive men. Is each case different, or is there a common pattern? How does the legal system respond? How does public opinion react?

Thinking about Connections

9. Traditionally, drama critics have distinguished between tragedy and comedy as the two major genres of drama. Tragedy solemnly chronicles the fall from high station or good fortune, either as the result of a character flaw or a hostile fate. Comedy pokes fun at human foibles but leads to a happy end. Can you stretch these definitions to show that Glaspell's *Trifles* might be considered a modern tragedy and Valdez' *Los Vendidos* a modern comedy?

12

Regained Roots:
Encountering Nature

The morning wind forever blows, the poem of creation is uninterrupted;
but few are the ears that hear it.

Henry David Thoreau

Once the trees are cut down, the water will wash the mountain away
and the river will be heavy with mud . . . We say look how the water
flows from this place and returns as rainfall; everything returns, we say,
and one thing follows another; there are limits, we say, on what can be
done and everything moves. We are all a part of this motion, we say,
and the way of the river is sacred, and this grove of trees is sacred, and
we ourselves, we tell you, are sacred.

Susan Griffin

You don't have to have any people when sunlight stands on the rocks
William Stafford, "Things That Happen When There Aren't Any People"

LITERATURE IN CONTEXT

"The groves were God's first temples," wrote the American nineteenth-century poet William Cullen Bryant. Like other Romantic poets, he sensed the grandeur of God in the healing calm of the forests. He felt the power of God in the thunderstorms, tornadoes, and hurricanes that dwarfed the power of human beings. The Romantic movement, first in Europe and then in this country, was rebelling against the crowded polluted cities and the violated landscape that were the legacy of the industrial revolution. Like writers and artists after them, they felt that it was unnatural for human beings to live in treeless congested cities or among slag heaps and belching smokestacks in the factory towns of the industrial age.

Meanwhile, the march of progress and professional killers like Buffalo Bill (William Cody) were exterminating the buffalo and the passenger pigeon. Native Americans, who had depended on the wildlife of the forests and prairies for survival, were driven from their hunting grounds to arid or inhospitable areas where no whites could make a living. For much of the nineteenth and twentieth centuries, progress meant leveling hills and blasting tunnels through mountains for railroads and highways, paving over the prairies for subdivisions, and bulldozing trees and creeks for parking lots and shopping malls. For many writers and artists, plastic became a symbol of a civilization cut off from nature, with plastic smiles and homogenized precooked food.

Today many again believe that, in order to remain sane, human beings have to stay in touch with their natural roots. We are learning a new respect for our fellow creatures in the animal kingdom. Greenpeace volunteers come between fishing crews and dolphins or between baby seals and those who would club them to death for their furs. "Ecofreaks" climb into trees to live there and defy the chainsaws of corporations that denude the landscape and then move on in search of other habitats to despoil.

Writers and artists have always helped us keep alive our sense of wonder at the mysterious natural world of which we are a part. Poets have looked in the mirror of nature for symbols of the cycles of growth and decay, of death and renewal, that shape our lives. Herman Melville's *Moby Dick,* his great mythical novel about the legendary white whale, confronts us with the beauty and terror of the natural world in which we live. American nature writers from Loren Eiseley to Annie Dillard have kept alive the habit of patient observation that keeps us in touch with the natural life around us.

CALIFORNIA HILLS IN AUGUST

Dana Gioia

> To the image merchants of the media, California calls up images of beaches, blondes, and Pepsi-Cola. To those who live there, it means sprawling metropolitan areas but also vast stretches of landscape with a harsh beauty, much of it semidesert, alive with wildflowers and new grass in the spring but parched and brown in the endless sun-scorched days of summer and autumn. Dana Gioia, born in Los Angeles, educated at Stanford and Harvard, knows both the West and the East.

I can imagine someone who found   1
these fields unbearable, who climbed
the hillside in the heat, cursing the dust,
cracking the brittle weeds underfoot,
wishing a few more trees for shade.   5

An Easterner especially, who would scorn
the meagreness of summer, the dry
twisted shapes of black elm,
scrub oak, and chaparral—a landscape
August has already drained of green.   10

One who would hurry over the clinging
thistle, foxtail, golden poppy,
knowing everything was just a weed,
unable to conceive that these trees
And sparse brown bushes were alive.   15

And hate the bright stillness of the noon,
without wind, without motion,
the only other living thing
a hawk, hungry for prey, suspended
in the blinding, sunlit blue.   20

And yet how gentle it seems to someone
raised in a landscape short of rain—
the skyline of a hill broken by no more
trees than one can count, the grass,
the empty sky, the wish for water.   25

The Responsive Reader

1. What images and ideas for you cluster around the word *nature?* Cluster the term, putting it in the center of your cluster and allowing ideas, memories, and associations it brings to mind to branch out from the

core. Then write a paragraph putting into words what the term *nature* brings to mind.

2. How is the natural world in this poem different from what many expect of nature? What are striking characteristic details?

3. How does the landscape look from the point of view of the imaginary Easterner? How does it look from the perspective of the poet?

Thinking, Talking, Writing

4. In some cultures, the sun is the central symbol, bringing warmth and life. In other cultures, water is the life-giving principle and source of fertility. In still other contexts, water is a symbol of the destructive force of nature. Have you encountered evidence of such differences in perspective? What for you is the symbolism of sun and water?

5. Some are drawn toward lush, rich beauty. Others prefer a sparse, harsh, or austere kind of beauty. What is your choice or preference?

HORSE AND TREE
Rita Dove

In 1993 at age forty, Rita Dove was chosen as the nation's new poet laureate, our youngest official national poet ever and the first African American appointed to the position. When she was chosen, Dove said that it was her aim to "keep poetry and the cause of literature in the national eye" and to help younger people find role models other than "sports figures who drive around in Porsches and have three-piece suits and silk jackets." Like other Americans from minority backgrounds, she found that libraries and reading was "our ticket to freedom." The following poem is from her collection Grace Notes *(1989).*

Poets have often related intuitively to the vital forces at work in nature. How does this poem carry on this tradition?

Everybody who's anybody longs to be a tree—   *1*
or ride one, hair blown to froth.
That's why horses were invented, and saddles
tooled with singular stars.

This is why we braid their harsh manes   *5*
as if they were children, why children
might fear a carousel at first for the way
it insists that life is round. No,

we reply, there is music and then it stops;
the beautiful is always rising and falling.   *10*
We call and the children sing back *one more time.*
In the tree the luminous sap ascends.

The Responsive Reader

1. For the poet, what makes a tree a good symbol of the vital forces in nature? What makes a horse for her a good symbol of natural vitality?
2. What does the speaker in the poet have in mind when she says, "there is music and then it stops;/the beautiful is always rising and then falling." Why do you think she feels this is something that children or young people should be told?

Thinking, Talking, Writing

3. What does a tree, a horse, or a merry-go-round symbolize for you?

A FINCH SITTING OUT A WINDSTORM

James Wright

James Wright was from a generation that remembered a simpler rural past when people lived closer to nature. He grew up in Ohio, and his father slaved for many years across the Ohio River in a glass factory in West Virginia. In Wright's poetry, nostalgic childhood scenes with large horses lazily munching little apples in dark barns contrast with memories of his father, grimy from working with machinery all day, living in a house close to the slag heaps piled up by smoke-belching steelworks, and haunted by the specter of the breadlines that awaited many of the industrials workers of the thirties.

Solemnly irritated by the turn   1
To cold air steals,
He puffs out his most fragile feathers,
His breast down,
And refuses to move.   5
If I were he,
I would not clamp my claws so stubbornly around
The skinny branch.
I would not keep my tiny glitter
Fixed over my beak, or return   10
The glare of the wind.
Too many Maytime snowfalls have taught me
The wisdom of hopelessness.

But the damned fool
Squats there as if he owned   15
The earth, bought and paid for.
Oh, I could advise him plenty
About his wings. Give up, drift,
Get out.

But his face is as battered   20
As Carmen Basilio's.°   *a boxer*
He never listens
To me.

The Responsive Reader

1. What do you expect in a poem about a bird? How is this poem different? What picture of nature does this poem create for the reader? What keeps the bird from being superficially pretty? Does the poem make you imagine a real bird?

2. What persona or assumed identity does the poet choose in this poem? How is he talking to the bird and why? What is the effect on you as the reader?

Thinking, Talking, Writing

3. Do we tend to have an anthromorphic view of the animal world—thinking and talking about animals as if they were human? Does this poem read too many human qualities into the bird?

TO CHRIST OUR LORD
Galway Kinnell

Part of poetry's usefulness in the world is that it pays some of our huge unpaid tribute to the things and creatures that share the earth with us.

Galway Kinnell

Galway Kinnell is a widely published poet who was born in Rhode Island of Irish and Scottish stock. He has lived and taught abroad in France and Iran, but he has done much of his writing in Vermont. He was active in the Civil Rights movement and in the movement opposing the Vietnam War. His nature poems may take the reader to a world of lakes and forests of spruce, cedar, and pine, where people still go about their logging, fishing, and hunting, sheltered for a time from development plans designed to "enrich the rich." Or a poem may ask the reader to imagine a native hunter, near starvation, stalking a bear slowly killed over the days by a sharpened wolf's rib that was coiled in frozen blubber and then uncoiled in the bear's maw.

In the nineteenth century, disciples of Charles Darwin thought of nature, "red in tooth and claw," as ruled by the principle of "kill or be killed." Modern biologists use the metaphor of the food chain, where the bigger and stronger feed on the small and weak. Have we become too civilized to play our role in this natural cycle?

The legs of the elk punctured the snow's crust   1
And wolves floated lightfooted on the land
Hunting Christmas elk living and frozen;
Inside snow melted in a basin, and a woman basted
A bird spread over coals by its wings and head.   5

Snow had sealed the windows; candles lit
The Christmas meal. The Christmas grace chilled
The cooked bird, being long-winded and the room cold.
During the words a boy thought, is it fitting
To eat this creature killed on the wing?   10

He had killed it himself, climbing out
Alone on snowshoes in the Christmas dawn,
The fallen snow swirling and the snowfall gone,
Heard its throat scream as the gunshot scattered,
Watched it drop, and fished from the snow the dead.   15

He had not wanted to shoot. The sound
Of wings beating into the hushed air
Had stirred his love, and his fingers
Froze in his gloves, and he wondered,
Famishing, could he fire? Then he fired.   20

Now the grace praised his wicked act. At its end
The bird on the plate
Stared at his stricken appetite.
There had been nothing to do but surrender,
To kill and to eat; he ate as he had killed, with wonder.   25

At night on snowshoes on the drifting field
He wondered again, for whom had love stirred?
The stars glittered on the snow and nothing answered.
Then the Swan spread her wings, cross of the cold north,
The pattern and mirror of the acts of earth.   30

The Responsive Reader

1. How did the speaker feel toward the bird? What are the speaker's hesitations or qualms about shooting and eating it? Do you share them?
2. How do the Christmas setting and the grace said at table complicate matters in this poem?
3. The title echoes the title of a famous nineteenth-century poem by the Jesuit priest Gerard Manley Hopkins. The poem made a glorious beautiful falcon an earthly emblem of the splendor and power of Christ. Why do you think Kinnell used this title?

Thinking, Talking, Writing

4. Are we too sensitive today about the slaughter of the animals that feed us?

DREAMS OF THE ANIMALS

Margaret Atwood

In that country the animals
have the faces of people.
Margaret Atwood, "The Animals in That Country"

> *The ecological movement and the Green parties in Europe and elsewhere have rekindled our sense of kinship with the animal world of which we are a part. Animal rights activists have protested the wretched unnatural conditions in which captive animals have lived in traditional zoos. They have started crusades to save animals once marked for extermination as predators or vermin. Margaret Atwood may be the Canadian writer best known in the United States. She published several volumes of poetry from the sixties though the eighties and has written on survival as the central theme in Canadian literature. Her novel* The Handmaiden's Tale *was made into a chilling movie projecting a dystopian, anti-Utopian future in which sexism has run amuck.*

Mostly the animals dream   1
of other animals   each
according to its kind

      (though certain mice and small rodents
      have nightmares of a huge pink   5
      shape with five claws descending)

: moles dream of darkness and delicate
mole smells

frogs dream of green and golden
frogs   10
sparkling like wet suns
among the lilies

red and black
striped fish, their eyes open
have red and black striped   15
dreams   defense, attack, meaningful
patterns

birds dream of territories
enclosed by singing.

Sometimes the animals dream of evil   20
in the form of soap and metal
but mostly the animals dream
of other animals.

There are exceptions:

> the silver fox in the roadside zoo 25
> dreams of digging out
> and of baby foxes, their necks bitten
>
> the caged armadillo
> near the train
> station, which runs 30
> all day in figure eights
> its piglet feet pattering,
> no longer dreams
> but is insane when waking;
>
> the iguana 35
> in the petshop window on St. Catherine Street
> crested, royal-eyed, ruling
> its kingdom of water-dish and sawdust
>
> dreams of sawdust

The Responsive Reader

1. In this poem, what is the difference between the animals in their natural habitats and those held captive? What are some striking or telling contrasts?
2. Which of these animals might normally be considered ugly or repulsive? How does the poet change or counteract the usual associations they might bring to mind?

Thinking, Talking, Writing

3. Which animals do humans tend to admire, and which do they look down upon, and why? How rational are our standards for what is beautiful or admirable in nature?
4. Are zoos obsolete? Or should something be said in defense of zoos?

RAIN OF GOLD

Victor Villaseñor

I began to see that maybe one person's reality was, indeed, another's fantasy.
                                                            Victor Villaseñor

Victor Villaseñor grew up in the barrio, or Mexican section of town, in Carlsbad, California. He remembers the stories his grandmother and his mother told him about the family's past in Mexico and the hardships they endured during the revolutionary war fought by the troops of Francisco Villa. As young Victor became more Americanized, these stories slowly receded into the past, becoming part of a world in which fantasy and reality intermingled. However, when he married and had his first child, Villaseñor decided to set out in search of the past, so he could tell his own children about their ancestral roots. He traveled in Mexico "by plane, by bus, by truck, by burro, by foot."

He says,

It took me two days to climb the mountains of La Barranca del Cobre where my mother was born. One morning, I saw Indians so shy that when I waved hello to them they froze like deer, then ran away from me with the agility and speed of a young antelope. I saw swarms of butterflies so vast that they filled the entire sky like dancing tapestry. I saw skies so clear and full of stars that I felt close to God.

In five years of research and writing and rewriting, Villaseñor put together a family history—Rain of Gold (1991)—that the original publisher wanted to hype as fiction but that he eventually published with a small noncommercial publisher as the story of real people, true places, and incidents that actually happened. He sees his book as "a history of a people—a tribal heritage, if you will—of my Indian-European culture as handed down to me by my parents, aunts, uncles and godparents."

The following modern parable is the opening section of the book. It recreates a modern myth of a lost paradise or Eden where people live close to nature. Greed and modern industry (North American industry) then gradually move in to destroy the people's link with the natural world.

High in the mountains in northwest Mexico, an Indian named Espirito   *1*
followed a doe and her fawn in search of water. The spring in the box canyon where Espirito and his tribe lived had dried up.

Following the deer through the brush and boulders, Espirito found a hidden spring on the other side of the box canyon at the base of a small cliff. Water dripped down the face of the cliff and the whole cliff glistened like a jewel in the bright mid-morning sunlight.

Once the deer were done drinking, Espirito approached the spring and drank, too. It was the sweetest water he'd ever tasted. Filling his gourd with water, Espirito pulled down a couple of loose rocks from the cliff and put them in his deerskin pouch. He knelt down, giving thanks to the Almighty Creator. He and his people weren't going to suffer the long, dry season, after all.

Then that winter came a torrent of rain and it got so cold that the raindrops froze and the mountaintops turned white. Espirito and his tribe grew cold and hungry. Desperately, Espirito went down to the lowlands to see if he could sell some of the sweet water that he'd found.

Walking into a small settlement alongside the great father river, El Rio Urique, Espirito told the store owner, Don Carlos Barrios, that he had the sweetest water in all the world to trade for food and clothing.

Laughing, Don Carlos said, "I'm sorry, but I can't trade for water, living here alongside a river. Do you have anything else to trade?"

"No," said Espirito, turning his purse inside out. "All I have are these little stones and this gourd of water."

Don Carlos's fat, grey eyebrows shot up. The stones were gold nuggets. Picking one up, Don Carlos put it to his teeth, marking it. "For these I can trade you all the food and clothing you want!" he screamed.

But Espirito was already going for the door. He'd never seen a man try to eat a stone before. It took all of Don Carlos's power to calm Espirito down and get him to come back into the store to trade.

Then, having traded, Espirito loaded the food and clothing into a sack, and he left the settlement as quickly as he could. He didn't want the crazy store owner to go back on their deal.

The winter passed and Espirito made a dozen trips down the mountain to trade stones for food and clothing. Don Carlos made so much money from the gold nuggets that he quit attending to his store and began having great feasts every evening. He begged Espirito to sell him the place where he got the nuggets. He offered to send his fat son up the mountain with his two burros loaded with merchandise every week so Espirito wouldn't have to come down the mountain anymore.

"I can't do that," said Espirito. "I don't own the stones or the spring any more than I own the clouds or the birds in the sky. The stones belong to my people who use the spring."

"Well, then, talk to them," said Don Carlos excitedly. "And offer them my deal!"

"All right," said Espirito. He went back up into the mountains and he talked it over with his people. They agreed to Don Carlos's deal, but only on the condition that he'd never dig into the cliff itself and ruin the spring which held the sweetest water in all the world.

Coming down from the box canyon after delivering the first two burro-loads of merchandise, Don Carlos's fat son was beside himself with joy.

"Papa," he said, "it's not just a pocket of gold. No, it's a whole cliff of gold raining down the mountainside!"

"How big a cliff?" asked Don Carlos, his eyes dancing with gold fever.

"As tall as twenty men standing on each other and twice as wide as our house."

Don Carlos bit his knuckles with anticipation. He began to send his fat son back up the mountain for more gold as soon as he'd come down.

Don Carlos's son lost all his soft flesh and grew as strong and slender as a deer. Espirito and his people came to like the boy and named him Ojos Puros because of his light blue eyes.

Years passed and all was going well in this enchanted box canyon of raining gold, until one day Ojos Puros came down the mountain and told his father that there wasn't any more gold. [20]

"What do you mean no more gold?" demanded Don Carlos, who now wore fine clothes from Mexico City and boots from Spain.

"All the loose nuggets are gone," said Ojos Puros. "To get more gold, we'd need to dig at the cliff, and that would ruin their spring."

"So do it!" ordered Don Carlos.

"No," said Ojos Puros. "We gave our word not to ruin their spring, Papa."

The rage, the anger, that came to Don Carlos's face would have cowed Ojos Puros a few years before. But it didn't now. So Don Carlos slapped his son until his hand was covered with blood, but still his son never gave in nor did he hit him back. That night Don Carlos drank and ate with such rage that he came down with a terrible stomachache. He slept badly. He had nightmares. And in his sleep he saw an angel of God coming to kill him for having tried to go back on his word. [25]

Three days later, Don Carlos awoke with a fever and he apologized to his son and wife for all the bad he'd done. Then he sold the mine to a local rancher who didn't know the meaning of the word "fear." This rancher's name was Bernardo Garcia. The next day Bernardo had a steer knocked down that Don Carlos still owed to the Indians and he had the animal skinned alive so he could keep the valuable hide. Then he forced the naked animal to run up the mountain to Espirito's encampment.

Seeing the naked animal come into their canyon, Espirito and his people were terrified. Bernardo himself cut the steer's throat in front of them, told the Indians that he'd bought the gold mine from Don Carlos, and he put a dozen men to work digging at the cliff. He ruined the spring and, when the Indians complained, he shot them and ran them out of their box canyon, even over Ojos Puros's protests.

In less than five years, Bernardo became a man so rich and powerful that he bought a home in Mexico City among the wealthiest of the world. He became a close friend of the great President Porfirio Diaz himself, and he took a second wife of European breeding, as Don Porfirio had done. Then, in 1903 he sold the mine to an American company from San Francisco, California, for unheard-of millions on Don Porfirio's advice for modernizing Mexico.

The American mining company came in with large equipment and dammed up the Urique River, put in a power plant, and built a road from the coast. The mine came to be officially known as La Lluvia de Oro, "The Rain of Gold," and thousands of poor Mexican people came to the box canyon hoping to get work.

Every six months the Americans loaded thirty-five mules with two sixty-pound bars of gold each and drove the mules out of the canyon and down the mountain to the railhead in El Fuerte. There, the Americans loaded the gold bars on trains and shipped them north to the United States.

30

The years passed, and the people who lived in the bottom of the box canyon made houses out of stone and lean-tos out of sticks and mud.

The American company prospered, grew, and built permanent buildings inside an enfenced area for their American engineers.

But then, in 1910, a huge meteorite came shooting out of the sky, exploding against the towering walls of the box canyon. The people who lived in the canyon thought it was the end of the world. They prayed and made love, asking God to spare them. And in the morning, when they saw the miracle of the new day, they knew God had, indeed, spared them. They thanked Him, refusing to go to work inside the darkness of the mine anymore.

The Americans became angry, but no matter how much they beat the people, they still could not get them to go back down into the darkness of the devil's domain. Finally, the Americans brought back Bernardo Garcia from Mexico City, and he threatened the people with God and the devil and got them back to work.

That same year, President Porfirio Diaz used La Lluvia de Oro as one of his examples to show to foreign dignitaries—whom he'd invited to celebrate his eightieth birthday—of how foreign investors could make a profit in helping him modernize Mexico.

35

The celebration for Don Porfirio's birthday lasted one month, costing the Mexican people more than twenty million dollars in gold. Bernardo Garcia stood alongside Don Porfirio in gold-plated *charro* dress, welcoming the different foreign dignitaries with a present made of pure gold.

Both Don Porfirio and Bernardo wore white powder on their dark Indian faces so that they'd look white-European. No Indians were allowed in Mexico City during the celebration. No mestizos or poor, dark-skinned people. So for thirty days the foreign dignitaries were driven in gold-studded carriages up and down the boulevard of La Reforma in Mexico City, which had been specially built by Don Porfirio to be an exact replica of the main boulevard in Paris, and the foreign visitors only saw beautiful homes, prosperous factories, well-cared-for haciendas and well-to-do European-looking people.

This, then, was the last straw that broke the burro's back. And the poor, hungry people of Mexico rose up in arms by the tens of thousands, breaking Don Porfirio's thirty-year reign, and the Revolution of 1910 began.

Broken-hearted, Espirito and his people watched from the top of the towering cliffs as their beloved box canyon—in which they'd lived peacefully for hundreds of years—turned first into a settlement of electric fences, grey stone buildings and terrible noises, and now into a bloodbath for the soldiers of the Revolution.

Then, one cold, clear morning, Ojos Puros and his Indian wife—he'd   40
married Espirito's youngest daughter—found the legendary Espirito dead up on the towering cliffs. It was said that Espirito had died of grief because he'd misled his people and brought them to ruin.

Ojos Puros and his wife buried Espirito where he'd died so that his soul could look down into their beloved box canyon for all eternity.

The Responsive Reader

1. A spring has often been a powerful symbol in earlier literature. What is the role of the spring in this account? What are its symbolic associations?
2. What are the role and the symbolic significance of the gold in this account? What are the different stages or major turning points in its exploitation? What is the author's implied comment on the economics of Third World countries?
3. What is Villaseñor's comment on the political power structure and the causes of the revolution?

Thinking, Talking, Writing

4. To judge from your reading or study, does what happens here seem representative of the political history of other Latin American countries?
5. A parable tells a story that can be applied to many different situations. Can this story be read as a parable for the way our modern technological civilization in general affects our relationship with nature?

MOBY DICK: FIRST DAY OF THE CHASE

Herman Melville

And God created great whales.
>Genesis

At a time when American merchant ships and naval vessels roamed the oceans, Herman Melville became famous with his tales of a sailor's life in the South Seas or on board an American battleship. In 1851 he published his masterpiece: Moby Dick, *his mythic tale of the obsessed Captain Ahab's hunt for the great white whale. He wrote when unhurried readers were used to seeing the great nineteenth-century novels take shape in many leisurely installments. His book had 135 chapters, with many detours through the history of whaling, life in the whaling towns, and preparation for the whaling trips that took crews to distant oceans.*

However, slowly the book closes in on its quarry: the great white whale that beckons and finally destroys its human tormentors. The crew of Melville's whaling ship, the Pequod, *was a strange cross-section of humanity. They were people of many ethnicities who, like a later multicultural America, were embarked on a common voyage. The captain was the fanatic Ahab, who had lost a leg in a previous confrontation with a whale. The first mate was Starbuck, an earnest New England Quaker. Of the three harpooners commanding the small rowboats giving chase to the whales, Queequeg was a South Sea islander practicing his own religious rites; Tashtego was a Native American from one of the last Indian villages to survive in the northeast, a pure-blood descendant of the "proud warrior hunters" who had hunted "the great New England moose" in the "aboriginal forests" of the continent; and Daggoo was a gigantic African ("six feet five in his socks"—a white man "standing before him seemed like a white flag come to beg truce of a fortress").*

The following chapter from the book at long last takes us to the first traumatic encounter with the great whale. In Melville's mysterious great book, much sooner or later acquires a symbolic meaning. The ocean from the beginning is the "image of the ungraspable phantom of life." The whale becomes a symbol of the maddening two-facedness, or ambivalence, of nature. At times, like in a passage included in the following excerpt, nature seems supremely calm and beautiful, promising everything that the harried, tension-ridden human heart desires. The whale floats, serenely beautiful, through a becalmed ocean. Thornton Wilder, one of America's most beloved dramatists, used to read this passage as one of the six or seven great magical passages in all of American literature.

All the time we know that nature may at any time show its capacity for destructive energy that dwarfs all human effort.

A NOTE ON MELVILLE'S LANGUAGE: Melville's readers are obviously expected to tune in to the way sailors talked in the age of sailing ships before floating whale-exploitation factories drove the great mammals to the brink

of extinction. Alert readers gather from the context what side of a ship leeward
*is, what the names of the different masts are on a three-master or four-master,
what the* gunwales *are in a rowboat, or what happens to a boat when it is
smashed, or* stove, *by a huge whale. (You may want to work with a group to
prepare a brief glossary of nineteenth-century nautical terms for the modern
reader.) Like many writers of his time, Melville uses many bookish or scholarly
words appealing to a book-loving public. Some of these words are archaic—old-
fashioned, or no longer in common use—even in his own time:* ere *for before,*
thither *for our current informal* thataway, twain *for two,* nigh *for near,* anon
*for in a minute. Other words are still current but have become dictionary words
or books words for most modern readers:* celerity *for speed,* confluent *for
flowing together,* succor *for help,* descried *for observed or noticed. With
some ingenuity, you can puzzle out what a word like* whelm *means (we still
use* overwhelm, *which also means something like* swamp). Lest, *in expressions like "be alert* lest *you be surprised," means "so that you won't . . ."*

"Man the mast-heads! Call all hands!"   *1*
    Thundering with the butts of three clubbed handspikes on the forecas-
tle deck, Daggoo roused the sleepers with such judgment claps that they
seemed to exhale from the scuttle, so instantaneously did they appear with
their clothes in their hands.
    "What d'ye see?" cried Ahab, flattening his face to the sky.
    "Nothing, nothing, Sir!" was the sound hailing down in reply.
    "T'gallant sails! stunsails! alow and aloft, and on both sides!"   *5*
    All sail being set, he now cast loose the life-line, reserved for swaying
him to the main royal-mast head; and in a few moments they were hoisting
him thither, when, while but two thirds of the way aloft and while peering
ahead through the horizontal vacancy between the main-top-sail and top-
gallant-sail, he raised a gull-like cry in the air, "There she blows! there she
blows! A hump like a snow-hill! It is Moby Dick!"
    Fired by the cry which seemed simultaneously taken up by the three
lookouts, the men on deck rushed to the rigging to behold the famous whale
they had so long been pursuing. Ahab had now gained his final perch, some
feet above the other lookouts, Tashtego standing just beneath him on the cap
of the top-gallant-mast, so that the Indian's head was almost on a level with
Ahab's heel. From this height the whale was now seen some mile or so ahead,
at every roll of the sea revealing his high sparkling hump and regularly jetting
his silent spout into the air. To the credulous mariners it seemed the same
silent spout they had so long ago beheld in the moonlit Atlantic and Indian
Oceans.
    "And did none of ye see it before?" cried Ahab, hailing the perched
men all around him.
    "I saw him almost that same instant, Sir, that Captain Ahab did, and I
cried out," said Tashtego.

"Not the same instant; not the same—no, the doubloon is mine, Fate   *10*
reserved the doubloon for me. *I* only; none of ye could have raised the White
Whale first. There she blows! there she blows! there she blows! There again!
there again!" he cried, in long-drawn, lingering, methodic tones, attuned to
the gradual prolongings of the whale's visible jets. "He's going to sound! In
stunsails! Down top-gallant-sails! Stand by three boats. Mr. Starbuck, remember, stay on board, and keep the ship. Helm there! Luff, luff a point! So;
steady, man, steady! There go flukes! No, no; only black water! All ready the
boats there? Stand by, stand by! Lower me, Mr. Starbuck; lower, lower—
quick, quicker!" and he slid through the air to the deck.

"He is heading straight to leeward, Sir," cried Stubb, "right away from
us; cannot have seen the ship yet."

"Be dumb, man! Stand by the braces! Hard down the helm! brace up!
Shiver her! shiver her! So, well that! Boats, boats!"

Soon all the boats but Starbuck's were dropped; all the boat-sails set—
all the paddles plying; with rippling swiftness, shooting to leeward; and Ahab
heading the onset. A pale, death-glimmer lit up Fedallah's sunken eyes; a
hideous motion gnawed his mouth.

Like noiseless nautilus shells, their light prows sped through the sea; but
only slowly they neared the foe. As they neared him, the ocean grew still
more smooth, seemed drawing a carpet over its waves—seemed a noon-
meadow, so serenely it spread. At length the breathless hunter came so nigh
his seemingly unsuspecting prey that his entire dazzling hump was distinctly
visible, sliding along the sea as if an isolated thing, and continually set in a
revolving ring of finest, fleecy, greenish foam. He saw the vast, involved
wrinkles of the slightly projecting head beyond. Before it, far out on the soft
Turkish-rugged waters, went the glistening white shadow from his broad,
milky forehead, a musical rippling playfully accompanying the shade; and
behind, the blue waters interchangeably flowed over into the moving valley
of his steady wake; and on either hand bright bubbles arose and danced by
his side. But these were broken again by the light toes of hundreds of gay
fowl softly feathering the sea, alternate with their fitful flight; and like to
some flag-staff rising from the painted hull of an argosy, the tall but shattered
pole of a recent lance projected from the White Whale's back; and at intervals
one of the cloud of soft-toed fowls hovering, and to and fro skimming like a
canopy over the fish, silently perched and rocked on this pole, the long tail
feathers streaming like pennons.

A gentle joyousness—a mighty mildness of repose in swiftness, invested   *15*
the gliding whale. Not the white bull Jupiter swimming away with ravished
Europa clinging to his graceful horns, his lovely leering eyes sideways intent
upon the maid, with smooth bewitching fleetness, rippling straight for the
nuptial bower in Crete—not Jove, not that great majesty Supreme—did
surpass the glorified White Whale as he so divinely swam.

On each soft side—coincident with the parted swell that but once
leaving him then flowed so wide away—on each bright side, the whale shed

off enticings. No wonder there had been some among the hunters who namelessly transported and allured by all this serenity had ventured to assail it, but had fatally found that quietude but the vesture of tornadoes. Yet calm, enticing calm, oh, whale! thou glidest on, to all who for the first time eye thee, no matter how many in that same way thou may'st have bejuggled and destroyed before.

And thus, through the serene tranquilities of the tropical sea, among waves whose hand-clappings were suspended by exceeding rapture, Moby Dick moved on, still withholding from sight the full terrors of his submerged trunk, entirely hiding the wrenched hideousness of his jaw. But soon the fore part of him slowly rose from the water. For an instant his whole marbleized body formed a high arch, like Virginia's Natural Bridge, and warningly waving his bannered flukes in the air the grand god revealed himself, sounded, and went out of sight. Hoveringly halting, and dipping on the wing, the white sea-fowls longingly lingered over the agitated pool that he left.

With oars apeak and paddles down, the sheets of their sails adrift, the three boats now stilly floated, awaiting Moby Dick's reappearance.

"An hour," said Ahab, standing rooted in his boat's stern; and he gazed beyond the whale's place, towards the dim blue spaces and wide wooing vacancies to leeward. It was only an instant, for again his eyes seemed whirling round in his head as he swept the watery circle. The breeze now freshened; the sea began to swell.

"The birds! the birds!" cried Tashtego.

In long Indian file, as when herons take wing, the white birds were now all flying towards Ahab's boat; and when within a few yards began fluttering over the water there, wheeling round and round, with joyous, expectant cries. Their vision was keener than man's; Ahab could discover no sign in the sea. But suddenly as he peered down and down into its depths, he profoundly saw a white living spot no bigger than a white weasel, with wonderful celerity uprising and magnifying as it rose, till it turned, and then there were plainly revealed two long crooked rows of white, glistening teeth, floating up from the undiscoverable bottom. It was Moby Dick's open mouth and scrolled jaw, his vast, shadowed bulk still half blending with the blue of the sea. The glittering mouth yawned beneath the boat like an open-doored marble tomb; and giving one sidelong sweep with his steering oar, Ahab whirled the craft aside from this tremendous apparition. Then, calling upon Fedallah to change places with him, went forward to the bows, and seizing Perth's harpoon, commanded his crew to grasp their oars and stand by to stern.

Now, by reason of this timely spinning round the boat upon its axis, its bow, by anticipation, was made to face the whale's head while yet under water. But as if perceiving this stratagem, Moby Dick, with that malicious intelligence ascribed to him, sidelingly transplanted himself, as it were, in an instant, shooting his pleated head lengthwise beneath the boat.

Through and through—through every plank and each rib, it thrilled

20

for an instant, the whale obliquely lying on his back, in the manner of a biting shark, slowly and feelingly taking its bows full within his mouth, so that the long, narrow, scrolled lower jaw curled high up into the open air and one of the teeth caught in a row-lock. The bluish pearl-white of the inside of the jaw was within six inches of Ahab's head, and reached higher than that. In this attitude the White Whale now shook the slight cedar as a mildly cruel cat her mouse. With unastonished eyes Fedallah gazed and crossed his arms, but the tiger-yellow crew were tumbling over each other's heads to gain the uttermost stern.

And now, while both elastic gunwales were springing in and out, as the whale dallied with the doomed craft in this devilish way—and from his body being submerged beneath the boat, he could not be darted at from the bows, for the bows were almost inside of him, as it were—and while the other boats involuntarily paused, as before a quick crisis impossible to withstand, then it was that monomaniac Ahab, furious with this tantalizing vicinity of his foe, which placed him all alive and helpless in the very jaws he hated—frenzied with all this, he seized the long bone with his naked hands and wildly strove to wrench it from its gripe. As now he thus vainly strove, the jaw slipped from him; the frail gunwales bent in, collapsed, and snapped, as both jaws, like an enormous shears, sliding further aft, bit the craft completely in twain and locked themselves fast again in the sea, midway between the two floating wrecks. These floated aside, the broken ends drooping, the crew at the stern-wreck clinging to the gunwales and striving to hold fast to the oars to lash them across.

At that preluding moment, ere the boat was yet snapped, Ahab, the 25 first to perceive the whale's intent, by the crafty upraising of his head, a movement that loosed his hold for the time at that moment his hand had made one final effort to push the boat out of the bite. But only slipping further into the whale's mouth and tilting over sideways as it slipped, the boat had shaken off his hold on the jaw, spilled him out of it as he leaned to the push, and so he fell flat-faced upon the sea.

Ripplingly withdrawing from his prey, Moby Dick now lay at a little distance, vertically thrusting his oblong white head up and down in the billows and at the same time slowly revolving his whole spindled body, so that when his vast wrinkled forehead rose—some twenty or more feet out of the water—the now rising swells, with all their confluent waves, dazzlingly broke against it; vindictively tossing their shivered spray still higher into the air. . . .

But soon resuming his horizontal attitude, Moby Dick swam swiftly round and round the wrecked crew, sideways churning the water in his vengeful wake, as if lashing himself up to still another and more deadly assault. The sight of the splintered boat seemed to madden him, as the blood of grapes and mulberries cast before Antiochus's elephants in the book of Maccabees. Meanwhile Ahab, half smothered in the foam of the whale's insolent tail, and too much of a cripple to swim—though he could still keep afloat, even in the heart of such a whirlpool as that—helpless Ahab's head was seen, like a tossed bubble which the least chance shock might burst. From the boat's fragmentary stern, Fedallah incuriously and mildly eyed him. The clinging crew, at the other drifting end, could not succor him; more than enough was it for them to look to themselves. For so revolvingly appalling was the White Whale's aspect, and so swift the ever-contracting circles he made, that he seemed horizontally swooping upon them. And though the other boats, unharmed, still hovered hard by, still they dared not pull into the eddy to strike, lest that should be the signal for the instant destruction of the jeopardized castaways, Ahab and all; nor in that case could they themselves hope to escape. With straining eyes, then, they remained on the outer edge of the direful zone, whose center had now become the old man's head.

Meantime, from the beginning all this had been descried from the ship's mast-heads; and squaring her yards, she had borne down upon the scene and was now so nigh, that Ahab in the water hailed her; "Sail on the"—but that moment a breaking sea dashed on him from Moby Dick and whelmed him for the time. But struggling out of it again and chancing to rise on a towering crest, he shouted, "Sail on the whale! Drive him off!"

The Pequod's prows were pointed; and breaking up the charmed circle, she effectually parted the White Whale from his victim. As he sullenly swam off, the boats flew to the rescue.

Dragged into Stubb's boat with blood-shot, blinded eyes, the white brine caking in his wrinkles, the long tension of Ahab's bodily strength did crack, and helplessly he yielded to his body's doom: for a time, lying all crushed in the bottom of Stubb's boat, like one trodden under foot of herds of elephants. Far inland, nameless wails came from him, as desolate sounds from out ravines. 30

But this intensity of his physical prostration did but so much the more abbreviate it. In an instant's compass, great hearts sometimes condense to one deep pang the sum total of those shallow pains kindly diffused through feebler men's whole lives. And so, such hearts, though summary in each one suffering; still, if the gods decree it, in their life-time aggregate a whole age of woe, wholly made up of instantaneous intensities; for even in their pointless centres, those noble natures contain the entire circumferences of inferior souls.

"The harpoon," said Ahab, half way rising, and draggingly leaning on one bended arm, "is it safe?"

"Aye, Sir, for it was not darted; this is it," said Stubb, showing it.

"Lay it before me—any missing men?"

"One, two, three, four, five—there were five oars, Sir, and here are five men." 35

"That's good. Help me, man; I wish to stand. So, so, I see him! there! there! going to leeward still; what a leaping spout!—Hands off from me! The eternal sap runs up in Ahab's bones again! Set the sail; out oars; the helm!"

It is often the case that when a boat is stove, its crew, being picked up by another boat, help to work that second boat; and the chase is thus continued with what is called double-banked oars. It was thus now. But the added power of the boat did not equal the added power of the whale, for he seemed to have treble-banked his every fin; swimming with a velocity which plainly showed, that if now, under these circumstances, pushed on, the chase would prove an indefinitely prolonged, if not a hopeless one. Nor could any crew endure for so long a period such an unintermitted, intense straining at the oar—a thing barely tolerable only in some one brief vicissitude. The ship itself, then, as it sometimes happens, offered the most promising intermediate means of overtaking the chase. Accordingly, the boats now made for her, and were soon swayed up to their cranes—the two parts of the wrecked boat having beeñ previously secured by her—and then hoisting everything to her side, and stacking her canvas high up, and sideways outstretching it with stun-sails, like the double-jointed wings of an albatross, the Pequod bore down in the leeward wake of Moby Dick. At the well known, methodic intervals, the whale's glittering spout was regularly announced from the manned mast-heads; and when he would be reported as just gone down, Ahab would take the time, and then pacing the deck, binnacle-watch in hand, so soon as the last second of the allotted hour expired, his voice was heard. "Whose is the doubloon now? D'ye see him?" and if the reply was, No, sir! straightway he commanded them to lift him to his perch. In this way the day wore on; Ahab now aloft and motionless, anon unrestingly pacing the planks.

The Responsive Reader

1. How does Melville create the impression of serene beauty and sublime calm that pervades his description of the whale moving through the smooth ocean? What are key details or key ingredients in his picture? How many words can you find that have positive connotations and that contribute to the magical overall effect?

2. What is the role of the classical allusion to Jupiter (also called Jove) and Europa?

3. What are the first hints or reminders of the whale's terrifying and destructive other side? What are key elements in Melville's description of the resurfacing whale? How has the author's language changed to words with ominous or sinister implications?

4. What glimpse do you get in this excerpt of the obsessed, "monomaniacal" Captain Ahab? What makes him a worthy antagonist, or worthy opponent, for the great white whale?

Thinking, Talking, Writing

5. What for you is the key to the whale's beauty? What seems to be the key to the fascination the whale has for the author?

6. Do you think the whale could be a symbol for all of nature? Or does it symbolize one part or aspect of nature?
7. With many animal species endangered, what reasons do you think account for the way the save-the-whales movement has captured the public's imagination?

TO BUILD A FIRE

Jack London

The oldest body of a human being ever discovered was found on the mountainside where he died, covered by snow and ice. He had on primitive clothing designed to shield him from the cold, he carried a bow and arrows to hunt for food, and he carried the means of making a fire. He furnished a perfect symbol of human beings struggling for survival on a planet where, as the following story says, they are "able only to live within certain narrow limits of heat and cold."

Jack London became immensely popular as a storyteller chronicling the struggle for survival. After a spotty education, he worked on a ship sailing to Japan and the Bering Sea, marched to Washington with the unemployed, and was jailed as a vagrant. He joined in the gold rush to the Klondike in 1897, and some of his best-known stories are set in the frozen North. The Call of the Wild (1903), which has been called "one of the world's great dog stories," made him internationally famous. Best known among his many other books are The Sea Wolf (1904) and White Fang (1906). His name became synonymous with a love of adventure and the rugged life; he served as a correspondent in the war between Russia and Japan in 1904 and in the Mexican revolution in 1914. His closeness to working people surviving against odds left him with little sympathy for the idle rich and made him an advocate of radical political causes.

The following story was first published in 1908, when writers in the tradition of naturalism prided themselves on their unretouched, unvarnished picture of nature in the raw. The story became a much-reprinted classic because of its uncompromising faithfulness to the harsh realities of life in the timber country of the American north. It is a story in which there are no tricks, no diversions, no surprise ending. You are meant to say: "That's exactly how it was." Is that how you react as a modern reader?

Day had broken cold and gray, exceedingly cold and gray, when the   1
man turned aside from the main Yukon trail and climbed the high earthbank, where a dim and little-travelled trail led eastward through the fat spruce timberland. It was a steep bank, and he paused for breath at the top, excusing the act to himself by looking at his watch. It was nine o'clock. There was no sun nor hint of sun, though there was not a cloud in the sky. It was a clear day, and yet there seemed an intangible pall over the face of things, a subtle gloom that made the day dark, and that was due to the absence of sun. This fact did not worry the man. He was used to the lack of sun. It had been days since he had seen the sun, and he knew that a few more days must pass before that cheerful orb, due south, should just peep above the sky line and dip immediately from view.

The man flung a look back along the way he had come. The Yukon lay a mile wide and hidden under three feet of ice. On top of this ice were as many feet of snow. It was all pure white, rolling in gentle undulations where the ice jams of the freeze-up had formed. North and south, as far as his eye could see, it was unbroken white, save for a dark hairline that curved and twisted from around the spruce-covered island to the south, and that curved and twisted away into the north, where it disappeared behind another spruce-covered island. This dark hairline was the trail—the main trail—that led south five hundred miles to the Chilcoot Pass, Dyea, and salt water; and that led north seventy miles to Dawson, and still on to the north a thousand miles to Nulato, and finally to St. Michael, on Bering Sea, a thousand miles and half a thousand more.

But all this—the mysterious, far-reaching hairline trail, the absence of sun from the sky, the tremendous cold, and the strangeness and weirdness of it all—made no impression on the man. It was not because he was long used to it. He was a newcomer in the land, a *chechaquo,* and this was his first winter. The trouble with him was that he was without imagination. He was quick and alert in the things of life, but only in the things, and not in the significances. Fifty degrees below zero meant eight-odd degrees of frost. Such fact impressed him as being cold and uncomfortable, and that was all. It did not lead him to meditate upon his frailty as a creature of temperature, and upon man's frailty in general, able only to live within certain narrow limits of heat and cold; and from there on it did not lead him to the conjectural field of immortality and man's place in the universe. Fifty degrees below zero stood for a bite of frost that hurt and that must be guarded against by the use of mittens, ear flaps, warm moccasins, and thick socks. Fifty degrees below zero was to him just precisely fifty degrees below zero. That there should be anything more to it than that was a thought that never entered his head.

As he turned to go on, he spat speculatively. There was a sharp, explosive crackle that startled him. He spat again. And again, in the air, before it could fall to the snow, the spittle crackled. He knew that at fifty below spittle crackled on the snow, but this spittle had crackled in the air. Undoubtedly it was colder than fifty below—how much colder he did not know. But the temperature did not matter. He was bound for the old claim on the left fork of Henderson Creek, where the boys were already. They had come over across the divide from the Indian Creek country, while he had come the roundabout way to take a look at the possibilities of getting out logs in the spring from the islands in the Yukon. He would be in to camp by six o'clock; a bit after dark, it was true, but the boys would be there, a fire would be going, and a hot supper would be ready. As for lunch, he pressed his hand against the protruding bundle under his jacket. It was also under his shirt, wrapped up in a handkerchief and lying against the naked skin. It was the only way to keep the biscuits from freezing. He smiled agreeably to himself as he thought of those biscuits, each cut open and sopped in bacon grease, and each enclosing a generous slice of fried bacon.

He plunged in among the big spruce trees. The trail was faint. A foot   *5*
of snow had fallen since the last sled had passed over, and he was glad he was
without a sled, traveling light. In fact, he carried nothing but the lunch
wrapped in the handkerchief. He was surprised, however, at the cold. It
certainly was cold, he concluded, as he rubbed his numb nose and cheekbones with his mittened hand. He was a warm-whiskered man, but the hair
on his face did not protect the high cheekbones and the eager nose that
thrust itself aggressively into the frosty air.

At the man's heels trotted a dog, a big native husky, the proper wolf
dog, gray-coated and without any visible or temperamental difference from
its brother, the wild wolf. The animal was depressed by the tremendous cold.
It knew that it was no time for traveling. Its instinct told it a truer tale than
was told to the man by the man's judgment. In reality, it was not merely
colder than fifty below zero; it was colder than sixty below, than seventy
below. It was seventy-five below zero. Since the freezing point is thirty-two
above zero, it meant that one hundred and seven degrees of frost obtained.
The dog did not know anything about thermometers. Possibly in its brain
there was no sharp consciousness of a condition of very cold such as was in
the man's brain. But the brute had its instinct. It experienced a vague but
menacing apprehension that subdued it and made it slink along at the man's
heels, and that made it question eagerly every unwonted movement of the
man as if expecting him to go into camp or to seek shelter somewhere and
build a fire. The dog had learned fire, and it wanted fire, or else to burrow
under the snow and cuddle its warmth away from the air.

The frozen moisture of its breathing had settled on its fur in a fine
powder of frost, and especially were its jowls, muzzle, and eyelashes whitened
by its crystalled breath. The man's red beard and mustache were likewise
frosted, but more solidly, the deposit taking the form of ice and increasing
with every warm, moist breath he exhaled. Also, the man was chewing
tobacco, and the muzzle of ice held his lips so rigidly that he was unable to
clear his chin when he expelled the juice. The result was that a crystal beard
of the color and solidity of amber was increasing its length on his chin. If he
fell down it would shatter itself, like glass, into brittle fragments. But he did
not mind the appendage. It was the penalty all tobacco chewers paid in that
country, and he had been out before in two cold snaps. They had not been
so cold as this, he knew, but by the spirit thermometer at Sixty Mile he knew
they had been registered at fifty below and at fifty-five.

He held on through the level stretch of woods for several miles, crossed
a wide flat . . . , and dropped down a bank to the frozen bed of a small
stream. This was Henderson Creek, and he knew he was ten miles from the
forks. He looked at his watch. It was ten o'clock. He was making four miles
an hour, and he calculated that he would arrive at the forks at half-past
twelve. He decided to celebrate that event by eating his lunch there.

The dog dropped in again at his heels, with a tail drooping discourage-
ment, as the man swung along the creek bed. The furrow of the old sled

trail was plainly visible, but a dozen inches of snow covered the marks of the last runners. In a month no man had come up or down that silent creek. The man held steadily on. He was not much given to thinking, and just then particularly he had nothing to think about save that he would eat lunch at the forks and that at six o'clock he would be in camp with the boys. There was nobody to talk to; and, had there been, speech would have been impossible because of the ice muzzle on his mouth. So he continued monotonously to chew tobacco and to increase the length of his amber beard.

Once in a while the thought reiterated itself that it was very cold and   10 that he had never experienced such cold. As he walked along he rubbed his cheekbones and nose with the back of his mittened hand. He did this automatically, now and again changing hands. But, rub as he would, the instant he stopped his cheekbones went numb, and the following instant the end of his nose went numb. He was sure to frost his cheeks; he knew that, and experienced a pang of regret that he had not devised a nose strap of the sort Bud wore in cold snaps. Such a strap passed across the cheeks, as well, and saved them. But it didn't matter much, after all. What were frosted cheeks? A bit painful, that was all; they were never serious.

Empty as the man's mind was of thoughts, he was keenly observant, and he noticed the changes in the creek, the curves and bends and timber jams, and always he sharply noted where he placed his feet. Once, coming around a bend, he shied abruptly, like a startled horse, curved away from the place where he had been walking, and retreated several paces back along the trail. The creek he knew was frozen clear to the bottom—no creek could contain water in that arctic winter—but he knew also that there were springs that bubbled out from the hillsides and ran along under the snow and on top the ice of the creek. He knew that the coldest snaps never froze these springs, and he knew likewise their danger. They were traps. They hid pools of water under the snow that might be three inches deep, or three feet. Sometimes a skin of ice half an inch thick covered them, and in turn was covered by the snow. Sometimes there were alternate layers of water and ice skin, so that when one broke through he kept on breaking through for a while, sometimes wetting himself to the waist.

That was why he had shied in such panic. He had felt the give under his feet and heard the crackle of a snow-hidden ice skin. And to get his feet wet in such a temperature meant trouble and danger. At the very least it meant delay, for he would be forced to stop and build a fire, and under its protection to bare his feet while he dried his socks and moccasins. He stood and studied the creek bed and its banks, and decided that the flow of water came from the right. He reflected awhile, rubbing his nose and cheeks, then skirted to the left, stepping gingerly and testing the footing for each step. Once clear of the danger, he took a fresh chew of tobacco and swung along at his four-mile gait.

In the course of the next two hours he came upon several similar traps. Usually the snow above the hidden pools had a sunken, candied appearance that advertised the danger. Once again, however, he had a close call; and once, suspecting danger, he compelled the dog to go on in front. The dog did not want to go. It hung back until the man shoved it forward, and then it went quickly across the white, unbroken surface. Suddenly it broke through, floundered to one side, and got away to firmer footing. It had wet its forefeet and legs, and almost immediately the water that clung to it turned to ice. It made quick efforts to lick the ice off its legs, then dropped down in the snow and began to bite out the ice that had formed between the toes. This was a matter of instinct. To permit the ice to remain would mean sore feet. It did not know this. It merely obeyed the mysterious prompting that arose from the deep crypts of its being. But the man knew, having achieved a judgment on the subject, and he removed the mitten from his right hand and helped tear out the ice particles. He did not expose his fingers more than a minute, and was astonished at the swift numbness that smote them. It certainly was cold. He pulled on the mitten hastily, and beat the hand savagely across his chest.

At twelve o'clock the day was at its brightest. Yet the sun was too far south on its winter journey to clear the horizon. The bulge of the earth intervened between it and Henderson Creek, where the man walked under a clear sky at noon and cast no shadow. At half-past twelve, to the minute, he arrived at the forks of the creek. He was pleased at the speed he had made. If he kept it up, he would certainly be with the boys by six. He unbuttoned his jacket and shirt and drew forth his lunch. The action consumed no more than a quarter of a minute, yet in that brief moment the numbness laid hold of the exposed fingers. He did not put the mitten on, but, instead, struck the fingers a dozen sharp smashes against his leg. Then he sat down on a snow-covered log to eat. The sting that followed upon the striking of his fingers against his leg ceased so quickly that he was startled. He had had no chance to take a bite of biscuit. He struck the fingers repeatedly and returned them to the mitten, baring the other hand for the purpose of eating. He tried to take a mouthful, but the ice muzzle prevented. He had forgotten to build a fire and thaw out. He chuckled at his foolishness, and as he chuckled he noted the numbness creeping into the exposed fingers. Also, he noted that the stinging which had first come to his toes when he sat down was already passing away. He wondered whether the toes were warm or numb. He moved them inside the moccasins and decided that they were numb.

He pulled the mitten on hurriedly and stood up. He was a bit frightened. He stamped up and down until the stinging returned into the feet. It certainly was cold, was his thought. That man from Sulphur Creek had spoken the truth when telling how cold it sometimes got in the country. And he had laughed at him at the time! That showed one must not be too sure of things. There was no mistake about it, it *was* cold. He strode up and down, stamping his feet and threshing his arms, until reassured by the returning warmth. Then he got out matches and proceeded to make a fire. From

15

the undergrowth, where high water of the previous spring had lodged a supply of seasoned twigs, he got his firewood. Working carefully from a small beginning, he soon had a roaring fire, over which he thawed the ice from his face and in the protection of which he ate his biscuits. For the moment the cold of space was outwitted. The dog took satisfaction in the fire, stretching out close enough for warmth and far enough away to escape being singed.

When the man had finished, he filled his pipe and took his comfortable time over a smoke. Then he pulled on his mittens, settled the ear flaps of his cap firmly about his ears, and took the creek trail up the left fork. The dog was disappointed and yearned back toward the fire. This man did not know cold. Possibly all the generations of his ancestry had been ignorant of cold, of real cold, of cold one hundred and seven degrees below freezing point. But the dog knew; all its ancestry knew, and it had inherited the knowledge. And it knew that it was not good to walk abroad in such fearful cold. It was the time to lie snug in a hole in the snow and wait for a curtain of cloud to be drawn across the face of outer space whence this cold came. On the other hand, there was no keen intimacy between the dog and the man. The one was the toil slave of the other, and the only caresses it had ever received were the caresses of the whip lash and of harsh and menacing throat sounds that threatened the whip lash. So the dog made no effort to communicate its apprehension to the man. It was not concerned in the welfare of the man; it was for its own sake that it yearned back toward the fire. But the man whistled, and spoke to it with the sound of whip lashes, and the dog swung in at the man's heels and followed after.

The man took a chew of tobacco and proceeded to start a new amber beard. Also, his moist breath quickly powdered with white his mustache, eyebrows, and lashes. There did not seem to be so many springs on the left fork of the Henderson, and for half an hour the man saw no signs of any. And then it happened. At a place where there were no signs, where the soft, unbroken snow seemed to advertise solidity beneath, the man broke through. It was not deep. He wet himself halfway to the knees before he floundered out to the firm crust.

He was angry, and cursed his luck aloud. He had hoped to get into camp with the boys at six o'clock, and this would delay him an hour, for he would have to build a fire and dry out his footgear. This was imperative at that low temperature—he knew that much; and he turned aside to the bank, which he climbed. On top, tangled in the underbrush about the trunks of several small spruce trees, was a highwater deposit of dry firewood—sticks and twigs, principally, but also larger portions of seasoned branches and fine dry last year's grasses. He threw down several large pieces on top of the snow. This served for a foundation and prevented the young flame from drowning itself in the snow it otherwise would melt. The flame he got by touching a match to a small shred of birch bark that he took from his pocket. This burned even more readily than paper. Placing it on the foundation, he fed the young flame with wisps of dry grass and with the tiniest dry twigs.

He worked slowly and carefully, keenly aware of his danger. Gradually, as the flame grew stronger, he increased the size of the twigs with which he fed it. He squatted in the snow, pulling the twigs out from their entanglement in the brush and feeding directly to the flame. He knew there must be no failure. When it is seventy-five below zero, a man must not fail in his first attempt to build a fire—that is, if his feet are wet. If his feet are dry, and he fails, he can run along the trail for half a mile and restore his circulation. But the circulation of wet and freezing feet cannot be restored by running when it is seventy-five below. No matter how fast he runs, the wet feet will freeze the harder.

All this the man knew. The old-timer on Sulphur Creek had told him   20 about it the previous fall, and now he was appreciating the advice. Already all sensation had gone out of his feet. To build the fire he had been forced to remove his mittens, and the fingers had quickly gone numb. His pace of four miles an hour had kept his heart pumping blood to the surface of his body and to all the extremities. But the instant he stopped, the action of the pump eased down. The cold of space smote the unprotected tip of the planet, and he, being on that unprotected tip, received the full force of the blow. The blood of his body recoiled before it. The blood was alive, like the dog, and like the dog it wanted to hide away and cover itself up from the fearful cold. So long as he walked four miles an hour, he pumped that blood, willy-nilly, to the surface; but now it ebbed away and sank down into the recesses of his body. The extremities were the first to feel its absence. His wet feet froze the faster, and his exposed fingers numbed the faster, though they had not yet begun to freeze. Nose and cheeks were already freezing, while the skin of all his body chilled as it lost its blood.

But he was safe. Toes and nose and cheeks would be only touched by the frost, for the fire was beginning to burn with strength. He was feeding it with twigs the size of his finger. In another minute he would be able to feed it with branches the size of his wrist, and then he could remove his wet footgear, and, while it dried, he could keep his naked feet warm by the fire, rubbing them at first, of course, with snow. The fire was a success. He was safe. He remembered the advice of the old-timer on Sulphur Creek, and smiled. The old-timer had been very serious in laying down the law that no man must travel alone in the Klondike after fifty below. Well, here he was; he had had the accident; he was alone; and he had saved himself. Those old-timers were rather womanish, some of them, he thought. All a man had to do was to keep his head, and he was all right. Any man who was a man could travel alone. But it was surprising, the rapidity with which his cheeks and nose were freezing. And he had not thought his fingers could go lifeless in so short a time. Lifeless they were, for he could scarcely make them move together to grip a twig, and they seemed remote from his body and from him. When he touched a twig, he had to look and see whether or not he had hold of it. The wires were pretty well down between him and his finger ends.

All of which counted for little. There was the fire, snapping and crack-ling and promising life with every dancing flame. He started to untie his moccasins. They were coated with ice; the thick German socks were like sheaths of iron halfway to the knees; and the moccasin strings were like rods of steel all twisted and knotted as by some conflagration. For a moment he tugged with his numb fingers, then, realizing the folly of it, he drew his sheath knife.

But before he could cut the strings, it happened. It was his own fault or, rather, his mistake. He should not have built the fire under the spruce tree. He should have built it in the open. But it had been easier to pull the twigs from the brush and drop them directly on the fire. Now the tree under which he had done this carried a weight of snow on its boughs. No wind had blown for weeks, and each bough was fully freighted. Each time he had pulled a twig he had communicated a slight agitation to the tree—an imper-ceptible agitation, so far as he was concerned, but an agitation sufficient to bring about the disaster. High up in the tree one bough capsized its load of snow. This fell on the boughs beneath, capsizing them. This process con-tinued, spreading out and involving the whole tree. It grew like an avalanche, and it descended without warning upon the man and the fire, and the fire was blotted out! Where it had burned was a mantle of fresh and disor-dered snow.

The man was shocked. It was as though he had just heard his own sentence of death. For a moment he sat and stared at the spot where the fire had been. Then he grew very calm. Perhaps the old-timer on Sulphur Creek was right. If he had only had a trail mate he would have been in no danger now. The trail mate could have built the fire. Well, it was up to him to build the fire over again, and this second time there must be no failure. Even if he succeeded, he would most likely lose some toes. His feet must be badly frozen by now, and there would be some time before the second fire was ready.

Such were his thoughts, but he did not sit and think them. He was busy all the time they were passing through his mind. He made a new foundation for a fire, this time in the open, where no treacherous tree could blot it out. Next he gathered dry grasses and tiny twigs from the high-water flotsam. He could not bring his fingers together to pull them out, but he was able to gather them by the handful. In this way he got many rotten twigs and bits of green moss that were undesirable, but it was the best he could do. He worked methodically, even collecting an armful of the larger branches to be used later when the fire gathered strength. And all the while the dog sat and watched him, a certain yearning wistfulness in its eyes, for it looked upon him as the fire provider, and the fire was slow in coming.

When all was ready, the man reached in his pocket for a second piece of birch bark. He knew the bark was there, and, though he could not feel it with his fingers, he could hear its crisp rustling as he fumbled for it. Try as he would, he could not clutch hold of it. And all the time, in his conscious-ness, was the knowledge that each instant his feet were freezing. This thought tended to put him in a panic, but he fought against it and kept calm. He pulled on his mittens with his teeth, and threshed his arms back and forth, beating his hands with all his might against his sides. He did this sitting down, and he stood up to do it; and all the while the dog sat in the snow, its wolf brush of a tail curled around warmly over its forefeet, its sharp wolf ears pricked forward intently as it watched the man. And the man, as he beat and threshed with his arms and hands, felt a great surge of envy as he regarded the creature that was warm and secure in its natural covering.

After a time he was aware of the first faraway signals of sensation in his beaten fingers. The faint tingling grew stronger till it evolved into a stinging ache that was excruciating, but which the man hailed with satisfaction. He stripped the mitten from his right hand and fetched forth the birch bark. The exposed fingers were quickly going numb again. Next he brought out his bunch of sulphur matches. But the tremendous cold had already driven the life out of his fingers. In his effort to separate one match from the others, the whole bunch fell in the snow. He tried to pick it out of the snow, but failed. The dead fingers could neither touch nor clutch. He was very careful. He drove the thought of his freezing feet, and nose, and cheeks, out of his mind, devoting his whole soul to the matches. He watched, using the sense of vision in place of that of touch, and when he saw his fingers on each side the bunch, he closed them—that is he willed to close them, for the wires were down, and the fingers did not obey. He pulled the mitten on the right hand, and beat it fiercely against his knee. Then, with both mittened hands, he scooped the bunch of matches, along with much snow, into his lap. Yet he was no better off.

After some manipulation he managed to get the bunch between the heels of his mittened hands. In this fashion he carried it to his mouth. The ice crackled and snapped when by a violent effort he opened his mouth. He drew the lower jaw in, curled the upper lip out of the way, scraped the bunch with his upper teeth in order to separate a match. He succeeded in getting one, which he dropped on his lap. He was no better off. He could not pick it up. Then he devised a way. He picked it up in his teeth and scratched in on his leg. Twenty times he scratched before he succeeded in lighting it. As it flamed he held it with his teeth to the birch bark. But the burning brimstone went up his nostrils and into his lungs, causing him to cough spasmodically. The match fell into the snow and went out.

The old-timer on Sulphur Creek was right, he thought in the moment of controlled despair that ensued: after fifty below, a man should travel with a partner. He beat his hands, but failed in exciting any sensation. Suddenly he bared both hands, removing the mittens with his teeth. He caught the whole bunch between the heels of his hands. His arm muscles not being frozen enabled him to press the hand heels tightly against the matches. Then he scratched the bunch along his leg. It flared into flame, seventy sulphur matches at once! There was no wind to blow them out. He kept his head to one side to escape the strangling fumes, and held the blazing bunch to the birch bark. As he so held it, he became aware of sensation in his hand. His flesh was burning. He could smell it. Deep down below the surface he could feel it. The sensation developed into pain that grew acute. And still he endured it, holding the flame of the matches clumsily to the bark that would not light readily because his own burning hands were in the way, absorbing most of the flame.

At last, when he could endure no more, he jerked his hands apart. The blazing matches fell sizzling into the snow, but the birch bark was alight. He began laying dry grasses and the tiniest twigs on the flame. He could not pick and choose, for he had to lift the fuel between the heels of his hands. Small pieces of rotten wood and green moss clung to the twigs, and he bit them off as well as he could with his teeth. He cherished the flame carefully and awkwardly. It meant life, and it must not perish. The withdrawal of blood from the surface of his body now made him begin to shiver, and he grew more awkward. A large piece of green moss fell squarely on the little fire. He tried to poke it out with his fingers, but his shivering frame made him poke too far, and he disrupted the nucleus of the little fire, the burning grasses and tiny twigs separating and scattering. He tried to poke them together again, but in spite of the tenseness of the effort, his shivering got away with him, and the twigs were hopelessly scattered. Each twig gushed a puff of smoke and went out. The fire provider had failed. As he looked apathetically about him, his eyes chanced on the dog, sitting across the ruins of the fire from him, in the snow, making restless, hunching movements, slightly lifting one forefoot and then the other, shifting its weight back and forth on them with wistful eagerness.

The sight of the dog put a wild idea into his head. He remembered the tale of the man, caught in a blizzard, who killed a steer and crawled inside the carcass, and so was saved. He would kill the dog and bury his hands in the warm body until the numbness went out of them. Then he could build another fire. He spoke to the dog, calling it to him; but in his voice was a strange note of fear that frightened the animal, who had never known the man to speak in such way before. Something was the matter, and its suspicious nature sensed danger—it knew not what danger, but somewhere, somehow, in its brain arose an apprehension of the man. It flattened its ears down at the sound of the man's voice, and its restless, hunching movements and the liftings and shiftings of its forefeet became more pronounced; but it would not come to the man. He got on his hands and knees and crawled toward the dog. This unusual posture again excited suspicion, and the animal sidled mincingly away.

The man sat up in the snow for a moment and struggled for calmness. Then he pulled on his mittens, by means of his teeth, and got upon his feet. He glanced down at first in order to assure himself that he was really standing up, for the absence of sensation in his feet left him unrelated to the earth. His erect position in itself started to drive the webs of suspicion from the dog's mind; and when he spoke peremptorily, with the sound of whip lashes

30

in his voice, the dog rendered its customary allegiance and came to him. As it came within reaching distance the man lost his control. His arms flashed out to the dog, and he experienced genuine surprise when he discovered that his hands could not clutch, that there was neither bend nor feeling in the fingers. He had forgotten for the moment that they were frozen and that they were freezing more and more. All this happened quickly, and before the animal could get away, he encircled its body with his arms. He sat down in the snow, and in this fashion held the dog, while it snarled and whined and struggled.

But it was all he could do, hold its body encircled in his arms and sit there. He realized that he could not kill the dog. There was no way to do it. With his helpless hands he could neither draw nor hold his sheath knife nor throttle the animal. He released it, and it plunged wildly away, with tail between its legs, and still snarling. It halted forty feet away and surveyed him curiously, with ears sharply pricked forward.

The man looked down at his hands in order to locate them, and found them hanging on the ends of his arms. It struck him as curious that one should have to use his eyes in order to find out where his hands were. He began threshing his arms back and forth, beating the mittened hands against his sides. He did this for five minutes, violently, and his heart pumped enough blood up to the surface to put a stop to his shivering. But no sensation was aroused in the hands. He had an impression that they hung like weights on the ends of his arms, but when he tried to run the impression down, he could not find it.

A certain fear of death, dull and oppressive, came to him. This fear *35* quickly became poignant as he realized that it was no longer a mere matter of freezing his fingers and toes, or of losing his hands and feet, but that it was a matter of life and death with the chances against him. This threw him into a panic, and he turned and ran up the creek bed along the old, dim trail. The dog joined in behind and kept up with him. He ran blindly, without intention, in fear such as he had never known in his life. Slowly, as he plowed and floundered through the snow, he began to see things again—the banks of the creek, the old timber jams, the leafless aspens, and the sky. The running made him feel better. He did not shiver. Maybe, if he ran on, his feet would thaw out; and, anyway, if he ran far enough, he would reach camp and the boys. Without doubt he would lose some fingers and toes and some of his face; but the boys would take care of him, and save the rest of him when he got there. And at the same time there was another thought in his mind that said he would never get to the camp and the boys; that it was too many miles away, that the freezing had too great a start on him, and that he would soon be stiff and dead. This thought he kept in the background and refused to consider. Sometimes it pushed itself forward and demanded to be heard, but he thrust it back and strove to think of other things.

It struck him as curious that he could run at all on feet so frozen that he could not feel them when they struck the earth and took the weight of his body. He seemed to himself to skim along above the surface, and to have no connection with the earth. Somewhere he had once seen a winged Mercury, and he wondered if Mercury felt as he felt when skimming over the earth.

His theory of running until he reached camp and the boys had one flaw in it: he lacked the endurance. Several times he stumbled, and finally he tottered, crumpled up, and fell. When he tried to rise, he failed. He must sit and rest, he decided, and next time he would merely walk and keep on going. As he sat and regained his breath, he noted that he was feeling quite warm and comfortable. He was not shivering, and it even seemed that a warm glow had come to his chest and trunk. And yet, when he touched his nose or cheeks, there was no sensation. Running would not thaw them out. Nor would it thaw out his hands and feet. Then the thought came to him that the frozen portions of his body must be extending. He tried to keep this thought down, to forget it, to think of something else; he was aware of the panicky feeling that it caused, and he was afraid of the panic. But the thought asserted itself, and persisted, until it produced a vision of his body totally frozen. This was too much, and he made another wild run along the trail. Once he slowed down to a walk, but the thought of the freezing extending itself made him run again.

And all the time the dog ran with him, at his heels. When he fell down a second time, it curled its tail over its forefeet and sat in front of him, facing him, curiously eager and intent. The warmth and security of the animal angered him, and he cursed it till it flattened down its ears appeasingly. This time the shivering came more quickly upon the man. He was losing in his battle with the frost. It was creeping into his body from all sides. The thought of it drove him on, but he ran no more than a hundred feet, when he staggered and pitched headlong. It was his last panic. When he had recovered his breath and control, he sat up and entertained in his mind the conception of meeting death with dignity. However, the conception did not come to him in such terms. His idea of it was that he had been making a fool of himself, running around like a chicken with its head cut off—such was the simile that occurred to him. Well, he was bound to freeze anyway, and he might as well take it decently. With this new-found peace of mind came the first glimmerings of drowsiness. A good idea, he thought, to sleep off to death. It was like taking an anesthetic. Freezing was not so bad as people thought. There were lots worse ways to die.

He pictured the boys finding his body next day. Suddenly he found himself with them, coming along the trail and looking for himself. And, still with them, he came around a turn in the trail and found himself lying in the snow. He did not belong with himself any more, for even then he was out of himself, standing with the boys and looking at himself in the snow. It certainly was cold, was his thought. When he got back to the States he could tell the folks what real cold was. He drifted on from this to a vision of the old-timer on Sulphur Creek. He could see him quite clearly, warm and comfortable, and smoking a pipe.

"You were right, old hoss; you were right," the man mumbled to the *40*
old-timer of Sulphur Creek.

Then the man drowsed off into what seemed to him the most comfortable and satisfying sleep he had ever known. The dog sat facing him and
waiting. The brief day drew to a close in a long, slow twilight. There were
no signs of a fire to be made, and, besides, never in the dog's experience had
it known a man to sit like that in the snow and make no fire. As the twilight
drew on, its eager yearning for the fire mastered it, and with a great lifting
and shifting of forefeet, it whined softly, then flattened its ears down in
anticipation of being chidden by the man. But the man remained silent. Later
the dog whined loudly. And still later it crept close to the man and caught
the scent of death. This made the animal bristle and back away. A little longer
it delayed, howling under the stars that leaped and danced and shone brightly
in the cold sky. Then it turned and trotted up the trail in the direction of the
camp it knew, where were the other food providers and fire providers.

The Responsive Reader

1. How does the beginning of the story make the setting and the prevailing conditions real for the reader? What are striking or especially significant details? What are touches that forewarn the reader of what
   might happen later?
2. What kind of person is the central character? Is he unprepared, over-
   confident, emotionally unsuited for the environment, absent-minded,
   careless? Does it matter that he is a newcomer to the territory? Is what
   happens to him his own fault? What, according to the author, is his
   flaw?
3. London wrote at a time when instinct and the instinctual basis of life
   were new and controversial topics. What role does the dog play in the
   story? How does London keep developing the contrast between the
   man and his animal companion? What seems to be his intention or
   major point?
4. What for you are key stages in this story? What for you is the turning point? When did you decide that the ending was a foregone
   conclusion?
5. What goes through the man's mind as the story unfolds? How does he
   meet his fate? Is the way he thinks and reacts meant to represent what
   normal human beings would think and feel? Would you call this an
   action story or a study in psychology?

Thinking, Talking, Writing

6. Naturalistic writers prided themselves on their hardnosed objective reporting of harsh reality, but they also often had a grim ironic sense of
   humor. Where does London's sense of irony show in this story? What
   are striking ironic contrasts?

7. Does this story have a meaning for the modern reader? Has the problem that this story focuses on become a thing of the past? Does this story have any meaning for people not living in extreme northern latitudes?
8. Is nature beautiful or ugly in this account?

Collaborative Projects

9. You may want to help your class set up groups exploring different dimensions of questions like the following: Many Americans have moved north attracted by economic development in Alaska; many Canadians live in a harsher climate than most Americans do. How much of a threat is the harsh climate to people living up north? How do they cope? How does the climate affect their outlook or mentality?

LOOKING SPRING IN THE EYE
Annie Dillard

Annie Dillard is an outstanding American naturalist—a writer who tries to keep alive our sense of wonder about the natural world. She has an uncanny gift for making us take a fresh look at nature, alerting us to the vital creative energy at work in the universe around us.

Dillard first became known to nature lovers when she published her Pulitzer Prize–winning Pilgrim at Tinker Creek *(1974), from which the following selection is taken. In this book, she recorded a year of observations of the natural environment around her house by Tinker Creek, in the Roanoke Valley of Virginia. She has the naturalist's gift for noticing things that others overlook—signs of the burgeoning life all around her, nature's small and big mysteries, and "quirky facts." She helps her readers see some of the fascinating and perturbing manifestations of the natural life around us without varnishing them or allowing them to be retouched.*

Although she says that she is not a scientist, she writes here as an expert, experienced observer—as a limnologist (student of freshwater life) who observes with infinite patience the animalcules (very small animal life) and plant life of her pond. She bears out the saying that "the expert has a word for it." She knows many of the microscopic creatures by their names, and she uses the technical terms needed to describe their body parts and motions. Which of the expert's terms do you recognize? Which can you make out from the context? Which are close to common language or have a poetic touch?

On an evening in late May, a moist wind from Carvin's Cove shoots down the gap between Tinker and Brushy mountains, tears along Carvin's Creek valley, and buffets my face as I stand by the duck pond. The surface of the duck pond doesn't budge. The algal layer is a rigid plating; if the wind blew hard enough, I imagine it might audibly creak. On warm days in February the primitive plants start creeping over the pond, filamentous green and blue-green algae in sopping strands. From a sunlit shallow edge they green and spread, thickening throughout the water like bright gelatin. When they smother the whole pond they block sunlight, strangle respiration, and snarl creatures in hopeless tangles. Dragonfly nymphs, for instance, are easily able to shed a leg or two to escape a tight spot, but even dragonfly nymphs get stuck in the algae strands and starve.

Several times I've seen a frog trapped under the algae. I would be staring at the pond when the green muck by my feet would suddenly leap into the air and then subside. It looked as though it had been jabbed from underneath by a broom handle. Then it would leap again, somewhere else, a jumping green flare, absolutely silently—this is a very disconcerting way to spend an evening. The frog would always find an open place at last, and break successfully onto the top of the heap, trailing long green slime from its back, and emitting a hollow sound like a pipe thrown into a cavern. Tonight I walked around the pond scaring frogs; a couple of them jumped off, going, in effect, eek, and most grunted, and the pond was still. But one big frog, bright green like a poster-paint frog, didn't jump, so I waved my arm and stamped to scare it, and it jumped suddenly, and I jumped, and then everything in the pond jumped, and I laughed and laughed.

There is a muscular energy in sunlight corresponding to the spiritual energy of wind. On a sunny day, sun's energy on a square acre of land or pond can equal 4500 horsepower. These "horses" heave in every direction, like slaves building pyramids, and fashion, from the bottom up, a new and sturdy world.

The pond is popping with life. Midges are swarming over the center, and the edges are clotted with the jellied egg masses of snails. One spring I saw a snapping turtle lumber from the pond to lay her eggs. Now a green heron picks around in the pondweed and bladderwort; two muskrats at the shallow end are stockpiling cattails. Diatoms, which are algae that look under a microscope like crystals, multiply so fast you can practically watch a submersed green leaf transform into a brown fuzz. In the plankton, single-cell algae, screw fungi, bacteria, and water mold abound. Insect larvae and nymphs carry on their eating business everywhere in the pond. Stillwater caddises, alderfly larvae, and damselfly and dragonfly nymphs stalk on the bottom debris; mayfly nymphs hide in the weeds, mosquito larvae wriggle near the surface, and red-tailed maggots stick their breathing tubes up from between decayed leaves along the shore. Also at the pond's muddy edges it is easy to see the tiny red tubifex worms and bloodworms; the convulsive jerking of hundreds and hundreds together catches my eye.

Once, when the pond was younger and the algae had not yet taken over, I saw an amazing creature. At first all I saw was a slender motion. Then I saw that it was a wormlike creature swimming in the water with a strong, whiplike thrust, and it was two feet long. It was also slender as a thread. It looked like an inked line someone was nervously drawing over and over. Later I learned that it was a horsehair worm. The larvae of horsehair worms live as parasites in land insects; the aquatic adults can get to be a yard long. I don't know how it gets from the insect to the pond, or from the pond to the insect, for that matter, or why on earth it needs such an extreme shape. If the one I saw had been so much as an inch longer or a shave thinner, I doubt if I would ever have come back.

The plankton bloom is what interests me. The plankton animals are all those microscopic drifting animals that so staggeringly outnumber us. In the spring they are said to "bloom," like so many poppies. There may be five times as many of these teeming creatures in spring as in summer. Among them are the protozoans—amoebae and other rhizopods, and millions of various flagellates and ciliates; gelatinous moss animalcules or byrozoans;

rotifers—which wheel around either free or in colonies; and all the diverse crustacean minutiae—copepods, ostracods, and cladocerans like the abundant daphnias. All these drifting animals multiply in sundry bizarre fashions, eat tiny plants or each other, die, and drop to the pond's bottom. Many of them have quite refined means of locomotion—they whirl, paddle, swim, slog, whip, and sinuate—but since they are so small, they are no match against even the least current in the water. Even such a sober limnologist as Robert E. Coker characterizes the movement of plankton as "milling around."

A cup of duck-pond water looks like a seething broth. If I carry the cup home and let the sludge settle, the animalcules sort themselves out, and I can concentrate them further by dividing them into two clear glass bowls. One bowl I paint all black except for a single circle where the light shines through; I leave the other bowl clear except for a single black circle against the light. Given a few hours, the light-loving creatures make their feeble way to the clear circle, and the shade-loving creatures to the black. Then, if I want to, I can harvest them with a pipette and examine them under a microscope.

There they loom and disappear as I fiddle with the focus. I run the eyepiece around until I am seeing the drop magnified three hundred times, and I squint at the little rotifer called monostyla. It zooms around excitedly, crashing into strands of spirogyra alga or zipping around the frayed edge of a clump of debris. The creature is a flattened oval; at its "head" is a circular fringe of whirling cilia, and at its "tail" a single long spike, so that it is shaped roughly like a horseshoe crab. But it is so incredibly small, as multicelled animals go, that it is translucent, even transparent, and I have a hard time telling if it is above or beneath a similarly transparent alga. Two monostyla drive into view from opposite directions; they meet, bump, reverse, part. I keep thinking that if I listen closely I will hear the high whine of tiny engines. As their drop heats from the light on the mirror, the rotifers skitter more and more frantically; as it dries, they pale and begin to stagger, and at last can muster only a halting twitch. Then I either wash the whole batch down the sink's drain, or in a rush of sentiment walk out to the road by starlight and dump them in a puddle. Tinker Creek where I live is too fast and rough for most of them.

I don't really look forward to these microscopic forays: I have been almost knocked off my kitchen chair on several occasions when, as I was following with strained eyes the tiny career of a monostyla rotifer, an enormous red roundworm whipped into the scene, blocking everything, and writhing in huge, flapping convulsions that seemed to sweep my face and fill the kitchen. I do it as a moral exercise; the microscope at my forehead is a kind of phylactery, a constant reminder of the facts of creation that I would just as soon forget. You can buy your child a microscope and say grandly, "Look, child, at the Jungle in a Little Drop." The boy looks, plays around with pond water and bread mold and onion sprouts for a month or two, and then starts shooting baskets or racing cars, leaving the microscope on the basement table staring fixedly at its own mirror forever—and you say he's growing up. But in the puddle or pond, in the city reservoir, ditch, or Atlantic Ocean, the rotifers still spin and munch, the daphnia still filter and are filtered, and the copepods still swarm hanging with clusters of eggs. These are real creatures with real organs leading real lives, one by one. I can't pretend they're not there. If I have life, sense, energy, will, so does a rotifer. The monostyla goes to the dark spot on the bowl: To which circle am I heading? I can move around right smartly in a calm; but in a real wind, in a change of weather, in a riptide, am I really moving, or am I "milling around"?

I was created from a clot and set in proud, free motion: so were they. *10* So was this rotifer created, this monostyla with its body like a light bulb in which pale organs hang in loops; so was this paramecium created, with a thousand propulsive hairs jerking in unison, whipping it from here to there across a drop and back. *Ad majorem Dei gloriam?* [To the greater glory of God.]

Somewhere, and I can't find where, I read about an Eskimo hunter who asked the local missionary priest, "If I did not know about God and sin, would I go to hell?" "No," said the priest, "not if you did not know." "Then why," asked the Eskimo earnestly, "did you tell me?" If I did not know about the rotifers and paramecia, and all the bloom of plankton clogging the dying pond, fine; but since I've seen it I must somehow deal with it, take it into account. "Never lose a holy curiosity," Einstein said; and so I lift my microscope down from the shelf, spread a drop of duck pond on a glass slide, and try to look spring in the eye.

The Responsive Reader

1. What for you are striking instances of Dillard's gift for making you see strange, quirky, or unforgettable sights? What striking imaginative comparisons does she use to help her describe the strange or unfamiliar?
2. What assumptions or attitudes about nature do you bring to this essay? Does this essay challenge your own assumptions? If visitors from a distant planet were to see only the cross-section of natural life that you see in this essay, how do you think they would describe and define life on this planet?
3. Does the author anywhere seem to sum up her own perspective on nature? Does her essay have a unifying thesis or a central philosophy?

Thinking, Talking, Writing

4. Is the natural world that Dillard makes you see beautiful or ugly? Or is this the wrong question to ask?
5. Melville looks at some of nature's largest creatures, Dillard at some of the smallest. For you, is there a connecting thread?

Collaborative Projects

6. Working with a group, study and sort out the technical biologist's language used in this essay. Present your findings in such a way that they would help the layperson understand and appreciate this essay.

THE JOURNEY'S END

Wendell Berry

When the despair of the world grows in me
and I wake in the night at the least sound
in fear of what my life and my children's life may be
I go and lie down where the wood drake
rests in his beauty on the water, and the great heron feeds.
Wendell Berry, "The Peace of Wild Things"

Wendell Berry is part of a tradition of American nature writing that turns to the healing influence of nature as the answer to the ills of our technological civilization. Writers from Henry David Thoreau to Loren Eiseley have encouraged their readers to leave the congestion and paranoia of the city behind at least for a time. They have taught their readers to refresh the spirit by putting themselves in touch with unspoilt nature. Like the Romantic poets of an earlier age, they ask us to look at the natural world in a spirit of love. They ask us to rekindle our sense of wonder and of awe.

Berry, a poet "rooted in the land" (Jonathan Yardly), has lived and farmed in Kentucky and has studied and taught at the University of Kentucky. He has published many collections of poems and essays, including To What Listens *(1975) and* Clearing *(1977). The following essay follows a pattern familiar to lovers of nature writing: Berry embarks on a journey of discovery. He shares with us the results of his gift for patient observation. These in turn inspire his thoughts about our relation to the natural world and about our destiny on this planet.*

Early in 1968 the state's newspapers were taking note of the discovery, in one of the rock houses in the Gorge, of a crude hut built of short split planks overlaying a framework of poles. The hut was hardly bigger than a pup tent, barely large enough, I would say, to accommodate one man and a small stone fireplace. One of its planks bore the carved name: "D. boon." There was some controversy over whether or not it really was built by Daniel Boone. Perhaps it does not matter. But the news of the discovery and of the controversy over it had given the place a certain fame.

The find interested me, for I never cease to regret the scarcity of knowledge of the first explorations of the continent. Some hint, such as the "Boone hut" might provide, of the experience of the Long Hunters would be invaluable. And so one of my earliest visits to the Gorge included a trip to see the hut.

The head of the trail was not yet marked, but once I found the path leading down through the woods it was clear to me that I had already had numerous predecessors. And I had not gone far before I knew their species:

scattered more and more thickly along the trail the nearer I got to the site of
the hut was the trash that has come to be more characteristic than shoeprints
of the race that produced (as I am a little encouraged to remember) such a
man as D. boon. And when I came to the rock house itself I found the
mouth of it entirely closed, from the ground to the overhanging rock some
twenty-five feet above, by a chain-link fence. Outside the fence the ground
was littered with Polaroid negatives, film spools, film boxes, food wrappers,
cigarette butts, a paper plate, a Coke-bottle.

And inside the fence, which I peered through like a prisoner, was the
hut, a forlorn relic overpowered by what had been done to protect it from
collectors of mementos, who would perhaps not even know what it was
supposed to remind them of. There it was, perhaps a vital clue to our history
and our inheritance, turned into a curio. Whether because of the ignorant
enthusiasm of souvenir hunters, or because of the strenuous measures necessary to protect it from them, Boone's hut had become a doodad—as had
Boone's name, which now stood for a mendacious TV show and a brand of
fried chicken.

I did not go back to that place again, not wanting to be associated with   5
the crowd whose vandalism had been so accurately foreseen and so over-
whelmingly thwarted. But I did not forget it either, and the memory of it
seems to me to bear, both for the Gorge and for ourselves, a heavy premo-
nition of ruin. For are those who propose damming the Gorge, arguing
convenience, not the same as these who can go no place, not even a few
hundred steps to see the hut of D. boon, without the trash of convenience?
Are they not the same who will use the proposed lake as a means of transporting the same trash into every isolated cranny that the shoreline will
penetrate? I have a vision (I don't know if it is nightmare or foresight) of a
time when our children will go to the Gorge and find there a webwork of
paved, heavily littered trails passing through tunnels of steel mesh. When
people are so ignorant and destructive that they must be divided by a fence
from what is vital to them, whether it is their history or their world, they are
imprisoned.

On a cold drizzly day in the middle of October I walk down the side
of a badly overgrazed ridge into a deep, steep hollow where there remains
the only tiny grove of virgin timber still standing in all the Red River
country. It is a journey backward through time, from the freeway droning
both directions through 1969, across the old ridge denuded by the agricultural policies and practices of the white man's era, and down into such a
woods as the Shawnees knew before they knew white men.

Going down, the sense that it is a virgin place comes over you slowly.
First you notice what would be the great difficulty of getting in and out,
were it not for such improvements as bridges and stairways in the trail. It is
this difficulty that preserved the trees, and that even now gives the hollow a
feeling of austerity and remoteness. And then you realize that you are passing

among poplars and hemlocks of a startling girth and height, the bark of their trunks deeply grooved and moss-grown. And finally it comes to you where you are; the virginity, the uninterrupted wildness, of the place comes to you in a clear strong dose like the first breath of a wind. Here the world is in its pure state, and such men as have been here have all been here in their pure state, for they have destroyed nothing. It has lived whole into our lifetime out of the ages. Its life is a vivid link between us and Boone and the Long Hunters and their predecessors, the Indians. It stands, brooding upon its continuance, in a strangely moving perfection, from the tops of the immense trees down to the leaves of the partridge berries on the ground. Standing and looking, moving on and looking again, I suddenly realize what is missing from nearly all the Kentucky woodlands I have known: the summit, the grandeur of these old trunks that lead the eyes up through the foliage of the lesser trees toward the sky.

At the foot of the climb, over the stone floor of the hollow, the stream is mottled with the gold leaves of the beeches. The water has taken on a vegetable taste from the leaves steeping in it. It has become a kind of weak tea, infused with the essence of the crown of the forest. By spring the fallen leaves on the stream bed will all have been swept away, and the water, filtered once again through the air and the ground, will take back the clear taste of the rock. I drink the cool brew of the autumn.

And then I wander some more among the trees. There is a thought repeating itself in my mind: This is a great Work, this is a great Work. It occurs to me that my head has gone to talking religion, that it is going ahead more or less on its own, assenting to the Creation, finding it good, in the spirit of the first chapters of Genesis. For no matter the age or the hour, I am celebrating the morning of the seventh day. I assent to my mind's assent. It *is* a great Work. It is a *great* Work—begun in the beginning, carried on until now, to be carried on, not by such processes as men make or understand, but by "the kind of intelligence that enables grass seed to grow grass; the cherry stone to make cherries."

Here is the place to remember D. boon's hut. Lay aside all questions of   10 its age and ownership—whether or not he built it, he undoubtedly built others like it in similar places. Imagine it in a cave in a cliff overlooking such a place as this. Imagine it separated by several hundred miles from the nearest white men and by two hundred years from the drone, audible even here, of the parkway traffic. Imagine that the great trees surrounding it are part of a virgin wilderness still nearly as large as the continent, vast rich unspoiled distances quietly peopled by scattered Indian tribes, its ways still followed by buffalo and bear and panther and wolf. Imagine a cold gray winter evening, the wind loud in the branches above the protected hollows. Imagine a man dressed in skins coming silently down off the ridge and along the cliff face into the shelter of the rock house. Imagine his silence that is unbroken as he enters, crawling, a small hut that is only a negligible detail among the stone rubble of the cave floor, as unobtrusive there as the nest of an animal or bird, and as he livens the banked embers of a fire on the stone hearth, adding wood, and holds out his chilled hands before the blaze. Imagine him roasting his supper meat on a stick over the fire while the night falls and the darkness and the wind enclose the hollow. Imagine him sitting on there, miles and months from words, staring into the fire, letting its warmth deepen in him until finally he sleeps. Imagine his sleep.

When I return again it is the middle of December, getting on toward the final shortening, the first lengthening of the days. The year is ending, and my trip too has a conclusive feeling about it. The ends are gathering. The things I have learned about the Gorge, my thoughts and feelings about it, have begun to have a sequence, a pattern. From the start of the morning, because of this sense of the imminence of connections and conclusions, the day has both an excitement and a comfort about it.

As I drive in I see small lots staked off and a road newly graveled in one of the creek bottoms. And I can hear chain saws running in the vicinity of another development on Tunnel Ridge. This work is being done in anticipation of the lake, but I know that it has been hastened by the publicity surrounding the effort to keep the Gorge unspoiled. I consider the ironic possibility that what I will write for love of it may also contribute to its destruction, enlarging the hearsay of it, bringing in more people to drive the roads and crowd the "points of interest" until they become exactly as interesting as a busy street. And yet I might as well leave the place anonymous, for what I have learned here could be learned from any woods and any free-running river.

I pull off the road near the mouth of a hollow I have not yet been in. The day is warm and overcast, but it seems unlikely to rain. Taking only a notebook and a map, I turn away from the road and start out. The woods closes me in. Within a few minutes I have put the road, and where it came from and is going, out of mind. There comes to be a wonderful friendliness, a sort of sweetness I have not known here before, about this day and this solitary walk—as if, having finally understood this country well enough to accept it on its terms, I am in turn accepted. It is as though, in this year of men's arrival on the moon, I have completed my own journey at last, and have arrived, an exultant traveler, here on the earth.

I come around a big rock in the stream and two grouse flush in the open not ten steps away. I walk on more quietly, full of the sense of ending and beginning. At any moment, I think, the forest may reveal itself to you in a new way. Some intimate insight, that all you have known has been secretly adding up to, may suddenly open into the clear—like a grouse, that one moment seemed only a part of the forest floor, the next moment rising in flight. Also it may not.

Where I am going I have never been before. And since I have no   15
destination that I know, where I am going is always where I am. When I come to good resting places, I rest. I rest whether I am tired or not because

the places are good. Each one is an arrival. I am where I have been going. At a narrow place in the stream I sit on one side and prop my feet on the other. For a while I content myself to be a bridge. The water of heaven and earth is flowing beneath me. While I rest a piece of the world's work is continuing here without my help.

Since I was here last the leaves have fallen. The forest has been at work, dying to renew itself, covering the tracks of those of us who were here, burying the paths and the old campsites and the refuse. It is showing us what to hope for. And that we can hope. And *how* to hope. It will always be a new world, if we will let it be.

The place as it was is gone, and we are gone as we were. We will never be in that place again. Rejoice that it is dead, for having received that death, the place of next year, a new place, is lying potent in the ground like a deep dream.

Somewhere, somewhere behind me that I will not go back to, I have lost my map. At first I am sorry, for on these trips I have always kept it with me. I brood over the thought of it, the map of this place rotting into it along with its leaves and its fallen wood. The image takes hold of me, and I suddenly realize that it is the culmination, the final insight, that I have felt impending all through the day. It is the symbol of what I have learned here, and of the process: the gradual relinquishment of maps, the yielding of knowledge before the new facts and the mysteries of growth and renewal and change. What men know and presume about the earth is part of it, passing always back into it, carried on by it into what they do not know. Even their abuses of it, their diminishments and dooms, belong to it. The tragedy is only ours, who have little time to be here, not the world's whose creation bears triumphantly on and on from the fulfillment of catastrophe to the fulfillment of hepatica blossoms. The thought of the lost map, the map fallen and decaying like a leaf among the leaves, grows in my mind to the force of a cleansing vision. As though freed of a heavy weight, I am light and exultant here in the end and the beginning.

The Responsive Reader

1. How do you think someone like Berry would compare the relation to the land and to nature of the Native Americans, of early white trappers and hunters, and of people of our own generation?
2. Both the trash left by tourists and the chain link fencing in this essay are to Berry closely related symbols of our current civilization. How and why?
3. Like other nature writers, Berry has a strong sense of the natural cycles of growth and renewal. What role do they play in this essay?
4. What is the difference between a *relic*, a *memento*, and a *curio*?

Thinking, Talking, Writing

5. Berry travels by car, and he approaches the outdoors map in hand. Is he himself too much a creature of our civilization to establish true contact with unspoiled nature? How close can we come to leaving our technological civilization behind for a cycle of spiritual renewal?

6. Writers like Berry are sometimes accused of idealizing or romanticizing nature, glossing over the cruelty and terror of the struggle for survival. How would you convict or clear him of such a charge?

7. When in your own experience have you felt closest to nature? What were your observations, thoughts, and feelings? Recreate the experience for your reader.

Collaborative Projects

8. Work with a group to research the following: What is the record of your state or your region in trying to conserve areas in their natural wilderness state?

Thinking about Connections

9. Ways to look at nature have ranged from a romantic view of nature as a benign, healing, or nurturing power to a naturalistic view of nature as the arena for the cruel struggle for survival. Among the writers in this chapter, which to you seem to incline most to the romantic view? Which seem to incline to the naturalistic view? Which would you place somewhere in between? What evidence would you choose to support your choices?

13

Writing About Literature

When you write about literature, you show how well you have read a poem, a story, or a play. However, you also show what special meaning the literature has for you as a person. Imaginative literature is an interaction between what you read and you as the reader. What you bring to your reading matters. Your own past history may help explain why one story grips you and another leaves you indifferent. Symbols in one poem or story may activate a rich range of memories and associations, while those in another selection may seem artificial or far-fetched. Successful writing about literature is a successful blend of close reading and the personal response.

THE RESPONSIVE READER

A responsive reader responds fully to the way imaginative literature acts out or embodies meanings. As a responsive reader, you are not obligated to like everything you read. But you make an effort to get out of a work what the writer put into it. You try to get into the spirit of a poem or story or play; you try to be receptive to what it has to offer. You develop the habit of close reading. You try to be open to what seems difficult, different, or disturbing. When you write about poetry, fiction, or drama, you want to show that you have entered fully into a writer's world.

Readers vary greatly in how they make the most of their reading. They may give a poem or story a quick first read and then go back over it slowly. They may develop their own system of highlighting or underlining key terms and crucial passages. They may scribble comments and notes in the margin. They may keep a reading journal as a record of their reading, using it as a source for class discussion or as a springboard for writing.

The following may be part of your own personal note-taking or journal writing:

CLUSTERING **Clustering** is a prewriting technique that helps you take stock of the memories or associations a poem or a story may trigger in your mind. You focus on a key phrase or central symbol, circling it and putting it at the center of your cluster. You then branch out from the core, following up different chains of associations. The more freely you let one thing lead to another, the more fully your cluster is likely to activate the full range of latent meanings.

The following cluster traces some of the possible associations of flowers as symbols carrying rich traditional freight. Many of these associations may be activated by a story like Steinbeck's "The Chrysanthemums," where flowers play a central role at turning points in the story. (Which of these associations do you think are relevant to Steinbeck's story?)

RUNNING COMMENTARY A good way of entering fully into a poem or story is to keep a running commentary. You note striking details, key quotations, or puzzling plot developments. You register queries and record first reactions. When you start working on a structured paper, you then have a backlog of key details and tentative ideas to sort out and draw on. Part of your running commentary on the Steinbeck story might read like this:

> Elisa has a particular talent for working with flowers. She puts her intelligence and passion to work in growing chrysanthemums. This is considered "woman's work," so no one interferes with her? She seems to put her energy into her garden because she is discontented with the rest of her life.
>
> The tinker provides a polar opposite for the farm family. The family stays fogbound while the tinker follows "the nice weather." The conventional cattle-tending chores of the husband contrast with the mismatched team pulling the strange wagon of the traveler.
>
> Elisa spills her passions to the tinker, who pretends to be interested in her gardening. She talks about the night and the stars, how they get "driven into your body . . . Hot and sharp and lovely." Apparently even this poor excuse for a man holds Elisa's attention enough to reach out to him.
>
> The tinker is looking only for some pots to mend; he cares little for the passions and desires of the woman. He throws out the chrysanthemum sprouts after he leaves the farm! Elisa sees her soil scattered in the road.
>
> The suppressed part of Elisa's personality surfaces when she shows an interest in the bloody and gory boxing matches? But in the end we see her "crying weakly, like an old woman."

THE PERSONAL CONNECTION   A reading journal may include running comments, character sketches, and brief plot summaries (especially when the plot line of a story seems to contain puzzling twists and turns). However, it also gives you a chance to explore your tentative personal reactions to your reading. How does a story touch your own life, your own experience? What in a poem or story has a special personal meaning for you? In the following journal entry, a student writer explains why the way Elisa dresses in the chrysanthemums story has a personal meaning for her:

> Steinbeck's story dealt with feminine emotions that can be very hard to understand. I was struck by the contrast between Elisa's mannish "working clothes" (her shapeless outfit, her heavy gloves) and the makeup and dress she puts on after her encounter with the tinker. Much of her thinking revolved around whether the men in her world would respect her work and desire her at the same time. Her change of clothes symbolizes the fact that in the male world the woman has to

play a dual role. She has to be a man's equal to survive in the world of work, yet on the other hand she is expected to be feminine and seductive. Today a woman has to look more like a man by wearing a dark "power" suit and practically no makeup to compete with men, or she may not be taken seriously. In a recent sitcom episode, I watched a sterile-looking businesswoman teaching a fashionable female how to dress for business success. Her pupil donned a blue suit, a buttoned white shirt, and a bandage-type thing to hide her breasts. Steinbeck's story points up this unresolved conflict: It is a sad but honest account of how women are taken advantage of when they expose their feminine selves.

WRITING ABOUT A POEM

You may be asked to write a paper based on a close careful reading of a poem. What did the poem as a whole mean to you as the reader? Since poetic language tends to be highly condensed, much of your paper may be devoted to tracing the meanings, implications, and associations of key words. However, ultimately your readers will expect you to show what the words in a poem contribute to the poem as a whole. Similarly, you may spend much time tracing the full implications of a symbol: a cup of water offered to a stranger, or perhaps a desert landscape allowing only the barest tumbleweed vegetation. Again, you will want to show what the symbol means in the context of the poem as a whole.

Poems do not mean the same way news bulletins or race results do. Rarely do poets make blunt statements like "Freedom is being able to do what you decide to do." They are more likely to say, "Freedom is not following a river./Freedom is following a river/though, if you want to" (William Stafford). Poets create images; they make something happen. They involve you in an experience that invites you to see, to feel, to think. To make the poem happen, you have to bring your own imagination and your own feelings into play. Ideally, the paper you write about the poem will help others to experience the poem more fully. It will help them become more responsive readers.

Look at the way you might move from a first exploratory reading of a poem to a structured paper exploring and interpreting the poem for your readers. Adrienne Rich wrote the following poem in 1951, when she was still a student.

Adrienne Rich
Aunt Jennifer's Tigers

Aunt Jennifer's tigers prance across a screen,   *1*
Bright topaz denizens of a world of green.
They do not fear the men beneath the tree;
They pace in sleek chivalric certainty.

Aunt Jennifer's fingers fluttering through her wool   *5*
Find even the ivory needle hard to pull.
The massive weight of Uncle's wedding band
Sits heavily upon Aunt Jennifer's hand.

When Aunt is dead, her terrified hands will lie
Still ringed with ordeals she was mastered by.   *10*
The tigers in the panel that she made
Will go on prancing, proud and unafraid.

As you read and reread the poem, you will want to start taking reading notes. You should pick up apparently important words and phrases, especially those that seem puzzling or different. (Why "topaz denizens"?) You should begin to note details that reinforce each other or begin to add up. (Words like *bright, green,* and *sleek* are all positive, upbeat words that make the animals seem healthy, vital, or attractive.) You will start charting the overall movement or development of the poem. (We first focus on the figures on a screen holding the panel with animals that Aunt Jennifer's needle is creating. Then we shift attention to Aunt Jennifer. Then, when she is gone, we are left contemplating the figures in the panel.)

As you expand and think about your notes, try to do justice to dimensions like the following:

POETIC LANGUAGE   In a short poem, each word counts. Each word is likely to carry more freight than a word does in ordinary talk; it is likely to bring into play a range of meanings, images, and associations. For instance, the tigers in this poem "prance." Why "prance"? The word *prance,* like much poetic language, creates a vivid image—it gives us something we can vividly imagine or see with the mind's eye. It carries with it feelings and associations (or **connotations**). *Prance* is a very different word from words like *slide, glide, slink, shuffle,* or *sneak:* People prance when they are in high spirits. To prance, they need elbow room to high-step and half-lift their arms. These tigers are full of energy, unafraid, delighting in their own vitality. They occupy their space without being crowded or held down.

Another weighty word in the poem, *chivalric,* implies an imaginative comparison. It is used figuratively rather than literally. The knights of chivalry were horsemen decked out in splendid armor and subscribing to a code of honor and nobility. (*Chivalry* was once the same word as *cavalry.*) The tigers are being compared to glamorous knights, not likely to fear the men lurking beneath the tree in the poem. When we call the animals knights (or when we call people animals), we are using a **metaphor,** a kind of figurative language that does without the *as* or *like* that would signal the coming of the comparison.

CENTRAL SYMBOL   To get a sense of a poem as a whole, we begin to ask: What is the poet focusing on? What does the poem dwell on? What seems most important or central to the poem? In "Aunt Jennifer's Tigers," the tigers keep prancing and pacing throughout the poem. They are in the title, in the opening lines, and in the concluding lines. They mean more than incidental decoration in the embroidery. If they had been pigeons, we would have a totally different poem. The tigers become a central **symbol:** they apparently represent something in Aunt Jennifer's consciousness, something that at some deep level matters to her.

Why would she be fascinated by tigers? Tigers are powerful, ferocious animals—terrible but also beautiful. They seem to symbolize some unreleased, frightening vital energy that dwells in the aging woman, as in all of us. On the surface, she is subdued, held down. But in her imagination, the tigers prance.

PATTERN Next to the tigers, what is a reader likely to remember from this poem? Next to the animals, the wedding band on Aunt Jennifer's finger literally weighs heavily in the poem. It is "massive," and it "sits heavily" upon her hand. Even in death her "terrified hands" will still be "ringed" by the ordeals, the challenges and sufferings, that the wedding rings symbolizes and that mastered and subdued her in life. The poem plays off these two opposites—the tigers symbolizing freedom and the ring symbolizing constraint. The poem as a whole plays off the untamed tigers against the restraining heavy wedding band symbolizing an oppressive marriage. It is this opposition that gives its shape to the poem as a whole.

POETIC FORM In form or appearance, the poem is very simple. Meter and rhyme are very regular. Each pair of two lines rhymes, with the rhymes marking off simple statements of equal length. There are no dramatic breaks in the middle of a line; neither are there passionate, sweeping sentences running through three or four lines or more. This outward simplicity suits the poem well. In this poem, there is no melodramatic rebellion, no passionate indictment. Aunt Jennifer apparently never rebelled. She found her escape in the realm of the imagination.

The central opposition in the poem between two contrasting symbols may suggest a strategy for your paper. You decide to focus first on the provocative, fascinating tigers. You then focus on the wedding band and what it tells us about Aunt Jennifer's life. You then come back to the tigers and their larger significance beyond the poem, beyond the life of one woman. Your overall plan can be summed up as follows:

tigers

wedding ring

tigers

Sample Student Paper

Study the following student paper, which employs this organizing strategy. Ask yourself:

- Where and how does the writer sum up her interpretation of the poem? (What is her thesis?)

- How much direct quotation from the poem does the writer use? Where does she use it well in strategic places?

- Where does the student writer provide needed explanation and interpretation in her own words?

- What transitions, or logical links, help the reader see the connection between major parts of the paper?

- How effective are title, introduction, and conclusion?

- Does the student writer's personal interest in or attitude toward the poem become clear? How?

- What questions does this paper leave unanswered?

Tigers and Terrified Hands

"When Aunt is dead, her terrified hands will lie/Still ringed with ordeals she was mastered by./The tigers in the panel that she made/ Will go on prancing, proud and unafraid." So ends the lush and very focused poem "Aunt Jennifer's Tigers" by Adrienne Rich. With memorable symbolism, the poet illuminates the tragedy of a woman who has lived the greater part of her life as the subordinate member in an unbalanced marriage.

The tiger has been symbolically used many times, and readers may assume that the presence of a tiger represents evil or darkness. In this poem, however, the tigers have an entirely different symbolic meaning. Aunt Jennifer's tigers, those "topaz denizens of a world of green" (2) are the brilliant jewellike embodiments of the faded shadows hiding in their creator's spirit. Their world of green, bursting with life, vitality, regeneration, receives its life-force from the crushed stirrings in Aunt Jennifer's defeated soul. Any shred of hope or victory or joy that somehow remains within her flows unconsciously through her fluttering fingers into the tapestry she so painfully sews. These wonderful tigers do not sidle or sneak or skulk; they stride "proud and unafraid" (12). With the natural confidence of knighthood, they "pace in sleek chivalric certainty" (4). And, perhaps most importantly, they "do not fear the men beneath the tree" (3). Aunt Jennifer stitches her defiance the only way she can, unconscious of her own vision.

Aunt Jennifer is the perfect foil for her creations, the gorgeous tigers. She is so fraught with anxiety, nervous confusion, exhausted resignation, fear, and defeat, that her fingers, which can only "flutter" through her wool (5), "find even the ivory needle hard to pull" (6). This shade of a woman is still weighed down by the "massive weight of Uncle's wedding band," which has doubtlessly drained her of any capacity for joy, celebration of life, or even peace. She is feeble, afraid, and "mastered." Even in death her "terrified hands will lie/Still ringed with ordeals she was mastered by" (9–10). She cannot escape the "ordeals" that were thrust upon her by her partner in marriage; the dominance and oppression that were her lot in marriage will always be part of who she was.

However, she has left a legacy. She has stitched a panel of glittering tigers that will "go on prancing, proud and unafraid" (12). Other women will come after Aunt Jennifer, and they may be inspired by her tigers to hold their heads up proudly and assume their rightful places as equals, rejecting any subordinate or humiliating roles. The tigers, often symbols of vitality, power, pride, fearlessness, here are those and more: They are the irrepressible human spirit and symbols of hope for woman's future.

The readers are not told of the particular ordeals in her marriage that defeated Aunt Jennifer. But they can make guesses and poke around for possibilities. The word *mastered* itself, used to describe Aunt Jennifer's situation, implies a "master." It is not a wild or unlikely conjecture that Aunt Jennifer's husband resembled other males who played the role of "master of the house," such as the poet's own father. Aunt Jennifer's husband, in the poet's mind, represents the traditional power of the male.

WRITING ABOUT A CHARACTER

When we read a story or see a play, we often become absorbed in a central character, or protagonist. We often come to think of the character as a flesh-and-blood person, forgetting that the character is a creation of the writer's imagination. A paper focused on a central character may show how a key trait, a childhood trauma, or an unfulfilled emotional need serves as the key to unlock the character's personality. Or a paper may trace the growth of a character as the person moves on to an important new stage in life in a story of initiation. Or a paper may show the character in conflict with opposing forces—another person, other people, tradition, poverty, or repressive institutions.

As you highlight passages in your reading or take notes, pay special attention to details that help you know and understand the central character. Sometimes, an author will let you know directly or by various hints about the character's background or past history. However, a character may also come into a story without background or introduction, coming to life as the author furnishes essential clues. Look for revealing things said by and about the character; note significant details and key events.

▪ *Listen to what the character says.* In Gilman's "The Yellow Wallpaper," for instance, you may note that the narrator's ideas are often at odds with those of her physician husband. Early in the story she starts to keep from him what she really thinks:

The narrator feels that "congenial work, with excitement and change, would do me good." The husband, however, prescribes "perfect rest." Because he is a "physician of high standing," she feels he must know what is best for her.

She wants a room "downstairs that opened on the piazza and had roses all over the window, and such pretty old-fashioned chintz hangings," but "John would not hear of it." She believes that writing "would relieve the press of ideas and rest me." Her husband insists that she stop. She writes a bit "in spite of them," but it is too exhausting "having to be so sly about it."

▪ *Listen to what other people say about the character.* However, use your judgment whether someone else sympathizes with the character—or looks at the person from a limited or biased point of view.

The husband calls the narrator "his little girl" and his "blessed goose." When she wants to have company, he tells her "he would as soon put fireworks in my pillow case as to let me have those stimulating people about now."

▪ *Study a character's habits, mannerisms, or preoccupations.* In Mason's "Shiloh," the husband builds miniature log cabins from model kits. His wife is interested in exercise and attends evening classes at the community college. This contrast is one of many hints that they may be in some ways very different people.

▪ *Look for key developments.* We learn something about people when we watch them react to adversity, to disappointment, to success, or to betrayal. There may be a turning point when the character understands something for the first time. There may be a high point when a character faces reality in a moment of insight or self-realization.

▪ *Look for symbolic gestures and other symbolic details.* The flowers in Steinbeck's "The Chrysanthemums" are symbols of burgeoning life. We focus on them at several key points in the story, as they come to symbolize the natural vitality for which the central character finds no outlet in her everyday life and in her relationship with her husband.

PUSHING TOWARD A THESIS   As you continue your note-taking, begin to look for a central question or a central issue that could help you focus your paper. Gender roles may turn out to be a central concern in a story of adolescence: What does it mean to be a girl? What does it mean to be a boy? Some people easily take to the role society has sketched out for them. They fit the mold. But the central character in a story may be an independent, adventurous, imaginative spirit, rebelling without success against his or her lot. Here is a paragraph presenting a student writer's thesis about such a character:

Children search for their identities and constantly run up against the wall of gender stereotypes to which they are made to conform. *The girl in the story reluctantly conforms to the stereotypes that will deny a part of her personality.* In her innocence, the girl in the story identifies with the outdoor work of her father, "red in the face with pleasure" when her father seems to praise and accept her as a co-worker. Her daydreams are about heroic rescues in which she plays the hero's part. However, her mother and grandmother conspire to drive home what is expected of a girl. It seems that after a last act of futile rebellion the invisible walls of the predestined gender roles will close in on her.

STRUCTURING THE PAPER   How will your paper be laid out? In a paper about a character's growing up, each part of your paper might focus on one major conflicting influence in the young person's life. Here is a scratch outline for a paper developing the thesis presented in the preceding paragraph:

spirited imaginative character—the prank played on kid brother, leadership, daydreams: "courage, boldness, and self-sacrifice"

the lure of the father's job

the mother and grandmother as voices of the stereotype

the climactic rebellion

pivotal role of younger brother—he will overtake her by virtue of the mere fact of being born male; he has the advantage

Sample Student Paper

Study the following sample paper. Is there a key question or key issue to help unify the paper? How did the writer structure the paper—what is the general plan or design? What details from the story did the student writer select as especially significant or revealing?

Yellow Women

Gilman's "The Yellow Wall-Paper" is a tragic story of a woman's attempt to recover from postpartum depression. This story represents the characteristic attitude toward woman and of women during the late 1800s and early 1900s. Gilman writes honestly of the isolated and confused feelings women were feeling. The woman in "The Yellow Wall-Paper" goes through three periods of change throughout the story. The story begins with the description of the woman as being sick, but there are no signs of mental illness, and she is aware of her environment and even believes she is not really sick. Then there is a curious change in her character, and she appears to be disillusioned and on the verge of becoming mentally insane. And in the end she does go over the edge, and her character is literally lost.

The woman in this story is taken to a summer house to rest and recuperate. Her husband, John, who is also her doctor, treats her as a child, and she says that "perhaps that is one reason I do not get well faster." She is apparently suffering from the baby blues, which is a depression some women experience after giving birth to a child. However, her husband sticks her in an atrocious nursery with barred windows and a wallpaper that she describes as

> dull enough to confuse the eye in following, pronounced enough to constantly irritate and provoke study, and when you follow the lame uncertain curves for a little distance they suddenly commit suicide—plunge off at outrageous angles, destroy themselves in unheard of contradictions.

Her description of the wallpaper represents her feelings about the paper, but it also symbolizes the feelings she has about herself. This confusing pattern could be a typical categorization of women, whereas a typical pattern for men might be straight and neat lines that meet at edges and appear to have an overall meaning. I say this because, in the story, John apparently knows all and has prescribed his wife's life as he sees fit. In a description of John's sister, the woman says she is "a perfect and enthusiastic housekeeper, and hopes for no better profession." This heartless description lacks praise for her sister-in-law's profession; it also symbolizes the status of women in the time the story was written.

Her husband, who calls her "his little girl" and his "blessed goose," forbids her to work until she is well; she disagrees, believing "congenial work, with excitement and change," would do her good. She believes she could recover from her baby blues if only she were able to keep active and do other things than sit alone in a nursery and stare at the wallpaper. She even asks her husband to have company for companionship, but he tells her, "he would as soon put fireworks in my pillow case as to let me have those stimulating people about now." She might not even have progressed to her second stage if it were not for her husband and sister-in-law constantly reminding her of how tired and sick she is.

Her second stage begins when she becomes "fond" of the wallpaper. She is losing contact with the outside world, instead spending her time trying, in a painstaking effort, to understand the overall pattern of the wall-paper. She sees a figure that looks like a "woman stooping down and creeping about behind that pattern." She also goes on to say, "I don't like it a bit. . . . I wish John would take me away from here." She is herself the woman "creeping" through the wallpaper. The woman creeping symbolizes women who are not allowed to stand tall and free and speak their minds. She "creeps" at night when her husband is asleep and, when she is caught "creeping," her husband tells her to get back in bed. Her husband, who has good intentions, keeps on assuring her that she is getting better, and when she disagrees with him by saying, "Better in body perhaps," he looks at her with such a "stern, reproachful" stare that she does not dare say another word.

She is alone in her own little world with no real support from anyone. She cannot be blamed for her condition and eventually insanity takes over her body. Here is another example of how the wallpaper symbolizes women:

> The front pattern does move—and no wonder! The woman
> behind shakes it! Sometimes I think there are a great many
> women behind, . . . And she is all the time trying to climb
> through. But nobody could climb through that pattern—it
> strangles so; I think that is why it has so many heads.

She realizes she is not the only woman who is lost but also many other women. This realization pushes her to her mental limit, and she tries to peel all of the wallpaper off so that the "strangled heads" can be free. She feels secure and safe in the room "creeping" and she says, "I don't want to go outside. . . . For outside you have to creep on the ground, and everything is green instead of yellow." She has no desire to live in the "green" world, and she chooses the "yellow" familiar world instead. She even locks herself in the room and throws away the key. This act symbolizes an instance of control over her own life. Comfortable in her "creeping" role, she does not want anyone to bother her. She is now mentally insane.

The woman in "The Yellow Wall-Paper" represents many women, even today, in the late twentieth century. There are many women who do not take advantage of their freedom, many who are also servants in life. I have seen this to be so in my grandmother's as well as in my mother's marriage. However, the wallpaper women are hiding behind is slowly being peeled off by both men and women.

WRITING ABOUT A THEME

The theme of a poem, story, or play is what the work as a whole seems to say. It is a statement about life, or about people, that the work seems to convey when we look back over it as a whole. Modern writers are often reluctant to state the theme of a story or play in so many words. Instead, their work dramatizes it, acts it out, and probes its human meaning. Earlier writers will sometimes directly or through the mouth of a character spell out the meaning of a story in a thematic passage, as the Easterner does in Stephen Crane's "The Blue Hotel." Crane here has the speaker present a modern view of evil as not the work of a single rotten person but as the end result of a chain of ignorance, stupidity, cowardice, self-righteousness, and neglect:

> Johnny was cheating. I saw him. . . . And I refused to stand up and be
> a man. I let the Swede fight it out alone. And you—you were simply
> puffing around the place and wanting to fight. And then only Scully
> himself! We are all in it! . . . Every sin is the result of a collaboration.
> We, five of us, have collaborated in the murder of this Swede.

Crane's theme in this story, summed up in a single sentence, is "Evil is the result of collaboration." Even so, we have to remember that a thematic passage might present only the *partial* view of a narrator or character caught up in the events.

When you write about theme, try to do justice to how a poem, story, or play acts out the writer's intended meaning. Think about how such elements as setting, character, plot, or symbol help shape the meaning of the literary text as a whole.

SETTING   The setting may play a major role in a story or play. It provides the context for people's lives and may help determine not only how they live but also how they think and act. It may shape their outlook. It may also provide a challenge, as they struggle against the limitations of their environment. You might say then that the setting becomes a major player in the developments that give meaning to a story as a whole. The writer of the following journal entry found a clue to the thematic meaning of Steinbeck's short story "Chrysanthemums" in the winter fog that closes off the valley.

> "The high grey-flannel fog of winter closed off the Salinas Valley
> from the sky and from all the rest of the world," Steinbeck
> begins. This introductory sentence points to one of the basic
> themes of the story. Something (in this case, the fog) is
> keeping something or someone "closed off"—held in, cut off.
> The fog covers the valley. Similarly, Elisa's situation closes in
> on her, keeps her trapped, holds her back. Neither her husband
> nor the itinerant tinker understands the energy and care she
> puts into the chrysanthemums, and her ability and potential go
> unrecognized and unappreciated; they are kept under wraps,
> "closed off." The fog is the lid that keeps the sun from
> penetrating; Elisa's circumstances put the "lid" on her vital
> energy and desires.

SYMBOL   A central symbol may help a writer give visible shape to the underlying theme of a poem, story, or play. In Hemingway's short story "In Another Country," the machines that play a central role in the physical therapy for the maimed soldiers assume a symbolic meaning. They are touted as highly effective by the physician, but too many harsh facts give the lie to their promise. The story as a whole says something about war as the graveyard of human hopes. The theme, as often in Hemingway's fiction, may be the loss of illusions, which leaves his characters suspicious of lofty ideals and big words.

KEY EVENT   The shooting of Boggs in Mark Twain's "A Day in Arkansaw" is a dramatic high point, but it also dramatizes a major point the author makes repeatedly in his work. In a way, the drunken, out-of-control Boggs "asked for it"; what happens to him is in a way "his own fault." And yet the way he is destroyed is brutally out of proportion with his guilt or his offense. This is Mark Twain's comment on what we today call "senseless violence." Maybe life at times give us provocation to revert to the stage of the killer ape. However, what makes us human is the ability to resist the impulse.

SUPPORTING DETAIL   Often minor characters or apparently peripheral events echo and parallel what goes on center stage. The death of the major's wife in "In Another Country" reinforces the idea that we live in a universe with little regard for human standards of loyalty and compassion.

Sample Student Paper

How does the following paper try to show that an underlying theme shapes the story as a whole? According to the student writer, how do different elements of the story serve the central theme?

Hemingway and the World of Illusion

Much of Hemingway's work concerns our struggle to cope in a world that is painful when stripped of illusions. His short story, "In Another Country," drawing on the author's own experiences, centers on wounded soldiers in Italy in World War I. In the story, people use different devices or contrivances to give themselves the illusion of physical and psychological well-being. These illusions are created so that no one will have to face squarely the realities of deterioration and death. The author makes us see our human need for illusion by contrasts in images, settings, and characters.

The opening paragraphs of the story present several such contrasts. The story takes place in Milan in Italy during World War I. It is fall, it is cold, and "dark comes early." *War, fall, dark,* and *cold* are words that suggest death or the ceasing of activity. Contrasted with these images are electric lights that come on at dark to shed light to the streets and shops. Light is a life image. Electric lights resurrect the cold, dark, dead world, making it appear beautiful and pleasant. The artificial light softens the reality that without these human contrivances the world is a cold, dark place where people deteriorate and die.

We soon encounter another death image: Hanging outside the shops are various kinds of game. Even if the snow picturesquely powders the fur of the dead foxes and even if the wind stirs the feathers of the birds, the fact remains that the animals are dead. "The deer hung stiff and heavy and empty" is a terse, blunt description of death. However, in the next paragraph, the men choose to get to the hospital by walking over a bridge where a woman sells roasted chestnuts. She roasts them over a charcoal fire (another human invention) that sheds warmth and light amidst the cold and darkness of the surroundings. Since the chestnuts stay warm in the men's pockets, they have the feeling of well-

being that warmth affords while they are walking the remainder of the
way to the hospital.

There is an old notion that people go to hospitals to die. The
initial description of the hospitals as "old and beautiful" lessens the
natural terror one might feel of such an institution.   However, the
sentences that follow offer no such comfort but explain in matter-of-fact
fashion that people usually walk in the front gate alive and are carried
out dead, by way of a funeral procession starting in the courtyard of
the "old and beautiful" hospital.   The only obstacle to this natural
progression of events seem to be the "machines" housed inside the
new brick pavilions, to the side of the hospital, where the men go for
physical therapy.

The doctor presiding over the pavilions perpetrates illusions of
healing by making the patients believe that they will be completely
cured.   He offers hope, with his "healing machines" and glib talk, to
those who will believe in the illusions.   To those with doubts, the doctor
shows photographs of cured wounds, pointing out how, by the miraculous
powers of the machines, badly wounded bodies have been resurrected so
that they function "better than ever."

The central character of the story would like to believe these
illusions.   He is a young man, and it is devastating to him to have to
face the reality of being badly deformed for the rest of his life.   He
wants to believe that he will be cured but notices contradictions between
what the doctor professes and the realities of the situation.   The doctor
tells him he will "play football again like a champion" in spite of the
fact that he has no calf and a knee that refuses to bend after months
of manipulation by the machines.   He also observes that the photograph
of a "cured" hand is only slightly larger than that of the withered hand
of the major, another patient.

The major, who takes treatment next to the young man, provides
the counterpoint to the young man's need for illusions.   The major is an
older man who knows that no one has control over death and infirmity.
His young wife has unexpectedly died after only a few days of illness.
No manufactured machine or medicine could help her while she was ill,
and nothing can resurrect her after her death.   The young wife's death
has taken from him the last tiny shred of belief in illusions.

The major's point of view offers a startling contrast to that of the
doctor.   Throughout the story, the young man is caught between those
who believe in illusions and those who discard illusion and attempt to
live with blunt reality.   He recognizes the foolishness and untruth of the
doctor's illusions, but he also notices the bitterness and resignation of
the major who has discarded all illusion.   After his wife's death, the
major returns to the hospital resigned to the fact that nothing we can
do will delay, for long, death.   He just sits on his therapy machine and
stares out of the window.   He seems to be marking time.   He does not
believe in the machines, yet he comes each day to use them.

Through the major's example and the many contrasts presented
in "In Another Country," Hemingway makes us see that, although life

based on illusion is dishonest, most of us cannot live as functioning human beings without some illusions. The blunt reality of death and infirmity is too painful and frightening for most human beings to face. Our capacity for illusion provides the minimum of hope we need to go on living.

COMPARING AND CONTRASTING

It is human nature to compare, to notice similarities and differences. We do not read a poem or a short story in isolation, as if we had never read a poem or a story before. Poems we have read before shape our expectations of what experience the reading of a new poem might provide. Short stories we have read on a similar subject or with a similar perspective may make it easier for us to enter into the world of a new story. As we read several poems or stories by the same author, we may begin to understand more fully the writer's point of view, her way of looking at people or at life.

Comparison is a good teacher; contrast is educational. When a similar image or the same symbol occurs again, we may conclude that it is more important than we first thought. When two stories look at the same subject from a different perspective, we may begin to appreciate more fully each writer's individual point of view. We may begin to explain to ourselves why they look at their world the way they do.

When you work on a **comparison-and-contrast** paper, you need to give special thought to how you will organize your material. You will have to develop a plan that helps your reader see the points of comparison. The reader has to see important connections—whether striking similarities or revealing differences. Your strategy may be to show basic underlying concerns that link works superficially unlike. Or you may want to highlight differences setting apart things that seem similar on the surface.

Consider familiar strategies for organizing a comparison and contrast of two or more works of literature:

- *You may choose to develop a* **point-by-point** *comparison.* For instance, you may want to begin by showing that two poets share a distrust of "big words." They do not use words like *freedom, justice, achievement, integrity, love, dedication.* It is as if, like many modern poets, they are allergic to uplifting words that can too easily be used by people who do not believe in them (and use them to get votes or sell soap). You may go on to show how both poets instead rely on startling, thought-provoking images. They may believe that the sight of an evicted family's furniture piled on the sidewalk does more to stir the reader's conscience than a lecture about social injustice. You may conclude by showing how both nevertheless in the end spell out the kind of thought that serves as an *earned* conclusion. They both tend to leave the reader with a thought or idea that the poem as a whole has worked out.

Simplified, the scheme for a point-by-point comparison might look like this:

Point 1—poem A and then B

Point 2—poem A and then B

Point 3—poem A and then B

▪ *You may want to develop a* **parallel-order** *comparison*. You start by doing justice to poem A: You show first the distrust of abstractions. Then you give examples of bold, provocative images. Finally, you show how the author of poem A spells out the conclusion that the poem as a whole suggests. You then take these three points up again in the same, or parallel, order for poem B: distrust of big words, love of bold images, willingness to make the implied ideas overt.

This way you may be able to give your reader a better sense of how each poem works on its own terms, as a self-contained whole. However, you will have to be sure to remind your readers of how each point you make about the second poem is parallel to or different from what you showed in the first.

▪ *You may want to start from a common base*. You emphasize similarities first. You then go on to the significant differences. You might vary this strategy by starting with surface similarities that might deceive the casual observer. You then go on to essential distinctions.

Much modern poetry has dealt with the subject of war. Of the two following poems, the first, by a British poet, was published in 1946 and the second, by an American poet, in 1947. The memory of World War II was still fresh in people's minds. From what point of view are you asked to look at war in these poems? Do they share a common perspective? Do they differ in how they come to terms with the war experience—in how the poets explain it to themselves and to their readers?

Henry Reed
Naming of Parts

Today we have naming of parts. Yesterday,   *1*
We had daily cleaning. And tomorrow morning,
We shall have what to do after firing. But today,
Today we have naming of parts. Japonica
Glistens like coral in all of the neighboring gardens,   *5*
    And today we have naming of parts.

This is the lower sling swivel. And this
Is the upper sling swivel, whose use you will see,
When you are given your slings. And this is the piling swivel,
Which in your case you have not got. The branches   *10*
Hold in the gardens their silent, eloquent gestures,
    Which in our case we have not got.

This is the safety-catch, which is always released
With an easy flick of the thumb. And please do not let me
See anyone using his finger. You can do it quite easy   15
If you have any strength in your thumb. The blossoms
Are fragile and motionless, never letting anyone see
    Any of them using their finger.

And this you can see is the bolt. The purpose of this
Is to open the breech, as you see. We can slide it   20
Rapidly backwards and forwards: we call this
Easing the spring. And rapidly backwards and forwards
The early bees are assaulting and fumbling the flowers:
    They call it easing the Spring.

They call it easing the Spring: it is perfectly easy   25
If you have any strength in your thumb: like the bolt,
And the breech, and the cocking-piece, and the point of balance,
Which in our case we have not got; and the almond-blossom
Silent in all of the gardens and the bees going backwards and forwards,
    For today we have naming of parts.   30

    In this poem, much of the talking is done by the drill instructor. There
is something spooky about the technical, impersonal descriptions of the mechanical parts: These mechanisms will be used by human beings to kill other
human beings. Where are the thoughts and feelings of the people who are
trained to use these weapons? Something else is strange about this poem:
While we listen to the instructions, our minds keep wandering to a world of
nature that is diametrically different from the world of lethal metal and preparation for killing. The technology of war and the world of nature provide a
steady play of point and counterpoint in this poem.
    What is similar and what is different in the following poem?

Richard Eberhart
The Fury of Aerial Bombardment

You would think the fury of aerial bombardment   1
Would rouse God to relent; the infinite spaces
Are still silent. He looks on shock-pried faces.
History, even, does not know what is meant.

You would feel that after so many centuries   5
God would give man to repent; yet he can kill
As Cain could, but with multitudinous will,
No farther advanced than in his ancient furies.

Was man made stupid to see his own stupidity?
Is God by definition indifferent, beyond us all?   10
Is the eternal truth man's fighting soul
Wherein the Beast ravens° in its own avidity?   *prowls*

Of Van Wettering I speak, and Averill,
Names on a list, whose faces I do not recall
But they are gone to early death, who late in school   *15*
Distinguished the belt feed lever from the belt holding pawl.

There is a striking similarity between the two poems. Like Reed's poem, this poem takes us to the school rooms of military training. (Eberhart himself was for a time an aerial gunnery instructor in World War II.) But Eberhart's use of the training experience is much shorter than Reed's. In this poem, the war experience leads the poet to raise questions about God's intentions. The poet also raises questions about our human responsibilities. (Why does the poet bring the **allusion** to Cain into the poem?)

Sample Student Paper

How does the following student paper trace the similarities and differences between these two poems? How does the paper use or adapt familiar organizing schemes for a comparison-and-contrast paper? How well does it use quotations and details to support its points?

Today We Have Naming of Parts
    Disillusioned by the experience of World War II, Henry Reed in "Naming of Parts" and Richard Eberhart in "The Fury of Aerial Bombardment" condemn and reject the horror of war. Both poems condemn our failure to see war as it is, attack our indifference, and reflect postwar antiwar feeling. We shall see that Eberhart's poem takes the attack on indifference one step further than Reed's poem does.
    Henry Reed's "Naming of Parts" satirically attacks the callousness of the military. By using impersonal, neutral words and phrases ("Today we have naming of parts. Yesterday/we had daily cleaning"), the speaker satirizes how precise and impersonal these lessons are. The trainee learns a process, without being taught or made aware how terrible and ugly practicing that process is. References to "the lower sling swivel," "the upper sling swivel," and the "slings" describe machinery. Such references to mechanical parts evoke neutral or even positive feelings, since most machines are used for the good of humanity. This technical language conceals the horror of using this particular machinery. Saying that "you can do it quite easy/If you have any strength in your thumb" obscures the possibility that it might be difficult emotionally to gun down a fellow human being.
    Reed uses a comparison to nature at the end of each stanza. Jumping from the mechanics of the gun to the beauty of the garden in consecutive sentences presents a contrast between the gun and the flower, the one a symbol of death and the other a symbol of life. The references in the first two stanzas stress the innocence of nature. The line "Japonica glistens like coral in all of the neighboring gardens" evokes an image of serenity and peace. The branches with "their silent, eloquent gestures" paint another image of bliss. The sterile descriptions

of the gun and the beautiful descriptions of nature proceed in a point-counterpoint fashion.

Richard Eberhart's "The Fury of Aerial Bombardment" shares the theme of "Naming of Parts" in that both poems attack indifference to violence and suffering. By saying that "History, even, does not know what is meant," the poet seems to lament that even painful experience does not teach us to prevent the senselessness of war. We are "no farther advanced," making the poet ask: "Was man made stupid?" Here again, as in Reed's poem, technical, impersonal references to the "belt feed lever" and the "belt holding pawl" imply a criticism of the callousness with which people handle the subject of war. A lesson about a belt feed lever might be more instructive if the part were named the genocide lever, for instance.

However, "The Fury of Aerial Bombardment" contrasts with "Naming of Parts" because Eberhart goes beyond attacking human indifference by attacking divine indifference to the horrors of war. The poet questions why God has not intervened to stop the aerial bombardment. The answer, that "the infinite spaces/Are still silent," is a criticism of God's looking passively upon "shock-pried faces." These are the faces of the people who have witnessed the horror of the bombing but to whom God offers no respite. The poet seems to expect a thinking, feeling entity to intervene, but no such intervention takes place. Men still kill with "multitudinous will." In the third stanza, the poet asks: "Is God by definition indifferent, beyond us all?"

Both of these poems were written half a century ago, yet their relevance remains undiminished today. In an age when we read daily of war and death, indifference is commonplace. The way in which a news reporter casually reads death tolls from current conflicts is reminiscent of the cold, sterile wording of "Naming of Parts." The casual and callous projections of the cost in human lives of "winning" a nuclear war are another example of what is under attack in these poems. And people who ponder such atrocities as Auschwitz and Hiroshima have cause to question divine indifference, for the earth is long on suffering.

WRITING THE DOCUMENTED PAPER

When you bring together material from a range of sources, you may be asked to provide **documentation.** In a documented paper, you supply the data a reader would need to verify your sources. Where can your reader find the lines or the passage you are quoting? In what book? Written or edited by whom? Published where, when, and by whom? On what page did this particular passage occur? If a poem or critical article appeared in a magazine, what was the date of the issue and the page number (or numbers)? If you are quoting from a newspaper review, in what edition (morning, evening, or regional) did it appear? In what section of the paper?

Documentation is for readers who do not like to settle for someone else's say-so. They like to check things out for themselves. You may be asked to provide documentation for writing situations like the following:

■ You compare different interpretations of a poem or story. Where and why do critics disagree in their reading of a poem? Is there nevertheless a common thread in their responses?

■ You explore the range of critical reactions to an author. What connecting thread of what major stages do critics see in the work of a major writer? What key theme do they see the author probing again and again?

■ You study biographical material shedding light on the connection between a writer's life and work. What key experience or private burdens help illuminate a writer's characteristic concerns?

■ You weigh conflicting views on the meaning of a historical document in its contemporary context. What now-forgotten issues triggered it? What did key terms or phrases mean in their historical setting?

FINDING PROMISING LEADS   To work up material for your paper, begin by checking in electronic or printed indexes for books, collections of critical articles, and individual articles in periodicals. For a writer like Emily Dickinson, John Steinbeck, or Alice Walker, most college libraries will have a wide range of critical and scholarly sources. Often critical studies will include bibliographies alerting you to other promising leads. Many magazines and Sunday magazine sections of major newspapers have reviews of current writers, ranging from short notices to full-length review articles.

TAKING NOTES   When working on a documented paper, you need to keep a detailed record of where you found your material. Writers develop their own ways of recording the materials for a documented research paper or library paper. You may use handwritten or typed note cards (which can be easily shuffled and put in the order in which you will use them in your paper). You may rely on files in your word processor (where you can transfer typed quotations and the like directly to the body of your paper, without the need for retyping). You may rely heavily on clippings from articles or photocopies of whole articles or key pages.

To assure maximum usefulness of your notes, remember:

■ *Start each note with a tag or "descriptor."* Show where the material tentatively fits into your paper. Use headings like the following:

NATURE—seasonal cycles

NATURE—interdependence of creatures

CIVILIZATION—uprooting rural populations

■ *Signal—with quotation marks—all direct quotation.* Distinguish clearly between direct quotation (material quoted exactly word for word) and paraphrase (where you put less important material in your own words, often in condensed form.)

QUOTATION: Maxine Hong Kingston attacks stereotypes about
Asians, including those of the wise elder and the dragon lady.
"Asians are not celestials, or Martians, nor are they ugly people
who don't have a beautiful voice or language."
PARAPHRASE: Maxine Hong Kingston attacks stereotypes about
Asians, including those of the wise elder and the dragon lady.
Asians are not divine beings or space aliens, nor are they
physically unattractive, speaking an ugly-sounding language.

▪ *Make each note show the exact source.* Include all publishing information
you will need later: exact names, titles and subtitles, publishers or publications, as well as dates and places. Register exact page numbers: the specific
page or pages for a quotation, but also the complete page numbers for an
article. Sample notes might look like this:

Self-contained Quotation

DICKINSON—SEXUAL IMAGERY
"Like her nature poetry, her use of female sexual imagery
suggests . . . not the 'subversion' of an existing male tradition,
nor the 'theft' of male power—but rather the assertion of a
concept of female sexuality and female creativity."

Paula Bennett, *Emily Dickinson: Woman Poet* (Iowa City: U of
Iowa P, 1990) 180.

Paraphrase (with partial direct quotation)

DICKINSON—FREUDIAN PERSPECTIVE
The prime motive in D.'s life and poetry was fear created by a
"bad child-parent relationship," specifically with her "cold and
forbidding father." This relationship shaped her view of men,
love, marriage, and religion. She viewed God as a forbidding
father-figure who spurned her.

Clark Griffith, *The Long Shadow: Emily Dickinson's Tragic Poetry*
(Princeton: Princeton UP, 1964) 78.

Note finer points: Even when you paraphrase, use quotation marks (as
in the sample note above) for striking phrases that you keep in the exact
wording of the author. Use **single quotation marks** for a phrase that appears as a quote-within-a-quote.

"To understand black Americans, one must, in the words of
Clarence Major, embrace irony as 'a key to the African
American experience.'"

Use the **ellipsis**—three spaced periods—to show an omission. (Use four periods when the periods include the period at the end of a sentence.)

> "Part of the American reality is . . . that black people and white people in America are kissing cousins."

Square brackets show that you have inserted material into the original quotation:

> "In this poem, based on the Emmett Till murder [1955], Brooks creates a surreal aura of hysteria and violence underlying an ostensibly calm domestic scene."

DOCUMENTATION STYLE   As you start to draft your paper, you will be grappling with familiar issues: What is going to be your focus? What will be your thesis—the point of your paper as a whole? What will be your organizing strategy? What material will you use to develop and support your points? How will you lay out your material in an order that will make sense to your readers?

However, in writing a documented paper, you will be paying special attention to matters of format and style. In the paper itself, you will use **parenthetical documentation:** You will put in parentheses exact page references—and quick identification of sources as needed. Then, at the end of your paper, you will provide an alphabetic list of **Works Cited,** giving complete information about your sources. Study the way parentheses, italics, quotation marks, colons, and other punctuation features are used in sample passages and sample entries.

Follow the current style of the Modern Language Association (MLA) unless instructed otherwise. This style no longer uses footnotes (though it still allows for **explanatory notes** at the end of a paper). Remember these key features:

- *Identify your sources briefly in your text.* Generally, introduce a quotation by saying something like the following:

> Mary Jo Salter says in her article "Puns and Accordions: Emily Dickinson and the Unsaid" that Dickinson "has inspired a massive critical industry rivaling that devoted to Shakespeare and Milton."

- *Give page references in parentheses in your text.* Usually, they will go at the end of the sentence and before the final period, for instance (73) or (42–45). If you have *not* mentioned the author, give his or her last name (Richter 187–90). If you are using *more than one* source by the same author, specify briefly which one (Richter, "Epiphanies" 187–90.)

Remember a few pointers: Italicize (underline on an old-fashioned typewriter) the titles of books and other complete publications: *The Color Purple*. Put in quotation marks the titles of poems, articles, and other pieces that are *part* of a publication: "Ringing the Bells."

Samples of Parenthetical Documentation

- simple page reference when you have identified the source:

Octavio Paz has called the meeting of the Indian and the Spaniard the key to the Mexican national character (138).

- author's name and page reference when you have not identified the source:

A prominent Latin American writer has called the meeting of the Indian and the Spaniard the key to the Mexican national character (Paz 138).

- more than one author:

Conservatives expect from literature "the staunch affirmation of a shared and stable culture" (Gibson and Lujo 56).

- abbreviated title added when you quote more than one source by the same author:

Rivera, who has written about the "dark energies" of misogyny and racism in Shakespeare's plays ("Dilemmas" 23), calls Ophelia and Queen Gertrude the "unheard voices" in *Hamlet* (*Reinterpretations* 69–71).

- a source you found quoted by someone else:

Steinbeck said he admired "strong, independent, self-reliant women" (qtd. in Barnes 201).

- a reference to preface or other introductory material, with page numbers given in lowercase Roman numerals:

In his preface to *The Great Mother*, Neumann refers to the "onesidedly patriarchal development of the male intellectual consciousness" (xliii).

Note: References to the Bible typically cite chapter and verse instead of page numbers (Luke 2.1); references to a Shakespeare play usually cite act, scene, and line (*Hamlet* 3.2.73–76). After block quotations, a parenthetical page reference *follows* a final period or other terminal mark. (See sample paper for examples.)

Sample Entries for "Works Cited"

Study sample entries for your alphabetical listing of Works Cited. Remember a few pointers:

- Use *italics* (or <u>underlining</u> on a typewriter) for the title of a whole publication—whether a book-length study, a collection or anthology of stories or essays, a periodical that prints critical articles, or a newspaper that prints reviews. However, use quotation marks for titles of poems or critical articles that are *part* of a collection.

- Leave *two* spaces after periods marking off chunks of information in the entry. Indent the second and following lines of each entry *five* spaces.

- Use ed. for editor; trans. for a translator.

- Abbreviate the names of publishing houses (Prentice for Prentice-Hall, Inc.; Southern Illinois UP for Southern Illinois University Press). Abbreviate the names of the months (Dec., Apr., Mar.). Abbreviate the names of states when needed to locate a little-known place of publication (CA, NY, NJ).

Items in Newspapers and Periodicals

- newspaper article with date and section of paper:

Alvarez, Cecilia.   "Jefferson's Heirs."   *Newport Times* 12 Aug.
    1994: B7–8.

- magazine article identified by date, with complete page numbers (the + sign shows that the article is continued later in the same issue):

Foote, Stephanie.   "Our Bodies, Our Lives, Our Right to Decide."
    The Humanist July–Aug. 1992: 2–8+.

- article with volume number (for a magazine with continuous page numbering through several issues):

Herzberger, David K.   "Narrating the Past: History and the Novel
    of Memory in Postwar Spain."   *PMLA* 106 (1991): 34–45.

- professional journal with separate page numbering for each issue of the same volume (volume number is followed by number of issue):

Winks, Robin W.   "The Sinister Oriental Thriller: Fiction and the
    Asian Scene."   *Journal of Popular Culture* 19.2 (1985):
    49–61.

- coauthored article (last name first for first author only):

Labov, Suleiman, and Mihail Naref. "Kate Chopin and Her
  Audience." *Studies in Short Fiction* July–Aug. 1994: 17–20.

▪ article with more than three authors—*et al.* for "and others":

Wilson, Brook, et al. "Today's Bilingual Poets." *Poet's Voice*
  23 Jan. 1994: 34–35.

▪ review (with edition and section of newspaper specified—article
  starts on page 1 and continues not on next page but later in the
  newspaper):

Montgomery, Karen. "Today's Minimalist Poets." *New York Times*
  22 Feb. 1992, late ed., sec. 2: 1+.

▪ untitled, unsigned review:

Rev. of *The Penguin Book of Women Poets,* ed. Carol Cosman, Joan
  Keefe, and Kathleen Weaver. *Arts and Books Forum* May
  1990: 17–19.

▪ unsigned editorial—author not identified (alphabetize under first
  word other than *A, An,* or *The*):

"At the Threshold: An Action Guide for Cultural Survival."
  Editorial. *Cultural Survival Quarterly.* Spring 1992: 17–18.

▪ letter to the editor:

Lubevic, Jacob. ["Poetry in the Schools."] Letter. *San Jose
  Mercury News* 12 Nov. 1994: C3.

Books and Parts of Books

▪ standard entry for a book:

Tan, Amy. *The Kitchen God's Wife.* New York: Putnam's, 1991.

▪ book with subtitle (published by a university press):

Johnson, Thomas H. *Emily Dickinson: An Interpretive Biography.*
  Cambridge: Harvard UP, 1966.

▪ material edited or collected by someone other than the author (or
  authors):

Shockley, Ann Allen, ed. *Afro-American Women Writers 1746–
  1933: An Anthology and Critical Guide.* Boston: G. K. Hall,
  1988.

Barrett, Eileen, and Mary Cullinan, eds. *American Women Writers: Diverse Voices in Prose Since 1845.* New York: St. Martin's, 1992.

- book of poems by the same author (editor's name first when editor's work of compiling or establishing texts is important):

Brooks, Gwendolyn. *The World of Gwendolyn Brooks.* New York: Harper, 1971.

Johnson, Thomas H., ed. *The Complete Poems of Emily Dickinson.* Boston: Little, Brown, 1960.

- poem printed in an anthology (with editor's name and with page number for the poem):

Colman, Cathy. "After Swimming in the Pacific." *New Poets: Women.* Ed. Terri Whetherby. Millbrae, CA: Les Femmes, 1976. 13.

- article in a collection (with inclusive page numbers):

Gutierrez, Irene. "A New Consciousness." *New Voices of the Southwest.* Ed. Laura Fuentes. Santa Fe, NM: Horizon, 1992. 123–34.

Spillers, Hortense J. "Gwendolyn the Terrible: Propositions on Eleven Poems." *A Life Distilled: Gwendolyn Brooks, Her Poetry and Fiction.* Ed. Maria K. Mootry and Gary Smith. Urbana: U of Illinois P, 1987. 224–35.

- later edition of a book:

Mayfield, Marlys. *Thinking for Yourself: Developing Critical Thinking Skills Through Writing.* 3rd ed. Belmont: Wadsworth, 1994.

- material translated from another language:

Neruda, Pablo. *Selected Poems of Pablo Neruda: A Bilingual Edition.* Trans. Ben Belitt. New York: Grove, 1961.

- special imprint (special line of books) of a publisher:

Acosta, Oscar Zeta. *The Revolt of the Cockroach People.* New York: Vintage-Random, 1989.

- one of several volumes:

Woolf, Virginia. *The Diary of Virginia Woolf.* Ed. Anne Olivier Bell. Vol. 1. New York: Harcourt, 1977. 5 vols. 1977–85.

- published interview:

Lorde, Audre. Interview. *Black Women Writers at Work.* Ed.
 Claudia Tate. Harpenden, Herts.: Oldcastle, 1985. 100–16.

- foreword by other than editor (with page numbers in small Roman numerals for introductory material):

Olsen, Tillie. Foreword. *Black Women Writers at Work.* Ed.
 Claudia Tate. Harpenden, Herts.: Oldcastle, 1985. ix–xxvi.

Nonprint sources

- personal interview:

Houghton, Adrienne. Personal interview. 18 Jan. 1994.

- talk by a poet:

Clifton, Lucille. Lecture. Visiting Poets Series. Tucson, AZ, 23
 Feb. 1992.

- audio or video source (may include writer, producer, or narrator of a program):

Poets of Protest. Narr. Joan Moreno. Writ. and prod. Lorna
 Herold. KSBM, Los Angeles. 8 Feb. 1992.

- computer software:

Naruba, Mark. *The Strategic Writer.* Vers. 1.3. Computer
 software. Pentrax, 1993. Macintosh, 128K, disk.

Special situations

- additional entry by same author (substitute three hyphens for name):

Steinem, Gloria. *Outrageous Acts and Everyday Rebellions.* New
 York: Holt, 1983.
———. *Revolution from Within: A Book of Self-Esteem.* Boston:
 Little Brown, 1992.

- title within title (title of poem is between single quotation marks in title of an article that is marked by double quotation marks):

Monteiro, George. "Dickinson's 'We Thirst at First.'" *The
 Explicator* 48 (1990): 193–94.

REVISING   The following revision strategies are especially to the point when you revise a paper that has brought together many quotations from literary sources and much critical commentary:

- *Strengthen the overall framework.* Do not make the reader feel lost in a forest of quotations. Make sure that the three or four major stages of your paper or the major steps in your argument are clear in your own mind, and that the reader can see how they structure your paper.

- *Strengthen transitions.* Highlight connections between one part of the paper and the next. Check whether a *however, on the other hand,* or *finally* is needed to clarify a logical link between two points.

- *Revise for clear attribution.* Who said what? Repeat the name of the quoted author if a *he* or *she* might point to the wrong person.

- *Integrate undigested chunk quotations.* If you have too many block quotations, break them up. (Readers in a hurry are sometimes tempted to skip long block quotations.) Work partial quotations into your own text for a smoother flow.

- *Do a final check of documentation style.* Teachers and editors of scholarly or research-based writing are sticklers for detail. Use capitals, indents, spacing, colons, parentheses, quotation marks, and the like exactly as the style guide for your class or for your publication specifies.

Sample Documented Paper

Study the following documented paper. How well does it bring the subject into focus? Does it have a thesis? How well does it support its main points? How clear and effective is its use of quotations from the poet and from the critics? Study the use of parenthetical documentation and the entries in the Works Cited, paying special attention to unusual situations or entries.

Emily Dickinson's Strange Irreverence

Religion in one guise or another pervades many of Dickinson's poems. It appears in the form of tender and not so tender prayers, skeptical questionings, and bitter confrontations. Critics have constructed a whole range of interpretations designed to provide a key to her changing, ambivalent religious attitudes. Some have cast her in the role of the rebel, rescuing her readers from the harshness of a rigid, constricted religious tradition, erecting for them a "citadel of art" and cultivating "the ego or consciousness" (Burbick 62). Others, however, see her as a "lone pilgrim" in the tradition of Puritan austerity and asceticism. She could not "allow herself the long luxury" of the evangelical movement of her own day, which was turning away from earlier, harsher versions of the Christian faith and promoting a sentimental attitude toward God as a "creature of caring, even motherly generosity" (Wolff 260). Still others attribute Dickinson's ambivalent, shifting religious attitudes to her need to keep her friends, to her "preoccupation with attachment" (Burbick 65). Some of Dickinson's dearest friends, to whom she wrote about her cherished hope for "one unbroken company in heaven," had experienced a religious conversion at

Mt. Holyoke Seminary, and she felt she had to follow their example so that the bonds of friendship that were so precious to her would not be dissolved.

Perhaps the closest to a connecting thread is Denis Donoghue's discussion of her as a truth-seeker, who in life as in poetry was *looking* for the truth. As Donoghue says, "In a blunt paraphrase, many of her poems would contradict one another; but her answers are always provisional." Her answers are tentative; "only her questions are definitive" (13). Although there are in her poems many references to the Old and New Testaments, "nothing is necessarily believed" but may be entertained only as a poetic or symbolic truth (17).

Because of the elusive, ambivalent nature of Dickinson's relation to religion, each poem must be interpreted individually in the quest to plumb her heart. Several of her poems are direct affirmations of her faith in Christ. In poem 698 in the Johnson edition ("Life—is what we make it"), she calls Christ a "tender pioneer," who blazed the trail of life and death for his "little Fellowmen":

> He—would trust no stranger—
> Others—could betray—
> Just his own endorsement—
> That—sufficeth me.
>
> All the other Distance
> He hath traversed first—
> No new mile remaineth—
> Far as Paradise—
>
> His sure foot preceding—
> Tender Pioneer—
> Base must be the Coward—
> Dare not venture—now—   (333–34)

In other poems, however, the faith that is supposed to provide a bridge to the hereafter proves a bridge with "mouldering" or "brittle" piers. In a famous poem, "I heard a Funeral in my Brain" (280 in the Johnson edition), the promise of faith seems unable to counteract the sense of the nothingness at the end of life. The Christian teachings of resurrection and an afterlife here do not seem to avail against the "plunge" into despair:

> And then I heard them lift a Box
> And creak across my Soul
> With those same Boots of Lead, again,
> Then Space—began to toll,
>
> As all the Heavens were a Bell,
> And Being, but an Ear,
> And I, and Silence, some strange Race
> Wrecked, solitary, here—

And then a Plank in Reason, broke,
And I dropped down, and down—
And hit a World, at every plunge,
And Finished knowing—then   (128–29)

Other poems seem to protest against the "ambiguous silence maintained by God" (Griffith 273). The following are the opening lines of poem 376 in Johnson's edition:

Of course—I prayed—
And did God Care?
He cared as much as on the Air
A Bird—had stamped her foot—
And cried "Give Me"—   (179)

Many of her poems seem to mourn the absence of God, as does the following stanza from poem 502 in Johnson:

Thou settest Earthquake in the South—
And Maelstrom, In the Sea—
Say, Jesus Christ of Nazareth—
Hast thou no Arm for Me?   (244)

In her most rebellious poems, she openly expresses defiance. She protests against the "tyranny" of God that forced Abraham to consent to offer his own son Isaac in sacrifice (Johnson 571). She rebels against commandments that keep us within a "magic prison," a limited and "constricted life," while we are within sight of the feast of happiness that is earthly pleasure—as if God were jealous of "the heaven on earth that is human happiness" (McNeil 60).

To read Emily Dickinson's poems is to see a poet's struggle for finding a meaning in her existence, rebelling at times against blind faith but also shrinking from complete doubt. She looked for evidence of the divine not in traditional revealed faith but in our earthly human existence. In a letter written several years before her death, she wrote: "To be human is more than to be divine . . . when Christ was divine he was uncontented until he had been human" (qtd. bin Wolff 519).

Works Cited

Burbick, Joan. "One Unbroken Company: Religion and Emily Dickinson."
      New England Quarterly 53 (1980): 62–75.
Donoghue, Denis. *Emily Dickinson*. U of Minnesota Pamphlets on
      American Writers. No. 81. 1969.
Griffith, Clark. *The Long Shadow: Emily Dickinson's Tragic Poetry*.
      Princeton: Princeton UP, 1964.
Johnson, Thomas H., ed. *The Complete Poems of Emily Dickinson*.
      Boston: Little, 1960.
McNeil, Helen. *Emily Dickinson*. New York: Pantheon, 1986.
Wolff, Cynthia Griffin. *Emily Dickinson*. Menlo Park, CA: Addison,
      1988.

A GLOSSARY OF TERMS

Abstraction a general idea that "draws us away" from the level of specific data or observations; large abstractions are concepts like justice, dignity, and freedom

Alliteration an echo effect produced by repeating identical consonants at the beginning of stressed syllables, as in Shakespeare's "When to the sessions of sweet silent thought / I summon up remembrance of things past"

Allusion a brief mention that brings a whole story or set of associations to the reader's mind

Analogy a close comparison traced into several related details, often used to explain the new in terms of the familiar

Anapestic in a line of poetry, sets of three syllables with the stress on the third and last syllable: "New RoCHELLE—New RoCHELLE—New Ro-CHELLE"; the following lines each have three anapestic feet: "For we KNEW | not the MONTH | was OcTOB|er / And we MARKED | not the NIGHT | of the YEAR" (Edgar Allan Poe)

Aphorism a pointed, memorable saying, like "A little learning is a dangerous thing"

Aside a comment made by a character in a play for the hearing of the audience but not the other characters on the stage

Brainstorming freely calling up memories, data, or associations relevant to a topic without at first editing or sorting them out

Cliché a tired, overused expression that may have been clever or colorful at one time but has long since lost its edge ("the tip of the iceberg," "we're all in the same boat")

Cluster a network or web of ideas centered in a key term or stimulus word, from which various strands of ideas and associations branch out

Comparison and contrast tracing connections to demonstrate similarities and differences

Connotation the attitudes, emotions, or associations a word carries beyond its basic factual meaning (or denotation); *sword* carries connotations of honor and valor; *dagger* carries connotations of stealth and treachery

Context what comes before and after a word or a statement and helps give it its full meaning; also, the setting or situation that helps explain what something means

Dactylic in a line of poetry, sets of three syllables with the stress on the first syllable, setting up a "ONE-two-three, ONE-two-three" or "BALTimore—BALTimore—BALTimore" pattern (as in Henry Wadsworth Longfellow's "THIS is the | FORest prim|EVal")

Definition staking out the exact meaning of a possibly vague, ambiguous, or abused term

Dialogue a verbal exchange by characters on the stage, supplemented by movement, body language, or gesture

729

Dialectic the kind of reasoning that makes ideas emerge from the play of pro and con; ideally, dialectic proceeds from thesis (statement) to antithesis (counterstatement) and from there to synthesis (a balanced conclusion)

Documentation in a library paper or research paper, providing complete information about quoted sources, including full names of authors, titles, and facts of publication

Ellipsis the use of three or four spaced periods to indicate an omission or deletion

Figurative language language using imaginative comparisons, such as calling someone a gadfly (metaphor) or punctual as a clock (simile)

Foot a segment of several syllables that has at least one stressed syllable, with several feet together making up a line of verse; according to the number of syllables and the position of the stressed syllable, feet are classified as iambic (DeTROIT), trochaic (BOSton), dactylic (BALtimore), or anapestic (New RoCHELLE).

Free verse poetry that abandons traditional rhyme and meter, developing its own unique pattern and rhythm

Genre a kind of literature with its own traditions or conventions, such as the novel, the short story, or the short lyrical poem; tragedy and comedy are traditional subdivisions of drama

Iambic an iambic line of poetry is made up of pairs of syllables with the stress or beat on the second syllable, setting up a "one-TWO, one-TWO" or "DeTROIT—DeTROIT—DeTROIT" pattern

Image something we can visualize; something that appeals vividly to our senses

Irony a wry comic effect produced when events develop, or people behave, counter to expectation; ironic situations or remarks deflate our naive hopes or optimistic assumptions

Literal literal-minded people take in only the plain surface meanings of words without responding to overtones, double meanings, or lurking ambiguities

Melodrama in the theater especially, giving the audience a steamy emotional workout by playing on their fear of villainy and their sympathy for persecuted virtue

Metaphor an imaginative comparison that treats one thing as if it were another, without using a signal such as *like* or *as* ("he *surfed* to the speaker's table on a *wave* of applause")

Meter the regularized beat or rhythm of traditional poetry; in much traditional poetry, the meter is regular enough to be charted or scanned

Monologue a long solo speech by a character in a play while other characters on the stage keep silent

Narrator in fiction, the person—real or imaginary—telling the story

Naturalism a turn-of-the-century literary movement (late 1900s and early twentieth century) that insisted on frank, unretouched treatment of the ugly or sordid side of life and of nature in the raw

Oratory the art of public speech; formal or highly conventionalized forms of oratory flourished in ancient Greece and Rome and in nineteenth-century America

Paradox an apparent contradiction that makes sense on second thought (why does it make sense on second thought for Octavio Paz to say that "all poems say the same thing, and each poem is unique"?)

Paraphrase putting a statement or passage into one's own words

Parody a humorous or mocking imitation

Peer review feedback given to a writer by classmates or fellow writers

Pentameter a five-beat line of verse; the basic underlying beat of much poetry in English is iambic pentameter, with five iambic feet ("They AL|so SERVE | who ON|ly STAND | and WAIT"—John Milton)

Persona the identity assumed or the public role played by a writer in a piece of writing (the persona may be different from the writer's private personality)

Point of view the angle or vantage point from which the events of a story are seen and narrated

Premise a shared assumption on which an argument is built

Quatrain a set of four lines of verse

Rhetoric the practice or the study of effective strategies for speech and writing (sometimes used negatively to mean empty or deceptive use of language)

Rhyme an echo effect used regularly in much traditional poetry; bonding two or more lines of verse by final syllables that start differently but end alike, as in *moon/June* or *fashion/passion*

Satire the use of humor as a weapon to deflate pomposity or ridicule abuses

Sentimentality giving in to a warm gush of emotion; cultivating emotions of tenderness or sorrow in order to bask in a glow of self-approval

Sestet a set of six lines of verse

Short short an exceptionally short short story, perhaps running to no more than one or two pages

Simile an imaginative comparison signaled by such words as *like* or *as* ("the library had bare solid walls *like a prison*")

Soliloquy a long solo speech while other characters are absent from the stage

Stanza in much traditional poetry, groups of lines following the same pattern, including perhaps the same variations in the length of lines and the same rhyme scheme (stanzas are to a poem what verses are to a song)

Symbol an object, person, or event that acquires a larger meaning beyond its literal significance, such as when the ice of Alpine mountain peaks becomes a symbol of burnt-out emotions

Theme a central concern or idea that a poem, story, or play as a whole explores or acts out; what a literary work as a whole seems to say

Thesis the central idea or unifying assertion that a piece of writing as a whole supports; the claim a paper stakes out and defends

Trochaic in a trochaic line of verse, each pair of syllables has the beat or stress on the first syllable, setting up a "ONE-two, ONE-two" or "BOSton—BOSton—BOSton" pattern

Understatement the playing down of emotions, making for a dry ironic style; the studied avoidance of sentimentality or melodrama

ACKNOWLEDGMENTS

Nelson Algren, "A Bottle of Milk for Mother," from *The Neon Wilderness.* Copyright 1941 by Nelson Algren. Used by permission of Doubleday, a division of Bantam Doubleday Dell Publishing Group, Inc.

Paula Gunn Allen, "Where I Come From Is Like This," from *The Sacred Hoop.* Copyright © 1986, 1992 by Paula Gunn Allen. Reprinted by permission of Beacon Press.

Margaret Atwood, "Dreams of the Animals," from *Selected Poems 1965–1975.* Copyright © 1976 by Margaret Atwood. Reprinted by permission of Houghton Mifflin Co. All rights reserved.

James Baldwin, "Notes of a Native Son," from *Notes of a Native Son.* Copyright © 1955, renewed 1983 by James Baldwin. Reprinted by permission of Beacon Press.

Toni Cade Bambara, "Raymond's Run," from *Gorilla, My Love.* Copyright © 1971 by Toni Cade Bambara. Reprinted by permission of Random House, Inc.

Donald Barthelme, "The School," copyright © 1976 by Donald Barthelme. Reprinted with the permission of Wylie, Aitken & Stone, Inc.

Stephen Berg, "Five Aztec Poems," from *Nothing in the Word.* Copyright © 1972 by Mushinkska Limited. Reprinted by permission of Eric Sackheim for the publisher.

Wendell Berry, excerpt from "The Peace of Wild Things," in *Openings.* Copyright © 1968 by Wendell Berry. Reprinted by permission of Harcourt Brace & Company.

Wendell Berry, from "The Journey's End," in *Recollected Essays 1965–1980* by Wendell Berry. Copyright © 1981 by Wendell Berry. Reprinted by permission of North Point Press, a division of Farrar, Straus & Giroux, Inc.

Ray Bradbury, "The Pedestrian." Copyright © 1951, renewed 1979 by Ray Bradbury. Reprinted by permission of Don Congdon Associates, Inc.

Gwendolyn Brooks, "The Boy Died in My Alley," from *Beckonings.* Copyright © 1975 by Gwendolyn Brooks. "Piano After the War" and "Mentors," from *Blacks.* Copyright © 1991 by Gwendolyn Brooks. Reprinted by permission of the author.

Diane Burns, "Sure You Can Ask Me A Personal Question." Copyright © 1989 by Diane Burns. Reprinted by permission of the author.

Olga Cabral, "Life and Death Among the Xerox People," by Olga Cabral from *We Become New,* edited by Iverson and Ruby, Bantam 1975. Copyright © 1975 by Olga Cabral. Reprinted by permission of the author.

Raymond Carver, "A Small, Good Thing," from *Cathedral.* Copyright © 1981, 1982, 1983 by Raymond Carver. Reprinted by permission of Alfred A. Knopf, Inc.

Lorna Dee Cervantes, "Refugee Ship." Reprinted with permission from the publisher of *A Decade of Hispanic Literature* (Houston: Arte Publico Press-University of Houston, 1982.)

Sandra Cisneros, "Mericans," from *Woman Hollering Creek.* Copyright © 1991 by Sandra Cisneros. Published in the United States by Vintage Books, a division of Random House, Inc., New York. Originally published in hardcover by Random House, Inc., New York in 1991. Reprinted by permission of Susan Bergholz Literary Services, New York.

Lucille Clifton, "The 1st" and excerpts from "Admonitions," in *Good Woman: Poems and a Memoir 1969–1980.* Copyright © 1987 by Lucille Clifton. Reprinted with the permission of BOA Editions, Ltd., 92 Park Ave., Brockport, NY 14420.

Countee Cullen, "For My Grandmother," from *Color* by Countee Cullen. Copyright © 1925 by Harper & Brothers; copyright renewed 1953 by Ida M. Cullen. Reprinted by permission of GRM Associates, Inc., Agents for the Estate of Ida M. Cullen.

Emily Dickinson, "A Bird Came Down the Walk," "'Hope' is the thing with feathers," "The Soul selects her own Society," "I'm Nobody! Who are you?" "Much Madness is divinest Sense," and Poem #1770, from *The Poems of Emily Dickinson*, edited by Thomas H. Johnson, Cambridge, Mass.: The Belknap Press of Harvard University Press. Copyright © 1951, 1955, 1979, 1983 by the President and Fellows of Harvard College. Reprinted by permission of the publishers and the Trustee of Amherst College.

Annie Dillard, "Looking Spring in the Eye," from "Spring" in *Pilgrim at Tinker Creek* by Annie Dillard. Copyright © 1974 by Annie Dillard. Reprinted by permission of HarperCollins Publishers, Inc.

Chitra Banerjee Divakaruni, "Indian Movie, New Jersey," from *Indiana Review*, Vol. 14, #1, Winter 1990. Reprinted by permission of the author.

John Dos Passos, "The House of Morgan," from *The 42nd Parallel*, 1919, and "Vag," from *The Big Money*, 1932 and 1936. Copyright Elizabeth H. Dos Passos. Reprinted by permission of Elizabeth H. Dos Passos, co-executor, Estate of John Dos Passos.

Rita Dove, "Horse and Tree," from *Grace Notes* by Rita Dove. Copyright © 1989 by Rita Dove. Reprinted with the permission of W. W. Norton & Company, Inc.

Louise Erdrich, "The Red Convertible," from *Love Medicine*, New and Expanded Version, by Louise Erdrich. Copyright © 1984, 1993 by Louise Erdrich. Reprinted by permission of Henry Holt and Company, Inc.

Martin Espada, "Latin Night at the Pawnshop," from *Rebellion is the Circle of a Lover's Hands / Rebelion es el giro de manos del amante*. Copyright © 1991 by Martín Espada. Distributed by InBook. Used with permission of Curbstone Press.

Mari Evans, excerpt from "Status Symbol" and "I Am a Black Woman," from *I Am a Black Woman*. Copyright © 1970 by Mari Evans. Reprinted by permission of the author.

William Faulkner, "The Tall Men," from *Collected Stories of William Faulkner*. Copyright © 1941 renewed 1969 by Estelle Faulkner and Jill Faulkner Summers. Reprinted by permission of Random House, Inc.

Dana Gioia, "California Hills in August." Originally published in *The New Yorker*, August 9, 1982. Reprinted by permission of *The New Yorker*. All rights reserved.

Nikki Giovanni, "Woman," from *Cotton Candy on a Rainy Day* by Nikki Giovanni. Copyright © 1978 by Nikki Giovanni. Reprinted by permission of William Morrow & Company, Inc.

Ellen Glasgow, "Only Yesterday," from *Vein of Iron*. Copyright 1935 by Ellen Glasgow and renewed 1963 by First and Merchants Bank of Richmond. Reprinted by permission of Harcourt Brace & Company.

Mary Gordon, "Eileen," from *Temporary Shelter* by Mary Gordon. Copyright © 1987 by Mary Gordon. Reprinted by permission of Random House, Inc.

Judy Grahn, excerpt from "Lesbians love to dance/inside the thunder." Originally published in *The Queen of Swords*, Beacon Press. Reprinted by permission of Judy Grahn.

Joy Harjo, "Leaving," from *She Had Some Horses* by Joy Harjo. Copyright © 1983 by Joy Harjo. Used by permission of the publisher, Thunder's Mouth Press.

Robert Hayden, Part I of "Runagate Runagate," from *Angle of Ascent, New and Selected Poems* by Robert Hayden. Copyright © 1975, 1972, 1970, 1966 by Robert Hayden. Reprinted by permission of Liveright Publishing Corporation.

John Heaviside, "A Gathering of Deafs," from the *Olivetree Review 8* (Fall 1989), Hunter College.

Ernest Hemingway, "In Another Country," from *Men Without Women* by Ernest Hemingway. Copyright 1927 by Charles Scribner's Sons. Copyright renewed 1955 by Ernest Hemingway. Reprinted with permission of Charles Scribner's Sons, an imprint of Macmillan Publishing Company.

Langston Hughes, "Pennsylvania Station." Copyright © 1963 by Langston Hughes. Reprinted by permission of Harold Ober Associates Incorporated.

David Henry Hwang, "The Dance and the Railroad," from *FOB and Other Plays* by David Henry Hwang. Copyright © 1981 by David Henry Hwang. Used by permission of Dutton Signet, a division of Penguin Books USA Inc.

Shirley Jackson, "The Lottery," from *The Lottery* by Shirley Jackson. Copyright © 1948, 1949 by Shirley Jackson, renewed © 1976, 1977 by Laurence Hyman, Barry Hyman, Mrs. Sarah Webster, and Mrs. Joanne Schnurer. Reprinted by permission of Farrar, Straus & Giroux, Inc.

Maxine Hong Kingston, "Twisters and Shouters," from *Tripmaster Monkey: His Fake Book* by Maxine Hong Kingston. Copyright © 1987, 1988, 1989 by Maxine Hong Kingston. Reprinted by permission of Alfred A. Knopf Inc.

Galway Kinnell, "To Christ Our Lord," from *What a Kingdom It Was* by Galway Kinnell. Copyright © 1960, renewed 1988 by Galway Kinnell. Reprinted by permission of Houghton Mifflin Company. All rights reserved.

Ursula K. Le Guin, "The Ones Who Walk Away from Omelas." First appeared in *New Dimensions 3*. Copyright © 1973 by Ursula K. Le Guin. Reprinted by permission of the author and the author's agent, Virginia Kidd.

Denise Levertov, "What Were They Like?" from *Poems 1968–1972*. Copyright © 1968 by Denise Levertov. "The Mutes," from *Poems 1960–1967*. Copyright © 1964 by Denise Levertov Goodman. Reprinted by permission of New Directions Publishing Corp.

Audre Lorde, "Sister Outsider," from *The Black Unicorn* by Audre Lorde. Copyright © 1978 by Audre Lorde. Reprinted by permission of W.W. Norton & Company, Inc.

Robert Lowell, "The Mouth of the Hudson," from *For The Union Dead* by Robert Lowell. Copyright © 1964 by Robert Lowell, renewed © 1988 by Harriet Lowell, Sheridan Lowell, and Caroline Lowell. Reprinted by permission of Farrar, Straus & Giroux, Inc.

Mary Mackey, "When I Was a Child I Played with the Boys." Originally published in *Split Ends*. Copyright 1974 by Mary Mackey. Reprinted by permission of the author.

Archibald MacLeish, From "To Thomas Jefferson, Esquire," in *Empire Builders, Collected Poems 1917–1982* by Archibald MacLeish. Copyright © 1985 by The Estate of Archibald MacLeish. Reprinted by permission of Houghton Mifflin Co. All rights reserved.

Bernard Malamud, "The Magic Barrel," from *The Magic Barrel* by Bernard Malamud. Copyright © 1954, 1958 and renewed © 1986 by Bernard Malamud. Reprinted by permission of Farrar, Straus & Giroux, Inc.

David Mamet, "The Rake: Scenes From My Childhood." First published in *Harper's*, June 1992. Copyright © by David Mamet. Used with the permission of Wylie, Aitken & Stone, Inc.

Bobbie Ann Mason, "Shiloh," from *Shiloh and Other Stories* by Bobbie Ann Mason. Copyright © 1982 by Bobbie Ann Mason. Reprinted by permission of HarperCollins Publishers, Inc.

Violet Kazue Matsuda, "Poetic Reflections of the Tule Lake Internment Camp 1944," by Violet Kazue Matsuda from *The Big Aiiieee!* edited by Jeffrey Paul Chan, et al. Reprinted by permission of Violet K. deCristofino (Matsuda).

Terry McMillan, "Quilting on the Rebound," by Terry McMillan, from *Voices Louder Than Words*, edited by William Shore. Copyright © 1991 by Share Our Strength. Reprinted by permission of Random House, Inc.

Czeslaw Milosz, "Incantation," from *The Separate Notebooks* by Czeslaw Milosz, first published by The Ecco Press in 1984. Copyright © 1984 by Czeslaw Milosz Royalties, Inc. Reprinted by permission of the Ecco Press.

N. Scott Momaday, excerpt from "Carriers of the Dream Wheel" and "New World," from *The Gourd Dancers*. Copyright © 1975 by N. Scott Momaday. Reprinted by permission of the author.

Gary Snyder, "After Work," from *The Back Country* by Gary Snyder. Copyright © 1959 by Gary Snyder. Reprinted by permission of New Directions Publishing Corp.

Cathy Song, "Lost Sister," from *The Picture Bride* by Cathy Song. Copyright 1983 by Yale University Press. Reprinted by permission of the publisher.

Gary Soto, "Oranges," from *New and Selected Poems*, by Gary Soto, published by Chronicle Books. Copyright © 1995 by Gary Soto. Reprinted by permission of Chronicle Books.

William Stafford, from "Things That Happen When There Aren't Any People," from *Things That Happen When There Aren't Any People* by William Stafford, BOA Editions, 1959, 1980. Originally published in *Western Humanities Review.* Copyright by William Stafford. Reprinted by permission of Dorothy Stafford.

John Steinbeck, "The Chrysanthemums," from *The Long Valley* by John Steinbeck. Copyright 1937, renewed © 1965 by John Steinbeck. Used by permission of Viking Penguin, a division of Penguin Books USA Inc.

Craig Strete, "Lives Far Child." First appeared in *Death Chants* by Craig Kee Strete, Doubleday 1988. Copyright © 1988 by Craig Kee Strete. Reprinted by permission of the author and Virginia Kidd Literary Agent.

Edna St. Vincent Millay, "Apostrophe to Man" and "Childhood is the Kingdom Where Nobody Dies," from *Collected Poems,* HarperCollins. Copyright © 1934, 1962 by Edna St. Vincent Millay and Norma Millay Ellis. Reprinted by permission of Elizabeth Barnett, literary executor.

Amy Tan, "Jing-Mei Woo: Two Kinds," from *The Joy Luck Club* by Amy Tan. Copyright © 1989 by Amy Tan. Reprinted by permission of G.P. Putnam's Sons.

Estela Portillo Trambley, "The Pilgrim," from *Trini* by Estela Portillo Trambley. Copyright © 1986 by the Bilingual Press/Editorial Bilingüe, Arizona State University, Tempe, AZ. Reprinted by permission of the publisher.

Richard Umans, "Speech." Originally appeared in the *James White Review*, 1984.

Luis Valdez, *Los Vendidos.* Copyright © 1967 by Luis Valdez. Reprinted by permission of the author.

Victor Villaseñor, from *Rain of Gold.* Copyright © 1991 by Arte Publico Press-University of Houston. Reprinted by permission of the publisher.

Alice Walker, "Roselily," from *In Love & Trouble: Stories of Black Women.* Copyright © 1972 by Alice Walker. "Women," from *Revolutionary Petunias & Other Poems.* Copyright © 1970 by Alice Walker. Reprinted by permission of Harcourt Brace & Company.

Douglas L. Wilson, "Jefferson and the Equality of Man," taken from a longer essay that originally appeared in *The Atlantic Monthly*, November 1992. Reprinted by permission of the author.

Richard Wright, "A Separate Road," from *Black Boy* by Richard Wright. Copyright 1937, 1942, 1944, 1945 by Richard Wright. Copyright renewed 1973 by Ellen Wright. Reprinted by permission of HarperCollins Publishers, Inc.

James Wright, "A Finch Sitting Out a Windstorm," from *This Journey* by James Wright. Copyright © 1977, 1978, 1979, 1980, 1981 by Anne Wright, Executrix of the Estate of James Wright. Reprinted by permission of Random House, Inc.

Mitsuye Yamada, "Marriage Was a Foreign Country," from *Camp Notes and Other Poems.* Copyright © 1986 by Mitsuye Yamada and Kitchen Table: Women of Color Press, P.O. Box 908, Latham, NY 12110. Reprinted by permission of the author and Kitchen Table: Women of Color Press.

INDEX OF AUTHORS AND TITLES